ZAGAT®

New York City Shopping
2008

EDITORS
Catherine Bigwood, Randi Gollin and Troy Segal

Published and distributed by
Zagat Survey, LLC
4 Columbus Circle
New York, NY 10019
T: 212.977.6000
E: nycshopping@zagat.com
www.zagat.com

ACKNOWLEDGMENTS

We thank Nancy Bilyeau, Michael Cohen, Jacques Dehornois, Angela Gaimari, Dana Gordon, Ki Hackney, Paul Himmelein, Faran Alexis Krentcil, Cheryl Locke, Laura Mitchell, Nancy Peretsman, Steven Shukow, Will Snyder, Neeraja Viswanathan and Mary Zubritsky, as well as the following members of our staff: Kelly Stewart (assistant editor), Christina Livadiotis (editorial assistant), Sean Beachell, Maryanne Bertollo, Sandy Cheng, Reni Chin, Larry Cohn, Carol Diuguid, Alison Flick, Jeff Freier, Michelle Golden, Karen Hudes, Roy Jacob, Natalie Lebert, Mike Liao, Dave Makulec, Chris Miragliotta, Andre Pilette, Josh Rogers, Kimberly Rosado, Becky Ruthenburg, Donna Marino Wilkins, Sharon Yates, Anna Zappia and Kyle Zolner.

Contents

Ratings & Symbols

					Zagat Ratings		
Zagat Top Spot	Name	Symbols			QUALITY	DISPLAY	SERVICE	COST

Area, Address, Subway Stop, Contact

Z Tim & Nina's ◑   ▽ 23 | 9 | 13 | I

W 50s | 4 Columbus Circle (8th Ave.) | 1/A/B/C/D to 59th St./Columbus Circle | 212-977-6000 | www.zagat.com

Review, surveyor comments in quotes

Paradoxically packed with both "prime pet products" and iPods (Nina's the pooch-lover, Tim handles the hardware), this "edgy" Columbus Circle canine/computer boutique attracts "bargain-hounds", who amble over for color-coordinated chew toys and chargers – plus bootlegged versions of 'How Much Is That Doggie in the Window?' to download; but even tail-waggers growl about the "snappish staff" and "doghouse decor."

Ratings

Quality, Display and **Service** are rated on the Zagat 0 to 30 scale. Newcomers or write-ins are listed without ratings.

0	–	9	poor to fair
10	–	15	fair to good
16	–	19	good to very good
20	–	25	very good to excellent
26	–	30	extraordinary to perfection
	▽		low response	less reliable

Cost reflects our surveyors' estimate of each store's price range.

I	Inexpensive
M	Moderate
E	Expensive
VE	Very Expensive

Symbols

Z	Zagat Top Spot (highest ratings, popularity and importance)
◑	usually open after 7 PM
S̶	closed on Sunday
M̶	closed on Monday
⊄	no credit cards accepted

Locations

For chains with over 10 locations in NYC, only the flagship address is listed.

About This Survey

This **2008 New York City Shopping Survey** is an update reflecting significant developments since our last Survey was published. It covers 2,463 of the city's best stores, including 167 important additions – a treasure trove of sources for everything from fashion to furniture, eyeglasses to undies, jeans to jewelry. We've also indicated new addresses, phone numbers and other major alterations.

WHO PARTICIPATED: Input from over 7,500 avid local shoppers forms the basis for the ratings and reviews in this guide (their comments are shown in quotation marks within the reviews). Their collective experience adds up to over one million shopping trips a year. We sincerely thank each of these participants – this book is really "theirs."

HELPFUL LISTS: Whether shopping for yourself or for the perfect gift, our top lists and indexes should help you find exactly the right store. See Key Newcomers (page 9), Most Popular (page 10), Top Ratings (pages 11–21) and Good Values (page 22). We've also provided 68 handy indexes.

OUR EDITORS: Special thanks go to our contributing editors, Donna Bulseco, a fashion editor who's been on staff at *WWD* and *W*; Erin Clack, a children's editor and shoe editor who has worked at *Children's Business* and *Footwear News*; and Kelly McMasters, who writes about home design for *CITY* and *Elle Decor,* among other publications.

ABOUT ZAGAT: This marks our 29th year reporting on the shared experiences of consumers like you. What started in 1979 as a hobby involving 200 of our friends has come a long way. Today we have well over 300,000 surveyors and now cover dining, entertaining, golf, hotels, movies, music, nightlife, resorts, shopping, spas, theater and tourist attractions worldwide.

SHARE YOUR OPINION: We invite you to join any of our upcoming surveys – just register at **ZAGAT.com,** where you can rate and review establishments year-round. Each participant will receive a free copy of the resulting guide when published.

AVAILABILITY: Zagat guides are available in all major bookstores, by subscription at **ZAGAT.com** and for use on web-enabled mobile devices via **ZAGAT TO GO** or **ZAGAT.mobi.** The latter two products allow you to contact any establishment by phone with one click.

FEEDBACK: There is always room for improvement, thus we invite your comments and suggestions about any aspect of our performance. Is there something more you would like us to include in our guides? Did we get anything wrong? We really need your input! Just contact us at **nycshopping@zagat.com.**

New York, NY
March 5, 2008

Nina and Tim Zagat

What's New

From exotic imports to all-American chains, retailers of every stripe emerged Uptown, way Downtown and all around this year, adding scores of new choices to this guide, which now covers 2,463 stores. While 60% of Zagat surveyors report that NYC shopping is more expensive than last year, Europeans armed with stronger currencies had a field day, hitting the town as if it were bargain-central and carting home suitcases stuffed with goodies.

DESIGNER DECADENCE: About 66% of our surveyors say they favor specific labels/designers and the latest exclusive enclaves provide plenty of high-end temptation. Deep-pocketed shoppers alighted in Allegra Hicks' jet-set heaven; Roberto Cavalli's spin-off Just Cavalli; Louis Féraud's French showcase; the newly reconceived Helmut Lang; and hot property 3.1 Phillip Lim.

PEACOCK ALLEY: A clear majority of surveyors – 63% – says it prefers shopping for wardrobe items vs. home goods. That figure includes the modern-day male who no longer needs to retread old turf since there's a raft of maverick arrivals, including music mogul Pharrell Williams' Billionaire Boys Club & Ice Cream; former pop-up (and now permanent) fashion provocateur Den; Hickey Freeman's spunky kid brother, hickey; designer John Bartlett's cool nook; the funky Marc Ecko Cut & Sew shop; and ex-Gucci goliath Tom Ford's namesake paean to posh. In addition, Buckler, Marc by Marc Jacobs and Lord Willy's expanded their reach with new branches.

THAT'S SHOE BIZ: The new Coach Legacy shop gave handbag addicts plenty of perusing pleasure, while the debuts of Michael Kors' SoHo showcase and Lambertson Truex did double duty, appealing to both purse and shoe fiends. In fact, footwear appears to be the 'it' accessory du jour. Bargainistas got their kicks at full-on phenomenon Crocs, trippy Irregular Choice and flip-flop king Rainbow Sandals. The well-heeled discovered the slightly subversive Brit men's brand Barker Black; Diana Broussard's sleek salon; the stately English affair Edon Manor; high-end haunt Iris; French buckle-meister Roger Vivier; and, of course, Saks' much-vaunted 10022-SHOE floor. Meanwhile, Castaner, the famed Spanish espadrille company, plans to hotfoot it into Manhattan this spring and Detny Footwear, a hip NYC-based outfit, will soon wedge its way into NoLita.

ROCK STARS: Leviev, the largest cutter and polisher of diamonds in the world, went retail with a new Madison Avenue flagship, while down the block the Donald's daughter Ivanka Trump opened her own namesake jewelry boutique, also specializing in the same sort of eye-popping precious stones.

GREENER PASTURES: Now that 'carbon footprint' is part of our everyday vocabulary, it's little wonder that Korres, the natural beauty hot spot from Greece, is making a splash in SoHo, while Urban Zen, Donna Karan's West Village oasis of calm purveying home furnishings and organic clothing, is luring laid-back loyalists. In fact, 45% of our surveyors claim they're now more eco-minded when buying merchandise than they were two years ago. Speaking of green, urban gardeners also grew closer to the land this year, prettifying pads with potted plants and sundry items from stores like Sprout Home and Tribbles Home & Garden.

ON THE HOME FRONT: SoHo (still voted the Survey's favorite shopping neighborhood) continues to hone in on the home sector with the arrival of three trendsetting shops: Moroso, an Italian icon ensconced within the ever-influential Moss; Luceplan, a cutting-edge lighting firm; and Japanese minimalist megastar Muji, which is drawing as many clamoring fans as a rock concert. SoHo is also the newest site of the more mainstream Mitchell Gold + Bob Williams furniture collection, while Uptown, decorating doyenne Charlotte Moss displays her patrician wares on five floors of a tony townhouse.

BREAK OUT THE BRAND: National chains and boldface names began their NYC blitz years ago, and now their offspring are pitching their tents too. In addition to Crate & Barrel's CB2, the Abercrombie & Fitch–owned company Hollister and J. Crew's jeans-centric adjunct Madewell (formerly a pop-up store) are setting their sights on SoHo, where mega-outfits from foreign shores, including Cotélac and Karen Millen, recently set up residence as well. Meanwhile, the J. Crew Collection, a store devoted to the luxe, limited-edition line of the casualwear standby, has designs on upper Madison; Free People, an Urban Outfitters–owned enterprise, arrived in the Flatiron District; and Threads, a childrenswear sibling of Pottery Barn Kids, opened in the East 70s.

LEAP AHEAD: Over the next year a host of newcomers are expected to stake their claim on the Big Apple. SoHo will soon be home to the highly anticipated Brit wonder-chain Topshop; German clothier Bogner; cheap-chic Russian fashion outfit Kira Plastinina; and Vera Wang's non-bridal contemporary womenswear concept, Lavender Label. The luxury Italian menswear honcho Canali will put down roots a stone's throw from Wall Street newcomers Hermès and Tiffany. And another status jeweler, the French legend Mauboussin, plans to open a five-story boutique on Madison Avenue in the East 60s.

New York, NY
March 5, 2008

Catherine Bigwood
Randi Gollin
Troy Segal

KEY NEWCOMERS

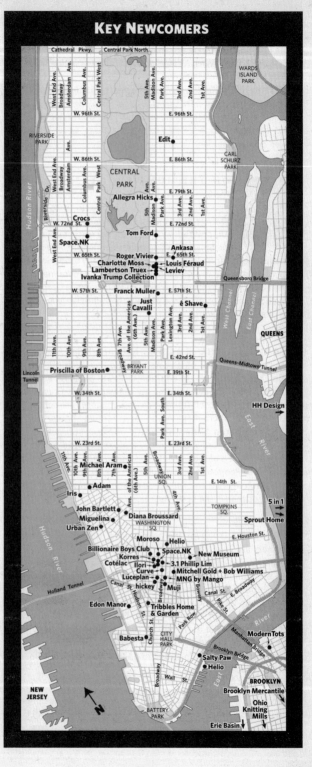

subscribe to ZAGAT.com

Key Newcomers

'If I can make it here, I can make it anywhere' – so goes one version of the song 'New York, New York,' and so seemingly goes the attitude of the newest retailers in town. Here's our take on the past year's most notable arrivals. (For a full list of additions to this book, see page 411.)

Adam	Just Cavalli
Allegra Hicks	Korres
Ankasa	Lambertson Truex
Babesta	Leviev
Billionaire Boys Club	Louis Féraud
Brooklyn Mercantile	Luceplan
Charlotte Moss	Michael Aram
Cotélac	Miguelina
Crocs	Mitchell Gold + Bob Williams
Curve	MNG by Mango
Diana Broussard	ModernTots
Edit	Moroso
Edon Manor	Muji
Erie Basin	New Museum
ê Shave	Ohio Knitting Mills
5 in 1	Priscilla of Boston
Franck Muller	Roger Vivier
Helio	Salty Paw
HH Design	Space.NK apothecary
hickey	Sprout Home
Ilori	3.1 Phillip Lim
Iris	Tom Ford
Ivanka Trump Collection	Tribbles Home & Garden
John Bartlett	Urban Zen

The year to come shows plenty of potential with a number of high-profile projects in the works. Designers and labels with loads of cachet continue to beef up the bounty in the Meatpacking District. **Hugo Boss** plans to add another notch to its belt, unveiling its latest offering near the newest Apple offshoot, while European iconoclast **Moschino** is slated to open its first retail venture just steps away. Coveted fashion brand **Ports 1961** is scheduled to make a splash with its multifloor concept, while celeb-favorite **Matthew Williamson** is said to be eyeing the desirable neighborhood for his premiere retail undertaking. And **Yohji Yamamoto** has two more stores in his arsenal – another namesake shop and a showcase for Y-3, his collaboration with Adidas.

Most Popular Stores

These places are also plotted on the map at the back of the book.

CHAINS

1. Bed Bath & Beyond
2. Banana Republic
3. H&M
4. Sephora
5. Met. Museum of Art
6. Williams-Sonoma
7. Tiffany & Co.
8. Anthropologie
9. Crate & Barrel
10. Ann Taylor
11. Ann Taylor Loft
12. Gap
13. Home Depot
14. Kiehl's
15. Pearl Paint
16. Brooks Brothers
17. buybuy Baby
18. Apple Store
19. Virgin Megastore
20. Coach
21. Talbots
22. Chico's
23. J.Crew
24. Old Navy

DEPARTMENT STORES

1. Bloomingdale's
2. Saks Fifth Ave.
3. Macy's
4. Bergdorf Goodman
5. Barneys New York
6. Lord & Taylor
7. Henri Bendel
8. Bergdorf Men's

DISCOUNTERS/MASS MERCHANTS

1. Century 21
2. B&H Photo-Video
3. Target
4. Costco Warehouse
5. J&R Music/Computer
6. Loehmann's
7. Daffy's
8. T.J. Maxx
9. Best Buy
10. DSW
11. Filene's Basement
12. Marshalls
13. Syms
14. Staples

INDEPENDENTS

1. Zabar's
2. Kate's Paperie
3. ABC Carpet & Home
4. Gracious Home
5. MoMA Store
6. Paragon
7. Takashimaya
8. Broadway Panhandler
9. Pearl River Mart
10. Bridge Kitchenware

While the above lists contain obvious big names, it's interesting that many of the stores, such as ABC Carpet & Home, B&H Photo-Video, Bergdorf Goodman, Broadway Panhandler, Gracious Home, Henri Bendel, Kate's Paperie and Zabar's, are of the "born in NY" variety, proof that New Yorkers love – and support – individuality in their shopping choices. What's more, if you turn to page 22 you'll see that shopping here can also be a world-class bargain.

Top Ratings (Based on a 30-pt. scale)

Excludes places with low votes, unless indicated by a ∇.
Department stores receive separate scores for different categories.

TOP QUALITY: FASHION/BEAUTY

29 Harry Winston
Van Cleef & Arpels
John Lobb
Chopard
Hermès
Fred Leighton
Mikimoto*
Balenciaga
A La Vieille Russie
Wempe
Loro Piana
Bergdorf Goodman
Cartier
Audemars Piguet
Chanel
Tod's
Bottega Veneta
Davide Cenci
Giorgio Armani
Akris

28 Turnbull & Asser
Salvatore Ferragamo
Belgian Shoes
Dior New York
Peter Fox Shoes*

Ermenegildo Zegna
Bergdorf Men's
Celine
Piaget*
Christian Louboutin
Oxxford Clothes
Manolo Blahnik
St. John
Brioni
Graff
Spring Flowers
J. Mendel*
Santa Maria Novella
Allen Edmonds
Leiber
Carolina Herrera
Giuseppe Zanotti*
La Perla*
Robert Clergerie*
Roger Vivier
H. Stern
Barbour/Peter Elliot
Valentino*
Bonpoint
Oscar de la Renta

BY CATEGORY

ACCESSORIES

28 Leiber
Marc Jacobs Access.
27 Dunhill
26 Porsche Design
Coach

ACTIVEWEAR

27 Patagonia
25 Orvis
24 North Face
JackRabbit Sports
Capezio

BRIDAL

28 Saks Fifth Ave.
27 Mark Ingram Bridal

Vera Wang Bridal
Amsale
25 Kleinfeld

CHILDRENSWEAR

28 Spring Flowers
Bonpoint
27 Petit Bateau
Jacadi
Magic Windows

DEPARTMENT STORES

29 Bergdorf Goodman
27 Barneys New York
Saks Fifth Ave.
26 Henri Bendel
23 Bloomingdale's

---

* Indicates a tie with store above

DESIGNER CLOTHING: MEN'S

28 Ermenegildo Zegna
Brioni
Tom Ford
26 John Varvatos
Hugo Boss

DESIGNER CLOTHING: MEN'S & WOMEN'S

29 Hermès
Giorgio Armani
28 Valentino
Etro
27 Louis Vuitton

DESIGNER CLOTHING: WOMEN'S

29 Balenciaga
Chanel
Akris
28 Dior New York
Celine

DISCOUNTERS/ MASS MERCHANTS

22 Century 21
20 Loehmann's
Gabay's Outlet
18 Syms
S&W

EYEWEAR

28 Morgenthal Frederics
Alain Mikli
27 Oliver Peoples
H.L. Purdy
Robert Marc

HANDBAGS: DESIGNER

29 Hermès
Chanel
Bottega Veneta
27 Louis Vuitton
Gucci

HOSE/LINGERIE

28 La Perla
Fogal/Switzerland
Wolford
Eres
27 Agent Provocateur

JEANS

28 Barneys CO-OP
26 AG Adriano Goldschmied
25 Rogan
Atrium
24 Diesel Denim Gallery

JEWELRY: COSTUME/ SEMIPRECIOUS

26 Michal Negrin
25 Swarovski
Alexis Bittar
Fragments
22 Magnificent Costume

JEWELRY: FINE

29 Harry Winston
Van Cleef & Arpels
Mikimoto
Cartier
28 Graff

JEWELRY: VINTAGE

29 Fred Leighton
A La Vieille Russie
James Robinson∇
27 Stephen Russell
26 Aaron Faber

MATERNITY

26 Veronique
25 Cadeau∇
23 Liz Lange Maternity
22 Destination Maternity
19 Mimi Maternity

MENSWEAR: CHAINS

26 Rochester Big/Tall
24 Brooks Brothers
21 Banana Republic Men
20 Express Men
19 Casual Male XL

MENSWEAR: CLASSIC

29 Davide Cenci
Bergdorf Men's
28 Oxxford Clothes
27 Paul Stuart
Hickey Freeman

MENSWEAR: CONTEMPORARY

29 Jeffrey
27 Barneys New York
24 Camouflage
23 Scoop Men's
Rothman's

MENS/WOMENSWEAR: CHAINS

24 Lacoste
22 J. McLaughlin
20 Kuhlman
Sisley
J.Crew

NEWCOMERS (RATED)

28 Roger Vivier
Louis Féraud
Tom Ford
27 Leviev
3.1 Phillip Lim

SHIRTS/TIES

28 Turnbull & Asser
Robert Talbott
26 Charles Tyrwhitt
Thomas Pink
25 Ascot Chang

SHOES: CHILDREN'S

26 Tip Top Kids
25 Little Eric
24 Lester's
23 Ibiza Kidz
22 Great Feet

SHOES: MEN'S

29 John Lobb
28 Allen Edmonds
27 Barneys New York
a. testoni
26 J.M. Weston

SHOES: MEN'S & WOMEN'S

29 Tod's
28 Salvatore Ferragamo
Belgian Shoes
Walter Steiger
Warren Edwards*

SHOES: WOMEN'S

29 Jeffrey
28 Peter Fox Shoes
Christian Louboutin
Manolo Blahnik
Robert Clergerie

SNEAKERS

27 New Balance
26 Super Runners Shop
24 Niketown NY
Alife
New York Running

SWIMWEAR

27 Vilebrequin
26 Malia Mills Swimwear
Canyon Beachwear
21 Quiksilver
Billabong

TOILETRIES: DEPT. STORES

29 Bergdorf Goodman
28 Takashimaya
27 Barneys New York
Saks Fifth Ave.
Henri Bendel

TOILETRIES: SPECIALISTS

28 Santa Maria Novella
Bond No. 9
27 Molton Brown
Penhaligon's
Bathroom

TWEEN/TEEN CLOTHING

24 Lester's
22 Infinity
21 Berkley Girl
18 Paul Frank
16 Yellow Rat Bastard

VINTAGE CLOTHING

26 Fisch for the Hip
25 Michael's/Consignment
Ina
24 Designer Resale
22 Tokyo Joe

WATCHES

29 Chopard
Wempe
Audemars Piguet
28 Piaget
27 Franck Muller

WOMENSWEAR: BOUTIQUES

27 Kirna Zabête
25 Emily's
Stella Gialla*
24 Searle
Lily

WOMENSWEAR CHAINS: CLASSIC

24 Eileen Fisher
22 Talbots
21 Ann Taylor
20 Chico's
Ann Taylor Loft

24	Intermix
23	Scoop NYC

	Calypso
22	BCBG Max Azria
20	Anthropologie

TOP QUALITY: HOME/GARDEN

29	Buccellati
	Bernardaud
	Steuben*
	Frette
	Baccarat
	Pratesi
	Bergdorf Goodman
	Cartier
	Lalique
	Scully & Scully
	Georg Jensen
28	Moss
	Bridge Kitchenware
	Tiffany & Co.
	Asprey
	Waterworks
	Takashimaya
	Stickley, Audi & Co.
	Ligne Roset
	Yves Delorme*
27	Schweitzer Linen
	Barneys New York
	Christofle
	Simon Pearce
	B&B Italia
	Ann Sacks

	Roche Bobois
	Broadway Panhandler
26	Zabar's
	Simon's Hardware
	Michael C. Fina
	Avventura
	Country Floors
	Dean & Deluca
	Williams-Sonoma
	Harris Levy
	Charles P. Rogers
	Aero
	Carlyle Convertibles*
	Maurice Villency
	Krup's Kitchen/Bath
	Artistic Tile
	Michael Aram
	Sur La Table
	Bellora
25	Alessi
	Pompanoosuc Mills
	Urban Archaeology
	Charlotte Moss
	MacKenzie-Childs
	S.Feldman Houseware*
	Signoria*

BY CATEGORY

ACCESSORIES

29	Scully & Scully
28	Moss
26	Michael Aram
25	Charlotte Moss
	ABC Carpet & Home

APPLIANCES

26	Krup's Kitchen/Bath
25	Gringer & Sons
24	Drimmers
23	Quintessentials
22	Bowery Kitchen

BATH FIXTURES

28	Waterworks
27	Ann Sacks
26	Country Floors
	Artistic Tile
23	Davis & Warshow

CHINA/CRYSTAL

29	Bernardaud
	Steuben*
	Baccarat
	Lalique
27	Simon Pearce

COOKWARE

28	Bridge Kitchenware
27	Broadway Panhandler
26	Zabar's
	Dean & Deluca
	Williams-Sonoma

DEPARTMENT STORES

29	Bergdorf Goodman
27	Barneys New York
	Saks Fifth Ave.
23	Bloomingdale's
19	Macy's

FURNITURE

28] Stickley, Audi & Co.
Ligne Roset
27] B&B Italia
Roche Bobois
26] Aero
Carlyle Convertibles*

GARDEN

29] Takashimaya
25] Gracious Home
Tribbles Home & Garden
24] Smith & Hawken
23] Chelsea Garden

HARDWARE

26] Simon's Hardware
24] Dykes Lumber
23] Vercesi Hardware
22] Janovic Plaza
Beacon Paint/Hardware

LIGHTING

25] Oriental Lamp Shade
24] Gracious Home
Just Bulbs
Lighting By Gregory
23] Lee's Studio

LINENS

29] Frette
Pratesi
28] Yves Delorme
27] Schweitzer Linen
26] Harris Levy

NEWCOMERS (RATED)

26] Michael Aram
25] Charlotte Moss
Tribbles Home & Garden
24] Ankasa
23] Luceplan

SILVER

29] Buccellati
Cartier
Georg Jensen
28] Tiffany & Co.
27] Christofle

TILE

28] Waterworks
27] Ann Sacks
26] Country Floors
Artistic Tile
25] Urban Archaeology

TOP QUALITY: LIFESTYLE

29] Ghurka

28] City Quilter
Tender Buttons
Lyric Hi-Fi
Mrs. John L. Strong*
Smythson of Bond St.
Purl
T. Anthony
TUMI
Il Papiro
Montblanc
Bang & Olufsen
Seaport Yarn*
Downtown Yarns
Fountain Pen
Harvey Electronics

27] Louis Vuitton
B&H Photo-Video
Bose
String
Crane & Co.
Apple Store
Dempsey & Carroll
Babeland
Kate's Paperie

Arthur Brown & Bro.
Other Music
Trixie and Peanut
Sound by Singer
Whiskers

26] Stereo Exchange
Canine Styles
Neue Galerie NY
International Photo
Leather Man
Museum Arts/Design
Mary Arnold Toys
Joon
Kidding Around
Tekserve*
Toga Bikes*
Sony Style
Rita's Needlepoint
B&J Fabrics
Pet Stop
Stitches East
Adorama Camera
Greenwich Letterpress
Yarn Co.*
EMS

BY CATEGORY

ART SUPPLIES

26 Pearl Paint
25 Lee's Art Shop
New York Central Art
Blick Art Materials
24 A.I. Friedman

AUDIO

28 Lyric Hi-Fi
Bang & Olufsen
Harvey Electronics
27 Bose
Sound by Singer

CAMERAS/VIDEO

27 B&H Photo-Video
26 Adorama Camera
23 Alkit
22 Camera Land
21 42nd St. Photo

COMPUTERS

27 Apple Store
26 Tekserve
Sony Style
24 J&R Music/Computer
21 DataVision

FABRICS

28 City Quilter
Tender Buttons
26 B&J Fabrics
25 M&J Trimming
23 Zarin Fabrics

GIFTS/NOVELTIES

24 Met. Opera Shop
Delphinium
22 Dylan's Candy Bar
19 Kiosk
Alphabets

KNITTING/NEEDLEPOINT

28 Purl
Seaport Yarn
Downtown Yarns
27 String
26 Rita's Needlepoint

LUGGAGE

29 Ghurka
28 T. Anthony
TUMI
27 Louis Vuitton
26 Crouch & Fitzgerald

MUSEUM SHOPS

26 Neue Galerie NY
International Photo
Museum Arts/Design
Rubin Museum
25 MoMA Store

MUSIC/DVDS

27 Other Music
25 Generation Records
24 J&R Music/Computer
Academy Records
Colony Music

NEWCOMERS (RATED)

23 ModernTots
22 Salty Paw
20 Helio
19 Homage∇

PETS

27 Trixie and Peanut
Whiskers
26 Canine Styles
Pet Stop
25 Barking Zoo

SEX TOYS

27 Babeland
26 Leather Man
24 Eve's Garden
22 Pleasure Chest
19 Pink Pussycat

SPORTS

26 Toga Bikes
EMS
25 Gerry Cosby
Tent and Trails
Burton Store

STATIONERY

28 Mrs. John L. Strong
Smythson of Bond St.
Il Papiro
Montblanc
Fountain Pen

TOYS

26 Mary Arnold Toys
Kidding Around
25 FAO Schwarz
24 West Side Kids
Scholastic Store

TOP QUALITY: BY LOCATION

CHELSEA

29 Balenciaga
28 City Quilter
   Stickley, Audi & Co.
26 Williams-Sonoma
   Comme des Garçons

EAST 40s

28 Allen Edmonds
   Bridge Kitchenware
   TUMI
27 Paul Stuart
   Robert Marc

EAST 50s

29 Buccellati
   Harry Winston
   Van Cleef & Arpels
   Bernardaud
   Baccarat

EAST 60s

29 Steuben
   Frette
   John Lobb
   Chopard
   Hermès

EAST 70s

28 Christian Louboutin
   Spring Flowers
   Carolina Herrera
   Il Papiro
   Morgenthal Frederics

EAST 80s

28 Lyric Hi-Fi
   Barbour/Peter Elliot
   TUMI
27 Petit Bateau
   H.L. Purdy
   Schweitzer Linen*

EAST 90s

28 Bonpoint
27 Robert Marc
   Jacadi
26 Veronique
25 Annie Needlepoint
   S. Feldman Housewares*

EAST VILLAGE

28 Downtown Yarns
27 Kiehl's
   Whiskers
25 Arche
   New York Central Art

FINANCIAL DISTRICT

29 Hermès
28 Tiffany & Co.
27 Hickey Freeman
26 DeNatale Jewelers
   Thomas Pink

FLATIRON DISTRICT

28 Bang & Olufsen
   Waterworks
   Ligne Roset
27 Ann Sacks
   Trixie and Peanut

GARMENT DISTRICT

27 B&H Photo-Video
   Tourneau
26 B&J Fabrics
25 M&J Trimming
   School Products*

GRAMERCY PARK

26 Simon's Hardware
24 Park Ave. Audio
23 Vercesi Hardware
22 City Opera Thrift
   Vintage Thrift

GREENWICH VILLAGE

27 Aedes De Venustas
   Kate's Paperie
   Broadway Panhandler
26 C.O. Bigelow
   Canine Styles

HARLEM

26 M.A.C. Cosmetics
24 Carol's Daughter
23 New York Public Library
   Davis & Warshow
21 Head over Heels

LOWER EAST SIDE

27 Babeland
26 Harris Levy
24 Alife
   Altman Luggage
   Lighting By Gregory

MEATPACKING DISTRICT

28 La Perla
   Alexander McQueen
   Jeffrey
27 Apple Store
26 Stella McCartney

MURRAY HILL

28 Bang & Olufsen
27 Roche Bobois
25 Morgan Library
23 Shoe Box
22 Yarn Connection

NOHO

28 Bond No. 9
27 Other Music
26 Stereo Exchange
25 Atrium
   Blick Art Materials

NOLITA

28 Santa Maria Novella
27 Selima Optique
26 Malia Mills Swimwear
   Fresh
25 Lilith

SOHO

29 Chanel
   Georg Jensen
28 Peter Fox Shoes
   Moss
   La Perla

SOUTH STREET SEAPORT

28 Seaport Yarn
25 Met. Museum of Art
   Firefly Children's
22 Talbots
   Salty Paw

TRIBECA

28 Fountain Pen
26 Bu and the Duck
25 Issey Miyake
   Pompanoosuc Mills
   Rogan*

UNION SQUARE

27 Sound by Singer
26 Country Floors
25 Paragon
24 JackRabbit Sports
23 Virgin Megastore

WEST 40s

28 Allen Edmonds
   TUMI
   Harvey Electronics
27 Crane & Co.
   Arthur Brown & Bro.

WEST 50s

28 Manolo Blahnik
   Smythson of Bond St.
27 Kate's Paperie
   Suarez
26 Leonard Opticians

WEST 60s

28 TUMI
   Morgenthal Frederics
   Wolford
27 Bose
   Kiehl's

WEST 70s

28 Bang & Olufsen
26 Malia Mills Swimwear
   Super Runners Shop
   L'Artisan Parfumeur
   Tip Top Kids

WEST 80s

27 Schweitzer Linen
   Patagonia
26 Zabar's
   Avventura
   Greenstones

WEST 90s/WEST 100s

25 Albee Baby Carriage
24 Kim's Mediapolis
20 Metro Bicycles
19 Petco
18 Planet Kids

WEST VILLAGE

28 Christian Louboutin
   Bonpoint
   Marc Jacobs Access.
   Bond No. 9
27 Bathroom

OUTER BOROUGHS

BRONX

[24] Dykes Lumber
[23] Davis & Warshow
[21] ABC Carpet/Whse. Outlet
[20] Athlete's Foot
Loehmann's

BROOKLYN: BAY RIDGE/DYKER HTS

[22] Century 21
[20] United Colors/Benetton
[19] Circuit City
Casual Male XL
[16] KB Toys

BROOKLYN: BOERUM HILL/DOWNTOWN

[24] Flight 001
[23] Something Else
Dig Garden
Lucky Brand Jeans
[21] DSW

BROOKLYN: CARROLL GDNS./COBBLE HILL

[24] Lily
[22] Home & Haven
Ohio Knitting Mills
[21] Néda
[17] LF Stores

BROOKLYN: HTS/DUMBO

[26] M.A.C. Cosmetics
[24] Design Within Reach
[23] ModernTots
[20] Neighborhoodies
Housing Works Thrift

BROOKLYN: PARK SLOPE

[26] Clay Pot
[25] Firefly Children's
[24] Lily

Lion in the Sun
Dykes Lumber
JackRabbit Sports*

BROOKLYN: WILLIAMSBURG/GREENPOINT

[24] Academy Records
[22] KCDC Skate
[21] Triple Five Soul
[20] HH Design
Brooklyn Industries

BROOKLYN: OTHER

[27] Jacadi
[24] Corduroy Kid
Drimmers
Lester's
Carol's Daughter

QUEENS: ASTORIA/L.I.C.

[26] Simon's Hardware
[24] Dykes Lumber
[22] Costco Warehouse
Metropolitan Lumber
[21] Mimi's Closet

QUEENS: OTHER

[25] Stella Gialla
Bare Escentuals
[23] Clarks
Geox
Lush

STATEN ISLAND

[27] Apple Store
[25] Swarovski
Emily's
[23] Ethan Allen
Crabtree & Evelyn

TOP DISPLAY

29 Moss
Bernardaud
Ghurka
J. Mendel

28 Oscar de la Renta
Cartier
Van Cleef & Arpels
Graff
Takashimaya
Harry Winston
Waterworks
Christian Louboutin
Manolo Blahnik
Apple Store
Trixie and Peanut
Bathroom
Steuben
John Lobb
Dior New York
Versace
Piaget

27 Hermès
Valentino
Chanel
Giorgio Armani

Chanel Jewelry
Baccarat
St. John
A La Vieille Russie
Alexander McQueen
Leiber
Louis Vuitton
Agent Provocateur
Tiffany & Co.
Comme des Garçons
Frette
Jo Malone
Bulgari
Room & Board*
Smythson of Bond St.*
Ralph Lauren Layette
Bottega Veneta
Fred Leighton*
Michal Negrin*
Scully & Scully*
Yohji Yamamoto*
Gucci
Aedes De Venustas
Brioni
Carolina Herrera

ARCHITECTURAL INTEREST

Alexander McQueen
Apple Store
Balenciaga
Billionaire Boys Club
Cartier
Charlotte Moss
Comme des Garçons
Conran Shop
ddc domus design
Dolce & Gabbana
Donna Karan
Fendi
Henri Bendel
Hugo Boss
Issey Miyake

Jacob & Co.
Just Cavalli
Louis Vuitton
Neue Galerie NY
New Museum
Paul Smith
Prada
Ralph Lauren
Roche Bobois
Stella McCartney
Tom Ford
Urban Zen
Versace
Vitra
Yves Saint Laurent

HOLIDAY DECORATION

ABC Carpet & Home
American Girl Place
Barneys New York
Bergdorf Goodman
Bloomingdale's
Cartier
FAO Schwarz
Henri Bendel

Lord & Taylor
Macy's
Paul Smith
Ralph Lauren
Saks Fifth Ave.
Sony Style
Takashimaya
Tiffany & Co.

TOP SERVICE

28 Babeland	Bulgari
Oscar de la Renta	**25** Town Shop
Van Cleef & Arpels	Mikimoto
Harry Winston	Steuben
27 Oxxford Clothes	Aedes De Venustas
John Lobb	H.L. Purdy
J. Mendel	Vercesi Hardware
Graff	Asprey
Buccellati	Calling All Pets
Fred Leighton*	Leonard Opticians
Piaget*	Robert Marc
26 Baccarat	Chanel Jewelry
City Quilter	Turnbull & Asser
Gianfranco Ferré	H. Stern
Cartier	A La Vieille Russie
Wempe	Bond No. 9*
Warren Edwards	Paul Stuart
Ghurka	Audemars Piguet
J.M. Weston	Kiehl's
Frette	Carolina Herrera
Mark Ingram Bridal	Fountain Pen*
Chopard	John Varvatos*
Giorgio Armani	Lalique*
DeBeers	Super Runners Shop*
Dunhill	Walter Steiger*

IN-STORE DINING

ABC Carpet & Home	Kiehl's
Alessi	Lord & Taylor
American Girl Place	Macy's
Am. Museum/Nat. Hist.	Met. Museum of Art
AsiaStore/Asia Society	MoMA Store
Barneys New York	Morgan Library
Bergdorf Goodman	Neue Galerie NY
Bergdorf Men's	Rubin Museum
Bloomingdale's	Saks Fifth Ave.
Bond No. 9	Takashimaya
Build-A-Bear	té casan
Dean & Deluca	202
DKNY	Virgin Megastore
Henri Bendel	Whitney Museum

GOOD VALUES

Aerosoles
Aldo
Altman Luggage
Am. Eagle Outfitters
American Apparel
Anbar
Ann Taylor Loft
Babies "R" Us
B&H Photo-Video
Bath & Body Works
Beacon's Closet
Best Buy
Bis Designer Resale
Blick Art Materials
Body Shop
Bolton's
Broadway Panhandler
Brooklyn Industries
Burlington Coat
Carol's Daughter
Casual Male XL
CB2
Century 21
Children's Place
Container Store
Costco Warehouse
Crate & Barrel
Crumpler Bags
Daffy's
Dave's Army Navy
David's Bridal
Drimmers
Dr. Jay's
DSW
Filene's Basement
Fishs Eddy
For Eyes
Fossil
Frock
Gabay's Home
Gabay's Outlet
Gentlemen's Resale
Goldy + Mac
H&M
Home Depot
Housing Works Thrift
Jam Paper
J&R Music/Computer
K&G Fashion
Kartell
Kiehl's
Kmart

Kohl's
Korres
Kuhlman
LeSportsac
Limited Too
Loehmann's
Lowe's
M&J Trimming
Marshalls
Mavi
Mish Mish
Missha
MNG by Mango
Moscot
Muji
My Glass Slipper
Natan Borlam's
Nat'l Wholesale Liquid
Necessary Clothing
Nemo Tile
Nine West
Old Navy
Orchard Corset
Origins
Oska
Payless Shoe
Pearl Paint
Pearl River Mart
Petco
Petland Discounts
Pippin
Pookie & Sebastian
Pottery Barn
Prato Fine Men's Wear
Rainbow Sandals
Ray Beauty Supply
RK Bridal
Roberta Freymann
S&W
SEE Eyewear
Skechers
Swatch
Sweet Tater
Syms
Target
Tiny Living
T.J. Maxx
Training Camp
Uniqlo
V.I.M.
William-Wayne
Zara

SHOPPING
DIRECTORY

A&G Merch

▽ 21 | 21 | 19 | E

Williamsburg | 111 N. Sixth St. (Berry St.) | Brooklyn | L to Bedford Ave. | 718-388-1779 | www.aandgmerch.com

Though only steps away from its envelope-pushing big sister, the gallerylike showcase The Future Perfect, this Williamsburg home furnishings hot spot feels worlds away; yes, the "very cool mix of cool, modern furniture" and "unique" accessories is also cultivated with a keen eye for the edgy and the quirky, but much of what fills the expansive modern space (comfy sofas, animal print pillows, funky stencil kits, sleek desks, novelty rugs) is "creative" *and* utilitarian – and prices are also down to earth.

Aaron Basha ☒

25 | 22 | 20 | VE

E 60s | 680 Madison Ave. (bet. 61st & 62nd Sts.) | 4/5/6/F/N/R/W to 59th St./Lexington Ave. | 212-935-1960 | www.aaronbasha.com

The "cute baby-shoe charms" are the most emblematic item at this Madison Avenue standby and "still the best gift for the newborn's mom" or granny, but others admire the array of "enameled" and "jewel-encrusted" pieces "with a sense of humor", including "bedazzled frogs", flowers and lucky ladybugs that turn up on necklaces and bracelets; however, detractors are disenchanted by "too much of the same thing" and not-so-cute price tags; N.B. also closed on Saturdays.

Aaron Faber Gallery ☒

26 | 24 | 24 | VE

W 50s | 666 Fifth Ave. (53rd St.) | E/V to 5th Ave./53rd St. | 212-586-8411 | www.aaronfaber.com

"Fresh and inspiring", this glass-and-chrome gallery on West 53rd Street makes for "a great stop on the way to MoMA"; its large vitrines display "the best art jewelry in New York" – an "unusual mix of handmade and custom-made" studio pieces by the "newest artists" – along with "interesting estate" gems, "covetable" vintage watches and a classic to contemporary collection of bridal bijoux.

◪ ABC Carpet & Home ◑

25 | 24 | 17 | VE

Flatiron | 888 Broadway (19th St.) | 4/5/6/L/N/Q/R/W to 14th St./Union Sq. | 212-473-3000 | www.abchome.com

This Flatiron "fantasyland for fancy furnishings" is a "quintessential New York shopping experience" for "fashionable" home goods; while the current emphasis is on all things Indian and ecologically correct (e.g. organic linens), the "eclectic mix of old and new" includes chandeliers, "rich fabrics" and "unique furniture" from all over the world (like chairs upholstered in vintage Suzani tapestries) and is displayed over seven "sprawling" floors of "sensory overload"; count on "beautiful creations", "boggling costs" and a "fairly invisible staff."

◪ ABC Carpet & Home (Carpets/Rugs) ◑

25 | 22 | 18 | E

Flatiron | 881 Broadway (bet. 18th & 19th Sts.) | 4/5/6/L/N/Q/R/W to 14th St./Union Sq. | 212-473-3000 | www.abccarpet.com

There's an "overwhelmingly huge inventory" of flat-weave, sisal, needlepoint and wall-to-wall carpeting at this "funky", three-floor Flatiron "bazaar" that's filled with a "never-disappointing" collection ("more than you can possibly look at in a day") of rugs; while some dissatisfied surveyors snipe "you'll have more luck finding a pork chop in a kosher deli than getting help" here, most say the "prices" are "fair", especially the "deals to be had" on closeouts and "great remnants" in the "bargain basement."

ABC Carpet & Home Warehouse Outlet
21 | 14 | 15 | E

Bronx | 1055 Bronx River Ave. (Bruckner Expwy.) | 6 to Whitlock Ave. | 718-842-8772 | www.abchome.com

"If you can find your way here through the potholes" to the Bronx, supporters say it's "worth it if you are looking for big-ticket items like leather sofas", rugs, bedding or other home furnishings featured at the two original Flatiron icons; but you may have to "dig deep" and "sort the treasures from the junk" "to find bargains" in the "overwhelming", "hit-or-miss" two-story space.

Abercrombie & Fitch
18 | 19 | 13 | M

E 50s | 720 Fifth Ave. (56th St.) | N/R/W to 5th Ave./59th St. | 212-306-0936 ◑
Seaport | Pier 17 | 199 Water St. (Fulton St.) | 2/3/4/5/A/C/J/M/Z to Fulton St./B'way/Nassau | 212-809-9000
888-856-4480 | www.abercrombie.com

Bet "if Paris Hilton opened a store", it might be something like this "staple brand" for "the young and the svelte" with a Fifth Avenue flagship and a South Street Seaport branch where "all-American" "preppy" tees, jeans and minis serve as "good backbones for wardrobes"; grinches gripe you have to have the "figure of a Popsicle stick", and snipe about the "thunderous" music and a "modelesque" staff that's more focused on "looking good" than offering assistance, but the "under-21" clientele barely notices.

Abitare Ⓜ
- | - | - | E

Brooklyn Heights | 309 Henry St. (bet. Atlantic Ave. & State St.) | Brooklyn | 1/2/4/5/M/N/R to Court St./Borough Hall | 718-797-3555 | www.abitareshop.com

Named after the Italian verb for 'to live', this modern all-white home accessories shop on the ground floor of a Brooklyn Heights brownstone features a well-edited collection of "lovely items" (mostly handmade and from small companies) ranging from ceramics, glassware, vases, bowls, blankets and rugs to an exclusive line of Italian linens.

About Glamour ◑
- | - | - | E

Williamsburg | 103 N. Third St. (bet. Berry St. & Wythe Ave.) | Brooklyn | L to Bedford Ave. | 718-599-3044 | www.aboutglamour.net

It's all about mixing it up at this wacky, multipurpose Williamsburg warehouse space where vintage and 21st-century apparel and accessories from Europe and Japan collide in a colorful hodgepodge; take home a proper tea set or quirky coffee mugs, drink in the artwork on the walls or lose yourself in the racks of eclectic clothing culled from visionaries in the vanguard of fashion.

Abracadabra
21 | 22 | 18 | M

Flatiron | 19 W. 21st St. (bet. 5th & 6th Aves.) | N/R/W to 23rd St. | 212-627-5194 | www.abracadabrasuperstore.com

"Not for the faint of heart", this "top-of-the-line" Flatiron District spook shop is haunted by Halloween revelers and thespians alike, looking to scare up wigs, masks, "costumes and props galore" – not to mention more than a few "gross effects" too ("like the occasional severed head"); magician's supplies, clown paraphernalia, swords and gags round out the "extensive collection" of "fun stuff" that's "dangling everywhere" you look.

A Brooklyn Table ⓜ

| - | - | - | E |

Cobble Hill | 140 Atlantic Ave. (bet. Clinton & Henry Sts.) | Brooklyn | F/G to Bergen St. | 718-422-7650 | www.abrooklyntable.com

Everything you need for a handsome table can be found at this elegant Cobble Hill shop that sets a stylish example with its vignette displays consisting of fine china, crystal and linen that combine rich, traditional lines and colors with sleek, contemporary accents.

Academy Records ❶

| 24 | 13 | 15 | I |

E Village | 77 E. 10th St. (bet. 3rd & 4th Aves.) | 6 to Astor Pl. | 212-780-9166 | www.academy-records.com

Flatiron | 12 W. 18th St. (bet. 5th & 6th Aves.) | 1 to 18th St. | 212-242-3000 | www.academy-records.com

Williamsburg | 96 N. Sixth St. (bet. Berry St. & Wythe Ave.) | Brooklyn | L to Bedford Ave. | 718-218-8200 | www.academyannex.com

A "world of music for a pocketful of change" awaits classical connoisseurs at this "excellent" Flatiron "treasure trove" of used and new CDs and LPs as well as its rock, jazz and soul campuses in the East Village and Williamsburg (each a "vinyl paradise"); sure, service is sometimes "snooty", and it may "take digging" to unearth "potluck" "treasures" in the "cramped quarters", but its rapt pupils proclaim it a "sanctuary."

a. cheng ❶

| ▽ 19 | 20 | 20 | E |

E Village | 443 E. Ninth St. (bet. Ave. A & 1st Ave.) | L to 1st Ave. | 212-979-7324 ⓜ

NEW Park Slope | 152 Fifth Ave. (bet. Douglass & Union Sts.) | Brooklyn | M/R to Union St. | 718-783-2826 www.achengshop.com

Expect "exquisite pieces worth trekking" Downtown – or over the bridge – for at this "easygoing yet elegant" East Villager and its new Park Slope offshoot; "lovely" owner-designer Alice Cheng's tasteful eye renders such standards as silk print blouses, versatile shirtdresses and cardigans and coats "unique" and "classy enough to wear to work."

Acorn ⓜ

| - | - | - | E |

Downtown | 323 Atlantic Ave. (bet. Hoyt & Smith Sts.) | Brooklyn | 2/3 to Hoyt St. | 718-522-3760 | www.acorntoyshop.com

Take a "trip down memory lane" at this "refreshing" Atlantic Avenue toy shop where, instead of "plastic" playthings, you'll discover a "nice" selection of classic, handcrafted wooden and tin toys reminiscent of your own childhood; shoppers also go nuts for the small array of clothing from local designers, all charmingly displayed in a woodsy setting, and praise the helpful owners' "insightful advice."

Active Wearhouse ❶

| ▽ 18 | 15 | 16 | M |

SoHo | 514 Broadway (bet. Broome & Spring Sts.) | 6 to Spring St. | 212-965-2284

"Grab trendy sneakers" and "traditional activewear" (i.e. gym shorts) at this SoHo spot that also boasts a "large, chic selection" of casual wardrobe essentials for men and women from "today's urban designers"; "it's just like Transit" muse comparative shoppers – perhaps "because it's run by the same company."

NEW Adam
| | | | E |

Meatpacking | 678 Hudson St. (bet. 13th & 14th Sts.) | A/C/E/L to 14th St./8th Ave. | 212-229-2838 | www.shopadam.com
Rising young designer Adam Lippes (an Oscar de la Renta protégé) makes his retail debut with this Meatpacking District store, decked out like a smart, modern bachelor's pad with dark parquet floors, gold metal-and-wood display cases and leather benches; glasses, books and bibelots are scattered throughout, but the emphasis is on the classic, casually chic separates – boys' to the left, girls' to the right – plus jewelry and, of course, the pima cotton tees that first made Lippes' name.

Add Accessories ◐
| ▽ 20 | 18 | 23 | M |

SoHo | 461 W. Broadway (bet. Houston & Prince Sts.) | B/D/F/V to B'way/Lafayette St. | 212-539-1439
"Add stands for addiction" quip acolytes who can't pass this "adorable" SoHo accessories shop without stopping in – what with the "lollipop-colored bags" and "sweet" staff, you feel like a kid in a "candy store"; the "cute scarves", gloves, jewelry and hats from international designers also "never disappoint", amounting to "great" wardrobe additions.

Addy & Ferro ◐
| | | | E |

Fort Greene | 672 Fulton St. (bet. S. Elliott Pl. & S. Portland Ave.) | Brooklyn | C to Lafayette Ave. | 718-246-2900 | www.addyandferro.com
Named after owner Erica Hutchinson's parents, this Fort Greene boutique mixes funky local designers with name brands like Earnest Sewn and Tracy Reese, along with a few men's pieces; it's worth the subway ride, especially when the courtyard is open.

Adidas Originals
| 23 | 23 | 19 | M |

SoHo | 136 Wooster St. (bet. Houston & Prince Sts.) | N/R/W to Prince St. | 212-673-0398

Adidas Sports Performance ◐

NoHo | 610 Broadway (Houston St.) | B/D/F/V to B'way/Lafayette St. | 212-529-0081
800-289-2724 | www.adidas.com
"Beautifully designed", the "garage-themed" "Wooster location is the mother ship for all of us Adidas freaks" addicted to the "impressively complete", "old-school" Originals collection of clothing and "sneakers with flair", plus the "so-fly-it-hurts hip-hop" music makes it "feel like a party"; the "name speaks for itself" at the sleek Sports Performance headquarters on Broadway offering "wonderful quality" trainers and "straightforward" athletic apparel along with service that's "attentive, not pushy."

☑ Adorama Camera
| 26 | 14 | 18 | M |

Flatiron | 42 W. 18th St. (bet. 5th & 6th Aves.) | 4/5/6/L/N/Q/R/W to 14th St./Union Sq. | 212-741-0052 | 800-223-2500 | www.adorama.com
"If you want it, it's probably here" at this veritable "camera cornucopia", a "legendary" Flatiron "gem" that "has everything" new or used "for beginners and professionals" alike; the "knowledgeable staffers" "know what they're talking about" and offer "some of the best deals in the city"; those who say "oy vey" about the "disheveled environment" and "cluttered", "crowded aisles" may be happy to hear a major expansion is underway; N.B. closed Saturdays.

| | QUALITY | DISPLAY | SERVICE | COST |

Adrien Linford
22 | 24 | 21 | E

E 70s | 927 Madison Ave. (bet. 73rd & 74th Sts.) | 6 to 77th St. | 212-628-4500
E 90s | 1339 Madison Ave. (bet. 93rd & 94th Sts.) | 6 to 96th St. |
212-426-1500

These Upper East Side sister spots showcase "elegantly presented" collections of contemporary decorative arts and home accessories, such as chests, occasional tables and lamps, as well as jewelry; inspired mainly by Asian designs, the items make "unusual" "engagement and housewarming gifts."

Adriennes 🗹 Ⓜ
▽ 24 | 22 | 21 | M

LES | 156 Orchard St. (bet. Rivington & Stanton Sts.) | F/V to Lower East Side/
2nd Ave. | 212-228-9618

Adriennes Bridesmaid 🗹 Ⓜ
LES | 155 Orchard St. (bet. Rivington & Stanton Sts.) | F/V to Lower East Side/
2nd Ave. | 212-475-4206
www.adriennesny.com

"Sort of like shopping for a gown in your friend's apartment, this cozy store on the LES" and its companion shop for bridesmaids offer a "welcoming environment" for brides who "don't want the typical" "experience"; the "chatty owner" and her staff are "professional and excellent at what they do" while aisle-wear from the house-label and designers like Saison Blanche, Alvina Valenta, Jim Hjelm and Lazaro "makes your special day really special."

🆉 Aedes De Venustas ●
27 | 27 | 25 | VE

G Village | 9 Christopher St. (bet. 6th & 7th Aves.) | 1 to Christopher St./
Sheridan Sq. | 212-206-8674 | 888-233-3715 | www.aedes.com

Celebrities and fashionistas frequent this hip haunt, a "charming" "little fragrance lover's sanctuary" in Greenwich Village known for its "well-edited selection of perfumes, soaps", skincare products and candles from statusy, hard-to-come-by European brands such as Serge Lutens and Costes; the "knowledgeable staff" is "generous with samples", and if you are buying a present, you should spring for the additional charge and "have them gift wrap it" in their "beautiful" black-and-gold boxes topped with fresh flowers, which adds to the "divine" experience.

🆉 Aero 🗷
26 | 24 | 20 | VE

SoHo | 419 Broome St. (bet. Crosby & Lafayette Sts.) | 6 to Spring St. |
212-966-1500 | www.aerostudios.com

"Thomas O'Brien rules!" declare devotees of this midcentury modern studio in SoHo that exudes "great taste"; a stylish mix of "beautiful" accessories and furnishings like lamps, chairs and sofas, as well as "one-of-a-kind" pieces and "reproductions" "at top-market prices", makes this high-design destination "a reason to make novenas to the lottery deity."

Aerosoles ●
18 | 17 | 17 | M

Garment District | 36 W. 34th St. (bet. 5th & 6th Aves.) | B/D/F/N/
Q/R/V/W to 34th St./Herald Sq. | 212-563-0610 | 800-798-9478 |
www.aerosoles.com
Additional locations throughout the NY area

Perfect "for the girl on the go" seeking "well-fitting" footwear at a "medium price", this "king of comfy shoes" hits the mark, offering a "wide range" of styles that "feel like butter"; sure, they're "not Manolo's", and a handful harrumph they're still "too grandma for me", but most applaud the chain's "360-degree turnaround" toward more "fashionable" looks.

AG Adriano Goldschmied
`26` `23` `21` `E`

SoHo | 111 Greene St. (bet. Prince & Spring Sts.) | C/E to Spring St. | 212-680-0581 | www.agjeans.com

Guy and gal hipsters who covet this California-based brand scoop up colorful cords and form-fitting jeans from an "amazing selection" at its first East Coast store, a sprawling, skylit SoHo space with "extremely helpful" employees who "aren't afraid to tell you if that pair makes your butt look too big"; should your new five-pockets need altering, head to the espresso bar while the complimentary in-house tailor nips and tucks your purchase; N.B. the lower level is reserved for VIP fittings.

Agatha Ruiz de la Prada ⌧
`24` `23` `21` `E`

SoHo | 135 Wooster St. (Prince St.) | N/R/W to Prince St. | 212-598-4078

"Fabulous colorful designs" for bright young things and women too fill this Spanish designer's slim white SoHo expanse, the perfect showcase in which to peruse her fanciful, heart- and flower-strewn baby and children's clothing, "great kids' shoes" and accessories, plus nightdresses and footwear for mom in vivacious hues; but others admit that while they enjoy eyeballing the vivid palette, they "just wouldn't wear" anything quite so startling.

Agent Provocateur
`27` `27` `23` `VE`

SoHo | 133 Mercer St. (bet. Prince & Spring Sts.) | N/R/W to Prince St. | 212-965-0229 | www.agentprovocateur.com

"Make your man blush" at this "delightfully decadent", "vampy" British import in SoHo, where the "come-hither lingerie" – ranging from "kinky" briefs with suspenders to "ooh-la-la" bras – transforms you into the "seductive" "star of your own blue movie"; sure, you may feel a "bit naughty" scooping up the "sexy wares", but the "awesome" scanties have a "humorous touch" and no matter which "erotic" unmentionable you buy, the "provocatively" dressed salespeople "don't bat an eye."

Agnès B.
`23` `22` `17` `E`

E 80s | 1063 Madison Ave. (bet. 80th & 81st Sts.) | 6 to 77th St. | 212-570-9333

SoHo | 103 Greene St. (bet. Prince & Spring Sts.) | N/R/W to Prince St. | 212-925-4649

Union Sq | 13 E. 16th St. (bet. 5th Ave. & Union Sq. W.) | 4/5/6/L/N/Q/R/W to 14th St./Union Sq. | 212-741-2585

888-246-3722 | www.agnesb.net

Left Bank lovers feel right at home perusing the "beautiful French duds" displaying "gorgeous fit" and "timeless styling with attention to details" in crisp shirts, striped tees and smartly cut suits at this trio; but *sceptiques* sigh this "once-so-edgy" brand is now just "boring stuff for lots of bucks", served by an often "uptight" staff; P.S. the "landmark SoHo" locale also sells men's clothes.

A.I. Friedman
`24` `22` `18` `M`

Flatiron | 44 W. 18th St. (bet. 5th & 6th Aves.) | 1 to 18th St. | 212-243-9000 | 800-736-5676 | www.aifriedman.com

Set in a landmark Flatiron building, this "polished" art supply store offers a "fabulous selection" of "high-quality paper", "good portfolios" and "cool gifts" along with "great frames"; some quibble it's "more for the hobbyist than the practicing artist", but even they admit the stock is "well organized", the service "courteous" and prices "competitive."

Airline Stationery Ⓢ | 21 | 13 | 19 | M |

E 40s | 284 Madison Ave. (40th St.) | 4/5/6/7/S to 42nd St./Grand Central | 212-532-6525 | 800-218-5815 | www.airlineinc.com

"One of the few oldies to survive the Staples challenge", this family-run, "unbelievably well-stocked workhorse" near Grand Central offers "nothing fancy", just a solid selection of paper supplies that meet "obscure office needs" along with popular brands like Filofax; but aesthetes assert the owners of the "cramped" store "don't even know that the concept of display exists"; N.B. also closed Saturdays.

Ⓩ Akris Ⓢ | 29 | 25 | 21 | VE |

E 60s | 835 Madison Ave. (bet. 69th & 70th Sts.) | 6 to 68th St. | 212-717-1170 | www.akris.ch

You're sure "to find one special piece that's the highlight of the season" at this luxuriously spare East 60s emporium housing Zurich designer Albert Kriemler's "stunning" women's line of slim separates, "business suits that travel well" and trim trench coats in plush double-face wool; while indulgences such as these are "expensive even on sale", they're meant "to be worn forever"; N.B. the savvy take a look-see at Akris punto, the won't-drain-the-Swiss-bank-account sportswear line as well.

Alain Mikli | 28 | 25 | 23 | VE |

E 50s | 575 Madison Ave. (bet. 56th & 57th Sts.) | E/V to 5th Ave./ 53rd St. | 212-751-6085 Ⓢ
E 70s | 986 Madison Ave. (bet. 76th & 77th Sts.) | 6 to 77th St. | 212-472-6085
www.mikli.com

"The French do know from fashionable faces" attest trendsetters who descend on this East 70s–East 50s duo with a "great atmosphere" for "distinctive", "cutting-edge" specs with a Gallic "flair" sold by a staff that's "extremely helpful, not snooty"; the "beautiful modern frames" are both "funky" and *très chic* – *mais oui*, it's the "only eyewear to be seen in" – ensuring you'll "always get compliments."

Ⓩ A La Vieille Russie Ⓢ | 29 | 27 | 25 | VE |

E 50s | 781 Fifth Ave. (59th St.) | N/R/W to 5th Ave./59th St. | 212-752-1727 | www.alvr.com

"For the czarina in all of us", this fifth-generation family emporium on Fifth Avenue "is the only place to go" for "Russian imperial treasures" "that are some of the most beautiful and rare things on earth"; whether it's "authentic Fabergé", vintage jewelry, silver or porcelain, they are "all one-of-a-kind" pieces presented by "a very informed staff", "but bring a couple of suitcases of cash" if you plan on purchasing.

Albee Baby Carriage Co. Ⓢ | 25 | 9 | 19 | M |

W 90s | 715 Amsterdam Ave. (95th St.) | 1/2/3 to 96th St. | 212-662-7337 | 877-692-5233 | www.albeebaby.com

"If you can handle the cluttered" and "chaotic" conditions, this "dependable" West 90s baby gear outfit, in business since 1933, is "the place to go for full service" infant shopping; while it "can't compete with the scale and offerings of the superstores", you'll find "all the essentials" here, from "brand-name" clothing and cribs to strollers and toys, and "what they don't have", the "knowledgeable" staff "will order for you."

Albertine ◑ | - | - | - | E |

G Village | 13 Christopher St. (bet. Greenwich Ave. & Waverly Pl.) | 1 to Christopher St./Sheridan Sq. | 212-924-8515

Shoppers sing the praises of this Greenwich Villager, which "may be small", but has a super-feminine stash of silky dresses, inventive knits and lacy extras that add up to "more than you'd find at stores 10 times the size" due to the unerring eye of owner Kyung Lee, who curates wares from new and local designers like Christina Hatler and Sir; N.B. check out Claudine, a sweet slip of a sister store at 19 Christopher, and its newer South Street Seaport sibling, Leontine.

Alcone ⧄ | ▽ 23 | 13 | 19 | M |

W 40s | 322 W. 49th St. (bet. 8th & 9th Aves.) | C/E to 50th St. | 212-757-3734 | 800-466-7446 | www.alconeco.com

"Forget fancy displays and fawning salespeople", this "professional makeup artist's paradise" in Hell's Kitchen is the "real deal" for a "great selection" of stage greasepaint like Mehron and Ben Nye, plus European brands such as Visiora that suit "civilians" as well; it's "small and cluttered", but it's stocked with a moderately priced "secret stash" that "no one else in New York has."

Aldo ◑ | 16 | 17 | 15 | M |

Garment District | 15 W. 34th St. (bet. 5th & 6th Aves.) | B/D/F/N/Q/R/V/W to 34th St./Herald Sq. | 212-594-6255 | 888-818-2536 | www.aldoshoes.com
Additional locations throughout the NY area

"Good stuff disappears fast" at this "shoe lover's dream" where "fashion-conscious" guys and gals flock for "trendy, sexy" styles that "don't bust the bank"; "party girls" go "crazy for clubbing" looks while nine-to-fivers latch onto "sassy heels for work" or "loafers with edge" – you "can always count on something different" at this chain; still, protestors pout they're "not the most comfy" and rarely "last more than a season."

Alessandro Dell'Acqua ⧄ | ▽ 26 | 23 | 21 | VE |

E 60s | 818 Madison Ave. (bet. 68th & 69th Sts.) | 6 to 68th St. | 212-253-6861 | www.alessandrodellacqua.com

The couture cognoscenti get the cinematic riffs behind the modernist interior of this Madison Avenue boutique where the Naples-born designer Alessandro Dell'Acqua celebrates the earthy sophistication of movie icons like Sophia Loren and Gina Lollobrigida with filmy chiffon blouses, curvaceous pantsuits and diva dresses for those "wanting something different from their friends"; bring along your Marcello – they sell menswear too, as well as accessories.

Alessi | 25 | 25 | 19 | E |

NEW **E 60s** | 30 E. 60th St. (bet. Madison & Park Aves.) | N/R/W to 5th Ave./59th St. | 212-317-9880
SoHo | 130 Greene St. (bet. Houston & Prince Sts.) | B/D/F/V to B'way/Lafayette St. | 212-941-7300
www.alessi.com

For "all Alessi, all the time", head to the Italian company's Hani Rashid-designed SoHo space that's as "sleek" as its stock of "high-quality designer stainless-steel products for the home"; "pick up all the Graves and Starck you can afford" or find "fun" "housewarming gifts" and gadgets ranging from "the whimsical to the utilitarian", whether it be coffeemakers, cookware or tableware, then take a break from all the "cool" stuff by hitting the Joe coffee bar in the front of the store; N.B. the new Upper East Side branch opened post-Survey.

Z Alexander McQueen   28 | 27 | 23 | VE

Meatpacking | 417 W. 14th St. (bet. 9th & 10th Aves.) | A/C/E/L to 14th St./8th Ave. | 212-645-1797 | www.alexandermcqueen.com
The designer who made dresses with leather harnesses hip delivers a "fashion-forward" Meatpacking District flagship for jet-set types bent on emulating a "super-vixenish Joan of Arc or modern-day Lucrezia Borgia" via skinny pants, zippered jackets or body-conscious gowns; naturally, you need a "serious trust fund" to afford such "couture cutting"-edge creations, but if you lack one, you "can always browse and pretend."

Alexandros ⑤   - | - | - | E

Chelsea | 345 Seventh Ave., 4th fl. (bet. 29th & 30th Sts.) | 1 to 28th St. | 212-868-1044
E 50s | 5 E. 59th St., 2nd fl. (5th Ave.) | 4/5/6/F/N/R/W to 59th St./Lexington Ave. | 212-702-0744
www.luxuryouterwear.com
While not as high-profile as some, this "wonderful furrier offers all of the latest styles" profess fans – though critics counter the looks are "a bit long in the tooth"; still, there's no debate that you can get the goods, plus shearlings and home accessories, "at downtown prices", whether you visit the Chelsea showroom (where pelts are produced) or Midtown.

Alexis Bittar   25 | 24 | 23 | E

SoHo | 465 Broome St. (bet. Greene & Mercer Sts.) | N/R/W to Prince St. | 212-625-8340 | www.alexisbittar.com
"A gem of a store", this "fantastic SoHo space" showcases the eponymous jewelry designer and his original, "vibrant" Lucite creations, along with "very wearable", "wonderfully creative" semiprecious and costume pieces that appeal to celebs like Cameron Diaz, Madonna and Mischa Barton; a "helpful" and "accommodating" staff adds to the "colorful" experience.

alice + olivia   22 | 23 | 19 | E

NEW **NoLita** | 219 Mott St. (bet. Prince & Spring Sts.) | 6 to Spring St. | 212-334-7815
W 40s | 80 W. 40th St. (6th Ave.) | 7/B/D/F/V to 42nd St./Bryant Park | 212-840-0887
www.aliceandolivia.com
"Finally there's a place to find all of this adorable" line – a spacious black-and-white tiled boutique opposite Bryant Park – and now a new NoLita branch too; converts keep chanting "cute, cute, cute" about the capris, pants that make "your butt look amazing" and "skimpy tank tops" that comprise designer Stacey Bendet's "body-conscious" brand; the styles, while "pricey", "are worth the money" – however, they're also seemingly "sized for teens", so stay clear of the Dylan's Candy Bar goodies in the corner.

	QUALITY	DISPLAY	SERVICE	COST

Alife

24 | 24 | 17 | E

LES | 158A Rivington St. (bet. Clinton & Suffolk Sts.) | F/J/M/Z to Delancey/Essex Sts. | 212-375-8116 | www.alifenyc.com

Alife Rivington Club

LES | 158 Rivington St. (bet. Clinton & Suffolk Sts.) | F/J/M/Z to Delancey/Essex Sts. | 212-375-8128 | www.rivingtonclub.com

"If you haven't been, just go" to this LES double whammy "hidden behind a tinted door, with a doorbell as the only identifying characteristic" – if, of course, you're a dude seeking one of the "best selections of kicks" (especially at the Club), house-label clothing, accessories or a few T-shirts for the ladies; you may not feel "cool enough to shop" at this "original concept", which is "ironic because it is completely unpretentious."

Alixandre Furs ⊠

▽ 24 | 16 | 22 | E

Garment District | 150 W. 30th St., 13th fl. (bet. 6th & 7th Aves.) | 1 to 28th St. | 212-736-5550 | www.alixandrefurs.com

Since the early days of the 20th century, this family-owned furrier has been luring ladies to its large Garment District showroom to try on a plethora of pelts in "au courant styles" (they're the licensees for several designers, including Oscar de la Renta), at "well below uptown prices"; the "excellent" staff may also steer you toward their fur-trimmed coats and shearlings for men; N.B. appointments are highly recommended.

Alkit Pro Camera ⊠

23 | 17 | 18 | E

Flatiron | 222 Park Ave. S. (18th St.) | 4/5/6/L/N/Q/R/W to 14th St./ Union Sq. | 212-674-1515 | 800-285-1698 | www.alkit.com

"When you need camera advice and you're willing to pay for it", go "elbow to reel with" the experts at this "easy-to-shop" family-owned Flatiron superstore offering "personalized service" and a "manageable" selection; shutterbugs snap up and rent "professional" equipment, while other photogs focus on the outfit's "great quality film developing"; N.B. also closed on Saturdays.

Allan & Suzi

20 | 16 | 15 | E

W 80s | 416 Amsterdam Ave. (80th St.) | 1 to 79th St. | 212-724-7445 | www.allanandsuzi.net

It's "like your eccentric-but-glamorous aunt's attic" at this Upper West Side vintage/consignment store that's "crowded" with "cool", "crazy fun stuff" "in every style from mostly the '50s on" ("they can't use your normal clothes"); while "expensive", "it's worth a visit for the vibe as well as the products" – just hope the owner is "in a good mood."

NEW Allegra Hicks ⊠

24 | 24 | 21 | VE

E 70s | 1007 Madison Ave. (78th St.) | 6 to 77th St. | 212-249-4241 | www.allegrahicks.com

"Fitting right in with the upper Madison Avenue boutiques", this British transplant offers "beautifully displayed" "bohemian luxury" for your "next beach trip anywhere from Miami to Mozambique" – including "fashion-forward swimwear" and "bold-print" caftans "too pretty to wear at the pool" – plus home furnishings and Murano glassware "perfect for cocktails"; but opinions split on the service: "sort of snooty" say some, "makes you feel like a celeb" crow others.

	QUALITY	DISPLAY	SERVICE	COST

☑ Allen Edmonds
28 | 23 | 25 | E

E 40s | 24 E. 44th St. (bet. 5th & Madison Aves.) | 4/5/6/7/S to 42nd St./
Grand Central | 212-682-3144
E 50s | 551 Madison Ave. (55th St.) | E/V to 5th Ave./53rd St. |
212-308-8305
NEW **W 40s** | Rockefeller Ctr. | 1250 Sixth Ave. (bet. 49th & 50th Sts.) |
B/D/F/V to 47-50th Sts./Rockefeller Ctr. | 212-262-4070 ●
877-817-7615 | www.allenedmonds.com

"You get what you pay for" agree "well-heeled" "conservative"
types keen on the "comfortable", "classically styled handmade"
men's shoes sold at this Midtown trio by an "accommodating" staff
that "takes fitting" footwear "seriously"; "good old American quality
still wins out" – in fact your purchase may "outlast most Manhattan
relationships if treated properly" since their "recrafting service is
second-to-none."

Alpana Bawa ●Ⓜ
- | - | - | E

E Village | 70 E. First St. (bet. 1st & 2nd Aves.) | F/V to Lower East Side/
2nd Ave. | 212-254-1249 | www.alpanabawa.com

Lush, "lovely colors" and embroidery galore characterize the namesake designer's India-inspired merchandise in her East Village shop,
be it the "nicely" designed shifts and tunics for women, easy-fitting
shirts in vibrant, painterly patterns for men or line of hot-hued pillows
and other furnishings for the home.

Alphabets ●
19 | 18 | 16 | M

E Village | 115 Ave. A (bet. 7th St. & St. Marks Pl.) | 6 to Astor Pl. |
212-475-7250
G Village | 47 Greenwich Ave. (bet. Charles & Perry Sts.) | 1/2/3 to
14th St. | 212-229-2966
800-419-3989 | www.alphabetsnyc.com

"Fun, fun, fun" giggle gift-givers – "last-minute" and otherwise – of
this duo offering "clever cards", "novelty tees", "funky" yet functional
housewares and classic toys that are a "trip down memory lane"; the
"witty" merch mix makes these shops a "great source for gifts both
gag and gracious" and a must-"stop before a party."

NEW Alter ●Ⓜ
- | - | - | M

Greenpoint | 109 Franklin St. (Greenpoint Ave.) | Brooklyn | G to
Greenpoint Ave. | 718-784-8818 | www.alterbrooklyn.com

Fashionable guys and gals reach an Alter-ed state without spending
stacks of greens at this hipster haunt in Greenpoint; the vibe is cozy-
comfy, with brick walls and wood trim, while the goods are super-cool,
ranging from vintage cowboy boots and Schmoove shoes to Cheap
Monday skinny jeans and cardigans.

Altman Luggage
24 | 13 | 20 | M

LES | 135 Orchard St. (bet. Delancey & Rivington Sts.) | F/J/M/Z to Delancey/
Essex Sts. | 212-254-7275 | 800-372-3377 | www.altmanluggage.com

Whether you're hunting "for that last-minute bag" or just a "fair price
on good luggage", this "crowded, out-of-the-way" "legend" "beats all
others' selection", making it "worth the trip to the Lower East Side";
"forget how it looks" and just turn to the "product savvy" staff for "advice" about suitcases, "pens and Filofax" organizers, and remember
there's "lots of room for negotiation"; N.B. closed Saturdays.

	QUALITY	DISPLAY	SERVICE	COST

Amadeo by M+M Scognamiglio 🅢
▽ 20 | 21 | 18 | E

E 70s | 958 Lexington Ave. (70th St.) | 6 to 68th St. | 212-737-4100 | www.cameos.com

This tiny fine jewelry boutique, an Upper East Side offshoot of an Italian-based business, is devoted exclusively to cameos and "makes you wish you had more than one neck"; since 1857, members of the family-owned firm have been carving classic portraits from seashells that also turn up on pins, earrings, bracelets, belts and bags, but for the ultimate ego trip, you can commission a custom piece in your own likeness.

NEW Amalia
▽ 20 | 21 | 21 | E

NoLita | 44 Prince St. (bet. Mott & Mulberry Sts.) | N/R/W to Prince St. | 212-966-6813 | www.amalianyc.com

"Young and trendy" types out to achieve the perfect degree of whimsical chic deem this spacious newcomer with roomy dressing rooms the "total neighborhood place"; whether you're hunting for "girlie dresses that aren't too ruffled, short or slutty", basic or novelty tees, super-skinny jeans or that special accessory, chances are you'll find it among the enticingly colorful, "creative" displays at this "definite must" on the NoLita shopping circuit.

Amarcord Vintage Fashion ●
- | - | - | E

E Village | 84 E. Seventh St. (bet. 1st & 2nd Aves.) | 6 to Astor Pl. | 212-614-7133 Ⓜ

SoHo | 252 Lafayette St. (bet. Prince & Spring Sts.) | B/D/F/V to B'way/Lafayette St. | 212-431-4161

Williamsburg | 223 Bedford Ave. (bet. N. 4th & 5th Sts.) | Brooklyn | L to Bedford Ave. | 718-963-4001

www.amarcordvintagefashion.com

Surveyors are in accord about this trio of vintage clothiers – each one is a "fashionista's dream", specializing in "well-selected" women's and men's duds, shoes and accessories bearing European designer labels (think Fendi, Fiorucci, Gucci) from the '40s through the '80s; if a few carp "prices are high for used clothes", diehards retort you'll "find at least a few things you'll love"; N.B. the Williamsburg offshoot was recently spruced up while the East Village branch has become more of an outlet.

Ambassador Luggage 🅢
22 | 20 | 21 | E

E 40s | 371 Madison Ave. (46th St.) | 4/5/6/7/S to 42nd St./Grand Central | 212-972-0965 | www.ambassadorluggage.com

This "swank" Madison Avenue luggage emporium has "everything from soup to nuts" agree traveling sorts who fly over for "wonderful" wheeled, carry-on, hardsided suitcases, satchels, garment bags, duffels, toiletry kits, briefcases and other "good-looking", "name-brand" "stuff that lasts" from the likes of Hartmann, Tumi, Samsonite and ZeroHalliburton at "all price ranges"; it's "got just what you need", but a few wallet-watchers warn there aren't a "whole lot of bargains" on hand.

American Apparel ●
19 | 20 | 17 | I

NoHo | 712 Broadway (Washington Pl.) | N/R/W to 8th St. | 646-383-2257 | 888-747-0070 | www.americanapparelstore.com

Additional locations throughout the NY area

"Stock up on reasonably priced", "super-comfy" T-shirts and knits in "every color under the sun" at this ever-expanding chain appreciated for its "simple" displays and "plain" but "slightly sexy" styling; "left-leaning" sorts "love the idea" of shopping "relatively guilt-free" – the goods are "made in the USA" with "no sweatshop labor" – though a number wonder "what's with all the porn-style photos" on the walls?

American Eagle Outfitters ◑

17 | 18 | 17 | M

Garment District | 40 W. 34th St. (bet. B'way & 5th Ave.) | B/D/F/N/Q/R/V/W to 34th St./Herald Sq. | 212-947-1677

SoHo | 575 Broadway (bet. Houston & Prince Sts.) | N/R/W to Prince St. | 212-941-9785

Union Sq | 17-19 Union Sq. W. (15th St. & Union Sq. W.) | 4/5/6/L/N/Q/R/W to 14th St./Union Sq. | 212-645-2086

Kings Plaza | Kings Plaza Shopping Ctr. | 5249 Kings Plaza (bet. Flatbush Ave. & Ave. U) | Brooklyn | B/Q to Newkirk Ave. | 718-377-0342

Bayside | 212-55 26th Ave. (Bell Blvd.) | Queens | 7 to Main St. | 718-279-0651

Elmhurst | Queens Ctr. | 90-15 Queens Blvd. (bet. 57th & 59th Aves.) | Queens | G/R/V to Woodhaven Blvd. | 718-699-2874

Staten Island | Staten Island Mall | 2655 Richmond Ave. (bet. Platinum Ave. & Richmond Hill Rd.) | 718-494-2885

888-232-4535 | www.ae.com

It's "*Dawson's Creek*" with a dash of *The OC* at this "frat-boy" (and -girl) chain offering "all-American preppy" clothing for "the teen set"; the "laid-back attire" suitable for everything from "safaris to Starbucks" leaves "pocketbooks happy", especially items from the sale racks that keep 'em coming back despite quality that's "sometimes wanting."

American Folk Art Museum

23 | 20 | 20 | M

W 50s | 45 W. 53rd St. (bet. 5th & 6th Aves.) | E/V to 5th Ave./53rd St. | 212-265-1040

W 60s | 2 Lincoln Sq., Columbus Ave. (bet. 65th & 66th Sts.) | 1 to 66th St./Lincoln Ctr. | 212-595-9533 ◑ Ⓜ

www.folkartmuseum.org

Folks who favor "one-of-a-kind" "treasures" with a "touch of whimsy" laud this "little" "hidden gem" in Midtown and its larger gallery near Lincoln Center; the "interesting books" and "special" handcrafted contemporary items and reproductions ring in at a "range of prices", and the "lovely ornaments" make it "great" for holiday shopping.

American Girl Place

24 | 27 | 22 | E

E 40s | 609 Fifth Ave. (49th St.) | B/D/F/V to 47-50th Sts./Rockefeller Ctr. | 212-371-2220 | 877-247-5223 | www.americangirl.com

Truly a "little girl's fantasy come true", this "over-the-top" Midtown "experience", based on the Chicago original, offers "entertainment" for "hordes of 10-and-unders" who "have a ball" shopping for dolls with "enough of an educational bent to keep parents happy"; take your tyke and her toy to the hair salon for a new 'do, then "treat" them to a "lovely lunch" and a "delightful show" in the theater; if cynics snarl those dollies should "do my laundry" for such "big bucks", enthusiasts rejoin it's "worth it" to "see such smiles."

American Kennels

17 | 13 | 16 | E

E 60s | 798 Lexington Ave. (bet. 61st & 62nd Sts.) | 4/5/6/F/N/R/W to 59th St./Lexington Ave. | 212-838-8460 | www.americankennels.com

"A peep show" for puppy and pussycat voyeurs, this UES pet shop attracts "crowds" with window displays of "adorable" animals; the "supplies are excellent" and "the name means a lot" to pedigree proponents, but a few stray opposers posit the four-legged offerings are "priced way over market value."

American Museum of Natural History 22 | 21 | 18 | M

W 70s | Central Park West & 79th St. | B/C to 81st St. | 212-769-5100 | www.amnh.org

From "reasonably priced" "doodads" ranging from "candy-coated bugs" to "beautiful jewelry" and "handcrafted African and Asian textiles", this "bustling" Upper West Side museum store has "something for everyone"; naturally, it's strong on "inspirational" "scientific toys" and books for "smart kids", and even if some lament the "less-than-helpful staff", the "amazing selection" "warrants a look."

Amsale ☒Ⓜ 27 | 24 | 21 | VE

E 50s | 625 Madison Ave. (bet. 58th & 59th Sts.) | N/R/W to 5th Ave./ 59th St. | 212-583-1700 | www.amsale.com

Expect "quite a presentation" of "gorgeous" bridal "gowns fit for a princess" at this "sleek", by-appointment-only Madison Avenue "loft space" that's "small enough to be intimate, but with enough choice" "so you don't feel limited"; Amsale Aberra "fulfills every woman's inner Cinderella" with her "heavenly dresses", "fantastic bridesmaids' ensembles that are comfy and classy" and a new line of couture eveningwear; while admirers applaud the staff, a few huff "for the price, they could be more accommodating."

Anbar ☒ 21 | 11 | 11 | M

TriBeCa | 60 Reade St. (bet. B'way & Church St.) | 1/2/3 to Chambers St. | 212-227-0253

"It's every woman for herself" at TriBeCa's two-floor "warehouse-esque" discount den, a "secret treat filled with designer" footwear and "organized by color, making it easy to navigate"; "don't let the look of the place turn you off" – ambiance and "service are not why you schlep Downtown" – it's the "surprise brands" at a "great price", like Biviel, Delman, Donald J Pliner and even Gucci and Prada "finds", "lurking next to the mall-variety" kicks that keep "shoeaholics" on their toes.

Andy's Chee-Pees ◐ 15 | 10 | 11 | M

E Village | 37 St. Marks Pl. (2nd Ave.) | 6 to Astor Pl. | 212-253-8404
NoHo | 691 Broadway (bet. 3rd & 4th Sts.) | 6 to Bleecker St. | 212-420-5980

"Andy ain't so cheap" anymore virtually every surveyor says about this "cramped", "punk" pair of used-clothing purveyors in NoHo and the East Village – and, argue the antagonistic, "nothing to shout about as far as selection" goes either ("old T-shirts passing as vintage"); still, "if you can stand fishing through the crowded racks", "you can find unique crinoline skirts, army jackets" and "authentic bell-bottoms from 1975."

Angela's Vintage Boutique ◐ - | - | - | M

E Village | 330 E. 11th St. (bet. 1st & 2nd Aves.) | L to 1st Ave. | 212-475-1571

In a neighborhood (the East Village) chockablock with boutiques selling vintage clothing, this small shop stands out for its oft-changing inventory; though it's famed for flapper dresses, there's also plenty of

'50–'70s formalwear, along with shoes, jewelry and other accessories to provide the perfect period look for ladies.

Angel Street Thrift Shop
17 | 16 | 16 | I

Chelsea | 118 W. 17th St. (bet. 6th & 7th Aves.) | 1 to 18th St. | 212-229-0546 | www.angelthriftshop.org

"Search well and you shall find" "some decent things" amid the "new clothes", "cool accessories", bric-a-brac and furniture – all "organized with eye appeal" or in "inventive window displays" at this Chelsea thrift whose proceeds benefit people with substance abuse problems, HIV and mental illness; patrons praise the plain but "pristine environs" and "considerate" staff, though skeptics shrug off its new "more up-market" efforts ("place thinks it's Barneys but it's more like Goodwill").

Anik ☻
21 | 18 | 14 | E

E 70s | 1355 Third Ave. (bet. 77th & 78th Sts.) | 6 to 77th St. | 212-861-9840
E 80s | 1122 Madison Ave. (bet. 83rd & 84th Sts.) | 4/5/6 to 86th St. | 212-249-2417

Upper East Siders "walk in and want everything" in this "cut-above" duo jam-packed with "trendy" casual wear, "stylish" suits and "core pieces" like cashmere sweaters; insiders promote the sale annex in back "full of good surprises" at the Third Avenue location – it's a "gem for great bargains"; still, a handful huff that the mood is "sometimes chaotic" and the service sort of "snotty."

NEW Ankasa
24 | 24 | 22 | E

E 60s | 135 E. 65th St. (Lexington Ave.) | 6 to 68th St. | 212-861-6800 | www.ankasa.com

The husband-and-wife team that owns this new home-furnishings store in an Upper East Side townhouse brings a fashion textile background with Vera Wang and Oscar de la Renta to the table and it shows in "stunning" and "unique" embroidered or beaded pillows, bed linens and headboards, along with furniture, lighting and accessories; the collection is "high quality", "but then again it should be when you're paying $300 for a cushion."

Anna ☻
– | – | – | E

E Village | 150 E. Third St. (bet. Aves. A & B) | F/V to Lower East Side/2nd Ave. | 212-358-0195 | www.annanyc.com

Owner Kathy Kemp may have studied anthropology, but what she really digs is designing the body-conscious togs that fill the racks and banquette of this East Villager; street-smart Downtowners say her funky silhouettes "get better all the time" as they scoop up her versatile 7-way top in 4-ply silk, a shapely lace skirt or striped rayon dress.

Anna Sui
23 | 23 | 20 | E

SoHo | 113 Greene St. (bet. Prince & Spring Sts.) | N/R/W to Prince St. | 212-941-8406 | www.annasui.com

"Boho chic" reigns at this designer's "little, dark and glam" SoHo boutique with an "always jolly" "vibe that feels like the '60s", what with the lavender-red-black color scheme, "the scent of patchouli" and the "kaleidoscope of psychedelia" emanating from the "inventive", hippie-ish garb and "drag-queen makeup at the front" – "what every NYU girl wants to wear when dressed up"; N.B. scores may not reflect a post-Survey expansion in size and into menswear.

	QUALITY	DISPLAY	SERVICE	COST

Ann Crabtree ⊠

	23	19	21	E

E 90s | 1260 Madison Ave. (bet. 90th & 91st Sts.) | 4/5/6 to 86th St. |
212-996-6499

Devotees of this "neighborhood jewel" include Carnegie Hill moms, who proclaim it's "very hard to pass by" the "elegant", "well-chosen selection of tasteful", "good quality" women's dresses, separates and "great accessories"; "it's not your usual boutique" – the vibe is oh-so-"low-key" and the mix "interesting" – and chances are you'll walk away with a "one-of-a-kind" find.

Anne Fontaine

	27	25	24	E

E 50s | 610 Fifth Ave. (bet. 49th & 50th Sts.) | B/D/F/V to 47-50th Sts./Rockefeller Ctr. | 212-489-1554
E 60s | 687 Madison Ave. (bet. 61st & 62nd Sts.) | 4/5/6/F/N/R/W to 59th St./Lexington Ave. | 212-688-4362
SoHo | 93 Greene St. (bet. Prince & Spring Sts.) | C/E to Spring St. | 212-343-3154
www.annefontaine.com

"If God were a woman", he'd go to this "blouse heaven" trio to "indulge in the chic simplicity of a classic white shirt" (plus some black and cream versions), whose "steep price tags" are "worth every penny"; loyalists laud the "lovely saleswomen" and how the shops, suffused with proprietary perfume, "even smell luxurious", so while some snap "the selections seem limited", most attest "*j'adore Anne.*"

Anne Klein ◐

	-	-	-	E

E 60s | 655 Madison Ave. (bet. 60th & 61st Sts.) | 4/5/6/F/N/R/W to 59th St./Lexington Ave. | 212-317-2731 | www.anneklein.com

As part of a push to rejuvenate this once-beloved brand, Jones Apparel is rolling out a series of sleek stores and higher-quality goods; the modern Madison Avenue representative, all chocolate-accented white floors and light woods (actually, wallpaper), emphasizes smart leather accessories – shoes, belts, gloves and bags – and womenswear (mostly neutral-toned basics now).

Annelore

	-	-	-	E

W Village | 636 Hudson St. (Horatio St.) | A/C/E/L to 14th St./8th Ave. | 212-255-5574

West Village waifs wander into this wee whitewashed wonderland for designer/co-owner Juliana Cho's "creative, edgy" femme fashions made from distinctive fabrics, including menswear textiles like twill and tuxedo cloth, and finished with TLC details like handmade buttons; it's a "delightful haven for the blouse maven" – not to mention seekers of superbly tailored women's jackets and coats, hand-knit pullovers and dresses, tunics and shirts in flirty prints.

Annie & Company Needlepoint

	25	24	24	E

E 90s | 1325 Madison Ave., 2nd fl. (bet. 93rd & 94th Sts.) | 6 to 96th St. | 212-360-7266 | 888-806-7200 | www.annieandco.com

Stocking a "vast selection of hand-painted canvases" "for every skill level" plus "all the yarns and supplies you could ever need", this Upper East Sider ranks as "one of NYC's best needlepoint stores"; free instruction at two central tables and "great" natural light from the front picture window make it a "wonderful" place to ply your plies, especially since the "super-friendly" staff delivers "expert" advice and "top-quality finishing"; N.B.the ground-level space beneath the store now caters to knitters.

☑ Ann Sacks ⊠ | 27 | 26 | 18 | VE |

E 50s | 204 E. 58th St. (bet. 2nd & 3rd Aves.) | 4/5/6/F/N/R/W to 59th St./Lexington Ave. | 212-588-1920

Flatiron | 37 E. 18th St. (bet. B'way & Park Ave.) | 4/5/6/L/N/Q/R/W to 14th St./Union Sq. | 212-529-2800

800-278-8453 | www.annsacks.com

"Search no further" – the "best place" for "luxurious, unusual" stone, mosaic and leather tiles in "phenomenal colors and patterns" as well as "magnificent sinks and other fixtures" is this duo in the Flatiron District and the East 50s; cynics say the "snooty help is no help" and the "staggering prices" mean "you'll have to sell your first born", but the smitten simply sigh "it doesn't get more beautiful than this"; N.B. also closed Saturdays.

☑ Ann Taylor ◐ | 21 | 21 | 19 | M |

E 60s | 645 Madison Ave. (60th St.) | 4/5/6/F/N/R/W to 59th St./Lexington Ave. | 212-832-9114 | 800-342-5266 | www.anntaylor.com
Additional locations throughout the NY area

"Like your best friend", this "conservative" chain is "always there if you need it", peddling "perfect attire for all things corporate" – i.e. "not for fashionistas, but for their lawyers" – in sizes to "fit average" women, "not just stick figures" (including "great options for petites"); the "willing", "helpful" service alone makes it "worth shopping here", even if trendsters yawn "still boring after all these years."

☑ Ann Taylor Loft ◐ | 20 | 20 | 19 | M |

E 40s | 150 E. 42nd St. (Lexington Ave.) | 4/5/6/7/S to 42nd St./Grand Central | 212-883-8766 | 800-342-5266 | www.anntaylor.com
Additional locations throughout the NY area

"A less-expensive alternative to Ann Taylor", this "ubiquitous" women's chain draws the "office"-oriented with its "business-casual" clothing (including a "satisfying" petites selection) that's perhaps "not very exciting" but can be had "without breaking the bank"; though to stylesetters it's "double-dull", "conservative" types swear by it, especially at sale time (they "really know how to mark down a garment").

☑ Anthropologie ◐ | 20 | 24 | 17 | E |

Flatiron | 85 Fifth Ave. (16th St.) | 4/5/6/L/N/Q/R/W to 14th St./Union Sq. | 212-627-5885

SoHo | 375 W. Broadway (bet. Broome & Spring Sts.) | C/E to Spring St. | 212-343-7070

W 50s | Rockefeller Ctr. | 50 Rockefeller Plaza (50th St. at 5th Ave.) | E/V to 5th Ave./53rd St. | 212-246-0386

www.anthropologie.com

Bringing a "French flea market-y" look to "the masses", these "boho chic" chain links brimming with "folkloric", "flirty, frilly" women's clothing, "vintage-inspired" jewelry, home accents and "wonderful trinkets" are the next best thing to "your funky aunt's attic"; the "kitschy" "creative" mix is a "dream" "for the fabulous girl" who's "tired of basics", and while it's "pricey", the "amazing" (if "chaotic") sale section provides "salvation" for those "on a shoestring budget"; N.B. the two-floor Rockefeller Center branch features an art gallery.

| | QUALITY | DISPLAY | SERVICE | COST |

Anya Hindmarch
25 | 21 | 20 | E

E 60s | 29 E. 60th St. (bet. Madison & Park Aves.) | N/R/W to 5th Ave./
59th St. | 212-750-3974 🖂
SoHo | 115 Greene St. (bet. Prince & Spring Sts.) | N/R/W to Prince St. |
212-343-8147
www.anyahindmarch.com

For "lovely handbags with a witty twist", turn to this British designer,
the "Kate Spade of the U.K.", whose shops in the East 60s and SoHo
boast "cute signature bow purses" along with "elegant leather goods"
and shoes; "check out" the be-a-bag service that allows for "fun
personalization" – you can "be your own celebrity" and have "your picture" or even your pooch's put on your tote or clutch "so long as you
have the kind of money celebs have to afford it."

Apartment 48
21 | - | 20 | M

G Village | 59 Greenwich Ave. (Perry St.) | 1 to Christopher St./Sheridan Sq. |
212-807-1391 | www.apartment48.com

Though recently relocated from the Flatiron District to the Village,
this home-furnishings store is still "brilliantly laid-out", with rooms
"arranged like an actual" apartment and filled with "practical" and
"beautiful" home and personal accessories aimed at men, women
and baby in the bed, bath, kitchen and dining departments; the "interesting" collection includes linens, decanters, decoupage platters,
pasta bowls and pitchers.

A.P.C.
21 | 22 | 17 | E

SoHo | 131 Mercer St. (bet. Prince & Spring Sts.) | N/R/W to Prince St. |
212-966-9685 | www.apc.fr

Amis agree this "light, airy" SoHo store with wood plank floors is "very
Left Bank", with designer Jean Touitou's "classic" men's and women's
trousers, tees and "killer" denim jackets imbued with a "dose of French
attitude" – which also applies, alas, to the "too-cool-for school" clerks;
it may be "more expensive than you'd expect" for "modern" "everyday-
wear", but most say *oui* to the tasteful "basics" "because they fit so
well"; N.B. a discount offshoot, A.P.C. Surplus, recently opened at 33
Grand Street in Williamsburg.

🆉 Apple Store ◐
27 | 28 | 21 | E

E 50s | 767 Fifth Ave. (59th St.) | N/R/W to 5th Ave./59th St. |
212-336-1440
NEW Meatpacking | 401 W. 14th St. (9th Ave.) | A/C/E/L to 14th St./
8th Ave. | 212-444-3400
SoHo | 103 Prince St. (Greene St.) | N/R/W to Prince St. |
212-226-3126
Staten Island | Staten Island Mall | 2655 Richmond Ave. (bet. Platinum Ave. &
Richmond Hill Rd.) | 718-477-4180
800-692-7753 | www.apple.com

"The promised land" "for Mac fans", this "seductive" spot in a former
SoHo post office – as well as its newer offshoots outside the 59th Street
GM building, Staten Island and now the Meatpacking District too –
sports "sleek, quality merchandise", including "beautifully laid-out",
"cool" computers that "you're allowed to touch", not to mention a
"knowledgeable" staff, "great free classes" and a "hipster vibe"; in short,
this Apple's got "polish" – even if the "craze" for iPods and iPhones has
made this outfit "as crowded as Times Square."

| | QUALITY | DISPLAY | SERVICE | COST |

Arcadia ●
Chelsea | 228 Eighth Ave. (bet. 21st & 22nd Sts.) | C/E to 23rd St. | 212-243-5358 | www.arcadianyc.com

▽ 25 | 26 | 24 | M

"Glory hallelujah – a fun, affordable place to shop" in Chelsea praise proponents of this "well-presented" gift/lifestyle and cosmetics boutique that successfully combines "old-world service with New Age products"; home accessories like candles, crystal and vases mingle with costume jewelry, aromatherapy treatments and "all types of salves and lotions for beautiful men and women" in a two-story space.

Archangela
Williamsburg | 340 Bedford Ave. (bet. S. 2nd & 3rd Sts.) | Brooklyn | L to Bedford Ave. | 718-785-5591 | www.archangela.com

- | - | - | E

Swoop down to this sparsely decorated shoe heaven tricked out with gold light fixtures and wood floors on the southside of Williamsburg for a well-edited selection of eclectic kicks from names like Dru, Foranina and Modern Vintage, plus a few guys' styles from Macbeth; complete your look with accessories and handbags crafted by local talent and womenswear from emerging lines like Candela and Rojas out of LA.

Archangel Antiques Ⓜ
E Village | 334 E. Ninth St. (bet. 1st & 2nd Aves.) | L to 1st Ave. | 212-260-9313

- | - | - | M

Divided into two sections, this dark, narrow East Villager carries a magpie's nest of vintage merchandise – from clothing to housewares to costume jewelry; but definitely ask to delve into the drawers of the various chests and cabinets, which house a huge collection of old buttons and cuff links.

Arche
E 60s | 1045 Third Ave. (bet. 61st & 62nd Sts.) | 4/5/6/F/N/R/W to 59th St./Lexington Ave. | 212-838-1933
E 70s | 995 Madison Ave. (77th St.) | 6 to 77th St. | 212-439-0700
E Village | 10 Astor Pl. (bet. B'way & Lafayette St.) | 6 to Astor Pl. | 212-529-4808 ●
W 50s | 128 W. 57th St. (bet. 6th & 7th Aves.) | N/Q/R/W to 57th St. | 212-262-5488
www.arche-shoes.com

25 | 20 | 20 | E

"Perfect city shoes from Paris" insist boosters who make a beeline to this "candy-store" quartet for "funky, European" footwear in "fabulous colors" and "soft leathers" with "supremely comfortable" natural Latex soles; they're so "inventive" "I could take every pair home in a heartbeat" – they should call it the "Arche de Triomphe!"; but those who skip to another beat archly retort it's a "one-note concept" and too "expensive."

Arden B. ●
E 60s | 1130 Third Ave. (66th St.) | 6 to 68th St. | 212-628-2003
Flatiron | 104 Fifth Ave. (bet. 15th & 16th Sts.) | 4/5/6/L/N/Q/R/W to 14th St./Union Sq. | 646-638-0361
SoHo | 532 Broadway (bet. Prince & Spring Sts.) | 6 to Spring St. | 212-941-5697
877-274-6722 | www.ardenb.com

17 | 19 | 17 | M

"On top of the fashions" and "unafraid to be a little glitzy", this "sweetly sexy" chain appeals to "younger women who haven't yet graduated to real boutiques" but seek "great going-out clothes" and "just-right accessories" to keep them "in vogue but not broke"; though it can be "a bit pricey for the quality", savvy regulars join the "shopper's reward program" so they can afford to "buy it, wear it and throw it away" after "a season or two."

Area   - | - | - | M

Carroll Gardens | 196 Court St. (Wyckoff St.) | Brooklyn | F/G to Bergen St. | 718-222-0869
Carroll Gardens | 233 Smith St. (bet. Butler & Douglass Sts.) | Brooklyn | F/G to Carroll St. | 718-522-6455
Carroll Gardens | 252 Smith St. (bet. Degraw & Douglass Sts.) | Brooklyn | F/G to Carroll St. | 718-246-9453
Carroll Gardens | 331 Smith St. (Carroll St.) | Brooklyn | F/G to Carroll St. | 718-624-2411
Park Slope | 103 Seventh Ave. (bet. President & Union Sts.) | Brooklyn | B/Q to 7th Ave. | 718-636-7235
Park Slope | 45 Fifth Ave. (Bergen St.) | Brooklyn | 2/3 to Bergen St. | 718-230-7495
www.areabrooklyn.com

Yoginis, health nuts and earthy mamas congregate at these children's emporiums sprinkled throughout Carroll Gardens and Park Slope – part of the Area spa, yoga studio and retail family – to check out the eclectic offerings; rifle through the racks of organic kids' apparel at some branches, then head to other links to check out the imported toys, including wooden guitars and ant farms, or test drive the Bugaboos.

Armani Casa Ⓜ   25 | 25 | 17 | VE

SoHo | 97 Greene St. (bet. Prince & Spring Sts.) | N/R/W to Prince St. | 212-334-1271 | www.armanicasa.com

"What doesn't Armani do well?" ask admirers of the Italian icon's "rarefied" take on home furnishings as displayed at this "sleek", skylit SoHo space; his "gorgeous minimalist" tableware, furniture and accessories include hand-blown Murano glass vases and leather side tables and make for "an art gallery of a store, with prices to match."

Artbag Ⓢ   24 | 17 | 23 | E

E 80s | 1130 Madison Ave. (84th St.) | 4/5/6 to 86th St. | 212-744-2720 | www.artbag.com

"Unique" handbags and accessories in "rich" Italian "leathers and exotic skins" at "all sorts of prices" line the maple cabinets of this East 80s brownstone; "even better" is the repair service declare loyalists who crown this 75-year-old family-run outfit "great merchants" thanks to a staff, including European-trained craftsmen, that's "not above" "giving that damaged bag new life" "rather than pushing a sale."

Artemide Ⓢ   ▽ 27 | 23 | 23 | E

SoHo | 46 Greene St. (bet. Broome & Grand Sts.) | A/C/E to Canal St. | 212-925-1588 | www.artemide.us

"If you like modern lighting, this is the place" swear supporters of this SoHo showroom for the "high-end" namesake Milanese company; many of its products, like the Boalum table lamp that's shaped like a snake, are in museum collections, so while it's expensive, even wallet-watchers window shop here "for design ideas."

	QUALITY	DISPLAY	SERVICE	COST

☒ Arthur Brown & Brother ☒ | 27 | 22 | 24 | E

W 40s | 2 W. 46th St. (bet. 5th & 6th Aves.) | B/D/F/V to 47-50th Sts./
Rockefeller Ctr. | 212-575-5555 | 800-772-7367 | www.artbrown.com
Since 1924, this "class act" stationer near Rockefeller Center has offered an "amazing selection of inks", "paper ephemera", art supplies
and "a great framing department"; still, some say the staff "can vary
from the service-oriented to the sales-oriented."

Arthur's Invitations and Prints ● | ▽ 21 | 19 | 23 | M

G Village | 13 E. 13th St. (bet. 5th Ave. & University Pl.) | 4/5/6/L/N/Q/R/
W to 14th St./Union Sq. | 212-807-6502 | www.arthursinvitations.com
Party animals as well as brides and grooms promise you'll find "everything but the caterer and florist" at this soaring Greenwich Village stationery shop offering custom invitations and printing, thank you notes
and table placecards, plus Larsen-Juhl designer framing; the staff is
"helpful but not intrusive", serving everyone from the graphically oriented Parsons crowd to locals like Susan Sarandon.

☒ Artistic Tile ☒ | 26 | 23 | 18 | E

E 50s | 150 E. 58th St. (bet. Lexington & 3rd Aves.) | 4/5/6/F/N/R/W to
59th St./Lexington Ave. | 212-838-3222
Flatiron | 38 W. 21st St. (bet. 5th & 6th Aves.) | 1 to 23rd St. | 212-727-9331
800-260-8646 | www.artistictile.com
"Artistic" vignette-style displays of glass, metal and porcelain tiles
"provide excellent design inspiration" and show off the "enormous
range" of "quality products" in these East 50s and Flatiron stores; still,
some say it's best to "know what you are looking for" because the
"snooty" staff is "not accommodating."

Artsee | - | - | - | VE

Meatpacking | 863 Washington St. (bet. 13th & 14th Sts.) | A/C/E/L to
14th St./8th Ave. | 212-414-0900 | www.artseeeyewear.com
"I could find fab frames for every day of the week" vow visionaries who
anoint this "service-oriented" Meatpacking District spectacle shop
one of "the greatest in the city" – and "one of the few that's not part of
a dreaded chain"; "not only can you shop for eyewear", choosing from
an "amazing selection" of vintage, designer and custom-made styles,
"you can also see great artwork" since it doubles as a gallery.

Ascot Chang ☒ | 25 | - | 24 | VE

W 50s | 110 Central Park S. (bet. 6th & 7th Aves.) | N/Q/R/W to 57th St. |
212-759-3333 | 800-486-9966 | www.ascotchang.com
"You surely pay a premium" at this "premier shirt shop" that recently
relocated to Central Park South, but most men say "the money's worth
it" to get a garment "as you like it", custom-made Shanghainese-style
from the "finest fabrics" and with "superior craftsmanship"; there's
also a "conservative collection" of ready-made button-downs and accessories including, yes, ascots.

NEW Asha Veza ●Ⓜ | - | - | - | E

Park Slope | 69 Fifth Ave. (bet. St. Marks Pl. & Warren St.) | Brooklyn |
2/3 to Bergen St. | 718-783-2742
Buy yourself a unique, brightly colored embroidered dress, waistcoat
or quilted jacket from Bosnian and Indian designers at this spacious
new Park Slope shop and you'll actually be doing the world some good;

the lively array of labor-intensive womenswear is made by former victims of human trafficking who've been trained as seamstresses and all of the profits go toward fighting this abusive practice.

AsiaStore at Asia Society and Museum | 24 | 22 | 20 | E |

E 70s | Asia Society and Museum | 725 Park Ave. (70th St.) | 6 to 68th St. | 212-327-9217 | www.asiastore.org

This renovated Park Avenue museum offers a "fantastic selection" of "upscale" "Pan-Asian goods" including "beautiful ceramics", "wonderful jewelry" and "lovely textiles" for the "discerning eye" along with "impressive books"; even though some whisper the wares are "overpriced", most agree it's a "unique" resource for "unusual gifts."

☑ Asprey ⑧ | 28 | – | 25 | VE |

E 70s | 853 Madison Ave. (bet. 70th & 71st Sts.) | 6 to 68th St. | 212-688-1811 | 800-883-2777 | www.asprey.com

"Oh, to be in England" – but if you're not, this "very British" 226-year-old retailer's American flagship, recently relocated to Madison Avenue, makes a most "stylish" substitute; it's "a delight to stroll through", perusing "everything from flawless diamonds" ("copies of the Queen's baubles") to the "mother lode of silver accessories", "scarves that last for decades", "well-designed" mens- and womenswear, "exquisite" leather goods and rare books; though a bit "pretentious", the "service matches the quality" of the merch – just be sure to "go loaded."

Atelier New York | – | – | – | VE |

SoHo | 125 Crosby St. (bet. Houston & Prince Sts.) | N/R/W to Prince St. | 212-941-8435 | www.ateliernewyork.com

"Rare finds for men" make this dark shop, adorned in black (leather) and white (marble) a favorite of the fashion-forward set with a penchant for European apparel à la Ann Demeulemeester, Raf Simons or Rick Owens; its "great buyers" stock up on "pieces that can't be found elsewhere", even among the swarms of other SoHo specialty boutiques; N.B. plans are underway to relocate to Hudson Street.

a. testoni | 27 | – | 23 | VE |

E 50s | Sherry-Netherland Hotel | 781 Fifth Ave. (bet. 59th & 60th Sts.) | N/R/W to 5th Ave./59th St. | 212-223-0909 | www.testoni.com

"Give your feet the shoes they deserve" urge devotees of this family-owned Italian leather-goods luxury purveyor, relocated to the Sherry-Netherland, that radiates a certain "panache"; the "incredibly beautiful high-quality" footwear for men and women with "somewhat conservative taste" comes at such "incredibly high prices" even admirers may find themselves gasping for air, but they're "so comfortable" you almost "don't mind" shelling out the big bucks.

Athlete's Foot, The | 20 | 16 | 15 | M |

Bronx | 2467 Grand Concourse (E. 188th St.) | B/D to 182nd/183rd Sts. | 718-733-1427 ☀

Bronx | 2918 Third Ave. (Westchester Ave.) | 2/5 to 3rd Ave./149th St. | 718-292-3390 ☀

Bronx | 300 E. Fordham Rd. (E. Kingsbridge Rd.) | 4 to Fordham Rd. | 718-367-2502 ☀

East NY | 1053-1055 Liberty Ave. (bet. Crescent & Hemlock Sts.) | Brooklyn | A to Grant Ave. | 718-235-3401

(continued)

(continued)

Athlete's Foot, The

Flushing | 136-92 Roosevelt Ave. (Main St.) | Queens | 7 to Main St. |
718-762-6684 ●

Jamaica | 163-11 Jamaica Ave. (163rd St.) | Queens | E/J/Z to
Jamaica Ctr. Parsons/Archer | 718-883-9300 ●
888-801-9157 | www.theathletesfoot.com

"The dizzying variety" of "all the latest sneakers" at these chain links
"is almost too much" assert sports buffs, "until you speak to a salesperson, who can narrow down the selection, based on your feet's
shape, and your personal needs"; but critics caution that the "personnel is not fully knowledgeable" and snipe that the stores are "unattrac-
tive", making it a low-on-the-rung "choice for New Yorkers."

Atrium ●   25 | 20 | 15 | E

NoHo | 644 Broadway (Bleecker St.) | 6 to Bleecker St. | 212-473-9200 |
www.atriumnyc.com

"Definitely one of the premier" "destinations" for "jeans fanatics", this
"clubby", "quintessential" his-and-hers NoHo "hot spot" staffed with
"attractive" help offers an "unrivaled selection" of "premium denim"
from the "most hyped brands" to the "more underground" labels; while
a few huff it's "organized by some mysterious system" and "madly expensive" to boot, most find the "amazing" assortment elevating – "if I
could pick one" stop "for my entire wardrobe, this would be it!"

Audemars Piguet   29 | 26 | 25 | VE

E 50s | 40 E. 57th St. (Madison Ave.) | N/R/W to 5th Ave./59th St. |
212-688-6644 | www.audemarspiguet.com

It's "a crystal-clear winner" declare devotees of this haute 1875 Swiss
horlogerie, with an outpost on East 57th Street; "exquisite timepieces"
(the "Royal Oak Offshore" sports watch is "a forever favorite") are
presented by a "gracious" and "informative" staff in a "class-act" atmosphere, making many "almost happy to drop $25k" on a purchase.

A Uno   ▽ 24 | 22 | 24 | E

TriBeCa | 123 W. Broadway (Duane St.) | 1/2/3 to Chambers St. |
212-227-6233

A Uno Walk

TriBeCa | 119 W. Broadway (bet. Duane & Reade Sts.) | 1/2/3 to
Chambers St. | 212-343-2040

Svelte, "trim women" and those with "full figures" saunter down to
this "wonderful" TriBeCa duo to peruse the "terrific" well-"curated
collection" of "avant-garde" puffy coats, unconstructed jackets,
cropped pants and sleek knitwear from labels like Annette Gortz,
Marithe + Francois Girbaud and Pierantonio Gaspari; the "competent
salespeople" help novices navigate the "edgier brands" so customers
always take home "pieces to keep forever"; N.B. A Uno Walk is
stocked with shoes from hard-to-find labels like Trippen.

auto ●   - | - | - | M

Meatpacking | 805 Washington St. (bet. Gansevoort & Horatio Sts.) |
A/C/E/L to 14th St./8th Ave. | 212-229-2292 | 866-568-2886 |
www.thisisauto.com

Husband-and-wife owners Renata Bokalo and Roman Luba apply an
artful eye to this minimalist Meatpacking District space stocked with

home furnishings ranging from boldly colored bedding to bath towels and pillows from John Robshaw and Missoni, as well as children's accessories like booties and hats; N.B. they've also expanded into the space next door to house their women's and men's jewelry and accessories.

Aveda Environmental Lifestyle Store | 26 | 24 | 24 | M |

E 40s | Grand Central, Park Ave. tunnel | 42nd St. (Vanderbilt Ave.) | 4/5/6/7/S to 42nd St./Grand Central | 212-682-5397 ☀
E 50s | 509 Madison Ave. (bet. 52nd & 53rd Sts.) | E/V to 5th Ave./53rd St. | 212-832-2416
E 60s | 1122 Third Ave. (bet. 65th & 66th Sts.) | 6 to 68th St. | 212-744-3113 ☀
Flatiron | 140 Fifth Ave. (19th St.) | 4/5/6/L/N/Q/R/W to 14th St./Union Sq. | 212-645-4797 ☀
SoHo | 456 W. Broadway (bet. Houston & Prince Sts.) | N/R/W to Prince St. | 212-473-0280 ☀
W 60s | The Shops at Columbus Circle, Time Warner Ctr. | 10 Columbus Circle, 3rd fl. (60th St. at B'way) | 1/A/B/C/D to 59th St./Columbus Circle | 212-823-9714 ☀
800-644-4831 | www.aveda.com
"Come for the products, stay for the tea" at this "eco-friendly", "moderately priced" beauty chain famed for "quality" products made from organic plants and flowers, "particularly the best shampoos and conditioners around" like the Sap Moss line "for taming frizzy locks" that's a Hollywood cult favorite; a "well-informed" staff presides over "soothing" settings that are "an instant escape from the stress" outside.

☑ Avventura | 26 | 20 | 18 | E |

W 80s | 463 Amsterdam Ave. (bet. 82nd & 83rd Sts.) | B/C to 81st St. | 212-769-2510 | 888-640-9177 | www.forthatspecialgift.com
It's clear that this Upper West Side purveyor of "unusual and distinctive" art glass and ceramics with an emphasis on "well-selected" Italian pieces from Murano and Deruta is a "perfect place" to find a "beautiful wedding gift"; the staff is "knowledgeable and nice", and while some say this "little gem" is "expensive", others reflect that "prices are high, but so is the quality"; N.B. closed Saturdays.

A.W. Kaufman | ▽ 26 | 9 | 21 | M |

LES | 73 Orchard St. (bet. Broome & Grand Sts.) | F/J/M/Z to Delancey/Essex Sts. | 212-226-1629 | www.awkaufman.com
"First impressions shouldn't scare you away from" this "too crowded", third-generation–run Lower East Sider that "may look like a rat's nest" but carries a "wide selection" of "top-of-the-line" European lingerie, undergarments, hosiery and "soft like buttah nightgowns" from "great names" like Chantelle, Hanro and La Perla at discount prices; the "schlep" Downtown is "worth the effort" – but only if you "don't mind changing without a formal dressing room"; N.B. the expanded inventory now also includes men's sleepwear and underwear and childrenswear.

A/X Armani Exchange ☀ | 19 | 19 | 16 | E |

E 50s | 645 Fifth Ave. (51st St.) | E/V to 5th Ave./53rd St. | 212-980-3037
Flatiron | 129 Fifth Ave. (bet. 19th & 20th Sts.) | N/R/W to 23rd St. | 212-254-7230
SoHo | 568 Broadway (Prince St.) | N/R/W to Prince St. | 212-431-6000
(continued)

(continued)

A/X Armani Exchange

W 60s | The Shops at Columbus Circle, Time Warner Ctr. |
10 Columbus Circle, 3rd fl. (60th St. at B'way) | 1/A/B/C/D to
59th St./Columbus Circle | 212-823-9321
Elmhurst | Queens Ctr. | 90-15 Queens Blvd. (bet. 57th & 59th Aves.) |
Queens | G/R/V to Grand Ave./Newtown | 718-271-4879
www.armaniexchange.com

For "a fun taste of the great Giorgio", hit "Armani's cheaper cousin", an
"urban-hip" men's and women's line that's an "edgier" version of
Emporio for those with "expensive tastes but not-so-big wallets"; perennial sales keep the "budget-conscious" coming back for "cool, casual"
clothing, but snobs suggest "X this out of your Rolodex" because
"what used to be a fabulous alternative" has "gone down-market."

Azaleas ●

`-` `-` `-` `M`

E Village | 223 E. 10th St. (bet. 1st & 2nd Aves.) | 6 to Astor Pl. |
212-253-5484 | www.azaleasnyc.com

"Cute, sassy" unmentionables share space with lingerie-inspired separates, loungewear, swimsuits and shoes at this "great" East Village
"neighborhood joint" featuring lots of "darling" designs like Deborah
Marquit's glow-in-the-dark undies, Wendy Glez's lace camis and hipster bikinis from Vix; add in plenty of fun accessories and it's easy to
see why brevity-boosters yell "yes!" to this one.

B8 ●

`-` `-` `-` `E`

Meatpacking | 27 Little W. 12th St. (bet. 9th Ave. & Washington St.) |
A/C/E/L to 14th St./8th Ave. | 212-924-8700

Purple-trimmed walls and sparkling chandeliers enchant customers at
this "undiscovered" Meatpacking "treasure" with a "cool downtown
vibe", where banker-turned–boutique owner Karine Bellil – who comes
from a family of eight (hence the name) – amasses menswear including
custom-made shirts and suits, jeans and organic cotton tees; she stocks
only one item per size, so you won't see yourself coming and going.

☑ Babeland ●

`27` `26` `28` `M`

LES | 94 Rivington St. (bet. Ludlow & Orchard Sts.) | F/J/M/Z to
Delancey/Essex Sts. | 212-375-1701
SoHo | 43 Mercer St. (bet. Broome & Grand Sts.) | 6/J/M/N/Q/R/W/
Z to Canal St. | 212-966-2120
800-658-9119 | www.babeland.com

"All questions and perversions are welcome" at New York's "best" sex
stores, a "delicious yet informative" woman-owned duo in SoHo and
on the Lower East Side, where "witty" signage, "beautiful displays",
"regular classes" and an "up-front" but "nonintimidating" staff (actually voted No. 1 for Service in this Survey) make browsing a "wide variety" of "quality" "erotica" a "stylish", "classy" experience; forget the
"dirty-old-man-in-a-raincoat" shtick – you'll "never feel sketchy" in
these shops that "take the smut out of intimate personal care."

ⓃⒺⓌ Babesta

`▽` `23` `16` `22` `E`

TriBeCa | 66 W. Broadway (bet. Murphy & Warren Sts.) | 1/2/3 to
Chambers St. | 212-608-4522 | www.babesta.com

The merch is "just so cute" it's tempting to buy everything" for the urban baby at this "hip" little TriBeCa tot shop, where even the most

jaded browsers are wowed by the "well-edited" assortment of teeny-tiny "rock 'n' roll" duds; get your shopping groove on with John Coltrane onesies, cheeky slogan tees, beanie hats and "kool", irreverent stuff from edgy brands like Monkeyboy, Pluto and Renegade Babe; yeah, it's "expensive", but it's all so "unique", plus the staff is "sweet."

Babies "R" Us ⊘

| 19 | 18 | 15 | M |

Union Sq | 24-30 Union Sq. E. (15th St.) | 4/5/6/L/N/Q/R/W to 14th St./ Union Sq. | 212-798-9905
Bensonhurst | 8973-95 Bay Pkwy. (W. 10th St.) | Brooklyn | D/M to Bay Pkwy. | 718-714-6400
Starrett City | Gateway Ctr. | 395 Gateway Dr. (bet. Erskine St. & Vandalia Ave.) | Brooklyn | A/C to Euclid Ave. | 718-277-3400
College Point | 139-19 20th Ave. (Whitestone Expwy.) | Queens | 7 to Main St. | 718-321-8166
888-222-9787 | www.babiesrus.com
This "all-under-one-roof" superstore chain is bursting with "everything for baby", including clothing for tots, furniture, toys, gear, diapers and other supplies at "moderate prices"; given its "warehouselike" proportions and "hard-to-find salespeople", though, it "can be a bit overwhelming for first-time parents" and registry customers, so the uninitiated should "shop with someone who knows what to look for."

NEW Baby Cottons

| 26 | 23 | 23 | E |

E 80s | 1236 Madison Ave. (89th St.) | 4/5/6 to 86th St. | 212-828-8979 | www.babycottons.com
Fashion purists herald the Madison Avenue arrival of this "lovely" South American import, specializing in simple, "luxurious", "good quality" Peruvian pima cotton newborn and infant clothing, crib bedding, bibs and blankets "softer than a baby's bottom", in "unusual patterns"; scoop up the "cute" goods along with silver spoons and keepsakes – what "great gifts"; sure, little ones "outgrow the stuff too fast" and the "prices may make you scream", but "it doesn't get much nicer than this."

babyGap ⊘

| 22 | 20 | 17 | M |

Garment District | 60 W. 34th St. (B'way) | B/D/F/N/Q/R/V/W to 34th St./Herald Sq. | 212-760-1268 | 800-427-7895 | www.gap.com
Additional locations throughout the NY area
"You can't go wrong" at this "shower or birthday gift" "mecca" for "adorable" "baby basics" that "wear well" and "don't break the bank"; "easy-to-browse" store setups mean it's a snap "to find something for each age" group, and bargain-hunters note there are "especially good deals" to be found on its ever-present "clearance racks", so never mind if service is "spotty" in some locations.

Babylicious

| – | – | – | E |

TriBeCa | 51 Hudson St. (bet. Duane & Jay Sts.) | 1/2/3 to Chambers St. | 212-406-7440 | www.babyliciousnyc.com
This "cute, little place" in TriBeCa carries just about everything a modern parent needs for bringing up baby in style from birth to four years, including a hefty helping of tees and onesies; gift-givers also appreciate the extensive selection of unique toys, books, bibs, blankets and other tiny trinkets.

	QUALITY	DISPLAY	SERVICE	COST

Ⓩ Baccarat ⊠
29 | 27 | 26 | VE

E 50s | 625 Madison Ave. (59th St.) | N/R/W to 5th Ave./59th St. |
212-826-4100 | 866-886-8003 | www.baccarat.com

For "the crystal of kings", connoisseurs head to this "elegant" East Side French "classic" whose "exquisite" and "exceptional" stemware, decanters, vases, candlesticks, chandeliers and jewelry set "the gold standard"; their pieces are "perfect for a wedding gift or corporate memento", but since prices are shattering you'll "need a large inheritance to buy anything."

Bag House, The
23 | 17 | 18 | M

G Village | 797 Broadway (bet. 10th & 11th Sts.) | N/R/W to 8th St. |
212-260-0940 | www.thebaghouse.com

Get your fill of "every bag you can think of and more" at the Village's "king of canvas" (and leather too) that's staffed with "cool, friendly" salespeople; choose from a "wide selection" of "utilitarian" backpacks, duffels, messenger bags and luggage from "well-known brand names" like Kipling, LeSportsac and Manhattan Portage; still, a smattering say the selection holds more appeal if you're "not too into fashion."

Baker Tribeca
▽ 28 | 29 | 25 | VE

TriBeCa | 129-133 Hudson St. (Beach St.) | 1 to Franklin St. | 212-343-2956 |
800-592-2537 | www.bakerfurniture.com

"A lovely store with gorgeous furniture", this 12,000-sq.-ft. TriBeCa duplex houses the more-than-100-year-old namesake Midwest manufacturer's collections, which range from traditional to the highly touted contemporary designs of Bill Sofield and Barbara Barry; many of the "quality" chairs, chests, sofas, tables and beds shine with old-world details such as hand-colored wood and gold-leaf, which are not tarnished by the high prices.

Ⓩ Balenciaga
29 | 26 | 21 | VE

Chelsea | 542 W. 22nd St. (bet. 10th & 11th Aves.) | C/E to 23rd St. |
212-206-0872 | www.balenciaga.com

It's a "cool" if slightly "strange garagelike" space in Chelsea that showcases the creations of Nicolas Ghesquière and reflects the tough-chic aesthetic he's applied to this venerable French fashion house; enthusiasts call the clothes "innovative and intellectual", but the real draw are the accessories – "ever heard of the motorcycle bag" sported by stars such as Uma Thurman and the Olsen twins? – that cause converts to "take the plunge for an incomparably designed" item that's "expensive but timeless (we hope!)."

Bally
28 | - | 24 | E

E 50s | 628 Madison Ave. (59th St.) | N/R/W to 5th Ave./59th St. |
212-751-9082 | www.bally.com

"Low-key consumers of high-end goods" fall for the "discreetly stylish and comfortable luxury footwear", what may be some of the "world's finest crocodile and ostrich accessories", "beautiful, classy" bags and even clothing at this his-and-hers "Swiss-made classic", now relocated back in their revamped orignal 59th Street digs; its "very conservative" image is bally-anced out with "some mod urban pieces intermixed" and an on-the-ball staff that's "efficient but not pushy."

	QUALITY	DISPLAY	SERVICE	COST

Bambini

27 | 18 | 20 | VE

E 80s | 1088 Madison Ave. (82nd St.) | 4/5/6 to 86th St. | 212-717-6742
The "classic", "beautiful" children's finery at this Madison Avenue establishment "sure beats what my parents dressed me in" agree admirers; the tony togs from Italian labels like Magil and pappa & ciccia reveal such "attention to detail" and are so darn "cute" they may even "make your baby say *ciao bella*"; still, the lire-lacking lament that the "out-of-this-world prices" are for "tiny billionaires only."

☑ Banana Republic ●

20 | 21 | 18 | M

E 50s | 626 Fifth Ave. (50th St.) | E/V to 5th Ave./53rd St. | 212-974-2350 |
888-277-8953 | www.bananarepublic.com
Additional locations throughout the NY area
Touted as "top Banana" by legions who consider it a "sure thing" for "basic business" staples with "easy classic styling", plus "cute accessories", this "ubiquitous" chain provides "lots of bang for the buck"; "easy-to-find-everything" store layouts and "usually helpful" service also contribute to its "standby" status, though even admirers concede "you'll see everyone else wearing" "the same clothes as you."

Banana Republic Men's ●

21 | 21 | 18 | M

Flatiron | 114 Fifth Ave. (17th St.) | 4/5/6/L/N/Q/R/W to 14th St./
Union Sq. | 212-366-4691
SoHo | 528 Broadway (Spring St.) | 6 to Spring St. | 212-334-3034
888-277-8953 | www.bananarepublic.com
A "safe place for men to buy clothing", these Flatiron-SoHo chain links allow guys to "stock up on work clothes" in styles ranging from "preppy staples" to "cookie-cutter metrosexual" office wear; trendsetters may yawn "boring", but for "clean-cut" types, the "well-made", "well-priced" "moderately cool" apparel and shoes are "a solid buy", especially during the "frequent sales", when staffers "keep the discount racks stuffed."

☑ B&B Italia

27 | 27 | 20 | VE

E 50s | 150 E. 58th St. (bet. Lexington & 3rd Aves.) | 4/5/6/F/N/R/W to
59th St./Lexington Ave. | 212-758-4046 | 🛇
SoHo | 137 Greene St. (bet. Houston & Prince Sts.) | N/R/W to Prince St. |
212-966-3514
800-872-1697 | www.bebitalia.it
"High-style Italian furniture" is the focus of this "very expensive", "classic modern" East 50s showroom, and its newer SoHo offshoot, which both feature "fabulous" designs, like the Charles sofa, in "great colors and forms", plus beds, armchairs and tables; but those who dwell in diminutive digs warn that most pieces are "scaled for an airport lobby."

☑ B&H Photo-Video-Pro Audio

27 | 20 | 21 | M

Garment District | 420 Ninth Ave. (bet. 33rd & 34th Sts.) | 1/2/3/A/
C/E to 34th St./Penn Station | 212-444-6615 | 800-606-6969 |
www.bhphotovideo.com
The "Disneyland of cameras", this "block-long" Garment District "oasis" boasts an "enormous", "fairly priced" selection managed with an inventive "tracking system" of "overhead bins" and overseen by an "educated sales force" that "turns the retail experience into an assembly line" (in a "great" way); still, some say the "staff is not always the friendliest",

while others claim the "busy-as-Grand-Central-at-rush-hour" setting makes them "feel like rats in a maze"; N.B. closed Saturdays.

⚡ B&J Fabrics ⑤   26 | 18 | 21 | M

Garment District | 525 Seventh Ave., 2nd fl. (38th St.) | 1/2/3/7/N/ Q/R/S/W to 42nd St./Times Sq. | 212-354-8150 | 866-354-8150 | www.bandjfabrics.com

"Well-organized" (with samples "on hangers so you can easily go through the racks") and "perfectly lit", this huge Garment District "mother of all fabric shops" offers a "stunning collection" of "upscale dress and theatrical" material ("interesting chiffons and sheers", "Liberty-print cottons"); the "helpful" "army of staffers" "really knows the trade", so it's "one of the best" options "for choice and service."

⚡ Bang & Olufsen   28 | 27 | 23 | VE

E 70s | 952 Madison Ave. (75th St.) | 6 to 77th St. | 212-879-6161
Flatiron | 927 Broadway (21st St.) | N/R/W to 23rd St. | 212-388-9792
Murray Hill | 200 Lexington Ave. (bet. 32nd & 33rd Sts.) | 6 to 33rd St. | 212-532-4787 ⑤
W 70s | 330 Columbus Ave. (bet. 75th & 76th Sts.) | 1 to 79th St. | 212-501-0926
www.bang-olufsen.com

Strictly "for the serious audio aficionado" who dreams of "stylishly sleek" "fantasy electronic toys" that are beyond "cutting-edge", this over-80-year-old "Danish firm has some of the most sophisticated" and "sinfully beautiful" audio-visual components around (the "clean look of the equipment" makes it "as fascinating 'off'" as when it's on); yes, the "prices are sky-high", but "wealthy" sorts insist the "personalized service" and "amazing" quality make it "worth every penny."

Barami ◐   16 | 16 | 16 | M

E 40s | 375 Lexington Ave. (41st St.) | 4/5/6/7/S to 42nd St./ Grand Central | 212-682-2550
E 40s | 535 Fifth Ave. (45th St.) | 4/5/6/7/S to 42nd St./Grand Central | 212-949-1000
E 50s | 136 E. 57th St. (Lexington Ave.) | 4/5/6/F/N/R/W to 59th St./ Lexington Ave. | 212-980-9333
Garment District | 485 Seventh Ave. (36th St.) | 1/2/3/A/C/E to 34th St./ Penn Station | 212-967-2990
www.barami.com

"Working babes" believe this brand is "worth checking out" because it "understands" that women want "sexy, but tasteful" clothes that "fit well and last", especially for petites; the "nice selection" includes "business-meeting"–"appropriate, but sassy" suits and "affordable dressy clothes"; P.S. if the salespeople get "pushy", just "tell them to back off."

Barbara Bui   27 | 26 | 21 | VE

SoHo | 115-117 Wooster St. (bet. Prince & Spring Sts.) | N/R/W to Prince St. | 212-625-1938 | www.barbarabui.fr

"Creative", "clever and a tad different" describes the style of this French-Vietnamese designer, whose gallerylike SoHo shop is as Zen-elegant as the "tall and sleek" followers who flock here for precisely cut pants, soigné suits, hip-high boots and heavenly handbags; "prices are a little high", *bien sûr*, but strapped-yet-smitten shoppers can always take home a bit of Bui in a perfume bottle.

| | QUALITY | DISPLAY | SERVICE | COST |

Barbara Feinman Millinery ⬤

23 | 21 | 23 | E

E Village | 66 E. Seventh St. (bet. 1st & 2nd Aves.) | 6 to Astor Pl. | 212-358-7092 | www.feinmanhats.com

Go for "stylish, edgy hats", "come out with jewelry" and "one-of-a-kind handbags" – "you never know what you'll find at this lovely little" East Villager done up with a chandelier and a "fun" retro flair; Fein-fans confide that the toppers are sometimes "eccentric but still very wearable", and what's more, they can be customized with "personal fittings", which exemplifies just one aspect of the "great service."

Barbara Shaum 🆂🅼

– | – | – | E

E Village | 60 E. Fourth St. (bet. Bowery & 2nd Ave.) | 6 to Astor Pl. | 212-254-4250

If you're finicky about your sandals, don't sidestep this East Villager, as it would be a shame to eschew Shaum's handcrafted numbers, many of which are custom-made to fit your tootsies to a tee; adding a personal touch to the experience, this cool, modern-day Geppetto cobbles her funky footwear in an on-site workshop, so take a peek, and while you're at it, pick up belts and buckles too.

🆉 Barbour by Peter Elliot

28 | 24 | 23 | E

E 80s | 1047 Madison Ave. (80th St.) | 6 to 77th St. | 212-570-2600 | www.barbour.com

Decked out like a hunting lodge – "all that's missing is the bird dog and the shotgun" – this "veddy" "preppy" upper Madison Avenue shop caters to "country gentlemen" and women who want to "nurse their nascent Anglophilia" with this impeccably made (since 1894) Brit brand of quilted jackets, tattersall scarves and the trademark waxed duffle coats; "there's nothing like" the "expensive but durable" microfiber macs concur acolytes – they're "all you can dream of" for "a drizzly weekend."

Bardith 🆉

– | – | – | VE

E 70s | 901 Madison Ave. (bet. 72nd & 73rd Sts.) | 6 to 68th St. | 212-737-3775 | www.bardith.com

For over 30 years the "knowledgeable staff" at this pricey Madison Avenue stalwart has been providing "fine pieces" of antique 18th-century and early-19th-century English and European porcelain and pottery, along with papier-mâché trays and period glassware, causing window-shoppers to proclaim "when I win the lottery, this will be one of my first buying stops."

Bare Escentuals ⬤

25 | 23 | 22 | M

E 60s | 1140 Third Ave. (bet. 66th & 67th Sts.) | 6 to 68th St. | 646-537-0070

Elmhurst | Queens Ctr. | 90-15 Queens Blvd. (bet. 57th & 59th Aves.) | Queens | G/R/V to Grand Ave./Newtown | 718-371-3724
800-227-3990 | www.bareescentuals.com

Its "like silk on my face" say supporters of the "excellent" makeup found at these East 60s and Elmhurst offshoots of the long-standing San Francisco–based chain; the focus is on their bareMinerals line featuring "natural-looking", preservative-free powder-based foundations, shadows and shimmers; "decent prices" and a "helpful staff" add to its appeal.

| | QUALITY | DISPLAY | SERVICE | COST |

Bark ⓜ

– | – | – | E

Downtown | 495 Atlantic Ave. (bet. Nevins St. & 3rd Ave.) | Brooklyn | A/C/
G to Hoyt/Schermerhorn Sts. | 718-625-8997 | www.barkshop.com

New design ideas come to light at this all-white gallerylike lifestyle
shop on Atlantic Avenue sparingly decorated with a fireplace and
fluffy throw rugs and boasting an eclectic array of finery for the home
or the discriminating owner; find the perfect gift among the Aarne
crystal glasses, Japanese tumblers, Laguiole wine openers and hand-
blown glass birds from Finland – then buy yourself a little something
too, like a standout piece of minimalist clothing.

Barker Black

25 | 24 | 21 | VE

NoLita | 198B Elizabeth St. (bet. Prince & Spring Sts.) | B/D/F/V to
B'way/Lafayette St. | 212-966-2166 | www.barkerblack.com

"Understated English good taste" is alive and kickin' at this black
brick-walled urban dandy's den, the NoLita stage for Ralph Lauren
alum Derrick Miller's much-heralded makeover of the 128-year-old
Barker Black footwear brand; on tap are "some of the finest handcrafted" "classic" wingtips, loafers, riding boots and spectators with
"a bit of grit" – slightly subversive "skull-and-crossbones" brogueing
and other "hip" rock 'n' roll–style twists, plus "edgy ties, hankies and
braces" carefully arranged on the coffee table.

Barking Zoo ❷

25 | 19 | 25 | M

Chelsea | 172 Ninth Ave. (bet. 20th & 21st Sts.) | C/E to 23rd St. |
212-255-0658 | www.thebarkingzoo.com

With the "best service" from a staff "as nice as your dog", it's no wonder
this "warm, cuddly" pet store is a "Chelsea institution" where even your
pooch is "ensured a fun shopping experience"; a "great selection" of specialty foods catering to "individual needs", unusual "duds" for fashion-
forward canines and "quality" supplies make it "worth every penny."

Barneys CO-OP

24 | 21 | 17 | E

Chelsea | 236 W. 18th St. (bet. 7th & 8th Aves.) | 1 to 18th St. |
212-716-8860 ❷

SoHo | 116 Wooster St. (bet. Prince & Spring Sts.) | N/R/W to Prince St. |
212-965-9964

W 70s | 2151 Broadway (75th St.) | 1/2/3 to 72nd St. | 646-335-0978 ❷
www.barneys.com

"Funky, fresh and for flat-bellied guys and gals" sums up the scene at this
trio, "the less intimidating" "side of Barneys", which offers relatively
"more affordable options" "for stylishly edgy fashion hawks" including
"by far the best denim selection in NYC", "hard-to-find" casual lines,
"the latest in accessories" and a "metrosexual paradise" of skincare;
those "over 30 with hips" opine it's "overpriced", and many slam a "staff
that's too hip to help the likes of you", but still, it's a treasure trove for
"trust-fund babies" "who want to look like downtown" types; N.B. the
Madison Avenue mother ship also boasts several CO-OP floors.

ⓩ Barneys New York ❷

27 | 26 | 20 | VE

E 60s | 660 Madison Ave. (61st St.) | N/R/W to 5th Ave./59th St. |
212-826-8900 | 888-822-7639 | www.barneys.com

Walking into this elite East 60s emporium is like "entering a cocktail
party – full of excitement and the possibility of naughty encoun-
ters" amid the "desirable goods and beautiful displays"; fashionis-

tas confirm it's like a "microcosm of the NY dream lifestyle", with "the edgiest looks from the best-known designers", "new" "pampering" cosmetics and "luxurious" accessories galore; some genuflect at the "slice of heaven" shoe floor, others kneel for the home furnishings department, and once "you convince the help that you're worthy, service can be quite good"; P.S. thanks to Simon Doonan, "the windows are beyond wonderful."

Bath & Body Works ◐

`19` `21` `20` `I`

Staten Island | Staten Island Mall | 2655 Richmond Ave. (bet. Platinum Ave. & Richmond Hill Rd.) | 718-982-8546 | 800-395-1001 |
www.bathandbodyworks.com
Additional locations throughout the NY area

Fans of this "bright", "fruity and fun" toiletries chain that's known for "a big variety of scents and body washes" that's "inexpensive" and "makes you feel like a kid again" are also pleased at the company's image upgrade, which includes a treatment line from Manhattan celeb dermatologist Dr. Patricia Wexler and the "brilliant addition of Bigelow products"; still, cynics sniff the stores' "sickly sweet smell" "overwhelms your olfactory senses'" and their cookie-cutter shelves make them "feel like a mall."

Bathing Ape, A
(aka Bape NY)

`▽` `21` `22` `15` `E`

SoHo | 91 Greene St. (bet. Prince & Spring Sts.) | N/R/W to Prince St. |
212-925-0222 | www.bape.com

This bright bi-level store in SoHo is as "cool as promised" profess both first-timers and bona fide sneakerheads; Japanese musician/designer/retailer Nigo's "limited-edition" T-shirts, streetwear, accessories and shiny conveyor belt of "hip, hip, hip" kicks attract men, women and kids who find the Wonderwall-designed interior, colorful merchandise and sometimes "silent staff" "intimidating and hilarious at the same time."

Bathroom, The ◐

`27` `28` `22` `E`

W Village | 94 Charles St. (bet. Bleecker & W. 4th Sts.) | 1 to Christopher St./Sheridan Sq. | 212-929-1449 | 800-856-9223 | www.inthebathroom.com

"Eye-catching" and "original" West Village bath-and-body boutique that's swimming in a sea of "the best brands" of "hard-to-find" "old-school and new-world" "upscale" beauty products; "everything is chicly presented" – from Lollia perfume, Olivina Napa Valley scrub and Gianna Rose Atelier seashell soaps to a cache of candles ranging from Rigaud to Seda France – and "the owner is a charmer."

Bblessing ◐

`▽` `21` `18` `18` `E`

LES | 181 Orchard St. (Stanton St.) | F/V to Lower East Side/2nd Ave. |
212-378-8005 | www.bblessing.com

"Young, hip men" say it's "surely a blessing to find" this Lower East Side boutique, with "cutting-edge fashion, art" and tunes from former music store occupant Breakbeat Science housed within its oxblood walls; fans applaud the tightly edited, "good-value-for-what-you-get" collection of Preen cashmere, denim from Surface to Air, Giacometti and Iliad and soft, cool tees, and dig the tongue-in-cheek sensibility – the upside-down objects suspended from the ceiling, the Parisian bar and a "secret back door" leading to a DJ-worthy stash of vintage vinyl.

| | QUALITY | DISPLAY | SERVICE | COST |

BCBG Max Azria

22 | 21 | 19 | E

NEW **E 40s** | 461 Fifth Ave. (40th St.) | 4/5/6/7/S to 42nd St./ Grand Central | 212-991-9777 🌓

E 60s | 770 Madison Ave. (66th St.) | 6 to 68th St. | 212-717-4225

Flatiron | 168 Fifth Ave. (22nd St.) | N/R/W to 23rd St. | 212-989-7307 🌓

SoHo | 120 Wooster St. (bet. Prince & Spring Sts.) | N/R/W to Prince St. | 212-625-2723

W 60s | 2003-2005 Broadway (bet. 68th & 69th Sts.) | 1 to 66th St./ Lincoln Ctr. | 212-496-1853 🌓

Staten Island | Staten Island Mall | 2655 Richmond Ave. (bet. Platinum Ave. & Richmond Hill Rd.) | 718-983-5938 🌓

866-518-2224 | www.bcbg.com

BCBG may be French slang for preppy, but the "conservative-with-an-edge" womenswear strikes a more seductive pose at this expanding chain where the staff usually "helps you buy the right thing"; while a "favorite" with "young-adult daughters", "most bodies are flattered" by the "colorful selection" of "party wear and office attire" ("although some suits are pretty risqué") and "ageless accessories" displayed in "high-energy presentations."

BDDW ⊠

- | - | - | VE

SoHo | 5 Crosby St. (bet. Grand & Howard Sts.) | 6/J/M/N/Q/R/W/ Z to Canal St. | 212-625-1230 | www.bddw.com

Under the arches of a high cathedral ceiling, this SoHo furniture showroom exhibits heirloom-quality beds, tables, chairs and floor lamps handcrafted out of American hardwood that proponents pine for; while this coveted collection is most certainly "not for the faint of wallet", enthusiasts assure that "what you can afford you will treasure" for a long time to come.

Beacon Paint & Hardware

22 | 15 | 23 | M

W 70s | 371 Amsterdam Ave. (bet. 77th & 78th Sts.) | 1 to 79th St. | 212-787-1090 | www.beaconpaint.com

The Stark family has helped Upper West Siders cover their walls for over 30 years, offering a full line of Benjamin Moore paints that can be custom color-matched from other brands, plus "reliable advice" to get novice DIYers started; it's a "cramped" beacon of convenience for "one-stop-shoppers" who stock up on everything from air conditioners to plumbing supplies, especially for early birds, who land at 7:30 AM for the weekday openings.

Beacon's Closet 🌓

19 | 15 | 13 | I

Park Slope | 220 Fifth Ave. (bet. President & Union Sts.) | Brooklyn | M/R to Union St. | 718-230-1630

Williamsburg | 88 N. 11th St. (bet. Berry St. & Wythe Ave.) | Brooklyn | L to Bedford Ave. | 718-486-0816

www.beaconscloset.com

"Bringing the best of the Midwest vibe to Williamsburg (the much larger of the two" locales) and Park Slope ("more mainstream"), these "hipster havens" offer "thrift shoppers" everything from "wacky party dresses to serious business suits"; while purists cavil the pieces "aren't actually vintage, just secondhand", most enjoy "fishing" through "rack upon rack" of "eye-poppers" for "dirt-cheap prices"; P.S. they buy used threads too, so you can "make and save a buck" at the same time.

| | QUALITY | DISPLAY | SERVICE | COST |

Beads of Paradise ⬤
| | 22 | 19 | 21 | M |

Flatiron | 16 E. 17th St. (bet. B'way & 5th Ave.) | 4/5/6/L/N/Q/R/W to 14th St./Union Sq. | 212-620-0642 | www.beadsofparadisenyc.com
"When you need a bead", heed the "awesome back room" of this "eclectic" Flatiron District "find" that beckons with "an overwhelming selection" that includes the largest collection of semiprecious stones in the city, as well as African and Asian artifacts hanging overhead; custom-made jewelry, plus re-stringing and repair services, are also part of the mix.

Beasty Feast ⬤
| | 24 | 20 | 25 | M |

W Village | 630 Hudson St. (bet. Horatio & Jane Sts.) | A/C/E/L to 14th St./8th Ave. | 212-620-7099
W Village | 680 Washington St. (bet. Charles & W. 10th Sts.) | A/B/C/D/E/F/V to W. 4th St. | 212-620-4055
www.beastyfeast.com
The "knowledgeable", "animal-loving" staff "never looks bored when proud 'pet parents' stop by to chat" at these two longtime West Village "favorites"; along with the "greatest selection" of chow and "all types of supplies", they offer grooming services and are affiliated with an adoption organization, Renaissance Project.

Beau Brummel ⬤
| | 22 | 22 | 19 | VE |

SoHo | 347 W. Broadway (bet. Broome & Grand Sts.) | C/E to Spring St. | 212-219-2666
W 70s | 287 Columbus Ave. (bet. 73rd & 74th Sts.) | 1/2/3 to 72nd St. | 212-877-3689
Named after the Regency dandy who popularized trousers over knee breeches in the early 1800s, these SoHo and Upper West Side men's stores offer "cutting-edge", "stylish European clothing", from ties to separates to suits with an "anti–Brooks Brothers" appeal; however, some find both prices and staff "a little too uppity."

bebe ⬤
| | 17 | 19 | 16 | M |

E 50s | 805 Third Ave. (50th St.) | E/V to 5th Ave./53rd St. | 212-588-9060
E 60s | 1127 Third Ave. (66th St.) | 6 to 68th St. | 212-935-2444
Flatiron | 100 Fifth Ave. (15th St.) | 4/5/6/L/N/Q/R/W to 14th St./Union Sq. | 212-675-2323
NEW **Murray Hill** | 1 W. 34th St. (bet. 5th & 6th Aves.) | B/D/F/N/Q/R/V/W to 34th St./Herald Sq. | 212-594-8205
W 60s | The Shops at Columbus Circle, Time Warner Ctr. | 10 Columbus Circle, ground fl. (60th St. at B'way) | 1/A/B/C/D to 59th St./Columbus Circle | 212-262-2690
Elmhurst | Queens Ctr. | 90-15 Queens Blvd. (bet. 57th & 59th Aves.) | Queens | G/R/V to Grand Ave./Newtown | 718-271-2323
Staten Island | Staten Island Mall | 2655 Richmond Ave. (bet. Platinum Ave. & Richmond Hill Rd.) | 718-697-0070
877-232-3777 | www.bebe.com
"If you want the 'in' look", this "young, fun" women's clothing chain "is the place" according to the "skinny minis" and "Pamela Anderson types" who sport its "dressed-up essentials" and racy "club wear"; down-to-earth detractors call the cut-"waaay-too-tight" threads "impractical" and complain that service "can be snooty", but even they concede when you want to "feel like a babe", this outfit's "bling and bedazzle" is hard to beat.

Beckenstein Fabrics & Interiors

- | - | - | M

Flatiron | 4 W. 20th St. (bet. 5th & 6th Aves.) | F/V to 23rd St. | 212-366-5142 | 800-348-1327 | www.beckensteinfabrics.com

Founded in 1918, this Flatiron dry-goods dealer specializes in custom draperies and reupholstered furniture (especially headboards), much of it constructed from scratch; the "selection is fab" and there's "a lot to look at" (remnants downstairs, special-ordered designer textiles upstairs), plus the staff is "willing and able to help you with questions and sample cuttings."

☑ Bed Bath & Beyond ◐

20 | 19 | 16 | M

E 60s | 410 E. 61st St. (1st Ave.) | 4/5/6/F/N/R/W to 59th St./Lexington Ave. | 646-215-4702

Flatiron | 620 Sixth Ave. (bet. 18th & 19th Sts.) | 1 to 18th St. | 212-255-3550

NEW TriBeCa | 270 Greenwich St. (Warren St.) | 1/2/3 to Chambers St. | 212-233-8450

W 60s | 1932 Broadway (65th St.) | 1 to 66th St./Lincoln Ctr. | 917-441-9391

Starrett City | Gateway Ctr. | 459 Gateway Dr. (bet. Erskine St. & Vandalia Ave.) | Brooklyn | A/C to Euclid Ave. | 718-235-2049

Elmhurst | 72-15 25th Ave. (72nd St.) | Queens | E/F/G/R/V to Roosevelt Ave. | 718-429-9438

Rego Park | 96-05 Queens Blvd. (Junction Blvd.) | Queens | G/R/V to 63rd Dr./Rego Park | 718-459-0868

Staten Island | 2700 Veterans Rd. W. (Englewood Ave.) | 718-984-2894

Staten Island | 2795 Richmond Ave. (Platinum Ave.) | 718-982-0071

800-462-3966 | www.bedbathandbeyond.com

"Household gadgets galore", all the "major brands" of bedding, a "newlyweds' dream" of cookware and "anything and everything else for the home" – "from Fido's food bowl to Hanukkah candles" – is "stacked to the ceiling" at this "warehouse-style" chain that's "like a 5-and-10 on steroids"; it's "forever popular" for its "forgiving return policy" and "long hours", and while "there are no bargains", "you won't take a bath" on prices either; still, some find the "cavernous" quarters "frightfully chaotic" – and sophisticates sneer the styles are "dorm-room chic" ("bed, bath and boring").

☑ Belgian Shoes ⓢ

28 | 22 | 25 | E

E 50s | 110 E. 55th St. (bet. Lexington & Park Aves.) | E/V to Lexington Ave./53rd St. | 212-755-7372 | www.belgianshoes.com

Like "slippers disguised as shoes", the "comfortable" his-and-hers "classics" at this East 50s "staple" (founded by Henri Bendel in 1956) are as "great for work as for around the city"; sure, "one hopes to own" many handmade loafers with tassels or bows "in any number of color combinations", but "if you can only splurge on one pair, you might want them to be Belgian"; P.S. they "keep banker's hours", closing at 4:30 PM and on Saturdays in summer.

Belle & Maxie ⓢ Ⓜ

- | - | - | E

Ditmas Park | 1209 Cortelyou Rd. (Westminster Rd.) | Brooklyn | Q to Cortelyou Rd. | 718-484-3302 | www.belleandmaxie.blogspot.com

From its retro tin ceiling to its neighborhood discussion nights, this Ditmas Park kids' outfitter strives to recapture the charm of an old-fashioned mom-and-pop shop; the merchandise is anything but old-school though, thanks to a generous serving of stylish picks, including snazzy shoes by See Kai Run and teeny-tiny graphic tees and patterned button-down shirts from indie labels like Fooey and Wonderboy.

Belle by Sigerson Morrison

| 22 | 22 | 21 | E |

NoLita | 242 Mott St. (bet. Houston & Prince Sts.) | 6 to Spring St. | 212-941-5404 | www.sigersonmorrison.com

When you "can't afford" the "real thing", strut over to this NoLita sliver of a shoe shop, home to Sigerson Morrison's diffusion line, dishing up a "funky" collection of "trendsetting" femme finds with "classic undertones", including the "cutest flats", that'll have you "looking good without completely blowing your budget"; there's "something for every stylish woman's wardrobe", but a few fuss that the pairs peddled here can "still leave the upper-middle-class person feeling broke."

Bellini

| 23 | 23 | 17 | E |

E 60s | 1305 Second Ave. (bet. 68th & 69th Sts.) | 6 to 68th St. | 212-517-9233

Staten Island | 363 New Dorp Ln. (bet. Clawson St. & Hylan Blvd.) | 718-667-0727
www.bellini.com

"If money is no object" when it comes to your little cherub, cruise over to these East 60s and Staten Island stores that peddle "amazing", Italian-crafted nursery and bedroom pieces made to "last long after kids need them"; still, the more price-sensitive scoff it's "not worth the investment."

Bellora

| 26 | 23 | 21 | VE |

SoHo | 156 Wooster St. (Prince St.) | N/R/W to Prince St. | 212-228-6651 | www.bellora.it

"Top-notch" luxurious linens and "pretty accessories" like waffle-weave robes in soft, sleep-inviting colors are "beautifully displayed" against whitewashed wood floors and walls in this soaring, sumptuously styled SoHo outpost of a Milanese establishment dating back to 1883; it boasts only the best for bed, bath and baby, but some wonder "can we afford to sleep in these sheets?" while they toss and turn over the "Euro prices."

Belly Dance Maternity

| - | - | - | E |

W Village | 548 Hudson St. (bet. Charles & Perry Sts.) | 1 to Christopher St./Sheridan Sq. | 212-645-3640 | 888-802-1133 | www.bellydancematernity.com

This Chicago-based chain with a branch in the West Village brings a boutique approach to pregnancy style, stocking an eclectic selection of figure-flattering maternity fashions from both established labels like Chaiken to up-and-coming brands like Juliet Dream; expectant moms can also scoop up skincare treats and diaper bags so fashionable they almost don't look like the real thing.

Beneath ●Ⓜ

| ▽ 22 | 19 | 21 | M |

E 70s | 265 E. 78th St. (2nd Ave.) | 6 to 77th St. | 212-288-3800 | www.allthingsbeneath.com

Whether you like your lingerie super-saucy or delicately demure, chances are you'll hit the jackpot at this "no intimidation" East 70s storefront, the brick-and-mortar companion to Karyn Riale's website; accent your assets with boldface designers including Anna Sui and mainstays like Eberjey and Hanky Panky, then top it all off with casual clothing and jewelry finds.

Ben Sherman ⓓ

23 | 21 | 19 | E

SoHo | 96 Spring St. (Mercer St.) | 6 to Spring St. | 212-680-0160 | www.benshermanusa.com

"London is still calling" for "wannabe mods" enamored of the "Swingin' '60s" (even if they were born in the '90s) who flock to this SoHo flagship of the "snappy" British brand; fans find it a "fab shoppe" full of "graphic patterns and slim cut" clothes ("better for blokes than gals", admittedly); the Mick (as in Jagger) mansion look of the place, with its crystal chandelier, faux antiques and endless English pop soundtrack, creates a "perfect" backdrop for "some fabulous eye candy, both shopping and working."

ⓩ Bergdorf Goodman ⓓ

29 | 27 | 24 | VE

E 50s | 754 Fifth Ave. (bet. 57th & 58th Sts.) | N/R/W to 5th Ave./59th St. | 212-753-7300 | 800-558-1855 | www.bergdorfgoodman.com

"There are department stores and then there's Bergdorf's", the "extravagant" emporium opposite The Plaza that's "every woman's" shopping "dream"; "the aura" "may seem intimidating", but "there's always someone to assist you" and a "wealth of riches" await, including "old-world and au courant" top designers "arranged in boutique-y sections", an "awe-inspiring shoe salon" for those "who can't live without the latest Louboutins" and jewelry that's "elegance under glass"; "heaven must buy its linens" in the revamped home department, whose wares now range from Leontine sheets to Deyrolle stuffed birds, while the cosmetics "basement is a must-do, if you want to be beautiful."

ⓩ Bergdorf Goodman Men's ⓓ

28 | 27 | 24 | VE

E 50s | 754 Fifth Ave. (58th St.) | N/R/W to 5th Ave./59th St. | 212-753-7300 | 800-558-1855 | www.bergdorfgoodman.com

When "you want to be treated like a king, make BG Men's your court" proclaim peacocks "who have arrived or want to look like they have" about this "silky smooth" "Fifth Avenue experience" whose "elegant" confines offer "designer suitings (Zegna, Brioni, etc.)", "traditional and just-trendy-enough" separates, a "grand cuff link collection", "incredible ties" and "an unusually broad shoe selection"; "you can leave looking like royalty, a rock star or anything in between", and while prices "run high" – "is that someone's zip code or the price of a suit?" – perhaps "if all men shopped here, the city would be a better place."

Berkley Girl

21 | 21 | 18 | E

E 70s | 1418 Second Ave. (74th St.) | 6 to 77th St. | 212-744-9507
W 70s | 410 Columbus Ave. (bet. 79th & 80th Sts.) | B/C to 81st St. | 212-877-4770
www.berkleygirl.com

"From the viewpoint of a tween", this "cute, well-done" West 70s boutique with an East 70s sidekick is "divine", in fact, you "need go no further for trendy wear"; the owner holds frequent focus groups with neighborhood kids to make sure she's stocking the "right" stuff, from Seven jeans and Lemon T-shirts to Sister Sam skirts and Monkey Wear party dresses, to piles of jewelry and accessories – so "if you're 10-13 years old", "you automatically love everything."

Berluti ⊠

-	-	-	VE

E 70s | 971 Madison Ave. (76th St.) | 6 to 77th St. | 212-439-6400 | www.berluti.com

"Truly a work of art" agree aesthetes who fall for these "beautiful" bespoke men's "shoes with a story" from the Berluti family whose company, now under the LVMH umbrella, dates back to 1895; sole-seekers with euros to spare make tracks to its Madison Avenue corner shop, a blue-walled gem offering a "gorgeous presentation" of the costly creations made from Venetia leather and meticulously rubbed with essential oils to attain the right patina.

☑ Bernardaud ⊠

29	29	24	VE

E 50s | 499 Park Ave. (59th St.) | 4/5/6/F/N/R/W to 59th St./Lexington Ave. | 212-371-4300 | 800-884-7775 | www.bernardaud.fr

Since 1863, this French "classic" has made "beautiful", "expensive" porcelain "almost too pretty to touch" that "dinner guests always compliment"; its well-appointed Park Avenue boutique also carries Baccarat and Hermès crystal and Christofle and Puiforcat sterling silver flatware, making the moneyed maintain "it's hard not to want everything" here.

☑ Best Buy ◑

20	17	14	M

E 80s | 1280 Lexington Ave. (86th St.) | 4/5/6 to 86th St. | 917-492-8870

Flatiron | 60 W. 23rd St. (6th Ave.) | F/V to 23rd St. | 212-366-1373

NoHo | 622 Broadway (bet. Bleecker & Houston Sts.) | 6 to Bleecker St. | 212-673-4067

W 40s | 529 Fifth Ave. (44th St.) | 7/B/D/F/V to 42nd St./Bryant Park | 212-808-0309

NEW W 60s | 1880 Broadway (62nd St.) | 1/A/B/C/D to 59th St./Columbus Circle | 212-246-9734

Bensonhurst | Caesar's Bay Shopping Ctr. | 8923 Bay Pkwy. (Shore Pkwy.) | Brooklyn | D/M to Bay Pkwy. | 718-265-6950

Elmhurst | Queens Pl. | 88-01 Queens Blvd. (bet. 55th & 56th Aves.) | Queens | G/R/V to Grand Ave./Newtown | 718-393-2690

LIC | 50-01 Northern Blvd. (bet. 50th St. & Newtown Rd.) | Queens | G/R/V to 46th St. | 718-626-7585

Staten Island | Staten Island Mall | 2795 Richmond Ave. (bet. Platinum Ave. & Richmond Hill Rd.) | 718-698-7546

888-237-8289 | www.bestbuy.com

Browsers love that "you can play" with the "large inventory" at these "mass-market" "electronics supermarkets", "one-stop shops" for "any device that plugs into a wall socket – from refrigerators to computers" and "all kinds of gadgets" in between; still, critics complain the "name is a misnomer" ("wait for a sale") and say "good luck finding help" since the "hit-or-miss staff" is often "nowhere to be found."

Betsey Bunky Nini ⊠

23	22	20	E

E 70s | 980 Lexington Ave. (bet. 71st & 72nd Sts.) | 6 to 68th St. | 212-744-6716

Visitors to the "happy environment" of this East 70s women's boutique warm to the "well-edited collection" of "high fashion" lines such as Alberta Ferretti, Ter et Bantine, Piazza Sempione and Paul Smith; "everything looks so good", but a nattering of naysayers squawk it's a bit "on the expensive side."

| | QUALITY | DISPLAY | SERVICE | COST |

Betsey Johnson
E 60s | 251 E. 60th St. (bet. 2nd & 3rd Aves.) | 4/5/6/F/N/R/W to 59th St./Lexington Ave. | 212-319-7699
E 80s | 1060 Madison Ave. (bet. 80th & 81st Sts.) | 6 to 77th St. | 212-734-1257
SoHo | 138 Wooster St. (bet. Houston & Prince Sts.) | N/R/W to Prince St. | 212-995-5048
W 70s | 248 Columbus Ave. (bet. 71st & 72nd Sts.) | 1/2/3/B/C to 72nd St. | 212-362-3364
www.betseyjohnson.com

21 | 22 | 20 | E

Every day is "party dress-up day" at this "wacky" "boudoirlike" quartet where the forever "young-at-heart" designer (the "pink punker of fashion") is "always a hit" with her "funky, feminine and sexy" dresses; the mature maintain that "only models and teens" "have the flair to pull off" the "trashy" "items that look cheaper than they are"; still, the "impossibly hip" staff is "attentive" and "honest – what a blessing."

Bettencourt ⊠
Williamsburg | 70 N. Sixth St. (Wythe Ave.) | Brooklyn | L to Bedford Ave. | 718-218-6737 | 800-883-7005 | www.bettencourtwood.com

– | – | – | E

Eco-conscious brownstoners, architects and developers alike hit pay dirt at Williamsburg's progressive building supply store tucked out of sight near the waterfront; house-proud patrons spruce up their digs with a wealth of green-minded choices ranging from bamboo counter-tops and all-natural cork flooring to clay plaster wall finishes and chemical-free paints.

Beverly Feldman
W 50s | 7 W. 56th St. (bet. 5th & 6th Aves.) | E/V to 5th Ave./53rd St. | 212-484-0000 | 877-776-5477 | www.beverlyfeldmanshoes.com

20 | 23 | 20 | E

"When your kooky mood strikes" bop over to this "kitschy" pink, gold and black West 50s shoe shop for an "over-the-top" "pick-me-up" to match your "glitz and bling" style; designer Beverly Feldman's "incred-ible pizzazz" translates into "fabulous" footwear for fashion heat-seekers who abide by the mantra "when more is not enuff"; still, subdued sorts chide "are you kidding?" – only if you're part of the "gold lamé crowd."

Bicycle Habitat
SoHo | 244 Lafayette St. (bet. Prince & Spring Sts.) | 6 to Spring St. | 212-431-3315 | www.bicyclehabitat.com

∇ 23 | 13 | 18 | M

"For quality, go" to this SoHo "source for custom and fixed-gear" bicy-cles, a "classic" "greasy, messy" shop that "professional riders" and park cruisers alike laud as just "what a bike shop should be", with "reasonably priced" items and repairs "done quickly"; still, while most find the "avid cyclists" on staff "knowledgeable", a few feel that "service is in decline"; N.B. a major expansion may not be reflected in the Display score.

Bicycle Renaissance
W 80s | 430 Columbus Ave. (bet. 80th & 81st Sts.) | 1 to 79th St. | 212-724-2350 | www.bicyclerenaissance.com

∇ 21 | 16 | 12 | E

Pedalers purport that this "urban bike shop" on the UWS is a "great place to trick out an ordinary" set of wheels and praise the "competent repair" department for "emergency" fix-ups; still, detractors switch to a different gear, griping that the "surly staff" is "not very helpful" and the offerings are "overpriced", advising head "elsewhere for a good deal."

Big Drop ❶ | 21 | 20 | 16 | E |

E 70s | 1321 Third Ave. (bet. 75th & 76th Sts.) | 6 to 77th St. |
212-988-3344
E 70s | 1325 Third Ave. (76th St.) | 6 to 77th St. | 212-472-3200
SoHo | 174 Spring St. (bet. Thompson St. & W. B'way) | C/E to Spring St. |
212-966-4299
SoHo | 425 W. Broadway (bet. Prince & Spring Sts.) | C/E to Spring St. |
212-226-9292
www.bigdropnyc.com

"Go on a skinny day" and "drop big bucks" on "hip" chick threads
from the "latest indie" and boldface designers like Gwen Stefani's
L.A.M.B. line, Ya-Ya and Rebecca Taylor at these "well-curated"
"trendsetters" that carry everything from a "going-out outfit" to "top-
of-the-line" jeans; but while supporters insist the staff "isn't aloof",
cynics snap they're "snobby"; N.B. the 1325 Third Avenue branch
sells menswear only.

Bike Works NYC ⊠ | – | – | – | I |

LES | 106 Ridge St. (Rivington St.) | F/J/M/Z to Delancey/Essex Sts. |
212-388-1077 | www.bikecult.com

Vintage models are an occasional draw at this Lower East Side bike
bodega, which carries fixed-gear and single-speed cycles for hipsters
and "messenger wannabes" looking to partake in the old-school
scene; service is anything but retro, though, with a staff of enthusiasts
who are "hard-core loisida."

ⓩ Billabong ❶ | 21 | 21 | 19 | M |

NEW Garment District | 112 W. 34th St. (bet. B'way & 7th Ave.) | B/D/
F/N/Q/R/V/W to 34th St./Herald Sq. | 212-967-2511
W 40s | 1515 Broadway (bet. 44th & 45th Sts.) | 1/2/3/7/N/Q/R/S/
W to 42nd St./Times Sq. | 212-840-0550
www.billabong.com

Wave-riders "love the Aussie style" of this "great quality brand" that
now has a home for its "surfer stuff", from board shorts to sunglasses;
the huge space also features the Element line of skateboard parts, giving "outdoor types" more reasons to coast over to Times Square – or
its new Garment Center branch.

NEW Billionaire Boys Club & Ice Cream | – | – | – | E |

SoHo | 456 W. Broadway (bet. Houston & Prince Sts.) | N/R/W to
Prince St. | 212-777-2225 | www.bbcicecream.com

Gentlemen, unleash your inner hip-hop with the hoodies, caps, tees
and kicks sold at this new SoHo store, co-owned by music mogul
Pharrell Williams; the candy-colored Ice Cream brand is on the gleaming white ground floor, with sneakers displayed in metal ice cream
containers; up past the neon-lit staircase lies a tubular moonscape,
where the astronaut- and robot-themed BBC merchandise sparkles
against the dark, starry walls; P.S. a ladies' line is coming in 2008; until
then, billionaire girls can join the club via the smaller sizes.

Billy Martin's Western Wear | 27 | – | 24 | E |

E 60s | 1034 Third Ave. (bet. 61st & 62nd Sts.) | 4/5/6/F/N/R/W to
59th St./Lexington Ave. | 212-861-3100 | www.billymartin.com

"If you're saddling up to go out West", this East 60th Street stockade,
newly relocated to Third Avenue but still gussied up with "memora-

bilia", a vintage bar and a Coca-Cola machine, is "the place to go" gush guys and gals in search of "fabulous" cowboy boots, "great belt buckles" and rodeo-ready attire "with pizzazz", favored by celebrities like Sheryl Crow and Billy Bob Thornton; the "workmanship is superior" – as are "Texas oil-men" prices.

Bird ●

▽ 25 | 25 | 25 | E

Cobble Hill | 220 Smith St. (Butler St.) | Brooklyn | F/G to Bergen St. | 718-797-3774
Park Slope | 430 Seventh Ave. (bet. 14th & 15th Sts.) | Brooklyn | F to 7th Ave. | 718-768-4940
www.shopbird.com
Fly into this Park Slope boutique – or its newer Cobble Hill perch – and you'll "want to come back again and again" coo "cutting-edge" chicks aflutter over the "feel-good vibe" and "unique" goods; former Barneys New York buyer Jennifer Mankins has a "great eye", mixing pieces from edgy labels like Tsumori Chisato with "quality designers" like 3.1 Phillip Lim and "established" lines like A.P.C., and to go-with, "such cool" accessories, jewelry and shoes; "trendy" doesn't come cheap – it's hard to "leave without spending a paycheck."

Birnbaum & Bullock ⊠ Ⓜ

- | - | - | E

Chelsea | 151 W. 25th St. (bet. 6th & 7th Aves.) | N/R/W to 23rd St. | 212-242-2914 | www.birnbaumandbullock.com
At this by-appointment-only Chelsea salon, the "extremely pleasant" namesake designers "custom fit dresses according to the bride's wishes", "making the experience extra special"; hit the sleek blue-and-silver showroom and slip into something sophisticated, like a silk chiffon number – whatever you choose, you can rely on the B&B team to offer "great recommendations for the entire ensemble."

Bisazza ⊠ Ⓜ

- | - | - | VE

SoHo | 43 Greene St. (bet. Broome & Grand Sts.) | A/C/E to Canal St. | 212-334-7130 | www.bisazzausa.com
The newly renovated outpost of this tony Italian tile company is a sparkling, gallerylike SoHo stunner displaying "gorgeous" glass mosaic designs; they'll make a big splash in your bath, kitchen or pool, but the prices may get you in hot water.

Bis Designer Resale

- | - | - | E

E 80s | 1134 Madison Ave., 2nd fl. (bet. 84th & 85th Sts.) | 4/5/6 to 86th St. | 212-396-2760 | www.bisbiz.com
The "inventory always looks immaculate" at this "wonderful consignment shop", which sells a "superb selection of high-end vintage" clothing and accessories (e.g. "Blahniks for a couple hundred" bucks) to ladies and, to some extent, gentlemen; labels like Chanel, Ferragamo and Vuitton suggest that it's "targeting an older crowd", but it *is* on the UES, after all – and a "must-visit if you're on a shopping spree."

Blacker & Kooby

25 | 17 | 19 | M

E 80s | 1204 Madison Ave. (88th St.) | 4/5/6 to 86th St. | 212-369-8308
Locals like this long-standing Upper East Side family-owned stationery store primarily because of its "great customer service and selection" of cards, invitations, pens, photo albums and picture frames, along with other "unique items."

	QUALITY	DISPLAY	SERVICE	COST

Blackman ⊠
▽ 26 | 18 | 16 | E

Flatiron | 85 Fifth Ave., 2nd fl. (16th St.) | 4/5/6/L/N/Q/R/W to 14th St./
Union Sq. | 212-337-1000
Flushing | 134-07 Northern Blvd. (bet. College Point Blvd. & Main St.) |
Queens | 7 to Main St. | 718-939-7200
Queens Village | 217-68 Hempstead Ave. (bet. Springfield Blvd. & 217th St.) |
Queens | E/J/Z to Jamaica Ctr. Parsons/Archer | 718-479-5533
800-843-2695 | www.blackman.com

The gigantic, "gorgeous" flagship in the Flatiron District displays "excellent lines" of kitchen and bath booty, including faucets, tubs, showers, sinks, hardware and every kind of designer plumbing imaginable "across a wide range of prices", but don't discount the Queens locations, where the establishment has been a fixture since 1921.

Blades Board and Skate ⦿
▽ 23 | 18 | 18 | M

Garment District | Manhattan Mall | 901 Sixth Ave. (bet. 32nd & 33rd Sts.) |
B/D/F/N/Q/R/V/W to 34th St./Herald Sq. | 646-733-2738
NoHo | 659 Broadway (bet. Bleecker & 3rd Sts.) | 6 to Bleecker St. |
212-477-7350
W 70s | 156 W. 72nd St. (bet. B'way & Columbus Ave.) | B/C to 72nd St. |
212-787-3911
888-552-5233 | www.blades.com

If shooting the slopes, catching a breaker or riding the halfpipe is your idea of R&R, hit this sports triplet for all things extreme; the stock seems to be more "boards than blades lately", but this outfit still "keeps it real" with a "good selection" of powder-shredding gear sold by a "young, fully pierced" staff that lives the lifestyle and "knows the product", adding to the "home-grown feel."

Blanc de Chine
24 | 24 | 24 | VE

E 50s | 673 Fifth Ave. (53rd St.) | E/V to 5th Ave./53rd St. | 212-308-8688 |
www.blancdechine.com

A "luxury" Chinese clothier makes its U.S. debut with this East 50s emporium, whose cool Zen-like digs – white walls, dark-wood floors and furnishings – are dominated by a spiral staircase; using sumptuous materials (velvets, cashmere, silk treated to look like leather), the mens- and womenswear offer an "elegant" East-meets-West fusion, i.e. mandarin-collar T-shirts, wool cheongsams and suits in Asian prints; scarves, jewelry, bed linens and pillows round out the collection.

Bleecker Bob's Golden Oldies Record Shop ⦿
20 | 12 | 18 | M

G Village | 118 W. Third St. (bet. MacDougal St. & 6th Ave.) | A/B/C/
D/E/F/V to W. 4th St. | 212-475-9677 | www.bleeckerbobs.com

"Get lost in the smell of old, dusty album covers" at this "legendary" Greenwich Village "relic" filled with "oddities", choice oldies, collectibles and even CDs; it's the "place to go for hard-to-find music", and though the "arrogant" staffers sometimes "act like the recording execs they never became", they're some of the "best record geeks in the world."

Bleecker Street Records ⦿
23 | 13 | 17 | M

G Village | 239 Bleecker St. (bet. Carmine & Leroy Sts.) | A/B/C/D/E/
F/V to W. 4th St. | 212-255-7899

"Hearkening back to the good old Village days", this "treat for music lovers" provides not only a "breath of nostalgia for the commercially wary" but an "eclectic and diverse collection" "including DVDs", "live CDs" and "hard-to-find old discs for your turntable"; despite the "self-serve atmosphere" and "somewhat crowded" presentation, it's "a classic spot" for late-night browsers.

Blibetroy ●🅼
- | - | - | E

LES | 100 Stanton St. (bet. Ludlow & Orchard Sts.) | F/V to Lower East Side/2nd Ave. | 212-979-5250 | www.blibetroy.com

Arm-candy connoisseurs seeking handbags hit the mother lode at this LES purse pantheon; though small in stature, it makes a big style statement with plyboo (plywood that looks like bamboo) walls and a cool console table, a modern dais for displaying architecturally inspired reversible leather shoulder bags, foldable clutches, male messenger bags and weekend totes.

⚡ Blick Art Materials ●
25 | 24 | 21 | M

NoHo | 1-5 Bond St. (bet. B'way & Lafayette St.) | 6 to Bleecker St. | 212-533-2444 | 800-828-4548 | www.dickblick.com

This "excellent", "well-organized" NoHo chain link offers a "wealth of supplies", "amazing papers" and "studio furniture" in a "bright, lofty" bi-level, pillar-accented space; "reasonable prices" and a "knowledge-able" staff composed of "helpful hipsters" add the final flourishes.

Bloch
- | - | - | M

W 70s | 304 Columbus Ave. (bet. 74th & 75th Sts.) | B/C to 72nd St. | 212-579-1960 | www.blochworld.com

"One of the few places to find" this Aussie dancewear-maker's clothes is this West 70s flagship outfitting professionals and dilettantes alike; scoop up leotards and leggings, then slip into pointe, tap or cutting-edge jazz or hip-hop shoes before ponying up to the barre for a preview on the plasma TV; even gym rats reveal "if you want to get looks, wear their work-out pants – they mold your butt beautifully."

Blockbuster Video ●
16 | 15 | 11 | I

W 50s | 829 Eighth Ave. (51st St.) | C/E to 50th St. | 212-765-2021 | www.blockbuster.com
Additional locations throughout the NY area

It's "movies for the masses" at this "reliable" chain whose "wide", if "predictable", selection of "big-budget Hollywood" flicks is well-suited to "family viewing"; still, cinéastes slam it as a "commercial" giant that can't "compete" when it comes to "older movies or obscure" titles, adding that its "clerks know utterly nothing about film."

Bloom 🅱
24 | 24 | 20 | M

E 40s | 361 Madison Ave. (bet. 45th & 46th Sts.) | 4/5/6/7/S to 42nd St./Grand Central | 212-370-0068 | www.bloom21llc.citysearch.com

Not to be confused with the Lexington Avenue flower shop, this Madison Avenue offshoot of a Japanese jewelry company sells "crisp", "clean-lined" fine steel, titanium and white gold chokers, chains, rings and bangles in a "sleek" white minimalist setting; if you're "looking for a gift but can't afford Cartier, this is the place."

⚡ Bloomingdale's ●
23 | 20 | 17 | E

E 50s | 1000 Third Ave. (bet. 59th & 60th Sts.) | 4/5/6/F/N/R/W to 59th St./Lexington Ave. | 212-705-2000

(continued)

☑ Bloomingdale's SoHo ●

SoHo | 504 Broadway (bet. Broome & Spring Sts.) | 6 to Spring St. |
212-729-5900
800-232-1854 | www.bloomingdales.com

"What can you say about a Manhattan institution?" – "from moderately priced merchandise to chic couture", "you can find everything you need" (except "knowledgeable sales help") at this East 50s "mother ship" and its "boutique"-like SoHo satellite; the "venerable" original is stocked with clothing, "baubles, bangles and beads" and "good-quality furniture", plus it's a "bridal shower mecca" for housewares; true, it teems with tourists and "overcrowded" aisles, but despite its sometimes "discombobulated state", it's voted NYC's Most Popular department store; N.B. star chef David Burke has an eatery in the flagship.

Blue

| | | | E |

E Village | 137 Ave. A (bet. 9th St. & St. Marks Pl.) | 6 to Astor Pl. |
212-228-7744

"There's a method" to owner-designer Christina Kara's "madness" declare devotees, who praise this East Village shop and its madcap proprietor for coming up with "the answer for curves" in her "dress-of-your-dreams" wedding gowns, "creative bridesmaid dresses", cocktail dresses and suits that fit "a real woman's body"; "even if you've got a smallish bridal gown budget", you won't leave singing the blues.

NEW Blue & Cream

| | | | E |

E Village | 1 E. First St. (Bowery) | F/V to Lower East Side/2nd Ave. |
212-533-3088 | www.blueandcream.com

Sleek and chic, like the spanking new condo building it's housed in, this offspring of the Hamptons duo seems to personify the gentrifying Bowery; the corner location with humongous windows, high ceilings, steel fixtures, low-slung tables and rotating artwork displayed gallery style houses casual and night-out threads from labels like Doo.Ri, Jenni Kayne, Nicholas K and Charlotte Ronson for her and Spurr and Ragg & Bone for him, plus accessories galore, like jewelry from Carlos de Souza.

Blue Bag

| | | | E |

NoLita | 266 Elizabeth St. (bet. Houston & Prince Sts.) | 6 to Spring St. |
212-966-8566

"Feel your troubles melt away" as you step inside this palm-studded, brick-walled, "St. Barts–inspired" NoLita boutique and peruse the "exquisite selection" of handbags displayed amid vintage furnishings; the "ever-changing" array of "very modern, chic" evening and day essentials includes "hard-to-find labels" and "independent designers", and it's all sold by a staff that "cares what you like" – no wonder it's a "favorite" of individualists who love being asked "where did you get that bag?"

Blue Bench M

| | | | VE |

TriBeCa | 159 Duane St. (bet. Hudson St. & W. B'way) | 1/2/3 to Chambers St. | 212-267-1500 | www.bluebenchnyc.com

This recently renovated TriBeCa treasure specializes in "the best in children's furniture" – everything from handmade, hand-painted cribs to bookshelves and beds, plus decorative trimmings like rugs, bedding, lamps, toy chests and picture frames; all this charm is costly, though, leaving the sticker-shocked wondering "who in their right mind would pay these prices?"

Blueberi ●M
— | — | — | E

Dumbo | 143 Front St. (bet. Jay & Pearl Sts.) | Brooklyn | A/C/F to Jay St./Borough Hall | 718-422-7724

For womenswear that has a "cool, 'mark of the hand' designer look", fashionistas duck into this Dumbo den of style, a larger, luxer sibling of owner Carlene Brown's Prospect Heights boutique, Redberi; the grottolike space boasts urban-chic finds from Jill Stuart and LaRok, plus a "treasure trove" of handbags and jewelry to complete the "sophisticated, sometimes funky" ensemble.

Blue in Green ●
▽ 21 | 21 | 20 | E

SoHo | 8 Greene St. (bet. Canal & Grand Sts.) | 6/J/M/N/Q/R/W/Z to Canal St. | 212-680-0555 | www.blueingreensoho.com

Break away from the Canal Street crowds and cruise into this "cool" SoHo spot where dudes who are into duds recognize the exclusive brands of British and Japanese casualwear; while there are a lot of "high-priced items" – especially the denim from labels like Johnbull – guys don't feel blue shelling out the green, cuz it's tough to find this limited-edition stuff stateside.

NEW Blue Ribbon General Store M
— | — | — | M

Boerum Hill | 365 State St. (Bond St.) | Brooklyn | A/C/G to Hoyt/Schermerhorn Sts. | 718-522-9848 | www.blueribbongeneralstore.com

The welcoming painted facade isn't the only spot of color at this new general store for urbanites set on a Boerum Hill corner; Brooklynite owner Ann Lopatin, who earned her retail stripes in the corporate trenches, strives to offer modern day goods deserving of a 'blue ribbon', from whimsical home and gift items to kiddy essentials like Silly Putty.

Blue Tree ⊠
24 | 22 | 20 | VE

E 90s | 1283 Madison Ave. (bet. 91st & 92nd Sts.) | 4/5/6 to 86th St. | 212-369-2583 | www.bluetreeny.com

It's the "kind of cute, quirky shopkeeper's boutique that doesn't exist in New York anymore" muse admirers who deem actress Phoebe Cates Kline's double-decker haunt in the East 90s a "unique" "place to browse"; choose from a "highly edited selection of toys, clothes, jewelry" and trinkets for kids, then shake the adult trees for diamonds, antiques, perfume, vintage LPs, chocolates and candles; still, a miffed few wail "everything looks great – until you look at the price tags."

blush ●
21 | 17 | 17 | E

W Village | 333 Bleecker St. (Christopher St.) | 1 to Christopher St./Sheridan Sq. | 212-352-0111

"Sexy and sometimes unusual" womenswear tempts at this West Village shop where the lovely wares include filmy tops, flirty knits and body-conscious suits "you must have a 24-inch waist" to wear; the only nays are for the "waaaay too pushy" staff, which may make you blush with its "overly complimentary" comments.

	QUALITY	DISPLAY	SERVICE	COST

Böc ◐
▽ 19 | 22 | 18 | E

W 80s | 491 Columbus Ave. (bet. 83rd & 84th Sts.) | B/C to 81st St. | 212-362-5405 | www.bocnyc.com

"Just what was needed on the Upper West Side" applaud admirers, who say bravo to the "downtown selection of modern, beautiful clothing" from labels like the owner's line, Lemon, along with finds from Vivienne Westwood and Rebecca Taylor and jeans from Citizens of Humanity; the "lofty, spacious" store offers "plenty of space to walk around" or park a stroller when searching for an "adorable" "last-minute Saturday night outfit."

Bochic ☒
- | - | - | VE

E 50s | The Crown Bldg. | 730 Fifth Ave. (bet. 56th & 57th Sts.) | N/R/W to 5th Ave./59th St. | 212-873-0707 | www.bochic.com

This jewelry showroom in The Crown Building lives up to its bohemian-chic name with a collection ranging from intricate inlaid rings and bracelets in Bakelite and enamel to vintage-looking lockets dusted with rose-cut diamonds; N.B. call ahead for an appointment.

BoConcept
17 | 22 | 18 | M

Chelsea | 144 W. 18th St. (bet. 6th & 7th Aves.) | 1 to 18th St. | 646-336-8188

NEW E 50s | 220 E. 57th St. (bet. 2nd & 3rd Aves.) | 4/5/6/F/N/R/W to 59th St./Lexington Ave. | 212-355-8188

Murray Hill | 105 Madison Ave. (30th St.) | 6 to 33rd St. | 212-686-8188

SoHo | 69 Greene St. (bet. Broome & Spring Sts.) | N/R/W to Prince St. | 212-966-8188

Dumbo | 79 Front St. (bet. Main & Washington Sts.) | Brooklyn | F to York St. | 718-246-8188

www.boconcept.us

"Modular" "Scandinavian furniture at a moderate price" is the point at this "well-laid-out" outfit where "stylish" "modern" pieces come in flexible designs – for example, one sofa style can be ordered in hundreds of variations in size, shape and color; still, skeptics question the quality of items that appear to have "more style than substance."

Body Shop, The ◐
20 | 19 | 19 | M

E Village | 747 Broadway (bet. Astor Pl. & 8th St.) | N/R/W to 8th St. | 212-979-2944 | 800-263-9746 | www.thebodyshop.com
Additional locations throughout the NY area

"The smell of mangos and coconut lures you" into "the original conscious cosmetics company" selling "reasonably priced", environmentally friendly "safe products" like the body butters that "are not tested on animals"; but cynics criticize the "overzealous staff", "hemp and hippie-ish" vibe ("bring your mood ring") and suggest "a face-lift" is in order.

Boffi SoHo ☒Ⓜ
- | - | - | VE

SoHo | 31½ Greene St. (Grand St.) | C/E to Spring St. | 212-431-8282 | www.boffi-soho.com

Located in a cavernous, multilevel SoHo showroom, this high-end Milan-based kitchen and bath manufacturer is a modernist's dream, with gleaming fixtures, sinks, appliances, custom-made cabinets, bathtubs and showers in materials ranging from steel and glass to wood; just note less costs more when it comes to the price here.

	QUALITY	DISPLAY	SERVICE	COST

Bolton's ◐

	14	11	11	I

W 50s | 27 W. 57th St. (bet. 5th & 6th Aves.) | F to 57th St. | 212-935-4431 | www.boltonsstores.com
Additional locations throughout the NY area

Though this "dingy" discounter definitely "has seen better days", you can still "score" "bargains if you search", rummaging through the racks of "color-coordinated clothing" – "a nice idea", especially since the staff is "not really interested in helping you"; there are "good, cheap accessories too", especially at the "well-located" West 57th Street flagship.

Bond No. 9

	28	26	25	E

E 60s | 680 Madison Ave. (61st St.) | N/R/W to 5th Ave./59th St. | 212-838-2780
E 70s | 897 Madison Ave. (73rd St.) | 6 to 68th St. | 212-794-4480
NoHo | 9 Bond St. (bet. B'way & Lafayette St.) | 6 to Bleecker St. | 212-228-1732 ◐
W Village | 399 Bleecker St. (11th St.) | A/C/E/L to 14th St./8th Ave. | 212-633-1641 ◐
877-273-3369 | www.bondno9.com

Those who've bonded with this "cool" "perfume line named for different NYC neighborhoods" like Nuits de Noho and Chelsea Flowers say it sells 30 "unique, sexy smells that you won't find on every other woman"(or guy), along with custom-blend options; N.B. the Bond Street flagship boasts a tearoom and library.

Bond 07 by Selima

	-	-	-	E

NoHo | 7 Bond St. (bet. B'way & Lafayette St.) | 6 to Bleecker St. | 212-677-8487 | www.selimaoptique.com

Some fancy her a Bond girl, but Selima Salaun, the creative designer, optician and optometrist behind star-magnet Selima Optique, offers up more than a Goldfinger's worth of glamour at this NoHo boutique, which boasts "gorgeous eyewear", an "eclectic" selection of new and vintage hats, handbags, dresses, lingerie and jewelry.

Bonne Nuit

	▽ 24	17	18	E

E 70s | 1193 Lexington Ave. (81st St.) | 6 to 77th St. | 212-472-7300 | www.bonnenuitonline.com

Shoppers are over the moon about the "wonderful selection of imported" ladies' lingerie and childrenswear at this Eastsider where you can snap up "sweet" undies and luxe sleepwear, crib-size quilts, mother-baby pajamas and old-fashioned little-girl dresses.

☒ Bonpoint

	28	26	19	VE

E 60s | 810 Madison Ave. (68th St.) | 6 to 68th St. | 212-879-0900 ☒
E 90s | 1269 Madison Ave. (91st St.) | 4/5/6 to 86th St. | 212-722-7720 ☒
W Village | 392 Bleecker St. (Perry St.) | 1 to Christopher St./Sheridan Sq. | 212-647-1700 ◐
www.bonpoint.com

"Ooh-la-la!" trumpet touters of this trio of "*très* chic" French children's clothiers, who fawn over the "magnificent", "beautifully made" layette, sportswear and special-occasion creations boasting "sophisticated fabrics and colors" – "mini-couture for the city's elite to drool over and on"; "prices are through the roof" but "it's hard to resist" such "divine" duds – especially when "every piece is a keepsake."

| | QUALITY | DISPLAY | SERVICE | COST |

Boomerang Toys
— | — | — | M

Financial District | 2 World Financial Ctr. (West Side Hwy.) | R/W to Rector St. | 212-786-3011
TriBeCa | 173 W. Broadway (Worth St.) | 1 to Franklin St. | 212-226-7650
www.boomerangtoys.com

You always "walk out with something" after visiting these Financial District and TriBeCa toy boxes, filled with "unique" playthings, including European imports like Ravensburger puzzles and Bruder trucks; they're "great to browse in", especially when you're hunting down "hard-to-find" items, plus they keep track of gifts bought for neighborhood parties.

Borrelli Boutique
— | — | — | VE

E 60s | 16 E. 60th St. (bet. 5th & Madison Aves.) | N/R/W to 5th Ave./ 59th St. | 212-644-9610 | www.luigiborrelli.com

On a swanky side street in the East 60s, a stone's throw from Barneys and Tod's, this small shop supplies *signore e signori* with some sunny sartorial style from Napoli, via colorful suits, separates, sweaters and shoes; it's "one of the best for custom shirts – though certainly at tailor-made prices" confide cognoscenti.

☑ Bose ◐
27 | 26 | 24 | VE

NEW SoHo | 465 Broadway (Grand St.) | N/R/W to Prince St. | 212-334-3710
W 60s | The Shops at Columbus Circle, Time Warner Ctr. | 10 Columbus Circle, 3rd fl. (60th St. at B'way) | 1/A/B/C/D to 59th St./Columbus Circle | 212-823-9314
800-999-2673 | www.bose.com

"Top-notch" home entertainment equipment that makes you think you're "walking into a fancy concert hall" has earned this sleek Time Warner Center staple – and a new SoHo branch – a rep for "great quality products" with "fabulous" acoustics (to wit, the Wave radio, which tops many an audiophile's wish list, and the iPod-compatible SoundDock); "excellent service" adds to the "confidence-building experience."

☑ Bottega Veneta
29 | 27 | 24 | VE

E 50s | 699 Fifth Ave. (bet. 54th & 55th Sts.) | E/V to 5th Ave./53rd St. | 212-371-5511 | www.bottegaveneta.com

Inhale the "smell of great leather" at this luxury label's mammoth Fifth Avenue flagship where the "presentation of goods" from accessories to shoes to clothing is "superb" and creative director Tomas Maier's "elegant" touch is evident everywhere; surveyors swoon over "mouthwatering" "soft, buttery" purses that "last forever" and "never go out of style", pronouncing them "worth every dear penny" they'll undoubtedly cost you; still, for most, "nothing beats" the "signature woven bags", which may be "extravagant", but "essential to the well-dressed wardrobe."

Botticelli
25 | 21 | 21 | E

E 40s | 522 Fifth Ave. (bet. 43rd & 44th Sts.) | 7/B/D/F/V to 42nd St./ Bryant Park | 212-768-1430
E 40s | 620 Fifth Ave. (49th St.) | B/D/F/V to 47-50th Sts./Rockefeller Ctr. | 212-582-6313
E 50s | 666 Fifth Ave. (53rd St.) | E/V to 5th Ave./53rd St. | 212-586-7421
www.botticellishoes.com

"Lush leathers with Italian elegance" – what "great stuff for the tootsies" – no wonder this Fifth Avenue "shoe heaven" was "Elaine from *Seinfeld*'s favorite" muse fans who also tune into the "soundly made" handbags and men's items; "excellent quality" and a staff with "unending patience" are its "hallmarks", plus "expensive" tags – but the goods "become affordable to mere mortals" at sale time.

Boucher ⓜ
20 | 20 | 21 | M

Meatpacking | 9 Ninth Ave. (Little W. 12th St.) | A/C/E/L to 14th St./8th Ave. | 212-206-3775 | www.boucherjewelry.com

If you love "delicate", colorful and "trendy" baubles in semiprecious and precious gemstones, especially lariats, earrings and briolette bracelets and necklaces, then this "jewel box" in the "super-hot" Meatpacking District is for you; "good prices" and "friendly service" are other reasons some call the shop their "favorite."

Bowery Kitchen Supplies
22 | 11 | 14 | I

Chelsea | Chelsea Mkt. | 75 Ninth Ave. (bet. 15th & 16th Sts.) | A/C/E/L to 14th St./8th Ave. | 212-376-4982 | www.bowerykitchens.com

Although no longer on the Bowery, this "bargain-priced", "cheaper-by-the-dozens" Chelsea store still serves up "restaurant-style supplies for the average home" and provides tools and equipment to the Food Network studio upstairs; most say the "cluttered" space is "full" of "everything you need for your kitchen", "except standing room."

Bowery Lighting
21 | 13 | 17 | M

LES | 148 Bowery (bet. Broome & Grand Sts.) | J/M/Z to Bowery | 212-941-8244 | www.liteelite.com

"It lights up my life!" assert admirers of this Bowery bastion, which offers "a dazzling array" of "mainstream choices" from "over-the-top crystal chandeliers to simple bathroom" fixtures; the endless rows of products leave some "overwhelmed" and with a "stiff neck" from all that looking up, but "fair prices" make it easier to focus.

B. Oyama Homme ●ⓑⓩ
– | – | – | E

Harlem | 2330 Seventh Ave. (bet. 136th & 137th Sts.) | 2/3 to 135th St. | 212-234-5128 | www.boyamahomme.com

Bernard Oyama's Parisian sensibility is everywhere in evidence at the Harlem haven for *hommes* near the 135th Street subway stop; there is a detailed elegance to the classy suits, slacks, shirts and knits that all seem to fit neatly into his cozy atelier decorated with old photos of style-setting African-American jazz and pop stars of yesteryear.

Bra Smyth
25 | 16 | 21 | E

E 70s | 905 Madison Ave. (bet. 72nd & 73rd Sts.) | 6 to 68th St. | 212-772-9400

W 70s | 2177 Broadway (77th St.) | 1 to 79th St. | 212-721-5111
www.brasmyth.com

With "old-fashioned fitters" who "figure out your perfect size" and make "free alterations on bras", the goods "feel custom-made" at this duo serving up "sexy lingerie" and swimwear that's "not super-luxury, but high-quality"; still, a few find the staff's attitude a tad "holier than thou."

Bra*Tenders ⓩ
– | – | – | M

W 40s | 630 Ninth Ave., 6th fl. (bet. 44th & 45th Sts.) | A/C/E to 42nd St./Port Authority | 212-957-7000 | www.bratenders.com

Overflowing with frilly goods, this by-appointment-only lingerie lair tucked away in a Theater District office building specializes in suiting up stage and screen sirens, but regular gals can get star treatment too via one-on-one bra-sizings; the impeccably fitting undergarments (including shapewear, sports bras and hosiery) don't come cheap, but even with no-pressure service, it's hard not to leave without a bagful of new favorites; N.B. also closed Saturdays.

Breguet ⊠ ▽ 29 | 28 | 27 | VE

E 60s | 779 Madison Ave. (bet. 66th & 67th Sts.) | 6 to 68th St. | 212-288-4014 | 800-331-1577 | www.breguet.com

"Amazing watches with an amazing history" from the Swiss luxury-brand horologist, dating back to 1775 and now part of Swatch, are the focus at this "fabulous" Madison Avenue boutique; whether you choose the timepiece brand worn by Napoléon Bonaparte and Marie Antoinette, select a glittering piece of fine jewelry or pick up a precision pen, the "exceptional staff" makes you "feel you are the most important customer that ever walked in" – "now, all you have to do is win the lottery."

Bric's ▽ 27 | 26 | 26 | E

E 50s | 535 Madison Ave. (bet. 54th & 55th Sts.) | E/V to 5th Ave./ 53rd St. | 212-688-4490 | 866-866-3390 | www.brics.it

If you want "skycaps to compliment your luggage as the nicest they've ever seen", but you also want something "well-made" and "well-priced", zip over to this Midtown shop and peruse the "tasteful selection" of "elegant", "practical" and "brilliantly conceived" Italian-designed travel gear; the "distinctive" pieces come in unconventional shades like lavender and are "very good-looking", and what's more, the staff is "supportive", dispensing "useful information."

Bridal Garden, The ●⊠ 18 | 10 | 15 | M

Flatiron | 54 W. 21st St., 9th fl. (bet. 5th & 6th Aves.) | N/R/W to 23rd St. | 212-252-0661 | www.bridalgarden.org

"You have to sift through" the "designer gowns at knockoff prices" and "pray they have your size, but if you're lucky" at this "cramped", by-appointment-only Flatiron District shop run by a not-for-profit children's charity, "ahhh . . . what a feeling!"; imagine "professing your love, looking great while you do it and giving back"; some dresses "need TLC before the big day" – but remember, it can be "quite the windfall" too.

Bridal Reflections ⊠Ⓜ 20 | 18 | 18 | E

Murray Hill | 286 Fifth Ave., 5th fl. (30th St.) | 6 to 28th St. | 212-764-3040 | 866-259-3678 | www.bridalreflections.com

Family-owned for 35 years, this Long Island wedding-gear retailer is looking to take Manhattan with its Murray Hill store; but Big Apple brides are being a bit skeptical: while there are "nice selections" among the 20-plus designers represented, ranging from the Thai silks of Avine Perucci to the bodacious styles of Stephen Yearick, the gowns seem "pricey for the quality", and the "aloof" "help is not so helpful."

⊠ Bridge Kitchenware ⊠ 28 | - | 19 | E

E 40s | 711 Third Ave., entry on 45th St. (bet. 2nd & 3rd Aves.) | 4/5/ 6/7/S to 42nd St./Grand Central | 212-688-4220 | 800-274-3435 | www.bridgekitchenware.com

Acolytes of this relocated East 40s "chef's heaven" swear that "in addition to the basics", "anything and everything you could ever want for your kitchen is here", including "odd gadgets", "hard-to-find, quality" equipment and other "uncommon things"; they also warn that "if you're not a professional cook, beware" as the staff can be "indifferent to or impatient with the ignorant."

Brief Encounters
- | - | - | E

W 70s | 239 Columbus Ave. (71st St.) | 1/2/3 to 72nd St. | 212-496-5649

Insiders with an intimate knowledge of this black-and-white Columbus Avenue corner lingerie shop say the "goods are high-quality", so whether you're looking for a slinky slip, luxe hosiery or silk pajamas, "wonderful" wares from labels like Elle Macpherson and Ralph Lauren await; the "very knowledgeable staff" is also "exceptional" – "no ill-fitting bras are allowed" to be sold.

☑ Brioni ⌧
28 | 27 | 25 | VE

E 50s | 55 E. 52nd St. (bet. Madison & Park Aves.) | E/V to 5th Ave./ 53rd St. | 212-355-1940

E 50s | 57 E. 57th St. (bet. Madison & Park Aves.) | 4/5/6/F/N/R/W to 59th St./Lexington Ave. | 212-376-5777

888-778-8775 | www.brioni.it

"Conservative, well-heeled gents" are well-served at this elegant East 50s pair that's "simply the best of the best" for "traditional Italian menswear", from the stunning suits to the "beautiful" ties; sure, "you pay top dollar", but the bill includes being made to feel "special" by a staff that can "do anything" – "the hunchback of Notre Dame could walk in and they would fit him."

British American House ⌧
▽ 22 | 19 | 16 | E

E 50s | 488 Madison Ave. (51st St.) | 6 to 51st St. | 212-752-5880

Oddly enough, considering its name, "a good selection of big-name" brands from Italy are the stock-in-trade of this Midtown men's store that's "been around for a long time"; though views vary on the service – some call it "high-pressure", others appreciate the "advice on appropriate looks" – all agree the contemporary-styled goods are "high-quality"; just "keep a stiff upper lip when you pay."

☑ Broadway Panhandler
27 | - | 21 | M

G Village | 65 E. Eighth St. (bet. B'way & University Pl.) | N/R/W to 8th St. | 212-966-3434 | 866-266-5927 | www.broadwaypanhandler.com

Your "culinary skills automatically increase upon entering" this "one-stop-shopping" "foodies' mecca" that's relocated from SoHo to Greenwich Village; supporters say it stocks "the best range of prices for good pots and pans", "top-of-the-line staples", "fun gadgets", bakeware and "more cookie cutters than you can imagine", and they're all sold by a "knowledgeable staff" "that's as sharp as the cutlery."

Brooklyn Collective ⌶
- | - | - | M

Red Hook | 198 Columbia St. (bet. Degraw & Sackett Sts.) | Brooklyn | F/G to Carroll St. | 718-596-6231 | www.brooklyncollective.com

Step off the beaten shopping trail and into this gallerylike boutique in emerging Red Hook, a showcase for a revolving roster of (mostly) local talent; co-owner/designers Tessa Phillips (slinky camis and dresses) and Rachel Goldberg (modern jewelry) spotlight their own collections and also curate an interesting inventory of edgy photographs and paintings, witty tees from Milton Carter and funky guitar straps.

Brooklyn General Store Ⓜ — | — | — | E

Carroll Gardens | 128 Union St. (Hicks St.) | Brooklyn | F/G to Carroll St. | 718-237-7753 | www.brooklyngeneral.com

Designed by and for crafty moms (it offers after-hours knitting, crocheting, quilting, sewing and spinning classes every weeknight), this "cute" and "friendly" West Carroll Gardens nook overflows with "interesting" specialty yarns, vintage fabrics, needlework notions, toys and clothing for women and kids; as similarly countrified knit competitors spring up all over town, though, the few who've found it feel it's "not that unique."

Brooklyn Industries ❶ 20 | 21 | 21 | M

Chelsea | 161 Eighth Ave. (18th St.) | A/C/E/L to 14th St./8th Ave. | 212-206-0477

SoHo | 286 Lafayette St. (bet. Jersey & Prince Sts.) | B/D/F/V to B'way/Lafayette St. | 212-219-0862

W Village | 500 Hudson St. (Christopher St.) | 1 to Christopher St./Sheridan Sq. | 212-206-1488

Boerum Hill | 100 Smith St. (bet. Atlantic Ave. & Pacific St.) | Brooklyn | F/G to Bergen St. | 718-596-3986

Park Slope | 206 Fifth Ave. (Union St.) | Brooklyn | M/R to Union St. | 718-789-2764

Park Slope | 328 Seventh Ave. (9th St.) | Brooklyn | F to 7th Ave. | 718-788-5250

Williamsburg | 162 Bedford Ave. (bet. N. 8th & 9th Sts.) | Brooklyn | L to Bedford Ave. | 718-486-6464

Williamsburg | 184 Broadway (Driggs Ave.) | Brooklyn | J/M/Z to Marcy Ave. | 718-218-9166

800-318-6061 | www.brooklynindustries.com

Now boasting five locations throughout its namesake borough plus three Manhattan outposts, this "funky" urban brand continues to keep "shallow-pocketed hipsters happy", offering artist-designed "limited-edition" silk-screened tees, "cool" neighborhood-pride hoodies "for the Brooklyn lover in you", "sturdy", "unique" messenger bags, belts, shoes and a line of premium denim that can "handle the wear and tear of the city"; P.S. the "cute staff" is "always helpful."

NEW Brooklyn Mercantile Ⓜ 21 | 20 | 19 | M

Park Slope | 335 Fifth Ave. (bet. 3rd & 4th Sts.) | Brooklyn | M/R to Union St. | 718-788-1233 | www.brooklynmercantile.com

"Love their stuff!" agree nesters who flock to this Park Slope newcomer filled with "cool" "wares for the Brooklyn abode"; "friendly" owner-film/video producer Tamara Lee knows a thing or two about setting the scene, as evidenced by the old-fashioned dry goods store feel and "offbeat" home furnishings including "very original" ceramic bowls, pillows and clocks, "irresistible" handcrafted furniture and "vintage collectibles", plus "special materials" like fabric, craft kits and handmade paper sure to "bring out your creative urge."

Brooklyn Museum Shop Ⓜ 22 | 19 | 18 | M

Prospect Heights | Brooklyn Museum | 200 Eastern Pkwy. (Washington Ave.) | Brooklyn | 2/3 to Eastern Pkwy. | 718-501-6259 | www.brooklynmuseum.org

"A shopping spree grows in Brooklyn" brag boosters of this "excellent museum shop" proffering a "wonderful hodgepodge" of merchandise including "quality materials thematically linked to the exhibitions", "wonderful" jewelry and crafts "from around the world" and "creative toys", all "imaginatively presented"; prices are "reasonable", and its "original selection" makes it "worth a trip"; N.B. also closed on Tuesdays.

⚡ Brooks Brothers

`24 | 22 | 22 | E`

E 40s | 346 Madison Ave. (44th St.) | 4/5/6/7/S to 42nd St./Grand Central | 212-682-8800

E 50s | 666 Fifth Ave. (53rd St.) | E/V to 5th Ave./53rd St. | 212-261-9440 ◐

TriBeCa | 1 Liberty Plaza (B'way) | R/W to Cortlandt St. | 212-267-2400

NEW **W 60s** | 1934 Broadway (65th St.) | 1 to 66th St./Lincoln Ctr. | 212-362-2374 ◐

800-274-1815 | www.brooksbrothers.com

"Classic with a capital 'C'", this "institution" remains the "gold standard in corporate wear" according to "button-down" sorts who seek out these chain links for "well-made" business suits, dress shirts and other "board room–appropriate" attire proffered by a "reliably old-school", "courteous" staff; the women's department "feels like an afterthought" to some and draws complaints about "stodgy" styles, but if you're looking to "channel your inner preppy", this "Wasp heaven" is the place to go.

Brookstone

`21 | 21 | 20 | E`

Garment District | Manhattan Mall | 901 Sixth Ave. (bet. 32nd & 33rd Sts.) | B/D/F/N/Q/R/V/W to 34th St./Herald Sq. | 212-947-2144 ◐

Seaport | Pier 17 | 18 Fulton St. (bet. Front & South Sts.) | 2/3/4/5/A/C/J/M/Z to Fulton St./B'way/Nassau | 212-344-8108 ◐

W 50s | 16 W. 50th St. (bet. 5th & 6th Aves.) | B/D/F/V to 47-50th Sts./Rockefeller Ctr. | 212-262-3237 ◐

W 50s | 20 W. 57th St. (bet. 5th & 6th Aves.) | F to 57th St. | 212-245-1405

Staten Island | Staten Island Mall | 2655 Richmond Ave. (bet. Platinum Ave. & Richmond Hill Rd.) | 718-982-1525 ◐

800-846-3000 | www.brookstone.com

Jam-packed with "tantalizing" toys that "dazzle the eye", this "fun novelty store" chain is perfect "for that quirky gift" thanks to scads of "unnecessary but enticing gadgets" and "oddball products" "you didn't even know existed" ("battery-powered nose-hair remover", anyone?); it seems "most people don't go there to buy as much as they do to play" and browse, though, or just to "sit on the massage chair" and unwind.

Brunello Cucinelli ◐

`- | - | - | VE`

W Village | 379 Bleecker St. (bet. Charles & Perry Sts.) | 1 to Christopher St./Sheridan Sq. | 212-627-9202 | www.brunellocucinelli.it

Imagine a rustic house in Umbria complete with white brick walls, wood floors, a twig-filled fireplace and state-of-the-art flat-screen TV, and you'll get a sense of this chic Bleecker Street shop for him and her; cashmere rules the day in plush sweaters, finely tuned skirts, tailored jackets and strictly cut trousers, all with the kind of attention to detail that reflects the quality and warm, gracious service you pay (dearly) for.

Bu and the Duck

`26 | 25 | 22 | E`

TriBeCa | 106 Franklin St. (bet. Church St. & W. B'way) | 1 to Franklin St. | 212-431-9226 | www.buandtheduck.com

"Unusual finds and splurges" abound at this "cute" TriBeCa mecca for "hip parents with cool kids", where "outrageous" prices and a sometimes "chilly" sales staff fail to deter determined shoppers from snapping up the "truly beautiful and unique", vintage-inspired children's clothes and accessories, handmade rag dolls and European shoes by the armful.

⚡ Buccellati ⚡

29	-	27	VE

E 50s | 46 E. 57th St. (bet. Madison & Park Aves.) | 4/5/6/F/N/R/ W to 59th St./Lexington Ave. | 212-308-2900 | 877-462-8223 | www.buccellati.com

This old-world Milanese manufacturer, which has moved back to its original American outpost on East 57th Street, is renowned for statusy, "substantial" and "strikingly beautiful" sterling silver serving pieces, flatware and tableware that is voted the Tops in this Survey's Home/Garden category, along with "magnificent" jewelry like "great rings"; "the two words that come to mind when you examine the fine work" will be "wow", immediately followed by "ow" when you get a glimpse of the "astronomical prices."

Buckler ⦿

-	-	-	E

Meatpacking | 13 Gansevoort St. (bet. 8th Ave. & Hudson St.) | A/C/ E/L to 14th St./8th Ave. | 212-255-1596
NEW SoHo | 93 Grand St. (bet. Greene & Mercer Sts.) | 6/J/M/N/ Q/R/W/Z to Canal St. | 212-925-1711
www.bucklershowroom.com

NYC blokes fulfill their buried rocker tendencies at designer Andrew Buckler's garage/band-room of a store in the subterranean surrounds of an old Meatpacking District factory – and at his newly opened, long-awaited SoHo leviathan too; feel like Franz Ferdinand or Tommy Lee (all fans of the brand) as you hang for a while playing the drums or flipping through the racks of jeans and leather jackets evoking that cooler-than-thou vibe.

Buffalo Exchange ⦿

17	16	16	I

Williamsburg | 504 Driggs Ave. (N. 9th St.) | Brooklyn | L to Bedford Ave. | 718-384-6901 | www.buffaloexchange.com

Buffalo are no longer extinct and neither are "good" deals at this offshoot of the Tucson-based chain, an "easy-to-navigate" factory building "trove of pre-worn goodies" where bargainistas "recycle the fashions of yesteryear" and semi-new stuff too and walk away with more used "treasures" or cold cash; it may be "grungier" than others of its ilk and it's usually a "crapshoot", but "cheap thrifting" opportunities abound, plus staffers have "less of the cooler-than-you attitude" than Billyburg competitors.

⚡ Build-A-Bear Workshop ⦿

22	26	23	M

E 40s | 565 Fifth Ave. (46th St.) | B/D/F/V to 47-50th Sts./Rockefeller Ctr. | 212-871-7080
Staten Island | Staten Island Mall | 2655 Richmond Ave. (bet. Platinum Ave. & Richmond Hill Rd.) | 718-698-1477
877-789-2327 | www.buildabear.com

"Kids love bringing their bear to life" at the Midtown and Staten Island branches of this "cute concept" chain where they can have a "great-quality" toy animal stuffed, stitched, fluffed and dressed "exactly to their liking" in "novel" outfits like NYPD uniforms; if Grizzly Adams types growl it's "fun to do once", soft touches shrug "what the heck, seems worth it"; N.B. older girls can create dolls at the Manhattan store's adjoining Friends 2B Made shop.

| | QUALITY | DISPLAY | SERVICE | COST |

Built by Wendy
| | - | - | - | E |

Little Italy | 7 Centre Market Pl. (bet. Broome & Grand Sts.) | 6 to Spring St. | 212-925-6538
Williamsburg | 46 N. Sixth St. (bet. Kent & Wythe Aves.) | Brooklyn | L to Bedford Ave. | 718-384-2882
www.builtbywendy.com

You'd expect a convergence of cool at the crossroads of Little Italy, NoLita and SoHo – and in this pale blue gem, you get it, along with the "hipster attitude" of designer-owner Wendy Mullin's edgy women's and men's sportswear; bargain-hunters can hit her Williamsburg branch for deals on older collections while nimble DIYers zero in on sewing patterns the proprietress created for Simplicity.

Bulgari
| | 28 | 27 | 26 | VE |

E 50s | 730 Fifth Ave. (57th St.) | F to 57th St. | 212-315-9000
E 60s | 783 Madison Ave. (bet. 66th & 67th Sts.) | 6 to 68th St. | 212-717-2300 ⊠
800-285-4274 | www.bulgari.com

"Showy", "distinctive" gold and gemstone jewelry, "unique" watches, small silver gifts and leather accessories are the luxury wares purveyed by this family-owned Italian firm with two East Side venues; sybarites sigh the only thing that tarnishes the experience is "extraordinary prices."

🆕 Bump Ⓜ
| | - | - | - | E |

Park Slope | 464 Bergen St. (bet. 5th & Flatbush Aves.) | Brooklyn | 2/3 to Bergen St. | 718-638-1960 | www.bumpbrooklyn.com

No need to skimp on style just because you're preggers – and you can skip the trip to the city too now that this spacious Park Slope maternity newcomer owned by two local moms has opened shop on burgeoning Bergen Street; the chic digs – brick walls, gleaming wood floors, black-and-white photos of expectant mothers – are a fitting backdrop for the hip booty including dresses, T-shirts and jackets, jeans and specialty skincare items.

Burberry
| | 27 | 24 | 22 | VE |

E 50s | 9 E. 57th St. (bet. 5th & Madison Aves.) | 4/5/6/F/N/R/W to 59th St./Lexington Ave. | 212-407-7100
SoHo | 131 Spring St. (bet. Greene & Wooster Sts.) | 6 to Spring St. | 212-925-9300
www.burberry.com

While they still sell "the best trenches this side of the pond", "they've come a long way from rainwear" at this historic British brand, whose Midtown and SoHo stores, with their "pitch-perfect layouts" and "lovely" if slightly "snooty" staff, supply men, women and even pets with "awesome" "basics and trendy collection pieces" sporting the familiar black, white and beige pattern (the Prorsum line is "as hip as plaid gets"); cynics cry it's "almost a cliché" – "like wearing a neon bulb for the status-oriented" – but none dispute that the "well-made" merch "measures up" to the "sky-high prices"; N.B. 57th Street also stocks children's clothing.

Burlington Coat Factory ☕
| | 15 | 9 | 8 | I |

Chelsea | 707 Sixth Ave. (bet. 22nd & 23rd Sts.) | F/V to 23rd St. | 212-229-2247

(continued)

Burlington Coat Factory

Downtown | Atlantic Ctr. | 625 Atlantic Ave. (bet. Ft. Greene Pl. & S. Portland Ave.) | Brooklyn | 2/3/4/5/B/D/M/N/Q/R to Atlantic Ave. | 718-622-4057
Staten Island | 1801 South Ave. (West Shore Expwy.) | 718-982-0300
800-444-2628 | www.coat.com

Calling all "bargain queens", kings and princelings to this discount chain, which carries "not just coats" – though those "really are their forte" – but "decent" adult, baby and kids' apparel, shoes and linens at "cheap prices"; but with its "dreary" decor, "piles of unrelated merchandise" and plethora of "last year's styles", it resembles "an indoor swap meet", and that – plus the "unhelpful assistants" – make naysayers nix it as "not worth the hunt."

Burton Store ◉   25 | 23 | 22 | E

SoHo | 106 Spring St. (Mercer St.) | C/E to Spring St. | 212-966-8068 | www.burton.com

"If you snowboard or ski", you'll "think you're in Arctic heaven" at this sports manufacturer's showcase and "cool concept store in SoHo"; in a space that mimics the slopes with tilted flooring, there's "the best gear" for snowboarding, plus "the most innovative, cutting-edge clothes anywhere"; staffers "know your questions before you ask", but don't take their word for it – put the goods to the test in the special 20-degree cold room.

Butik Ⓜ   - | - | - | E

W Village | 605 Hudson St. (bet. Bethune & W. 12th Sts.) | A/C/E/L to 14th St./8th Ave. | 212-367-8014

The name means 'shop' in old Danish, and that's exactly what supermodel Helena Christensen and pal Leif Sigersen have created in this cozy boutique, which brings the Scandinavian spirit to the West Village with an eclectic mix of "bohemian bric-a-brac", including antique furniture, modern and vintage clothing, flowers and organic chocolates that are all "beautifully presented."

Butter   ▽ 23 | 23 | 17 | VE

Downtown | 389 Atlantic Ave. (bet. Bond & Hoyt Sts.) | Brooklyn | A/C/G to Hoyt/Schermerhorn Sts. | 718-260-9033

"Everything is breathtaking" at this expansive Atlantic Avenue mecca owned by stylemeister-sisters Robin and Eva Weiss agree admirers who melt at the "exquisitely edited selection" of "unique must-haves" from Dries Van Noten, Marni, Tucker, Veronique Branquinho and Rick Owens, all arranged by color, along with super-"stylish" jewelry, handbags and shoes in a modern "gallerylike" setting; but the price-sensitive pout that the "lovely" looks are too "expensive for words", "especially in Downtown Brooklyn."

NEW Butterflies &   23 | 24 | 23 | E
Zebras & Moonbeams ⊠

TriBeCa | 104 Reade St. (bet. Church St. & W. B'way) | 1/2/3 to Chambers St. | 212-227-2902 | www.bzmny.com

Like the Jimi Hendrix classic from whence it gets its name (and proclivity for psychedelic fuchsia wallpaper), this expansive TriBeCa boutique with a "really nice" staff takes ladies under its wing to outfit them in "hip clothes with a hard rock edge" (e.g. Twinkle, Ya-Ya) as well as indie scents and pretty but no-nonsense jewelry.

🛂 buybuy BABY ⦿ | 23 | 21 | 19 | M |

Chelsea | 270 Seventh Ave. (bet. 25th & 26th Sts.) | 1 to 23rd St. | 917-344-1555 | www.buybuybaby.com

"Bed Bath & Beyond meets the baby world" at Chelsea's "one-stop shop" "wonderland" – a "welcome suburban intrusion" that "covers all categories with ease", offering the "broadest assortment" of clothing, furniture, gear, toys and supplies; throw in a well-oiled, "awesome registry" process, a staff that "knows its products (how refreshing)" and prices "for everyone's wallet" and "all you want to do is buy, buy, buy."

By Boe | – | – | – | M |

(fka Annika Inez)

SoHo | 172 Prince St. (bet. Sullivan & Thompson Sts.) | C/E to Spring St. | 212-226-5200 | www.byboe.com

Though the name changed, this understated SoHo shop still keep devotees coming back for Swedish designer Annika Salame's clean-lined, simple jewelry – from a sliver of a gold crescent pendant and thin, wire-styled earrings to chunky vintage bead necklaces and colored enamel chains; though quantities are limited, the reasonably priced gems and accessories are always changing, and the service is laid-back.

Caché | 18 | 19 | 18 | E |

E 40s | 805 Third Ave. (bet. 49th & 50th Sts.) | 6 to 51st St. | 212-588-8719

W 60s | The Shops at Columbus Circle, Time Warner Ctr. | 10 Columbus Circle, ground fl. (60th St. at B'way) | 1/A/B/C/D to 59th St./Columbus Circle | 212-823-9693 ⦿

Staten Island | Staten Island Mall | 2655 Richmond Ave. (bet. Platinum Ave. & Richmond Hill Rd.) | 718-370-8843 ⦿

800-788-2224 | www.cache.com

Make a beeline for this "black-tie" bonanza to emulate your favorite *Dynasty* diva via "flashy", spangly, "dressy" eveningwear in "all lengths, all colors and all styles", all "on the pricy side"; though it's a standard chain-stop on the hunt for a "great prom dress", "larger-size women" chide "not everyone is a size 2 or 4."

Cadeau | ▽ 25 | 23 | 23 | E |

NoLita | 254 Elizabeth St. (bet. Houston & Prince Sts.) | N/R/W to Prince St. | 212-674-5747 | 866-622-3322 | www.cadeaumaternity.com

Expectees who can't part with their pre-pregnancy style head to this "amazing" NoLita maternity shop offering some of the "most beautiful, well-made" and on-trend clothing for those all-important nine months; yes, the "chic" Italian garments are "expensive", but moms-to-be believe that "feeling hip" "rather than frumpy" makes the dent in the wallet "worthwhile."

Calling All Pets | 24 | 16 | 25 | M |

E 70s | 301 E. 76th St. (bet. 1st & 2nd Aves.) | 6 to 77th St. | 212-734-7051
E 80s | 1590 York Ave. (bet. 83rd & 84th Sts.) | 4/5/6 to 86th St. | 212-249-7387

"Loved by all two- and four-legged critters in the neighborhood", this "cozy" UES duo boasts the "nicest", most "informed" staff as well as the "best selection of top pet products" at "good prices"; in addition to their "awesome" free delivery service, they can also special-order birthday cakes and cookies to help your creatures celebrate in style.

Calvin Klein

25 | 26 | 22 | VE

E 60s | 654 Madison Ave. (60th St.) | N/R/W to 5th Ave./59th St. | 212-292-9000 | 877-256-7373 | www.calvinklein.com

The "austere rooms are a perfect showcase for the clean lines" of the "subtle", "sexy, American" men- and womenswear offered at this trendsetting designer flagship in the East 60s; "as a New Yorker, you should always dress in black and they have plenty" of it – though Francisco Costa, who took over a few years ago, has added color to the clothes; the Calvin clan also "loves to browse" the "wonderful home section", aided by "salespeople who help when needed."

Calvin Klein Underwear ●

21 | 19 | 17 | M

SoHo | 104 Prince St. (bet. Greene & Mercer Sts.) | N/R/W to Prince St. | 212-274-1639 | 877-258-7646 | www.cku.com

"If you're comfortable in your 'Calvins'" head to this minimalist shop in SoHo kitted out with captivating photos of scantily clad models and start from the first layer, picking up "sexy" "casual-to-dressy" undies for men and women, plus "nicely styled" sleepwear; the "staff makes you feel welcome" and "prices are reasonable", so acolytes are in-Kleined to "definitely return."

Calvin Tran

- | - | - | E

NoLita | 246 Mulberry St. (bet. Prince & Spring Sts.) | 6 to Spring St. | 212-431-2576 | www.calvintran.com

The Zen-garden aura at this NoLita boutique invites shoppers to contemplate the "chic and refined" threads of this young designer, whose "terrific staff is ready to help but not harass" the female clientele (which has included Iman, Drew Barrymore and Brooke Shields); patrons praise the "pieces that can go just about anywhere", be they "well-priced" slinky gowns, ruffly face-framing jackets, Red Engine denim or "multifunctional" garments, like shirts that turn into skirts.

Calypso

23 | 24 | 18 | E

E 60s | 815 Madison Ave. (bet. 68th & 69th Sts.) | 6 to 68th St. | 212-585-0310

E 70s | 935 Madison Ave. (74th St.) | 6 to 77th St. | 212-535-4100

NoLita | 280 Mott St. (bet. Houston & Prince Sts.) | B/D/F/V to B'way/ Lafayette St. | 212-965-0990

SoHo | 191 Lafayette St. (Broome St.) | B/D/F/V to B'way/Lafayette St. | 212-941-6512

SoHo | 424 Broome St. (bet. Crosby & Lafayette Sts.) | 6 to Spring St. | 212-274-0449

TriBeCa | 137 W. Broadway (bet. Duane & Thomas Sts.) | 1/2/3 to Chambers St. | 212-608-2222

W Village | 654 Hudson St. (bet. Gansevoort & W. 13th Sts.) | A/C/E/L to 14th St./8th Ave. | 646-638-3000

www.calypso-celle.com

No "matter which outpost" of this "dreamy" boutique you visit, you'll uncover "boho chic by the boatload" with the help of a "gorgeous", "caring" staff; owner-designer Christiane Celle creates a "visual feast", "dressing" each shop "like a rainbow" – "you feel the beat of the islands" as you sift through the "breezy", "floaty" tunics and dresses, "au courant" cashmere sweaters and "girlie" fashions from "hard-to-find" labels that walk the line between "urban vintage and tropical exoticism"; even her sexy trademark "perfumes brighten up" your mood; N.B. the 424 Broome Street branch is now a Calypso outlet.

Calypso Bijoux ▽ 25 | 26 | 22 | E

NoLita | 252 Mott St. (bet. Houston & Prince Sts.) | N/R/W to Prince St. | 212-334-9730 | www.calypso-celle.com

This NoLita jewel in the Christiane Celle network of "great, hip stores" for everything from resort wear to home furnishings is "a great place to send your boyfriend for a winning present", whether it's a costume or semiprecious piece; though on the "expensive" side, "there are some great finds" in the high-end selection from around the world, including signature silver or gold ID disc necklaces that can be engraved.

Calypso Home - | - | - | E

NoLita | 199 Lafayette St. (Broome St.) | 6 to Spring St. | 212-925-6200 | www.calypso-celle.com

If you want to "channel St. Barts' style into your home", hit this "gorgeous" NoLita shop, part of Christiane Celle's wildly popular, ever-expanding Caribbean-inspired consortium; it's a well-edited showcase for handmade wooden furniture and international accessories like gold leather ottomans, Mexican silver bowls, snake quilts from India, Italian pottery and colorful cashmere throws; P.S. the "relaxing" space makes fans feel as if they're "in a spa", so no wonder they "want to move in."

Calypso Kids & Home 26 | 23 | 21 | E

SoHo | 407 Broome St. (bet. Centre & Lafayette Sts.) | 6 to Spring St. | 212-941-9700 | www.calypso-celle.com

The apple doesn't fall far from the tree at this "beautiful" SoHo kids' offshoot of the "trendy" Calypso women's empire; there are "mini-me" versions of the signature beachy duds and "amazing cashmere sweaters" along with furniture finds and limited-edition toys.

Camera Land ⊠ 22 | 15 | 23 | E

E 50s | 575 Lexington Ave. (bet. 51st & 52nd Sts.) | 6 to 51st St. | 212-753-5128 | 866-967-8427 | www.cameralandny.com

"There are not that many real camera stores" of the "traditional neighborhood" variety left and this "surprisingly price-competitive" East 50s standby is one of "the best NY can offer" attest photo fiends; the "professional, competent" staff provides "great service and advice", while the space boasts "the latest" equipment to purchase or rent, digital printing kiosks and a gallery of "attractive picture frames."

Camilla Dietz Bergeron ⊠⊅ - | - | - | VE

E 60s | 818 Madison Ave., 4th fl. (bet. 68th & 69th Sts.) | 6 to 68th St. | 212-794-9100 | www.cdbltd.com

This Madison Avenue charmer, tucked away on the fourth floor, feels so "personal" it's almost like "family" to fans who turn to the owners for their "exquisite taste" and "high level of knowledge" when looking for "beautiful" estate and antique jewelry with "pizzazz" from Cartier, Van Cleef & Arpels, Paul Flato, Jean Schlumberger and Mauboussin, as well as the eponymous designer's own pieces; N.B. by appointment only.

	QUALITY	DISPLAY	SERVICE	COST

Camouflage
24 | 24 | 22 | E

Chelsea | 139 Eighth Ave. (17th St.) | A/C/E/L to 14th St./8th Ave. | 212-691-1750

Chelsea | 141 Eighth Ave. (17th St.) | A/C/E/L to 14th St./8th Ave. | 212-741-9118

A "neighborhood asset" since the '70s, these Chelsea twins project sophistication with their "nice mix" of men's dress-up-or-down design-ers like Etro and Marc Jacobs that are always "of the moment" but also "thoughtfully chosen" "with an eye to what a [regular] guy wants to wear"; N.B. the branch on the 'uptown' side of Eighth Avenue carries more familiar labels, while the 'downtown' site's sportswear is edgier.

Camper ●
23 | 21 | 17 | E

SoHo | 125 Prince St. (Wooster St.) | N/R/W to Prince St. | 212-358-1841 | www.camper.com

"Love the way" the "buttery leather" "styles are laid out" – they're so "easy to see and touch" at this "nicely designed" SoHo stomping ground showcasing his-and-hers "match-everything shoes" from the "eccentric Spanish label"; "hipsters with deep pockets" "don't come here looking for high heels and pointy toes", but they do come for "unique Euro" looks with "splashes of color and whimsy", sold by a staff that's "cool" but still "helpful."

Canal Hi-Fi
16 | 10 | 13 | M

Chinatown | 319 Canal St. (bet. Greene & Mercer Sts.) | 6/J/M/N/Q/R/W/Z to Canal St. | 212-925-6575 | www.canalhifi.com

"Typifying Canal Street's bargain-basement reputation" for "cheap electronics", this "mom-and-pop" fixture features "help that can lead you to the right choices" in DJ equipment and home-audio components (and since some "stuff is connected", you might get a demo); still, the cash-conscious caution you'd "better know how much you should be paying before going" so you can "haggle to get the best bargains."

Canal Jean Company ●
17 | 13 | 13 | M

Flatbush | 2236 Nostrand Ave. (bet. Aves. H & I) | Brooklyn | 2/5 to Brooklyn College/Flatbush Ave. | 718-421-7590

For a "funky selection" of "eclectic jeans" and "everything you need for your wardrobe, from lingerie to shoes", to "unique used clothing, some head for this Flatbush standby; Brooklyn's warehouse-style haunt yields "great buys if you dig for them", plus it's especially "awe-some" for "teenagers" on the hunt for "trendy" threads; N.B. the Lower Broadway behemoth is now closed.

⊠ Canine Styles
26 | 25 | 21 | VE

E 60s | 830 Lexington Ave. (bet. 63rd & 64th Sts.) | F to Lexington Ave./63rd St. | 212-838-2064

E 80s | 1195 Lexington Ave. (bet. 81st & 82nd Sts.) | 6 to 77th St. | 212-472-9440 ⊠

G Village | 43 Greenwich Ave. (bet. Charles & Perry Sts.) | A/B/C/D/E/F/V to W. 4th St. | 212-352-8591 ●

www.caninestyles.com

The "cute" Downtown pet shop for the "style-conscious" formerly known as Fetch recently joined forces with this East 80s canine cou-ture club – and even spawned an East 60s offspring, all offering a "beautiful selection" of "unique" goods for beloved bowwows; the vibe is still "Gucci for poochie" so expect to "dish out a fortune" for "fancy beds", "adorable" catwalk-worthy "doggy duds", "superb" toys and "colorful collars and leashes."

Cantaloup
22 | 19 | 18 | E

E 70s | 1036 Lexington Ave. (74th St.) | 6 to 77th St. | 212-249-3566
NEW **Gravesend** | 514 Kings Hwy. (bet. E. 2nd & 3rd Sts.) | Brooklyn | F to Kings Hwy. | 718-336-4733
Cantaloup: Destination Denim
E 70s | 1359 Second Ave. (72nd St.) | 6 to 77th St. | 212-288-3569
Cantaloup Luxe ●
E 70s | 1217 Third Ave. (bet. 70th & 71st Sts.) | 6 to 68th St. | 212-249-1241
A "cute stop" for "chic" clothing, this "friendly" East 70s trio appointed with antique tables and chandeliers and its new Gravesend sibling ap-peel to women with a fine-tuned sense of "their own style"; the Destination Denim shop boasts an LA vibe, stocked with "all the jeans" you could possibly need, including "fun", of-the-moment labels like Earnest Sewn, Rock & Republic and True Religion, while the Lexington Avenue standby and Luxe shop carry lots of "unique pieces from the trendiest up-and-coming designers."

Canyon Beachwear ●
26 | 18 | 21 | E

E 60s | 1136 Third Ave. (66th St.) | 6 to 68th St. | 917-432-0732 | 800-863-6681 | www.canyonbeachwear.com
For those who have a "hard time finding swimwear to fit" and "nice cover-up choices", this East 60s "nirvana" "is the place to go" agree the sea-and-sand set who promise "you won't feel intimidated" here; the staff is "attentive" and "knowledgeable", bringing you a "wonderful selection" of the "latest styles" that "flatters even the most bathing-suit averse"; it's "worth every penny", and what's more, you "leave feeling like Elle Macpherson."

Capezio
24 | 18 | 19 | M

E 60s | 136 E. 61st St. (Lexington Ave.) | 4/5/6/F/N/R/W to 59th St./Lexington Ave. | 212-758-8833
E 90s | 1651 Third Ave., 3rd fl. (93rd St.) | 6 to 96th St. | 212-348-7210
W 50s | 1650 Broadway, 2nd fl. (51st St.) | 1 to 50th St. | 212-245-2130 ●
W 50s | 1776 Broadway, 2nd fl. (57th St.) | 1/A/B/C/D to 59th St./Columbus Circle | 212-586-5140
877-532-6237 | www.capeziodance.com
"If you dance or want to look like you do", give this "legendary" "lifesaver" a twirl; sure it's twinkle-toe "heaven", offering "work-out clothes that dancers crave", with "fine-quality" footwear and leotards in every "color you need for any show", but the "great gear" also "wows" "stylish gym-goers who want to look sexy while sweating."

Capitol Fishing Tackle Co. ▣
– | – | – | M

Garment District | 132 W. 36th St. (bet. B'way & 7th Ave.) | B/D/F/N/Q/R/V/W to 34th St./Herald Sq. | 212-929-6132 | 800-528-0853 | www.capitolfishing.com
Reeling in tyros and experts alike for nearly four decades, this vintage Chelsea anglers' paradise recently relocated to the Garment District, but brought its refreshingly raffish neon sign along for the ride; according to fin fans who hook "excellent equipment for salt-" and fresh-water fishing – from Penn to Shimano – from its well-stocked shelves

and appreciate its staff of *Old Man and the Sea* types who dole out tackle tips, it remains the "best in New York" City.

Cappellini

-	-	-	VE

SoHo | 152 Wooster St. (Houston St.) | N/R/W to Prince St. | 212-620-7953 | www.cappellini.it

Decked out in floor-to-ceiling red, this SoHo space showcases modern chairs, sofas, beds, dressers and lighting accessories, all of which are made by the venerable Italian design house that was founded in the 1930s; "cutting-edge" fashion for your home comes at a "large price", but when you "fall in love" with this furniture as some of our respondents did, cost seems inconsequential.

Capucine ●

-	-	-	E

TriBeCa | 20 Harrison St. (bet. Greenwich & Hudson Sts.) | 1/2/3 to Chambers St. | 212-219-4030 | www.capucinemaman.com

Svelte trendseekers as well as expectant women unwilling to see their style vanish along with their waistlines count on Capucine Vacher's TriBeCa shop to keep them in top fashion form; the first camp covets finds from lines like Diane von Furstenberg while pregos scout out "beautiful, original" maternity clothing from labels like Belly Basics, Home Mummy and yes, DvF too; rounding out the mix: kids clothing, furniture, bedding and home furnishings.

Caravan ●

▽ 20	24	16	M

NoHo | 2 Great Jones St. (B'way) | 6 to Astor Pl. | 212-260-8189 | www.shopcaravan.com

Embrace the vagabond spirit at this airy NoHo shop (the now stationary home of a formerly moving store on wheels), where indie designers like Sretsis and Rojas showcase their "beautiful clothing" for both sexes in a "very original, very chic" high-ceilinged space; you can also catch up with these fashionable gypsies in their original van (weekends-only), or at the by-appointment offshoot at 128 East 91st Street.

Cardeology ●

19	15	15	I

W 70s | 314 Columbus Ave. (bet. 74th & 75th Sts.) | B/C to 72nd St. | 212-579-9310
W 80s | 452 Amsterdam Ave. (bet. 81st & 82nd Sts.) | 1 to 79th St. | 212-873-2491

Thank god there's "no Hallmark here" exhale admirers who converge at this "cute" West Side stationery duo carrying a "creative selection of cards and gifts" ranging from journals and calendars to Crabtree & Evelyn toiletries.

Carlos Miele

-	-	-	E

Meatpacking | 408 W. 14th St. (bet. 9th Ave. & Washington St.) | A/C/E/L to 14th St./8th Ave. | 646-336-6642 | www.carlosmiele.com.br

It's not only the São Paulo sexpots who dig this Brazilian designer's Meatpacking shop with its "amazing" curvy walls and rows of "gorgeous" dresses that "fit like a dream"; NYC fashionistas also flock here for the red-carpet–worthy eveningwear, stylish suits, shoes and clutches.

☑ Carlyle Custom Convertibles

26	19	24	E

Chelsea | 122 W. 18th St. (bet. 6th & 7th Aves.) | 1/2/3 to 14th St. | 212-675-3212

(continued)

(continued)

Carlyle Custom Convertibles

E 60s | 1056 Third Ave. (bet. 62nd & 63rd Sts.) | 4/5/6/F/N/R/W to 59th St./Lexington Ave. | 212-838-1525
www.carlylesofas.com

Sellers of sofa beds since the '60s, this Chelsea and UES duo has a "reputation for being the best of any convertibles" available, with a "great selection", "good upholstery", "excellent mattresses" and "lovely fabrics", as well as an option to work with your own material; the only thing about these sleepers that will keep you awake is the "high price."

ⓩ Carolina Herrera ⓢ | 28 | 27 | 25 | VE |

E 70s | 954 Madison Ave. (75th St.) | 6 to 77th St. | 212-249-6552 | www.carolinaherrera.com

"Get dressed to go" to the "most elegant house of chic on [upper] Madison Avenue", where you'll encounter "refined, can't-go-wrong" dresses and suits in a "classic style like the designer herself", as well as an expanded floor of wedding gowns for "brides who want the best"; the "ladies who lunch" also love the "luxurious" alterations process and "personal service (they know your name every time)", which help offset the "ouch"-inducing prices.

Carol's Daughter ◗ | 24 | 22 | 21 | M |

Harlem | 24 W. 125th St. (bet. 5th & Lenox Aves.) | 2/3 to 125th St. | 212-828-6757
Downtown | Atlantic Terminal | 139 Flatbush Ave. (Atlantic Ave.) | Brooklyn | 2/3/4/5/B/D/M/N/Q/R to Atlantic Ave. | 718-622-4514
Fort Greene | 1 S. Elliot Pl. (DeKalb Ave.) | Brooklyn | G to Fulton St. | 718-596-1862
877-540-2101 | www.carolsdaughter.com

Owner Lisa Price started out by mixing lotions in her kitchen sink for pals and family, and her "positive-vibe" Fort Greene original shop, Atlantic Terminal kiosk and Harlem offshoot continue the tradition with homemade "natural products that are great for glowing skin" and making tresses "do what they are supposed to do"; fans like Will Smith and Jay-Z have invested big bucks in the brand – and yes, Oprah loves it too.

ⓩ Cartier | 29 | 28 | 26 | VE |

E 50s | 653 Fifth Ave. (52nd St.) | E/V to 5th Ave./53rd St. | 212-753-0111
E 60s | 828 Madison Ave. (69th St.) | 6 to 68th St. | 212-472-6400 ⓢ
800-227-8437 | www.cartier.com

In 1917, Pierre Cartier traded a string of pearls plus $100 for a Fifth Avenue neo-Renaissance mansion, which is still the U.S. headquarters for this jeweler that's joined by a renovated East 60s spin-off; an "extraordinary" staff purveys the "best baubles", bangles and beads, watches, silver *objets* and stationery, all "status symbols" of "classic elegance"; sure, you "shell out big bucks for small things", but "nothing says 'I love you' like that red box."

Cassina USA ⓢ | - | - | - | VE |

E 50s | 155 E. 56th St. (bet. Lexington & 3rd Aves.) | 4/5/6/F/N/R/W to 59th St./Lexington Ave. | 212-245-2121 | 800-770-3568 | www.cassinausa.com

For those who feel that "classic is best", this sexy, high-voltage red-and-white East 50s showroom for the famed Italian furniture manufacturer features The Masters Collection from industry icons like Le Corbusier and Charlotte Perriand, as well as pieces from newer luminaries like Piero Lissoni and Philippe Starck; although prices range "from high to extra high", enthusiasts applaud the "impressive quality" and a buying option that promises 10-day delivery of select beds, chairs, lounges and tables straight from The Boot.

Castor & Pollux
| | | | E |

W Village | 238 W. 10th St. (bet. Bleecker & Hudson Sts.) | 1 to Christopher St./Sheridan Sq. | 212-645-6572 | www.castorandpolluxstore.com

Owner-designer Kerrilynn Pamer moved her "lovely little" women's boutique from Prospect Heights into a West Village space that's twice the size but no less charming thanks to its glam retro vibe; choose from hip-girl goodies from Filippa K, Mint and 3.1 Phillip Lim – and don't forget to peruse the display cases filled with jewelry and beauty finds like Poppy King's coveted Lipstick Queen line.

Casual Male XL
| 19 | 16 | 20 | M |

Gramercy | 291 Third Ave. (bet. 22nd & 23rd Sts.) | 6 to 23rd St. | 212-532-1415
Bronx | Bay Plaza Shopping Ctr. | 2094 Bartow Ave. (CoOp City Blvd.) | 6 to Pelham Bay Park | 718-379-4148 ●
Canarsie | 1110 Pennsylvania Ave. (bet. Cozine & Flatlands Aves.) | Brooklyn | L to Canarsie/Rockaway Pkwy. | 718-649-2924
Dyker Heights | 527 86th St. (bet. 5th Ave. & Fort Hamilton Pkwy.) | Brooklyn | R to 86th St. | 718-921-9770
Mill Basin | 2435 Flatbush Ave. (bet. Aves. T & U) | Brooklyn | 2/5 to Brooklyn College/Flatbush Ave. | 718-252-1313 ●
Staten Island | 2295 Richmond Ave. (bet. Nome & Travis Aves.) | 718-370-7767 ●
866-844-6595 | www.casualmale.com

This chain for larger-than-average men carries casual "hard-to-find" items for the big boys including suits, shirts, jeans and tees from brands like Polo, Cutter & Buck and Levi's; the "good selection" and "not-so-fancy" offerings make this store "the Jeep of clothing" dispensing practical, somewhat "mundane" items that "will wear for years."

Caswell-Massey
| 25 | 23 | 22 | M |

E 40s | 518 Lexington Ave. (48th St.) | 6 to 51st St. | 212-755-2254 | 800-326-0500 | www.caswellmassey.com

In 1752, Great Britain still owned America, Ben Franklin was flying his kite and this company was selling its first cologne, called Number Six and favored by George Washington; "America's oldest chemist and perfumer" still purveys soaps, fragrances and lotions that are "classic" like the "wonderful almond-scented" potions, plus shaving gear and children's items at this Lexington Avenue shop.

Catbird ●
| | | | E |

Williamsburg | 219 Bedford Ave. (N. 4th St.) | Brooklyn | L to Bedford Ave. | 718-599-3457
Williamsburg | 390 Metropolitan Ave. (Marcy Ave.) | Brooklyn | L to Bedford Ave. | 718-388-7688
www.catbirdnyc.com

Shoppers on the prowl for well-priced finds, recognizable boutique labels, jeans from J Brand and Wrangler and a smart selection of shoes and accessories score big time at the original robins-egg-blue Metropolitan Avenue branch of this Williamsburg duo; the newer outpost on Bedford provides plenty of catnip for jewelry junkies, showcasing delicate necklaces, bold earrings and more from local artisans like Bing Bang and St. Kilda in whitewashed antique china cabinets.

Catherine Angiel
25 | 23 | 23 | E

G Village | 43 Greenwich Ave. (bet. Charles & Perry Sts.) | 1 to Christopher St./Sheridan Sq. | 212-924-4314 | www.catherineangiel.com
This long-standing namesake jeweler in a gallerylike space in the Village carries a collection that ranges from "edgy" (think black diamond dragons inspired by tattoos) to more ethereal, vintage-looking necklaces, engagement rings and bands; N.B. Courteney Cox-Arquette and Anne Heche are Angiel admirers.

Catherine Malandrino
24 | 24 | 20 | VE

SoHo | 468 Broome St. (Greene St.) | C/E to Spring St. | 212-925-6765
W Village | 652 Hudson St. (13th St.) | A/C/E/L to 14th St./8th Ave. | 212-929-8710
www.catherinemalandrino.com
"Paris takes NYC by storm" at this duo in SoHo and on the West Village/Meatpacking border filled with "printed tunics, flowy skirts" and "romantic, flirty frocks" that Demi Moore, Heidi Klum and "young women of style and substance" love since they "make you feel feminine" "in a modern way"; but while most find the French designer's styles "flattering", a few deem them "ill-fitting" – unless you're "six feet tall and rich."

Catherine Memmi
- | - | - | VE

SoHo | 45 Greene St. (bet. Broome & Grand Sts.) | N/R/W to Prince St. | 212-226-8200 | www.catherinememmi.com
Laid out like a large, lavish apartment, this SoHo home furnishings and accessories shop showcases the eponymous Parisian designer's warm, neo-minimalist collection; tables in precious woods like wenge, lavish linens in unusual colors like chocolate and room sprays and candles in refreshing scents like white orchid and cucumber make it a haunt for well-heeled Francophiles.

Catimini
26 | 25 | 18 | VE

E 80s | 1125 Madison Ave. (bet. 84th & 85th Sts.) | 4/5/6 to 86th St. | 212-987-0688 | www.catimini.com
City parents who want their offspring "to look different than all the other Gap toddlers" and kiddies on the playground frequent this Madison Avenue shop, the sole U.S. branch of the popular French childrenswear chain whose forte is "unique" "but don't-let-your-child-eat-a-bite-in-this" clothing; the "stylish" and "adorable tot togs" come in "cute mix-and-match outfits", making shopping a snap for the time-pressed.

Catriona Mackechnie ◑
- | - | - | E

Meatpacking | 400 W. 14th St. (9th Ave.) | A/C/E/L to 14th St./8th Ave. | 212-242-3200 | 800-901-3310 | www.catrionamackechnie.com
For unmentionables your partner won't stop talking about and you probably won't see anywhere else, head to this Meatpacking District den of desire and linger over "very sexy lingerie" from unique Italian, French and British labels including Damaris, Dolce & Gabbana and Guia La Bruna; order custom-made knickers, then

get in the swim of showing off your hot bod with brazen bathing suits from handpicked European designers.

CB I Hate Perfume 🗷Ⓜ

-	-	-	VE

Williamsburg | 93 Wythe Ave. (N. 10th St.) | Brooklyn | L to Bedford Ave. | 718-384-6890 | www.cbihateperfume.com

Owner Christopher Brosius (ex Kiehl's and Demeter) considers himself an artist and, accordingly, his Williamsburg storefront looks more like a gallery than a *parfumerie*, but what's lining the shelves are bottles of handmade, non-alcohol-based original scents like The Fir Tree, Lavender Tea and Gathering Apples, and cutting-edge aromas including custom-blends are in the air.

NEW CB2 🌑

-	-	-	I

SoHo | 451 Broadway (bet. Grand & Howard Sts.) | 6/J/M/N/Q/R/W/Z to Canal St. | 212-219-1454 | www.cb2.com

Crate & Barrel's younger, hipper new spin-off lands in SoHo, the first offshoot located outside its Chicago hometown; the affordably priced, apartment-sized home goods range from midcentury style furniture in bright, bold colors to glassware, lighting, rugs and bedding-, bath- and office accessories in materials other than the plywood and plastic purveyed by some competitors.

Cécile et Jeanne

∇ 24	24	23	M

E 80s | 1100 Madison Ave. (bet. 82nd & 83rd Sts.) | 4/5/6 to 86th St. | 212-535-5700
SoHo | 436 W. Broadway (bet. Prince & Spring Sts.) | C/E to Spring St. | 212-625-3535 🌑
www.cecilejeanne.com

"It's great that I can indulge my obsession without having to fly to Paris" assert admirers of this French jeweler with Uptown and Downtown offshoots; "wearable" handcrafted pieces – like the signature doves, "spectacularly colored" resin gems or the newer Renaissance-like Opera styles – are offered by a "friendly" staff at reasonable prices.

🟅 Celine

28	24	24	VE

E 60s | 667 Madison Ave. (bet. 60th & 61st Sts.) | N/R/W to 5th Ave./59th St. | 212-486-9700 | www.celine.com

"Ladies who lunch do their thing" at this Upper East Side boutique, which houses "high-end", "sophisticated Parisian" goods from the established French luxury label; some suggest it "can't decide if it wants to cater to the young and stylish or the old" "since Michael Kors left" as the designer of the line; still, it's perfect for "people with expense accounts" who find the "understated, timeless elegance" of the nipped-in suits, lusted-after Inca loafers and Lirine bags "worth the investment."

Cellini 🗷

27	23	24	VE

E 40s | Waldorf-Astoria | 301 Park Ave. (bet. 49th & 50th Sts.) | 6 to 51st St. | 212-751-9824
E 50s | 509 Madison Ave. (53rd St.) | E/V to 5th Ave./53rd St. | 212-888-0505
www.cellinijewelers.com

Whether it's the Waldorf-Astoria shop or the pint-sized Madison Avenue branch a few blocks uptown, watch aficionados say "you can't go wrong" with this "great place for the very best" brands like Franck Muller and Richard Mille; the "knowledgeable staff" is "surprisingly friendly," and "treats regulars like family"; N.B. check out the chic pink and yellow diamond jewelry.

Centricity ●

`- | - | - | I`

E Village | 63 E. Fourth St. (bet. Bowery & 2nd Ave.) | 6 to Bleecker St. | 212-979-7601

It helps "to be a garage/tag sale person", but even vintage-savvy East Villagers find this nook "a fun, different place to browse", to the tune of two chirping parakeets; most of the merch seems straight from the malls of the '70s and '80s: polyester jumpsuits, woolly purses and pouf dresses, plus costume jewelry and racks crammed with kitchen items and tchotchkes; prices for the menswear and womenswear are as friendly as the owner; N.B. closed Tuesdays.

Ⓩ Century 21 ●

`22 | 10 | 9 | M`

Financial District | 22 Cortlandt St. (bet. B'way & Church St.) | R/W to Cortlandt St. | 212-227-9092

Bay Ridge | 472 86th St. (bet. 4th & 5th Aves.) | Brooklyn | R to 86th St. | 718-748-3266

www.c21stores.com

This "Downtown discount destination" and its Bay Ridge relative is "a financially strapped fashionista's dream", with "designer duds" "at pauper prices", "plus undies and accessories galore", "orgasmic discoveries" in shoes and "a veritable cornucopia" of cosmetics, housewares and electronics; get ready to "do some hunting" – "shoving when necessary" – and "be in a patient, forgiving mood" with the "infuriatingly disorganized" displays, "tight, open fitting rooms", "busloads of tourists" and near-"useless staff", because "when you find a treasure, you'll be bragging for years."

Challengher NYC Ⓢ Ⓜ

`- | - | - | M`

Williamsburg | 555 Metropolitan Ave. (bet. Lorimer St. & Union Ave.) | Brooklyn | L to Lorimer St. | 718-387-6228

Owner-designer Christine Ryan can usually be found at her sewing machine inside this under-the-radar Williamsburg shop showcasing her small seasonal collections, which include such carefully tailored, handmade pieces as flowered button-down shirts, tweed jackets and fitted corduroy skirts, many of them priced below $100; tees, pillows and undies silkscreened with her pin-up logo are for sale as well.

Champs ●

`17 | 16 | 14 | M`

Harlem | 208 W. 125th St. (bet. 7th & 8th Aves.) | A/B/C/D to 125th St. | 212-280-0296

W 40s | 5 Times Sq. (42nd St. & 7th Ave.) | 1/2/3/7/N/Q/R/S/W to 42nd St./Times Sq. | 212-354-2009

Elmhurst | Queens Ctr. | 90-15 Queens Blvd. (bet. 57th & 59th Aves.) | Queens | G/R/V to Woodhaven Blvd. | 718-760-0095

Staten Island | Staten Island Mall | 2655 Richmond Ave. (bet. Platinum Ave. & Richmond Hill Rd.) | 718-698-1560

www.champssports.com

Bargain boosters cheer this chain for its "low prices" on sports equipment, including bats, balls, helmets and shoes as well as a "good selection of team merchandise"; in short, most "would shop here again", even if foes find the merely "decent products" and "sketchy service" "disappointing."

	QUALITY	DISPLAY	SERVICE	COST

☒ Chanel
29 27 23 VE

E 50s | 15 E. 57th St. (bet. 5th & Madison Aves.) | N/R/W to 5th Ave./
59th St. | 212-355-5050

E 60s | 737 Madison Ave. (bet. 64th & 65th Sts.) | N/R/W to 5th Ave./
59th St. | 212-535-5505 ⑤

SoHo | 139 Spring St. (Wooster St.) | N/R/W to Prince St. |
212-334-0055

800-550-0005 | www.chanel.com

The "doorman almost dares you to enter" these havens of "haute logo
couture" to peruse Karl Lagerfeld's "traditional tweeds", quilted bags,
signature shoes and eyewear that, whether "fabulous or silly", are the
"embodiment of perfection"; some suggest that "unless you're dropping mega-cash" and dressed "in your best", the otherwise-"helpful"
staff may not even "acknowledge your presence"; but even if "you
have to be 20 to wear it and 70 to afford it", Coco's brand's been the
"epitome of taste, trends and snob appeal" "for almost a century."

Chanel Fine Jewelry ⑤
27 27 25 VE

E 60s | 733 Madison Ave. (64th St.) | F to Lexington Ave./63rd St. |
212-535-5828 | 800-550-0005 | www.chanel.com

For the "ultimate in classy flash", whether it's very-Mademoiselle-
Chanel masses of pearls, the signature quilted Matelessé line or a bijoux
from the Eléments Célesté collection, this Madison Avenue outpost
offers "grandly proportioned breathtaking pieces"; of course, "jewelry
for the stars" comes at "out-of-this-world prices."

Charles Nolan ◑
- - - E

Meatpacking | 30 Gansevoort St. (Hudson St.) | A/C/E/L to 14th St./
8th Ave. | 212-924-4888 | 888-996-6526 | www.charlesnolan.com

In the still-hot Meatpacking District, how refreshing to find an "adorable store" with a "friendly, knowledgeable staff" say the few familiar
with this American designer (best-known for rejuvenating the Anne
Klein label); the colorful, spacious boutique houses his signature chic
tees, silk gowns, tailored wool jackets and pencil skirts, as well as
"one-of-a-kind treasures from resin bangles to lace-up gloves", along
with furniture, housewares and even books.

☒ Charles P. Rogers ◑
26 21 23 E

Flatiron | 55 W. 17th St. (bet. 5th & 6th Aves.) | 4/5/6/L/N/Q/R/W
to 14th St./Union Sq. | 212-675-4400 | 800-582-6229 |
www.charlesprogers.com

"From sleigh beds to day beds", in wood, wrought iron, brass or leather,
there's a "great selection of styles" at this Flatiron manufacturer that
dates back to 1855; "excellent and attentive" customer service, including "right-on-time delivery", also adds to the relaxed experience.

Charles Tyrwhitt ◑
26 24 23 E

E 40s | 377 Madison Ave. (46th St.) | 4/5/6/7/S to 42nd St./Grand Central |
212-286-8988

W 50s | 745 Seventh Ave. (50th St.) | N/R/W to 49th St. | 212-764-4697
www.ctshirts.com

Whether "for work or formal occasions", "comfortable", colorful,
"classy shirts in the English tradition" are available at these Midtown
shops for men (and women); an ample selection of "gorgeous ties"
"and cuff links makes putting an outfit together a snap", and while the

"lovely" goods are "a bit on the expensive side", "there are always terrific sales" going on.

NEW Charlotte Moss 🛇

| 25 | 25 | 18 | VE |

E 60s | 20 E. 63rd St. (bet. 5th & Madison Aves.) | 4/5/6 to 59th St. | 212-308-3888 | www.charlottemoss.com

This "beautifully restored and decorated" five-story East Side townhouse is filled with the patrician interior designer's "well-edited" and very "expensive" collection of "all things unnecessary and fabulous" for the high-end home, from "great vintage books" and antiques to French hand-embroidered linens, throws, William Yeoward crystal and Elsie de Wolfe inspired china, all displayed in vignette room settings; *pour madame*, there's also a choice selection of faux tortoise, vermeil and woven jewelry from the South of France along with equally exquisite pieces from the Sorab & Roshi line.

Charlotte Russe ❶

| 10 | 13 | 11 | I |

Garment District | Manhattan Mall | 901 Sixth Ave. (bet. 32nd & 33rd Sts.) | B/D/F/N/Q/R/V/W to 34th St./Herald Sq. | 212-465-8425
Elmhurst | Queens Ctr. | 90-15 Queens Blvd. (bet. 57th & 59th Aves.) | Queens | G/R/V to Grand Ave./Newtown | 718-271-5807
Staten Island | Staten Island Mall | 2655 Richmond Ave. (bet. Platinum Ave. & Richmond Hill Rd.) | 718-761-0020
www.charlotte-russe.com

"Teens on a limited budget" swamp these "flashy" Manhattan Mall, Queens and Staten Island chain links offering "disposable junior-size duds" and "inexpensive accessories" perfect for gals looking to put together a "last-minute outfit" while only "dropping a few bucks"; sure, they "could use more salespeople to assist and clean up" (watch out for the "piles of clothing dumped around"), but given that they're "packed" with "trendy stuff for cheap", most don't mind much.

Cheap Jack's ❶

| 14 | 12 | 12 | M |

Garment District | 303 Fifth Ave. (31st St.) | B/D/F/N/Q/R/V/W to 34th St./Herald Sq. | 212-777-9564 | www.cheapjacks.com

"Though not as cheap as the name would suggest", this "fairly large" Garment District used-clothing purveyor is a "place to find the quirky and antique" among its vast variety of vintage mens- and womenswear, from "lazy weekend tees" to "leather '70s-era coats"; but critics carp that while "there's a huge inventory, there's not enough good stuff", and "you need to be in the mood to look at overloaded racks" and deal with "help that isn't terribly helpful."

Chelsea Garden Center

| 23 | 20 | 19 | M |

Chelsea | 580 11th Ave. (44th St.) | A/C/E to 42nd St./Port Authority | 212-727-7100
NEW Red Hook | 444 Van Brunt St. (bet. Beard & Reed Sts.) | Brooklyn | F/G to Smith/9th Sts. | 718-875-2100
www.chelseagardencenter.com

Located on the Red Hook waterfront and "in the middle of apartment-centric" Chelsea, this "neighborly" "go-to" duo has "everything for small" pad "plant needs", "huge terrace foliage" and outdoor greenery too; the "dedicated staff" "understands urban gardener issues", plus you can also pick up essential tools and a "nice selection of stuff" like teak window boxes, cast stone planters, "interesting" statues, fountains, birdbaths and patio furniture; still, a few feel "you pay through the nose" for "nothing special."

Chelsea Girl
`- | - | - | E`

SoHo | 63 Thompson St. (bet. Broome & Spring Sts.) | C/E to Spring St. | 212-343-1658

Chelsea Girl Couture

SoHo | 186 Spring St. (bet. Sullivan & Thompson Sts.) | C/E to Spring St. | 212-343-7090
www.chelsea-girl.com

"Vintage vixens seeking fabulous" finds "should flock to this adorable" store on a "sleepy" stretch of Thompson Street, whose intimate, "creaky wood" environs are literally covered with century-spanning clothes and accessories; their current emphasis is on American labels from the '20s –'70s, and there's "a particularly solid collection of handbags" too; N.B. Chelsea Girl Couture nearby features upscale designers like YSL.

Cherry ●
`- | - | - | E`

W Village | 19 Eighth Ave. (bet. Jane & W. 12th Sts.) | A/C/E/L to 14th St./8th Ave. | 212-924-1410

Cherry Men ●

W Village | 17 Eighth Ave. (bet. Jane & W. 12th Sts.) | A/C/E/L to 14th St./8th Ave. | 212-924-5188
www.cherryboutique.com

Whether you patronize the original store, now devoted solely to women, or the newer adjacent men's branch, this Village vintage clothing pair is a "great couture and near-couture designerwear resource"; both are crammed with "cool-looking" mannequins and displays (many featuring the wares of custom shoemaker Joseph LaRose), but if you don't have a weakness for flamboyant, rock 'n' roll rags and costume-y creations from the '60s–'80s, the prices may seem "crazy."

Chico's ●
`20 | 19 | 21 | M`

E 70s | 1310 Third Ave. (75th St.) | 6 to 77th St. | 212-249-9105
NEW **W 80s** | 2300 Broadway (83rd St.) | 1 to 86th St. | 212-579-4572
Bayside | Bay Terrace Shopping Ctr. | 23-60 Bell Blvd. (24th Ave.) | Queens | 7 to Main St. | 718-224-1256
888-669-4911 | www.chicos.com

"Made for me!" cry "forgotten over-40s" of these chain links in Manhattan and Bayside catering to "non-model-shaped women" with "reasonably priced", "stylish" yet "forgiving" suits, separates and dresses in "mix-and-match" styles, many of them "machine-washable"; the "nicest salesladies in the world" ensure "great shopping" despite interiors that are often "too crowded", so never mind if upstarts dismiss its "no-wrinkle" duds as strictly "frumpy."

Children's General Store
`∇ 27 | 21 | 21 | E`

E 40s | Grand Central | 42nd St. (Vanderbilt Ave.) | 4/5/6/7/S to 42nd St./Grand Central | 212-682-0004 ●
E 90s | 168 E. 91st St. (bet. Lexington & 3rd Aves.) | 6 to 96th St. | 212-426-4479

A popular "stopover" for Grand Central commuters and now East 90s residents too, this "old-fashioned" toy duo steers clear of "commercial brands" in favor of items that "emphasize learning" like puzzles and science kits, making it "every intelligent parent's dream"; there are "no bargains", but the "cute gift-wrapping" compensates.

Children's Place, The ◑ — 16 | 16 | 15 | M

Garment District | Manhattan Mall | 901 Sixth Ave. (bet. 32nd & 33rd Sts.) | B/D/F/N/Q/R/V/W to 34th St./Herald Sq. | 212-268-7696 | 800-527-5355 | www.childrensplace.com
Additional locations throughout the NY area

"Considering how fast children grow", it's nice to have a chain where "cheerful" duds for the little ones are "inexpensive enough to stock up on", especially staples like jeans and T-shirts; some report hit-or-miss quality (some things "wear well, others fall apart"), but with "prices this cheap", no one complains too loudly.

Chip & Pepper ◑ — 23 | 22 | 20 | E

NoLita | 250 Mulberry St. (bet. Prince & Spring Sts.) | 6 to Spring St. | 212-343-4220 | www.chipandpepper.com
Complete with a deer antler chandelier, pine-wood shelving and fishing rods, the vibe at twin brothers Chip and Pepper Foster's NoLita nook is more log cabin than designer boutique, emphasizing the lived-in look of their "flattering" "vintage-inspired" jeans; fans (including Naomi Campbell, who allegedly whacked her maid with a BlackBerry over a lost pair) judge the brand a "winner in the overcrowded high-end denim market" and also collect California-cool T-shirts and hoodies.

Chloé ⊠ — 26 | 25 | 20 | VE

E 70s | 850 Madison Ave. (70th St.) | 6 to 68th St. | 212-717-8220 | www.chloe.com
"Everything the twentysomething with a handbag of cash would want" crows the chorus of Chloé converts, who single out the "fantastic fit" and "gamine styling" of this "so-cool" French label for the "younger jet set" housed in a glossy Madison Avenue boutique; the "boho-chic" line is now designed by Paulo Melim Andersson (ex Marni), who replaced creative director Phoebe Philo, which may outdate the above scores.

⊠ Chopard ⊠ — 29 | - | 26 | VE

E 60s | 709 Madison Ave. (bet. 62nd & 63rd Sts.) | 6 to 68th St. | 212-223-2304 | www.chopard.com
"If you love bling", you'll find dazzlers aplenty at the larger, newly relocated Madison Avenue outpost of the 1860 Swiss firm known for "gorgeous" watches like the signature Happy Diamond timepieces with loose gems floating inside the face, as well as fine jewelry; needless to say, "time is money", so the "beautiful merchandise ranges from very expensive to ridiculously expensive."

⊠ Christian Louboutin — 28 | 28 | 24 | VE

E 70s | 965 Madison Ave. (bet. 75th & 76th Sts.) | 6 to 77th St. | 212-396-1884 ⊠
W Village | 59 Horatio St. (bet. Greenwich & Hudson Sts.) | A/C/E/L to 14th St./8th Ave. | 212-255-1910
www.christianlouboutin.fr

"The red soles are the giveaway . . . you spent a fortune!"; *mais oui*, it's "worth every penny" because the French designer's "killer stilettos" and "incredibly sexy", "luxurious footwear" for the "shoe fetishist" showcased at the recently relocated East 70s shop and West Village "gem" are "beyond chic"; "can't live without" his "beautifully crafted" "high-fashion" heels vow the wowed – they're among the "most comfortable and the most sublime" "classy styles" around, plus the staff's "low on attitude."

☑ Christofle ⊠   27 | 26 | 24 | VE

E 60s | 680 Madison Ave. (62nd St.) | N/R/W to 5th Ave./59th St. | 212-308-9390 | www.christofle.com

For "gorgeous everything" in "heavy-weight, beautiful silver", head to the crisp rosewood interior of this Madison Avenue mecca that's particularly known for its "clean-lined" flatware; you can find other "exquisite gifts" in silver plate, crystal and porcelain, but no matter what the material, the prices are consistently "not for the faint of wallet."

Christopher Fischer   ▽ 23 | 27 | 23 | VE

SoHo | 80 Wooster St. (bet. Broome & Spring Sts.) | N/R/W to Prince St. | 212-965-9009 | www.christopherfischer.com

This knitwear designer's namesake SoHo shop may be pristine white, but there's nothing muted about the "many gorgeous colors" of cashmere goods that fill the shelves and racks; the ultramodern, "stunning presentation" offsets the "to-die-for sweaters", both "conservative" and cut down to there, kittenish crocheted cardigans, flirty skirts and high-style wraps, plus there's a cache of colorful luxe accessories and soft-touch items for men, kids and the home.

Christopher Totman   - | - | - | E

NoLita | 262 Mott St. (bet. Houston & Prince Sts.) | N/R/W to Prince St. | 212-925-7495

Urbanites ready to go natural applaud this American designer's "genius way of recycling materials [like kimono fabrics] into high fashion" at his NoLita shop; fans "love the atmosphere", which features a fish tank and actual tree-trunk shelves to hold the harvest of nubby knit pullovers, bright gauzy tops and a few smart-looking separates for men; prices seem "decent", given the "extremely high quality" and "great service."

Chrome Hearts ⊠   ▽ 28 | 28 | 24 | VE

E 60s | 159 E. 64th St. (bet. Lexington & 3rd Aves.) | 6 to 68th St. | 212-327-0707 | www.chromehearts.com

A garden with a fish-pond fountain separates the wings of this "mysterious little company" in an unmarked brownstone on East 64th Street "with a loyal, almost cult following" that includes "rock stars"; "alternate" signature sterling silver that is "hot" and Goth ("great crosses") and loads of bling like diamond-studded dog tags dominate, but don't overlook the watches, flexi-lense sunglasses and "exquisite" leather goods in the "too cool for school" handmade mix.

Chuckies ●   25 | 21 | 15 | VE

E 60s | 1073 Third Ave. (bet. 63rd & 64th Sts.) | F to Lexington Ave./ 63rd St. | 212-593-9898
E 80s | 1169 Madison Ave. (86th St.) | 4/5/6 to 86th St. | 212-249-2254
877-693-9898 | www.chuckiesnewyork.com

It's "like visiting a museum of shoes" agree aesthetes who amble over to this Upper East Side duo to view a "wealth" of the "hottest styles" from "top" names like Marc Jacobs and Jimmy Choo as well as "unique" "stuff" from "lesser-knowns"; but while a handful find "the help de-lightful", most are put off by the "nose-in-the-air" 'tude, huffing they're "not so friendly unless you're dressed in designer duds."

Church's Shoes

| | 25 | 21 | 21 | E |

E 60s | 689 Madison Ave. (62nd St.) | 6 to 68th St. | 212-758-5200
"Fine English shoes for fine English men" and Anglophiles-in-the-making are the backbone of this "top-caliber", "friendly" Madison Avenue shop; "don't look for trendy" stuff here, instead, zero in on the "impeccable", "handcrafted" "super-establishment" footwear that "wears like iron – you'll pass them on to your grandchildren" – and "never goes out of style"; if a few wail "it ain't what it used to be", wor-shipers retort this "classic" is a keeper.

Circuit City ●

| | 19 | 15 | 12 | M |

E 80s | 232 E. 86th St. (bet. 2nd & 3rd Aves.) | 4/5/6 to 86th St. | 212-734-1786
Union Sq | 52 E. 14th St. (bet. 4th & 5th Aves.) | 4/5/6/L/N/Q/R/W to 14th St./Union Sq. | 212-387-0730
W 80s | 2232 Broadway (80th St.) | 1 to 79th St. | 212-362-9850
Bay Ridge | 502-12 86th St. (5th Ave.) | Brooklyn | R to 4th Ave. | 718-748-1021
Clinton Hill | Atlantic Ctr. | 625 Atlantic Ave. (bet. Ft. Greene Pl. & S. Portland Ave.) | Brooklyn | 2/3/4/5/B/D/M/N/Q/R to Atlantic Ave. | 718-399-2990
Starrett City | Gateway Ctr. | 369 Gateway Dr. (bet. Fountain & Vandalia Aves.) | Brooklyn | A/C to Euclid Ave. | 718-277-1611
College Point | 136-03 20th Ave. (Whitestone Expwy.) | Queens | 7 to Main St. | 718-961-2090
Rego Park | 96-05 Queens Blvd. (Junction Blvd.) | Queens | G/R/V to 63rd Dr./Rego Park | 718-275-2077
Staten Island | 2505 Richmond Ave. (Richmond Hill Rd.) | 718-982-1182
800-843-2489 | www.circuitcity.com
"Good values" are the draw for fans of this "mass-market chain" offer-ing "all those electronics that we can no longer live without" – "from computers to microwave ovens" – within a "warehouse atmosphere"; just "do your research first" and "don't expect in-depth answers", for "when it comes to customers", the "know-nothing help" forgot to "plug in their circuit."

City Cricket

| | – | – | – | E |

W Village | 555 Hudson St. (Perry St.) | 1 to Christopher St./Sheridan Sq. | 212-242-2258 | www.citycricket.com
"There's always something adorable to buy here" chirp acolytes who fly over to this "perfect little West Village spot", newly relocated from West 10th Street to Hudson; it's a haven for "gift-givers", filled with a "unique" array of old-fashioned toys, handmade quilts, silver and pewter keepsakes and even kiddie-sized wing and Adirondack chairs.

City Opera Thrift Shop

| | 22 | 20 | 17 | M |

Gramercy | 222 E. 23rd St. (bet. 2nd & 3rd Aves.) | 6 to 23rd St. | 212-684-5344
"A theater buff's trash may be your treasure" at this Gramercy thrift shop run by the New York City Opera, whose digs – dominated by a wrought-iron staircase – are rather "serene and elegant" compared to the usual charity outlet; though "the stock is limited, you can always

find something" among "the well-organized" items, "especially books, jewelry", "costume castoffs" and "new designer stuff, tags and all"; critics carp that the "highbrow" goods sometimes come with "high-end prices", "but think of it as an investment in your inner diva."

⊠ City Quilter, The Ⓜ   28 | 24 | 26 | M

Chelsea | 133 W. 25th St. (bet. 6th & 7th Aves.) | 1 to 23rd St. | 212-807-0390 | www.cityquilter.com

"What a store!" proclaim pieceniks who prize this "welcoming" Chelsea specialist where "quilting enthusiasts" can get square deals on a "fantastic selection" of fabrics, notions and other supplies or take the "best classes"; it can be "somewhat expensive" since it's the "only game in town", but the "friendly" staffers "care" enough to "want you to get what you need for perfect results"; P.S. it's a "great place to buy gifts for quilters" too.

City Sports ◐   20 | 15 | 17 | M

E 50s | 153 E. 53rd St. (bet. Lexington & 3rd Aves.) | E/V to Lexington Ave./53rd St. | 212-317-0541
Murray Hill | 390 Fifth Ave. (36th St.) | 6 to 33rd St. | 212-695-0171
www.citysports.com

"Your plain-Jane, gym-rat stores for when you want practical, not flashy" activewear and gear agree urbanites who sprint to these Midtown and East 30s links of a Boston-based chain; "show your ID" from select NYC sports clubs "for an on-spot discount" and score a "great sneaker deal" too – "if you buy two pairs"; still, a few feel the "presentation is nothing to write home about" and find the staff "helpful – if you can locate them."

CK Bradley   24 | 23 | 23 | E

E 70s | 146 E. 74th St. (bet. Lexington & 3rd Aves.) | 6 to 77th St. | 212-988-7999 | www.ckbradley.com

Almost as "preppy as a grosgrain headband", this "whimsical" East 70s boutique lures loyalists with its "weekends in Connecticut essentials" including "fabulous totes", "colorful belts", "feminine" "summer cocktail dresses" and "fun patterned skirts", all designed by owner Camilla Bradley; the "Wasp-cubed" clothing is such a "guilty pleasure" – all you "need is a house in" Greenwich "to go with your wardrobe."

Claire's Accessories   8 | 11 | 11 | I

Garment District | 1385 Broadway (bet. 37th & 38th Sts.) | B/D/F/N/Q/R/V/W to 34th St./Herald Sq. | 212-302-6616 | www.claires.com
Additional locations throughout the NY area

"Cash-strapped" "teenyboppers" "trying to look flashy" "play all day" among a "mishmash maze" of "cheap jewelry and accessories", from chandelier earrings to fake tattoos, headbands and makeup; "you get what you pay for" so "don't expect their items to last forever."

Clarins ◐   26 | 25 | 24 | E

E 80s | 1061 Madison Ave. (bet. 80th & 81st Sts.) | 6 to 77th St. | 212-734-6100
SoHo | 146 Spring St. (Wooster St.) | C/E to Spring St. | 212-343-0109
W 70s | 247 Columbus Ave. (bet. 71st & 72nd Sts.) | 1/2/3 to 72nd St. | 212-362-0190
www.clarins.com

This "high-end French line" with a trio of outlets around town has a "no-nonsense, botanical approach" to beauty that "really works"; besides their famous self-tanner (known for no streaks and "no carrot"-like color), fans favor items like Le Rouge lipstick and Line Prevention Cream; an "attentive" staff adds to the "terrific top-to-toe experience."

Clarks

23 | 18 | 19 | M

E 40s | 363 Madison Ave. (45th St.) | 4/5/6/7/S to 42nd St./Grand Central | 212-949-9545
NEW **E 50s** | 993 Third Ave. (59th St.) | 4/5/6/F/N/R/W to 59th St./Lexington Ave. | 212-207-4115 ◐
Elmhurst | Queens Ctr. | 90-15 Queens Blvd. (bet. 57th & 58th Aves.) | Queens | G/R/V to Woodhaven Blvd. | 718-271-7505 ◐
www.clarksusa.com

If you "gotta walk", slip on a pair of "well-wearing casual shoes" from this "friendly", "fun place to shop" in Manhattan and Queens; "here, as in the U.K.", the "great conservative" men's and women's styles are some of the "most comfortable on the planet, especially if that planet is the desert" and the footwear of choice is the signature "desert boot."

Classic Kicks ⊠

▽ 25 | 23 | 21 | E

NoHo | 298 Elizabeth St. (bet. Bleecker & Houston Sts.) | 6 to Bleecker St. | 212-979-9514 | www.classickicks.com

"As the name implies, a classic collection" of "awesome" "old-school sneaks", in imported, limited-edition, collectible and fashion-forward versions, "keeps hipsters coming back" to this NoHo haunt; sneaker buffs scoop up footwear from faves like Adidas, Nike, Lacoste, Puma and Vans "in all-new styles and colors" and to-go-with, way-"trendy threads", all dispensed by "wonderful, warm owners."

Classic Sofa

▽ 23 | 17 | 20 | E

Flatiron | 5 W. 22nd St. (bet. 5th & 6th Aves.) | N/R/W to 23rd St. | 212-620-0485 | www.classicsofa.com

There are "lots of choices" at this "high-quality" sofa store in the Flatiron District, which offers couches constructed out of hardwood and down-fill in modern and traditional styles, and "if you don't see what you want", they'll custom-design it for you; loyalists like the "quick turnaround" time of about two weeks average, although the sticker-shocked wonder "what is this stuff made of, gold?"

Claudia Ciuti

25 | 24 | 20 | E

E 70s | 955 Madison Ave. (75th St.) | 6 to 77th St. | 212-535-3025 | www.claudiaciuti.com

"Bella bella bella" – "have I made my point clear?" – "Ms. Ciuti is a genius!" agree adoring fans of the Florentine footwear designer, who fall head over heels for the "divine, utterly feminine" suede stiletto boots, T-straps, platform pumps and "hot bling sandals" at her "lovely" East 70s shop; add in exotic leathers, alluring color combos and "excellent service" and it's plain to see these luxe kicks are "worth the money."

Claudine ◐

22 | 23 | 22 | E

G Village | 19 Christopher St. (bet. Greenwich Ave. & Waverly Pl.) | A/B/C/D/E/F/V to W. 4th St. | 212-414-4234

"Feminine, without being precious", this quaint, "friendly" Christopher Street shop, currently decorated with old bird cages, watercolors and shabby-chic plates, offers a "carefully curated" selection of "up-and-coming" "designers who are in demand"; part of a trio of "adorable" boutiques all named for characters in *Bonjour Tristesse* (Albertine and Leontine are the other two), it's "where your personal shopper – if you had one – would shop."

Clay Pot ◗

26 | 24 | 23 | E

Park Slope | 162 Seventh Ave. (bet. 1st St. & Garfield Pl.) | Brooklyn | B/Q to 7th Ave. | 718-788-6564 | 800-989-3579 | www.clay-pot.com

"Beautiful crafts chosen with a classy eye" are the draw at this "cute", "eclectic" Park Slope mainstay representing 75 different U.S. artists and specializing in handblown glass and "great handmade jewelry", including engagement rings and wedding bands; though it's "a little on the high side", devotees declare the "diverse" selection makes it the "perfect" place for a "special one-of-a-kind gift."

Clea Colet 🖾 M

▽ 26 | 21 | 20 | E

E 70s | 960 Madison Ave. (bet. 75th & 76th Sts.) | 6 to 77th St. | 212-396-4608 | www.cleacolet.com

You'll have a "wonderful time trying on the beautiful" bridalwear at this by-appointment-only Madison Avenue salon where you'll be looked after by an "easygoing staff"; the "well-made" gowns come in a "variety of materials from Duchess satin to silk organza" and work well "for any shape" especially since the namesake designer (who "specializes in simpler styles" – sans-"glitz") will custom-"fit the dress to your body type"; P.S. "such great sample sales" too.

Clio

- | - | - | E

SoHo | 92 Thompson St. (bet. Prince & Spring Sts.) | C/E to Spring St. | 212-966-8991 | www.clio-home.com

This "stylish" SoHo tabletop shop sells "unique" international accessories ranging from teardrop vases from San Francisco and bone china dinnerware from Germany to handblown glass lighting from Brooklyn and palm wood trays from Bali; no wonder supporters say it's a "great resource for wedding and housewarming gifts."

Cloak ◗

- | - | - | VE

SoHo | 10 Greene St. (Canal St.) | C/E to Spring St. | 212-625-2828 | www.cloakdesign.com

A "dark" "moody ambiance" reigns at this librarylike lair in SoHo, the flagship for designer Alexandre Plokhov's label that's also big in Japan; men wishing to shroud themselves in "high-fashion" mystery uncover Gothic coats galore, "sharply tailored" suits, special-order fabrics and somber separates with dashing details; a bookcase that features coffee-table titles from DAP also conceals a dressing room – just a touch of cloak-and-dagger mystique.

Cloth ◗ M

- | - | - | E

Fort Greene | 138 Fort Greene Pl. (Hanson Pl. & Lafayette Ave.) | Brooklyn | C to Lafayette Ave. | 718-403-0223 | www.clothclothing.com

For womenswear that's not cut from the same old cloth, stylehounds duck into Zoe van de Wiele's cozy, brick-walled Fort Greene gem in the burgeoning BAM Cultural District; the owner's fashion training has made her a stickler for construction and the result is an unassumingly chic selection including hip labels like Loomstate and Matta, plus knockout jewelry and beauty wares from Rhode Island's Farmaesthetics.

| | QUALITY | DISPLAY | SERVICE | COST |

Club Monaco ◑
18 | 20 | 16 | M

E 60s | 1111 Third Ave. (65th St.) | 6 to 68th St. | 212-355-2949
Flatiron | 160 Fifth Ave. (21st St.) | N/R/W to 23rd St. |
212-352-0936
SoHo | 121 Prince St. (bet. Greene & Wooster Sts.) | N/R/W to Prince St. |
212-533-8930
SoHo | 520 Broadway (bet. Broome & Spring Sts.) | N/R/W to Prince St. |
212-941-1511
W 50s | 6 W. 57th St. (bet. 5th & 6th Aves.) | F to 57th St. | 212-459-9863
NEW **W 60s** | 211 Columbus Ave. (bet. 69th & 70th Sts.) | B/C to
72nd St. | 212-724-4076
W 80s | 2376 Broadway (87th St.) | 1 to 86th St. | 212-579-2587
Elmhurst | Queens Ctr. | 90-15 Queens Blvd. (bet. 57th & 59th Aves.) |
Queens | G/R/V to Woodhaven Blvd. | 718-760-9282
www.clubmonaco.com

When you "don't feel like shelling out for the real designer outfit" hit this "cleanly" styled men's and women's clothing chain that draws "young" "trendsetters" and others with its "runway" "knockoffs" and "hip, but not slick" suits, dresses and jeans that amount to "great value" considering the overall "quality"; the service, however, is perhaps best-suited for those "with low expectations."

Clyde's ◐
27 | 23 | 22 | E

E 70s | 926 Madison Ave. (74th St.) | 6 to 77th St. | 212-744-5050 |
800-792-5933

"Classy right down to the shopping bags", this Upper East Sider remains among "the last of the old-world drug and beauty stores" that's "great for hard-to-find and imported items" like Versace makeup, Boucheron fragrance and almost anything else that "keeps the ladies who lunch looking good"; most maintain "the sales people are generally great", so the only issue is the cost, which leads customers to complain the establishment "could double as a comedy club with those prices!"

☒ Coach ◐
26 | 24 | 22 | E

E 50s | Fuller Bldg. | 595 Madison Ave. (57th St.) | N/R/W to 5th Ave./
59th St. | 212-754-0041 | 888-262-6224 | www.coach.com
Additional locations throughout the NY area

"Durable" "bags that age better than some people do" in "timeless" styles you'll "will to your daughters" and "trendy" designs are "displayed in an appealing way" at this "marvelous" chain where the staff "meets and greets" "addicts" of all ages; the "craftsmanship is apparent" – "nothing beats the leather line" of accessories and jackets, plus their "warranty is one of the best in the business"; if critics coach "ease up" on the "logo-ed" merchandise, and find the stores "ubiquitous", even they may reassess after visiting the new boutique-like Coach Legacy store at 372-374 Bleecker Street.

C.O. Bigelow Chemists ◐
26 | 21 | 21 | M

G Village | 414 Sixth Ave. (bet. 8th & 9th Sts.) | A/B/C/D/E/F/V to
W. 4th St. | 212-533-2700 | 800-793-5433 |
www.bigelowchemists.com

Founded in 1838 as an apothecary, this Greenwich Village institution "is a gold mine for toiletry divas" with common brands crammed alongside Greek body scrubs from Propoline, jasmine and ginger toothpaste from Marvis and their own in-house line of face and body products in vintage packaging along with oodles of hair accessories and "products you never knew existed"; though it's "stuffed to the gills", it has a "cool, old-school feel" leading loyalists to exclaim "if I could, I would live upstairs."

Coclico ⊘

| | - | - | - | E |

NoLita | 275 Mott St. (bet. Houston & Prince Sts.) | B/D/F/V to B'way/ Lafayette St. | 212-965-5462 | www.shopcoclico.com

Europe rules at this cute, colorful NoLita shop where fashionistas flock for "fabulous" east-of-the-pond labels; choose from lesser-known names, including the house brand and finds from the likes of Leopoldo Giordana, then try on accessories to complete the head-to-toe look.

CoCo & Delilah ⊘ Ⓜ

| | - | - | - | E |

E Village | 115 St. Marks Pl. (bet. Ave. A & 1st Ave.) | 6 to Astor Pl. | 212-254-8741 | 866-881-2626 | www.coco-nyc.com

Smack dab in the "funky" East Village sits this pretty shop, complete with a crystal chandelier and coveted womenswear (Alice & Olivia), super-cool denim (Joe's Jeans) and tees (Three Dots); followers of owner Collette LoVullo's website feel "thrilled" to have a go-to spot for her inspired choices that "run the gamut" of getups for "work and weekends."

Cog & Pearl ⊘ Ⓜ

| | 21 | 21 | 15 | M |

Park Slope | 190 Fifth Ave. (Sackett St.) | Brooklyn | M/R to Union St. | 718-623-8200 | www.cogandpearl.com

Crafty Slopers make a beeline to this "lovely venue" on Fifth Avenue to peruse the gallerylike "showcase" of "unique items" from "local talent and amazing artisans" including "one-of-a-kind" handmade jewelry, "very cute" handbags, accessories, journals, T-shirts and "original" ceramics and home knickknacks, like John Derian decoupage; while many of the "edgy products" are made from recycled materials, "happily" they don't have that "crunchy, reused-burlap feel."

Cohen's Fashion Optical ⊘

| | 19 | 16 | 16 | M |

E 60s | 767 Lexington Ave. (60th St.) | 4/5/6/F/N/R/W to 59th St./ Lexington Ave. | 212-751-6652 | 800-393-7440 | www.cohensfashionoptical.com
Additional locations throughout the NY area

"The same wherever you go", this "Woolworth's of eyewear" ("glasses for the masses") can "come through with the goods" and some "decent" "deals"; but "wary" customers caution that the "final price" rarely "lives up to the ads" and find the service "lame", concluding "this isn't your store if you wanna resemble Paris Hilton."

Cole Haan ⊘

| | 25 | 23 | 22 | E |

E 50s | 620 Fifth Ave. (50th St.) | B/D/F/V to 47-50th Sts./Rockefeller Ctr. | 212-765-9747

E 60s | 667 Madison Ave. (61st St.) | 4/5/6/F/N/R/W to 59th St./ Lexington Ave. | 212-421-8440

W 60s | The Shops at Columbus Circle, Time Warner Ctr. | 10 Columbus Circle, ground fl. (60th St. at B'way) | 1/A/B/C/D to 59th St./Columbus Circle | 212-823-9420
800-488-2000 | www.colehaan.com

"Talk about a reinvention!" this "high-quality" outfit boasting "solidly crafted" footwear, bags and outerwear "isn't your mama's store anymore!"; the staff is "patient" and what's more, "you'll be hooked" on the "hip and trendy (but in a good way)" shoes and the "amazingly comfortable, sexy" styles from the "funky" "G-series, designed with Nike"; if a few pout it's become "more generic", most retort just "treat your feet" – "you can wear them next season too."

Colony Music ●

| 24 | 15 | 19 | E |

W 40s | 1619 Broadway (49th St.) | 1 to 50th St. | 212-265-2050 | www.colonymusic.com

Broadway babies boast this "fantastic" Theater District "original" in the Brill Building has "stuff no one else has" in the way of "obscure sheet music", "vintage vinyl", "fun memorabilia" and karaoke machines; sure, the "know-it-all staff" and "laughably high prices" can strike a sour note, but the "remarkable selection" and late hours make it just the ticket for most; N.B. a refurb may outdate the Display score.

Comme des Garçons

| 26 | 27 | 24 | VE |

Chelsea | 520 W. 22nd St. (bet. 10th & 11th Aves.) | C/E to 23rd St. | 212-604-9200

"Even veteran shoppers are surprised" by this Chelsea boutique with its tunnel leading to a "womblike space" filled with Japanese designer Rei Kawakubo's "fantastic", if "way, way out", his-and-hers garments; critics cry "the clothes are more a curiosity than something to be worn in public", "but if you feel daring and have money to burn", these "avant-garde" "art pieces" could become "an addictive acquired taste" – or else, "display them as textile sculptures."

Compact Impact ●▣

| - | - | - | E |

Financial District | 71 Broadway (Trinity Pl.) | R/W to Rector St. | 212-677-0500 | www.compact-impact.com

This innovative, by-appointment-only electronic-gadget gallery in the Financial District offers the latest in trendy Tokyo technology and urban lifestyle design, from Japanimation-inspired gizmos and solar-powered backpacks that'll juice up your cell phone to conceptual contraptions like an iDog whose byte is all digital, but whose bark is all music.

Concord Chemists

| 23 | 19 | 20 | E |

E 50s | 485 Madison Ave. (bet. 51st & 52nd Sts.) | 6 to 51st St. | 212-486-9543 | www.concord-chemists.com

An "upscale Madison Avenue crowd" has been heading to this "old-school" "institution" and apothecary in Midtown since 1979; a "helpful" multilingual staff "reminds you of what service was like before Duane Reade" and can direct you to "anything you need to pamper yourself with beauty or nurture yourself for health", ranging from hair-care products and perfumes to vitamins and homeopathic remedies.

Conran Shop, The ●

| 23 | 25 | 18 | E |

E 50s | Bridgemarket | 407 E. 59th St. (1st Ave.) | 4/5/6/F/N/R/W to 59th St./Lexington Ave. | 212-755-9079 | 866-755-9079 | www.conranusa.com

English style icon Sir Terence Conran's "cool, slick store" is "like a museum of design" where there are "stunning displays" of "beautiful modern" furniture and housewares ranging from "dishes to divans, from towels to telephones"; it's "waaaay out of the way", tucked beside the 59th Street Bridge, but enthusiasts insist it's worth the schlep.

| | QUALITY | DISPLAY | SERVICE | COST |

Consignment

| - | - | - | E |

Downtown | 371 Atlantic Ave. (bet. Bond & Hoyt Sts.) | Brooklyn | A/C/G to Hoyt/Schermerhorn Sts. | 718-522-3522

Shoppers toast the arrival of this cutting-edge consignment haunt on Atlantic Avenue, hauling home never-been-worn clothing that once graced the racks of Butter, its fashion-forward big sister, along with gently used and still-pricey finds from labels like Gucci, Isabel Marant, Mayle and Rick Owens; natch, the decor is spare but chic, all the better to show off the accessibly arranged threads, tasteful jewelry, sunglasses, shoes and bags and select pieces of furniture.

Container Store, The ❶

| 22 | 22 | 21 | M |

Chelsea | 629 Sixth Ave. (bet. 18th & 19th Sts.) | 1 to 18th St. | 212-366-4200

E 50s | 725 Lexington Ave. (58th St.) | 4/5/6/F/N/R/W to 59th St./Lexington Ave. | 212-366-4200

800-733-3532 | www.containerstore.com

"First-timers walk around dazed", but pros know how to navigate this Chelsea "nirvana" for nesters "with small apartments" that's an "organizational dreamland" "containing everything you need to contain anything" – including "a great closet line" – and all sold by staffers that are "so friendly you think they're part of a cult"; it's an "addictive" "place that was made for Manhattan" and, with any luck, the crushing "crowds" of fellow "obsessive-compulsives" will be minimized now that there's a second city store in the East 50s.

Cooper-Hewitt National Design Museum Shop Ⓜ

| 24 | 21 | 17 | M |

E 90s | Cooper-Hewitt | 2 E. 91st St. (5th Ave.) | 4/5/6 to 86th St. | 212-849-8355 | www.cooperhewitt.org

Devotees of both "classic and innovative design" delight in this Upper East Side "find" offering a "great selection" of "modern housewares" and "decorative accessories" from "top" names as well as "fantastic books" at "varied prices"; the space is "nicely laid out", and though a few gripe the goods are "sometimes uninspired" and "disappointing", more maintain it's "one of the best of the museum shops."

NEW Corduroy Kid Ⓜ

| 24 | 22 | 22 | M |

Prospect Heights | 613 Vanderbilt Ave. (bet. Bergen St. & St. Marks Ave.) | Brooklyn | B/G to 7th Ave. | 718-622-4145 | www.corduroykid.com

"Love the layout" proclaim mamas and papas who find the "cutest" clothing for their offspring at this Prospect Heights infants' and children's shop; the Aussie owner who does double time as a fashion stylist zeroes in on "excellent value", colorful, sassy designer favorites from Down Under complemented by utilitarian yet super-stylish gear including Micralite Fastfold strollers and kicky diaper bags.

Cosmophonic Sound

| - | - | - | E |

E 80s | 1622 First Ave. (84th St.) | 4/5/6 to 86th St. | 212-734-0459 | www.cosmophonic.com

Whether you need "same-day service for a complicated television hookup" or "to repair your old Betamax", head to this East 80s home-theater specialty shop, a family-run biz with a staff that forgoes the "high-pressure sale pitch"; audiophiles also turn to the "wonderful" help to customize a multiroom automated system to specifications or to purchase a plasma TV, confiding, "they know their products intimately."

⚄ Costco Warehouse ●

QUALITY	DISPLAY	SERVICE	COST
22	12	12	I

Sunset Park | 976 Third Ave. (39th St.) | Brooklyn | D/M/N/R to 36th St. | 718-965-7603
LIC | 32-50 Vernon Blvd. (B'way) | Queens | N/W to Broadway | 718-267-3680
Staten Island | 2975 Richmond Ave. (Staten Island Expwy.) | 718-982-9525
www.costco.com

Ah, "the joys of buying in bulk" for all your household and personal needs, "from batteries to steaks", this "essential" "big-box" chain "has everything" attest addicts who also adore the "excellent optical and pharmacy departments" and the "great brand names" from Cartier to Canon; it all makes the $50 annual "membership fee pay for itself" – that is, if you have "storage space in your home" ("everything's large, except the prices"); don't expect anything in the way of amenities, unless you count the "endless samples" of snacks.

Costume National

QUALITY	DISPLAY	SERVICE	COST
▽ 26	29	23	VE

SoHo | 108 Wooster St. (bet. Prince & Spring Sts.) | N/R/W to Prince St. | 212-431-1530 | www.costumenational.com

Embrace the dark side in the ebonized interior of this sophisticated SoHo boutique with its "great shoes" and "funky, cool, chic pieces" for men and women designed by Ennio Capasa in "shiny monochromatic fabrics, most of them black" and tailored so cleverly that they would even make Darth Vader "the paradigm of sexiness."

NEW Cotélac

QUALITY	DISPLAY	SERVICE	COST
-	-	-	M

SoHo | 92-94 Greene St. (bet. Prince & Spring Sts.) | N/R/W to Prince St. | 212-219-8065 | www.cotelacusa.com

Making its NYC debut, this popular French label seeks to take on Manhattan with a *très moderne* space – silvery gray walls, sculptural furniture and bleached wood floors – that houses a sizable array of clothing for men (downstairs) and women (up); the casual, crinkly separates, plus a few party dresses, should perfectly suit the SoHo bobos (bohemian-bourgeois), especially given the moderate prices.

Council Thrift Shop

QUALITY	DISPLAY	SERVICE	COST
18	13	12	M

E 80s | 246 E. 84th St. (bet. 2nd & 3rd Aves.) | 4/5/6 to 86th St. | 212-439-8373 | www.ncjwny.org

If you feel "Upper East Side thrift stores are the place to be", then this veteran, established by the National Council of Jewish Women in 1952, is definitely one "to check out", thanks to its "frequently changing", "very good selection" of "brand-name" clothes, furniture, housewares and china; some say the staff's "on the snobbish side", "but it's worth it" to "find that discarded pair of $600 shoes selling for $50."

⚄ Country Floors ⊠

QUALITY	DISPLAY	SERVICE	COST
26	26	18	VE

Union Sq | 15 E. 16th St. (bet. 5th Ave. & Union Sq. W.) | 4/5/6/L/N/Q/R/W to 14th St./Union Sq. | 212-627-8300 | www.countryfloors.com

Proof that "you don't have to go to Italy to find wonderful tiles", this "dream store" in Union Square has provided connoisseurs with a "fabulous place to troll for ideas" for over 40 years; terra-cotta, natural stone and glass with unusual textures and finishes mix with mosaic designs from the 17th century and "magnificent hand-painted" pieces, making this a "favorite place for over-the-top" purchases "if you have the budget for them"; N.B. also closed Saturdays.

C.P.W. ☻

∇ 22 | 19 | 19 | E

W 80s | 495 Amsterdam Ave. (84th St.) | 1 to 86th St. | 212-579-3737
After stocking up on must-haves like J Brand jeans for yourself, pick up shrunken versions of all the latest adult styles for the youngest members of your clan at this West 80s boutique for women and kids; tiny trendseekers also find it hard to resist C&C California tees, denim duds from Joe's Jeans and Lacoste polo shirts in a rainbow of colors.

Crabtree & Evelyn

23 | 22 | 21 | M

E 40s | Rockefeller Ctr. | 620 Fifth Ave. (bet. 49th & 50th Sts.) | B/D/F/V to 47-50th Sts./Rockefeller Ctr. | 212-581-5022
E 50s | 520 Madison Ave. (bet. 53rd & 54th Sts.) | E/V to 5th Ave./53rd St. | 212-758-6419 🖂
W 60s | The Shops at Columbus Circle, Time Warner Ctr. | 10 Columbus Circle, ground fl. (60th St. at B'way) | 1/A/B/C/D to 59th St./Columbus Circle | 212-823-9584 ☻
Staten Island | Staten Island Mall | 2655 Richmond Ave. (bet. Platinum Ave. & Richmond Hill Rd.) | 718-982-8252 ☻
800-272-2873 | www.crabtreeandevelyn.com
An "oasis" "for the woman who's outgrown candy-scented products", this English chainlet and "blast from the past" founded in 1800 offers soaps, scents, potpourri and room sprays that rely on "classic" ingredients like lavender and "don't smell syrupy sweet"; prices are moderate and there are "excellent sales", but cutting-edge it ain't.

▣ Crane & Co., Paper Makers

27 | 23 | 21 | E

W 40s | Rockefeller Ctr. | 59 W. 49th St. (bet. 5th & 6th Aves.) | B/D/F/V to 47-50th Sts./Rockefeller Ctr. | 212-582-6829 | www.crane.com
For "beautiful, traditional paper" that's "pricey but worth it" and the "finest quality engraved stationery" that will "make an impression", "you can't go wrong" at this small Rockefeller Center branch of an "American classic" dating back to 1801; fashionistas claim they can't find "trendy" designs, but admirers insist "no one's ever turned down any of the invitations" they've bought here.

▣ Crate & Barrel ☻

21 | 24 | 20 | M

E 50s | 650 Madison Ave. (59th St.) | N/R/W to 5th Ave./59th St. | 212-308-0011
NoHo | Cable Bldg. | 611 Broadway (Houston St.) | B/D/F/V to B'way/Lafayette St. | 212-780-0004
800-967-6696 | www.crateandbarrel.com
"Lock, stock and barrel", these NoHo and Midtown "you-want-it-they-got-it" "from furniture to flower pots" housewares mega-stores are "popular for a reason" – a "wide range" of "nicely laid-out", "high-quality" "chic designs" and "terrific value" make them "great for a first apartment or home" and "bring good taste to the masses."

Crembebè ☻

- | - | - | E

E Village | 68 Second Ave. (bet. 3rd & 4th Sts.) | F/V to Lower East Side/2nd Ave. | 212-979-6848 | www.crembebe.com
Trendsetters are sweet on this Second Avenue confection, well-stocked with all of the ingredients needed to "dress your baby in East Village

funk from head-to-toe" like cute finds from Appaman and other new designers high on the most-wanted list; P.S. for a bona fide sugar high, indulge in "cool" accessories, toys and other gift-worthy goodies.

Crew Cuts ●

-|-|-| M

SoHo | J.Crew | 99 Prince St. (Greene St.) | N/R/W to Prince St. | 212-966-2739 | www.jcrew.com

J.Crew courts the milk-and-cookies crowd with this splurge-inducing kids' shop, tucked inside its SoHo adults' store, which serves up tiny takes on its signature collegiate styles; tomorrow's prepsters score everything from classic candy-colored cableknit sweaters and corduroy pants to rugby shirts and tartan kilts, plus shoes, slippers and rainboots to match; the icing on the cake: prim party dresses and spiffy gold-buttoned blazers and bow ties for dress-up occasions.

NEW Crocs

-|-|-| M

W 70s | 270 Columbus Ave. (bet. 72nd & 73rd Sts.) | 1/2/3 to 72nd St. | 212-362-1655 | 866-306-3179 | www.crocs.com

Get your fix of the now-ubiquitous, kicky-colored resin clogs at this West 70s newcomer, another notch in the Boulder, Colorado, company's mushrooming empire; whatever your age or gender you'll find something super-comfy to pull off the racks, from the closed-toe, slip-resistant Bistro style flogged by celeb chef/ardent fan Mario Batali to spin-offs of the odor-resistant original, including MaryJanes, fleece-lined strapless slip-ons and funky Frankenstein-ish rainboots.

C. Ronson

∇ 16 | 18 | 20 | E

NoLita | 239 Mulberry St. (bet. Prince & Spring Sts.) | B/D/F/V to B'way/Lafayette St. | 212-625-9074 | www.cronson.com

Always good for a girlie-girl fix, designer Charlotte Ronson's NoLita boutique reveals her groovy-gal-about-town sensibility with "cute" "but not cheap" finds like "casualwear with hearts and cherries", undies and iPod-pocketed hoodies; while you're there, check out the "fun" clothing and accessories with a downtown vibe from other "emerging" lines.

Crouch & Fitzgerald

26 | 21 | 22 | E

E 40s | 400 Madison Ave. (bet. 47th & 48th Sts.) | B/D/F/V to 47-50th Sts./Rockefeller Ctr. | 212-755-5888 | 800-627-6824 | www.crouchandfitzgerald.com

A "NYC tradition among the moneyed crowd" since 1839, this "dependable" Madison Avenue luggage leviathan is the "real thing", "one of those rare places that make shopping a fulfilling treat"; loyalists insist that the "outstanding range" of "classy leather items", including "chic" suitcases, handbags and accessories "at top prices", "age better than" themselves; still, a few Crouch-grouchers wonder "what has happened to the venerable" store, the "one my mother" patronized?

Crumpler Bags ●

24 | 19 | 20 | M

NoLita | 45 Spring St. (bet. Mott & Mulberry Sts.) | 6 to Spring St. | 212-334-9391

W Village | 49 Eighth Ave. (bet. Horatio & W. 4th Sts.) | A/C/E/L to 14th St./8th Ave. | 212-242-2535

www.crumplerbags.com

"Proof" that "superb functional utility" accessories "don't have to be in black", or cross the "over-designed" line, the totable "wonders from

Down Under" at this Downtown duo come in "odd color pairings that work", including custom creations at the newer West Village shop; choose from "sturdy" camera bags, laptop cases and "backpacks galore" "full of useful" details, like the third leg strap, an "invention bicycle messengers have been waiting for."

Crunch ●
15 | 16 | 14 | M

E Village | 404 Lafayette St. (bet. Astor Pl. & 4th St.) | 6 to Astor Pl. | 212-614-0120 | 888-227-8624 | www.crunch.com
Additional locations throughout the NY area

"Hip" hoodies, sweats, leggings and T-shirts so "playful and unique" you may "live in" them draw muscle-meisters to the "crowded retail areas" of this urban-gym chain; if a few sniff this outfit "should stick to exercise and leave" the activewear to "experts", for most it's crunchy "fun."

NEW Curve
19 | 19 | 18 | E

SoHo | 83 Mercer St. (Spring St.) | N/R to Prince St. | 212-966-3626 | www.shopcurve.com

Touches of haberdashery, antique brass fixtures and a rustic chandelier lend an English air to Bulgarian-born tastemaker Nevena Borissova's brick-walled womenswear haunt in SoHo; lookswise it bears no resemblance to its minimalist, celeb-magnet LA sibling, but merchandising- and saleswise, it mirrors the West coast, with staffers who moonlight as stylists offering personal service and curated racks filled with the next big thing from the European catwalks, hard-to-find designers like Preen and Unconditional and even a rack of vintage evening attire.

Custo Barcelona
21 | 23 | 20 | E

SoHo | 474 Broome St. (bet. Greene & Wooster Sts.) | C/E to Spring St. | 212-274-9700 | www.custo-barcelona.com

The brothers Dalmau originally made a name for themselves with their "exuberantly creative" "paper-thin T-shirts" for "funky" gals and guys, and they've evolved and extended their line at this sleek SoHo boutique, whose decor changes with the seasons; the "hip" apparel "with Euro flair" delivers "bold prints", "color and pattern" galore in suits and separates "that always exude sexiness and garner compliments."

Cynthia Rowley ●
23 | 22 | 22 | E

W Village | 376 Bleecker St. (bet. Charles & Perry Sts.) | 1 to Christopher St./Sheridan Sq. | 212-242-3803 | www.cynthiarowley.com

Slip into this silvery little West Village gem to pick up "girlie-girl-to-the-max" garb from the *Swell* book series co-creator whose "vibrant" styles, from sweet coats to party dresses, "look so cute" and make "material girls" "feel pretty as a princess"; unfortunately, the "price tags can be pretty pricey too" – though several "middle-income" mademoiselles maintain they're "decent" enough.

Ⓩ Daffy's ●
17 | 10 | 9 | M

Garment District | 1311 Broadway (34th St.) | B/D/F/N/Q/R/V/W to 34th St./Herald Sq. | 212-736-4477 | 877-933-2339 | www.daffys.com
Additional locations throughout the NY area

"For those with a strong hunter's gene", it's "possible to find outstanding labels at bargain prices" at this "crowded discount" chain carrying "wacky Euro styles" for men and women, "Italian clothing for infants", accessories and home decor items; but even "if you're willing to dig", "you can never find salespeople", and the merch "seems to be in a constant state of disarray", leading foes to fume you're "daft" to shop here.

Dalaga NYC ●Ⓜ | ▽ 19 | 22 | 18 | E |

Greenpoint | 150 Franklin St. (bet. Greenpoint Ave. & Kent St.) | Brooklyn | G to Greenpoint Ave. | 718-389-4049

The displays in the plate-glass windows are just the icing on the cake at this boudoirlike boutique in Greenpoint, a lovely style-lair for men and women decorated with tin ceilings, a Victorian bedroom set and framed photos and filled with the owner-designer's colorful, textural creations, plus a "nice variety" of finds from local talent; the selection caters to every fashion whim, running the gamut from jeans and casual pieces to cocktail wear.

Damiani Ⓩ | - | - | - | VE |

E 60s | 796 Madison Ave. (67th St.) | 4/5/6/F/N/R/W to 59th St./ Lexington Ave. | 212-375-6474 | www.damiani.com

"Italians know about good jewelry" according to admirers of this third-generation, family-owned, Milan-based business dating back to 1924; its Madison Avenue outpost offers the sleek, D-Side collection co-designed with Brad Pitt and more opulent diamond- and gemstone-encrusted pieces with plenty of eye appeal.

Dana Buchman | 25 | 23 | 23 | E |

E 50s | 65 E. 57th St. (bet. Madison & Park Aves.) | N/R/W to 5th Ave./ 59th St. | 212-319-3257 | 800-522-3262 | www.danabuchman.com

A master at careerwear for the nine-to-five crowd, this American maker's "designs are changing" from "very conservative" to "well-made, not ultra-expensive" wide-leg trousers, colorful suede jackets and tile-print tunics at her East 50s boutique; skeptics still say it's "stuffy", but devotees "love the fit" and all applaud the employees who, while "not obsequious", are "eager to find you what you want."

D & G ● | 24 | 24 | 21 | VE |

SoHo | 434 W. Broadway (bet. Prince & Spring Sts.) | C/E to Spring St. | 212-965-8000 | www.dolcegabbana.it

Housed in a "sparse" concrete jungle of a boutique in SoHo, what some call "the slutty younger sister of Dolce & Gabbana" holds sway with both sexes, and "if you're looking to add something tight in a leopard print to your closet, this is the place"; while the body-baring tops and plastered-on jeans may be a bit "bizarre for those past 30", the "Italian-with-an-attitude" apparel keeps the "young and hip" happy; N.B. divas-in-training can shop for D & G Junior childrenswear here too.

Danskin ● | 23 | 18 | 19 | M |

W 60s | 159 Columbus Ave. (bet. 67th & 68th Sts.) | 1 to 66th St./ Lincoln Ctr. | 212-724-2992 | 800-288-6749 | www.danskin.com

Find "just the right tutu at just the right price" at this "tried-and-true" women's and children's "standby" set "close to Lincoln Center for performers'" convenience; sure, it's "been known for its ballet" apparel since 1882, but gym buffs are "happy" to find "comfortable" activewear here too; if a few bemoan the "boring" displays, most applaud the "great selection of clothing that looks great in or out of the studio."

	QUALITY	DISPLAY	SERVICE	COST

Darling ◐
| | - | - | - | E |

W Village | 1 Horatio St. (8th Ave.) | A/C/E/L to 14th St./8th Ave. | 212-367-3750 | www.darlingnyc.com

Devotees whisper that former Broadway costume designer Ann French Emont's "charming boutique" is "possibly the best-kept shopping secret in the West Village"; the "extremely friendly" owner sets the stage for "flirtation" with "dreamy", "vintage and vintage-inspired" "girlie-girl" party dresses and sexy separates that "flatter all figures, not just underfed models'", from designers like Nieves Lavi, Shoshanna and Zola; P.S. on warm Thursday nights, treat yourself, darling, to "champagne in the back" garden.

Daryl K
| | ▽ 23 | 19 | 23 | E |

NoHo | 21 Bond St. (bet. Bowery & Lafayette St.) | B/D/F/V to B'way/ Lafayette St. | 212-529-8790 | www.darylk.com

"Downtown dressing for city girls" describes the duds of Daryl Kerrigan, a designer idolized as "still an innovator" – or perhaps a contemporary-minded nostalgist, since cheeky minis, sexy short shorts and naughty-girl baby-dolls never go out of style in her ice-cool world; so channel your inner Edie Sedgwick at her stripped-to-the-necessities NoHo shop, which also features vintage boots and bags.

DataVision ◐
| | 21 | 14 | 12 | M |

Murray Hill | 445 Fifth Ave. (39th St.) | 4/5/6/7/S to 42nd St./ Grand Central | 212-689-1111 | www.datavis.com

"They have everything you could want in electronics", including a "wide selection of computer items", at this "great place" near the 42nd Street Library; critics contend that management "could clean up" the "cluttered, claustrophobic" layout and complain that the "variable" staff is "either all over you or totally absent", but "if you know your stuff", "you can bargain a bit here and get a good deal."

Daum ▣
| | ▽ 27 | 25 | 25 | VE |

E 60s | 694 Madison Ave. (bet. 62nd & 63rd Sts.) | N/R/W to 5th Ave./ 59th St. | 212-355-2060 | www.daum.fr

For some of "the most unique crystal around", this "small" Upper East Side shop offers "one-of-a-kind" French glassware including *pâte de verre* vases, perfume bottles, bowls, lamps and jewelry with signature frosted floral, animal and insect-inspired motifs.

Dave's Army Navy
| | 21 | 12 | 18 | I |

Chelsea | 581 Sixth Ave. (bet. 16th & 17th Sts.) | F/L/V to 14th St./ 6th Ave. | 212-989-6444 | 800-543-8558 | www.davesnewyork.com

"Rock 'n' roll and join the army – they got all the authentic stuff" you need at this "longtime Chelsea favorite"; surveyors hail it for having "hands down, the best selection of work-clothes brands like Carhartt and Levi's" "at great prices"; sure, the digs are "basic", but just think of it as a store that serves "steak without the sizzle."

Dave's Quality Meat ◐
| | - | - | - | E |

E Village | 7 E. Third St. (bet. Bowery & 2nd Ave.) | F/V to Lower East Side/ 2nd Ave. | 212-505-7551 | www.davesqualitymeat.com

It may look like a retro butcher shop, but the prime pickings hanging from the metal meat racks at this "very cool" East Village spot owned by three skateboarders happen to be limited-edition sneakers, not steaks, from "boss" labels like Adidas, Converse, Nike and Vans; adding gravy to the mix: house-brand T-shirts, shrink-wrapped and displayed in a refrigerator case, plus clothing from other grade-A labels.

⊠ Davide Cenci

29	22	24	VE

E 60s | 801 Madison Ave. (bet. 67th & 68th Sts.) | 6 to 68th St. |
212-628-5910 | www.davidecenci.com

Men who appreciate a full-service shop will find a most "enjoyable experience" at this multilevel townhouse whose "fine merchandise" includes "classic Italian threads", ready-made and made-to-measure shirts, coats, ties and "Tod's shoes to boot", along with a smaller selection of womenswear that also gets "high marks"; the sterling "service can be a little stuffy, but hey, this *is* Madison Avenue."

David Lee Holland Ⓜ

-	-	-	E

SoHo | 69 Sullivan St. (bet. Broome & Spring Sts.) | C/E to Spring St. |
212-925-1944 | www.davidleeholland.com

The eponymous owner-designer of this serene SoHo jewelry "oasis" says he is inspired by nature and proves it with "unique" pieces like 18-karat gold oncidium orchid earrings, a laurel leaf necklace and a beech burr pendant appointed with a black Tahitian pearl; for the younger set, there's a collection of silver pieces mixed with oversized, brightly colored gem stones; "excellent one-on-one service" adds to its appeal.

David's Bridal ❶

13	12	14	I

LIC | 35-00 48th St. (Northern Blvd.) | Queens | G/R/V to 46th St. |
718-784-8200 | 888-480-2743 | www.davidsbridal.com

Penny-pinchers proclaim "it's hard to pass up" the mostly inexpensive wedding regalia found at this LIC chain link that feels like a "department store for the bride"; if "you have the patience and don't need to be catered to" it's "great for quicky shopping", but most blast the "run-of-the-mill" dresses and would "rather pay more to go somewhere else."

David Webb ⊠

▽ 25	24	25	VE

E 60s | 789 Madison Ave. (bet. 66th & 67th Sts.) | 6 to 68th St. |
212-421-3030 | www.davidwebb.com

"Quintessentially New York", this Upper East Side gem dating back to 1948 is still home to sparkling signature tiger-, zebra- and armadillo-inspired jewelry in enamel, gold or gemstones, plus other "overscaled, overpriced and unique" designs that are the "Palm Beach–chic" "alternative to Kenny Lane" "for the truly affluent."

David Yurman ⊠

25	24	23	VE

E 60s | 729 Madison Ave. (64th St.) | 6 to 68th St. | 212-752-4255 |
877-226-1400 | www.davidyurman.com

Loyalists "love" this "right-on-the-money" Madison Avenue jeweler, including his signature "silver and gold look", plus pearls with sterling or gem-set bijoux that are "not for the faint of heart"; but detractors dub the designs "overly expensive", "stylish suburban soccer-mom" stuff, and give the staff "mixed reviews."

David Z. ❶

19	14	15	M

G Village | 821 Broadway (12th St.) | 4/5/6/L/N/Q/R/W to 14th St./
Union Sq. | 212-253-5511

Murray Hill | 384 Fifth Ave. (bet. 35th & 36th Sts.) | 6 to 33rd St. |
917-351-1484

(continued)

David Z.

NoHo | 620 Broadway (Houston St.) | B/D/F/V to B'way/Lafayette St. | 212-477-3826

SoHo | 487 Broadway (Broome St.) | 6 to Spring St. | 212-625-9391

SoHo | 556 Broadway (bet. Prince & Spring Sts.) | 6 to Spring St. | 212-431-5450

Union Sq | 12 E. 14th St. (bet. 5th Ave. & University Pl.) | 4/5/6/L/N/Q/R/W to 14th St./Union Sq. | 212-229-4790

www.davidz.com

It's a "good resource for sneakers" and the "latest in urban", "trendy" footwear with "lots of choices" and "deals to be found" attest throngs of shoppers who swarm to this "hectic" chain around town; "it's a zoo, but someone will eventually help you", though "you better take a seat" and you may have to put up with attitude that's either "nonchalant" or as "aloof as a bad nightclub crowd."

DaVinci Artist Supplies

23 | 19 | 20 | E

Chelsea | 132 W. 21st St. (bet. 6th & 7th Aves.) | 1 to 23rd St. | 212-871-0220 | www.davinciartistsupply.com

"With a name like that it has to be good" concur creative sorts who feel like "Alice in an artists' wonderland" at this "lovely" Chelsea art supply shop offering brushes, paints, pads, paper and canvas by the yard and a custom framing department too; "selection, quality and experienced help – a great combination" – and "DaVinci's got it!"; but it's different strokes for less-impressed folks who sigh "nothing special here."

Davis & Warshow, Inc. ⊠

23 | 18 | 19 | E

E 50s | A&D Bldg. | 150 E. 58th St., 4th fl. (bet. Lexington & 3rd Aves.) | 4/5/6/F/N/R/W to 59th St./Lexington Ave. | 212-980-0966

Harlem | 207 E. 119th St. (bet. 2nd & 3rd Aves.) | 6 to 116th St. | 212-369-2000

Harlem | 251 W. 154th St. (bet. 8th Ave. & Macombs Pl.) | B/D to 155th St. | 212-234-5100

NEW **SoHo** | 96 Spring St. (bet. B'way & Mercer St.) | 6 to Spring St. | 212-680-9000

Bronx | 3150 Jerome Ave. (bet. Bedford Park Blvd. & Mosholu Pkwy.) | 4 to Bedford Park Blvd. | 718-584-1351

Maspeth | 57-22 49th St. (bet. 56th Rd. & Maspeth Ave.) | Queens | 718-937-9500

www.daviswarshow.com

A favorite of the wholesale set, this well-stocked "one-stop-shopping" sextet of showrooms is "the jumping-off point" for 150 products for the kitchen and bath – from bronze basins and Japanese tubs to saunas and bar sinks from the likes of Kohler and Kallista; N.B. also closed on Saturdays.

DC Shoes ⦁

22 | 21 | 19 | M

SoHo | 109 Spring St. (bet. Greene & Mercer Sts.) | 6 to Spring St. | 212-334-4500 | www.dcshoes.com

Skate rats, snowboarders, surfers and rally racers all roll into this slick SoHo spot to scope out the sweet selection of "cool" sneakers, boots, hoodies, parkas and caps with an arty spin at "reasonable" prices; the gnarly goods are displayed amid a futuristic "teen"-perfect atmosphere featuring free-floating chrome fixtures and 16 plasma screens beaming the brand's edgy film projects and team tour footage.

ddc domus design collections 🖂 ▽ 27 | 28 | 24 | VE

Murray Hill | 181 Madison Ave. (34th St.) | 6 to 33rd St. | 212-685-0800 | www.ddcnyc.com

If it's sleek and chic, it can probably be found at this three-story Murray Hill showroom featuring contemporary furniture, lighting and accessories that's housed in a landmark building designed by Grand Central Station architects Warren & Wetmore.

DDC Lab - | - | - | E

Meatpacking | 427 W. 14th St. (bet. 9th & 10th Aves.) | A/C/E/L to 14th St./8th Ave. | 212-414-5801 | www.ddclab.com

Technology pays off in "superbly designed" trendy wear at this sleek Meatpacking District hot spot where the "innovative urban styles" of owners Roberto Crivello and Savania Davies-Keiller draw those in search of premium Japanese jeans, washable suede or leather separates and climate-control hoodies that regulate the body temperature of the guy and gal hotties who shop here.

⛉ Dean & Deluca ❶ 26 | 24 | 18 | E

SoHo | 560 Broadway (Prince St.) | N/R/W to Prince St. | 212-226-6800 | 800-781-0450 | www.deandeluca.com

Truly a "SoHo pioneer", this "high-end" "specialty gourmet store" where "beautiful" "produce is arranged like a still life" and "brownies are the size of a small child" also sells "posh cookware", cutlery, housewares and serving pieces; the practical point out that "prices are beyond belief", so you better "have Bloomberg's wallet."

Dear Fieldbinder ❶ - | - | - | E

Cobble Hill | 198 Smith St. (bet. Baltic & Warren Sts.) | Brooklyn | F/G to Bergen St. | 718-852-3620 | www.dearfieldbinder.com

It's a "pleasure" to "find what you want" amid the "well-edited selection of hipster clothes" claim fashionistas who write love letters to this "awesome" Cobble Hill emporium, a retro-modern mecca filled with "feminine" looks from both style stalwarts (Cynthia Rowley, Ted Baker) and lesser-known labels like Mona & Holly and Porridge; Lara Fieldbinder, "the owner, is always at your service", which helps mitigate the fact that her wares "demand my whole paycheck."

Debbie Fisher Ⓜ - | - | - | M

Carroll Gardens | 461 Court St. (bet. 4th Pl. & Luquer St.) | Brooklyn | F/G to Carroll St. | 718-625-6005 | www.debbiefisher.com

Inspired by museum collections of ancient and ethnic art, this Carroll Gardens jewelry shop mainly features the "beautiful" work of its eponymous owner-designer whose "unique, understated and feminine" pieces are crafted from precious and semiprecious stones, Thai, Indian and African beads or 18- or 22-karat gold and silver.

DeBeers 🖂 27 | 23 | 26 | VE

E 50s | 703 Fifth Ave. (55th St.) | E/V to 5th Ave./53rd St. | 212-906-0001 | 800-929-0889 | www.debeers.com

A joint venture between the eponymous South African firm and prestigious Louis Vuitton, this jewelry store brings "amazing diamonds from the source" to Fifth Avenue; of course, there are "sell-your-house-before-going-shopping-here" pieces like enormous engagement rings, but for those intimidated by the price of all that ice, the "beautiful presentation" also includes a clearly marked under-$1,000 section.

de Grisogono ⚠

`-` `-` `-` `VE`

E 60s | 824 Madison Ave. (69th St.) | 6 to 68th St. | 212-439-4220 | www.degrisogono.com

This wildly expensive Geneva-based fine jewelry company is housed in a dramatic black and lime-green Madison Avenue space (complete with spiral staircase) – an apt backdrop for their bold designs; glittering gemstones in colorful, often arresting contrasting combinations (emerald with amethyst for example) turn up in witty pieces like eggplant or apple earrings, floral rings and spiraling snake neckaces.

delfino ◐

`22` `20` `18` `M`

E 70s | 1351A Third Ave. (bet. 77th & 78th Sts.) | 6 to 77th St. | 212-517-5391
W 50s | Rockefeller Ctr. | 56 W. 50th St. (bet. 5th & 6th Aves.) | B/D/F/V to 47-50th Sts./Rockefeller Ctr. | 212-956-0868
www.delfinoshop.com

Loyalists "love to wander" this pair of "stylish" spots in the East 70s and West 50s searching for "unique" "of-the-moment" handbags and accessories "not everyone has", including the house line and "delicious" brands from Europe (Longchamp, Hervé Chapelier, etc.) that take you "from day to play"; it's just too bad the "bored sales staff" doesn't help you navigate the "excellent array."

Delphinium Cards & Gifts ◐

`24` `20` `22` `M`

W 40s | 358 W. 47th St. (bet. 8th & 9th Aves.) | C/E to 50th St. | 212-333-7732

Delphinium Home ◐

W 40s | 653 Ninth Ave. (bet. 45th & 46th Sts.) | A/C/E to 42nd St./Port Authority | 212-333-3213 | www.delphiniumhome.com

These "cute" "hole-in-the-wall" Hell's Kitchen shops with "helpful service" are "full of cool stuff for your home and kitchen" (or someone else's for a "last-minute gift") that isn't "found on every other corner", like umbrellas with imprints of blue skies on their underbellies and matte silver leaf Zen photo albums; "it can get cramped but it's worth getting shoved for" their "delightful", moderately priced "small things."

DeMask

`▽ 22` `-` `18` `E`

LES | 144 Orchard St. (bet. Rivington & Stanton Sts.) | F/J/M/Z to Delancey/Essex Sts. | 212-466-0814 | www.demask.com

Rubber lovers reveal you'll be "hot, hot, hot", literally and figuratively, squeezed into a "top-quality latex" ensemble from this European import, which relocated from Chelsea to the Lower East Side, where it still peddles "the world's finest fetishwear"; the "awesome", fashion-forward selection is only for females, but guys can perch on a red leather couch and let their "imaginations run wild" while their lady friends model duds that are "divine for the dominatrix."

Demolition Depot/
Irreplaceable Artifacts ⚠⊠

`-` `-` `-` `E`

Harlem | 216 E. 125th St. (bet. 2nd & 3rd Aves.) | 4/5/6 to 125th St. | 212-860-1138 | www.demolitiondepot.com

For "great finds from back in time", hit this Harlem outlet for all things old whose inventory of unique architectural works and ornaments changes daily, as pieces are switched in and out of the numerous New England warehouses operated by this salvage sultan; antique elevator and entrance doors are popular, as are the plentiful plumbing fixtures, but there are smaller pieces like deco door knockers too.

☑ Dempsey & Carroll ☒

| | 27 | 22 | 24 | VE |

E 50s | 136 E. 57th St., 4th fl. (bet. Lexington & 3rd Aves.) | 4/5/6/F/N/R/W to 59th St./Lexington Ave. | 212-750-6055 | 877-750-1878 | www.dempseyandcarroll.com

"Mingle with socialites" at this "old-world" (since 1878) East 57th Street shop where "Edith Wharton would feel at home"; a "dignified staff" purveys "classy", "traditional engraved stationery", wedding invitations and address books in a "postage-stamp-size" space; "you pay for what you get" – "premium products" that "others aren't likely to be using."

NEW Den ☽

| | 22 | 19 | 19 | E |

E Village | 330 E. 11th St. (bet. 1st & 2nd Aves.) | L to 1st Ave. | 212-475-0079 | www.dennewyork.com

"If you see something you like, buy it before it's replaced with another brand" shriek "chic" supporters of this "small", stark East Villager, which displays a different "sharp, modern" men's and sometimes women's collection every six weeks or so; the wares can be "hit-or-miss, depending on the particular designer "of the moment" – but "it can't hurt to pop in while shopping next door at Odin" (which owns it).

DeNatale Jewelers, Inc. ☒

| | 26 | 25 | 24 | E |

E 50s | 7 W. 51st St. (bet. 5th & 6th Aves.) | E/V to 5th Ave./53rd St. | 212-317-2955

Financial District | 170 Broadway (Maiden Ln.) | 2/3/4/5/A/C/J/M/Z to Fulton St./B'way/Nassau | 212-349-2355
www.denatale.com

Whether you're searching for a gold-link bracelet or a radiant-cut canary diamond engagement ring, you "can always find what you're looking for" at this family-owned and -operated Wall Street and Midtown jewelry duo dating back to 1908; "quality" "in all price ranges" and "friendly", "old-world service" help guarantee you'll have "a good shopping experience"; they also do custom designs and repairs and offer a full selection of china, crystal and other giftware; N.B. also closed Saturdays.

Dennis Basso

| | ▽ 24 | 26 | 22 | VE |

E 60s | 765 Madison Ave. (bet. 65th & 66th Sts.) | 6 to 68th St. | 212-794-4500 | www.dennisbasso.com

"You'll be a showstopper" in one of the "warm, extravagant" shearlings and furs, including "the ne plus ultra of sables", produced by this black-and-gold-accented, elegant East 60s salon whose "beautifully hand-embroidered" "styles are exquisite" without "nodding to what is supposedly 'in'"; not surprisingly, they're also "super-duper expensive – don't expect to pay any less than a year of college tuition" (but do "the kids really need to learn", anyway?).

Dernier Cri ☽

| | - | - | - | E |

Meatpacking | 869 Washington St. (bet. 13th & 14th Sts.) | A/C/E/L to 14th St./8th Ave. | 212-242-6061

The store's name translates to the 'latest fashion' or 'newest discovery', which is just what you'd expect to find at this Meatpacking District

spot owned by MTV alum Stacia Valle who knows how to keep it real –
and "worth a look", kitting the space out with celery-green walls, industrial "metal racks" and a rebellious mix of renegade silhouettes
and rocker tees for righteous babes from lines including Sonia by Sonia
Rykiel, Preen and Vivienne Westwood.

Designer Resale
24 | 20 | 18 | E

E 80s | 311 E. 81st St. (bet. 1st & 2nd Aves.) | 6 to 77th St. |
212-734-2836
E 80s | 324 E. 81st St. (bet. 1st & 2nd Aves.) | 6 to 77th St. |
212-734-3639
www.resaleclothing.net

Set in two facing townhouses on 81st Street, this "grande dame of
thrift shops" offers a "well-presented", "impressive selection of upscale designer threads" and accessories of a "definitely Upper East
Side" nature ("nothing too trendy or too cool"); however, the "haughty
sales clerks" "are not so helpful", and some find the consigned goods
"overpriced" – although the "twice-annual sales can be phenomenal"
("Coach and Kate Spade at knockoff prices!").

Design Within Reach
24 | 22 | 20 | E

E 60s | 27 E. 62nd St. (bet. Madison & Park Aves.) | 4/5/6/F/N/R/W to
59th St./Lexington Ave. | 212-888-4539
Flatiron | 903 Broadway (20th St.) | 6 to 23rd St. | 212-477-1155
Meatpacking | 408 W. 14th St. (bet. 9th & 10th Aves.) | A/C/E/L to
14th St./8th Ave. | 212-242-9449
SoHo | 142 Wooster St. (bet. Houston & Prince Sts.) | N/R/W to Prince St. |
212-475-0001
TriBeCa | 124 Hudson St. (bet. Beach & N. Moore Sts.) | 1 to Franklin St. |
212-219-2217
W 70s | 341 Columbus Ave. (76th St.) | 1/2/3 to 72nd St. |
212-799-5900
Brooklyn Heights | 76 Montague St. (Hicks St.) | Brooklyn | 1/2/4/5/
M/N/R to Court St./Borough Hall | 718-643-1015
800-944-2233 | www.dwr.com

Within the space of four years, this San Francisco–based furniture firm
has exploded across the city and in Brooklyn, opening seven locations,
and democratizing the "midcentury" modern mystique by offering
"haute design for the masses"; a "well-informed staff" can talk you
through classics from Charles and Ray Eames and Isamu Noguchi or
newer pieces from Karim Rashid and Philippe Starck; still, surveyors
are split on the cost, with proponents praising "almost reasonable
prices", while critics who call the store's name a "misnomer" declare
that tabs are only "within reach of the well-heeled"; N.B. they've also
introduced a children's line.

Desiron
▽ 22 | 26 | 24 | VE

SoHo | 151 Wooster St. (bet. Houston & Prince Sts.) | N/R/W to
Prince St. | 212-353-2600 | 888-337-4766 | www.desiron.com

"Wonderful lines", "custom-made quality" and "beautiful finishes and
detail" make aesthetes aspire to the "absolute minimalism" of this
"high-fashion" furniture shop in SoHo that spans over 6,000 sq. ft.
and showcases the Carfaro brothers' collection of tables, seating,
beds, bureaus and storage pieces; everything here is stylishly spare
except the prices.

Destination ●

▽ 23 | 25 | 22 | E

Meatpacking | 32-36 Little W. 12th St. (bet. 9th Ave. & Washington St.) | A/C/E/L to 14th St./8th Ave. | 212-727-2031 | www.destinationny.net

The plaster pig on the sidewalk outside signals that this Meatpacking District destination is no ordinary fashionista stomping ground; clotheshorses and art-lovers alike wander the large, contemporary shop that doubles as an art gallery, perusing the "well-curated selection" of apparel, shoes and accessories from an international coterie of under-the-radar designers – this is definitely "not run-of-the-mill stuff."

Destination Maternity ●

22 | 20 | 22 | M

E 50s | 28 E. 57th St. (Madison Ave.) | E/V to 5th Ave./53rd St. | 212-588-0220 | 800-291-7800 | www.destinationmaternity.com

It's the "mother ship for expectant mothers, literally" proclaim pregnant patrons who find an Edamame spa, Pea in the Pod, Mimi Maternity and Motherhood Maternity clothing and accessories "all at your fingertips" at this three-level Madison Avenue mecca; you "feel like a fashion plate" whether you "pick up a cheap top or glam it up" – there's something for "everyone in every price range"; still, a few grumble it's "somewhat understaffed, which can make a cranky prego impatient."

NEW Diabless ●

- | - | - | E

E 60s | 1138 Third Ave. (bet. 66th & 67th Sts.) | 6 to 68th St. | 212-744-0290 | www.diabless.com

Now that this French label has made its stateside debut, opening this petite East 60s charmer (and a shop in LA too), you no longer have to seek out its flirty knitwear and feminine, fashion-forward silhouettes in boutiques about town or on jaunts to Paris; the collection of sweet-but-sexy minis, rompers, cropped jackets, night-out dresses, cashmere sweaters and other Gallic-girl essentials are all arranged by color on racks and low, modern tables for easy mixing and matching.

NEW Diana Broussard

22 | 21 | 19 | E

G Village | 22 Christopher St. (bet. Gay St. & Waverly Pl.) | 1 to Christopher St./Sheridan Sq. | 646-336-6365 | www.dianabroussard.com

"What beautiful shoes" gush groupies of this Village newcomer, where owner-designer Diana Broussard's chic, "individual approach" to shoemaking is showcased in a "perfectly pleasant" atmosphere inspired by an Italian palazzo, replete with chandeliers and antique furnishings; mixed in with the "gorgeous" evening sandals, flats, stilettos and boots are unusual "jewelry" and photographs by Steve Pyke and Todd Burris that can be bought from right off the walls.

Diana Kane ●

- | - | - | E

Park Slope | 229B Fifth Ave. (bet. Carroll & President Sts.) | Brooklyn | M/R to Union St. | 718-638-6520

Park Slope | 78A Seventh Ave. (bet. Berkeley & Union Sts.) | Brooklyn | B/Q to 7th Ave. | 718-638-5674
www.dianakane.com

"Diana's got the best taste" – and now fashionistas can reap the benefits of the namesake owner's clean, elegant style at two Park Slope locations; the Fifth Avenue original can be "torture" for those who "want it all", including "great lingerie" (Cosabella, Skin) and womenswear (Edun, Velvet), Repetto ballet flats, Vix swimsuits and Kane's own "gorgeous handmade jewelry", but can "afford little"; the all-white Seventh Avenue offshoot traffics in similar temptations, plus choice pieces from Lewis Cho and Only Hearts.

Diane T ● Ⓜ — | — | — | E

Cobble Hill | 174 Court St. (bet. Amity & Congress Sts.) | Brooklyn | F/G to Bergen St. | 718-923-5777

"Displaced Manhattan fashionistas" can forgo the F train and make tracks to this gleaming white, "stylish outpost" in Cobble Hill, where owner Diane Tkacz stocks plenty of desirables from Rebecca Taylor and Marc by Marc Jacobs along with the latest jeans from Juicy Couture and 7 for All Mankind; it's also "an excellent resource" for smart stuff from Milly, Paul & Joe, Vanessa Bruno and emerging designers, and, to go-with, "pricey" handbags and shoes.

Diane von Furstenberg 24 | — | 22 | E
(aka DVF the Shop)

Meatpacking | 874 Washington St. (14th St.) | A/C/E/L to 14th St./8th Ave. | 646-486-4800 | www.dvf.com

When craving "eye candy for your wardrobe" from Ms. Furstenberg, the "Manhattan maven of comfortable, chic, body-conscious" design, head west to her relocated boutique, a pink-and-white showcase with a zebra rug now set on the ground floor of the DVF Studio, a multifloor Meatpacking District complex; while cultists clamor for her "feminine and flattering" wrap dresses that "can handle many figure shapes", there's lots more on hand, plus you may see "the queen" herself, as she "treats this store as if it's her own closet."

Didi's Children's Boutique — | — | — | E

E 80s | 1196 Madison Ave. (bet. 87th & 88th Sts.) | 4/5/6 to 86th St. | 212-860-4001 | 800-707-8895 | www.didis.com

A nice alternative to the big-box behemoths, this "friendly, welcoming" East 80s emporium (with an elder sibling in Bedford, NY) aims to please with its imaginative, albeit "pricey", inventory of playthings for tykes, ranging from "adorable wooden European toys", train sets, puppet theaters and picture books to "cute" clothing, accessories and even mother-daughter tote bags.

Diesel 23 | 21 | 17 | E

E 60s | 770 Lexington Ave. (60th St.) | 4/5/6/F/N/R/W to 59th St./Lexington Ave. | 212-308-0055 ●

SoHo | 135 Spring St. (bet. Greene & Wooster Sts.) | C/E to Spring St. | 212-625-1555

Union Sq | 1 Union Sq. W. (14th St.) | 4/5/6/L/N/Q/R/W to 14th St./Union Sq. | 646-336-8552 ●
www.diesel.com

It's the "king" of "everything denim" declare denizens who worship the "always hip" label that helped "start it all" at these huge Lex, SoHo and Union Square outposts; if you're "lucky enough to have a Diesel body", these "high-priced", "cutting-edge" styles "deliver" and "keep you coming back"; but a miffed minority fumes about the staff of "absolute prima donnas", grumbling "just remember you're not allowed to touch" the "carefully stacked inventory."

	QUALITY	DISPLAY	SERVICE	COST

Diesel Denim Gallery
24 23 18 E

SoHo | 68 Greene St. (bet. Broome & Spring Sts.) | C/E to Spring St. | 212-966-5593 | www.diesel.com

"If you want sharp, unique, imported limited-edition jeans" that make your butt "look super", this "trendy", half-gallery, half-shop is the SoHo "spot for you"; some pairs "seem to fit better than others" and service veers from "helpful" to "terribly hip", but instead of singing the blues, remember that "buying new" denim "isn't supposed to be easy", plus there's a silver lining: "great" options to "suit anyone's body."

Diesel Kids
▽ 25 23 19 E

SoHo | 414-416 W. Broadway (bet. Prince & Spring Sts.) | C/E to Spring St. | 212-343-3863 | www.dieselkids.com

Budding fashionistas get their fill of the Italian fashion phenomenon at this spacious SoHo shop done up with stainless-steel fixtures and chocolate-colored wood floors; the "very friendly staff" helps steer you through the selection of seasonal streetwear and footwear and, of course, the giant jeans wall, stuffed to the seams with its highly covetable premium denim for babies through teens.

Dig Garden Shop ●Ⓜ
23 21 22 M

Downtown | 479 Atlantic Ave. (bet. Nevins St. & 3rd Ave.) | Brooklyn | 2/3/4/5/B/D/M/N/Q/R to Atlantic Ave. | 718-554-0207 | www.gardendig.com

What a "lovely gardening store!" sigh nature lovers who dig into the "broad assortment" of indoor and outdoor plants, "beautiful selection of vases", whimsical topiaries and mega planters, plus handy tools and supplies at this "neighborhood destination" on Atlantic Avenue; it's "not fancy" but it boasts "nice flourishes" like a botanical theme and an outdoor space, plus the "owner is lovely and very helpful."

DIGS ●
19 20 18 E

E 60s | 1079 Third Ave. (64th St.) | 4/5/6 to 59th St. | 212-308-3447 | www.glamorousdigs.com

Mavens maintain they've hit pay dirt with this "trendy", "30-and-under" women's boutique on an otherwise conservative retail stretch on the UES; all of the "eclectic" "edgy" clothing – ranging from contemporary looks like ruffled tunics and sequined turtlenecks to vintage-inspired items like faux-leopard fur jackets – is designed by the owner and displayed against a backdrop of velvet-damask wallpaper and calfskin rugs.

Dinosaur Designs
- - - E

NoLita | 250 Mott St. (bet. Houston & Prince Sts.) | B/D/F/V to B'way/Lafayette St. | 212-680-3523 | www.dinosaurdesigns.com

The three Aussies behind this Sydney-based business with an offshoot in NoLita began with organic-inspired, brightly colored and "quirky" resin jewelry like rings, bangles and necklaces and have branched out using the same modern material to shape housewares, vases and bowls in equally vibrant shades.

Dinosaur Hill
▽ 24 24 24 M

E Village | 306 E. Ninth St. (2nd Ave.) | 6 to Astor Pl. | 212-473-5850 | www.dinosaurhill.com

"Expect the unexpected" at this "simply marvelous" East Village "wonderland", where every "nook and cranny" is filled with "magical" toys, making it "fun to wander through with a child"; it has "all the basics", but it's also jammed with the "sort of stuff you would've gone nuts for when you were" a kid like kaleidoscopes, marionettes from around the world, stained-glass fairies, wooden dollhouses, steel drums and figurines.

Dior Homme

▽ | 26 | 26 | 21 | VE

E 50s | 17 E. 57th St. (bet. 5th & Madison Aves.) | N/R/W to 5th Ave./ 59th St. | 212-421-6009 | www.diorhomme.com

Hip *hommes* "highly recommend" the slim suits, narrow ties and jewelry at this sleek, polished sliver of a store next to Dior's main 57th Street boutique; the black slate floors and white laminated shelving show off the merch, which is "good value, given the quality"; nevertheless, some caution that considering the costs and the cuts, these clothes are "only for the rich and skinny."

☒ Dior New York

28 | 28 | 23 | VE

E 50s | 21 E. 57th St. (bet. 5th & Madison Aves.) | N/R/W to 5th Ave./ 59th St. | 212-931-2950 | www.dior.com

"If you're on an expense account", "start shopping here" at this luxury-laden, multifloor East 50s haven for logo-loco ladies with "displays that are some of the best in NY" and an "unpretentious staff"; not many designers alive today can "match designer John Galliano's wit, visual flair and pure madness" of design – be it in bustier bikinis or corseted gowns – all of which enable "your days to be a continuous Sarah-Jessica-Parker-in-*Sex-and-the-City* moment."

Disc-O-Rama Music World

20 | 9 | 14 | I

G Village | 186 W. Fourth St. (bet. 6th & 7th Aves.) | A/B/C/D/E/F/V to W. 4th St. | 212-206-8417 ☻

G Village | 44 W. Eighth St. (bet. MacDougal St. & 6th Ave.) | A/B/C/D/E/F/V to W. 4th St. | 212-477-9410 ☻

Union Sq | 40 Union Sq. E. (bet. 16th & 17th Sts.) | 4/5/6/L/N/Q/R/W to 14th St./Union Sq. | 212-260-8616

866-606-2614 | www.discorama.com

"New releases" of "top CDs" plus "current videos and games" can be found at this "no-frills" trio; the "crowded", "small spaces" are "difficult to browse" and some of the "knowledgeable" staffers are "nasty", but with such "low prices" you'll think the merchandise "must have fallen off the truck" – strike quickly, though, as "popular product goes fast."

Disrespectacles

▽ | 27 | 27 | 27 | E

TriBeCa | 117 W. Broadway (bet. Duane & Reade Sts.) | 1/2/3 to Chambers St. | 212-608-8892

W Village | 82 Christopher St. (bet. Bleecker St. & 7th Ave. S.) | 1 to Christopher St./Sheridan Sq. | 212-741-9550

www.disrespectacles.com

At this "cool" TriBeCa–West Village duo, a "learned", "extremely accommodating" staff proffers "the most unique eyewear in the city" ranging from "understated to outlandish" with "hard-to-find vintage" and "funky" eyeglasses in between; you'll have "hours of fun trying on" the "excellent quality" specs that "get more compliments than your jewelry" and make "New Yorkers the envy of mall-bound" vision-questers.

	QUALITY	DISPLAY	SERVICE	COST

Diva

| | - | - | - | E |

Midwood | 1409 Ave. M (bet. 14th & 15th Sts.) | Brooklyn | Q to Ave. M | 718-645-9797

Little fashion plates with big appetites for style make pilgrimages to this pink-and-chocolate-colored Midwood boutique, which aims to bring out the inner diva in every girl, particularly tweens, with its racks of runway-worthy sportswear and special-occasion finery from hip European labels like Miss Blumarine, Parrot and Simonetta, and its stockpile of snazzy shoes from designers like D & G Junior and Moschino.

DKNY ◑

| | 21 | 22 | 18 | E |

E 60s | 655 Madison Ave. (60th St.) | N/R/W to 5th Ave./59th St. | 212-223-3569
SoHo | 420 W. Broadway (bet. Prince & Spring Sts.) | C/E to Spring St. | 646-613-1100
www.dkny.com

Whether they're sipping a smoothie at the Madison Avenue shop's organic cafe or sampling the fruity Be Delicious fragrance at the SoHo site, disciples declare Donna Karan's "got it down" with her lower-priced line, aka "staple urbanwear" for men and women seeking "stylish" items for work or play; but views vary on the clothes' price-value ratio ("excellent" vs. "not always affordable") and whether the staff comes with or "without any attitude."

D/L Cerney ◑

| | - | - | - | M |

E Village | 13 E. Seventh St. (bet. 2nd & 3rd Aves.) | 6 to Astor Pl. | 212-673-7033

Retro works best when it's well made – and a bit cheeky – which is why this East Village fixture attracts guys and gals with a weakness for the house label's "unusual, top-quality", vintage-inspired rayon gabardine shirts and silk wrap skirts, ratcheted up a style notch with "details like special antique buttons", '40s-esque prints and topstitching.

Doggystyle

| | - | - | - | E |

SoHo | 73 Thompson St. (bet. Broome & Spring Sts.) | C/E to Spring St. | 212-431-9200 | www.doggystylenyc.com

"Pampered pooches" make tracks for this "amazing" SoHo shop showcasing an "excellent selection of hip apparel" and "unique" accessories; "special" services like pet portraiture are other reasons some say it's the "best" boutique for "spoiled puppies."

Dö Kham ◑

| | ∇ 22 | 21 | 22 | M |

NoLita | 51 Prince St. (bet. Lafayette & Mulberry Sts.) | N/R/W to Prince St. | 212-966-2404

This NoLita shop features the "best of Tibet in Manhattan" with its "amazing array of boho-chic" fashion ranging from "unique chandelier earrings" and vibrant tunics to tiered skirts "embellished with sequins"; devotees can also decorate their digs with "perennially fashionable" Silk Road must-haves, including colorful bedspreads and pillows.

Dolce & Gabbana

| | 27 | 26 | 22 | VE |

E 60s | 825-827 Madison Ave. (bet. 68th & 69th Sts.) | 6 to 68th St. | 212-249-4100 | www.dolcegabbana.it

The dynamic duo of Domenico Dolce and Stefano Gabbana never disappoints those types – "tall, skinny and a bit loud in their taste" – who visit this East 60s showcase (snazzily and recently redone with huge black chandeliers, black mirrors and lava stone floors) for the label synonymous with "pure sex appeal"; an "amazing staff" offers help with the "original", corsetry-inspired collections for her and "edgy suits" for him, inspiring those who live to "imagine their inner rock star" to declare "when money is no object, this is the place to shop – even when it *is* an object, this is the place to shop."

Dolce Vita ☻

23 | 19 | 18 | E

LES | 149 Ludlow St. (bet. Rivington & Stanton Sts.) | F/J/M/Z to Delancey/Essex Sts. | 212-529-2111

DV ☻

LES | 159½ Ludlow St. (bet. Rivington & Stanton Sts.) | F/J/M/Z to Delancey/Essex Sts. | 212-529-2111
www.shopdolcevita.com

No "sticker shock" here – just "trendy" women's shoes for less greens than similar styles at "neighboring stores" marvel admirers of this Lower East Sider; check out the house-brand boots, T-straps and wedges on the tiered display, then move on to the "great selection" of hip, pricier threads from Vince and Tsesay – there's lots of sweet "stuff" to pine for; N.B. tiny sister shop DV boasts a mod living room feel and less footwear.

Domain

20 | 20 | 18 | E

E 60s | Trump Palace | 1179 Third Ave. (69th St.) | 6 to 68th St. | 212-639-1101

Flatiron | 938 Broadway (22nd St.) | N/R/W to 23rd St. | 212-228-7450

W 60s | 101 West End Ave. (65th St.) | 1 to 66th St./Lincoln Ctr. | 917-441-2397

800-888-1388 | www.domain-home.com

Trio of home stores that is the domain of European-inspired, "oversized" "traditional furniture" such as armoires, couches, chaises, bookcases and beds with "ornate" decorative elements like wrought-iron flourishes, fluted pilasters, hand-painted details and other frills as well as "antiquey accessories"; modernists maintain the styles can be a "little foofie", but bargain-hunters boast that "good deals can be had at sale time."

Domenico Vacca

– | – | – | VE

E 50s | 781 Fifth Ave. (bet. 59th & 60th Sts.) | 4/5/6/F/N/R/W to 59th St./Lexington Ave. | 212-759-6333

E 60s | 702 Madison Ave. (bet. 62nd & 63rd Sts.) | 6 to 68th St. | 212-421-8902

SoHo | 367 W. Broadway (Broome St.) | C/E to Spring St. | 212-925-0010 ☻
www.domenicovacca.com

Sartorial sybarites feel right at home at this threesome of high-end haberdasheries where well-dressed CEOs go for alligator shoes hand-crafted in Naples, overcoats lined in cashmere and colorful, custom-made suits and eveningwear that reflect their prestigious bank accounts; intelligent salespeople and plush surroundings – wool-paneled walls and soft leather couches – add to the allure.

Donna Karan

25 | 25 | 23 | VE

E 60s | 819 Madison Ave. (bet. 68th & 69th Sts.) | 6 to 68th St. | 212-861-1001 | www.donnakaran.com

Art imitates life at this "clever" multilevel Madison Avenue store, "which mixes clothing and objects in a magical manner", placing this admired American designer's his-and-hers collections in "silks and natural fibers that titillate the senses" against the backdrop of a bamboo and Japanese sculpture garden; a few feel the line's "lost some of its glamour" of late, but most "monotone-dressing NYers" maintain these "consistently excellent pieces become never-dated classics", and applaud the "amazing service."

Don the Verb ◐

∇ 16 | 15 | 17 | E

LES | 61 Delancey St. (bet. Allen & Eldridge Sts.) | F/J/M/Z to Delancey/Essex Sts. | 212-219-7633 | www.dontheverb.com

On a desolate stretch of Delancey Street lies this little black pearl, offering "the ultimate in vintage" clothing for femmes; the postmodern decor – steel-paneled wall and bare wood-beamed floor – belies the ladylike, time-defying designs (mostly late '60s and on) from the likes of Yves Saint-Laurent and Jean-Paul Gaultier, plus "pristine" Italian bags and heels; some declare a need "for deep pockets" to buy, but this is "only the finest designer wear"; N.B. there's also a house label that includes leggings and tunics made of vintage, gossamer-silk fabrics.

Donzella ⌧

- | - | - | VE

TriBeCa | 17 White St. (bet. 6th Ave. & W. B'way) | 1 to Franklin St. | 212-965-8919 | www.donzella.com

You'll find "high-end furnishings with all the trimmings" (including "very expensive" price tags) at this TriBeCa store; "a helpful staff" guides you through the museum-worthy collection of vintage or period furniture and accessories from Europe and America, ranging from ebonized mahogany seating from Edward Wormley and cork-top side tables circa 1950 from Paul Frankl to Murano glassware from Italy.

Dooney & Bourke

25 | 23 | 22 | E

E 60s | 20 E. 60th St. (bet. Madison & Park Aves.) | 4/5/6/F/N/R/W to 59th St./Lexington Ave. | 212-223-7444 | 800-347-5000 | www.dooney.com

"Even if D.B. aren't your initials", the "lovely" leather backpacks, "preppy" "colorful" drawstring purses and other luxe accessories at this "great" East 60s store will have you "obsessed"; the "cheerful", "helpful" staff may be another reason why loyalists "own almost every handbag they've made."

Door Store

17 | 16 | 17 | M

Chelsea | 123 W. 17th St. (bet. 6th & 7th Aves.) | 1 to 18th St. | 212-627-1515
E 50s | 969 Third Ave. (bet. 58th & 59th Sts.) | 4/5/6/F/N/R/W to 59th St./Lexington Ave. | 212-421-5273
Gramercy | 1 Park Ave. (33rd St.) | 6 to 33rd St. | 212-679-9700
W 80s | 601 Amsterdam Ave. (89th St.) | 1 to 86th St. | 212-501-8699
Downtown | 475 Atlantic Ave. (bet. Nevins St. & 3rd Ave.) | Brooklyn | 2/3/4/5/B/D/M/N/Q/R to Atlantic Ave. | 718-237-6888 ◐
www.doorstorefurniture.com

"Decent-quality furniture" "at great prices" is "the reason this chain's been around for 52 years"; it's "not known for the coolest" presentation, and "there's not a door in sight", but "practical" pieces like "casual sofas", bedroom sets, tables and entertainment units that are "attractive" and appropriate for a "first apartment" keep customers coming back.

	QUALITY	DISPLAY	SERVICE	COST

Dosa 🖼
▽ 24 | 23 | 23 | E

SoHo | 107 Thompson St. (bet. Prince & Spring Sts.) | C/E to Spring St. | 212-431-1733 | www.dosainc.com

"Pretty, bohemian, arty" are adjectives that all apply to the womens-wear in this nearly "unnoticeable" SoHo shop, whose eco-friendly owner-designer, Christina Kim, specializes in "better-quality" cotton and silk pieces (pajamas are particularly popular), accessories and home furnishings; she employs hand-loomed fabrics, organically grown wool, natural pigments and metallic threads – so "be prepared for high prices."

Douglas Cosmetics ⬤
22 | 18 | 18 | M

E 40s | Grand Central | 42nd St. (Vanderbilt Ave.) | 4/5/6/7/S to 42nd St./ Grand Central | 212-599-1776 | 800-770-0081 | www.douglascosmetics.com

"When you forget that last-minute hostess gift or your makeup bag on your way to a weekend rendezvous", this cosmetics purveyor in Grand Central gets an "A for commuter convenience"; at other times, "limited space" and "service that's offhand at best" aren't nearly as impressive.

🄯 Downtown Yarns
28 | 25 | 25 | E

E Village | 45 Ave. A (bet. 3rd & 4th Sts.) | F/V to Lower East Side/2nd Ave. | 212-995-5991 | www.downtownyarns.com

"The screen door is a clue" to the "laid-back" vibe of this "inviting" "Vermont country store on Avenue A", a neighborhood knitters' "re-treat" where classes are offered, the "kind" staff is "willing to help you on all fronts" and the "beautiful" wools and tools "spur [one's] creativ-ity"; though a few frown on the "tiny" confines, there's one big plus: "you'll pay less here than at some more upscale joints."

Doyle & Doyle 🅼
▽ 25 | 27 | 28 | E

LES | 189 Orchard St. (bet. Houston & Stanton Sts.) | F/V to Lower East Side/2nd Ave. | 212-677-9991 | www.doyledoyle.com

"Charming" and "helpful" sister-owners Pamela and Elizabeth Doyle have a "great eye" and it shows at this "small", "laid-back" Lower East Side shop with "fantasyland" displays of "gorgeous" and "eclectic" vintage and estate jewelry; styles range from Georgian to art deco, and prices from "affordable to extravagant."

Drimmers
24 | 12 | 20 | M

Midwood | 1608 Coney Island Ave. (bet. L & M Aves.) | Brooklyn | Q to Ave. M | 718-773-8483 | 877-338-3500 | www.drimmers.com

"If you are ready for the ultimate kitchen", head to this family-owned, 30-plus-year-old Coney Island Avenue appliance stalwart that still of-fers "some of the best prices" on high-end domestic and European re-frigerators, dishwashers, washer/dryers and ovens, as well as "great service"; the store itself is "not much to look at", but it's "filled with stuff" you need, making it worth the "trek", plus there's no charge for delivery in Brooklyn or any of the boroughs.

Dr. Jay's ⬤
18 | 14 | 12 | M

Garment District | 33 W. 34th St. (bet. 5th & 6th Aves.) | B/D/F/N/Q/R/V/W to 34th St./Herald Sq. | 212-695-3354 | www.drjays.com
Additional locations throughout the NY area

"Hip-hoppers" of all ages and sexes find "all things streetwear" from "urban" powerhouse labels like Ecko and Evisu at this "mega-shop" with branches throughout NYC; yes, the "lines are usually long" and the service "lax", but your "cred will be impeccable" in these "ultra-cool" threads that won't "break your bank account."

ⓩ DSW ◐

21 | 16 | 11 | M

Financial District | 102 N. End Ave. (Vesey St.) | A/C to Chambers St. | 212-945-7419
Union Sq | 40 E. 14th St., 3rd fl. (bet. B'way & University Pl.) | 4/5/6/L/N/Q/R/W to 14th St./Union Sq. | 212-674-2146
Downtown | Atlantic Terminal | 139 Flatbush Ave. (bet. Atlantic & 4th Aves.) | Brooklyn | 2/3/4/5/B/D/M/N/Q/R to Atlantic Ave. | 718-789-6973
Elmhurst | Queens Pl. | 88-01 Queens Blvd. (bet. 55th & 56th Aves.) | Queens | G/R/V to Grand Ave./Newtown | 718-595-1361
800-477-8595 | www.dswshoe.com

"If you don't mind last year's styles" from labels like "Coach and Carlos Santana", you can let "your inner Imelda run wild" at this chain, which carries "row after row" of "everything from stilettos to sneakers" – "oh, and they have men's too"; though it's all discounted, "check the clearance rack first" for the "really good deals"; P.S. it's especially rewarding "if you're a fan of self-serve: there's no waiting for someone to fetch your shoes because they're all out on the floor."

Dudley's Paw 🖂

- | - | - | E

TriBeCa | 327 Greenwich St. (bet. Duane & Jay Sts.) | 1/2/3 to Chambers St. | 212-966-5167

A "teeny-weeny shop with a big heart", this TriBeCa longtimer "barks and meows NYC" "neighborhood store"; the staff "couldn't be nicer", and even if the "small space" means the "selection is minimal", it offers "all the essentials" and the pet food's "good quality."

Dulcinée ◑

- | - | - | M

LES | 127 Stanton St. (bet. Essex & Norfolk Sts.) | F/V to Lower East Side/2nd Ave. | 212-253-2534 | www.dulcineenyc.com

At this streamlined LES vintage clothier, the selection is small but chic: women's couture labels like YSL, Alaïa and Ungaro, mostly from the '60s-'80s (though you may discover a "mint Claire McCardle with tags, from – what, 50 years ago?" or even a treasure from the 1880s); the only drawback is the dressing room – actually, a corner with a ringed curtain; N.B. closed Mondays and Tuesdays in the summertime.

Duncan Quinn ◐Ⓜ

- | - | - | E

NoLita | 8 Spring St. (bet. Bowery & Elizabeth St.) | J/M/Z to Bowery | 212-226-7030 | www.duncanquinn.com

Make an appointment at this "candy-box" of a shop for "the dandy in your life", who'll relish this cheeky namesake Brit who's made his rep applying Savile Row refinement to rather racy clothes (the "boldest pinks and purples"); though it's about the size of a walk-in closet, the NoLita digs offer ready-made and bespoke suits and shirts, luggage and all sorts of accessories, from suspenders to sterling silver collar stays, plus custom-tailored haberdashery for her.

Dunderdon Workshop

- | - | - | E

SoHo | 272 Lafayette St. (Prince St.) | B/D/F/V to B'way/Lafayette St. | 212-226-4040 | www.dunderdon.com

It may be super-small in size, but this "wonderful" SoHo Swedish import is big on style, supplying trendsetting guys – and now gals too –

with functional yet fashion-forward finds; the detail-happy don't have to dig deep to uncover "the best" sturdy, multipocketed canvas and denim pants, plus pile-lined casual jackets, and to go-with, cool hoodies, T-shirts and accessories.

Dune ⊠

-	-	-	E

TriBeCa | 88 Franklin St. (bet. B'way & Church St.) | 1 to Franklin St. | 212-925-6171 | www.dune-ny.com

Housed in a soaring former painting studio in TriBeCa is this "minimalist" showroom for made-to-order, cutting-edge American contemporary furniture like funky ottomans and sectional sofas; if you don't see what you need, "just ask for what you want – they'll make it."

Dunhill

27	27	26	VE

E 50s | 711 Fifth Ave. (bet. 55th & 56th Sts.) | E/V to 5th Ave./53rd St. | 212-753-9292 | 800-776-4053 | www.dunhill.com

"Bringing the refined style of the English elite" to Midtown, this "bastion of civilized living" offers men of means an "absolutely marvelous shopping experience", from the "impeccable service" to the "totally unnecessary but totally desirable objects"; "check out" the "high-quality" bespoke clothing, shoes and "genuine gentlemen's accessories" including leather goods, watches and "lighters that'll last a lifetime" (a flashback to its cigar-specialist past); it's the "best – if you can afford it."

Dusica Dusica ●

-	-	-	E

SoHo | 67 Prince St. (Crosby St.) | N/R/W to Prince St. | 212-966-9099 | www.dusicadusica.com

Cultists who consider footwear art get their culture fix at designer Dusica Sacks' playfully minimalist SoHo boutique set in, what else, a former gallery, with the "unique" shoes, boots and handbags displayed against a dramatic white backdrop enhanced by 20-ft.-high curtains; you "won't see yourself coming and going" in these colorful heels and flats decked out with straps, buckles, fur and other "inventive" details.

Dykes Lumber ⊠

24	13	22	M

W 40s | 348 W. 44th St. (bet. 8th & 9th Aves.) | 1/2/3/7/N/Q/R/S/W to 42nd St./Times Sq. | 212-246-6480
Bronx | 1777 W. Farms Rd. (174th St.) | 2/5 to W. Farms Sq. | 718-784-3920
Park Slope | 167 Sixth St. (bet. 2nd & 3rd Aves.) | Brooklyn | F/M/R to 4th Ave./9th St. | 718-624-3350
LIC | 26-16 Jackson Ave. (bet. 44th & Purves Sts.) | Queens | E/V to 23rd St./Ely Ave. | 718-784-3920
www.dykeslumber.com

"When you need wood" "delivered fast" for that home project or "molding for your pre-war apartment", head to this borough-wide "mom-and-pop lumberyard" outfit staffed with "friendly" folk "who know their stuff" and put first-time DIYers "at ease"; constructionists confide that you can also nail down windows from specialists like Andersen or Marvin, and even order custom millwork or "doors and the like" here – "who'd a thunk it?"

Dylan's Candy Bar ●

22	26	16	M

E 60s | 1011 Third Ave. (60th St.) | 4/5/6/F/N/R/W to 59th St./Lexington Ave. | 646-735-0078 | www.dylanscandybar.com

Devotees drool over this East 60s "sugary wonderland" whose colorful, "chaotic" premises promise the sweet-toothed and "chocoholics every conceivable fix", from "your favorite childhood bar" to "the latest craze", from "hard-to-find flavors" to "ordinary" brands in bulk; some get a toothache from the prices (it "costs how much"?), but most agree "this is what's at the end of the rainbow"; N.B. check out the candy-hued clothing and accessories too.

Earnest Cut & Sew, An
▽ 25 | 19 | 19 | VE

NEW LES | 90 Orchard St. (Broome St.) | B/D to Grand St. | 212-979-5120 ☾

Meatpacking | 821 Washington St. (bet. Gansevoort & Little W. 12th Sts.) | A/C/E/L to 14th St./8th Ave. | 212-242-3414
www.earnestsewn.com

The Earnest Sewn jeans "people always ask about" with "just the right amount of distress and whimsy" can be found at this Meatpacking District concept shop with a library, espresso bar and general store decor that reveals its rustic "taste and philosophy" – and at its new offshoot in the former Lower East Side Tenement Museum space; these "top-quality", label-less must-haves from the co-founder of Paper Denim & Cloth are "pricey", particularly the "custom-fit-for-your-bum" styles, made within hours, but there's lots to "love."

E.A.T. Gifts
23 | 21 | 17 | E

E 80s | 1062 Madison Ave. (bet. 80th & 81st Sts.) | 6 to 77th St. | 212-861-2544 | www.elizabar.com

Eli Zabar's "crowded" Madison Avenue kids' mecca is the "perfect" place to "get stuck on a rainy afternoon", especially if you relish "rummaging through the bins" for "obsession-worthy knickknacks and toys"; you'll find "whimsical, fun" "finds in every nook and cranny", from "Tin-Tin to Olivia to creative gifts for adults" to "last-minute" "party favors"; sure, some "prices are insane, but they do have some cute" "tchotchkes."

E. Braun & Co. ⌧
- | - | - | E

E 60s | 717 Madison Ave. (bet. 63rd & 64th Sts.) | F to Lexington Ave./63rd St. | 212-838-0650 | 800-372-7286 | www.ebraunandco.co

Since 1943, this Madison Avenue "classic" has been providing "beautifully detailed linens" imported from Europe for the bed, dining table and bath; if the luxury of embroideries, appliqués and scalloped edges on Egyptian cotton, silk and linen is not enough to lure you in, there's also a myriad of customization options – monogramming, patterning, quilting and coloring – offered.

Edge nyNoHo Ⓜ
24 | 20 | 21 | M

NoHo | 65 Bleecker St. (bet. B'way & Lafayette St.) | B/D/F/V to B'way/Lafayette St. | 212-358-0255 | www.edgeny.com

"An impressive gathering of independent designers" – "all eager to spill every detail about how their goods were made" – collects in miniboutiques at this large, bright bazaar created by Market NYC founder Nicholas Petrou in NoHo's historic Louis Sullivan building; it's "the best place to pick up something unique" and "not too expensive", whether your needs run to "one-of-a-kind" jewelry or "something new" in men's and women's apparel and accessories; N.B. closed Tuesdays too.

Ed Hardy ☾
21 | 21 | 18 | E

Meatpacking | 425 W. 13th St. (bet. 9th Ave. & Washington St.) | A/C/E/L to 14th St./8th Ave. | 212-488-3131

(continued)

Ed Hardy

NEW SoHo | 49 Mercer St. (bet. Broome & Grand Sts.) | 6/J/M/N/
Q/R/W/Z to Canal St. | 212-431-4500
www.donedhardy.com

From its doorman ropes to its "eclectic clientele
of rock stars and star stalkers" and the like, this "Meatpacking
District hideaway" (and its new SoHo sidekick) feels more nightclub than store – but that's to be expected from designer Christian
Audigier, who tapped legendary inker Don Ed Hardy to create "flashy
and cashy" clothes ("tattoo chic for the needle phobic"); "if you're
looking for skull design" merchandise, it's probably here, so "grab a T-
shirt", rhinestone cap, sneakers or energy drink, while it's "still the fad
of the moment."

NEW Edit ⊠Ⓜ

`-│-│-│E`

E 90s | 1368 Lexington Ave. (bet. 90th & 91st Sts.) | 4/5/6 to 86th St. |
212-876-1368 | www.editfashion.com

Everything's black-and-white, down to the little poodle frisking about,
at this elegant women's boutique carved out of a narrow Carnegie Hill
townhouse; the ground floor carries a smart selection of separates,
short coats and dresses from the likes of Michael Kors and Tuleh –
ideal for an on-staff editor; her freelance sister might ascend the spiral
staircase for more casual wear from Paul & Joe and Alara or to peruse
the jeans stacked in the 'library', with its sofas, fireplace and TV; the
sweetly attentive staff will fetch coordinating shoes, jewelry or snakeskin bag too.

Edith Machinist ❶

`-│-│-│M`

(fka Edith and Daha)

LES | 104 Rivington St. (bet. Essex & Ludlow Sts.) | F/J/M/Z to
Delancey/Essex Sts. | 212-979-9992

Edith Machinist may have taken over the Lower East Side basement-
level boutique she once shared with biz partner Sara Daha but the
threads and the boatload of shoes and handbags are sure to be familiar to fans who've long considered this clothier "truly the best" resource for "great vintage" at "vintage prices"; what's changed: the
owner-designer now features more feminine silk dresses and "cool
original pieces" from her own label.

Edith Weber ⊠

`-│-│-│VE`

E 70s | 994 Madison Ave. (77th St.) | 6 to 77th St. | 212-570-9668

Edith Weber at the Carlyle ⊠Ⓜ

NEW E 70s | Carlyle Hotel | 987 Madison Ave. (bet. 76th & 77th Sts.) |
6 to 77th St. | 212-570-1033
www.edithweber.com

Family-owned for 50 years, this pair of jewel-box boutiques, kitty-
cornered from each other across Madison Avenue, literally sparkles
with a centuries-spanning array of antique and period pieces (the
newer store in the Carlyle Hotel carries a larger selection of 'important' items, as well as contemporary baubles); though not low, prices
are fair, given the uniqueness and history of the jewelry – about which
the owners will happily offer a crash course (president Barry Weber
often appears on *Antiques Roadshow*).

NEW Edon Manor

-|-|-| VE

TriBeCa | 391 Greenwich St. (bet. Beach & N. Moore Sts.) | 1 to Franklin St. | 212-431-3890 | www.edonmanor.com

Kitted out with a huge white bookcase, rolling ladders, pale-green drapes and classical canapés, this playfully theatrical TriBeCa stomping ground owned by recent Parsons grad Davinia Wang offers a fresh-faced take on a British country manor, a fitting stage for a well-edited selection of luxurious footwear and accessories; treat yourself royally and walk away with shoes and boots from Laurence Decade, Nina Ricci and Vivienne Westwood and lesser-known talents like Rupert Sanderson, along with Chloé sunglasses and Derek Lam handbags.

Eidolon ●M

-|-|-| M

Park Slope | 233 Fifth Ave. (bet. Carroll & President Sts.) | Brooklyn | M/R to Union St. | 718-638-8194 | www.eidolonbklyn.com

Yes, it's "microscopic" in size, but discriminating sorts still consider this Park Slope cooperative a "treat", touting the "trendy" womenswear, "great concept" and "personal service"; choose from an array of local designers including co-owners Andrea Fisher's "beautifully sewn", "1940s-inspired" dresses, Amara Felice's harmoniously hued separates, Yukie Ohta's unusual handbags, plus retro-inspired shoes from Lisa Nading/Gentle Souls.

Eileen Fisher

24 | 23 | 23 | E

E 50s | 521 Madison Ave. (bet. 53rd & 54th Sts.) | E/V to 5th Ave./ 53rd St. | 212-759-9888

E 70s | 1039 Madison Ave. (bet. 79th & 80th Sts.) | 6 to 77th St. | 212-879-7799

E Village | 314 E. Ninth St. (bet. 1st & 2nd Aves.) | 6 to Astor Pl. | 212-529-5715 ●

Flatiron | 166 Fifth Ave. (bet. 21st & 22nd Sts.) | N/R/W to 23rd St. | 212-924-4777

SoHo | 395 W. Broadway (bet. Broome & Spring Sts.) | C/E to Spring St. | 212-431-4567

W 60s | The Shops at Columbus Circle, Time Warner Ctr. | 10 Columbus Circle, 2nd fl. (60th St. at B'way) | 1/A/B/C/D to 59th St./Columbus Circle | 212-823-9575 ●

W 70s | 341 Columbus Ave. (bet. 76th & 77th Sts.) | 1 to 79th St. | 212-362-3000

800-345-3362 | www.eileenfisher.com

This "comfy" chain "offers new things without straying from its core concept" – "beautiful clothing that never dates" – pleasing "women of a certain age" who appreciate the "forgiving", "unstructured" fit of its basics made to "flatter figures that are less than (or perhaps more than) perfect" as well as "fabulous salespeople"; never mind if a few dis its "upscale frump"-wear as "formless"; N.B. the original East Ninth Street branch carries samples and discounted merchandise.

Einstein-Moomjy

24 | 20 | 21 | E

E 50s | 155 E. 56th St. (bet. Lexington & 3rd Aves.) | 4/5/6/F/N/R/ W to 59th St./Lexington Ave. | 212-758-0900 | 800-864-3633 | www.einsteinmoomjy.com

"What a range of rugs" – from Aubusson, Arts & Crafts, tribal and traditional hand-knotted ones to broadloom Berbers and a kids' collection – can be found at this East 50s emporium that also offers furniture like leather ottomans and sofas.

Eisenberg & Eisenberg ▽ 22 | 16 | 20 | M

Flatiron | 16 W. 17th St. (bet. 5th & 6th Aves.) | F/L/V to 14th St./6th Ave. | 212-627-1290 | www.eisenbergandeisenberg.com

"Been buying clothes here for 50 years" declare loyalists about this family-owned Flatiron fixture that dates back to 1898; it's still renowned for "very good values" in men's formalwear purchases and rentals, whether you favor forward styles from Joseph Abboud or traditional looks from Ralph Lauren; amid a simple warehouse setting, all the appropriate accessories are available too, from patent-leather shoes to cummerbunds; N.B. closed Sundays in January and February.

Ekovaruhuset ●Ⓜ - | - | - | E

LES | 123 Ludlow St. (Rivington St.) | F to Delancey St. | 212-673-1753 | www.ekovaruhuset.se

"Amazed" skeptics evolve into enthusiasts upon entering this tiny Stockholm satellite on the Lower East Side, an avant-garde house of hemp and cotton that "turns organic [materials] into edgy", "off-the-runway-looking" designs; and "even if it's spendy, it's worth it" for a clear conscience, plus the pleasure of shopping in a boutique made of sustainable materials (though the eco-origins of the disco ball overhead are debatable).

Elgot Ⓩ ▽ 25 | 19 | 16 | VE

E 60s | 937 Lexington Ave. (bet. 68th & 69th Sts.) | 6 to 68th St. | 212-879-1200 | www.elgotkitchens.com

For half a century, this "reliable" Upper East Side kitchen and bath showroom has featured some of "the best" quality manufacturers like Gaggenau, Wolf and Sub-Zero, as well as custom and semi-custom cabinetry and countertops.

Elie Tahari ● 24 | 22 | 21 | E

SoHo | 417 W. Broadway (bet. Prince & Spring Sts.) | C/E to Spring St. | 212-334-4441 | www.elietahari.com

A sparkling ballroom-sized chandelier welcomes women to waltz right into this sweeping SoHo store where Elie Tahari's "well-tailored" "classics with a kick" please "ladies with curves" who collect the "well-made" silk-lined coats, brocade jackets and "sassy, sexy" separates; "expensive embellishments" like filigree buttons, plus "attentive service", make purchases "worth the extra dollars."

Elizabeth Charles ●Ⓜ - | - | - | E

Meatpacking | 639½ Hudson St. (bet. Gansevoort & Horatio Sts.) | A/C/E/L to 14th St./8th Ave. | 212-243-3201 | www.elizabeth-charles.com

The "decor and layout are the best" assert insiders, who, much like celeb customers Gemma Ward and Hilary Swank, covet everything about Melbourne-born tastemaker Elizabeth Charles' Meatpacking District shop bordering the West Village; antiques and midcentury-modern furniture create a madcap living-room–like feel while the Down Under designs from Alice McCall, Camilla & Marc and Zambesi, rarely found outside of Oz, inspire unbridled lust; try on the goodies in the huge boudoir to the rear while reflecting on the splendor of the garden.

	QUALITY	DISPLAY	SERVICE	COST

Elizabeth Locke 🗷
∇ 29 | 29 | 26 | VE

E 70s | 968 Madison Ave. (bet. 75th & 76th Sts.) | 6 to 77th St. | 212-744-7878 | www.elizabethlockejewels.com

"Gorgeous" "handmade" earrings, brooches, chokers and charm bracelets are adorned with miniature "mosaics, Venetian glass intaglios", Roman coins and precious or semiprecious stones and set in signature hammered 19-karat gold; the palazzolike interior of the East 70s shop is an appropriate backdrop for the designer's "supreme artistry."

Ellen Christine
- | - | - | E

Chelsea | 255 W. 18th St. (bet. 7th & 8th Aves.) | 1 to 18th St. | 212-242-2457 | www.ellenchristine.com

"Booming personality Ellen Christine has created a little" Chelsea "nook filled with crannies" that boast "amazing vintage creations" and "contemporary" finds, from pre-1920s toppers and chic modern-day cloches to Victorian-inspired capelets and jewelry that "complete a look"; this milliner/costumer/stylist custom-makes "fun, wacky" hats too, and the *chapeaux*-crazed confide "she knows what works on people"; N.B. Mondays by appointment only.

El Museo Del Barrio 🅼
∇ 20 | 18 | 20 | M

E 100s | 1230 Fifth Ave. (104th St.) | 6 to 103rd St. | 212-831-7272 | www.elmuseo.org

From "superb jewelry" to "lovely ceramics" to "interesting" crafts such as *santos* and masks, "hidden treasures" abound at this "small shop" in an Upper East Side museum focused on Latin American and Caribbean art and history; the "great products" also include books, posters and CDs, and its amigos report some "incredible deals"; N.B. closed Tuesdays too.

Emanuel Ungaro 🗷
28 | 26 | 23 | VE

E 60s | 792 Madison Ave. (67th St.) | 6 to 68th St. | 212-249-4090 | www.emanuelungaro.fr

Some things never change – like the "beautiful creations" at this "so-chic" Madison Avenue fixture – and that's a good thing for Gallic-crazy gals who "love, love, love this line" with its bustiers, poufy skirts and sensuous gowns in a mélange of sun-drenched florals or geometric prints; the "out-of-this-world prices" mean "if your last name is Trump, you'll be a regular"; otherwise, you best Ungar-go elsewhere.

EMc2 ◑
23 | 24 | 21 | E

NoLita | 240 Elizabeth St. (Houston St.) | N/R/W to Prince St. | 212-431-4134 | www.emmettmccarthy.com

A "haven for those who need their *Project Runway* fix", this "cute" NoLita shop carries "gorgeous" womenswear from a "mix and match of [the show's] winners and losers", including designers Chloe Dau, Kara Janx and the store's owner, Emmett McCarthy; "never knowing when you might run into Tim Gunn" (McCarthy designed his bobblehead doll) "makes it even more fun", even if some would wave *auf Wiedersehen* to a scene they call "tragically hip (more tragic than hip)."

Emily's 🗷
25 | 24 | 22 | E

Staten Island | 1654 Richmond Rd. (bet. Buel Ave. & Four Corners Rd.) | 1 to South Ferry | 718-351-0979 | www.emilysny.com

For 25 years, this top-notch Staten Island boutique has brought bold-face women's designer names as well as fresh fashion faces to the borough; look for contemporary sportswear ranging from Tory Burch to Tracy Reese, along with an extensive evening collection that counts Carmen Marc Valvo among its luxe lineup.

Emmelle
▽ 21 | 22 | 18 | E |

E 70s | 1042 Madison Ave. (bet. 79th & 80th Sts.) | 6 to 77th St. | 212-570-6559

E 80s | 123 E. 89th St. (bet. Lexington & Park Aves.) | 4/5/6 to 86th St. | 212-289-5253

W 70s | 311 Columbus Ave. (75th St.) | 1/2/3 to 72nd St. | 212-580-0457

www.emmelledesign.com

"Park Avenue" types head to this Upper East Side duo and its Westside sidekick to peruse the rows and rows of "lovely" "classic designs" including "great special-occasion dresses", and "truly timeless" suits that fit well, even "if you're not stick thin" – and chances are you won't "see someone else wearing the same thing"; still, "service varies" – "you take the good with the bad and the rude."

Emporio Armani
23 | 23 | 20 | E |

E 50s | 601 Madison Ave. (bet. 57th & 58th Sts.) | N/R/W to 5th Ave./ 59th St. | 212-317-0800

SoHo | 410 W. Broadway (Spring St.) | C/E to Spring St. | 646-613-8099

www.emporioarmani.com

"Beginner Armani"-ites of both sexes can savor the great Giorgio's "sophisticated, yet simple" secondary line, sold in stand-alone stores in SoHo and the East 50s; but while the "impeccably tailored" slouchy jackets and crêpe separates sell "for a fraction of his black label", many moan the "prices keep getting steeper", and sometimes the "distinct, flamboyant" styles "can turn heads both toward and away from you."

EMS (Eastern Mountain Sports) ◐
26 | 21 | 21 | M |

SoHo | 591 Broadway (bet. Houston & Prince Sts.) | N/R/W to Prince St. | 212-966-8730 | 888-463-6367 | www.ems.com

"You can almost smell the fresh pine" at this SoHo shop that caters to both experienced nature "sporting enthusiasts" and "aspiring outdoorsy" types "looking to gear up" with a "phenomenal selection" of "camping, whitewater", "hiking and climbing stuff" (as well as "workout clothes" for dedicated urbanites); plus, the "friendly, knowledgeable staffers" are so "helpful" they'll even "put up a tent in the middle of the store if you ask."

Encore
20 | 14 | 13 | M |

E 80s | 1132 Madison Ave. (bet. 84th & 85th Sts.) | 4/5/6 to 86th St. | 212-879-2850 | www.encoreresale.com

"If you like upscale designer merchandise", "great resale finds are possible at this second-floor Upper East Side institution", which for over 50 years has been supplying women and men with "conservative" consignment clothing, costume jewelry and "more shoes than my girlfriend should be looking at"; on the downside, the staff can seem "hostile" and the "surroundings are not very pleasant", particularly the "curtainless communal dressing room"; N.B. closed Sundays in the summertime.

Eneslow
▽ 28 | 23 | 24 | E |

Murray Hill | 470 Park Ave. S. (bet. 31st & 32nd Sts.) | 6 to 33rd St. | 212-477-2300

(continued)

(continued)

Eneslow

Little Neck | Little Neck Shopping Ctr. | 254-61 Horace Harding Expwy. (Little Neck Pkwy.) | Queens | 718-357-5800
www.eneslow.com

There's nary a flimsily constructed stiletto to be found at this "source for comfort and superb fit" on Park Avenue South and the Little Neck Shopping Center, home of solid-to-the-ground footwear from the house label, plus names like Birkenstock, MBT and New Balance; "if you have foot problems", "walk no farther", as the "knowledgeable staff" tends to "special needs."

environment337

| - | - | - | E |

G Village | 56 University Pl. (10th St.) | 4/5/6/L/N/Q/R/W to 14th St./ Union Sq. | 212-254-3400 🖂
Carroll Gardens | 337 Smith St. (Carroll St.) | Brooklyn | F/G to Carroll St. | 718-522-1767 Ⓜ
www.environment337.com

It's still "worth the extra time to go way down Smith" to get to this "pleasant" lifestyle emporium that opened long "before a million housewares stores" converged on the Carroll Gardens strip – and with another offshoot in Greenwich Village, Gothamites have their own home furnishings environment within reach; the "unique" collection ranging from offbeat pillows and lamps to midcentury modern furniture is edited with a "great eye", making it the go-to source for "one-of-a-kind gifts."

Enzo Angiolini ◐

| 20 | 18 | 18 | M |

Garment District | Manhattan Mall | 901 Sixth Ave. (bet. 32nd & 33rd Sts.) | B/D/F/N/Q/R/V/W to 34th St./Herald Sq. | 212-695-8903 |
www.enzoangiolini.com

"On-trend", "office-worthy" shoes for the "sexy corporate woman" rule at this Garment Center chain link that footwear fans find a "significant step up" from its "Nine West brethren"; it's "always dependable for affordable prices" that "won't break the bank", "decent comfort and current fashions" that "aren't too out there", but "if you're looking for something more fun and flashy, it's not the place to go."

Equinox Energy Wear ◐

| 22 | 19 | 17 | E |

E 60s | 140 E. 63rd St. (Lexington Ave.) | 4/5/6/F/N/R/W to 59th St./ Lexington Ave. | 212-752-5360 | www.equinoxfitness.com
Additional locations throughout the NY area

"Hip activewear that you'd expect from an equally hip club" is what proponents posit who are pumped over this gym chain's "trendy" selection that's as "stylish and comfy for running errands as it is for working out"; if it's "a little overpriced", check out the "discount bin."

Eres

| 28 | 25 | 22 | VE |

E 50s | 621 Madison Ave. (bet. 58th & 59th Sts.) | 4/5/6/F/N/R/W to 59th St./Lexington Ave. | 212-223-3550 🖂
SoHo | 98 Wooster St. (bet. Prince & Spring Sts.) | C/E to Spring St. | 212-431-7300
800-340-6004 | www.eresparis.com

"The thing to wear" when you want to "feel like a sophisticated Paris jet-setter" – and spend like one too – jest Francophiles who gladly "break the bank" at the "fabulous" French lingerie chain's sleek Madison Avenue and SoHo branches; the bras, panties and "wonderful swimsuits" are "elegant and sexy" (and guys, just right for your "wife or significant other"), and while the designs are "subtle, they're never boring" – *oui*, they make any "woman look great."

Eric | 24 | 19 | 22 | E |

E 70s | 1333 Third Ave. (bet. 76th & 77th Sts.) | 6 to 77th St. | 212-288-8250
E 80s | 1222 Madison Ave. (bet. 88th & 89th Sts.) | 4/5/6 to 86th St. | 212-289-5762

It's "dangerous to live" within strolling distance of this Upper East Side duo declare shoehounds who exult in the "good variety" of "classy" footwear finds; choose from some of the "best flats!" imbued "with a great sense of style", designer "looks" from the retro-inspired line Bettye Muller and house-label "knockoffs of very expensive brands"; while it "can be pricey" you can always score at the "frequent sales."

Erica Tanov | - | - | - | E |

NoLita | 204 Elizabeth St. (bet. Prince & Spring Sts.) | 6 to Spring St. | 212-334-8020 | www.ericatanov.com

This huge white shop with quirky lighting "makes you feel a lot cooler than usual" confide insiders, who "soak in the NoLita-ness of it", perusing the namesake designer's dreamy collection for women, which includes fluttery dresses and "beautiful" jackets, pants and skirts imbued "with a sense of earnestness, in spite of the very New York prices"; splurge on compatible lines like John Smedley knitwear along with "especially lovely linens, children's clothing", jewelry and delicate lingerie.

NEW Erie Basin Ⓜ | - | - | - | E |

Red Hook | 388 Van Brunt St. (Dikeman St.) | Brooklyn | F/G to Smith/9th Sts. | 718-554-6147 | www.eriebasin.com

Sink your teeth into Victorian-era necklaces, rings and earrings and ultracontemporary interpretations bearing offbeat insect and animal motifs, claws, Egyptian scarabs and other designs that recall jewelry obsessions of those buttoned-up times at this Red Hook newcomer; owner Russell Whitmore also turns his curator's eye to off-kilter pieces like pendants strung with tartan fabric-covered beads and metal pins, bronze bird feet candlesticks and other eerie *objets* sure to add a Goth edge to your next séance, er, soiree.

Ⓩ Ermenegildo Zegna | 28 | 26 | 24 | VE |

E 50s | 663 Fifth Ave. (bet. 52nd & 53rd Sts.) | E/V to 5th Ave./53rd St. | 212-421-4488 | www.zegna.com

"Who needs A to Z when Z is all you need" ask the well-appointed who zip over to this "elegant" mecca for "dress-to-impress" menswear (plus a little for ladies), which plans to move from its temporary Madison quarters back to its newly renovated home at 663 Fifth Avenue in early 2008; "sure, it's expensive", but "if clothes make the man, Zegna makes them immortal", thanks to "beautiful fabrics" and silhouettes "with a subtle hint of Euro-style"; if you can't "buy your entire wardrobe here, at least get a tie", or try the lower-priced Z Zegna and Zegna Sport lines.

| | QUALITY | DISPLAY | SERVICE | COST |

Erwin Pearl
20 | 22 | 20 | M

E 40s | Grand Central, Lexington Ave. passage | 42nd St. (Vanderbilt Ave.) | 4/5/6/7/S to 42nd St./Grand Central | 212-922-1106 ◐
E 60s | 697 Madison Ave. (bet. 62nd & 63rd Sts.) | 4/5/6/F/N/R/W to 59th St./Lexington Ave. | 212-753-3155
Financial District | Winter Garden | 3 World Financial Ctr. (West St.) | R/W to Rector St. | 212-227-3400
W 50s | Rockefeller Ctr. | 70 W. 50th St. (bet. 5th & 6th Aves.) | B/D/F/V to 47-50th Sts./Rockefeller Ctr. | 212-977-9088
800-379-4673 | www.erwinpearl.com

Costume-jewelry quartet specializing in "fantastic fakes", from "the best faux pearls" to "cubic-zirconium studs in every size and color" starting at under $100 "so there are no tears if you lose one"; a few question the "disappointing quality", but most praise their "good-looking" "classic pieces at modest prices."

Escada
27 | 26 | 24 | VE

E 50s | 715 Fifth Ave. (56th St.) | N/R/W to 5th Ave./59th St. | 212-755-2200 | www.escada.com

"For the woman with a little Ivana in her", this Midtown boutique stands ready to supply "sexy socialite" garb (structured suits, fur- and leather-trimmed sportswear) and accessories (crystal-encrusted cell phones); some call the look a bit "aggressive", like the help (though they do "find exactly what looks best on you"), but most marvel the "clothing is runway-worthy, you just need the body for it" – not to mention the bucks.

NEW ê Shave ⊠
23 | 24 | 22 | E

E 50s | 993B First Ave. (54th St.) | 4/5/6/F/N/R/W to 59th St./Lexington Ave. | 212-838-0807 | www.eshave.com

This polished new "men's mecca" for grooming in the East 50s offers "high-quality", "attractively designed" shaving accoutrements like razors, badger-haired brushes and white tea shaving cream; gals even frequent the black-and-white contemporary space because "it's a great place for that 'special man' gift."

Eskandar ⊠
- | - | - | VE

G Village | 33 E. 10th St. (bet. B'way & University Pl.) | N/R/W to 8th St. | 212-533-4200 | www.eskandar.com

"Understated, quiet and refined" describes this British designer's collection showcased at his light-filled, loftlike Greenwich Village shop; guys and girls alike fall for his "forever pieces" including cowlneck tops, drawstring trousers and tunics that achieve an "almost monklike perfection" in "gorgeous" wool, cashmere and silk "fabrics and knits" that help "justify" the prices; penny-pinchers who "pray for the euro/dollar ratio to make it viable" can content themselves with a vase or a bottle of ginger-blossom body wash.

Esprit ◐
17 | 19 | 17 | M

NEW E 40s | 600 Fifth Ave. (bet. 48th & 49th Sts.) | E/V to 5th Ave./53rd St. | 212-247-9899
SoHo | 583 Broadway (bet. Houston & Prince Sts.) | N/R/W to 8th St. | 646-823-0183
Union Sq | 110 Fifth Ave. (16th St.) | 4/5/6/L/N/Q/R/W to 14th St./Union Sq. | 212-651-2121

(continued)

Esprit

W 60s | The Shops at Columbus Circle, Time Warner Ctr. |
10 Columbus Circle, 2nd fl. (60th St. at B'way) | 1/A/B/C/D to
59th St./Columbus Circle | 212-823-9922
Staten Island | Staten Island Mall | 2655 Richmond Ave. (bet. Platinum Ave. &
Richmond Hill Rd.) | 347-745-3020
www.esprit.com

Fans who feel like they've "grown up alongside" this San Francisco label
"are glad to see it back", hailing the "relatively inexpensive" items in
"great colors" with a "classic flair" that "keeps pace with trends without going overboard"; but critics kvetch that the "weird sizing" and
only "nice-ish" clothes are "not as cutting-edge as in days of yore."

Essentials ● | 20 | 16 | 16 | M |

E 70s | 1392 Third Ave. (79th St.) | 6 to 77th St. | 212-517-4447
Flatiron | 123 E. 19th St. (5th Ave.) | 4/5/6/L/N/Q/R/W to 14th St./
Union Sq. | 212-228-8141
W 80s | 2259 Broadway (81st St.) | 1 to 79th St. | 212-721-2818
www.essentialsplus.com

Customers "could die happy (and well moisturized)" at this "really essential" trio of "resources for beauty supplies", from cosmetics to
haircare products and appliances; plus you're guaranteed to "find
what they tried to sell you at your fancy salon at a fraction of the price",
so "what more could you ask for?"

Estella | ▽ 25 | 25 | 22 | E |

G Village | 493 Sixth Ave. (bet. 12th & 13th Sts.) | F/L/V to 14th St./
6th Ave. | 212-255-3553 | 877-755-3553 | www.estella-nyc.com

Fetching window displays draw passersby into this Village children's
shop where a thoughtfully assembled selection of "adorable" clothing
from Belgium, England and Italy - along with a smattering of Bugaboo
strollers and "unique" furniture - awaits, displayed on an antique table or
minimalist racks; but party-poopers put off by the "shockingly expensive" sticker prices decree "gimme a break" and "wait for the sales."

Etcetera ● | - | - | - | M |

Murray Hill | 481 Third Ave. (bet. 33rd & 34th Sts.) | 6 to 33rd St. |
212-481-6527 | www.etceteragiftsny.com

Cute children's outfits share space with sparkly purses, costume jewelry
jostles pretty painted pottery and overall a cornucopia of "great finds"
draws gift-givers into this Murray Hill haunt; the dizzying displays can
"overwhelm the eyes", but not the budget - though the classy "wrapping alone will make friends and family think you spent a fortune."

Ethan Allen | 23 | 23 | 22 | E |

E 60s | 1107 Third Ave. (65th St.) | 4/5/6/F/N/R/W to 59th St./
Lexington Ave. | 212-308-7703
W 60s | 103 West End Ave. (bet. 64th & 65th Sts.) | 1 to 66th St./
Lincoln Ctr. | 212-201-9840
Forest Hills | 112-33 Queens Blvd. (76th Rd.) | Queens | F to 75th St. |
718-575-3822
Staten Island | 2935 Veterans Rd. W. | 718-984-6882
888-324-3571 | www.ethanallen.com

"Well-made furniture" that is "not one-of-a-kind but still lovely" sums
up this chain offering "pricey" but "lasts forever" sofas, tables, beds,

bureaus, lighting and other home accessories; still, sophisticates sniff the pieces "shout suburbia" and "won't fit into the average NYC apartment", and add they "hate the assigned salesperson" policy that means a staff member "follows you around" everywhere; N.B. plans are afoot to consolidate the Manhattan and Queens branches.

Etherea ●

`- | - | - | M`

E Village | 66 Ave. A (bet. 4th & 5th Sts.) | F/V to Lower East Side/2nd Ave. | 212-358-1126 | www.etherea.net

Specializing in "obscure titles", this East Village music "mecca" satisfies "your electronic music needs", and when it comes to indie rock they "have all the new releases"; though sometimes "snobby", the "knowledgeable" staff will allow you to preview any CD in stock, even "if you aren't wearing the right clothes."

Etro ⊠

`28 | 27 | 23 | VE`

E 60s | 720 Madison Ave. (bet. 63rd & 64th Sts.) | F to Lexington Ave./63rd St. | 212-317-9096 | www.etro.it

"For the cognoscenti of color, paisley and pattern-mixing", this East 60s boutique holds "so much under one roof", from "beautiful quality" his-and-hers clothing to "awesome printed" scarves, leather goods and home furnishings "with flair"; "it takes a special sort of fashionista to pull off" this "high-Renaissance" look – "only the Italians understand" "the art of how it all fits together" – but happily the "discreet" staff helps offset the "drama" of the designs.

Eve's Garden ⊠Ⓜ

`24 | 19 | 24 | M`

W 50s | 119 W. 57th St., 12th fl. (bet. 6th & 7th Aves.) | N/Q/R/W to 57th St. | 212-757-8651 | 800-848-3837 | www.evesgarden.com

"You can go in to buy a dildo, and people will think you are just visiting an office" when you hit this "discreet and comfortable" "femme-friendly" "paradise" of "pleasure" devices on the 12th floor of a West 57th highrise; the "no-storefront entry" also makes for a "non-pervy environment" in which to browse merch for "all levels of knowledge and sexuality."

Express ●

`16 | 17 | 15 | M`

Garment District | 7 W. 34th St. (bet. 5th & 6th Aves.) | B/D/F/N/Q/R/V/W to 34th St./Herald Sq. | 212-629-6838 | www.expressfashion.com
Additional locations throughout the NY area

"Good staples for work and play" are the province of this "fun" chain whose "moderately priced" pieces run the gamut from "conservative" suits to "throwaway trend" wear; though the "quality of some pieces is decent enough for the office", the goods may "not be built to last", leading a few to complain it's "expensive for what you get" – but then again, "items don't stay full price very long", so just "wait for the sales."

Express Men ●

`20 | 18 | 19 | M`

Seaport | Pier 17 | 89 South St. (Fulton St.) | 2/3/4/5/A/C/J/M/Z to Fulton St./B'way/Nassau | 212-766-5709
Kings Plaza | Kings Plaza Shopping Ctr. | 5100 Kings Plaza (bet. Flatbush Ave. & Ave. U) | Brooklyn | B/Q to Newkirk Ave. | 718-258-2254
www.expressfashion.com

Polished basics ("go for the jeans") plus some "edgier" items "to make a man look good" occupy the racks at this male counterpart to Express with links in Kings Plaza and the South Street Seaport; critics fail to find "much flair" in the styling and pout that the "items are a bit pricey" for the quality, but even they suggest you should "run, not walk" when the "slash-and-burn monthly sale" is going on.

Eye Candy ☻

	QUALITY	DISPLAY	SERVICE	COST
	∇ 24	24	20	M

NoHo | 329 Lafayette St. (bet. Bleecker & Houston Sts.) | 6 to Bleecker St. | 212-343-4275 | www.eyecandystore.com

"Their name says it best" profess fans who feast on the "sparkly, sparkly" "faux jewels, bags", hats and "tremendous selection of shoes" at this moderately priced NoHo specialist in antique accessories; while generally known as a place for "the downtown set" "to get its fix" on "funky, edgy vintage items", "they also carry stunning [things] by new designers."

Eye Man, The

	∇ 25	21	26	E

W 80s | 2264 Broadway (bet. 81st & 82nd Sts.) | 1 to 79th St. | 212-873-4114 | www.eyeman.com

"An institution on the West Side", this "warm and cozy" "neighborhood store" maintains a faithful following for its "dozens of colorful frames coming out of neat rows of drawers", including "prescription and non-prescription glasses from top designers" and lots of children's options; perhaps even better is the "helpful" staff of opticians that takes such "excellent care" of customers – "once you shop here you'll never go elsewhere."

Fabulous Fanny's ☻

	-	-	-	M

E Village | 335 E. Ninth St. (bet. 1st & 2nd Aves.) | 6 to Astor Pl. | 212-533-0637 | www.fabulousfannys.com

Stocking the "absolute best in vintage frames", this "true" eyewear "find" in the East Village offers a "fabulous", "fairly priced" selection from the 1700s to the present, and also does custom rhinestone work on glasses; "the owners are great guys" who're "pretty excited to show you the coolest stuff", some of which is snapped up for Broadway productions (*Spamalot*) and movies (*Little Miss Sunshine*).

FACE Stockholm

	22	24	22	M

SoHo | 110 Prince St. (Greene St.) | N/R/W to Prince St. | 212-966-9110
W 60s | The Shops at Columbus Circle, Time Warner Ctr. | 10 Columbus Circle, ground fl. (60th St. at B'way) | 1/A/B/C/D to 59th St./Columbus Circle | 212-823-9415 ☻
W 70s | 226 Columbus Ave. (bet. 70th & 71st Sts.) | 1/2/3/B/C to 72nd St. | 212-769-1420
888-334-3223 | www.facestockholm.com

Mother-and-daughter-owned Swedish cosmetics chain that's famed for its "vast selection" of colors and moderately priced, "no-frills" products like Pearl Eyeshadow and Aura Blush, but the brand's big secret weapon is undoubtedly the "super-durable nail polish that's a must for manicure mavens."

Facial Index

	-	-	-	VE

SoHo | 104 Grand St. (bet. Greene & Mercer Sts.) | 6/J/M/N/Q/R/ W/Z to Canal St. | 646-613-1055 | www.facial-index.com

Hipsters on the hunt for "something different" to frame their peepers hit the jackpot at this "immaculate" eyewear emporium where the handmade specs and sunglasses come in a variety of fashion-forward hues, shapes and materials; "let the expert staff pick a frame" to suit your face, and turn a blind eye to the fact that its consumer price index is commensurate with the "sleek" SoHo digs.

Façonnable ◐

| 27 | 25 | 24 | E |

E 50s | 636 Fifth Ave. (51st St.) | E/V to 5th Ave./53rd St. | 212-319-0111 | www.faconnable.com

Though now "owned by Nordstrom", a "discreet French flair" still pervades this Gallic label that specializes in "Euro-hip meets preppy" looks for men and women; whether you're seeking "jet-set–casual" separates, "super-proper" accessories or "timeless" tailored garments, the two-floor beaux arts flagship in Rockefeller Center "has it all", including a "smile and a helping hand" from the staff; sure, it's "expensive", but the "sophisticated" clientele gladly shells out for "Côte d'Azur chic with American comfort."

Family Jewels, The

| - | - | - | E |

Chelsea | 130 W. 23rd St. (bet. 6th & 7th Aves.) | F/V to 23rd St. | 212-633-6020 | www.familyjewelsnyc.com

For an "undeniably great selection" of "good condition" clothing and accessories for men and women ranging from Victorian petticoats and vintage hats, shoes and jewelry to '50s beaded sweaters to '70s ties make tracks to this "crowded" Chelsea standby; however, if the vibe's "hipper-than-thou", the staff's "unfriendlier than most", and malcontents mutter its popularity among fashion and show-biz stylists means "unforgivable prices" for "mediocre finery."

FAO Schwarz

| 25 | 26 | 20 | E |

E 50s | 767 Fifth Ave. (58th St.) | N/R/W to 5th Ave./59th St. | 212-644-9400 | www.fao.com

Still the "ultimate playground" for "tourists and New Yorkers alike" following a face-lift, this "rare" Fifth Avenue "treat" "brings out the little kid in everyone" with its "magical", "overwhelming" assortment; "live out your *Big* fantasy" with spectacles like the 22-ft. floor piano and the "pricey ice cream parlor that must be tried", then "be prepared to knock over Fort Knox to pay for" "out-of-this-world" "specialty toys" from the newborn doll nursery and Hot Wheels custom car factory; still, the price-sensitive snipe "nice place to visit, wouldn't want to buy here."

Fat Beats ◐

| - | - | - | M |

G Village | 406 Sixth Ave., 2nd fl. (bet. 8th & 9th Sts.) | A/B/C/D/E/F/V to W. 4th St. | 212-673-3883 | www.fatbeats.com

Scratch the competition cuz the "best place" for rap and hip-hop "vinyl junkies" may well be this Greenwich Village vanguard with outposts in Amsterdam and Los Angeles; collectors sing the praises of a "better-quality" queue of CDs and records and "excellent selection of DJ mixes" and beat a path for the "great" in-store events.

Federico de Vera ⊠Ⓜ

| - | - | - | E |

SoHo | 1 Crosby St. (Howard St.) | 6/J/M/N/Q/R/W/Z to Canal St. | 212-625-0838 | www.deveraobjects.com

"You didn't know you wanted or needed it until you saw it" at this "beyond comparison" SoHo gallery where antique *objets* share space with jewelry, much of which is made in-house; one-of-a-kind pieces include intricate Japanese lacquer boxes, Buddhas, Indian dagger hilts and cameos carved from lava rock.

Femmegems Nolita

▽ 17 | 19 | 19 | M

NoLita | 280 Mulberry St. (bet. Houston & Prince Sts.) | 6 to Bleecker St. | 212-625-1611 | www.femmegems.com

NoLita *bijouterie* that draws DIYers, fashionistas and celebrities alike who applaud the "fun" idea of "creating their own jewelry", choosing from a bountiful inventory of colorful beads, gemstones and findings to create unique necklaces, bracelets and earrings; for the craft-impaired, founder Lindsay Cain keeps a supply of ready-made styles on hand.

Fendi

27 | - | 23 | VE

E 50s | 677 Fifth Ave. (bet. 53rd & 54th Sts.) | E/V to 5th Ave./53rd St. | 212-759-4646 | 800-336-3469 | www.fendi.com

Following a major redo and the closing of its Madison Avenue store, this venerable Italian label's Fifth Avenue showcase was reconceived as a cool, high-tech affair, complete with a digital 'waterfall' over the staircase and movies playing on the walls – and now, more than ever, it's a "must-stop" in Midtown for femme-fatale fans who favor Karl Lagerfeld's "fun styles" in furs, frilly dresses or a statusy, "well-made" purse; granted, the goods are geared to "those who don't have to ask 'how much'" – but those who do needn't Fendi for themselves, since the staff makes anyone feel "like a queen."

NEW 55DSL

19 | 21 | 18 | E

SoHo | 281 Lafayette St. (bet. Houston & Prince Sts.) | B/D/F/V to B'way/Lafayette St. | 212-226-5055 | www.55dsl.com

This SoHo "offshoot of Diesel" offers the "newest zip-up sweat-shirts" and other "sporty" duds in "wild colors" to bring out the skater in all of us; the "cool threads" at "half the price" of the main label make it "a must-visit", as does the prescient staff, who "knows exactly what will look good on you", to which we say (in our best Spicoli impersonation), whoa!

Fila ◑

23 | 20 | 19 | E

E 40s | 340 Madison Ave. (bet. 43rd & 44th Sts.) | 4/5/6/7/S to 42nd St./Grand Central | 646-502-2100 | 866-758-3452 | www.fila.com

"Bright and airy", this modern East 40s shop designed by Palermo-born visionary architect Giorgio Borruso "makes you look" at this "solid" Italian activewear label "with new eyes"; "love" the "preppy but fun" finds like the "hip tennis line" ("retro is back in fashion") as well as the "unique, practical" golf and running apparel, accessories and custom-configured sneakers – it seems this "old favorite" has "come back to life."

☑ Filene's Basement ◑

18 | 10 | 9 | I

Flatiron | 620 Sixth Ave. (18th St.) | 1 to 18th St. | 212-620-3100
Union Sq | 4 Union Sq. S. (14th St.) | 4/5/6/L/N/Q/R/W to 14th St./Union Sq. | 212-358-0169
W 70s | 2222 Broadway (79th St.) | 1 to 79th St. | 212-873-8000
Flushing | 18704 Horace Harding Expwy. (188th St.) | Queens | 7 to Main St. | 718-479-7711
888-843-8474 | www.filenesbasement.com

So maybe "it's better in Boston" where it began, but NYers still file in to this "mother of discount department stores" – especially the Union

Square behemoth, whose "real quality" items have earned admirers; "the others leave a little to be desired", with their "cramped quarters" and often "hard-to-find employees"; still, if you're "prepared to dig", "you can grab great deals here on everything from socks to jewelry" to bath items, with special praise going to "the Vault area for designer brands that mere mortals don't often see in real life."

Firefly Children's Boutique
25 | 23 | 22 | E

NEW Seaport | 224 Front St. (bet. Beekman St. & Peck Slip) | 2/3/4/5/A/C/J/M/Z to Fulton St./B'way/Nassau | 646-416-6560
Park Slope | 240 Seventh Ave. (bet. 4th & 5th Sts.) | Brooklyn | F to 7th Ave. | 718-965-3535
www.fireflychildrensboutique.com

Buzz over to this "cute new store" in the South Street Seaport or its older Park Slope sibling for "adorable" discounted brand-name children's attire from around the world (with an emphasis on South America), plus wooden toys, science kits and Phil & Ted's sport strollers; with 17 clothing and shoe sizes for boys and girls, there's something for every age range among the "good quality", "colorful" offerings, though a few wallet-watchers whine it's "no bargain."

Fisch for the Hip
26 | 21 | 19 | E

Chelsea | 153 W. 18th St. (bet. 6th & 7th Aves.) | 1 to 18th St. | 212-633-9053

"Heads above the other consignment" places is this "classy" Chelsea clothier chock-full of "the current season's latest and greatest" discoveries from some of "the best" labels for both genders, plus shoes and "more Hermès bags than Hermès itself"; some "prices are high", particularly the purses' ("the rationale is, you avoid designer waiting lists"), but that doesn't deter devotees who declare "I could've bought the whole store."

Fishs Eddy ☻
18 | 18 | 17 | I

Flatiron | 889 Broadway (19th St.) | N/R/W to 23rd St. | 212-420-9020 | 877-347-4733 | www.fishseddy.com

"Unusual dinnerware" dotted with "odd monograms or names of schools and clubs" as well as "funky" cutlery and glasses from restaurants and diners are some of the options for "avoiding traditional" table settings at this "non-snob's paradise of possibilities" for cute, inexpensive kitchen "kitsch" in the Flatiron District; although some say the store has "lost some of its unique flavor" and gone a bit "mainstream", you can still "buy a set of martini glasses for less money than the liquor you fill them with."

NEW 5 in 1 Ⓜ
- | - | - | E

Williamsburg | 60 N. Sixth St. (bet. Kent & Wythe Aves.) | Brooklyn | L to Bedford Ave. | 718-384-1990 | www.studio5in1.com

The Williamsburg brainchild of creative director Norman Rabinovich, this multitentacled coterie of fashion and graphic designers blurs the lines between the creative process and the commercial; style sleuths shop for eclectic womenswear (from lines like Eventide and Uluru), far-out footwear (Tashkent by Cheyenne) and Goth-esque jewelry (Made Her Think) at the front of the high-ceilinged, plank-floored 19th-century warehouse space while the talented faces behind the labels toil away in the work area to the rear.

	QUALITY	DISPLAY	SERVICE	COST

NEW Flight Club
| | 21 | 21 | 18 | E |

Financial District | 120 Nassau St. (bet. Ann & Beekman Sts.) | 2/3/4/5/A/C/
J/M/Z to Fulton St./B'way/Nassau | 212-233-7178 | www.flightclubny.com
Serious kicks collectors jet to this Financial District "megastore" that's
laced up a loyal following thanks to what may be one of the city's "largest" selections of "vintage", "exclusive", "limited-edition" and "hard-
to-find sneakers" – including ultrarare Nike Air Force1 styles and
Adidas Superstars that can run up to $4,500; those not in the Club find
it a little "overhyped" and "chaotic", but "true sneakerheads" "fly"
high over all the "old-school", "tricked-out trainers."

Flight 001 ●
| | 24 | 24 | 20 | E |

W Village | 96 Greenwich Ave. (bet. Jane & W. 12th Sts.) | A/C/E/L to
14th St./8th Ave. | 212-989-0001
Boerum Hill | 132 Smith St. (bet. Bergen & Dean Sts.) | Brooklyn | F/G to
Bergen St. | 718-243-0001
NEW Park Slope | 58 Fifth Ave. (bet. Bergen St. & St. Marks Pl.) |
Brooklyn | 2/3 to Bergen St. | 718-789-1001
877-354-4481 | www.flight001.com
"There's something here for every jet-lagged soul – even those who
just traversed the NYC" subway quip "hipster" voyagers who get carried away at this "must-go" outfit for "design-conscious, streamlined
travel goods" in the Village, Boerum Hill and now Park Slope too (plus
branches in Chicago, Los Angeles and San Francisco); "these guys get
it, with style", packing a punch with "funky luggage", "unique passport
holders", "practical miniature kits of things you'll forget" and even
"going-away presents" with "creative gift-wrapping."

Flirt ●Ⓜ
| | - | - | - | M |

Carroll Gardens | 252 Smith St. (bet. Degraw & Douglass Sts.) | Brooklyn | F/
G to Carroll St. | 718-858-7931
Park Slope | 93 Fifth Ave. (bet. Baltic & Warren Sts.) | Brooklyn | 2/3 to
Bergen St. | 718-783-0364
www.flirt-brooklyn.com
Unusual, feminine clothing is the come on at this Smith Street staple
with its shabby-chic decor and its Fifth Avenue sidekick, both stuffed
with a cornucopia of kicky pieces; coquettes snatch up the house line
of custom snap skirts (and now the snap jumpers too) and local designers' finds, including reconstructed vintage pieces; DIYers should
check out Home Ec, the owners' new Gowanus studio offering pattern
making, knitting and craft classes.

flora and henri
| | ▽ 23 | - | 20 | E |

E 70s | 1023 Lexington Ave. (bet. 73rd & 74th Sts.) | 6 to 77th St. |
212-249-1695 | www.florahenri.com
Parents with a penchant for "classics with a hip, modern twist" "love
buying" essentials for their little ones like "ribbed tees" and "pleated"
skirts at this standby, which moved from Madison to Lexington Avenue;
European fabrics, soft colors and traditional details give the collection a
vintage charm that's sweet, but not too twee, and while it's sure "expensive", the craftsmanship and "quality are excellent."

Florsheim Shoe Shops
| | 20 | 18 | 18 | M |

E 50s | 444 Madison Ave. (50th St.) | 6 to 51st St. | 212-752-8017
(continued)

(continued)

Florsheim Shoe Shops

Garment District | 101 W. 35th St. (6th Ave.) | B/D/F/N/Q/R/V/W to 34th St./Herald Sq. | 212-594-8830 ◑
www.florsheim.com

After clocking 116 years, this "service-oriented" outfit with Midtown links deserves its "classic" crown, and some men still swear by its "solid", "well-made" footwear that stands up to "years of wear"; but while it's a "great first-paycheck place" for young bucks, some say these shoes are "not made to impress", adding it's "gliding on its faded laurels."

Flou | - | - | - | VE

SoHo | 42 Greene St. (bet. Broome & Grand Sts.) | C/E to Spring St. | 212-941-9101 | www.flou.com

The slickest of clever, contemporary Italian beds (more than 40 models including ones with stylish storage space options) are showcased at this SoHo specialist housed in an old converted factory with brick walls and tin ceilings; bedroom-oriented items, likes linens, lighting, mattresses and even pajamas, also make it a one-stop shop for sleep.

Flying A | 17 | 18 | 14 | E

SoHo | 169 Spring St. (bet. Thompson St. & W. B'way) | C/E to Spring St. | 212-965-9090 | www.flyinganyc.com

There are "volumes of vintage for the hipster set" at this SoHo shop that also carries a "cool mix" of retro to brand-new his-and-hers "finds" from their house line, "unique" indie names and "great stuff" from Fred Perry and Petit Bateau; whether you scoop up Birkenstocks or Spitfire shades, remember, "getting the free vinyl totebag is worth almost any purchase!"

Flying Squirrel, The | - | - | - | M

Williamsburg | 96 N. Sixth St. (bet. Berry St. & Wythe Ave.) | Brooklyn | L to Bedford Ave. | 718-218-7775 | www.flyingsquirrelbaby.com

If you want your kid to look like a million bucks without spending a lot of greens, scurry over to this wallet-friendly Williamsburg boutique, which peddles new and nearly new children's clothes, shoes, toys, books and baby gear; there's lots to go nuts for, plus if you buddy up with the "helpful" sales people, "they'll call you" when fresh goods arrive.

F.M. Allen 🖼 | - | - | - | M

E 70s | 962 Madison Ave. (bet. 75th & 76th Sts.) | 6 to 77th St. | 212-737-4374 | www.fmallen.com

Named after a safari outfitter from the '40s, this intriguing UES shop for all things African Colonial is replete with antique campaign furniture, Victorian-era whips, pith helmets and brass compasses, as well as new canvas and leather luggage and clothing; "everything is so Indiana Jones" that "you'll want to take a trip just to be able to sport the gear."

🛡 Fogal of Switzerland | 28 | 24 | 25 | VE

E 50s | 515 Madison Ave. (53rd St.) | E/V to 5th Ave./53rd St. | 212-355-3254 🖼
NEW E 50s | 611 Madison Ave. (58th St.) | N/R/W to 5th Ave./59th St. | 212-207-3080
www.fogal.com

You'll find "Swiss quality all the way around" at these Madison Avenue outposts of the European lingerie outfit, from the "cool" sales staff to the "neatly arranged" "sexy" stockings and textured opaque legwear that run the "rainbow gamut" to men's socks; "wow, I didn't know pantyhose could cost this much" whisper the wide-eyed, to which savvy sorts retort yes, but these "last for years."

Foley + Corinna ●

21	22	20	E

LES | 114 Stanton St. (bet. Essex & Ludlow Sts.) | F/V to Lower East Side/ 2nd Ave. | 212-529-2338 | www.foleyandcorinna.com

It's a Lower East Side "shopping gem" agree devotees of owners Anna Corinna and Dana Foley's "really pretty" flea-markety space; the "great mix of vintage finds" and "new stuff" boasting an "eclectic, feminine" feel (e.g. "gorgeous Grecian-inspired tops", "satiny, classy" creations in "fantastic colors") elicits "endless compliments", making it a "hipster-chick" "favorite."

Foot Locker ●

21	18	15	M

Garment District | 120 W. 34th St. (bet. 6th & 7th Aves.) | 1/2/3/A/C/E to 34th St./Penn Station | 212-629-4419 | 800-991-6815 | www.footlocker.com
Additional locations throughout the NY area

The "place to go for all sports footwear" say supporters who "stand by" this "classic" chain "found all over NYC"; "if you want to run, walk or just look stylish the variety is there to choose from", including the "current must-have sneaker"; but an unhinged handful huffs it's a "cookie-cutter" outfit with "lackadaisical service."

Forever 21 ●

10	13	9	I

Garment District | 50 W. 34th St. (B'way) | B/D/F/N/Q/R/V/W to 34th St./Herald Sq. | 212-564-2346
NEW SoHo | 568 Broadway (bet. Houston & Prince Sts.) | N/R/W to Prince St. | 212-941-5949
Union Sq | 40 E. 14th St. (bet. B'way & University Pl.) | 4/5/6/L/N/Q/ R/W to 14th St./Union Sq. | 212-228-0598
Kings Plaza | Kings Plaza Shopping Ctr. | 5250 Kings Plaza (bet. Flatbush Ave. & Ave. U) | Brooklyn | B/Q to Newkirk Ave. | 718-434-9368
Elmhurst | Queens Ctr. | 90-15 Queens Blvd. (bet. 57th & 59th Aves.) | Queens | G/R/V to Woodhaven Blvd. | 718-699-5630
Staten Island | Staten Island Mall | 2655 Richmond Ave. (bet. Platinum Ave. & Richmond Hill Rd.) | 718-477-2121
800-966-1355 | www.forever21.com

"No trend is below the style radar" at this "cheap, cheerful" and "sometimes trashy" chain where the "dizzying array" of "snazzy" runway knockoffs and accessories for "young lads and lasses" "changes from one day to the next"; sure, the "long lines at the fitting rooms and registers" can make you "feel like you'll be there forever", but for "party-girl" garb and other "disposable" duds, it's hard to beat.

For Eyes ☒

∇ 23	21	21	M

E 40s | Graybar Bldg. | 420 Lexington Ave. (bet. 43rd & 44th Sts.) | 4/ 5/6/7/S to 42nd St./Grand Central | 212-697-8888 | 800-367-3937 | www.foreyes.com

Right "next to Grand Central" – a "great location for commuters" – this Midtown eyewear chain outpost offers a "two-for-$99 deal" (you "can't beat it") that's ideal for those seeking "an extra pair or two of glasses for a different look"; maybe the frames "won't be top-of-the-line", but they're "nice enough" considering the "great price."

Forréal

19	14	14	M

E 70s | 1335 Third Ave. (bet. 76th & 77th Sts.) | 6 to 77th St. | 212-734-2105 | www.forrealnyc.com

"Trendy" Upper East Side high-schoolers and the "young at heart" latch onto this "teenybopper paradise" where "you can find everything you need" from babe-a-licious basics and "your favorite jeans" from the label-likes of Big Star and Hudson to dressier options (BCBG, Nicole Miller) "to go clubbing"; even "moms shop here", because this standby is "fair" with its "price points" – and that's for real.

Fort Street Studio 🖼⇌

-	-	-	VE

SoHo | 578 Broadway, Ste. 506 (bet. Houston & Prince Sts.) | N/R/W to Prince St. | 212-925-5383 | www.fortstreetstudio.com

The fine, hand-knotted wild-silk carpets found at this fifth-floor SoHo showroom are based on ethereal abstract watercolor designs created by husband-and-wife owners Brad Davis and Janis Provisor; of course, the wildly expensive prices will leave some spinning; N.B. closed Saturdays and Sundays.

Fortunoff ◑

24	-	21	M

NEW | **W 50s** | 3 W. 57th St. (bet. 5th & 6th Aves.) | F to 57th St. | 212-292-8800 | 800-367-8666 | www.fortunoff.com

"No one gets taken" at this "trustworthy" source that recently shuttered its long-standing Fifth Avenue store in favor of this mammoth, new three-story flagship on 57th Street; there are "excellent quality and prices" on diamond, pearl and gold jewelry as well as on china, crystal, silver and flatware that make wedding attendees "come here like lemmings" for "classy gifts"; "informed" and "polite service" also means "it's a more pleasant place to shop" than others of its ilk.

45rpm 🖼

▽ 23	23	20	E

E 70s | 17 E. 71st St. (bet. 5th & Madison Aves.) | 6 to 68th St. | 212-737-5545

R by 45rpm

SoHo | 169 Mercer St. (bet. Houston & Prince Sts.) | N/R/W to Prince St. | 917-237-0045
www.rby45rpm.com

Über-premium jeans with a "Japanese aesthetic" made from "environmentally" friendly fabrics (and woven on antique looms) lure acolytes to these spare Shinto shrines to denim on the Upper East Side and in SoHo; though the "beautiful line" and "amazing environments" may be "like nothing you've ever seen before", the stratospheric prices prompt a few to label the brand "R for rip-off."

42nd Street Photo ◑

21	14	14	M

Garment District | 378 Fifth Ave. (bet. 35th & 36th Sts.) | B/D/F/N/Q/R/V/W to 34th St./Herald Sq. | 212-594-6565 | 888-810-4242 | www.42photo.com

"Been a-shopping here since I was a kid" and it's still "a pleasure to stop in" to this "gigantic" Garment District "mail-order icon" that fulfills "all of your electronic needs", from cameras, cell phones and iPods to "the latest gadgets"; "educate yourself and check prices online beforehand or you may find them as inflated as a hot-air balloon" – but bear in mind that there's wiggle room since the

"brusque", "hard-sell" staff is oftentimes "willing to bargain";
N.B. closed Saturdays.

Fossil ❶ | 19 | 19 | 18 | M

E 40s | 530 Fifth Ave. (bet. 44th & 45th Sts.) | 4/5/6/7/S to 42nd St./
Grand Central | 212-997-3978
Elmhurst | Queens Ctr. | 90-15 Queens Blvd. (bet. 57th & 59th Aves.) |
Queens | G/R/V to Woodhaven Blvd. | 718-592-2528
800-449-3056 | www.fossil.com
This Dallas-based chainlet with links in Midtown and Queens Center
features lots of "cute", "inexpensive novelty watches" "for every time
and place at startlingly good prices" so "you can wear a different one
every day of the week"; strap one on, then check out the "cool handbags", sunglasses and other accessories.

☒ Fountain Pen Hospital ☒ | 28 | 21 | 25 | E

TriBeCa | 10 Warren St. (bet. B'way & Church St.) | R/W to City Hall |
212-964-0580 | 800-253-7367 | www.fountainpenhospital.com
Proponents proclaim it's "Pen central" at this "high-quality", "old New
York" TriBeCa shop with a "mind-boggling selection" that ranges
"from the everyday" to "rarefied" vintage models to calligraphy pens
with 14-karat-gold nibs, as well as an "excellent repair" service ("if it
writes or used to they can fix it"); the "incredibly knowledgeable" staff
also leaves an indelible impression.

4PlayBK | - | - | - | M

Park Slope | 360 Seventh Ave. (bet. 10th & 11th Sts.) | Brooklyn | F to
7th Ave. | 718-369-4086
Tweens, teens and twentysomethings congregate at this "cute,
kitschy", "strictly-for-the-under-30-set" South Slope hangout; gab
and gobble up the "cool, eclectic mix of trend-right" hoodies, jeans,
jackets and accessories at wallet-friendly prices from faves like Le
Tigre and Paul Frank, then share your borough pride and pick up "T-
shirts for all your Brooklyn-crazed friends."

Fragments | 25 | 24 | 20 | E

E 70s | 997 Madison Ave. (77th St.) | 6 to 77th St. | 212-537-5000
SoHo | 116 Prince St. (bet. Greene & Wooster Sts.) | N/R/W to Prince St. |
212-334-9588
888-637-2463 | www.fragments.com
"It's almost impossible to walk away empty handed from these stores"
in SoHo and on Madison Avenue – just ask J. Lo, Britney, Debra
Messing or anyone else who's looking for "stellar designs" "by everyone who's who in jewelry" (both costume and fine) that is "hard to find
elsewhere"; loyalists like the warm "compliments" they get when
wearing their goods, but service with "attitude" leaves critics cold.

NEW Franck Muller ☒ | 27 | 26 | 25 | VE

E 50s | 38 E. 57th St. (bet. Madison & Park Aves.) | N/R/W to 5th Ave./
59th St. | 212-355-3736 | www.franckmullerusa.com
The renowned Geneva-based firm has opened a new East 57th Street
store "for watch connoisseurs" showcasing styles from the "classic"
rounded square Curvex to those with calendars and multiple-time
zones to "over-the-top designs" in green or lavender diamonds; so
whether you're a blueblood or a bling king, "if you've got the money,

honey, they've got the time"; N.B. the shop also carries the collections of subsidiaries like Barthelay and Pierre Kunz.

Frank Stella, Ltd. | 22 | 19 | 19 | E |

E 70s | 1326 Third Ave. (bet. 75th & 76th Sts.) | 6 to 77th St. | 212-744-5662 ◑

W 50s | NY Athletic Club | 921 Seventh Ave. (58th St.) | N/Q/R/W to 57th St. | 212-957-1600

W 80s | 440 Columbus Ave. (81st St.) | B/C to 81st St. | 212-877-5566 ◑

When "looking for a little style, the business-casual set" finds this trio "a great place to splurge" on suits and sportswear from the likes of Robert Graham and Nat Nast as well as Mason and Ben Sherman; "in a city of ever-larger department stores, it's one of the few small men's shops left" – like "the haberdasher your mother told you to have" – and those who buy gifts here find they've "never had one item returned."

Fratelli Rossetti | 27 | 24 | 23 | E |

E 50s | 625 Madison Ave. (58th St.) | 4/5/6/F/N/R/W to 59th St./ Lexington Ave. | 212-888-5107 | www.rossetti.it

Shoe aficionados have turned to this name brand since 1953 for "pricey", "good-fitting" footwear constructed by "Italian cobbling masters" and you can still slip into the results of such craftsmanship at this Madison Avenue standby staffed with "excellent" help; the luxe men's and women's "shoes wear on and on", plus the Flexa comfort line is "like walking on air", and to top it off, the handbags and "leather coat selection have fabulous style."

☒ Fred Leighton ⑤ | 29 | 27 | 27 | VE |

E 60s | 773 Madison Ave. (66th St.) | 6 to 68th St. | 212-288-1872 | www.fredleighton.com

"Glitz and glamour" abound at this Madison Avenue über-jeweler where the "drool" factor is sky-high; a 1920s-style salon is the backdrop for "wonderful gems from old India", "beautiful" "$10,000 baubles at the bracelet counter", old-mine and cushion-cut diamond estate and antique engagement rings and opulent art deco designs that all go for "buckets of bucks"; P.S. "there really is a Fred, and he's a charmer."

Freemans Sporting Club ◑ | - | - | - | E |

LES | 8 Rivington St. (bet. Bowery & Christie St.) | F/V to Lower East Side/ 2nd Ave. | 212-673-3209 | www.freemanssportingclub.com

Sartorial studs with a PC bent appreciate the union-made, hand-tailored menswear at this understated LES address; it's part barbershop (haircuts and straight razor shaves available in vintage chairs upstairs), part haberdasher (made-to-measure and ready-to-wear suits, classic work shirts, limited number of house-label jeans and Quoddy moccasins), part apothecary (grooming goods from Geo F. Trumper and D.R. Harris) and yes, part social club for the owners of the nearby hipster hangout Freemans restaurant right down the alley.

NEW Free People ◑ | - | - | - | M |

Flatiron | 79 Fifth Ave. (bet. 15th & 16th Sts.) | 4/5/6/L/N/Q/R/W to 14th St./Union Sq. | 212-647-1293 | www.freepeople.com

Twentysomething stylesetters hankering for Urban Outfitters' popular, once-private label–turned–mini-chain can now find the creative, quirky collection at this new Flatiron link; the sprawling two-floor shop done up with bright, zany fixtures and decorations evoking a fiesta-ish feel sets the scene for spirited, modern-day hippie-chick finds, from babydoll dresses, folkloric print tops and Nordic-style sweater coats to flirty undies and swimwear and embroidered backpacks.

French Connection ●

20 | 19 | 17 | M

NoHo | 700 Broadway (4th St.) | N/R/W to 8th St. | 212-473-4486
SoHo | 435 W. Broadway (Prince St.) | N/R/W to Prince St. | 212-219-1197
W 50s | 1270 Sixth Ave. (bet. 50th & 51st Sts.) | B/D/F/V to 47-50th Sts./ Rockefeller Ctr. | 212-262-6623
888-741-3285 | www.frenchconnection.com

"Find a staple" or perhaps an "of-the-moment add-on" for your wardrobe at this Brit chain that's "worth a pass-through"; but detractors who "don't get the hype" declare the clothing "far too expensive for what it's worth" and exhort "don't bother if you're above a size 10" – and even admirers aver it's time to "drop the FCUK logo ("the shock value is gone")."

French Sole

▽ 24 | 13 | 15 | M

E 70s | 985 Lexington Ave. (bet. 71st & 72nd Sts.) | 6 to 68th St. | 212-737-2859 | www.frenchsoleshoes.com

It's as if "you've gone to ballet-flat heaven" at this East 70s "shoebox" that may be a "little crammed-in, but makes you feel like you've discovered something" truly "adorable"; nothing compares to "walking the city streets" in any of the 300 variations, from "beautiful" quilted leather to "one-of-a-kind" metallic numbers, so swan on over.

Fresh ●

26 | 25 | 22 | E

E 70s | 1367 Third Ave. (78th St.) | 6 to 77th St. | 212-585-3400
Flatiron | 872 Broadway (18th St.) | 4/5/6/L/N/Q/R/W to 14th St./ Union Sq. | 212-477-1100
NoLita | 57 Spring St. (bet. Lafayette & Mulberry Sts.) | 6 to Spring St. | 212-925-0099
W 60s | 159A Columbus Ave. (67th St.) | 1 to 66th St./Lincoln Ctr. | 212-787-3505
W Village | 388 Bleecker St. (bet. Perry & W. 11th Sts.) | 1 to Christopher St./ Sheridan Sq. | 917-408-1850
800-373-7420 | www.fresh.com

"The cleanest store you've ever seen" is this "chic" chain known for skincare, haircare and fragrances based on "ingredients like sugar and lychee fruit that smell so good, you want to eat them"; a "knowledgeable staff" sells "beautifully packaged", "ahead-of-the-pack" products that are "Fresh and original without being overpowering."

Fresh Kills Ⓜ

– | – | – | M

Williamsburg | 50 N. Sixth St. (bet. Kent & Wythe Aves.) | Brooklyn | L to Bedford Ave. | 718-388-8081 | www.freshkillsforthepeople.com

Two former set decorators set the quirky tone at this sprawling home-furnishings purveyor in a split-level converted warehouse/garage in Williamsburg's burgeoning design district; midcentury modern sofas from stalwarts like Thayer Coggin along with lighting, mirrors, consoles and chairs share space with a cache of Milo Baughman tables and frames and fresh pieces from Brooklyn-based designers.

☑ Frette

29 | 27 | 26 | VE

E 60s | 799 Madison Ave. (bet. 67th & 68th Sts.) | 6 to 68th St. | 212-988-5221 | www.frette.com

Posh patrons demanding the "ultimate" in "luxurious" Italian sheets that make you feel like you're "sleeping on a cloud" tuck in to this East 60s shop that also sells table linens, robes, home fragrances and candles; while fans of the "crisp cotton bedding" include the Vatican and "royalty and their consorts", most who "Frette over" "the ridiculously expensive cost" can only sigh "ah to have money!"

Frick Collection Ⓜ

22 | 18 | 18 | M

E 70s | 1 E. 70th St. (5th Ave.) | 6 to 68th St. | 212-547-6848 | www.frick.org

Housed in an "intimate museum" with a "high masterpiece-per-square-footage quotient", this "small" shop at the UES Frick Collection offers a "precise", "classy", "moderate-sized" selection of "art objects" and "reference volumes"; though a few rue it's "unremarkable" and even a bit "boring", more generous sorts insist it's "great" for "unique gifts."

Frock

- | - | - | M

LES | 148 Orchard St. (bet. Rivington & Stanton Sts.) | F/J/M/Z to Delancey/Essex Sts. | 212-594-5380 | www.frocknyc.com

The '60s, '70s and '80s live on – sartorially, at least – within the clean, white confines of this LES women's boutique; explore the vintage styles of Azzedine Alaïa, Ossie Clark, Norma Kamali, Calvin Klein (when Calvin still designed it) and Stephen Sprouse, all arrayed on the walls, with Roger Vivier and Stuart Weitzman shoes to go-with; returns are limited, but the owners are happy to consult about a garment's fit (yes, pants once sat at the waist, not the hip).

Furla

25 | 23 | 21 | E

E 50s | 598 Madison Ave. (57th St.) | N/R/W to 5th Ave./59th St. | 212-980-3208
E 60s | 727 Madison Ave. (64th St.) | 6 to 68th St. | 212-755-8986
www.furla.com

A trip to either the renovated East 60s link or its East 50s sibling will "transport you" to Europe laud leather-fiends who claim that a "well-deserved splurge" on this Bologna-based Italian outfit's "timeless bags and gorgeous shoes" "last forever"; better yet, the "no-pressure" service "with a smile" makes it all "worth the price."

Furry Paws ❶

21 | 15 | 19 | M

E 50s | 1036 First Ave. (bet. 56th & 57th Sts.) | 4/5/6/F/N/R/W to 59th St./Lexington Ave. | 212-486-8661
E 90s | 1705 Third Ave. (bet. 95th & 96th Sts.) | 6 to 96th St. | 212-828-5308
Gramercy | 310 E. 23rd St. (bet. 1st & 2nd Aves.) | 6 to 23rd St. | 212-979-0920
G Village | 9 E. Eighth St. (bet. 5th Ave. & University Pl.) | 6 to Astor Pl. | 212-979-0685
Murray Hill | 120 E. 34th St. (bet. Lexington & Park Aves.) | 6 to 33rd St. | 212-725-1970
W 60s | 141 Amsterdam Ave. (66th St.) | 1 to 66th St./Lincoln Ctr. | 212-724-9321

Proponents of this paws-itively ubiquitous Manhattan mini-chain maintain it's a "great source" for "natural pet foods and products" and hail the "helpful staff" and "reasonable prices"; sure, some snarl the stock is "hit-or-miss" and the service "impersonal", but diehards demur "the free delivery makes it worthwhile."

Future Perfect, The

| – | – | – | E |

Williamsburg | 115 N. Sixth St. (Berry St.) | Brooklyn | L to Bedford Ave. | 718-599-6278 | www.thefutureperfect.com

Early adopters get a glimpse of directional trends at this "cutting-edge" Williamsburg home-furnishings shop, a showcase for the industry's emerging talents; you never know what you'll stumble upon – Lladró figurines from the edgy Re-Deco collection, intensely graphic wallpaper and/or recycled wood furniture – but chances are it's "not necessarily practical", making it the perfect landing spot for the avant-garde set.

f.y.e. ◐

| 18 | 16 | 13 | M |

Astoria | 31-63 Steinway St. (B'way) | Queens | G/R/V to Steinway St. | 718-545-1883

Jackson Heights | 3736 82nd St. (Roosevelt Ave.) | Queens | 7 to 82nd St./ Jackson Hts. | 718-639-1441

www.fye.com

This chain "sometimes gets it right" maintain media-hounds who hunt down "current CDs and DVDs" at branches in Queens; still, critics cavil that "full-price" offerings mean there's "no incentive to shop" at this "cookie-cutter" outfit, while "esoteric" sorts seeking "obscure" titles blast the "dull", "Top 40" choices.

Gabay's Home

| 15 | 10 | 14 | M |

E Village | 227 First Ave. (bet. 13th & 14th Sts.) | L to 1st Ave. | 212-529-4036 | www.gabaysoutlet.com

"Sometimes you find" "great values" on merchandise like Calvin Klein linens, Waterford tableware, Cuisinart appliances, cappuccino machines and "unusual pieces of furniture" confide bargain-hunters who score "deals" at this industrial-looking East Village home-furnishings outlet next door to its discount designer "clothing sister"; but naysayers retort it's a total "crapshoot" and "probably not worth the detour."

Gabay's Outlet

| 20 | 7 | 14 | M |

E Village | 225 First Ave. (bet. 13th & 14th Sts.) | L to 1st Ave. | 212-254-3180 | www.gabaysoutlet.com

With its "amazing bargains, particularly on top brands of shoes and handbags" (think Gucci, Fendi, Marc Jacobs), this East Village discounter is "a treasure trove for label-astute fashionistas" who've vowed "never to pay retail again"; "the store's not much to look at and it can be hit-or-miss", but "they seem to get new merchandise regularly", so "keep stopping in."

Galo

| 22 | 20 | 21 | E |

E 60s | 825 Lexington Ave. (bet. 63rd & 64th Sts.) | 6 to 68th St. | 212-832-3922

E 70s | 1296 Third Ave. (bet. 74th & 75th Sts.) | 6 to 77th St. | 212-288-3448

E 70s | 895 Madison Ave. (72nd St.) | 6 to 68th St. | 212-744-7936

www.galoshoes.com

"I gallivant everywhere in my Galo shoes" gloat gals about town who "treat their feet" – and their kids' too – to "something special" at this Upper East Side trio; the "fashionable but not way-out" variety of boots, pumps and sandals is "perfect for someone who likes" their shoes "stylish yet classic", but you'll also find "pricey", "glamorous surprises" peeking out from among the more "practical" offerings.

Gant

22	20	20	E

E 50s | 645 Fifth Ave. (bet. 51st & 52nd Sts.) | B/D/F/V to 47-50th Sts./Rockefeller Ctr. | 212-813-9170 | www.gant.com

From its tailored dress shirts to its V-necked sweaters, this American label (now foreign-owned) has, for half a century, epitomized "good taste" for men, and women and kids too; so what if the rugby shirts "lack genuine ruggedness" – "you get what you pay for" at its multifloor Midtown shop: "excellent quality" wares, "nice" service and now, thanks to a major image revamp and jaw-dropping renovation, a modern, artful steel-and-glass environment in which to peruse the "stylish" collections.

Z Gap ●

18	17	16	M

Garment District | 60 W. 34th St (B'way) | B/D/F/N/Q/R/V/W to 34th St./Herald Sq. | 212-760-1268 | www.gap.com
Additional locations throughout the NY area

"Always worth a look-see", this "inexpensive" wonder-chain remains a "reliable" resource for "classic", "easygoing" men's and women's "wardrobe staples" from jeans to T-shirts – even those with a "Gap in their wallets" can "afford these prices"; if more daring sorts declare the fashions too "vanilla ice cream", perhaps they may reevaluate after devouring the one-off designer capsule collections (like Pierre Hardy's spring 2008 shoe offerings) and the fresh looks from Patrick Robinson, the new head of design.

GapKids ●

21	19	17	M

Garment District | 60 W. 34th St. (B'way) | B/D/F/N/Q/R/V/W to 34th St./Herald Sq. | 212-760-1268 | www.gap.com
Additional locations throughout the NY area

"Dress your little darling" in "well-made, good-looking" "basics" from this chain outfitting kids, tweens and teens in "versions of adult clothes" that they'll "actually wear"; the "fair prices" become even more so during its "fantastic sales", so "what would we do without them?"

Garrard & Co. ▣

–	–	–	VE

SoHo | 133 Spring St., 3rd fl. (bet. Greene & Wooster Sts.) | C/E to Spring St. | 212-688-2209 | www.garrard.com

The official Crown jeweler to Britain's Royal family for six successive monarchs, this dowager dating back to 1722 has been given a face-lift since creative director Jade Jagger took the reins; both fashion-forward customers and traditionalists converge at this homey salon in SoHo, reveling in the gold, platinum, enamel or gem-studded pieces that run the gamut from charms to tiaras.

G.C. William

∇ 20	14	16	E

E 80s | 1137 Madison Ave. (bet. 84th & 85th Sts.) | 4/5/6 to 86th St. | 212-396-3400
W 70s | 111 W. 72nd St. (bet. Amsterdam & Columbus Aves.) | 1/2/3 to 72nd St. | 212-873-2314

Once a magnet for trendsetting tweens, these bookend boutiques on the Upper East and West Sides are gearing their merchandise more toward teenagers and twenty- and thirtysomethings, dishing up funky fare from the likes of Hudson and True Religion; still, some profess to a "love-hate thing" for the place, since they're intrigued by the inventory but put off by the "expensive" prices and "unfriendly staff."

Geminola Ⓜ | - | - | - | E |

W Village | 41 Perry St. (bet. 7th Ave. S. & W. 4th St.) | A/B/C/D/E/F/V to W. 4th St. | 212-675-1994 | www.geminola.com

Just down the block from hot eatery Sant Ambroeus sits this "quirky" shop that "exemplifies West Village cool" with its tulle skirts, candy-colored satins, repurposed tweed jackets and reworked frocks made from vintage fabrics and hand-dyed to enchanting effect by British designer Lorraine Kirke and favored by stars like Nicole Kidman and Sarah Jessica Parker; fashionistas also indulge in finds like La Voleuse flats and Rogan jeans.

Generation Records ◑ | 25 | 19 | 19 | M |

G Village | 210 Thompson St. (bet. Bleecker & W. 3rd Sts.) | A/B/C/D/E/F/V to W. 4th St. | 212-254-1100 | www.generationrecords.com

"Hardcore" and "indie" rock fans "who like their music with an edge" swear this Greenwich Village haunt has "the city's best selection" of "affordable" LPs and CDs (DVDs too), including "rare recordings" and other "fabulous finds" you "couldn't buy on the Internet"; just "don't expect courteous service" from the "too-cool-for-school" staff.

Gentlemen's Resale | ▽ 24 | 22 | 19 | M |

E 80s | 322 E. 81st St. (bet. 1st & 2nd Aves.) | 4/5/6 to 86th St. | 212-734-2739

"Fashionable suits, dress shirts and ties" from A(rmani) to Z(egna) are "nicely presented" in this Upper East Side townhouse, one of the few consignment stores devoted to guys (they're a male relation of Designer Resale down the block); "other than the occasional wrinkle" or "minor flaw", "the wares are as you'd find them at Saks – just a lot less costly."

George Smith ⑤ | - | - | - | VE |

SoHo | 315 Hudson St. (Spring St.) | 1 to Canal St. | 212-226-4747 | www.georgesmith.com

"Great goods" and more than 70 silhouettes of the "most fabulous" bespoke furniture, including "lovely overstuffed" sofas, chaises and chairs, are available at this London transplant's sprawling showroom on Hudson Street in West SoHo; much of the handmade-to-order selection is based on original 19th-century designs with beech or birch wood framing and the finest natural fabrics, and while the "first-class quality" doesn't come cheap, respondents remind "you get what you pay for."

Ⓩ Georg Jensen | 29 | 27 | 24 | VE |

E 60s | 685 Madison Ave. (bet. 61st & 62nd Sts.) | 4/5/6/F/N/R/W to 59th St./Lexington Ave. | 212-759-6457 ⑤

SoHo | 125 Wooster St. (Prince St.) | C/E to Spring St. | 212-343-9000

800-546-5253 | www.georgjensen.com

Supporters swear the "gold standard for silver" is to be found at these Upper East Side and SoHo shops purveying a "unique selection" of "striking" cutlery, hollowware and jewelry crafted with "Scandinavian simplicity and elegance", whether in "classic old-style or cutting-edge contemporary" designs; yes, these "magnificent" objects are "expensive", but enthusiasts also extol their "excellent value."

Geox

23 | 20 | 19 | M

E 50s | 575 Madison Ave. (57th St.) | E/V to 5th Ave./53rd St. | 212-319-3310
E 50s | 731 Lexington Ave. (bet. 58th & 59th Sts.) | 4/5/6/F/N/R/W to 59th St./Lexington Ave. | 212-319-3321 ☻
NEW Flatiron | 862 Broadway (bet. 17th & 18th Sts.) | 4/5/6/L/N/Q/R/W to 14th St./Union Sq. | 212-993-5850 ☻
Elmhurst | Queens Ctr. | 90-15 Queens Blvd. (bet. 57th & 59th Aves.) | Queens | G/R/V to Woodhaven Blvd. | 718-760-1002 ☻
800-992-4369 | www.geox.com

You "can't beat the technology" of these shoes – it's like "walking on marshmallows" sigh comfort-seeking families who step lightly to this Italian innovator's "sleek" branches in Midtown, Queens, and now the Flatiron District, for "stylish" patented "breathable" footwear that's "air-cooled from the sole"; if a few wail "waited for ages" for "unfriendly" help, insiders retort go to the Madison Avenue flagship – the "staff is knowledgeable", the space-shuttle–like presentation is "inviting" and they stock the "full selection."

Gerry Cosby & Co. ☻

25 | 14 | 18 | E

Garment District | Madison Square Garden | 3 Penn Plaza (7th Ave. & 32nd St.) | 1/2/3/A/C/E to 34th St./Penn Station | 212-563-6464 | 877-563-6464 | www.cosbysports.com

"A hockey oasis in the concrete jungle", this Madison Square Garden "landmark" is a "mecca" for puck proponents looking to find "any jersey or [piece of] equipment"; true, the "cramped" space is "a zoo" when it's crowded, making a visit feel like spending time in the penalty box, but it's worth the roughing up to be "properly fitted by professionals"; N.B. baseball, basketball and football gear is also offered.

Gerry's ☻

24 | 19 | 21 | E

Chelsea | 110 Eighth Ave. (bet. 15th & 16th Sts.) | A/C/E/L to 14th St./8th Ave. | 212-243-9141
Chelsea | 112 Eighth Ave. (bet. 15th & 16th Sts.) | A/C/E/L to 14th St./8th Ave. | 212-691-2188
G Village | 474 Sixth Ave. (bet. 11th & 12th Sts.) | F/L/V to 14th St./6th Ave. | 212-691-0636

Though it's "not exactly a destination", admirers say this Downtown trio is "excellent" for "neighborhood shopping": at the recently relocated Village branch, men find business and casual essentials from labels like Ben Sherman and Ted Baker among others, while the Chelsea branches – one for him, the other for her – stock an array of "practical yet cool" brands (True Religion, Gwen Stefani's L.A.M.B. line, plus Puma and Adidas sneakers).

⦿ Ghurka

29 | 29 | 26 | VE

E 60s | 683 Madison Ave. (bet. 61st & 62nd Sts.) | N/R/W to 5th Ave./59th St. | 212-826-8300 | 800-587-1584 | www.ghurka.com

What "great stuff" – you'll "want every piece" of the "well-crafted" luggage from this "high-end" Madison Avenue shop, voted No. 1 in this guide's Lifestyle category; the "excellent goods", ranging from leather carry-ons to duffels and travel bags, have moved further away from "classic styling" into more exotic terrain, thanks to the use of über-expensive skins like alligator, a beefed-up selection of luxury handbags and the expansive vision of creative director John Bartlett, who recently opened his own menswear shop in the West Village.

Gianfranco Ferré 🖾   27 | 26 | 26 | VE

E 70s | 870 Madison Ave. (bet. 70th & 71st Sts.) | 6 to 68th St. | 212-717-5430 | www.gianfrancoferre.com

This Italian-born designer who passed away in June 2007, was long lauded for his "sexy" shapes, "amazing fabrics", and "sophisticated" construction and indeed his East 70s boutique is still "the place to have your fashion dreams come true" if you have a penchant for luxurious womenswear and menswear; Swede Lars Nilsson, formerly of Nina Ricci, recently took over as creative director and word has it that he will adhere to Ferré's architectural sensibility while pushing the collection forward into the 21st century.

Giggle   25 | 26 | 23 | E

E 70s | 1033 Lexington Ave. (74th St.) | 6 to 77th St. | 212-249-4249

SoHo | 120 Wooster St. (bet. Prince & Spring Sts.) | N/R/W to 8th St. | 212-334-5817

800-495-8577 | www.egiggle.com

Owner Allison Wing brings her infants' lifestyle concept from "San Fran to the Big Apple", specifically SoHo and the East 70s, wowing "trendy NYC parents" with "well-edited merch that makes choosing stylish baby items a breeze"; leave your stroller on the 'parking meters', then wander through the "modern" digs filled with "colorful" organic clothing, crib bedding, furniture and all-natural skincare products – "it's the perfect place to dream about how cute your kids can be."

NEW Gilan   25 | 23 | 20 | VE

E 50s | 743 Fifth Ave. (bet. 57th & 58th Sts.) | N/R/W to 5th Ave./ 59th St. | 212-949-4350 | www.gilan.com

"Dainty and everyday they are not", but if you are looking for "very expensive, unique jewels", this new Midtown outpost of a well-known Istanbul firm may be the place; "creative designs" that evoke an opulent Ottoman aesthetic include large, colorful precious stone bracelets and necklaces caressed by pavéed diamonds and elaborate chandelier earrings that are miniature versions of the crystal lighting fixtures found in the harem rooms of the legendary Topkapi Palace; N.B. by appointment only.

Z Giorgio Armani 🖾   29 | 27 | 26 | VE

E 60s | 760 Madison Ave. (65th St.) | 6 to 68th St. | 212-988-9191 | www.giorgioarmani.com

Now in his 70s, this "top-of-the-list" designer still has his finger on the pulse of what celebs like Cate Blanchett, Heidi Klum and Julia Roberts love "for those red-carpet moments"; the "four floors of absolute perfection" of his East 60s store boasts his-and-hers "drool, drool, pant, pant" "tailored and timeless" suits and separates, "elegant" accessories and "runway clothing at runaway prices", plus "service is impeccable"; N.B. plans are underway to open a gigantic new flagship at 717 Fifth Avenue in 2008.

	QUALITY	DISPLAY	SERVICE	COST

Giorgio Fedon 19 ❶
| | - | - | - | E |

W 40s | Rockefeller Ctr. | 30 Rockefeller Ctr. (49th St.) | B/D/F/V to 47-50th Sts./Rockefeller Ctr. | 212-582-3232 | www.giorgiofedon1919.it

Add a touch of Euro style to your work space or wardrobe with orange, black, brown or red accessories from this dramatic-looking Rock Center shop, the Italian stalwart's first U.S. branch; while craftsmanship is key, the small leather (and leatherlike) luxury goods, including men's and women's totes, briefcases and wallets, along with desk accoutrements, still manage to convey an urbane 21st-century elegance.

Giraudon ❶
| | ▽ 22 | 20 | 19 | E |

Chelsea | 152 Eighth Ave. (bet. 17th & 18th Sts.) | 1 to 18th St. | 212-633-0999 | 800-278-1552 | www.giraudonnewyork.com

"Nice and airy", Chelsea's "go-to place for cool (but not too cool) shoes" lures fashion-conscious men and women with its pointy-toed ankle boots, Victorian-inspired side-button styles and more casual, sportier numbers with cushy soles; diehards declare that this "good-quality" footwear, all made by the French company that's been a style staple since 1977, is among the "best and most fabulous" around.

Girl Props ❶
| | 11 | 14 | 13 | I |

SoHo | 153 Prince St. (bet. Thompson St. & W. B'way) | C/E to Spring St. | 212-505-7615 | 877-932-7244 | www.girlprops.com

"Take your bored tween or teen daughter" to this "funky" SoHo spot for "sweatshop baubles" to "flash around" like "zillions of sparkly" necklaces and "sassy" earrings, beaded barrettes, feather boas, bags and belts; this outfit may not be long on quality or service, but it definitely provides "cheap thrills."

Girly NYC ❶
| | 21 | 22 | 21 | M |

E Village | 441 E. Ninth St. (bet. Ave. A & 1st Ave.) | L to 1st Ave. | 212-353-5366

Femme-finds are the name of the game at this "fun and flirty" lingerie boutique full of "East Village flair" and done up with a Pucci-esque patterned floor and art for sale on the walls; channel vixens of yore with noirish nighties or play the gamine with cute-as-heck camis, then pick up "trendy" accessories and clothing essentials that also work the feminine angle; N.B. closed Tuesdays and Wednesdays.

❷ Giuseppe Zanotti Design
| | 28 | 26 | 22 | VE |

E 60s | 806 Madison Ave. (bet. 67th & 68th Sts.) | 6 to 68th St. | 212-650-0455 | www.giuseppe-zanotti-design.com

Not just for "high-style" trophy wives and *Sex and the City* disciples coo cultists who go cuckoo for the "unusual, gorgeous" footwear at this "fab" Madison Avenue stomping ground, which recently underwent a facelift; "if you want shoes that are a piece of art" – think "hot" boots "with lots of gems", specifically Swarovski crystals, jewel-encrusted sandals and "over-the-top" stilettos in eye-popping colors – and don't want to see "yourself coming and going", this "beautiful" shop is a "real find."

Global Table
| | - | - | - | M |

SoHo | 107-109 Sullivan St. (bet. Prince & Spring Sts.) | C/E to Spring St. | 212-431-5839 | www.globaltable.com

To immediately "improve" your home's "style", hit this Asian-influenced Sullivan Street spot for an "unusual selection" of "cute" tabletop things like bamboo bowls, blue-and-white pineapple vases from Thailand and black ceramic tea sets from Japan; it's "the perfect place to find a gift", especially since the prices are "moderate" "by SoHo standards."

Goldy + Mac ❂

| | ∇ 22 | 23 | 22 | M |

Park Slope | 219 Fifth Ave. (bet. President & Union Sts.) | Brooklyn | M/R to Union St. | 718-230-5603 | www.goldyandmac.com

Macki

TriBeCa | 146 Reade St. (bet. Greenwich & Hudson Sts.) | A/C to Chambers St. | 212-226-2268 | www.mackinyc.com

Pals, partners and jewelry designers Ashley Gold and Susan McInerney and their "wonderful" staff lure style-mavens to this gilt-mirrored Park Slope haunt offering "fashion-forward" clothing from the likes of Free People, Gold Hawk and Rebecca Beeson at "won't-break-the-bank" prices; McInerney's TriBeCa offshoot, Macki, also carries a "well-priced", "comfortable mix" of womenswear that dispenses with the "sticker shock of most Downtown" shops.

Golfsmith

| | 23 | 21 | 19 | E |

E 50s | 641 Lexington Ave. (bet. 54th & 55th Sts.) | 4/5/6/F/N/R/W to 59th St./Lexington Ave. | 212-317-9720 | www.golfsmith.com

"Everything you need is in one place" at this East 50s sports "super-market" specializing in "golf stuff galore" and "impressive tennis offerings" too; prices for the "newest gear" and "top-notch equipment" are "competitive", if "not cheap"; and while the "service is uneven, ranging from old pros" to those who "think there are 14 holes on a course", the "fun indoor driving range" hits "a hole in one" with most.

gominyc ❂

| | - | - | - | M |

E Village | 443 E. Sixth St. (bet. Ave. A & 1st Ave.) | F/V to Lower East Side/ 2nd Ave. | 212-979-0388 | www.gominyc.com

The unofficial motto of this East Village eco-conscious boutique is 'it's not cheesy being green', and the store puts its money where its mouth is by stocking pieces made from environmentally friendly materials; while the emphasis is on women's clothing like organic cotton jeans from Del Forte and tops from Perfectly Imperfect, there are also vegetable-tanned leather shoes and housewares made from recycled goods.

Good, the Bad & the Ugly, The ❂

| | - | - | - | E |

NoLita | 85 Kenmare St. (Mulberry St.) | 6 to Spring St. | 212-473-3769 | www.goodbaduglynyc.com

Loyalists "love the name" of this psychedelic NoLita lair because it encapsulates all that owner-designer Judi Rosen has to offer, like high-waisted blue jeans, slouchy, sexy knit tops and on-the-mark accessories from her Miss Dater line, including gauntlet-style gloves and thigh- and knee-highs, plus trendy totes, sexy 1950s-inspired mules and a new men's collection of skinny-fit denim that's just right for bad boys.

Goodwill Industries ❂

| | 12 | 9 | 11 | I |

Downtown | 258 Livingston St. (Bond St.) | Brooklyn | A/C/G to Hoyt/ Schermerhorn Sts. | 718-923-9037 | www.goodwillny.org
Additional locations throughout the NY area

In between the often "messy" displays and sometimes "seriously un-savory items" ("the clothes scare me"), this century-old chain of "pretty cheap" charity stores may represent the "lowest common denominator of thrift shopping", "but still, God bless 'em" say those willing "to really rummage" "through a lot of junk" "to find the occasional treasure"; P.S. "truly dedicated bargain"-hunters hail the East 23rd Street branch as "having more to offer, better presented."

Gotham Bikes

∇ 24 | 18 | 22 | E

TriBeCa | 112 W. Broadway (bet. Duane & Reade Sts.) | 1/2/3 to Chambers St. | 212-732-2453 | www.gothambikes.com

The staff "sure knows" and "loves their bikes" at this TriBeCa boutique, "Toga's twin", that's especially "great for mountain and hybrid" models; the combination of a "no-bull atmosphere" and a "no-hard-sell" approach adds up to "terrific service", making it a good place for your inner Lance to find the right wheels with "all the accoutrements."

Gothic Cabinet Craft

15 | 9 | 13 | M

W 40s | 730 11th Ave. (51st St.) | C/E to 50th St. | 212-246-9525 | www.gothiccabinetcraft.com
Additional locations throughout the NY area

"They will build it if you come" to these finished and unfinished "starter" furniture stores featuring bookcases, beds and dressers for "a fraction" of what their painted and primped brethren cost; but critics counter "don't expect master craftsmanship", and add the "aggravation of the terrible customer service is not worth the bang for your buck."

Gotta Knit

21 | 15 | 12 | E

G Village | 498 Sixth Ave., 2nd fl. (bet. 12th & 13th Sts.) | F/L/V to 14th St./ 6th Ave. | 212-989-3030 | 800-898-6748 | www.gottaknit.net

Trendy NYU and New School students who've gotta knit swarm this "convenient", sunny second-floor shop in the Village, where the cubbyholed yarns are "high-end" and "fabulous" and custom-created patterns can be ordered but "the prices are intimidating" ("what if you look awful in it?"); despite "great classes", many maintain this place "disappoints" due to "disorganization" and "attitude" ("the staff needs smiling lessons").

⚡ Gracious Home

25 | 18 | 20 | E

E 70s | 1201 Third Ave. (bet. 69th & 70th Sts.) | 6 to 68th St. | 212-517-6300
E 70s | 1217 & 1220 Third Ave. (70th St.) | 6 to 68th St. | 212-517-6300
W 60s | 1992 Broadway (67th St.) | 1 to 66th St./Lincoln Ctr. | 212-231-7800 ◑
800-338-7809 | www.gracioushome.com

"From a $10 screw to a $1,000 vacuum", "everything the well-maintained home" requires resides at these "premier hardware/ houseware stores" offering a "tempting" array and free delivery (in Manhattan) with a "smile"; sure, quarters are "claustrophobic", some merch "may be cheaper" elsewhere and you sometimes have to "wait while others get the gracious service" but "if you need it, they have it" and "if you can't find it here – you really don't need it" (the 1201 Third Avenue branch focuses on lamps, lighting and bathroom fixtures while 1217 is devoted to bed and bath); N.B. a new Chelsea branch is scheduled to open later in the year.

	QUALITY	DISPLAY	SERVICE	COST

☑ Graff Ⓢ
| | 28 | 28 | 27 | VE |

E 60s | 721 Madison Ave. (bet. 63rd & 64th Sts.) | 6 to 68th St. | 212-355-9292 | www.graffdiamonds.com

Devotees "can't walk past the window without stopping to drool over the dazzlers" at this London-based jeweler lighting up Madison Avenue with rainbows of enormous, "beautifully displayed and designed" diamonds – think one to 100+ karats, in colors ranging from deep-yellow to icy white; the "nice staff is helpful", but ordinary oglers assert that "overwhelming" applies both to the stone size and their "money-is-no-object" price – and come summer 2008, it may also pertain to its larger new two-story quarters when it moves to 710 Madison Avenue.

Grand Central Racquet
| | - | - | - | E |

E 40s | 341 Madison Ave. (44th St.) | 4/5/6/7/S to 42nd St./Grand Central | 212-292-8851 Ⓢ
E 40s | Grand Central, 45th St. passageway | 42nd St. (Vanderbilt Ave.) | 4/5/6/7/S to 42nd St./Grand Central | 212-856-9647 Ⓢ
Flushing | USTA National Tennis Ctr., Flushing Meadows Park | 11101 Corona Ave. (Saultell Ave.) | Queens | 7 to Main St. | 718-760-6227 ◑ www.grandcentralracquet.com

Rail-riding racquet-eers report that the "excellent stringing service" at this East 40s outfit is the "best" for commuters thanks to "knowledge-able staffers", same-day service and convenient locations – a "cramped" kiosk "in a hallway between train tracks" on Grand Central Terminal's main floor and a Madison Avenue big brother boasting shoes, equipment and a "great pro-shop atmosphere"; the NTC Pro shop branch inside Flushing's USTA National Tennis Center also sells clothing.

Granny-Made
| | 24 | 20 | 23 | E |

W 70s | 381 Amsterdam Ave. (bet. 78th & 79th Sts.) | 1 to 79th St. | 212-496-1222 | 877-472-6691 | www.grannymade.com

Purl-seekers pop by this 21-year-old West 70s steady-eddy to scoop up "wonderful" hand-knit children's sweaters and hats just like "your granny made but you don't have the time to", along with "whimsical" Polar fleece scarves, "unusual" blankets, slippers, toys and even "nice knitware" for women; still, Granny's not everyone's bag: a handful jab that it's a "bit pricey" – "unless daddy's a Trump."

GRDN Bklyn
| | ▽ 23 | 25 | 21 | M |

Boerum Hill | 103 Hoyt St. (bet. Atlantic & Pacific Sts.) | Brooklyn | 2/3/4/5/B/D/M/N/Q/R to Atlantic Ave. | 718-797-3628 | www.grdnbklyn.com

Exuding "country charm in the city", this "delightful" Boerum Hill haunt stocks "healthy plants", plus seeds, topiaries, trees, tools and containers; it's run by "lovely staffers" who are experts on organic farming, but "even those without a garden" find plenty of "beautiful, itch-ing-to-be-bought items" like French soaps, scents, chimes, cards and carafes, along with Francis Palmer Pearl tableware and vases.

Great Feet
| | 22 | 19 | 17 | M |

E 80s | 1241 Lexington Ave. (84th St.) | 4/5/6 to 86th St. | 212-249-0551 | www.striderite.com

Parents who want their wee ones well-heeled swear by this "great all-around" East 80s standby, which stocks a "diverse selection" of footwear for newborns to age 12, from "sneakers to rain boots and everything in between" from brands like Stride Rite, Merrell and Primigi; the "knowledgeable" staff "knows how to fit your child" – "just make sure you have plenty of time" if you stop in "before school starts in September."

Green Onion, The 🖼️Ⓜ️

∇ 24 | 20 | 10 | E

Cobble Hill | 274 Smith St. (bet. Degraw & Sackett Sts.) | Brooklyn | F/G to Carroll St. | 718-246-2804

You're "always sure to find something new and interesting" at this "sweet" Cobble Hill kiddie shop avow admirers aflutter over its hand-picked, "unique assortment of clothes, toys and books" at a variety of price points, all housed inside antique armoires and other unique display pieces; however, a few "neighborhood moms" who gripe about the "off-putting" sales help "dub it The Mean Onion."

Greenstones

26 | 18 | 21 | E

E 70s | 1410 Second Ave. (bet. 73rd & 74th Sts.) | 6 to 77th St. | 212-794-0530

E 80s | 1184 Madison Ave. (bet. 86th & 87th Sts.) | 4/5/6 to 86th St. | 212-427-1665

W 80s | 442 Columbus Ave. (bet. 81st & 82nd Sts.) | B/C to 81st St. | 212-580-4322

For "lovely high-end and European children's" togs "with a modern twist" or the "perfect baby gift", trek to these "excellent" crosstown cousins Uptown, which also boast one of the "best assortments of play clothes"; if a handful huff that the racks are "not well organized", the green team points out that the "staff helps you make selections", which "makes shopping here a delight."

Greenwich Letterpress

26 | 23 | 23 | E

W Village | 39 Christopher St. (bet. 6th & 7th Aves.) | 1 to Christopher St./Sheridan Sq. | 212-989-7464 | www.greenwichletterpress.com

"Oh-so-civilized, so lovely" and yes, oh-so-"great for cards" and "whimsical gifts" too, this "highly recommended" bright pink-and-brown wallpapered West Village stationer with a "wonderful, knowledgeable staff" oozes "vintage-style charm"; the "cute, handmade stock and special papers" "make you wish it weren't so easy to e-mail" concur wistful correspondents who also practice their penmanship with "unique", custom-made invitations that elicit "compliments from guests."

Gringer & Sons 🖼️

25 | 11 | 18 | M

E Village | 29 First Ave. (2nd St.) | F/V to Lower East Side/2nd Ave. | 212-475-0600 | www.gringerandsons.com

Since 1918, this East Village "expert on making the most of cramped city spaces" has been offering a "huge selection" of "fairly priced" appliances spanning low-end to "midrange to luxe" manufacturers, i.e. from Frigidaire to Viking; "it's not a pretty" place and you "don't always get helped right away", but eventually a "know-their-stuff staff" can show you "everything you would ever want for your dream kitchen" or bath.

Groupe

– | – | – | E

(aka Groupe 16sur20)

NoLita | 267 Elizabeth St. (bet. Houston & Prince Sts.) | B/D/F/V to B'way/Lafayette St. | 212-343-0007 | www.groupe1620.com

If James Bond were a bit nerdy, he'd feel at home in this spacious garagelike NoLita storefront (a casual menswear cousin of nearby Seize sur Vingt) where edgy classics – think wide-wale cord jackets, bespoke cotton shirting, two-tone shoes – from house brands like Troglodyte Humongous, 16sur20 and Wolf Rayet hang next to a black 1983 Aston Martin parked at the front; ponder the latest photo exhibit on the wall, while deciding which trouser style makes your behind look oh-so-sexy.

Gruen Optika
25 | 21 | 23 | E

E 50s | 599 Lexington Ave. (52nd St.) | 6 to 51st St. | 212-688-3580 🖂
E 60s | 1076 Third Ave. (64th St.) | 6 to 68th St. | 212-751-6177 🖂
E 60s | 740 Madison Ave. (bet. 64th & 65th Sts.) | 6 to 68th St. | 212-988-5832 🖂
E 80s | 1225 Lexington Ave. (83rd St.) | 4/5/6 to 86th St. | 212-628-2493 🖂
W 60s | 2009 Broadway (bet. 68th & 69th Sts.) | 1 to 66th St./Lincoln Ctr. | 212-874-8749 🖂
W 80s | 2384 Broadway (87th St.) | 1 to 86th St. | 212-724-0850
www.grueneyes.com

This "upscale" eyewear outfit stands out with its "well-edited", "beautiful collection of designer frames" and sunglasses from Chanel, Oakley, Prada, Tag Heuer and Vera Wang that "varies from store to store"; some feel "you're paying for" the "overpriced" "aura of German optical excellence", but even though it's "not the mom-and-pop optician it started out as", the "always-helpful" salespeople add value because they "know what you want even if you don't."

G-Star Raw ☾
▽ 23 | 20 | 19 | E

NEW Flatiron | 873 Broadway (18th St.) | N/R/W to 18th St. | 212-253-1117
SoHo | 270 Lafayette St. (Prince St.) | B/D/F/V to B'way/Lafayette St. | 212-219-2744
www.g-star.com

"Rock-star clothes", particularly "gorgeous" raw-denim jeans with distinctive details, form the backbone of this Netherlands-based company's two-floor SoHo showcase awash in cement, steel and raw wood and its handsome new Flatiron hangout boasting camel-colored walls and utilitarian shelving; if a handful huff it's a "li'l too trendy" and "slightly overpriced", true-blue "believers" "spend the money", "tight budget" be damned, because these threads are "worth it!"

Gucci
27 | 27 | 23 | VE

E 50s | 685 Fifth Ave. (54th St.) | E/V to 5th Ave./53rd St. | 212-826-2600
E 60s | 840 Madison Ave. (bet. 69th & 70th Sts.) | 6 to 68th St. | 212-717-2619
www.gucci.com

"You definitely feel like you're shopping on Fifth Avenue" (Madison too) at this "beautifully appointed" modernistic duo where all "runs like clockwork" from the "impressive entrance" to salespeople who "cherish their customers"; "stop by and view" the "simply chic" clothing, "snobbissimo" leather goods and "everything from shoes to ice trays" stamped with the ubiquitous logo or horse-bit; if kvetchers quibble it's "lost its edge" "post–Tom Ford", most retort with creative director Frida Giannini holding the reins it's still "happening"; N.B. plans are afoot to open a Trump Tower leviathan in 2008.

Guess ☾
21 | 20 | 19 | M

SoHo | 537 Broadway (bet. Prince & Spring Sts.) | N/R/W to Prince St. | 212-226-9545

(continued)

(continued)

Guess

Seaport | Pier 17 | 23-25 Fulton St. (Water St.) | 2/3/4/5/A/C/J/M/Z to Fulton St./B'way/Nassau | 212-385-0533
Kings Plaza | Kings Plaza Shopping Ctr. | 5351 Kings Plaza (bet. Flatbush Ave. & Ave. U) | Brooklyn | B/Q to Newkirk Ave. | 718-421-5075
Staten Island | Staten Island Mall | 2655 Richmond Ave. (bet. Platinum Ave. & Richmond Hill Rd.) | 718-370-1594
800-394-8377 | www.guess.com

The "true test" of how "flattering" this chain's "cool" "moderately priced" jeans are is "walking down the street and watching the heads turn" as you strut by; while there's no question that the "nice selection" has "teen set"–appeal, and even some adults find it has a "bit of edge", snobs simply pass, pointing to "cheap-looking ads."

Guggenheim Museum Store
22 | 19 | 17 | M

E 80s | Guggenheim Museum | 1071 Fifth Ave. (89th St.) | 4/5/6 to 86th St. | 212-423-3615 | 800-329-6109 | www.guggenheimstore.org

Echoing this Museum Mile's gem of a building, the Guggenheim store's offerings are "well rounded", featuring "arty scarves, books and jewelry" as well as "great gadgets and mobiles" along with "decorative accessories"; some frankly fret over the "too-tight" space with "limited" merch, but more report the "esoteric" selection has the Wright stuff.

NEW Gus Modern
20 | 16 | 17 | E

Chelsea | 207 W. 18th St. (bet. 7th & 8th Aves.) | 1 to 18th St. | 212-206-7065 | www.gusmodern.com

This Toronto-based design team has opened a Chelsea offshoot showcasing their own line of "tightly constructed" "utilitarian" furniture with an industrial, "mostly masculine" feel that turns up on sofas, chairs and tables, along with accessories like lighting; in addition, they also carry a selection of Kartell and Atlantico goods.

Gymboree
22 | 20 | 20 | M

E 70s | 1332 Third Ave. (bet. 76th & 77th Sts.) | 6 to 77th St. | 212-517-5548
E 80s | 1120 Madison Ave. (bet. 83rd & 84th Sts.) | 4/5/6 to 86th St. | 212-717-6702
W 80s | 2271 Broadway (81st St.) | 1 to 79th St. | 212-595-9071 ◑
Glendale | The Shoppes at Atlas Park | 80-28 Cooper Ave. (bet. 80th & 83rd Sts.) | Queens | 718-386-6139 ◑
Staten Island | Staten Island Mall | 2655 Richmond Ave. (bet. Platinum Ave. & Richmond Hill Rd.) | 718-370-8679 ◑
877-449-6932 | www.gymboree.com

"Mommies and mommies-to-be go wild" for the "durable", "ever-adorable" kids' duds, accessories and toys at this "delightful" chain that's always "stocked to the rafters"; "casual", "colorful" "reasonably priced" clothing with "very cute themes (especially for girls)" mean for many it's the "first stop for shower and birthday presents" sure to make a tot "look like a million bucks."

Gym Source
▽ 26 | 23 | 26 | VE

E 50s | 40 E. 52nd St. (bet. Madison & Park Aves.) | 6 to 51st St. | 212-688-4222 | 888-496-7687 | www.gymsource.com

Fans turn back flips for this "excellent resource" in Midtown for "top-quality gym equipment" – "both residential and commercial" varieties –

including Cybex, Nautilus and Stairmaster brands; athletes ranging from bodybuilders to runners appreciate the "knowledgeable" salespeople and "great delivery service", even if they come at "high prices"; N.B. a recent refurb may impact the Decor score.

Hable Construction ⊠

- | - | - | E

W Village | 117 Perry St. (bet. Hudson & Greenwich Sts.) | A/C/E/L to 14th St./8th Ave. | 212-989-2375 | www.hableconstruction.com
Sister-owners Susan and Katharine Hable offer a wealth of screen-printed canvas and linen totes, baskets, pillows, oven mitts and sun hats in "original, artistic fabrics" at their charming West Village nook; choose from "wonderful" light-hearted prints like Charcoal Checker and Scarlet Flower, plus matching desk accessories, colorful alpaca throws, embroidered cotton voile quilts and a smattering of vintage jewelry; N.B. also closed Wednesdays.

Habu Textiles ⊠

- | - | - | E

Chelsea | 135 W. 29th St., 8th fl. (bet. 6th & 7th Aves.) | 1 to 28th St. | 212-239-3546 | www.habutextiles.com
For an "amazing selection" of "wonderful" Japanese "yarns and fabrics you will find nowhere else" (made from substances like pineapple, bamboo and a stainless-steel-and-silk combo), artists and fashionistas wend their way to this textile specialist on the eighth floor of a Chelsea building near FIT, which also houses a weaving studio and gallery; the "minimalist" space displays hand-dyed pieces for garments or home furnishings that are also fabu as artworks in their own right.

Hairy Mary's

- | - | - | I

LES | 149 Orchard St. (bet. Rivington & Stanton Sts.) | F/V to Lower East Side/2nd Ave. | 212-228-8989 | www.hairymarysvintage.com
With blue, pink and fuchsia walls enlivened by the proprietor's own vibrant paintings, this "way cool", pint-size boutique presents a pretty picture to LES passersby; roughly one side consists of vintage womenswear – mostly everyday garb from the '70s and '80s and slightly older coats and fur stoles; the other carries reconstructed items – "really, some lovely things" – while rows of timeless shoes and boots line the floor.

halcyon the shop ●Ⓜ

- | - | - | M

Dumbo | 57 Pearl St. (Water St.) | Brooklyn | F to York St. | 718-260-9299 | www.halcyonline.com
One-stop shopping for hipsters, this high-concept Dumbo music store/boutique/gallery offers the latest in electronica, house, techno, soul, funk, avant-garde, Afrobeat and bossa lounge, plus a slew of vintage and used records; the groovy, eco-themed interior, complete with bark-accented walls and sod-and-stone flooring, also showcases local art, cool clothing and pro DJ accessories as well as in-store happenings; N.B. Mondays are appointment only.

Half Pint

- | - | - | M

Dumbo | 55 Washington St. (bet. Front & Water Sts.) | Brooklyn | F to York St. | 718-875-4007 | 877-543-7186 | www.babybazaar.com
The brick-and-mortar offshoot of Babybazaar.com, this spacious Dumbo shop, blocks from the Brooklyn Bridge, stocks an A to Z assortment of loot for little people, from furniture, bedding and strollers to

toys, diaper bags and gifts; it's also home to an impressive selection of clothing from both old favorites like Levi's and Zutano and of-the-moment labels like Appaman and Small Paul.

Hammacher Schlemmer & Co.

25 | 25 | 22 | E

E 50s | 147 E. 57th St. (bet. Lexington & 3rd Aves.) | 4/5/6/F/N/R/W to 59th St./Lexington Ave. | 212-421-9000 | 800-421-9002 | www.hammacher.com

An "oasis of the unlikely and improbable", this "high-tech gift" store in the East 50s "keeps up with the latest outlandish items", many of which are destined for the "Gadget Hall of Fame"; penny-wise perusers protest that the "cool" "toys for big boys" can be as "expensive" as a "vacation to Paris" ("$4,000 for a massage chair?"), but it's nevertheless "a fun place to browse", "try out new items" and "dream."

H&M ●

12 | 14 | 9 | I

E 50s | 640 Fifth Ave. (51st St.) | E/V to 5th Ave./53rd St. | 212-489-0390 | www.hm.com
Additional locations throughout the NY area

How to handle this "cheap, cheap, cheap" ever-expanding Swedish chain: "shop before noon" (when the "mob" descends and the "messiness begins"), buy without trying on to avoid "ridiculous fitting-room lines" and "bring armloads of patience" to endure staff attitude that's "demanding at best"; "annoyances" aside, though, most "cannot resist" its "of-the-moment" fashions "for the whole family" – including one-off lines from top designers (like Roberto Cavalli) – packing "huge bang for the buck."

Hannah Clark Ⓜ

- | - | - | M

E Village | 60 E. Fourth St. (bet. Bowery & 2nd Ave.) | 6 to Bleecker St. | 212-539-1970 | www.hannah-clark.com

After stints at Parsons School of Design and an internship with popular potter Jonathan Adler, Clark opened this atmospheric jewelry shop in the East Village; her affordable, eclectic, slightly bohemian pieces range from signature bird earrings and flower bud necklaces to lion's head studs and good-luck, "cross-your-fingers" pendants; there's also a selection of vintage bijoux and accessories from other like-minded artists.

Harris Levy

26 | 13 | 19 | M

LES | 98 Forsyth St. (bet. Broome & Grand Sts.) | B/D to Grand St. | 212-226-3102 | 800-221-7750 | www.harrislevy.com

"My mother brought me here when I was getting married and I brought my kids here when they started college" is a typical statement from supporters who frequent this fourth-generation, family-owned Lower East Side purveyor of "very good quality" "discount bedding" (especially Italian 600-thread-count sheets) as well as towels, shower curtains and comforters; there's a "good selection", but "know what you want beforehand", as the space "isn't great for browsing"; N.B. closed Saturdays.

Harry's Shoes

24 | 16 | 18 | M

W 80s | 2299 Broadway (83rd St.) | 1 to 86th St. | 212-874-2035 | 866-442-7797 | www.harrys-shoes.com

Staffed with "efficient" folks "who measure your feet", this "crowded", "chaotic" "old-school" West 80s "standard" offers a "staggering inventory" of "trendy and traditional" footwear for men and an even more extensive selection for women; forget Jimmy Choos – instead, think "sturdy sport shoes" from Timberland, Merrill and Teva offset by "excellent" offerings from Camper, Frye and Puma.

Harry's Shoes for Kids
`- | - | - | M`

W 80s | 2315 Broadway (83rd St.) | 1 to 86th St. | 212-874-2034 | www.harrys-shoes.com

Just a skip and a hop from its parent store, this old-guard West 80s children's shoe shop sticks to its winning formula: customer service, expert fitting and an A-to-Z assortment of American and European brands, including Aster, Geox, Ecco, Kenneth Cole, Mod8, Nike and Skechers; while the lines can stretch long, especially on Saturdays, the staff knows how to treat kids' feet, making it well worth the wait.

⚠ Harry Winston ⌧
`29 | 28 | 28 | VE`

E 50s | 718 Fifth Ave. (56th St.) | N/R/W to 5th Ave./59th St. | 212-245-2000 | 800-988-4110 | www.harrywinston.com

"Who isn't wild about Harry?" ask acolytes of this "exceptional", "elegant, expensive" and "imposing" Fifth Avenue icon voted this Survey's No. 1 for Fashion/Beauty that's known for "amazing diamonds" that are the "best there is"; since 1920 they've had a "rich, famous" and "red-carpet" following, including stars like Gwyneth Paltrow and Halle Berry, and "once they open the gates for you, you'll feel like royalty too."

⚠ Harvey Electronics ⌧
`28 | 24 | 20 | VE`

W 40s | 2 W. 45th St. (bet. 5th & 6th Aves.) | B/D/F/V to 47-50th Sts./Rockefeller Ctr. | 212-575-5000 | 800-254-7836 | www.harveyonline.com

"Audiophiles are at home" at this "gold-standard" electronics outlet in the West 40s with "nice sound rooms" for novices looking to "learn" and a staff of "audio specialists" that is "a pleasure to deal with"; in fact, the main gripe about this "high-end", "high-quality" hi-fi haven is its "high prices", though sound zealots insist you "suck up the expense" – "you won't be disappointed."

Hasker Ⓜ
`- | - | - | E`

Carroll Gardens | 333 Smith St. (bet. Carroll & President Sts.) | Brooklyn | F/G to Carroll St. | 718-222-5756 | www.haskerhome.com

It may be a few blocks away from the heart of "Smith Street's home furnishings row", but this "spectacular" modern mecca in Carroll Gardens featuring unexpected finds from innovative Brooklyn and Scandinavian designers is worth seeking out; ponder the art on the exposed-brick walls, then imagine how much chicer your next dinner party might be if you toted home fine china, linens, carafes or even a handsome dining room table from this decorating dynamo.

Hastens
`- | - | - | VE`

SoHo | 80 Greene St. (bet. Broome & Spring Sts.) | C/E to Spring St. | 212-219-8022 | www.hbeds.com

If you don't loose sleep at the thought of investing five figures in a mere mattress then a purchase at this SoHo offshoot of the 156-year-old Swedish firm may be a dream come true; only natural materials such as cotton, flax, wool and purified hand-flailed, hypo-allergenic horsehair are used on the handmade beds, which are bound in signature blue-and-white gingham; but some just keep on counting sheep when it comes to the price tag, which can climb to $49,500.

Hastings Tile & Bath Collection ⊠
(fka Hastings Tile & Il Bagno Collection)

QUALITY	DISPLAY	SERVICE	COST
▽ 26	–	19	VE

E 50s | A&D Bldg. | 150 E. 58th St., 10th fl. (bet. Lexington & 3rd Aves.) | 4/5/6/F/N/R/W to 59th St./Lexington Ave. | 212-674-9700 | 800-351-0038 | www.hastingstilebath.com

The name may have been spruced up, but this top-notch East 50s showroom now in the A&D Building remains a "museum for tiles, plus kitchen and bath" accessories including faucets and basins praise proponents; renovators on the hunt for trendsetting styles (think chic crocodile-patterned squares) reveal that the collection is packed with "great stuff" – but of course "you'll pay dearly" for the edgy designs; N.B. also closed Saturdays.

Hat Shop, The

QUALITY	DISPLAY	SERVICE	COST
24	24	24	E

SoHo | 120 Thompson St. (bet. Prince & Spring Sts.) | C/E to Spring St. | 212-219-1445 | www.thehatshopnyc.com

"J'adore – there's nothing else like it in NYC" declare devotees who descend on this SoHo "favorite" for "fabulous", "top-notch" quality toppers (including an expanded array of men's lids) from over 30 local milliners; chances are you'll find "just the right" headgear with "just the right fit" but don't forget to ask the "lively, informative", "hands-on owner" about Chapeau Chateau, the house line of "great" hats available with custom details.

NEW Head over Heels ◗

QUALITY	DISPLAY	SERVICE	COST
21	21	20	E

Harlem | 270 St. Nicholas Ave. (124th St.) | A/C to 125th St. | 212-222-2804
Fort Greene | 366 Myrtle Ave. (bet. Adelphi St. & Clermont Ave.) | Brooklyn | A/C to Lafayette Ave. | 718-237-8880
www.headoverheelsnyc.com

"Wow – love the look" of this "modern" new stomping ground in Fort Greene and Harlem for women's shoes (and a few men's kicks too) boasting striking white walls and dark wood shelves and flooring; footwear fetishists fall head over heels for the "very sophisticated" array, confiding you're "sure to find something" "great", be it hand-painted treasures from John Ashford, showstoppers from Courtney Crawford or handbags from Marie Elaine for Allison Designs, plus the staff really "tries to please."

Heidi Klein ⊠

QUALITY	DISPLAY	SERVICE	COST
–	–	–	E

E 70s | 1018 Lexington Ave. (bet. 72nd & 73rd Sts.) | 6 to 77th St. | 212-327-1700 | www.heidiklein.com

It's a "vacation just to shop" at this "charming UES" boutique, a breezy British import filled with everything you need to jump-start your warm-weather holiday – no matter when you're jetting to the tropics; the resort-bound flip for "beautiful" bikinis, sarongs, swim trunks, sunglasses and totes, plus "cute sundresses and cover-ups" sure to "wow the East Hampton crowd", from labels like Apsara, Diane von Furstenberg, Emamo, Eres, Vilebrequin and Vix.

Heights Kids

QUALITY	DISPLAY	SERVICE	COST
–	–	–	E

Brooklyn Heights | 85 Pineapple Walk (bet. Cadman Plaza & Henry St.) | Brooklyn | 2/3 to Clark St. | 718-222-4271 | www.heightskids.com

For over two decades, this "excellent", 3,000-sq.-ft. Brooklyn Heights emporium has remained a "reliable" source for all things *enfant*; the "wonderful selection of toys" comprises half of the stock, with plenty of educational choices too, and there's also more in store, from French and Italian clothing and all-natural bath products that scale the heights of expectations to "high-end" stroller brands like Bugaboo and Silver Cross.

Helen Ficalora

- | - | - | E

NoLita | 21 Cleveland Pl. (bet. Kenmare & Spring Sts.) | 6 to Spring St. | 212-219-3700 | 877-754-2676 | www.helenficalora.com

For "sweet pieces" of fine jewelry like alphabet- or nature-inspired charm necklaces and delicate diamond and gemstone rings boasting bloom designs like daffodils and dogwood, follow in the footsteps of celebs like Sarah Jessica Parker and Katie Holmes and head to designer Helen Ficalora's pink-and-gold bandbox on the NoLita/SoHo border; "complement your unique style" with a "unique" gold or platinum find – what a "wonderful way to mark a special occasion for a woman."

Helen Wang

- | - | - | E

SoHo | 69 Mercer St. (Broome St.) | N/R/W to Prince St. | 212-997-4180 | www.helenwangny.com

Browsers of Barneys and Bergdorf who know the Shanghai-born Wang's wares now also alight at this designer's own shop, an airy SoHo loft brimming with her characteristic cute, colorful dresses, classic coats and cashmere cardigans that channel an updated Doris Day; there's also kids' wear named after her daughter, Mina, and a smattering of pillows, candles and fragrant soaps.

NEW Helio ◗

20 | 22 | 17 | M

NoHo | 626 Broadway (bet. Bleecker & Houston Sts.) | 1 to Houston St. | 212-358-7090

Seaport | Pier 17 | 89 South St. (bet. Beekman & Fulton Sts.) | 2/3/4/5/A/C/J/M/Z to Fulton St./B'way/Nassau | 212-608-3605

www.helio.com

"What's not love?" – the "awesome phones feel like toys", the staff at these "beautiful" NoHo and South Street Seaport chain links "seem very professional, not like those electronics stores where the kids they hire don't even know what anything means", the displays are "very cool", plus it's stocked with "all the latest gadgets" declare wireless wags; if a few shrug "nothing blows your mind" even they allow that these gizmos offer "good quality at a reasonable price."

NEW Helmut Lang

- | - | - | E

Meatpacking | 819 Washington St. (bet. Gansevoort & Little W. 12th Sts.) | A/C/E/L to 14th St./8th Ave. | 212-242-3240 | www.helmutlang.com

Helmut Lang decamped from his Prada-owned label in 2005 but the spirit of his minimalist aesthetic lives on thanks to the iconic brand's relaunch and the opening of this brick-walled gallerylike Meatpacking newcomer; Link Theory Holdings Co. Ltd., the Tokyo-based firm behind Theory, now holds the purse strings while Michael and Nicole Colovos, the former heads of clothing line Habitual, are at the design helm, offering uniquely detailed, 21st-century menswear and womenswear – somewhat more affordable renditions that riff on the namesake visionary's trademark stylings.

Z Henri Bendel ☾

26 | 25 | 21 | VE

E 50s | 712 Fifth Ave. (bet. 55th & 56th Sts.) | N/R/W to 5th Ave./
59th St. | 212-247-1100 | 800-423-6335 | www.henribendel.com

The feel is "more like a boutique than a department store" at this Fifth
Avenue *femmes* favorite that's "always up on the latest styles"; it's a
browsers' "heaven", from the "hard-to-find indie designer" goods nestled near house-label "cashmere sweaters at reasonable prices" to the
"amazing" accessories, "cutting-edge skincare" and new scent bar from
Memoire Liquide Bespoke Perfumery; "service is friendly", if *un peu*
pushy, and while the lachrymose lament the "lost edge" of elegance to
"teenybopper-time" threads, at least navigating the "confusing multilevel maze" lets you "look at the beautiful Lalique windows."

Henry Beguelin

- | - | - | E

Meatpacking | Gansevoort Hotel | 18 Ninth Ave. (13th St.) | A/C/E/L to
14th St./8th Ave. | 212-647-8415 | www.henrybeguelin.it

"Boho-luxe leatherwear for those most in-the-know" is on show at this
tiny shop adjacent to the Gansevoort Hotel, where nearly everything –
from the floor to the furnishings to the "arty" his-and-hers clothing
and signature Spazzatura and Tribu belts – is made of handcrafted
cowhide; and while some ask "what's up with the prices?", the "understated, anti-Louis (Vuitton)" crowd confides this is "the ultimate in
paying a lot to look like you've paid very little."

Henry Lehr

▽ 24 | 21 | 22 | E

NoLita | 11 Prince St. (bet. Bowery & Elizabeth St.) | 6 to Spring St. |
212-274-9921
NoLita | 9 Prince St. (bet. Bowery & Elizabeth St.) | 6 to Spring St. |
212-274-9921

It may be "well-edited", but the "manageable" denim and cord selection at this NoLita nook is one of the "best in town" according to fit-
minded guys and girls; the "part-guru/part-genius" staff "will put you
in the hottest" styles from Earnest Sewn to Joe's Jeans – they "know
what looks best on you the minute you walk in the door", so go ahead,
"trust them" – then duck through the doorway to 11 Prince Street for
T-shirts to match.

Here Comes the Bridesmaid ⊠ Ⓜ

17 | 9 | 14 | M

Chelsea | 238 W. 14th St. (bet. 7th & 8th Aves.) | A/C/E/L to 14th St./
8th Ave. | 212-647-9686 | www.bridesmaids.com

If you're looking for a "moderately priced gown that your bridesmaids
won't hate you for picking out", wedding dresses, flower girl outfits
and prom options too, "roll up your sleeves" and sift through "tons" of
finery "shoved onto racks" at this by-appointment Chelsea nook;
while some frocks are "beautiful", the "worn-out" "samples require
imagination", plus "service is as good as it could be in such a closet."

Z Hermès ⊠

29 | 27 | 23 | VE

E 60s | 691 Madison Ave. (62nd St.) | N/R/W to 5th Ave./59th St. |
212-751-3181
NEW Financial District | 15 Broad St. (Exchange Pl.) | 2/3 to Wall St. |
212-785-3030
800-441-4488 | www.hermes.com

"Be prepared to drop your inheritance" at this "exceptional" Parisian
"status store" and "tourist magnet" on Madison Avenue that luxury

lovers "worship" as a "temple of high-quality" apparel and consider the "holy grail of accessories" – and its new *frère* in the Philippe Starck-designed Financial District condo building; "go, gawk and gasp" at the wait-listed Birkin and Kelly bags, "gorgeous" "investment scarves", leather goods "that will outlast our lives" and "crème de la crème" ties; while most feel service is "*fantastique*", some retort "Oprah wasn't entirely wrong" about the "haughty" help.

NEW HH Design: Shop ●Ⓜ

20	19	19	E

Greenpoint | 211 Franklin St. (Freeman St.) | Brooklyn | G to Greenpoint Ave. | 718-349-2247 | www.haydenharnett.com

Hayden-Harnett may not be a household name – yet – but the Brooklyn designers are making inroads with the arrival of this new Greenpoint source for their hot handbags boasting "lovely" linings and details that keep "NYC hipsters coming back for more"; sure, they're "expensive, but that's a relative term these days" when it comes to arm candy, plus there are more enticements at hand, like the partners' witty womenswear collection and must-have accessories like clutch wallets, corset belts and leather cuff bracelets.

H. Herzfeld Ⓢ

▽	26	20	22	VE

E 50s | 118 E. 57th St. (bet. Lexington & Park Aves.) | 4/5/6/F/N/R/W to 59th St./Lexington Ave. | 212-753-6756 | www.hherzfeld.com

The East 50s digs may be a mere four years old, but this venerable haberdasher, established in 1890, still has that "bygone age" feel thanks to its "quiet" air, custom clothes, "nice selection" of accessories, from Briggs umbrellas to Zimmerli underwear, and "salesmen of an antediluvian tradition"; "discriminating men" head here for "classic goods" (Sea Island cottons, Scottish cashmeres), but "don't go if you have to ask about the prices", which reflect the "rarity" of the tailoring tradition.

NEW hickey

-	-	-	E

SoHo | 96 Grand St. (bet. Greene & Mercer Sts.) | 6/J/M/N/Q/R/W/Z to Canal St. | 212-219-0230 | www.hickeystyle.com

A skull-emblazoned black tee nestled next to a three-piece pinstriped suit sums up the sensibility of this new SoHo men's store, the self-styled 'rebellious younger brother' of Hickey Freeman; within its whitewashed brick walls, eclectically furnished (a ram's head here, a huge red wheel there), are tailored goods in traditional fabrics, but with distinctly contemporary cuts and mischievous touches (e.g. buttons with a marijuana-leaf emblem), plus shirts, sweaters and whimsical accessories displayed under bell jars; bear in mind, though, that while prices are one-third of the parent label's, this baby boy's wares still require a trust fund.

Hickey Freeman

27	24	24	VE

E 50s | 666 Fifth Ave. (bet. 52nd & 53rd Sts.) | E/V to 5th Ave./53rd St. | 212-586-6481
Financial District | 111 Broadway (Thames St.) | 4/5 to Wall St. | 212-233-2363 Ⓢ
888-603-8968 | www.hickeyfreeman.com

The style's "a little old-school" ("makes a 30-year-old look like a 50-year-old" jesters jibe), but "if you want an American-made" suit, "hand-tailored" from the "finest" fabric (off-the-rack or made-to-measure), plus a "very good selection of accessories" and sportswear, this

Midtown–Financial District duo is "what a quality men's haberdasher should be"; prices are "not for the faint of wallet", but the "business-crowd" clientele amortizes the cost, knowing their purchase "will last forever"; N.B. hickey, its hip new offshoot, recently opened in SoHo.

Highway

| - | - | - | M |

NoLita | 238 Mott St. (bet. Prince & Spring Sts.) | 6 to Spring St. | 212-966-4388 | www.highwaybuzz.com

"The street-chic factor hasn't" changed since its Hiponica days – reason enough for cutting-edgers to continue cruising this Highway in NoLita for "colorful", "quirky" shoulderbags, "cool" laptop totes and other accessories in "fun" materials like textured nylon, patent leather and leather accents; it's the wheel deal declare diehards who wear the gear "for years", so expect to be "complimented by everyone from Japanese tourists to New Zealand shopgirls."

Hippototamus

| 22 | 22 | 20 | E |

NEW **E 80s** | 1163 Madison Ave. (bet. 85th & 86th Sts.) | 4/5/6 to 86th St. | 212-249-6182
NEW **W 50s** | 30 Rockefeller Plaza, Concourse level (on 50th St., bet. 5th & 6th Aves.) | B/D/F/V to 47-50th Sts./Rockefeller Ctr. | 212-246-0480 ⓢ
W 80s | 451 Amsterdam Ave. (bet. 81st & 82nd Sts.) | B/C to 81st St. | 212-787-1029
www.hippotots.com

Big Apple parents on the hunt for "adorable", "well-made" "everyday" "sweet things" for kids that are "European in look" wander over to this delightful" threesome; choose from "unique but classic" wrap dresses and tweed skirts for girls and corduroy cargo pants and peacoats for boys at relatively "moderate" prices; if a few sniff the duds are "not very imaginative", fans retort it's "functional and not too frilly" – plus sales are "frequent."

hip-squeak Ⓜ

| ▽ 23 | 24 | 22 | E |

Bay Ridge | 8119 Third Ave. (bet. 81st & 82nd Sts.) | Brooklyn | R to 77th St. | 718-745-3705 | www.hip-squeak.com

"Need to pinch myself to not go in every single time I walk by" this "adorable" little pipsqueak in Bay Ridge festooned with a blue awning and a festive chandelier confide customers tempted to coddle their children with "fun", colorful clothing for all occasions; what an "excellent selection" – there are "lots of choices", from Converse sneakers and rocker tees to Tea Collection separates and Diesel jeans, and natch, prices can be "high."

H.L. Purdy ⓢ

| 27 | 25 | 25 | VE |

E 50s | 501 Madison Ave. (52nd St.) | E/V to 5th Ave./53rd St. | 212-688-8050
E 80s | 1171 Madison Ave. (86th St.) | 4/5/6 to 86th St. | 212-249-3997
E 80s | 1195 Lexington Ave. (81st St.) | 6 to 77th St. | 212-737-0122
www.hlpurdy.com

"Beautiful", "elegant" specs presented by a "superb" and "profoundly knowledgeable" staff have eye-ficionados tagging this Uptown troika the "Harry Winston" of eyewear; "skillful" on-site opticians can finesse even the "trickiest lenses" and cater to fashion-forward kiddies (Lexington location), and even if it's admittedly "expensive", the selection and service are "worth the extra cost."

	QUALITY	DISPLAY	SERVICE	COST

Hogan
	26	26	21	VE

SoHo | 134 Spring St. (bet. Greene & Wooster Sts.) | C/E to Spring St. | 212-343-7905 | 888-604-6426 | www.hogancatalog.com
Pick up a "dream bag" with "great classic style and lines" at this funky, "friendly" SoHo sibling to Tod's that "makes shopping a real pleasure"; the "beautifully presented" goods by designer Diego Della Valle include "high-quality" footwear too but budget-watchers warn the "tried-and-true" finds can "cost a great deal."

Hollander & Lexer M
	-	-	-	E

Boerum Hill | 358 Atlantic Ave. (bet. Bond & Hoyt Sts.) | Brooklyn | A/C/G to Hoyt/Schermerhorn Sts. | 718-797-9190
With its curio-shop vitrines and stuffed roosters, this black-as-night Boerum Hill menswear boutique feels like a cross between Atlantic Avenue's antiques shops and a London haberdashery; still, a closer look at its wares reveals a hipness factor in the shape of its own house line, Rag & Bone tweed jackets, Steven Alan cardigans and Santa Maria Novello toiletries cool enough to satisfy the snobbiest of metrosexuals.

Hollywould ⬲
	24	23	21	VE

NoLita | 198 Elizabeth St. (bet. Prince & Spring Sts.) | 6 to Spring St. | 212-219-1905 | www.ilovehollywould.com
"Where's Holly [Dunlap] been all our lives?" wonder admirers who "can't get enough" of the owner-designer's "funky" pumps, "hot, hot, hot!" stilettos for that "go-out outfit", "classic flats-made-sexy – an 'it' girl staple" – and "Palm Beach"–perfect sandals, all showcased at her "convenient", cabana-striped NoLita shop; but there's more: she also offers a "clothing line with style" and "fun bags" too; if a handful huff "too expensive", others wait for the "insane sales."

NEW Homage ◐M
	▽ 19	17	19	M

Boerum Hill | 151 Smith St. (Bergen St.) | Brooklyn | F/G to Bergen St. | 718-596-1511
Step up your skills and style at this "true neighborhood store" on Smith Street owned by a former Burton creative director and an experienced skater; the highly coveted selection of helmets, goggles and customized skateboards, plus clothing and sneakers from Etnies, Fourstar and UXA and an organic cafe are just a few reasons why it's become hangout central for locals and teens; also in the pipeline: snowboarding essentials and a backyard ramp.

Homboms Inc. ⬲
	-	-	-	M

E 70s | 1500 First Ave. (78th St.) | 6 to 77th St. | 212-717-5300
"Great doesn't say enough" about this East 70s "stalwart" that's now under new ownership; playful patrons pronounce it one of the "best toy stores in NYC", citing a really "nice selection" including Lego sets, dolls, arts-and-crafts kits and puzzles and a staff that "never steers you wrong"; humbugs who once grumbled that "everything is crowded and smushed together" may want to revisit now that it's been remodeled.

Home & Haven M
	22	21	18	E

Cobble Hill | 177 Smith St. (bet. Warren & Wyckoff Sts.) | Brooklyn | F/G to Bergen St. | 718-875-1775 | www.homehavennyc.com
Feather your nest at this "funky, cool" Cobble Hill home furnishings haven stocked with an ever-changing array of "fun, bright, cheerful

home and garden items" from around the globe, all showcased in roomlike vignettes; perk up your bedroom with a "unique" made-to-order Habutai silk quilt or colorful throw pillows, "pick up a housewarming gift", say, modern leather coasters, and complete the table tableau with Hungarian wine goblets sure to add that "personal touch."

Z Home Depot ◑

19 | 16 | 14 | M

Flatiron | 40 W. 23rd St. (bet. 5th & 6th Aves.) | F/V to 23rd St. | 212-929-9571 | 800-430-3376 | www.homedepot.com
Additional locations throughout the NY area

"Forget the suburbs, we've got doormen" at the chain's Flatiron flagship, anyway, quip "home-handy" "hardware-starved New Yorkers" who "feed" their DIY "fantasies" at this "big-box" "superstore"; "whether you need screws, toilet seats" or "how-to classes" or want to "finish" renovating "your apartment without leaving Manhattan" it's a "godsend" with a "surprisingly deep inventory"; but detractors suggest "packing survival supplies" before hitting the "interminable check-out lines" and deem the staff a "bunch of amateurs", adding, "for expert advice shop late when the contractors go."

Homer ⊠

- | - | - | E

E 50s | 150 E. 58th St., 3rd fl. (bet. Lexington & 3rd Aves.) | 4/5/6/F/N/R/W to 59th St./Lexington Ave. | 212-744-7705 | www.homerdesign.com
Named after American artist Winslow Homer, this modern space – recently relocated to Midtown – showcases contemporary tables, desks, seating, lighting and accessories from American and European designers alongside owner-architect Richard Mishaan's signature collection of elegant offerings in exotic woods; N.B. closed weekends.

NEW Honey in the Rough ◑

∇ 21 | 20 | 20 | E

LES | 161 Rivington St. (bet. Clinton & Suffolk Sts.) | F/V to Delancey St. | 212-228-6415 | www.honeyintherough.com
"Trendy" types claim a sweet victory for discovering this new Lower East Side boutique that's devoted to the dress, since "you won't see yourself coming or going" in "different" indie looks from local designers (Sue Stemp) and international ones like Tsumori Chisato; throw in imported fine jewelry, a cosmetics line and a rustic, relaxing worn-brick backdrop and no wonder there's a bit of buzz about the place.

Honora ⊠

- | - | - | E

E 50s | 30 E. 57th St. (Madison Ave.) | N/R/W to 5th Ave./59th St. | 212-308-8707 | www.honora.com
If you have a passion for pearls, you won't feel stranded at this East 50s jewelry store that's a first in New York City for the 60-year-old company; Chinese freshwater cultured pearls as well as specimens from the South Seas may be combined with silver, gold or leather and turn up in everything from bracelets, belts, necklaces, earrings and watches, in prices ranging from $50–$50,000.

Hooti Couture ◑Ⓜ

∇ 21 | 21 | 23 | M

Prospect Heights | 321 Flatbush Ave. (7th Ave.) | Brooklyn | B/Q to 7th Ave. | 718-857-1977 | www.hooticouture.com
"Pretty cool place" purr Prospect Heights patrons of this "funky shop" whose owner not only "has a great eye" for "good vintage bags", clothing (mostly midcentury) and furs, but is "so entertaining to watch" as

she zips around the Victorian storefront, offering "attentive service" and even price adjustments; you'll hoot with laughter at the phrases scrawled on the tags hanging from the "quality goods."

Hot Toddie Ⓜ
-	-	-	E

Fort Greene | 741 Fulton St. (bet. S. Elliott Pl. & S. Portland Ave.) | Brooklyn | C to Lafayette Ave. | 718-858-7292 | www.hottoddieonline.com

Bridget Williams' Fort Greene children's boutique beckons with an arsenal of sizzling sportswear brands, including Bu and the Duck, Lipstik and Marie Chantel, along with Diesel and Levi's denim and sweet shoes and accessories; everything is artfully displayed within a cozy, chandelier-lit space, peppered with antique prams, doll carriages and tricycles.

House of Oldies Ⓢ Ⓜ
-	-	-	E

G Village | 35 Carmine St. (bet. Bedford & Bleecker Sts.) | A/B/C/D/E/F/V to W. 4th St. | 212-243-0500 | www.houseofoldies.com

"What an amazing selection" sing "pop-music fans" who're "happy to pay" the prices at this "expensive" record store, a Greenwich Village fixture since 1968 specializing in rare mint-condition vinyl from the '50s on up (no CDs or cassettes); true, most folks' "closet is bigger" than the minuscule digs, but speak up if you can't find that "obscure 45" because they may have it in their off-limits block-long basement or Long Island storage annex.

Housing Works Thrift Shop
20	17	16	I

Chelsea | 143 W. 17th St. (bet. 6th & 7th Aves.) | 1 to 18th St. | 212-366-0820
E 70s | 202 E. 77th St. (bet. 2nd & 3rd Aves.) | 6 to 77th St. | 212-772-8461
E 80s | 1730 Second Ave. (90th St.) | 4/5/6 to 86th St. | 212-722-8306
Gramercy | 157 E. 23rd St. (bet. Lexington & 3rd Aves.) | 6 to 23rd St. | 212-529-5955
W 70s | 306 Columbus Ave. (bet. 74th & 75th Sts.) | 1/2/3/B/C to 72nd St. | 212-579-7566
W Village | 245 W. 10th St. (bet. Bleecker & Hudson Sts.) | 1 to Christopher St./Sheridan Sq. | 212-352-1618
Brooklyn Heights | 122 Montague St. (Henry St.) | Brooklyn | A/C/F to Jay St./Borough Hall | 718-237-0521
www.housingworks.org

Known for "witty windows" "you want to move into", this "benchmark of thrifts" around NYC draws crowds for its "interesting mix" of "high-quality" "clothes, furniture, books and bric-a-brac" "previously owned by folks with good taste"; "prices are ok, not cheap", "some stores have friendly staffers and some don't", and impulse-buyers are irritated that "the most coveted pieces are always on auction", but isn't it nice to know "the money you spend on a Burberry coat goes directly toward helping others"?

Ⓩ H. Stern Ⓢ
28	26	25	VE

E 50s | 645 Fifth Ave. (51st St.) | E/V to 5th Ave./53rd St. | 212-688-0300 | 800-747-8376 | www.hstern.net

Brazilian-based jeweler, with over 150 international branches, that mines and designs its own precious and semiprecious pieces and is particularly known for "beautiful colored stones" like aquamarine, tourmaline and citrine and "modern" shapes that "make a statement", although they are starting to add some "daintier" things;

the Fifth Avenue store is "accessible", "nicely organized" and run by an "attentive", "gracious" staff.

H2O Plus ◑

QUALITY	DISPLAY	SERVICE	COST
23	22	21	M

E 50s | 511 Madison Ave. (53rd St.) | E/V to 5th Ave./53rd St. | 212-750-8119 | 800-242-2284 | www.h2oplus.com

This water-oriented chain with a Madison Avenue link relies on "natural ingredients without naturally high prices", and specializes in hydration as "fresh products" with names like Ebb Tide Shower Gel and Natural Spring Cream attest; the aqueous theme continues with white-and-blue settings that are as "soothing" as the sea.

Hugo Boss

26	25	22	VE

SoHo | 132 Greene St. (bet. Houston & Prince Sts.) | N/R/W to Prince St. | 212-965-1300

W 60s | The Shops at Columbus Circle, Time Warner Ctr. | 10 Columbus Circle, ground fl. (60th St. at B'way) | 1/A/B/C/D to 59th St./Columbus Circle | 212-485-1900 ◑

800-484-6267 | www.hugoboss.com

Executive wizards looking to "land a spot on *The Apprentice*" or just "strut in the latest power suits" stop at the Time Warner Center standby for "beautifully cut" businesswear; it's also the go-to spot for "stylish" sportswear and for Boss ladies who covet the "crisp" designs showcased upstairs; the SoHo branch sells trendier threads from the red label line, but whichever you prefer, take a "wad of money" "if you want to look great"; N.B. the Fifth Avenue flagship closed but a Meatpacking District branch is slated to open in summer 2008.

Hunting World

-	-	-	E

SoHo | 118 Greene St. (bet. Prince & Spring Sts.) | N/R/W to Prince St. | 212-431-0086 | www.huntingworld.com

Urban adventurers and jungle trekkers alike head to this SoHo shop for luggage, carryalls and handbags made of sturdy canvas or lightweight, durable Battue nylon, and to go-with safari-inspired attire; the functional, fashionable pieces are based on the vision of the company's founder who created the first line of resilient travel gear following an African expedition over 40 years ago.

NEW Hus ◑

-	-	-	E

G Village | 11 Christopher St. (bet. Greenwich Ave. & Waverly Pl.) | 1 to Christopher St./Sheridan Sq. | 212-620-5430 | www.husliving.com

It seems fitting that this "airy", new gallerylike space in Greenwich Village features rotating art exhibits, but it's also a *hus* (or "home") for all things sourced from Scandinavia; the main focus is on men's and women's wear like Tiger of Sweden clothing and Tretorn sneakers, but the signature clean-lined design sense is also expressed in sterling-silver jewelry and sleek stainless-steel housewares like thermal carafes.

Hyman Hendler & Sons ⊠

∇ 28	-	19	M

Garment District | 21 W. 38th St. (bet. 5th & 6th Aves.) | B/D/F/N/Q/R/V/W to 34th St./Herald Sq. | 212-840-8393 | www.hymanhendler.com

"Good enough even for Martha Stewart", this multigenerational ribbon specialist (now in new, larger Garment District digs) peddles an "exquisite selection" of "absolutely gorgeous" grosgrains, laces, straps, strings, tassels and novelty trims (including "fantastic antique" versions) that "stir the imagination"; sure, the staff includes some "disinterested clerks"; nevertheless, this "NYC classic" remains a "favorite retreat" of dressmakers, florists, milliners and crafters.

Ibiza Kidz ⦿

23 | 23 | 21 | E

G Village | 42 University Pl. (bet. 9th & 10th Sts.) | N/R/W to 8th St. | 212-505-9907

G Village | 61 Fourth Ave. (9th & 10th Sts.) | 6 to Astor Pl. | 212-228-7990
www.ibizakidz.com

"Crammed with fun stuff", these "relaxed", "friendly" Greenwich Village tot shops help "you turn your babies, toddlers and children into the New York City style mavens they ought to be"; the relocated University Place branch specializes in "high-quality" European items "just funky enough that your kids will love them", while its Fourth Avenue sidekick zeroes in on toys and "colorful shoes"; but shoppers "not only love what's inside – the windows are always so inviting" too.

Ibiza NY ⦿

21 | 23 | 18 | E

G Village | 46 University Pl. (bet. 9th & 10th Sts.) | N/R/W to 8th St. | 212-533-4614

It's "one of my favorite neighborhood stores" vow Villagers who covet this boutique's "wonderful hippiesque" women's apparel imbued with a "one-of-a-kind" vibe; drink in the "fabulous funk" of its tanks, skirts and jewelry, some of which seems "more Marrakech- than Ibiza"-inspired, and pat yourself on the back for looking "creative and cool at the same time!"

IC Zinco

- | - | - | E

SoHo | 85 Mercer St. (bet. Broome & Spring Sts.) | 6 to Spring St. | 212-680-1414 | www.zincozone.com

The beefier the cardigan, the higher the price at this Italian import in SoHo, a 'bottega'-type concept shop that charges by the weight of the Mongolian cashmere (and come summer, the Sea Island cotton); choose men's and women's styles from wooden baskets affixed to the walls of the modern, loftlike space, then hit the digital scales, paying by the ounce for solid and novelty patterned sweaters, hats and scarves; N.B. wool items are sold at set prices.

Ideal Tile ▨

∇ 20 | 16 | 19 | M

E 50s | 405 E. 51st St. (1st Ave.) | 6 to 51st St. | 212-759-2339 | www.idealtileimporting.com

"Go to the high-end places to get your ideas" suggest some, then head to this "enlarged" East 50s franchise outpost that stocks floor and wall tiles made of granite, marble and porcelain, as well as bathroom faucets and sinks; while some feel the selection is a bit "limited", chances are "if they have what you are looking for, the price is good."

IF

- | - | - | VE

SoHo | 94 Grand St. (bet. Greene & Mercer Sts.) | 6/J/M/N/Q/R/W/ Z to Canal St. | 212-334-4964

Look in the fashion dictionary under "avant-garde at its best", and you'll find this SoHo pioneer, which established its "cutting-edge" roots over 30 years ago and continues to lure stylesetters today in an unassuming, tin-ceilinged space lined with one-of-a-kind pieces and rarefied wear for him and her from a roll call of the finest, including

Comme des Garçons, Dries Van Noten, Ivan Grundahl, Junya Watanabe, Martin Margiela, Paul Harden and Veronique Branquinho.

I Heart ◐

| - | - | - | E |

NoLita | 262 Mott St. (bet. Houston & Prince Sts.) | B/D/F/V to B'way/ Lafayette St. | 212-219-9265 | www.iheartnyc.com

Descend "several feet below ground level" to this NoLita cavern, a "best-kept secret" boasting a smartly edited, "interesting collection of hip foreign labels" including an ever-changing stash of "indie designers" (Sunshine & Shadow, Perks and Mini) and names that are "well-known", at least in certain fashion circles (Isabel Marant, Lover, United Bamboo); don't miss the art on the walls, the Phaidon books or the re-purposed china by Sarah Cihat.

Il Bisonte

| ∇ 27 | 22 | 24 | E |

SoHo | 120 Sullivan St. (bet. Prince & Spring Sts.) | C/E to Spring St. | 212-966-8773 | 877-452-4766 | www.ilbisonte.com

Invest in "classic" bags made of "subtle, sublime hides" that "look better as they age" say bullish boosters of the "beautiful" vacchetta leather offerings at the SoHo branch of this Florence-based brand; the briefcases, totes, luggage, small goods and a new line of tapestries are presented in an airy space decorated with antique bison figures.

Il Makiage

| ∇ 23 | - | 18 | E |

E 50s | 830 Third Ave. (bet. 50th & 51st Sts.) | E/V to Lexington Ave./ 53rd St. | 212-371-3993 | www.il-makiage.com

Founded by makeup guru Ilana Harkavi in 1972, this cosmetics maven, which relocated from the East 60s to the East 50s, is "still one of the best" in the city, with "great stuff for the artist or Joe Schmo off the street"; although professionals receive discounts on products like non-smearing lip pencils and brow-lash brushes, "good prices" are a draw for everyone; N.B. closed Saturdays.

NEW Ilori ◐

| - | - | - | E |

SoHo | 138 Spring St. (Wooster St.) | C/E to Spring St. | 212-226-8276 | www.iloristyle.com

Shades and more shades, as far as you can see, that's the lure at this sleek optical honcho in SoHo, the flagship of Luxottica, a Milan-based luxury eyewear brand poised for a major U.S. expansion; sunglass temptations abound, with exclusive eye candy in every shape and color from the house label, Badgley Mischka, Chanel and Tom Ford, plus collections from iconic image maker Fabien Baron and Loree Rodkin lining the illuminated white shelves accented by colorful, Mondrianlike squares.

Ⓩ Il Papiro ▣

| 28 | 25 | 23 | E |

E 70s | 1021 Lexington Ave. (bet. 73rd & 74th Sts.) | 6 to 77th St. | 212-288-9330 | www.ilpapirofirenze.it

"Cheaper than a trip to Florence", this 26-year-old Upper East Side staple is the source for "beautiful", "elegant" marbleized papers *fatto a mano* in Italy, as well as desk accessories, photo albums and picture frames that are "great for gifts" – for yourself or others.

Ina

| 25 | 19 | 13 | E |

E 70s | 208 E. 73rd St. (bet. 2nd & 3rd Aves.) | 6 to 68th St. | 212-249-0014

(continued)

Ina

NoHo | 15 Bleecker St. (Elizabeth St.) | 6 to Bleecker St. | 212-228-8511 ●
NoLita | 21 Prince St. (bet. Elizabeth & Mott Sts.) | B/D/F/V to B'way/
Lafayette St. | 212-334-9048
NoLita | 262 Mott St. (bet. Houston & Prince Sts.) | 6 to Spring St. |
212-334-2210
SoHo | 101 Thompson St. (bet. Prince & Spring Sts.) | C/E to Spring St. |
212-941-4757
www.inanyc.com

"Top-notch" "trendy labels find a home" at this string of consignment shops for her and, at Mott Street, just him; "although priced higher than you'd expect for 'used'", the "precisely selected" clothes "from recent seasons" are "in great shape" – "many worn only once in fashion shoots" – and "attractively presented"; true, the "staff couldn't be more haughty", but most "deal with it" 'cuz "where else can you get a Dries Van Noten cardigan to go with your patent leather Helmut Lang shoes?"

Infinity ⌧ | 22 | 10 | 14 | E

E 80s | 1116 Madison Ave. (83rd St.) | 4/5/6 to 86th St. | 212-517-4232 |
www.infinitynyc.com

This "terrific" East 80s shop is overrun by "trendy NY teens" and tweens armed with "daddy's credit card", combing through the "hottest" "of-the-minute fashions" from Free People and ordering custom tees, sweats and jeans affixed with their name; if a few sulk that "you must be a regular" to receive attention from the "attitudinal help", others counter "have patience" – "if I was that age I'd shop here too."

In God We Trust ●Ⓜ | - | - | - | E

NEW **NoLita** | 265 Lafayette St. (bet. Prince & Spring Sts.) | 6 to
Spring St. | 212-966-9010
Williamsburg | 135 Wythe Ave. (bet. 7th & 8th Sts.) | Brooklyn | L to
Bedford Ave. | 718-388-2012
www.ingodwetrustnyc.com

Shana Tabor's tiny Williamsburg charmer with an appealing curio shop feel has long been a style beacon for Brooklynites; now that she's opened a somewhat larger Lafayette Street lair, Manhattanites can also revel in her quirky-cool aesthetic, shopping for the owner's fanciful charm jewelry, menswear and womenswear, plus well-crafted threads and accessories from like-minded designers.

Ingo Maurer Making Light Ⓜ | - | - | - | VE

SoHo | 89 Grand St. (Greene St.) | A/C/E to Canal St. | 212-965-8817 |
www.ingo-maurer.com

"I see the light!" exclaim electrical enthusiasts when they look at some of the "best creative" modern pieces – like the flotation hanging lamp with a three-tiered paper shade – from this eponymous German designer; his "witty" works, which are often on display at museums around the world, are sold in a soaring SoHo landmark building.

In Living Stereo ●Ⓜ | - | - | - | E

NoHo | 13 E. Fourth St. (bet. B'way & Lafayette St.) | 6 to Astor Pl. |
212-979-1273 | www.inlivingstereo.com

The exclusive NYC retailer for many top lines, this elite electronics showroom in NoHo has an experienced staff that'll demo the different "options available, even for beginning audiophiles"; the patient pros give the same attention to patrons purchasing an all-out home entertainment center as those choosing connecting cables.

Innovation Luggage
20 | 14 | 16 | M

E 40s | 300 E. 42nd St. (2nd Ave.) | 4/5/6/7/S to 42nd St./Grand Central | 212-599-2998

Flatiron | 134 Fifth Ave. (bet. 18th & 19th Sts.) | 4/5/6/L/N/Q/R/W to 14th St./Union Sq. | 212-924-0141 ◑

W 50s | 1392 Sixth Ave. (bet. 56th & 57th Sts.) | B/D/F/V to 47-50th Sts./Rockefeller Ctr. | 212-586-8210

W 50s | 1755 Broadway (bet. 56th & 57th Sts.) | 1/A/B/C/D to 59th St./Columbus Circle | 212-582-2044 ◑

W 60s | 2001 Broadway (68th St.) | 1 to 66th St./Lincoln Ctr. | 212-721-3164 ◑

800-903-8728 | www.innovationluggage.com

"They always seem to have everything in stock" at this "reliable", "not fancy" outfit carrying "important luggage names" like Samsonite, Tumi and Victorinox, but critics counter there are "no great deals here."

Innovative Audio
▽ 29 | 26 | 24 | VE

E 50s | 150 E. 58th St. (bet. Lexington & 3rd Aves.) | 4/5/6/F/N/R/W to 59th St./Lexington Ave. | 212-634-4444 | www.innovativeaudiovideo.com

A sound experience "you won't forget" can be found at this East 50s "high-end stereo store" that's been a "favorite" "for the audiophile" since its Brooklyn-basement beginnings; aficionados are addicted to its "truly fine" home-entertainment systems and "great service" from a "nice" staff that "takes time to work with customers" and "will let you linger with the equipment" in a listening room "until you decide."

Intermix
24 | 21 | 15 | E

E 70s | 1003 Madison Ave. (bet. 77th & 78th Sts.) | 6 to 77th St. | 212-249-7858

Flatiron | 125 Fifth Ave. (bet. 19th & 20th Sts.) | N/R/W to 23rd St. | 212-533-9720 ◑

SoHo | 98 Prince St. (bet. Greene & Mercer Sts.) | N/R/W to Prince St. | 212-966-5303 ◑

W 60s | 210 Columbus Ave. (bet. 69th & 70th Sts.) | B/C to 72nd St. | 212-769-9116 ◑

W Village | 365 Bleecker St. (Charles St.) | 1 to Christopher St./Sheridan Sq. | 212-929-7180 ◑

www.intermixonline.com

"My go-to place" for that "sexy night out" outfit or "that one pair of jeans" vow fashionistas who count on these "hipster destinations" for "hot, of-the-moment pieces" sure to invite the "envy of girlfriends"; there's "lots of bling", making it the "best place to go broke" – hey, dressed in Geren Ford, Matthew Williamson and Robert Rodriguez, "at least you'll look good in bankruptcy court"; still, service can be "frosty", which is "just plain mixed up"; N.B. the Madison Avenue branch recently expanded, making it the largest location.

☒ International Center of Photography
26 | 19 | 20 | M

W 40s | 1133 Sixth Ave. (43rd St.) | 7/B/D/F/V to 42nd St./Bryant Park | 212-857-9725 | www.icp.org

"Photojournalism enthusiasts" celebrate this Midtown museum's "first-rate" selection of "wonderful" and otherwise "hard-to-find" "coffee-table" books as well as "fun, inexpensive" novelty cameras and other "good photography-related items" such as frames and albums; "helpful service" makes it a snap to sort through the "great variety" of "gems."

Intimacy

∇ 28 | 21 | 27 | E

E 90s | 1252 Madison Ave. (90th St.) | 4/5/6 to 86th St. | 212-860-8366 | www.myintimacy.com

With the "nicest pj's and robes", "tons" of underthings and a "discreet" staff that "won't sell you a bra without a proper fitting", this "intimate" pink-colored Madison Avenue shop is a "great resource" for "basic to tarty" lingerie; fans who "keep coming back" say you may have to "wait your turn" for the "excellent" service.

NEW Iris

23 | 21 | 20 | VE

Meatpacking | 827 Washington St. (bet. Gansevoort & Little W. 12th Sts.) | A/C/E/L to 14th St./8th Ave. | 212-645-0950

Now that this "delectable" Italian import has planted roots in the Meatpacking District, shoe lovers can shop the full footwear collections of six tony designer labels – Chloé, Paul Smith, Viktor & Rolf, Marc Jacobs, John Galliano, Veronique Branquinho – no cherry-picking: "if you can't find it here, you can't find it anywhere"; what a "thrill" to choose your "pricey" "work of art" from the gallerylike shelves, sink into a low-slung silver seat and slip into the "dreamy" femme finds; even if you can't afford the eye candy, "go for the sheer lux of it!"

Irma

- | - | - | E

W Village | 378 Bleecker St. (bet. Charles & Perry Sts.) | A/B/C/D/E/F/V to W. 4th St. | 212-206-7475

At this stripped-down West Village womenswear boutique, the seductive threads seem sewn for arty individualists who embrace the moody, anarchistic beauty of labels like Vivienne Westwood, Dark Shadow by Rick Owens and Philosophy di Alberta Ferretti, as well as va-va-vroom motorcycle and aviator gear from Belstaff; if you don't see your size, do ask – the just-friendly-enough staff will gladly fetch a frock from the back if you need it.

NEW Irregular Choice ◑

- | - | - | M

SoHo | 276 Lafayette St. (bet. Jersey & Prince Sts.) | N/R/W to Prince St. | 212-334-3404 | www.irregularchoice.co.uk

With a lone carousel horse as the centerpiece and a trippy Candyland-gone-amuck decor, you know you're in for a zany, anything-but-vanilla shopping experience at this SoHo newcomer, the first retail venture from this much-coveted shoe label owned by Brit designer Danny Sullivan; the funky women's footwear (plus a handful of men's styles too) may be functional, nevertheless the bold colors, unconventional shapes and unexpected details make each pair look like wearable art.

IS: Industries Stationery

- | - | - | M

SoHo | 91 Crosby St. (bet. Prince & Spring Sts.) | N/R/W to Prince St. | 212-334-4447 | www.industriesstationery.com

If you care as much about the look of your journals as what goes into them, this SoHo store is "the best" for sleek, chic styles, along with stationery and note cards with colorful, modern graphics that change with the seasons; also in stock here are über-stylish Nava desk accessories.

	QUALITY	DISPLAY	SERVICE	COST

Issey Miyake
25 | 25 | 23 | VE

E 60s | 802 Madison Ave. (bet. 67th & 68th Sts.) | 6 to 68th St. |
212-439-7822 | www.isseymiyake.com
TriBeCa | 119 Hudson St. (bet. Franklin & N. Moore Sts.) | 1 to Franklin St. |
212-226-0100 | www.tribecaisseymiyake.com

Followers of this "cool-as-it-gets" Japanese "genius" plan a pilgrimage
to the Frank Gehry–designed TriBeCa flagship or the Madison Avenue
branch to revel in the "unusual but beautifully made" male and female
garb designed by Dai Fujiwara; admittedly, one woman's "wearable art"
is another's "weird clothes", but those "looking for something edgy"
enjoy it, and certainly the "wow" fragrances "never go out of style."

NEW Ivanka Trump Collection 🖼
- | - | - | VE

E 60s | 683A Madison Ave. (bet. 61st & 62nd Sts.) | N/R/W to 5th Ave./
59th St. | 212-756-9912 | www.ivankatrumpcollection.com

The Donald's savvy daughter has apparently decided that along with real
estate diamonds are a girl's best friend so she's opened her own glittering jewel box of a coral, black and white shop for them on Madison
Avenue; the emphasis is on eye-popping stones encrusted with rock
crystal, onyx and agate and executed in signature oval and tassel shapes.

Jacadi
27 | 24 | 20 | VE

E 60s | 787 Madison Ave. (67th St.) | 6 to 68th St. | 212-535-3200
E 70s | 1260 Third Ave. (72nd St.) | 6 to 68th St. | 212-717-9292
E 90s | 1296 Madison Ave. (92nd St.) | 6 to 96th St. | 212-369-1616
W 60s | 1841 Broadway (60th St.) | 1/A/B/C/D to 59th St./Columbus Circle |
212-246-2753
Borough Park | 5005 16th Ave. (bet. 50th & 51st Sts.) | Brooklyn | D/
M to 50th St. | 718-871-9402
www.jacadiusa.com

"Darling clothes from France for baby" and kids that "really hold up"
are the focus of these "lovely" chain links with a Parisian pedigree,
where you can find everything from "chic", "one-of-a-kind" dresses
and coats to "beautiful" bedding for the nursery; still, a miffed few
mutter that service can be "apathetic" and are put off by "laugh-out-
loud prices", suggesting "catch them at seasonal sales" instead.

Jackie Rogers 🖼
- | - | - | VE

E 70s | 1034½ Lexington Ave. (bet. 73rd & 74th Sts.) | 6 to 77th St. |
212-535-0140 | www.jackierogers.com

Within her cozy East 70s atelier, this seasoned couturier caters to
pampered party gals (who also patronize her Palm Beach and East
Hampton shops); her "elegant" eveningwear dishes out a "definite
look" that devotees describe as "high drama in organza and satin."

JackRabbit Sports ◑
24 | 18 | 22 | M

Union Sq | 42 W. 14th St. (bet. 5th & 6th Aves.) | 4/5/6/L/N/Q/R/W to
14th St./Union Sq. | 212-727-2980
Park Slope | 151 Seventh Ave. (bet. Carroll St. & Garfield Pl.) | Brooklyn |
B/Q to 7th Ave. | 718-636-9000
www.jackrabbitsports.com

"Thank goodness they made it over to Manhattan!" rejoice runners
and triathletes who hop over to the "great" Union Square flagship (as
well as the smaller Park Slope sibling) for "expert advice and high-
quality" activewear; vaunters vow you'll "never buy running shoes

anywhere else" after staffers who "actually look like they exercise" "pop you on a treadmill for a test drive", complete with a video analysis that lets you compare kicks.

Jack Spade
25 | 23 | 20 | E

SoHo | 56 Greene St. (bet. Broome & Spring Sts.) | C/E to Spring St. | 212-625-1820 | www.jackspade.com

"Kate's hubby (Andy) follows her recipe", "dishing out" "classic style with a mod attitude" "in Spades" at this SoHo haunt with a "cool, at-home atmosphere"; "practical and affordable", the "snazzy" yet "subtle designs" appeal to "guys who want to look hip without pushing it"; the "trump" card: these "beautiful leather", canvas or nylon messenger styles and briefcases can take "abuse and still look fantastic."

Jacob & Co. ⊠
▽ 24 | 26 | 23 | VE

E 50s | 48 E. 57th St. (bet. Madison & Park Aves.) | 4/5/6/F/N/R/W to 59th St./Lexington Ave. | 212-398-1224 | www.jacobandco.com

"Calling all ballers and shot callers" to this four-story building on East 57th Street that's home to Jacob Arabo, who was discovered by Faith Evans and her late husband, Notorious B.I.G., and dubbed "Jacob the Jeweler" by Sean "Diddy" Combs; huge diamond crosses and signature Multi Time Zone watches are just two of the oversized, "bling is blinging" styles favored by the rock, rap and sports sets.

Jaded
▽ 25 | 25 | 22 | E

E 80s | 1048 Madison Ave. (80th St.) | 6 to 77th St. | 212-288-6631 | www.jadedjewels.com

"Consistently interesting" styles, "good quality" and a "nice selection" are the hallmarks of this veteran Upper East Side jeweler with a celeb and social register clientele; its owner-designers still make 22-karat-gold-plated pieces by the "lost wax" process and use heaps of lustrous pearls and colorful semiprecious stones like quartz, carnelian and peridot to produce items that often look like antiques.

Jaime Mascaró ❶
▽ 21 | 21 | 18 | E

SoHo | 430 W. Broadway (bet. Prince & Spring Sts.) | C/E to Spring St. | 212-965-8910 | www.jaimemascaro.com

"What's Spanish for 'I spent my whole paycheck on shoes'?" quip customers who stake out "highly styled" artfully showcased kicks and handbags from this SoHo mainstay; this family-owned European find may be the "best-kept secret in the city" confide acolytes enchanted by colorful pumps festooned with bows, floral-trimmed ballet flats and leopard-print numbers.

James Perse ❶
24 | 22 | 21 | M

W Village | 361 Bleecker St. (bet. Charles & W. 10th Sts.) | 1 to Christopher St./Sheridan Sq. | 212-255-5801
W Village | 411 Bleecker St. (W. 11th St.) | 1 to Christopher St./Sheridan Sq. | 212-620-9991
www.jamesperse.com

"Cotton never looked and felt so good" than it does at this West Village duo, which lays out its "super-soft", "easy-to-wear" basics for her (at 411 Bleecker Street) and for him (a few blocks down) in a "minimalist" nature-inspired setting; the "more-than-willing-to-help" staff and the "mix-and-match color palette" of the hip wares, which include the "coolest T-shirts on the planet", "make life simple" for the "fashion-impaired"; N.B. the women's store now stocks infant and toddlers' wear too.

James Robinson

▽ 29 | 26 | 28 | VE

E 50s | 480 Park Ave. (58th St.) | 4/5/6/F/N/R/W to 59th St./
Lexington Ave. | 212-752-6166 | www.jrobinson.com

"Very pricey" Park Avenue aristocrat that's "the epitome of classical good taste", from the "outstanding selection of vintage jewelry", particularly 19th-century gems, 20th-century art deco pieces, signature cuff links and engagement rings, to the "best sterling silver flatware" ("made the old-fashioned way – by hand in England"), prestigious European porcelain dinner services and antique table glass; the atmosphere is "super-swanky", but the "staff is friendly."

Jamin Puech

- | - | - | E

NoLita | 247 Elizabeth St. (bet. Houston & Prince Sts.) | 6 to Bleecker St. |
212-431-5200 | www.jamin-puech.com

What a "little jewel" sigh tastemakers smitten by the French designer's "quirky" handbag "treasures" with a decidedly "boho flair" showcased at this "warm, inviting", intimate NoLita nook; peruse the big old-fashioned cabinets filled with "tiny evening" purses, rock-chick satchels and tony totes bearing "super-luxurious embellishments" like beads, feathers and embroidery in a riot of color and leather combos, and be prepared to get carried away.

Jammyland ❶

- | - | - | I

E Village | 60 E. Third St. (bet. 1st & 2nd Aves.) | F/V to Lower East Side/
2nd Ave. | 212-614-0185 | www.jammyland.com

"One of those shops that makes you proud to live in this city", this East Village music store slakes the thirst of both "hard-core enthusiasts and newbies" faster than a Red Stripe with "excellent" reggae, ska, rock steady and dub as well as African and Carib grooves; rude boys also give big ups to the "niche"-like digs jammed with vintage LP covers and posters.

Jam Paper & Envelope

18 | 10 | 11 | I

Gramercy | 135 Third Ave. (bet. 14th & 15th Sts.) | 4/5/6/L/N/Q/R/W to
14th St./Union Sq. | 212-473-6666 | 800-801-0526 | www.jampaper.com

Crafters, students and arty types of all stripes swear by the "deep but not large" selection of funky colored "paper, paper everywhere" (including stationery, folders, portfolios, gift-wrapping, boxes and "oddsized envelopes") at this "cluttered" "warehouse" east of Irving Place; sure, it's "cheap", but some "frustrated" fans fume the "self-serve" attitude means "they just Jam it in and don't help you pull it out."

❚ J&R Music & Computer World ❶

24 | 17 | 17 | M

Financial District | 1-34 Park Row (bet. Ann & Beekman Sts.) | R/W to
City Hall | 212-238-9000 | 800-221-8180 | www.jr.com

"You name it" – you can probably find it at this "Park Row legend" whose "great selection of electronics, appliances, music, movies", "etc." seems to include "every techie gadget under the moon", all peddled by a "brusque" but "efficient" staff; the "bustling", "Byzantine" complex "spread out in multiple buildings" "can be overwhelming", so insiders advise "go early" or "use the online store and avoid the lines" altogether.

	QUALITY	DISPLAY	SERVICE	COST

Jane ⑤
– – – E

E 70s | 1025 Lexington Ave. (bet. 73rd & 74th Sts.) | 6 to 77th St. | 212-772-7710 | www.janeboutique.com

Rest assured there's no plain-Jane garb at this elegant boutique that feels like a dream closet where the color-coded womenswear from European labels, including Blumarine and Hess Intropia, play off an artistic pale pink backdrop; while the look is classically stylish, there's a smart edginess to the silhouettes – and attentive customer service – to keep fans returning to this Upper East Sider.

NEW Jane Eadie
– – – E

NoLita | 248 Elizabeth St. (bet. Houston & Prince Sts.) | N/R/W to Prince St. | 212-334-7975 | www.janeeadie.com

This NoLita newcomer's eponymous owner is a British expat who worked for HRH The Prince of Wales and Polo Ralph Lauren before opening her dream emporium where she sells original jewelry from South America and Italy; "high-quality materials, great designs and presentation" mean that the charm necklaces, rings and earrings of Murano glass beads and gemstones at less-than-break-the-bank prices are "perfect for that special gift."

Jane's Exchange
21 16 21 M

E Village | 191 E. Third St. (bet. Aves. A & B) | F to 2nd Ave. | 212-677-0380 | www.janesexchangenyc.com

"Seek and you will find" an "abundance of great baby/kids stuff" at this East Village consigner that consists entirely of children's wear, toys and some furniture; it has the air of a day-care center, with brightly painted walls, a play area and hand-lettered signs ('we need cribs'); in the back are maternity togs from such makers as A Pea in the Pod, so mom can "look hip at a fraction of the price."

Jane Wilson-Marquis ⑤Ⓜ
– – – E

E 70s | 42 E. 76th St. (bet. Madison & Park Aves.) | 6 to 77th St. | 212-452-5335 | www.bridalgowns.net

Brides and social butterflies who want custom-made choices that aren't "just what Vera Wang is showing this season", plus affordable ready-to-wear gowns, make an appointment at this namesake designer's atelier, now located in the East 70s; the "romantic", "vintage-looking" couture creations seem straight out of a fairy tale, while the lower-priced off-the-rack line appeals to women with more modern – and retro-modern – sensibilities; N.B. guys can also dress the part with big-day essentials from the JWM collection.

Janovic Plaza ●
22 17 17 M

E 60s | 1150 Third Ave. (67th St.) | 6 to 68th St. | 212-772-1400 | 800-772-4381 | www.janovic.com
Additional locations throughout the NY area

If you "need to refresh your home or apartment", this is "the place to go for paint, wallpaper and window treatments" assert "city dwellers" who find this outfit "convenient", "well stocked" and "easy" to "comb through"; however, servicewise, it's different strokes for different folks, with fans hailing the salespeople as "helpful" and others sniping that they're "knowledgeable but not forthcoming" – "it would be great if they'd be more willing to share it."

| | QUALITY | DISPLAY | SERVICE | COST |

Jay Kos 🛇

| - | - | - | VE |

E 50s | 475 Park Ave. (bet. 57th & 58th Sts.) | 4/5/6/F/N/R/W to 59th St./Lexington Ave. | 212-319-2770

This "pricey but excellent" shop in the East 50s has earned a devoted following over the past decade for its superior selection of classic, old-world men's business attire enlivened by "lots of color" for a kind of "edgy conservative" feel; besides brand-name and bespoke suits, "interesting" ties, hats, cuff links and cigars abound at the boutique whose "friendly owner" often offers style advice.

Jazz Record Center 🛇

| - | - | - | M |

Chelsea | 236 W. 26th St., 8th fl. (bet. 7th & 8th Aves.) | 1 to 28th St. | 212-675-4480 | www.jazzrecordcenter.com

There's nothing "run-of-the-mill" about the world-class selection at this eighth-floor Chelsea hideaway with "drawers of great CDs" and "lots of vinyl"; whether "you want jazz", Latin, gospel, blues or fusion, fans insist "there's no better place" to score that coveted recording, and an extensive assortment of T-shirts, books and ephemera such as magazines, posters and "great photos" completes the experience.

J.Crew ◐

| 20 | 21 | 18 | M |

E 40s | 347 Madison Ave. (45th St.) | 4/5/6/7/S to 42nd St./Grand Central | 212-949-0570

Flatiron | 91 Fifth Ave. (bet. 16th & 17th Sts.) | 4/5/6/L/N/Q/R/W to 14th St./Union Sq. | 212-255-4848

SoHo | 99 Prince St. (bet. Greene & Mercer Sts.) | N/R/W to Prince St. | 212-966-2739

Seaport | Pier 17 | 203 Front St. (bet. Beekman & Fulton Sts.) | 2/3/4/5/A/C/J/M/Z to Fulton St./B'way/Nassau | 212-385-3500

W 50s | Rockefeller Ctr. | 30 Rockefeller Ctr. (bet. 5th & 6th Aves.) | B/D/F/V to 47-50th Sts./Rockefeller Ctr. | 212-765-4227

W 60s | The Shops at Columbus Circle, Time Warner Ctr. | 10 Columbus Circle, 2nd fl. (60th St. at B'way) | 1/A/B/C/D to 59th St./Columbus Circle | 212-823-9302

800-562-0258 | www.jcrew.com

Complete your "prepster look" at this "traditional" chain that's "never been better" with its "quality cashmere sweaters in fun colors", "flirty dresses with a vintage bent", bathing suits and other "classics that are easily funkied up"; plus, who can resist its "classy-looking" stores sporting "reasonable" prices, a "great return policy" and "helpful staff"?

Jean Shop

| - | - | - | VE |

Meatpacking | 435 W. 14th St. (9th Ave.) | A/C/E/L to 14th St./8th Ave. | 212-366-5326

NEW **SoHo** | 424 W. Broadway (bet. Prince & Spring Sts.) | C/E to Spring St. | 212-334-5822 ◐

www.worldjeanshop.com

"If you could put a price on cool", then this "grand" Meatpacking District destination (with a new SoHo sibling) is "pretty darn cool" – so "be prepared to shell out a pretty penny for some of the finest" his-and-hers Japanese denim around confide hipsters; "don't bother looking for Diesel or Earl jeans here" because the spare, sprawling confines contain their own label goods with a few styles distressed to your specifications.

	QUALITY	DISPLAY	SERVICE	COST

Jeffrey New York ●
28 23 22 VE

Meatpacking | 449 W. 14th St. (bet. 9th & 10th Aves.) | A/C/E/L to 14th St./8th Ave. | 212-206-1272 | www.jeffreynewyork.com

"*La crème de la crème*" of his-and-hers "high fashion, with an accent on the high" is hosted by this "shopping heaven" in the Meatpacking District with "too-chic-to-be-chic atmosphere" and an "eager", slightly "intrusive" staff; it "shines in shoes", with "unique models" from all the names, but the wares also include "edgy" threads (bound to "raise eyebrows at even the most open-minded" offices) and "seductive" jewelry; malcontents moan "prices are exorbitant" but "if you're sufficiently thin and adventurous", it's worth it for what converts call "the best-curated clothing collection in the city."

Jennifer Convertibles ●
13 12 13 M

Flatiron | 902 Broadway (20th St.) | N/R/W to 23rd St. | 212-677-6862 | www.jenniferfurniture.com
Additional locations throughout the NY area

Wallet-watchers maintain that this chain offers "decent" sofa beds, love seats and cocktail tables "for a starter home" at "insanely cheap prices", but the unconverted tersely assert that "poor workmanship" makes for "disposable furniture."

Jennifer Miller Jewelry 🖼
- - - M

E 70s | 972 Lexington Ave. (bet. 70th & 71st Sts.) | 6 to 68th St. | 212-734-8199 | www.jewelsbyjen.com

Whether you're a fan of the faux or the fine, you'll find it at this tiny UES jewelry boutique; the store's namesake designer offers a "lovely selection" of contemporary and classic looks in precious stones as well as a popular collection of replicas in man-made diamonds; N.B. there's also a small sampling of handbags, clothing and tabletop accessories.

Jensen-Lewis
19 18 16 M

Chelsea | 89 Seventh Ave. (15th St.) | 1/2/3 to 14th St. | 212-929-4880 | www.jensen-lewis.com

For almost 40 years this Chelsea showroom has sold "functional" "contemporary furniture" "at a decent price"; choices range from canvas to metal, wood and leather so "you are sure to find something" here, except perhaps for consistent service.

Jeri Cohen Fine Jewelry 🖼
∇ 27 27 25 VE

E 60s | Trump Plaza | 1036 Third Ave. (bet. 61st & 62nd Sts.) | 4/5/6/F/N/R/W to 59th St./Lexington Ave. | 212-750-3172 | www.jericohenjewelry.com

Trained in the arts, jeweler Jeri Cohen loves what she does, and while she might be playing with her pugs when you step into her bright shop in the East 60s, her passion for "beautiful" "quality" diamonds is certainly on display – especially understated ones for daytime – from stacks of glittering, slightly oval bangles to signature flower studs and pendants that she also produces in miniature for the younger set; all tagged as "fairly" as possible in this pricey medium.

NEW Jessie James ●
- - - E

W Village | 95 Greenwich Ave. (bet. Bank & W. 12th Sts.) | 1/2/3 to 14th St. | 212-217-9944 | www.jessiejamesonline.com

From the moment you lay eyes on the twig chandelier and pale green walls you know there's something a bit different about this West Villager, an offshoot of the Hoboken original; fashion followers and dare-to-be different outlaws all revel in the smoking hot womenswear from labels like Madison Marcus, Plastic Island, Shoshanna and Walter, displayed by color in closetlike compartments; within easy grasp of the on-target looks: well-priced jewelry and accessories.

Jewish Museum Stores, The   25 | 22 | 20 | M

E 90s | The Jewish Museum | 1109 Fifth Ave. (92nd St.) | 6 to 96th St. | 212-423-3211

W 70s | Jewish Community Ctr. | 334 Amsterdam Ave. (76th St.) | 1 to 79th St. | 646-505-5730

www.thejewishmuseum.org

"Browse to the tunes of *Fiddler on the Roof*" at the "lovely" shops within the Jewish Museum, one that specializes in "high-end" Judaica and ceremonial objects and another filled with "gorgeous" jewelry, "wonderful books" and art exhibit–related items "with a Jewish bent" – or find the whole "interesting" *megillah* at the Upper West Side offshoot; though a few kvetch over sometimes "expensive" tabs, with such "quality" and a "helpful" staff to boot, "what's not to like?"; N.B. closed Saturdays.

Jill Platner Ⓜ   - | - | - | E

SoHo | 113 Crosby St. (bet. Houston & Prince Sts.) | N/R/W to Prince St. | 212-324-1298 | www.jillplatner.com

A "stark" SoHo space is an apt backdrop for the designer's "bold", "organic", hammered silver and gold jewelry that's a sculptural "modern" take on nature – from a 19-karat forget-me-not pendant on a string to wild-bean earrings; though "a bit pricey", the pieces are "striking", and "when you wear them, you can't stop touching them."

Jill Stuart   ▽ 22 | 19 | 17 | E

SoHo | 100 Greene St. (bet. Prince & Spring Sts.) | N/R/W to Prince St. | 212-343-2300 | www.jillstuart.com

It's an Edwardian-inspired combo of innocence and sensuality that's the calling card of this American designer, whose "uncluttered" SoHo digs trips the light fantastic with its '60s Mod and baby-doll dresses and "fun, girlie" separates lined in lace, tulle, crochet and chiffon; insiders collect her "extraordinary shoes" or descend downstairs to shop collections past; N.B. the Display score may not reflect a recent redo.

Jil Sander Ⓧ   25 | - | 22 | VE

E 70s | 1042 Madison Ave. (bet. 79th & 80th Sts.) | 6 to 77th St. | 212-838-6100 | 800-704-7317 | www.jilsander.com

"How can one resist" when "you feel just wonderful" in the plush fabrics and "elegant", subtle stylings of this visionary mens- and womenswear house, which moved last fall into Upper East Side digs; still, some miss the "true eye" of the namesake designer, saying the line is "not as well-designed as it used to be" since she left.

Jimmy Choo   28 | 27 | 23 | VE

E 50s | 645 Fifth Ave. (51st St.) | E/V to 5th Ave./53rd St. | 212-593-0800

E 60s | 716 Madison Ave. (bet. 63rd & 64th Sts.) | 4/5/6/F/N/R/W to 59th St./Lexington Ave. | 212-759-7078

www.jimmychoo.com

"If I don't make it to heaven, I'll opt for" my "favorite place on the planet" fawn "fashion-lovers" who feed their "addictive habit" with designers Tamara Mellon and Sandra Choi's "sexy", "ultra-expensive eye candy" at this East Side duo; "comfortable stilettos? somehow JC makes it happen" – "you'll want every pair" (it's "worth the extra cashola") – and if a few scoff "who can walk in stilts?", groupies gush "gimme Jimmy!"

J.J. Hat Center Ⓢ

▽ 27 | 23 | 25 | E

Garment District | 310 Fifth Ave. (bet. 31st & 32nd Sts.) | B/D/F/N/Q/R/V/W to 34th St./Herald Sq. | 212-239-4368 | 800-622-1911 | www.jjhatcenter.com

Perhaps the "only place in NYC for a man to buy a real hat", this topper titan, established in 1911, housed in the fresco-filled former IBM building and staffed with some of the "most knowledgeable" help "in town", makes you feel like "you've stepped into the past"; slip on a Borsalino fedora or a porkpie number and embrace your inner nostalgist; N.B. there are some women's styles too.

J.J. Marco Ⓢ

▽ 24 | 23 | 24 | VE

E 80s | 1070 Madison Ave. (81st St.) | 4/5/6 to 86th St. | 212-744-3202 | www.jjmarco.com

"Nothing says I'm sorry like a designer piece of 18-karat gold" and "if you really mean it, throw in some diamonds" too, just like those found on the "classic", "colorful and beautiful" earrings and necklaces at this elegant little Upper East Side shop fitted out with cherry cabinets filled with their own brand of eye candy.

J. Lindeberg Stockholm ◗

26 | 23 | 20 | E

SoHo | 126 Spring St. (Greene St.) | N/R/W to Prince St. | 212-625-9403 | www.jlindeberg.com

Hard to believe it's been 10 years since Johan Lindeberg left Diesel to launch his vision of contemporary sports- and activewear that continues to earn "cool points with those in-the-know"; the "stylish duds" – kind of a "Swedish take on the preppy look" – for men are served up amid the sleek, black and white environment of his SoHo store, one of only two in the U.S.

J. McLaughlin

22 | 21 | 21 | E

E 70s | 1008 Lexington Ave. (72nd St.) | 6 to 68th St. | 212-879-9565
E 90s | 1311 Madison Ave. (bet. 92nd & 93rd Sts.) | 6 to 96th St. | 212-369-4830
www.jmclaughlin.com

Ivy Leaguers unsure of what to wear to the dean's house for dinner head to this Carnegie Hill townhouse – and now a new East 70s offshoot too – where the "nice, classic" sportswear, "proper" skirts, "country-club" pants and rich cashmere cable knits "in every color of the rainbow" are "just conservative enough" to satisfy; but edgier sorts sneer the styling is exclusively for "frumpy preps or preppy frumps" and rather "pricey for what it is."

ⓏJ. Mendel Ⓢ

28 | 29 | 27 | VE

E 60s | 723 Madison Ave. (bet. 63rd & 64th Sts.) | 4/5/6/F/N/R/W to 59th St./Lexington Ave. | 212-832-5830 | www.jmendel.com

The "furs are without peer" at this East 60s "branch of a Parisian classic", whose "novel, whimsical creations" represent the "ultimate in self-indulgence" – as does the "smart" clothing; "salespeople who know what they're talking about" and a salon decorated with a dramatic, curved staircase create a "luxurious" shopping experience; of course, you better "bring your bank account with you" to cover the "incredible prices" – but "who can argue when you're getting the Rolls-Royce of designer" skins?

J.M. Weston

26 | 23 | 26 | VE

E 60s | 812 Madison Ave. (68th St.) | 6 to 68th St. | 212-535-2100 |
877-493-7866 | www.jmweston.com

"If you can afford it you should have at least one pair" of "wonderful quality" hand-sewn shoes from this 120-year-old famed French company opine men "in-the-know" who shop at this East 60s emporium for footwear made the old-world way; what "excellent craftsmanship and great service" exclaim big spenders who tout the "tony", "very expensive" collection, opting for "classic" loafers and wingtips or more contemporary offerings like Chelsea boots and trainers designed by Michel Perry, all made from naturally tanned leathers.

Joan Michlin Gallery

∇ 27 | 26 | 24 | E

SoHo | 449 W. Broadway (bet. Houston & Prince Sts.) | N/R/W to
Prince St. | 212-475-6603 | 800-331-1335 | www.joanmichlin.com

"You won't see yourself coming and going" if you're wearing a piece of this pioneering SoHo designer's "unique", "well-crafted" jewelry in gold or gold with gemstones; still, some wish her "aggressive" sales staff weren't like "piranhas in a feeding frenzy" when it comes to pursuing customers.

Joël Name Optique de Paris

– | – | – | E

SoHo | 448 W. Broadway (Prince St.) | N/R/W to Prince St. |
212-777-5888

This longtime SoHo specialty retailer excels at "eyewear with flair", including frames and sunglasses from boldface brands like Chanel, Judith Leiber and Silhouette; although there's "no same-day service", they do "quality work" according to regulars – and what's more, you "can always find a pair" of specs that "will earn compliments."

Joe's Fabrics and Trimmings

– | – | – | M

LES | 102-110 Orchard St. (Delancey St.) | F/J/M/Z to Delancey/
Essex Sts. | 212-674-7089 | www.joesfabrics.com

Located at the corner of Orchard and Delancey, this Lower East Side draper displays a "fantastic selection" of "upholstery fabrics, lace and diaphanous sheers", plus trims and tassels; owing to "aisles and aisles of fabric" this place is "not easy" to browse, but worthwhile if "you're going for one particular thing" – especially since you can consult the "human encyclopedias" who staff the store; N.B. closed Saturdays.

NEW John Bartlett Ⓜ

23 | 23 | 21 | VE

W Village | 143 Seventh Ave. S. (Charles St.) | 1 to Christopher St./
Sheridan Sq. | 212-633-6867 | www.johnbartlettny.com

The namesake menswear designer's first flagship is this new West Village boutique displaying a "well-made" collection ranging from preppie cable knit v-neck sweaters and vests to made-to-order suits that's a "favorite of metrosexuals everywhere"; the decor is urban general store, replete with exposed rafters, white birches, fieldstone walls and a funky light fixture.

	QUALITY	DISPLAY	SERVICE	COST

John Derian Ⓜ
E Village | 6 E. Second St. (bet. Bowery & 2nd Ave.) | F/V to Lower East Side/
2nd Ave. | 212-677-3917
| | - | - | - | E |

John Derian Dry Goods Ⓜ
E Village | 10 E. Second St. (bet. Bowery & 2nd Ave.) | F/V to Lower East Side/
2nd Ave. | 212-677-8408
www.johnderian.com

The eponymous owner of this "artistic" East Village shop offers his
own "expensive" and "unique" decoupage designs – fanciful flowers,
birds, bats and insects – on tableware, lamps, coasters and paperweights, along with exotic items like giant clam shells and sea
sponges; an offshoot, just two doors down, showcases softer goods
such as bedding and pillows, along with vintage Pakistani quilts and
refurbished sofas, all "perfect for the person with everything."

John Fluevog Shoes ◑
| 23 | 21 | 20 | E |

NoLita | 250 Mulberry St. (Prince St.) | N/R/W to Prince St. | 212-431-4484 |
800-381-3338 | www.fluevog.com

If you want "funky, baby", as in "super-sturdy", "kickin' shoes" with a
"cool edge" that "can take anything that the mean streets of New York
throws at them", follow the "downtown crowd" to this Canadian outfit's way-"different" NoLita nook; it's "easy" for dudes and dolls alike
"to become addicted to Fluev's friendly attitude" and "consistently
creative" "leather-lined and well-designed" "trendy styles" ranging
from "clunky to diva"-esque to flat-out "unique" numbers.

☒ John Lobb ▣
| 29 | 28 | 27 | VE |

E 60s | 680 Madison Ave. (bet. 61st & 62nd Sts.) | 4/5/6/F/N/R/W to
59th St./Lexington Ave. | 212-888-9797 | www.johnlobb.com

"Simply the best, if you can afford them" agree well-shod aesthetes
who fall head over heels over the "amazing craftsmanship" of the
"beautiful" ready-to-wear collection of men's shoes, handmade in
England by this Hermès Group outfit and sold by an "extremely knowledgeable" sales staff at this Madison Avenue mecca; while that line,
ranging from classic oxfords and loafers to contemporary ankle boots,
is undoubtedly "excellent", the made-to-measure styles, crafted in
Paris, each pair involving 300 steps, reach unparalleled "perfection."

Johnston & Murphy
| 25 | 22 | 22 | E |

E 40s | 345 Madison Ave. (44th St.) | 4/5/6/7/S to 42nd St./Grand Central |
212-697-9375
E 50s | 520 Madison Ave. (54th St.) | E/V to 5th Ave./53rd St. | 212-527-2342
800-424-2854 | www.johnstonmurphy.com

"For the businessman in" you, turn to this Madison Avenue twosome
offering "real classic", "well-made", "excellent men's shoes that last"
and are "worth every penny"; if a few quip that a "Greenwich zip code
is a must in order to purchase" a pair, for most, these "straight-laced"
"styles can't be matched", and ditto for the apparel and leather goods.

John Varvatos
| 26 | - | 25 | VE |

SoHo | 122 Spring St. (bet. Greene & Mercer Sts.) | N/R/W to Prince St. |
212-965-0700 | 800-689-0151 | www.johnvarvatos.com

"How 21st-century man is intended to dress" declare the "designer-
shy" of the "understated" collection – a "well-edited balance of color
and cut with no gimmicks" – developed by this alum of Calvin Klein

and Ralph Lauren; in late 2005, the store relocated to SoHo, taking its "easygoing sportswear and business attire" and the "best staff anywhere" along, and plans are underway to open a new shop in 2008 in music club CBGB's former Bowery space with a merch mix that, natch, appeals to rockers.

Jo Malone
27 | 27 | 24 | E

E 70s | 946 Madison Ave. (bet. 74th & 75th Sts.) | 6 to 77th St. | 212-472-0074

Flatiron | Flatiron Bldg. | 949 Broadway (23rd St.) | N/R/W to 23rd St. | 212-673-2220 ●

866-566-2566 | www.jomalone.com

"Perfection in a bottle" is found at these "pricey but exquisite" scent shops in the Flatiron District and Upper East Side with 18 naturally inspired fragrances like Lime Basil and Mandarin that can be "mixed and matched", along with a line of "good facial products" and candles; "elegant packaging" adds visual impact to the "olfactory adventure."

Jonathan Adler
▽ 26 | 24 | 20 | E

E 80s | 1097 Madison Ave. (83rd St.) | 4/5/6 to 86th St. | 212-772-2410

NEW **G Village** | 37 Greenwich Ave. (Charles St.) | A/B/C/D/E/F/V to W. 4th St. | 212-488-2803

SoHo | 47 Greene St. (bet. Broome & Grand Sts.) | C/E to Spring St. | 212-941-8950

877-287-1910 | www.jonathanadler.com

Design devotees can now shop for "cult" pottery pop star Jonathan Adler's collection at his SoHo original, younger Madison Avenue locale and the new Village addition, all offering a "lively" "carnival of kitsch and color" for the "young at heart"; the "awesome" line of lacquered furniture is "as appealing" as his "pricey" "trademark" ceramics, textiles and pillows – what an "aesthetic delight."

☑ Joon
26 | 21 | 23 | E

E 40s | Grand Central | 42nd St. (Vanderbilt Ave.) | 4/5/6/7/S to 42nd St./Grand Central | 212-949-1700 ●

E 50s | Trump Tower | 725 Fifth Ave. (bet. 56th & 57th Sts.) | 4/5/6/F/N/R/W to 59th St./Lexington Ave. | 212-317-8466

E 60s | 795 Lexington Ave. (bet. 61st & 62nd Sts.) | 4/5/6/F/N/R/W to 59th St./Lexington Ave. | 212-935-1007 ☒

800-782-5666 | www.joonpens.com

Serious scribes jones for Joon – "a palace" for an "astonishing selection" of "quality" pens, from a simple Sheaffer to a mighty Montblanc, and "hard-to-find refills" presented by a "patient" staff.

Jos. A. Bank ●
18 | 19 | 20 | M

E 40s | 366 Madison Ave. (46th St.) | 4/5/6/7/S to 42nd St./Grand Central | 212-370-0600 | 800-285-2265 | www.josabank.com

Part of a nationwide chain, this bi-level building in the East 40s offers "inexpensive" but "decent" "work dress clothes" that are "perfectly ok if you wanna look like every other businessman" some sophisticates sneer; still, the average Jos. can bank on a "knowledgeable staff" presenting plenty of suits, separates, golfwear and accessories for all sizes that are seemingly "always on sale."

Joseph
23 | 20 | 21 | E

E 60s | 816 Madison Ave. (bet. 68th & 69th Sts.) | 6 to 68th St. | 212-570-0077

(continued)

Joseph

SoHo | 106 Greene St. (bet. Prince & Spring Sts.) | N/R/W to Prince St. | 212-343-7071

Shoppers of both sexes, start your search for "beautifully cut pants" and "great knits" at this earthy, wood-and-leather SoHo shop (but it's ladies' apparel only at the Madison Avenue branch); though a few fear "my American bottom will never fit" this British line's low-rise rockers, supporters say the other "practical", "professional" styles are quite "flattering."

Joseph Edwards

▽ 22 | 18 | 18 | E

E 40s | 50 E. 42nd St. (Madison Ave.) | 4/5/6/7/S to 42nd St./Grand Central | 212-730-0612

Since 1978, this Midtowner has been a staple for an "outstanding" array of "middle-tier watches", but what really charges fans' batteries is "more reasonable pricing than their competitors"; Swarovski crystals add sparkle to their fine jewelry collection; N.B. plans are underway to relocate to 452 Fifth Avenue in summer 2008.

NEW Journelle ◑

- | - | - | E

Flatiron | 3 E. 17th St. (5th Ave.) | F/L/V to 14th St./6th Ave. | 212-255-7800 | www.journellenyc.com

Large and lovely with gallerylike displays of fetching little nothings lining the entranceway and dark-wood floors, light walls and purple accents throughout, this Flatiron newcomer opens its arms to both moderate-minded and price-be-damned lingerie-lovers; choose from bras, panties, robes, slips and loungewear from names like Elle Macpherson Intimates, Le Mystère and Princess Tam-Tam, then slip into the boudoirlike dressing rooms with comfy seating and imagine your next move.

Joyce Leslie

8 | 9 | 7 | I

G Village | 20 University Pl. (8th St.) | N/R/W to 8th St. | 212-505-5419 ◑

Bay Ridge | 2147 86th St. (bet. Bay Pkwy. & 21st Ave.) | Brooklyn | D/M to Bay Pkwy. | 718-266-0100 ◑

Kings Plaza | Kings Plaza Shopping Ctr. | 5225 Kings Plaza (bet. Flatbush Ave. & Ave. U) | Brooklyn | B/Q to Newkirk Ave. | 718-252-6488 ◑

Mill Basin | Georgetown Shopping Ctr. | 2109 Ralph Ave. (Ave. K) | Brooklyn | 2/5 to Brooklyn College/Flatbush Ave. | 718-251-3219 ◑

Flushing | 37-28 Main St. (38th Ave.) | Queens | 7 to Main St. | 718-359-8419 ◑

Ridgewood | 56-48 Myrtle Ave. (bet. Catalpa & Hancock Sts.) | Queens | L/M to Myrtle/Wycoff Aves. | 718-381-3031

Staten Island | Staten Island Mall | 2655 Richmond Ave. (bet. Platinum Ave. & Richmond Hill Rd.) | 718-370-1705 ◑

www.joyceleslie.com

"A paradise for noncommittal fashionistas on a budget", this "teen hot spot" chain peddles "cheap" "party clothes" and accessories that may be "poor quality", but then they'll "only be trendy for a few weeks" anyway; young things willing to "plow through the mess" and endure "rude salespeople" are rewarded with "astoundingly low prices" and the occasional "interesting" "impulse item."

J. Press ⊠

23 | - | 22 | E

E 40s | 380 Madison Ave. (bet. 46th & 47th Sts.) | 4/5/6/7/S to 42nd St./ Grand Central | 212-687-7642 | 877-450-5845 | www.jpressonline.com

"Old school is the only school" at this East 40s "bastion" of "classic Ivy League style" and formalwear, which recently moved to Madison Avenue; double-majoring in "beautiful blazers" and "first-year ties" for undergrads as well as plentiful knits and "preppy accessories" for the "post-college set", it offers a look that's "stylish but not hip."

Jubilee ◐

∇ 16 | 17 | 21 | M

E 50s | 649 Lexington Ave. (bet. 54th & 55th Sts.) | E/V to Lexington Ave./ 53rd St. | 212-308-5505

E 70s | 1331 Third Ave. (76th St.) | 6 to 77th St. | 212-327-4555

G Village | 57 W. Eighth St. (bet. 5th & 6th Aves.) | A/B/C/D/E/F/V to W. 4th St. | 212-598-1050

W 70s | 2169 Broadway (bet. 76th & 77th Sts.) | 1 to 79th St. | 212-875-0095

Forest Hills | 71-54 Austin St. (bet. Continental & 71st Aves.) | Queens | E/F/G/R/V to Forest Hills/71st Ave. | 718-575-0650

When beset with the blues, buying new shoes can be like a shot of St. John's Wort, and the aptly named Jubilee, now flying its flag around town, provides a cheerful "fashion fix" with its "young" looks; latch onto "lots of flats", wedges and boots – "so many different" kicks and none "budget busters" – from the house label, Durango and Seychelles; N.B. the Forest Hills and East Side shops stock women's styles only.

Judith Ripka

25 | 24 | 22 | VE

E 60s | 673 Madison Ave. (61st St.) | 4/5/6/F/N/R/W to 59th St./ Lexington Ave. | 212-355-8300

E 60s | 777 Madison Ave. (bet. 66th & 67th Sts.) | 6 to 68th St. | 212-517-8200 ⊠

800-575-3935 | www.judithripka.com

Once inside either the recently renovated 673 Madison Avenue boutique or the grander jewelry salon slightly further uptown, "even the most self-controlled shopper will have difficulty leaving empty-handed, despite the prices"; whether it's a trademark loop-and-toggle bracelet, a glittering gold-and-colored crystal Lola ring or a sterling silver something from the secondary line, pros praise her "gorgeous", "wearable pieces" that emit "enough sparkle to elevate your outfit to *Vogue* standards."

Juicy Couture

20 | 21 | 17 | E

E 70s | 860 Madison Ave. (bet. 70th & 71st Sts.) | 6 to 68th St. | 212-327-2398

Flatiron | 103 Fifth Ave. (bet. 17th & 18th Sts.) | 4/5/6/L/N/Q/R/W to 14th St./Union Sq. | 212-727-8029 ◐

W Village | 368 Bleecker St. (Charles St.) | 1 to Christopher St./Sheridan Sq. | 646-336-8151 ◐

www.juicycouture.com

"What took them so long?" cry converts of this California brand that hit NYC with "a juicy explosion" of "brightly colored" Uptown and Downtown shops; you'll have "no arguments with your teens and pre-teens" – or "mothers who dress like teens" – as they wiggle into the signature "cute" velour sweatsuits and "sweet jeans"; but while the smitten swear "you're never too old or fat" for a fix, opponents of the "over-priced" garb opine "isn't their 15 minutes up yet?"; N.B. the Bleecker Street mother ship offers goodies for the whole family.

| | QUALITY | DISPLAY | SERVICE | COST |

Julian & Sara
`-` | `-` | `-` | **E**

SoHo | 103 Mercer St. (bet. Prince & Spring Sts.) | N/R/W to Prince St. | 212-226-1989 | www.julianandsara.com

This "great little neighborhood" nook, located in an old SoHo carriage house, is chock-full of "charm and character" – "unlike those huge chain stores"; shop here for your tot or teen, picking from a parade of "pretty" things from some of Europe's most exclusive labels, among them Kenzo, Lili Gaufrette and Miniman.

Jumelle ◑
`-` | `-` | `-` | **E**

Williamsburg | 148 Bedford Ave. (bet. N. 8th & 9th Sts.) | Brooklyn | L to Bedford Ave. | 718-388-9525 | www.shopjumelle.com

Browse by the light of the black chandelier, pondering the unstudied chic of emerging and established designers ranging from Alexander Wang and Isabelle Marant to Sonia by Sonia Rykiel and 3.1 Phillip Lim at this cool Williamsburg haunt, a style magnet for many a boho babe; complete the look with delicate jewelry from Camille Hempel, handbags from Rebecca Minkoff and funky boots from Devotte, all unusual enough to stop you in your tracks.

Just Bulbs
24 | `-` | 20 | **M**

E 60s | 220 E. 60th St. (bet. 2nd & 3rd Aves.) | 4/5/6/F/N/R/W to 59th St./Lexington Ave. | 212-888-5707

"From Christmas lights to fridge bulbs", this 2,500-sq.-ft. behemoth space, now screwed into an East 60s socket, stocks 26,000 specimens, making for a "great selection", including "odd things like fluorescent kitchen rings" or "wacky" items like party strings decorated with Sponge Bob, palm trees or flamingos.

NEW Just Cavalli
25 | 24 | 21 | **E**

E 50s | 665 Fifth Ave. (bet. 52nd & 53rd Sts.) | E/V to 5th Ave./53rd St. | 212-888-4333 | www.robertocavalli.it

Whether the decor at this enormous new, less-expensive East 50s spin-off of Roberto Cavalli's designer line is all marble and mirrors or merely smoke and mirrors depends on your party-going perspective: fans feel the "show-stopping" his-and-hers club wear and "butt-flattering" jeans are "funky", "young" and fun"; but cynics cite "glitzy to garish" "clothes that scream 'I'm dating a Russian mobster!'", and as for "the help, they're not helpful" "unless you look like you will be spending a million bucks."

Just Shades ⓈⓂ
▽ 24 | 16 | 22 | **M**

NoLita | 21 Spring St. (Elizabeth St.) | 6 to Spring St. | 212-966-2757 | www.justshadesny.com

Since 1966, this NoLita "specialty store" has provided ready-made and custom shades for those New Yorkers tired of bare-bulbing it; decorative finials and bespoke options allow you to fashion a one-off creation, which is a good thing opine opponents, who find the selection "limited."

Jutta Neumann ◑
`-` | `-` | `-` | **E**

LES | 158 Allen St. (bet. Rivington & Stanton Sts.) | F/V to Lower East Side/2nd Ave. | 212-982-7048 | www.juttaneumann-newyork.com

If you fancy your leather sandals, handbags, belts, wallets and wristbands "handmade" and "earthy", in an "overwhelming" variety of vivid and natural colors, look no further than this Lower East Side boutique;

trained by an old-school craftsman, the German-born namesake designer has her "own vibe going on", which translates to understated pieces that stand out in their simplicity.

J.W. Cooper ◑   - | - | - | VE

W 60s | The Shops at Columbus Circle, Time Warner Ctr. | 10 Columbus Circle, ground fl. (60th St. at B'way) | 1/A/B/C/D to 59th St./Columbus Circle | 212-823-9380 | www.jwcooper.com

Whether you want to "be a cowboy, New York–style" or just stand out in the crowd, dig deep into your trust fund then head to this "lovely" Time Warner Center shop specializing in luxury accessories; well-heeled habitués "find plenty of gifts" including exotic leather belts, sterling silver, 14-karat and 18-karat buckles, some inlaid with jade or turquoise, alligator wallets and some of the "best Western boots" around.

Kaas GlassWorks Ⓜ   - | - | - | E

W Village | 117 Perry St. (bet. Greenwich & Hudson Sts.) | 1 to Christopher St./Sheridan Sq. | 212-366-0322 | www.kaas.com

Husband-and-wife-team Chris and Carol Kaas combine the art of decoupage with their love of vintage prints and the result is a distinctive handmade collection brimming with glass trays, coasters, plates and paperweights decorated with playful parrots, ferns, flowers and the like and displayed in a sweet, shoebox-sized West Village shop whose antique fixtures and tin ceilings reflect the old-fashioned aesthetic.

Kaight ◑   - | - | - | E

LES | 83 Orchard St. (bet. Broome & Grand Sts.) | B/D to Grand St. | 212-680-5630 | www.kaightshop.com

Take a page from Kermit – it's easy bein' green nowadays, or rather, finding cool green garb – just hightail it to owner Kate McGregor's eco-conscious LES womenswear boutique; everything in the airy, spacious space is made from recycled and/or organic materials, from the dark brown bamboo floors to the stylish (no-crunch) clothing from Stewart + Brown to the Lulu Frost jewelry and Beyond Skin footwear.

K & G Fashion Superstore ◑   15 | 13 | 12 | I

E 40s | 122 E. 42nd St. (Lexington Ave.) | 4/5/6/7/S to 42nd St./ Grand Central | 212-682-9895

Harlem | 2321 Eighth Ave. (bet. 124th & 125th Sts.) | D to 125th St. | 212-222-2389

www.kgmens.com

"Bargain-hunters who don't want to hunt too hard" have a field day at this multifloor East 40s discounter (with a Harlem offshoot) where a "vast assortment" of "moderately priced work and casual clothes" ("from items that look like Kmart to low-end designer collections") for guys and gals awaits; but the "not very helpful" clerks dissuade foes, who also find the merchandise "unappealing" ("bring a sense of fashion – you won't find it here"); N.B. the Midtown shop reopened in November 2007 after a fire, possibly outdating the Display score.

Kangol Columbus Ave. ◑   23 | 21 | 19 | M

W 60s | 196 Columbus Ave. (bet. 68th & 69th Sts.) | 1 to 66th St./ Lincoln Ctr. | 212-724-1172

"Friendly and helpful", the staff "never makes you feel creepy for trying on 73 different hats" at this "fad-fabulous" West 60s accessories haunt; sure, you'll find the "ubiquitous cap", but this "candy store" also stocks a "wide range" of the British label's toppers from the "sporty" to the "trendy" in "every color and size", plus a clutch of "cute purses" too.

NEW Karen Millen — | - | - | E

SoHo | 112-114 Prince St. (bet. Greene & Wooster Sts.) | N/R/W to Prince St. | 212-334-8492 | www.karenmillen.com

Finally hitting the shores of SoHo, this U.K.-based chain offers a variety of clothing for birds who want to look hip (but not too-too) in high-waisted pants, shiny dresses, striped shirts and colorful sweaters (or 'jumpers', as the tags say); to go-with, there are high heels and leather goods galore in the glittery, glass-and-marble space, which once housed the Mimi Ferzt Gallery.

Karim Rashid Shop Ⓜ — | - | - | M

Chelsea | 137 W. 19th St. (bet. 6th & 7th Aves.) | 1 to 18th St. | 212-337-8078 | www.karimrashidshop.com

Colorful Chelsea lifestyle shop showcasing the omnipresent Cairo-born, Canadian-bred designer's take on gifts and everyday objects for the home from garbage cans to tabletop and dinnerware pieces, as well as limited-edition furniture and art; still, the less-impressed assert "innovation for the sake of innovation doesn't do a thing for me."

Kartell — | - | - | E

SoHo | 39 Greene St. (bet. Broome & Grand Sts.) | C/E to Spring St. | 212-966-6665 | 866-854-8823 | www.kartell.it

SoHo home-furnishings showroom featuring "great plastic" pieces that are relatively "cheap but stylish"; floor-to-ceiling displays include Philippe Starck's best-selling Bubble Club and Louis Ghost chairs, along with tables, stools, storage units and shelving.

Kate Spade 24 | 25 | 20 | E

NEW **Flatiron** | 135 Fifth Ave. (20th St.) | N/R/W to 23rd St. | 212-358-0420 ◗
SoHo | 454 Broome St. (Mercer St.) | N/R/W to Prince St. | 212-274-1991
www.katespade.com

"My love affair started with the bags, and now I love" the renovated, super-"spacious" SoHo shop too, with its "polite" staff and "perfect presentation" of "whimsical" "adorable" accessories; "it seems impossible to be hip, country-club-ish, quirky and classic at the same time" but most maintain "Kate does it", albeit at "mind-boggling prices"; N.B. the new Flatiron branch opened post-Survey.

ⓩ Kate's Paperie 27 | 26 | 20 | E

E 70s | 1282 Third Ave. (bet. 73rd & 74th Sts.) | 6 to 77th St. | 212-396-3670
G Village | 8 W. 13th St. (bet. 5th & 6th Aves.) | F/L/V to 14th St./6th Ave. | 212-633-0570 ◗
SoHo | 72 Spring St. (bet. Crosby & Lafayette Sts.) | 6 to Spring St. | 212-941-9816 ◗
W 50s | 140 W. 57th St. (bet. 6th & 7th Aves.) | N/Q/R/W to 57th St. | 212-459-0700 ◗
888-941-9169 | www.katespaperie.com

These "arty" "must-stops" for the "serious writer and inviter" feature the "most beautiful selection of paper goods" from stationery, "thoughtful cards", scrapbooks and "buttery leather journals" to hundreds of "lush" handmade decorative papers, "exquisite ribbons" and a custom gift-wrapping service; it's "pricey", but proponents proclaim "the quality and quantity" of "unique merchandise" are "worth it."

Katz in the Cradle

- | - | - | M

Midwood | 2920 Ave. L (bet. Nostrand Ave. & 29th St.) | Brooklyn | 2/5 to Brooklyn College/Flatbush Ave. | 718-258-1990

Its "small" size can't tarnish the appeal of this Midwood mainstay where you can furnish your child's bedroom under the guiding hand of the store's "extremely knowledgeable and polite sales staff"; for those on the prowl for an "excellent deal" on brand-name wooden cribs, beds, dressers, armoires, mattresses and more, this place is the 'Katz' meow.

Kavanagh's Ⓢ Ⓜ

- | - | - | VE

E 40s | 146 E. 49th St. (bet. Lexington & 3rd Aves.) | 6 to 51st St. | 212-702-0152

The "highest-quality designer stuff" – think Chanel suits and Valentino dresses – from seasons past is carried by this elegant East 40s consignment shop, decorated with antiques and artwork (and that's not counting the Hermès bags lining the walls); those used to thrift-shop tags note "this is not for bargains, but you know what you're getting" – and it's still well below the retail prices at, say, Bergdorf Goodman, where owner Mary Kavanagh worked as director of personal shopping.

KB Toys ⬤

16 | 10 | 9 | I-

Garment District | Manhattan Mall | 901 Sixth Ave. (bet. 32nd & 33rd Sts.) | B/D/F/N/Q/R/V/W to 34th St./Herald Sq. | 212-629-5386
Bay Ridge | 424 86th St. (bet. 4th & 5th Aves.) | Brooklyn | R to 86th St. | 718-745-7994
Flushing | 136-45 Roosevelt Ave. (bet. Main & Union Sts.) | Queens | 7 to Main St. | 718-460-6092
Jackson Heights | 37-48 82nd St. (bet. Roosevelt & 37th Aves.) | Queens | 7 to 82nd St./Jackson Hts. | 718-803-3702
Ridgewood | 56-29 Myrtle Ave. (Catalpa Ave.) | Queens | L/M to Myrtle/Wycoff Aves. | 718-418-9388
Staten Island | Staten Island Mall | 2655 Richmond Ave. (bet. Platinum Ave. & Richmond Hill Rd.) | 718-698-8686
877-552-8697 | www.kbtoys.com

They're real "madhouses" but shoppers with the stamina to "sift through the mess" and deal with "cramped" conditions at these "budget" chain links score "terrific deals" on the "fad toys" "every kid wants" and a few "classics" too; "if you want ambiance, go to FAO Schwarz" but "if all you need is a cheap" game "for a birthday present, this is where to find it."

KCDC Skateshop ⬤

22 | 20 | 18 | M

Williamsburg | 90 N. 11th St. (Wythe Ave.) | Brooklyn | L to Bedford Ave. | 718-387-9006 | www.kcdcskateshop.com

The lode star of the skateboarding scene, this Williamsburg haunt strives to create a sense of community, luring young and old, gals and guys, novices and diehards, with its art gallery, on-site mini ramp and hands-on help from experienced skater-owner Amy Gunther and her equally skilled staff; there's lots of "good stuff" on hand, including T-shirts from local designers, "awesome", crazy colorful boards, racks of sneakers and capping it off, a truckload of hats.

| | QUALITY | DISPLAY | SERVICE | COST |

KD Dance & Sport ◗
| | - | - | - | M |

NoHo | 339 Lafayette St. (Bleecker St.) | 6 to Bleecker St. | 212-533-1037 | www.kddance.com

Performers and would-bes striving for a limelight-worthy look head to this tranquil NoHo corner nook for high-style, body-conscious dance and sports clothing ranging from sexy knit wrap tops, shrugs and stretchy leotards in a cache of colors just right for stage- or streetwear.

Kenjo ⊠
| | 25 | 22 | 21 | E |

Financial District | 40 Wall St. (Broad St.) | 2/3 to Wall St. | 212-402-7000
W 50s | 40 W. 57th St. (bet. 5th & 6th Aves.) | N/Q/R/W to 57th St. | 212-333-7220
www.kenjo.net

"One of the most helpful and engaging watch stores in the city", this 57th Street staple stocks "hard-to-find" items like a "full line of Fortis" styles, as well as popular tickers like Omega and Breitling; its "post-purchase care is excellent", as the "knowledgeable" staff includes a watchmaker; N.B. the Wall Street offshoot is younger and smaller.

Kenneth Cole New York ◗
| | 21 | 21 | 20 | M |

E 40s | 107 E. 42nd St. (bet. Lexington & Park Aves.) | 4/5/6/7/S to 42nd St./Grand Central | 212-949-8079
E 40s | Rockefeller Ctr. | 610 Fifth Ave. (49th St.) | B/D/F/V to 47-50th Sts./Rockefeller Ctr. | 212-373-5800
E 50s | 130 E. 57th St. (Lexington Ave.) | 4/5/6/F/N/R/W to 59th St./Lexington Ave. | 212-688-1670
Flatiron | 95 Fifth Ave. (17th St.) | 4/5/6/L/N/Q/R/W to 14th St./Union Sq. | 212-675-2550
SoHo | 597 Broadway (Houston St.) | B/D/F/V to B'way/Lafayette St. | 212-965-0283
W 70s | 353 Columbus Ave. (77th St.) | B/C to 81st St. | 212-873-2061
800-536-2653 | www.kennethcole.com

"Feel like a New Yorker" from head to toe at this "easy-to-navigate" "lifestyle" chain specializing in "great hip men's and women's basics with flair", "handbags that last an eternity" and, of course, "unbeliev-ably feet-friendly" footwear for "young, sophisticated professionals", all from the designer who's as recognized for his "infamous" "social-conscience" ads; if quibblers snap "he still makes much better shoes than he does clothing", there's no controversy when it comes to the "courteous", "good-looking" staff.

Key
| | - | - | - | E |

SoHo | 41 Grand St. (bet. Thompson St. & W. B'way) | C/E to Spring St. | 212-334-5707 | www.shopkeynyc.com

Head off SoHo's main drag and hit this spacious skylit shop that's trend-central for "J Brand jeans, vintage bags, slouchy cashmere sweaters" and pieces from under-the-radar designers like Manoush; the "personnel are personable", and your guy can chill comfortably on the "cute" canvas couches or out on the back patio while you're looking.

☒ Kidding Around
| | 26 | 24 | 22 | M |

Flatiron | 60 W. 15th St. (bet. 5th & 6th Aves.) | F/L/V to 14th St./6th Ave. | 212-645-6337 | www.kiddingaround.us

For arguably "the best selection of traditional" playthings "this side of the North Pole", look no further than this Flatiron favorite, which proffers an "unusual mix of merchandise you don't see elsewhere", with an emphasis on "smart" toys like chemistry sets and educational games and a "great dress-up section"; the "friendly" staff can even assemble party favor bags, pulling from their stash of "adorable" trinkets.

kid o.
22 | 23 | 18 | E

G Village | 123 W. 10th St. (Greenwich Ave.) | F/L/V to 14th St./6th Ave. | 212-366-5436 | www.kidonyc.com

Design diehards descend on this "wonderful", "friendly" Greenwich Village children's shop to drool over the über-contemporary eye candy, including kid-size Eames and Bertoia chairs, Oeuf cribs, arty mobiles and wall hangings, Montessori "high-quality educational" toys and other "creative", "one-of-a-kind" gifts that "will wow moms and please kids"; no kidding - the "stylish selection" is "enough to keep you returning" again and again.

Kid Robot ⦿
- | - | - | E

SoHo | 126 Prince St. (bet. Greene & Wooster Sts.) | N/R/W to Prince St. | 212-966-6688 | 877-762-6543 | www.kidrobot.com

More like a museum than a toy store, this "cool, little" SoHo shop "for the Japanese toy enthusiast" offers a cache of limited-edition collectibles; two-inch-tall treasures like action figures of all the current covetable Asian characters share space with old-school classics and apparel.

Kids Rx ⊠
- | - | - | M

W Village | 523 Hudson St. (W. 10th St.) | 1 to Christopher St./Sheridan Sq. | 212-741-7111 | www.kidsrx.com

If your kid seems to be coming down with something, bundle him up and trundle him into this West Village pharmacy catering to children with such healthcare, bath and body products as California Baby calming massage oil; while you're consulting with the druggist, your little one is being distracted by a toy train that chugs around the store and a Thomas the Tank table.

Kidville Boutique
22 | 19 | 18 | E

E 80s | 163 E. 84th St. (bet. Lexington & 3rd Aves.) | 4/5/6 to 86th St. | 212-772-8435

NEW **TriBeCa** | 200 Church St. (Duane St.) | 1/2/3 to Chambers St. | 212-362-3923

W 80s | 466 Columbus Ave. (82nd St.) | B/C to 81st St. | 212-362-7792 www.kidvilleny.com

What a "nice addition to the kiddie parade" muse parents who "can't stop shopping for adorable clothes" at this retail arm of this pre-school franchise in the East and West 80s and now TriBeCa too; if a few find the offerings "limited" and "overpriced", most retort there are "gems within the mix", including "wonderful" togs from "trendy" labels like Shoshanna, Kule, Splendid and Tea Collection.

⊿ Kiehl's ⦿
27 | 23 | 25 | M

E Village | 109 Third Ave. (13th St.) | 4/5/6/L/N/Q/R/W to 14th St./ Union Sq. | 212-677-3171

W 60s | 154 Columbus Ave. (bet. 66th & 67th Sts.) | 1 to 66th St./ Lincoln Ctr. | 212-799-3438
800-543-4571 | www.kiehls.com

"As New York as cheesecake", this "classic" toiletries duo Downtown and Uptown is a "favorite" of "moms, models and more"; it's "a terrific place" that "makes you feel as if you're in an old-fashioned drug store" with a "beyond helpful" staff that talks you through "no-frills" "quality products that work" like Protein Chamomile Shampoo and "the best lip balm this side of the Nile"; prices are "affordable" and there's a "liberal sample policy", leading loyalists to lament "I would Kiehl myself without Kiehl's!"

QUALITY | DISPLAY | SERVICE | COST

Kieselstein-Cord

▽ 28 | - | 23 | VE

E 80s | 1058 Madison Ave. (80th St.) | 6 to 77th St. | 212-744-1041 | www.kieselstein-cord.com

Anyone who can attract a clientele as diverse as Oprah and Armani must be offering "some of the most original jewelry and accessories" around, and this designer, who moved from Downtown to Uptown, does; his "gorgeous works of art" (all signed, dated and copyrighted) include silver belt buckles, ornate animal jewelry like signature alligators in matte-finish green-gold, as well as trophy handbags and shades; "absolutely stunning" applies to the products and the prices.

Kiki de Montparnasse

25 | 26 | 22 | VE

SoHo | 79 Greene St. (bet. Broome & Spring Sts.) | N/R/W to Prince St. | 212-965-8150 | 888-965-5454 | www.kikidm.com

"Get your kink on" at this "naughty" but "tasteful" SoHo salon named after Man Ray's muse and mistress where black-and-white erotic photographs line the walls and "gorgeous" "high-end European lingerie" dominates the display racks; "saucy" shoppers seek out the "classy", "very expensive" (ahem) "adult" products displayed like museum pieces in glass cases, while shyer sorts peruse the selection of luxurious house brand body products and candles.

Kim's Mediapolis ●

24 | 16 | 14 | M

W 100s | 2906 Broadway (bet. 113th & 114th Sts.) | 1 to 110th St. | 212-864-5321

Kim's Video ●

W Village | 89 Christopher St. (Bleecker St.) | 1 to Christopher St./Sheridan Sq. | 212-242-4363

Mondo Kim's ●

E Village | 6 St. Marks Pl. (3rd Ave.) | 6 to Astor Pl. | 212-505-0311 www.kimsvideo.com

The "video stores to end all video stores", this triumvirate features a film collection that seemingly spans "every hard-to-find", "rare or foreign" title; though the West Village branch solely supplies DVDs, the East Village and Uptown outposts also offer videocassettes, LPs, books and a "fabulous CD selection" that'll "please a wide variety of musical palates", all at "college-student" prices – if only the "snotty", "pretentious" staffers weren't "so damn mean."

Kiosk 🚫Ⓜ

19 | 19 | 18 | M

SoHo | 95 Spring St. (bet. B'way & Mercer St.) | N/R to Prince St. | 212-226-8601 | www.kioskkiosk.com

"Quirky but relevant", this "charming" "playland" tucked away in SoHo is stocked with "exotic versions of everyday things from around the world"; there's "so much interesting stuff" – it's "heaven" for "great gifts you can't find anywhere else" (maybe for your "long-forgotten sibling"); you can't help but be "totally immersed" in "inexpensive items" like Finnish dart sets and tar shampoo, Japanese carpenter knives, Swedish garden tools, German xylophones and Mexican bobby pins, most done up in "cute" packaging.

Kipepeo

- | - | - | M

NoLita | 250 Elizabeth St. (bet. Houston & Prince Sts.) | N/R/W to Prince St. | 212-219-7555 | www.kipepeo74.com

More is more at this pink-and-cream NoLita accessories haven bursting with Lucite bangles, earrings and vintage-y lockets (like the one worn by Lindsay Lohan); once you have jewelry in the bag, hunt down affordable arm candy like the standout Nairobi tote.

Kirna Zabête

27 | 26 | 15 | VE

SoHo | 96 Greene St. (bet. Prince & Spring Sts.) | N/R/W to Prince St. | 212-941-9656 | www.kirnazabete.com

Stylesetters hungering for "lovely, trendy" clothing "priced in the outer limits" need look no further than SoHo's candy-colored, Nick Dine-designed double-decker destination that "pioneered the boutique as interior-design-mecca" concept; with-it owners Beth Buccini and Sarah Easley "sway" tastemakers with an "amazing", "well-edited selection" of "high-end" European and American designers including Chloé, Proenza Schouler and Rick Owens, leading sybarites to sigh "wish my closet looked like this"; if a few quibble that the staff doesn't "go out of its way" to help, others applaud the "no-pressure" service.

Kiton ⊠

- | - | - | VE

E 50s | 4 E. 54th St. (bet. 5th & Madison Aves.) | E/V to 5th Ave./53rd St. | 212-813-0272 | www.kiton.it

Head to this East 50s brownstone for Neapolitan made-to-measure menswear, finely tailored women's clothes and handmade shoes; the superb cuts and meticulous details of these "greatest-ever" garments, plus a staff that's "better" than any department store's, underscore the couture sensibility and pricing, but some wonder "who can afford this?"

Kiwi

22 | 22 | 23 | E

Park Slope | 119 Seventh Ave. (bet. Carroll & President Sts.) | Brooklyn | B/Q to 7th Ave. | 718-622-5551 | www.kiwidesignco.com

So "sweet" exclaim enthusiasts of this spacious Park Slope boutique staffed with "salespeople who know their stuff" and filled with "distinctive", "beautiful" womenswear; rounding out the selection of Autumn Cashmere sweaters, funky Sanctuary pants, lingerie and jewelry, there's a "custom-couture" capsule collection of "unique items" from co-owner/designer Christine Alcalay, who draws her inspiration from Hollywood style icons like Audrey Hepburn.

Kleinfeld ⓜ

25 | 19 | 20 | E

Chelsea | 110 W. 20th St. (bet. 6th & 7th Aves.) | C/E to 23rd St. | 212-352-2180 | www.kleinfeldbridal.com

"The cadillac of bridal salons" is "finally in Manhattan!" – "thanks for crossing the river" gush those who are gleeful over the Brooklyn "icon's" "awesome" by-appointment-only Chelsea digs; "grandmothers, mothers, daughters – what a tradition" – "there's a reason they've been in business" since 1941: the selection of "sensational" gowns is "huge", and the "patient staff" "takes care of every need" – "I thought it would be too posh but it was everything you could ask for and more"; still, the put-off pout that the salespeople "push too hard."

	QUALITY	DISPLAY	SERVICE	COST

Kmart ●

| | 12 | 10 | 7 | I |

Garment District | 250 W. 34th St. (bet. 7th & 8th Aves.) | 1/2/3/A/ C/E to 34th St./Penn Station | 212-760-1188
G Village | 770 Broadway (Astor Pl.) | 6 to Astor Pl. | 212-673-1540
Bronx | 1998 Bruckner Blvd. (bet. Pugsley Ave. & White Plains Rd.) | 6 to Parkchester | 718-430-9439
Bronx | 300 Baychester Ave. (bet. Bartow Ave. & Hutchinson River Pkwy.) | 6 to Pelham Bay Park | 718-671-5377
Middle Village | 66-26 Metropolitan Ave. (bet. Audley St. & Grosvenor Rd.) | Queens | M to Middle Vill./Metropolitan Ave. | 718-821-2412
Staten Island | 2660 Hylan Blvd. (Ebbitts St.) | 718-351-8500
Staten Island | 2875 Richmond Ave. (Yukon Ave.) | 718-698-0900
866-562-7844 | www.kmart.com

"If you can find it – a big if – you can get good value at this chain of barnlike" megastores that carry "all the basic things" – "and Martha Stewart, of course" – for the home and person; supporters single out the "wide selection" of "going-off-to-college" cookware, "cheap bed and bath needs" and "simple" watches; even so, given the "glacial-in-speed service", "junky" looks and the fact they're often "out of what you came for", most say they're pretty "sad to shop in."

Knit-A-Way of Brooklyn

| | - | - | - | M |

Boerum Hill | 398 Atlantic Ave. (bet. Bond & Hoyt Sts.) | Brooklyn | A/ C/G to Hoyt/Schermerhorn Sts. | 718-797-3305 | www.knitaway.com
This bi-level Boerum Hill boutique offers "hours of yarn browsing" thanks to wares that range from budget brands (Brown Sheep) to loftier labels (Karabella, Tahki); frequent classes, held in the basement, cover basic technique as well as specialized skills, while regular onsite knitting and crocheting circles give learners the chance to click with a likeminded clique.

Knit New York ●

| | 25 | 23 | 20 | E |

E Village | 307 E. 14th St. (2nd Ave.) | L to 1st Ave. | 212-387-0707 | www.knitnewyork.com
At this "super-hip" yet "comfortable" 14th Street "wonderland for knitters", the "unusual" range of "gorgeous yarns" and "excellent pattern collection" are supplemented by a "wonderful cafe" where stitchers can "have a coffee while browsing the books" or "chatting about future projects"; the "good product" and lessons can be "expensive", however, and service seems somewhat "inconsistent" – fans find staffers "easy-going" and "knowledgeable" but foes fret "prepare to be ignored."

Knitting 321 ⊠ Ⓜ

| | - | - | - | E |

E 70s | 321 E. 75th St. (bet. 1st & 2nd Aves.) | 6 to 77th St. | 212-772-2020 | www.knitting321.com
Knit-wits head to this "small" basement-level shop in the East 70s for trendy natural-fiber yarns from around the world; the few who've found this nook say service is "good", but prices can be "crazy."

Knoll ⊠

| | - | - | - | VE |

Chelsea | 76 Ninth Ave., 11th fl. (bet. 15th & 16th Sts.) | A/C/E/L to 14th St./8th Ave. | 212-343-4000 | www.knoll.com
"Modern equals Knoll" assert aesthetes about this furniture pioneer that holds the license for midcentury masters such as Mies; its appointments-preferred Chelsea showroom (formerly open to the

trade only) showcases iconic residential and office seating and tables that are the "real deal"; N.B. also closed Saturdays.

Kohl's ◑
- | - | - | M

Bensonhurst | Caesar's Bay Shopping Ctr. | 8973 Bay Pkwy. (Shore Pkwy.) | Brooklyn | D/M to Bay Pkwy. | 718-266-6357
Fresh Meadows | 6111 188th St. (Long Island Expwy.) | Queens | 718-454-5770
Staten Island | Staten Island North | 2239 Forrest Ave. (Mersereau Ave.) | 718-447-7101
www.kohls.com

Price-conscious shoppers head to these Bensonhurst, Fresh Meadows and Staten Island links of the ever-expanding mass-merchant to snap up Simply Vera womenswear, the much vaunted lower-priced collection from Vera Wang, along with the designer's bed and bath lines; name-brand goods abound, from Dockers for the dudes and Fisher-Price toys for tots to cooking essentials from Cuisinart and Farberware.

Koh's Kids
- | - | - | E

TriBeCa | 311 Greenwich St. (bet. Chambers & Reade Sts.) | 1/2/3 to Chambers St. | 212-791-6915

Despite its shoebox size, this TriBeCa treasure manages to stuff a surprisingly vast selection of children's clothing and accessories within its walls – you'll love sampling all of the European fashion eye candy here; for something truly one-of-a-kind, check out the store's own original collection of colorful, handknit sweaters, dresses and hats.

NEW Korres
- | - | - | M

SoHo | 110 Wooster St. (bet. Prince & Spring Sts.) | N/R/W to Prince St. | 212-219-0683 | www.korres.com

This airy, eye-catching SoHo newcomer showcases the cult Greek toiletries brand that began life in an Athens apothecary and still relies on all-natural ingredients for its impact; the extensive, reasonably priced line ranges from hair, face and skin products like guava body butter and wild rose moisturizer to homeopathic herbal remedies; gullible gals and guys who've been burned once too often with bogus beauty claims will bless the kits that come with trial sizes; N.B. a Brooklyn Heights branch is slated to open early 2008.

Kraft Hardware ⌧
∇ 26 | 23 | 23 | E

E 60s | 315 E. 62nd St. (bet. 1st & 2nd Aves.) | 4/5/6/F/N/R/W to 59th St./Lexington Ave. | 212-838-2214 | www.kraft-hardware.com

For 70 years, this "wonderful" two-story UES has been known for a "great selection" of hardware, plumbing fixtures, faucets and cast-iron tubs ranging in price "from moderate to expensive"; enthusiasts also appreciate the "great" attentive staff; N.B. also closed Saturdays.

Kreiss Collection ⌧
∇ 26 | 26 | 21 | VE

E 50s | 215 E. 58th St. (bet. 2nd & 3rd Aves.) | 4/5/6/F/N/R/W to 59th St./Lexington Ave. | 212-593-2005 | www.kreiss.com

Custom-made "California modern" sectional couches, chairs and tables in neutral tones and all-natural fibers are showcased in the company's East 50s store alongside accessories like bed linens and lamps; the big, "beautiful" pieces are "perfect for your place in the Hamptons", and "worth the large price tags."

| | QUALITY | DISPLAY | SERVICE | COST |

Kremer Pigments 🗒

∇ 29 | - | 24 | E

Chelsea | 247 W. 29th St. (bet. 7th & 8th Aves.) | 1 to 28th St. |
212-219-2394 | 800-995-5501 | www.kremer-pigmente.com

For the "finest selection of ground pigments, resins and varnishes available" make tracks to this painters' outpost, relocated to Chelsea, which still evokes a "medieval apothecary", with shelves showcasing jars of "superb" raw materials for "real artists" and restorers; a "patient" staff helps you find any hue "imaginable" at this sole American satellite of a Germany-based company, though take note: "it's not for novices."

Krizia 🗒

- | - | - | E

E 60s | 769 Madison Ave. (66th St.) | 6 to 68th St. | 212-879-1211 |
www.krizia.it

Follow your animal instincts to Mariuccia Mandelli's Madison Avenue boutique where her label's iconic tiger adorns "young, sexy designs" such as fluttery chiffon dresses, trendy-with-a-twist suits and signature, you'll-have-'em-"forever" knits; your Tarzan can get into the swing of things too, as the airy limestone premises also houses cashmere coats, silk ties and a sensual scent for him.

🌣 Krup's Kitchen & Bath, Ltd. 🗒

26 | 14 | 19 | E

Flatiron | 11 W. 18th St. (bet. 5th & 6th Aves.) | 1 to 18th St. |
212-243-5787 | www.krupskitchenandbath.com

This long-standing, family-owned Flatiron store features "quality" kitchen appliances from the likes of Bosch and Sub-Zero and custom-made cabinets and countertops as well as bathroom and plumbing fixtures; the "overcrowded" space "needs renovation", but "good prices" and a "helpful" staff help straighten things out.

Ksubi ◑

22 | 22 | 18 | E

(fka Tsubi)

NoLita | 219C Mulberry St. (bet. Prince & Spring Sts.) | 6 to Spring St. |
212-334-4690 | www.ksubi.com

The 'T' may have morphed into a 'K' but true-blue fashionistas "who love this brand" created by edgy Aussie surfers remain "very loyal", skipping down to this NoLita shop for its "hip", limited-edition, signature "skinny jeans"; but denim isn't the only way to get a "taste of the Down Under in NYC" – acolytes also score "cool" retro sunglasses (favored by celebs like Ashley Olsen) along with "wonderful" tees and dresses.

Kuhlman Company ◑

20 | 18 | 20 | M

G Village | 484 Sixth Ave. (bet. 12th & 13th Sts.) | F/L/V to 14th St./
6th Ave. | 212-414-4678 | www.kuhlmancompany.com

Many a Manhattanite is "impressed" by this Minneapolis-based chain with a Greenwich Village offshoot, as it offers suits and separates that are "colorful and flashy, but still office-wearable" for "guys and girls alike"; maybe the merchandise is "not of the best quality", but you can't beat" their "won't-break-the-bank" prices.

La Boutique Resale

∇ 23 | 18 | 20 | M

E 60s | 803 Lexington Ave., 2nd fl. (62nd St.) | 4/5/6/F/N/R/W to
59th St./Lexington Ave. | 212-588-8858
E 70s | 1045 Madison Ave., 2nd fl. (bet. 79th & 80th Sts.) | 6 to 77th St. |
212-517-8099

(continued)

(continued)

La Boutique Resale

W 70s | 160 W. 72nd St., 2nd fl. (bet. B'way & Columbus Ave.) | 1/2/
3 to 72nd St. | 212-787-3098
www.laboutiqueresale.com

"If you hit it right" you'll "find hidden treasures" at this trio – perhaps
a piece of Prada, or a St. John suit, or a chemise among the Chanels;
prices are "reasonable", given the "high-quality goods", but what really makes it "one of the best of its kind" is its "friendly staff";
P.S. there's "interesting vintage" stock at the Madison Avenue mother
ship, and the Upper West Side branch now carries menswear.

La Brea ◗　　　　　　　　　　　18 | 18 | 13 | M

E 60s | 1321 Second Ave. (bet. 69th & 70th Sts.) | 6 to 68th St. |
212-879-4065
E 80s | 1575 Second Ave. (bet. 81st & 82nd Sts.) | 6 to 77th St. | 212-772-2640
W 70s | Beacon Hotel | 2130 Broadway (bet. 74th & 75th Sts.) | 1/2/
3 to 72nd St. | 212-873-7850
www.labrea.com

These "essential resources" for "witty, funny cards" (think "upscale
Hallmark") also house "an eclectic assortment" of gifts and gag items
from T-shirts to Freud bobbleheads; the "wonderful variety" of products makes browsing "always interesting"; however, some shrug off
the "cute stuff" as "too cute for me."

La Cafetière ◗Ⓜ　　　　　　　　－ | － | － | M

Chelsea | 160 Ninth Ave. (20th St.) | C/E to 23rd St. | 646-486-0667 |
866-486-0667 | www.la-cafetiere.com

"Charming" Chelsea shop that sells "beautiful housewares and linens"
in a "setting that makes you feel like you've traveled abroad" to the
South of France; "unusual items" include peg-and-groove constructed
furniture in over 20 patinas, hand-blown glassware and mohair throws
that will make you and your *maison* smile.

Lacoste　　　　　　　　　　　24 | 22 | 19 | E

E 40s | 608 Fifth Ave. (49th St.) | E/V to 5th Ave./53rd St. | 212-459-2300 ◗
E 50s | 575 Madison Ave. (bet. 56th & 57th Sts.) | 4/5/6/F/N/R/W to
59th St./Lexington Ave. | 212-750-8115
SoHo | 134 Prince St. (bet. W. B'way & Wooster St.) | N/R/W to Prince St. |
212-226-5019
800-452-2678 | www.lacoste.com

"Anyone can pull off a simple polo", but it helps if it has a "cute little
crocodile" as a logo and "fits great", like this "classic" brand's versions, which come "in every color and permutation"; though the
"shirts are still its staple", the "styles are updated" and accessorized
with leather bags, sporty watches and sneakers; but you might need a
serve like supporter/tennis champ Andy Roddick's to "get help" in the
often "overcrowded stores."

LaCrasia Gloves ⌧　　　　　　　25 | － | 18 | M

Chelsea | 1181 Broadway, 8th fl. (28th St.) | N/R/W to 28th St. |
212-803-1600 | www.lacrasia.com

"Your fingers can find fashionable coverage all year round" at this
"great focused resource" that moved to this new address in Chelsea
that offers every "glove you can imagine" from "arm-length" numbers

"for that black-tie outfit" to "racy fine leather driving" styles; hand mavens vow "this place is a trip", even if your digits don't need protection; N.B. the Grand Central shop of the same name carries their merchandise but is separately owned.

LaDuca Shoes

-	-	-	E

Garment District | 534 Ninth Ave. (bet. 39th & 40th Sts.) | A/C/E to 42nd St./Port Authority | 212-268-6751 | www.laducashoes.com

Broadway hoofers and studio savants consider choreographer Phil LaDuca's "beautiful", flexible Italian-made character shoes displayed in his vintagey-looking Garment District stomping ground the "most coveted dance" numbers "in the city"; nothing "makes you look like a star" and "tells people you are serious" about your floor moves like these custom-crafted or off-the-shelf designs made for jazz, tap or can-can classes and performances.

Lady Foot Locker ⏺

22	19	17	M

Garment District | 120 W. 34th St. (B'way) | B/D/F/N/Q/R/V/W to 34th St./Herald Sq. | 212-629-4626

SoHo | 523 Broadway (Spring St.) | 6 to Spring St. | 212-965-0493

Kings Plaza | Kings Plaza Shopping Ctr. | 5364 Kings Plaza (bet. Flatbush Ave. & Ave. U) | Brooklyn | B/Q to Newkirk Ave. | 718-253-9631

Sunset Park | 5314 Fifth Ave. (bet. 53rd & 54th Sts.) | Brooklyn | R to 53rd St. | 718-439-4669

Elmhurst | Queens Ctr. | 90-15 Queens Blvd. (bet. 57th & 59th Aves.) | Queens | G/R/V to Woodhaven Blvd. | 718-760-3271

Staten Island | Staten Island Mall | 2655 Richmond Ave. (bet. Platinum Ave. & Richmond Hill Rd.) | 718-370-0505

800-991-6815 | www.ladyfootlocker.com

There's "always something new on the shelves" assert sneaker fans who also find this chain is "getting better with activewear"; the "good selection and prices make for a pleasant shopping experience", and the "salespeople are willing and able to get you the right size"; still, it doesn't rock everyone's locker – a handful wail it "seems to fall short, from its lack of style diversity to its bland presentations."

Laila Rowe ⏺

14	18	17	I

E 40s | 8 E. 42nd St. (5th Ave.) | 7/B/D/F/V to 42nd St./Bryant Park | 212-949-2276 | www.lailarowe.com

Additional locations throughout the NY area

If you've "outgrown plastic jewelry" but don't want to "blow a month's rent", head to this "well-laid-out" "cheap thrill" of a local chain for "bling-bling without the ka-ching"; be it "colorful baubles" or "bohemian trinkets", "you'll find just the thing for pennies and look like you've spent lots more"; the "rapidly changing stock" gives you reasons to visit anew and "makes it hard to leave empty-handed."

Laina Jane

-	-	-	E

G Village | 45 Christopher St. (bet. 7th Ave. & Waverly Pl.) | 1 to Christopher St./Sheridan Sq. | 212-807-8077 ⏺

W 80s | 416 Amsterdam Ave. (80th St.) | 1 to 79th St. | 212-875-9168

www.lainajane.com

"I always find something" at these "small" "attitude-free" shops in the Village and on the Upper West Side – "it's my favorite place to buy" "fine lingerie" laud loyalists who take a shine to the stash of "sweet nothings" fashioned from silk and lace or delicate cotton; "from engagement and bridal shower gifts" to unmentionables "for myself" from brands such as Chantelle and Cosabella to "hard-to-find" labels, "everything they carry is sophisticated and pretty."

Lalaounis ⊠   ▽ 29 | 24 | 23 | VE

E 60s | 739 Madison Ave. (bet. 64th & 65th Sts.) | 6 to 68th St. | 212-439-9400 | www.lalaounis.com

Ancient civilizations are the inspiration for this fourth-generation Greek jeweler in a cozy, burgundy-and-beige bijouterie in the East 60s; "magnificent", "very original" and very expensive designs of hand-hammered 18- and 22-karat gold incorporate classical techniques such as granulation, filigree and repoussé.

Z Lalique ⊠   29 | 26 | 25 | VE

E 60s | 712 Madison Ave. (bet. 63rd & 64th Sts.) | 6 to 68th St. | 212-355-6550 | 800-214-2738 | www.lalique.com

"Madison Avenue is the right place" to house this "elegant" "museum" of "beautiful", "incomparable quality" opalescent French "crystal that will stand the test of time" and "should be handed down from generation to generation", whether it's vases, barware, perfume bottles or jewelry; while "nothing here is cheap", respondents remind "you're buying art."

NEW Lambertson Truex ⊠   - | - | - | VE

E 60s | 692 Madison Ave. (62nd St.) | F to Lexington Ave./63rd St. | 212-750-4895 | www.lambertsontruex.com

Long coveted by luxury lovers, this high-end handbag and shoe line designed by Richard Lambertson and John Truex finally gets its own retail platform on Madison Avenue, and what a stage it is; from its cushy decor – leather couches, Tibetan rugs, spiral staircase and two-story crystal chandelier – to its sumptuous footwear, purses, briefcases and leather goods, many made from exotic skins and displayed on two floors, everything here bespeaks fine taste and opulence.

Lana Marks ⊠   ▽ 28 | 29 | 21 | VE

E 60s | 645 Madison Ave. (bet. 59th & 60th Sts.) | N/R/W to 5th Ave./59th St. | 212-355-6135 | www.lanamarks.com

"Where else can you buy a handbag to match your dog's eyes" and find over 150 styles in ostrich, alligator, crocodile and lizard ask aficionados who pledge their loyalty to the Palm Beach–based designer (aka the "queen of leather goods") and her Madison Avenue shrine; the "simplicity of design", "fabulous quality" and "craftsmanship speak for themselves" – just ask celeb customers like Oprah Winfrey and Julianne Moore – but your wallet may be rendered speechless.

Lancôme ●   26 | 24 | 22 | E

W 60s | 201 Columbus Ave. (69th St.) | B/C to 72nd St. | 212-362-4858 | www.lancome.com

The first NYC outpost of the French firm and "a pleasant addition to the Upper West Side's" beauty row is this "bright and airy" "place to indulge one's self" with "pick-me-up" cosmetics, fragrances and "classic" skincare "products that serve a wide range of ages"; a "supportive" staff that can "help you find your look" also adds to its appeal.

| | QUALITY | DISPLAY | SERVICE | COST |

LaoLao Handmade ●Ⓜ
- | **-** | **-** | **M**

E Village | 149 Ave. C (bet. 9th & 10th Sts.) | L to 1st Ave. | 212-979-1855 | www.laolaohandmade.com

Adding a welcome hint of Southeast Asian spice to Avenue C is this bright boutique full of "gorgeous" handmade silk textiles and accessories for women, men and the home that's named after the traditional moonshine of Laos; the luxurious but affordable loot also includes a proprietary line of striking hand-painted porcelain dishes and platters from Vietnam.

☒ La Perla
28 | **25** | **23** | **VE**

E 60s | 803 Madison Ave. (bet. 67th & 68th Sts.) | 6 to 68th St. | 212-570-0050

Meatpacking | 425 W. 14th St. (bet. 9th Ave. & Washington St.) | A/C/E/L to 14th St./8th Ave. | 212-242-6662

SoHo | 93 Greene St. (bet. Prince & Spring Sts.) | C/E to Spring St. | 212-219-0999

866-527-3752 | www.laperla.com

"If God wears underwear, she shops here" proclaim parishioners who worship at this "amazingly indulgent" trio that traffics in "classy", "high-end lacy" thongs, bustiers, garter belts and other "beautiful" unmentionables that act like "Kryptonite for men"; while you're indulging "all the senses", pour yourself into "sexy" swimwear and hosiery that will "make him want to touch" your "perfect body" – but remember that in order to drive this "incredible" "Mercedes of lingerie", you may need to "rob a bank."

La Petite Coquette
26 | **23** | **23** | **E**

G Village | 51 University Pl. (bet. 9th & 10th Sts.) | 6 to Astor Pl. | 212-473-2478 | 800-240-0308 | www.thelittleflirt.com

From the "littlest creation to full-body lace coverings", Rebecca Apsan's "delightfully naughty" "lingerie candy store" for "women of exquisite taste and deep pockets" is "a great place to watch celebrities" (Sarah Jessica Parker, Winona Ryder) buying "barely there" unmentionables from designers like Aubade and Myla; with a "friendly" "gossipy" staff on hand, you'll always "find the perfect thing" at this Village boudoir – or "spend your last dollar" trying to.

Lara Hélène Ⓢ
- | **-** | **-** | **VE**

E 60s | 13 E. 69th St. (bet. 5th & Madison Aves.) | 6 to 68th St. | 212-452-3273 | www.larahelene.com

"Definitely worth a stop by all brides", this by-appointment-only atelier on the UES offers its own customized collection – the work of a sisterly duo; samples of the sophisticated gowns hang from the ceiling in the airy, elegant space, shimmering against the dark-wood floor and furniture, along with a garden backdrop.

Larry & Jeff's Bicycle Plus
- | **-** | **-** | **M**

E 70s | 1400 Third Ave. (bet. 79th & 80th Sts.) | 6 to 77th St. | 212-794-2929 | www.bicyclesnyc.com

This pedal peddler on the Upper East Side offers a "good selection" of wheels, including "specialized road" rigs; whether you're looking for big bikes from names such as Cannondale and Giant or Kettler tricycles for toddlers graduating from strollers, the "helpful", "courteous" staff will match the perfect ride to your specs.

| | QUALITY | DISPLAY | SERVICE | COST |

L'Artisan Parfumeur

26 | 25 | 23 | E

E 80s | 1100 Madison Ave. (bet. 82nd & 83rd Sts.) | 6 to 77th St. | 212-794-3600

SoHo | 68 Thompson St. (Spring St.) | C/E to Spring St. | 212-334-1500 ●

NEW W 70s | 222 Columbus Ave. (70th St.) | 1/2/3/B/C to 72nd St. | 212-787-4400 ●

www.artisanparfumeur.com

These SoHo and UES boutiques are the first U.S. offshoots of this premier French fragrance house; they showcase pretty gold-capped bottles filled with "unique" scents based on natural ingredients like almond milk, figs and orange blossoms, along with candles and body creams concocted from fruit and flower extracts; the products are pricey but "you'll never smell like the person next to you"; N.B. the Upper West Side branch opened post-Survey.

Layla Ⓜ

- | - | - | E

Downtown | 86 Hoyt St. (bet. Atlantic Ave. & State St.) | Brooklyn | A/C/G to Hoyt/Schermerhorn Sts. | 718-222-1933

At this "great" Brooklyn homage to all things Indian just off of Atlantic Avenue, shoppers discover brightly colored bed linens, cushions and quilted silk coverlets, most of them handmade and detailed; delicate jewelry, including unique earrings and bangle bracelets, plus an eponymous clothing line using all natural materials add to the earthy ethnic emphasis; N.B. also closed Tuesdays.

Laytner's Linen & Home ●

20 | 18 | 16 | M

E 80s | 237 E. 86th St. (bet. 2nd & 3rd Aves.) | 4/5/6 to 86th St. | 212-996-4439

W 80s | 2270 Broadway (82nd St.) | 1 to 79th St. | 212-724-0180

800-690-7200 | www.laytners.com

Many locals laud these long-standing Upper East and West Side home-furnishings emporiums for being "convenient", "decently priced" "saviors" "when you need something in a pinch", including sheets, towels, candles, place mats, folding chairs and Shaker-style furniture; "the selection isn't huge" and "nothing is out of this world or unique", but "frequent sales help makes up for shortcomings in the coolness factor."

Ⓩ Leather Man, The ●

26 | 22 | 24 | E

W Village | 111 Christopher St. (bet. Bleecker & Hudson Sts.) | 1 to Christopher St./Sheridan Sq. | 212-243-5339 | 800-243-5330 | www.theleatherman.com

"Even experts periodically have to ask 'what the hell is that for?'" when they peruse the "wicked stuff" at this duplex "leather S/M" shop in the "gay central" section of the West Village; "the store is overflowing with goods" "packed in every nook and cranny" – speaking of which, "young guys" in particular "should prepare for manhandling" by the staff, whose "touchy-feely"approach is "helpful" to "fetishists" being fitted for custom-made apparel.

Le Chien Pet Salon

∇ 23 | 23 | 17 | VE

E 60s | Trump Plaza | 1044 Third Ave. (bet. 61st & 62nd Sts.) | 4/5/6/F/N/R/W to 59th St./Lexington Ave. | 212-861-8100 | 800-532-4436 | www.lechiennyc.com

Fashionistas who "can afford to schlep Fifi" in Chanel-like carriers frequent this "luxurious" Trump Plaza fixture boasting digs reminiscent of a "museum", but down-to-earth doggies and kitties declare "you have to own a very well-off human" to handle the "high price" tags.

Lederer de Paris ⌧
25 19 20 E

E 50s | 457 Madison Ave. (51st St.) | 6 to 51st St. | 212-355-5515 | 888-537-6921 | www.ledererdeparis.com

It's a mixed bag for this "classic" Madison Avenue leather goods shop that's been a staple since the 1940s: proponents predict "when all else fails, you'll find something" amid its "always dependable" purses and luggage, but faultfinders fume there's "attitude for no reason" since the prices make "you feel like you're just paying their rent."

Lee Anderson
- - - VE

E 70s | 988 Lexington Ave. (bet. 71st & 72nd Sts.) | 6 to 68th St. | 212-772-2463 | www.leeandersoncouture.com

Each season, discriminating women make an appointment at this namesake designer's custom-made clothing boutique that recently moved from the East 60s to larger Lexington Avenue digs; they peruse the chic samples, choose from an "abundant" array of special high-end European fabrications (brocade, silk faille, chiffon) and walk away six weeks later with one-of-a-kind creations ranging from corduroy coats that look like fur to sophisticated mother-of-the-bride dresses.

Lee's Art Shop ❶
25 23 19 E

W 50s | 220 W. 57th St. (bet. B'way & 7th Ave.) | N/Q/R/W to 57th St. | 212-247-0110 | www.leesartshop.com

"Hours of browsing" await at this multilevel West 50s "wonderland", which "got even better as it got bigger"; "you can't beat" the "staggering selection" of "fantastic art supplies", "terrific writing instruments" and other "fun finds", plus there's also a "great framing department"; "solicitous service" completes the picture, though bashers brush off the "uptown" prices (hence the "term 'starving artist'").

Lee's Studio ❶
23 19 17 E

W 50s | 220 W. 57th St., 2nd fl. (bet. B'way & 7th Ave.) | N/Q/R/W to 57th St. | 212-581-4400 | 877-544-4869 | www.leesstudio.com

Located above Lee's Art Shop in Midtown, this 20,000-sq.-ft. space features furniture and fans, but the main focus is on lighting from the likes of Leucos, Flos and Artemide; however, "expensive" prices and "indifferent" salespeople "with attitude" leave many customers in the dark.

Le Fanion ⌧
- - - E

W Village | 299 W. Fourth St. (Bank St.) | 1 to Christopher St./Sheridan Sq. | 212-463-8760 | www.lefanion.com

Small West Village home-furnishings shop that evokes the French countryside with pretty pieces ranging from antique armoires and zinc weathervanes to rustic pitchers, platters and delicate bronze chandeliers dripping with crystal fruits.

⛉ Leiber
28 27 23 VE
(fka Judith Leiber)

E 60s | 680 Madison Ave. (61st St.) | 4/5/6/F/N/R/W to 59th St./Lexington Ave. | 212-223-2999 | 866-542-7167 | www.judithleiber.com

"You feel like a million" carrying one of this designer's "tiny treasures" – animal-shaped, "expensive minaudières" "encrusted with Austrian crystals" that are basically "handbag bling for ladies who lunch" and the "favored clutches at most black-tie events"; these "works of art", all on display at the "gorgeous" Madison Avenue shop, add "dazzle" to "any outfit", but take note, she's also "got the skinny" on "exotic skins" and some of the "best shoes to boot."

Le Labo | − | − | − | VE |

NoLita | 233 Elizabeth St. (bet. Houston & Prince Sts.) | 6 to Spring St. | 212-219-2230 | www.lelabofragrances.com

At this atmospheric, interactive NoLita perfume lab, clients sniff from giant glass apothecary jars containing 10 fragrances – many based on essences from Grasse, France's olfactory capital – and choose a scent that a "helpful" staff member will blend and pour into plain-Jane packaging with your hand-lettered name and an expiration date; it's a "cool concept", but of course all this personalization comes at a price.

Leonard Opticians ⊠ | 26 | 23 | 25 | E |

E 70s | 1264 Third Ave. (bet. 72nd & 73rd Sts.) | 6 to 68th St. | 212-535-1222
W 50s | 40 W. 55th St. (bet. 5th & 6th Aves.) | F to 57th St. | 212-246-4452
www.leonardopticians.com

"You're guaranteed the best quality" at this longtime UES and Midtown pair of spectacle shops stocking the "latest styles" from top international designers alongside "tried-and-true classics"; the "terrific" staff "won't sell it to you if it doesn't flatter", and "prices are fair" for what you get.

Leontine ●Ⓜ | − | − | − | E |

Seaport | 226 Front St. (bet. Beekman St. & Peck Slip) | 2/3/4/5/A/C/J/M/Z to Fulton St./B'way/Nassau | 212-766-1066

With her latest undertaking, a warmly lit beacon on the South Street Seaport waterfront, Kyung Lee (owner of the Village boutiques Albertine and Claudine) goes where few specialty shopkeepers have gone to date; her handpicked finds range from Kathy Kemp dresses and jewelry from Delphine to delicate toile linens and antique furnishings, making visitors feel like they've wandered into a charming brownstone rather than a boutique – except that everything's for sale.

Léron ⊠ | ▽ 29 | 24 | 25 | VE |

E 60s | 804 Madison Ave. (bet. 67th & 68th Sts.) | 6 to 68th St. | 212-753-6700 | 800-954-6369 | www.leron.com

Since 1910, this Upper East Side doyenne has been purveying "beautiful and classic" bath, bed, baby and table linens; they can also "custom-make anything" in the aforementioned categories, plus lingerie; while wallet-watchers warn "don't even enter this store unless you just robbed a bank", the only thing enthusiasts advise is "love what you purchase because it will be around for a long, long time."

Le Sabon and Baby Too ● | 23 | 23 | 18 | E |

E 60s | 834 Lexington Ave. (63rd St.) | F to Lexington Ave./63rd St. | 212-319-4225 | www.lesabon.com

When you "can't hold back on your little one" or need a "nattily packaged" baby shower gift, head to this "tiny" East 60s shop and scoop up "cute" stuff like leather bibs and onesies, plus "fragrant creams", soy candles and Dead Sea bath products from the "eye-catching displays"; if a handful get in a lather about "hard to come by" help, most retort it's a "great stop after shopping Bloomie's."

| | QUALITY | DISPLAY | SERVICE | COST |

Les Petits Chapelais
▽ 25 | 23 | 20 | E

SoHo | 86 Thompson St. (Spring St.) | C/E to Spring St. | 212-625-1023 | www.lespetitschapelais.com

"Reminds me of shopping in French baby stores" reminisce browsers who tip their hats to this SoHo tot shop named for designer Nathalie Simonneaux's generations-old family farm in Brittany; the whimsical wearables "for kids go beyond the Gap" with "beautiful fabrics", bright colors and creative combinations – just what you'd expect from the visionary who once dreamed up costumes for Le Cirque du Soleil.

LeSportsac
20 | 19 | 17 | M

E 80s | 1065 Madison Ave. (bet. 80th & 81st Sts.) | 6 to 77th St. | 212-988-6200

SoHo | 176 Spring St. (bet. Thompson St. & W. B'way) | C/E to Spring St. | 212-625-2626

877-397-6597 | www.lesportsac.com

For "funky", "inexpensive" "knockaround" ripstop parachute-nylon satchels and suitcases that "wear forever", stop by these SoHo and Upper East Side branches where you'll find selections that are "perfect when your shoulder hurts from 50-lb. designer bags"; a forthcoming new collection for them from PETA-supporting designer and non-leather lover Stella McCartney seems like it should be a perfect match.

Lester's
24 | 19 | 19 | E

E 80s | 1534 Second Ave. (80th St.) | 6 to 77th St. | 212-734-9292

Gravesend | 2411 Coney Island Ave. (Ave. U) | Brooklyn | Q to Ave. U | 718-645-4501

www.lestersnyc.com

"Why aren't there more stores like this?" ponder parents bewitched by this "been-around-forever" "one-stop shopping" destination in the East 80s and Gravesend boasting "cute kids' clothing" "from dress-up to camp-trunk" essentials; the "trendy" juniors section is "teenybopper heaven", and "you can't beat the selection" in the stellar shoe department; still, it gets "zoo-y" – "your child may grow a size while waiting."

NEW Leviev ⧄
27 | 22 | 23 | VE

E 60s | 700 Madison Ave. (bet. 62nd & 63rd Sts.) | F to Lexington Ave./63rd St. | 212-763-5300 | 877-453-8438 | www.leviev.com

The largest cutter and polisher of diamonds in the world has opened its first American retail store on Madison Avenue, where you'll be dazzled by the "beautiful selection" of "extraordinary" rare white and colored (think pink, red, green and blue) stones in all shapes and sizes; owned by billionaire Lev Leviev, it's a given that this store is only "for those with very deep wallets."

Levi's Store, The ◑
23 | 18 | 18 | M

E 50s | 750 Lexington Ave. (59th St.) | 4/5/6/F/N/R/W to 59th St./Lexington Ave. | 212-826-5957

Flatiron | 25 W. 14th St. (bet. 5th & 6th Aves.) | F/L/V to 14th St./6th Ave. | 212-242-2128

SoHo | 536 Broadway (bet. Prince & Spring Sts.) | N/R/W to Prince St. | 646-613-1847

800-872-5384 | www.levisstore.com

"Keep your designer jeans – this is the real deal" pledge the true-blue who pick up their "perennial favorite" brand at this "attitude-free" denim trio; whether "you've got a rumpshaker like J.Lo's" or just want an "all-American" "classic" cut, the "personable staff" is "willing to pull and pull" from the "very organized", "right-on-trend" selection until you find your "extremely well-fitting" pair.

Lexington Gardens ⊠
`- | - | - | E`

E 70s | 1011 Lexington Ave. (bet. 72nd & 73rd Sts.) | 6 to 68th St. | 212-861-4390 | www.lexingtongardensnyc.com

Long-standing Upper East Sider providing "super-fine", "top-of-the-line custom-made dried flower arrangements" for local patricians and visiting princes and heads of state; interspersed among the bespoke bouquets are "unique" outdoors-inspired antiques like urns, which add to the atmospheric setting.

Lexington Luggage
`21 | 10 | 21 | M`

E 60s | 793 Lexington Ave. (bet. 61st & 62nd Sts.) | 4/5/6/F/N/R/W to 59th St./Lexington Ave. | 212-223-0698 | 800-822-0404 | www.lexingtonluggage.com

If prices seem high "at first blush", just rely on your "old-fashioned haggling" skills advise insiders who consider this Lex luggage haunt a "find"; trust the "patient" staff that's "willing to go the extra mile to help find the perfect gear" and you'll wheel away "incredible deals."

LF Stores
`17 | 14 | 17 | E`

Flatiron | 150 Fifth Ave. (bet. 19th & 20th Sts.) | 4/5/6/L/N/Q/R/W to 14th St./Union Sq. | 212-645-1334 ◗

SoHo | 149 Spring St. (bet. W. B'way & Wooster St.) | C/E to Spring St. | 212-966-5889 ◗

Cobble Hill | 227 Court St. (bet. Baltic & Warren Sts.) | Brooklyn | F/G to Bergen St. | 718-797-3626

www.lfstores.com

This trifecta of trendiness is housed in "cool digs" – and dig you must, through a "cluttered closet"-like inventory of "fun, young clothes to mix, match and layer", à la the Olsen twins; still, some sigh that these "items that look like what you'd make yourself if you were a crafty girl", cost "three times what they should."

Liberty House
`▽ 25 | 20 | 21 | E`

W 100s | 2878A Broadway (112th St.) | 1 to 116th St. | 212-932-1950 | www.libertyhousenyc.com

Located on Upper Broadway, this "socially conscious" store features "funky", "politically correct" clothing with an emphasis on natural fibers for women, men and children, plus "globally" sourced "tchotchkes."

Lightforms
`▽ 23 | - | 23 | E`

Chelsea | 142 W. 26th St. (bet. 6th & 7th Aves.) | 1 to 28th St. | 212-255-4664 ⊠

W 80s | 509 Amsterdam Ave. (bet. 84th & 85th Sts.) | 1 to 86th St. | 212-875-0407

www.lightformsinc.com

The enlightened head to this duo for a swell selection of "funky to sedate" lighting from over 200 companies such as Halo, Kovacs, Flos, Juno, Lightolier and Leucos, plus bulbs, shades and dimmers; the Amsterdam Avenue store is more traditional, but "good service and prices" keep respondents returning to both places; N.B. the Chelsea branch recently moved to the larger location listed above.

	QUALITY	DISPLAY	SERVICE	COST

Lighting By Gregory
24 | 16 | 19 | M

LES | 158 Bowery (bet. Broome & Delancey Sts.) | J/M/Z to Bowery | 212-226-1276 | 888-811-3267 | www.lightingbygregory.com

Supporters say it's "worth the trek" to the Bowery for this "fairly priced" lighting store's "great selection" of over 155 different lines ranging "from contemporary to traditional", plus ceiling fans; but while some are satisfied with the "knowledgeable" service, detractors take a dimmer view and dub the staff "surly."

☑ Ligne Roset
28 | 25 | 21 | VE

Flatiron | 250 Park Ave. S. (bet. 19th & 20th Sts.) | 6 to 23rd St. | 212-375-1036

SoHo | 155 Wooster St. (Houston St.) | N/R/W to Prince St. | 212-253-5629
800-297-6738 | www.ligne-roset-usa.com

"Sleek" and "sexy" French home-furnishings stores in the Flatiron District and SoHo selling "beautiful" beds, tables, seating, accessories and other "first-rate quality designs" with "clean modern lines" but "without an icy cold attitude"; Antoine Roset founded the business in 1860, and today his great-grandsons oversee the production of "almost flawless" pieces at "very expensive" prices.

Lilith
25 | 23 | 24 | E

NoLita | 227 Mulberry St. (bet. Prince & Spring Sts.) | 6 to Spring St. | 212-925-0080 | www.lilith.fr

Housed in a warm red NoLita boutique, this "French designer brand" by Lily Bareth includes "beautiful", "drapey", "cosmopolitan clothes" with "unusual cuts", "original" colors and "luxe fabrics"; the "attentive staff provides a high level of service" "for hip women of a certain age", "a certain style" and definitely "with deep pockets."

Lilliput
- | - | - | E

NoLita | 265 Lafayette St. (bet. Prince & Spring Sts.) | 6 to Spring St. | 212-965-9567 Ⓢ

SoHo | 240 Lafayette St. (bet. Prince & Spring Sts.) | 6 to Spring St. | 212-965-9201
www.lilliputsoho.com

Named for that land of little people in *Gulliver's Travels,* these sibling stores – situated a stone's throw across Lafayette – are filled to the gills with "cute" children's clothing, shoes and toys from all of the top brands; but neat freaks snap it's so cluttered that it "would be a miracle to find anything"; N.B. the 265 branch offers more newborn–toddler sizes.

Lily
24 | 23 | 22 | E

Cobble Hill | 209 Court St. (bet. Warren & Wyckoff Sts.) | Brooklyn | F/G to Bergen St. | 718-858-6261

NEW Park Slope | 435 Seventh Ave. (15th St.) | Brooklyn | F to 7th Ave. | 718-832-1805 Ⓜ
www.lilybrooklyn.com

What a "bright, fun, happy environment" cheer cohorts of this Cobble Hill resource and its spanking-new Park Slope sidekick, stocking scads of "terrific", colorful clothing choices for adolescents and young women, all arranged on handy racks and tables; reach for the Michael Stars T-shirts and Free People pieces, darling undies from Hanky Panky and Only Hearts and colorful clogs, or just let the "helpful salespeople guide you."

| | QUALITY | DISPLAY | SERVICE | COST |

Limited, The ⬤

- | - | - | M

Kings Plaza | Kings Plaza Shopping Ctr. | 5301 Kings Plaza
(bet. Flatbush Ave. & Ave. U) | Brooklyn | B/Q to Newkirk Ave. |
718-951-6621

Staten Island | Staten Island Mall | 2655 Richmond Ave. (bet. Platinum Ave. &
Richmond Hill Rd.) | 718-982-7192

www.thelimited.com

Much like its cousin Express, this womenswear chain with links in Kings
Plaza and the Staten Island Mall is the go-to source for au courant fashion pieces to spice up your work-a-day wardrobe without going broke;
the selection isn't limited to office garb, though – you can also score
well-priced finds for stepping out at night or just plain hanging out.

Limited Too ⬤

16 | 16 | 14 | M

Kings Plaza | Kings Plaza Shopping Ctr. | 5301 Kings Plaza
(bet. Flatbush Ave. & Ave. U) | Brooklyn | B/Q to Newkirk Ave. |
718-951-7830

Elmhurst | Queens Ctr. | 90-15 Queens Blvd. (bet. 57th & 59th Aves.) |
Queens | G/R/V to Woodhaven Blvd. | 718-592-2857

Staten Island | Staten Island Mall | 2655 Richmond Ave. (bet. Platinum Ave. &
Richmond Hill Rd.) | 718-698-6207

www.thelimited.com

A little slice of "tween heaven", these "always reliable" chain links are
stuffed with "trendy", "well-priced" "cute disposables" including
clothes, shoes, accessories and other "plastic delights" for the "budding fashionista" who changes or "outgrows her wardrobe every two
weeks"; while a few grouches gripe of "crowded" conditions and
"sloppy displays", most young girls love the "shrunken teen togs."

Linda Derector Ⓜ

- | - | - | E

NoLita | 211 Mott St. (bet. Prince & Spring Sts.) | 6 to Spring St. |
212-680-3023 | www.lindaderector.com

Even fashion visionaries may be blindsided by stylehound Linda
Derector's sleek red NoLita nook featuring an expertly curated collection of vintage eyeglass frames and sunglasses from boldface and under-the-radar names dating back to the '60s along with covetable costume
jewelry; channel your favorite silver-screen icon or rock star with purr-fect cat eye specs, Italian aviators and enormous '70s styles.

Linda Dresner Ⓢ

▽ 25 | 21 | 23 | VE

E 50s | 484 Park Ave. (bet. 58th & 59th Sts.) | 4/5/6/F/N/R/W to
59th St./Lexington Ave. | 212-308-3177 | www.lindadresner.com

This serene Park Avenue space appeals to "NYC matrons" "who can
afford" to comfortably contemplate on which Tuleh dress, Balenciaga
blouse or Dsquared suit they might buy; the refined interior and tasteful selection of "classy choices" reveal the sharp eye of owner Linda
Dresner, who keeps her clientele "delighted with everything about the
experience and the purchase."

Lingerie on Lex

▽ 24 | 20 | 22 | E

E 60s | 831 Lexington Ave. (bet. 63rd & 64th Sts.) | 6 to 68th St. |
212-755-3312

With a "wide selection" of mostly European lingerie, sleepwear and
hosiery from "popular" labels like Lise Charmel and La Perla, plus a
"sweet" staff, this Lexington lair is a favorite for the wedding-bound

bent on "big-ticket items" as well as those looking for "moderately priced" "basics"; it's "small", but with "lots of storage", they'll "find your size."

Links of London

24 | 22 | 22 | E

E 40s | MetLife Bldg. | 200 Park Ave. (45th St.) | 4/5/6/7/S to 42nd St./ Grand Central | 212-867-0258 ⑤

E 50s | 535 Madison Ave. (bet. 54th & 55th Sts.) | E/V to Lexington Ave./ 53rd St. | 212-588-1177

SoHo | 402 W. Broadway (bet. Broome & Spring Sts.) | C/E to Spring St. | 212-343-8024

800-210-0079 | www.linksoflondon.com

It's the men's cuff links that inspired the name of this trio, but they also offer classic gold and silver jewelry for women and a wide array of charms; supporters say its "reliable" quality makes it "good for gifts."

Lion in the Sun

24 | 20 | 21 | M

Park Slope | 232 Seventh Ave. (4th St.) | Brooklyn | F to 7th Ave. | 718-369-4006 | www.lioninthesunps.com

"Even better since moving to a more visible location" agree *paperie* tigers who "love to impulse-buy their way through" this "neighborly, friendly", family-owned Park Slope "treasure"; scribes scope out the "lovely cards", "beautiful stationery" and gift items like photo albums and scrapbooks while party-throwers and the nuptials-bound order "creative" custom-printed invitations to the rear, attended by a staff that's "helpful, but not too in-your-face."

Lisa Levine Jewelry ●Ⓜ

- | - | - | E

Williamsburg | 536 Metropolitan Ave. (bet. Lorimer St. & Union Ave.) | Brooklyn | G/L to Metropolitan Ave./Lorimer St. | 718-349-2824 | www.lisalevinejewelry.com

The namesake designer's store-cum-workroom in Williamsburg displays her delicate copper, silver, oxidized silver and gold jewelry; the clean, organic shapes range from long hoop earrings to multirow necklaces, some incorporating intricate miniaturized chains that may be threaded with feathers or capped with a colored stone or coins.

Little Eric

25 | 21 | 24 | E

E 80s | 1118 Madison Ave. (bet. 83rd & 84th Sts.) | 4/5/6 to 86th St. | 212-717-1513

Put your kid's best foot forward at this East 80s stomping ground, which boasts a "really nice assortment you may not see elsewhere" from Italy including "first-time walkers", boots, loafers, sneakers, Mary Janes and party shoes, in styles that span the spectrum from "classic" to "avant-garde"; still, budget-minded shoppers turn up their heels, quipping "they're only shoes, not Fabergé eggs."

NEW Little Marc Jacobs ●

- | - | - | E

W Village | 298 W. Fourth St. (bet. Bank & W. 11th Sts.) | 1 to Christopher St./Sheridan Sq. | 212-206-6644 | www.marcjacobs.com

Set on a picturesque West Village corner a skip and a jump away from Marc Jacobs' retail wonderland (aka Bleecker Street), this new addition for fashionista juniors feels like a unique discovery, complete with vintage toys standing guard in the windows – but of course, it's a destination for faithful fans and their offspring; bust open the piggybank and splurge on darling toddler- and childrenswear must-haves like waffle-weave cashmere hoodies and itty-bitty bomber jackets, all boasting the designer's Midas touch.

Little Stinkers Shoe Company ◕

QUALITY	DISPLAY	SERVICE	COST
-	-	-	M

E Village | 280 E. 10th St. (bet. Ave. A & 1st Ave.) | L to 1st Ave. | 212-253-0282 | www.thelittlestinkersshoeco.com

An alternative to pricey tot shops, this East Villager takes the sticker shock out of shopping for kids' shoes by stocking wallet-friendly American finds, ranging from Bobux baby booties to Kidorable rain boots; they also stock socks, hats and gloves geared to little stinkers.

Living on Fifth ◑

QUALITY	DISPLAY	SERVICE	COST
-	-	-	M

Park Slope | 231 Fifth Ave. (bet. Carroll & President Sts.) | Brooklyn | M/R to Union St. | 718-499-0098

Living on Seventh

Park Slope | 219 Seventh Ave. (bet. 3rd & 4th Sts.) | Brooklyn | F to 7th Ave. | 718-788-1651

Living on Smith Ⓜ

Carroll Gardens | 289 Smith St. (bet. Sackett & Union Sts.) | Brooklyn | F/G to Carroll St. | 718-222-8546

Nearly everything you need for nesting with flair can be found at this modern Park Slope–Carroll Gardens lifestyle trio filled with home furnishings and women's casualwear; accent your pad with handcrafted vases and ceramics, pendant lamps, decorative pillows and custom-made rugs, then treat yourself to Calypso sweaters, Claus Porto candles and soaps and Cosabella undies; N.B. the Fifth Avenue offshoot recently relocated to number 231.

Livi's Lingerie

QUALITY	DISPLAY	SERVICE	COST
▽ 20	7	24	M

E 80s | 1456 Third Ave. (bet. 82nd & 83rd Sts.) | 4/5/6 to 86th St. | 212-879-2050

Owner "Livi is a legend" declare devotees of this "old-fashioned corsetiere" who can "tell you're a 34B from one block away" – or from the "tight quarters" of her East 80s shop where her staff will also "take time" with you; designer and specialty lingerie, including bodyshapers, are at your fingertips, but you'll have to "ask for the racey stuff"; N.B. closed Saturdays.

Liz Lange Maternity

QUALITY	DISPLAY	SERVICE	COST
23	24	23	VE

E 70s | 958 Madison Ave. (bet. 75th & 76th Sts.) | 6 to 77th St. | 212-879-2191 | 888-616-5777 | www.lizlange.com

One trip to the namesake designer's Madison Avenue boutique and "you'll keep your style during nine tough months" proclaim pregnant patrons who pay "high prices" for "fabulous-looking" jeans, tailored trousers, blouses and suits that are "great for working moms"; most praise the "intelligent" staff that "understands what you're going through", but a "disappointed" few find "nothing special."

L'Occitane ◑

QUALITY	DISPLAY	SERVICE	COST
25	24	22	E

SoHo | 92 Prince St. (Mercer St.) | N/R/W to Prince St. | 212-219-3310 | www.loccitane.com
Additional locations throughout the NY area

Provençal phenomenon with a "European-meadow vibe" purveying "high-qualtiy soaps, creams and candles", whose supporters single out "the excellent shea butter products"; still, snobs sniff "it was better when it didn't seem to be in every mall in the country."

Z Loehmann's ◐ | 20 | 11 | 9 | M |

Chelsea | 101 Seventh Ave. (bet. 16th & 17th Sts.) | 1 to 18th St. | 212-352-0856
NEW W 70s | Ansonia Bldg. | 2101 Broadway (bet. 73rd & 74th Sts.) | 1/2/3 to 72nd St. | 212-882-9990
Bronx | 5740 Broadway (236th St.) | 1 to 238th St. | 718-543-6420
Coney Island | 2807 E. 21st St. (Emmons Ave.) | Brooklyn | Q to Sheepshead Bay | 718-368-1256
NEW Rego Park | 97-77 Queens Blvd. (bet. 64th Rd. & 65th Ave.) | Queens | G/R/V to 63rd Dr./Rego Park | 718-289-2590
www.loehmanns.com

"Don't put that sweater down, even for an instant" lest you lose it amid the "garage-sale atmosphere" of this chainster where insiders beat a path to the Back Room for the "bonanza of bargains" on designers "from Jean-Paul Gaultier to Anne Klein"; the communal dressing rooms are "like boarding school, with lots of sharing", and if the "lack of service" leaves fans lamenting it's "not like the old days", most maintain it still delivers "damn good" deals.

NEW Lola | 22 | 22 | 20 | E |

Park Slope | 383 Seventh Ave. (bet. 11th & 12th Sts.) | Brooklyn | F to 7th Ave. | 718-499-0753

When you "want a standout outfit that's truly unique", step right up to this "lovely" new Park Slope coquette boasting a well-edited selection of womenswear; "love everything in there" – the owner has such "nice taste" sigh boutique browsers who embrace upbeat lines like Calypso and Miss Sixty and sophisticated finds from Graham & Spencer; fleshing out the fashionista fare: impulse-buy merch like Savon de Marseille soaps and Junior Drake handbags.

Lolli by Reincarnation ◐⊄ | 20 | 19 | 18 | E |

LES | 85 Stanton St. (bet. Allen & Orchard Sts.) | F/V to Lower East Side/2nd Ave. | 212-529-2030 | www.lolli-reincarnation.com

"Interesting in its concept and setup", this Lower East Sider with a flea market feel offers an "eclectic" array of vintage clothing along with custom-made leather or suede handbags (the "hobos are so cute"), plus obi-style belts, sandals and boots in a veritable rainbow of 56 colors; while you flip through the racks, your significant other can relax on the couch from the late 1800s, flip through magazines dating back to the 1940s or wave to the birds flitting about the old-fashioned cage.

Longchamp | 26 | 23 | 21 | E |

E 60s | 713 Madison Ave. (bet. 63rd & 64th Sts.) | 6 to 68th St. | 212-223-1500 ⑤
SoHo | 132 Spring St. (bet. Greene & Wooster Sts.) | 6 to Spring St. | 212-343-7444
866-566-4242 | www.longchamp.com

Addicts of this Paris-based line's Le Pliage bag "buy a new color every year" even though the "always-in-style" lightweight nylon totes "great for traveling" hold up so "fabulously" you can carry one "from now to eternity"; this Madison Avenue "favorite" offers "fashionable" accessories, a "can't-be-beat repair policy" and a staff of champs "willing to go that "extra mile" – and the SoHo flagship offers even more of the same, plus a new collection of womenswear.

Loom ●   ▽ 23 | 19 | 21 | M

Park Slope | 109A Seventh Ave. (bet. Carroll & President Sts.) | Brooklyn | B/Q to 7th Ave. | 718-789-0061

Park Slope | 115 Seventh Ave. (bet. Carroll & President Sts.) | Brooklyn | B/Q to 7th Ave. | 718-789-0061

"You're sure to find that little gift you need" for everyone from "babies to grandmothers" at this "friendly", modern Park Slope stop that fills its birch-wood shelves with "reliably funky" wares, from "fun hand-bags" in unique colors, to unusual jewelry, soaps, candles, home accessories, toys and "great cards", plus clothing from casual favorites like Ella Moss and Velvet; N.B. the closet-size offshoot at 109A Seventh Avenue sells primarily women's apparel.

Loopy Mango ●   - | - | - | E

Dumbo | 117 Front St. (bet. Adams & Washington Sts.) | Brooklyn | F to York St. | 718-858-5930 | www.loopymango.com

There's nothing loopy about the "one-of-a-kind garments" at this Dumbo den of desire done up with "really cool" gold-framed mirrors and antique furniture (also for sale); spring for über-feminine separates, party dresses and hip finds from coveted labels like Deener, Mike & Chris and Borne; the goods cost more than a few mangoes, but it's "well worth the prices" given the "tons of compliments" you'll receive on "anything you buy"; N.B. the Jay Street original closed.

☑ Lord & Taylor ●   22 | 20 | 19 | M

Murray Hill | 424 Fifth Ave. (bet. 38th & 39th Sts.) | 4/5/6/7/S to 42nd St./Grand Central | 212-391-3344 | 800-223-7440 | www.lordandtaylor.com

"One of the last of the old-guard NY department stores", "focusing on American-made products", this "quiet" Murray Hill "mainstay" "contains level after level of clothing and accessories for men, women and children"; while it's trying "to accommodate younger looks", "people perceive it as fuddy-duddy" – perhaps because many styles reflect "not high fashion, but good middle-of-the-road taste"; still, if you need "professional" garb, "classic" shoes or ("pardon the oxymoron") "the biggest petite section", this "grande dame" "is a great place to find something that fits and is probably marked-down"; P.S. "don't miss the Christmas windows."

Lord Willy's Ⓜ   - | - | - | E

NEW **W Village** | 102 Christopher St. (bet. Bedford & Bleecker Sts.) | 1 to Christopher St./Sheridan Sq. | 212-691-0888

NoLita | 223 Mott St. (bet. Prince & Spring Sts.) | B/D to Grand St. | 212-680-8888

www.lordwillys.com

Owners Alex and Betty Wilcox and their two Jack Russell terriers hold court in this NoLita matchbook-size wonder, which produces bespoke, English-tailored suits and coats in vintage wools; signature three-button-cuff or French cuff men's shirts in "bold designs" and hues line the tasteful interior, along with a few inches devoted to candy-colored ties; hot lads hail it as all "good, if pretentious" – though "if you're not a *GQ*-er, skip it"; N.B. the West Village branch is ready-to-wear only.

	QUALITY	DISPLAY	SERVICE	COST

☑ Loro Piana ⑤
29 | 25 | 23 | VE

E 60s | 821 Madison Ave. (bet. 68th & 69th Sts.) | 6 to 68th St. |
212-980-7961 | www.loropiana.com

Catering to the "oh-so-affluent" with a variety of "luxurious fibers", this
Upper East Side brick-front shop carries "cashmere that will ruin you for
anyone else's", be it in the shape of "gorgeous" his-and-hers sweaters, "a
bit staid" "but eminently wearable sportswear" and even blankets; admittedly, the staff can seem "disinterested" at times, and "prices are
steep – but better [to buy] one fabulous piece than 10 mediocre ones."

NEW Louis Féraud ⑤
28 | 25 | 24 | VE

(aka Féraud)

E 60s | 717 Madison Ave. (63rd St.) | F to Lexington Ave./63rd St. |
212-980-1919 | 800-227-5863 | www.feraud.com

"Sometimes its worth the splurge" for "exceptional quality and style"
declare devotees of the late French designer, who was Brigitte Bardot's
couturier back in the '50s; at this Madison Avenue outpost, "beautiful
classics" including "fabulous suits" with "elegant" "refined" details
endure – so much so say some that "you will go out of style before
the clothes do."

Louis Vuitton
27 | 27 | 22 | VE

E 50s | 1 E. 57th St. (5th Ave.) | N/R/W to 5th Ave./59th St. | 212-758-8877
SoHo | 116 Greene St. (bet. Prince & Spring Sts.) | N/R/W to Prince St. |
212-274-9090
866-884-8866 | www.vuitton.com

Vuitton vixens "swear by" the world's biggest, "never-to-be-topped"
luxury brand designed by Marc Jacobs, which "has grown with the
times" by ensuring its "simply stunning" flagship on 57th Street and
SoHo sister are "dream-come-true" draws for stars like Uma Thurman
and Salma Hayek; you "feel like royalty" ogling the "to-die-for" rich-
girl garb, "impeccable" menswear, collectible purses "costing more
than a car" and leather goods that "last a lifetime (and maybe even
your daughter's too)"; while some voters lament the "logo overload"
and slam the "snooty-to-anyone-not-a-celebrity" salespeople, the
consensus is "everyone should own a piece" of Louis.

Lounge ◐
19 | 21 | 15 | E

SoHo | 593 Broadway (bet. Houston & Prince Sts.) | N/R/W to Prince St. |
212-226-7585 | www.loungesoho.com

"Come for the music, the fun and the cool setup" say the "wealthy teenyboppers" who frequent SoHo's "large multifloor" lifestyle store offering an "eclectic mix of labels" from Sacred Blue and Junk Food to
True Religion and Antik Denim; troll through the fringe-y CD bar and
"listen to music", "get a drink" in the Casablanca tearoom, a trim in the
hair salon or shop till you drop during the sales – otherwise, the
"trendy-to-the-max" merchandise will max out your credit line.

Love Brigade CoOp ◐⑤Ⓜ
- | - | - | E

Williamsburg | 230 Grand St. (bet. Driggs & Roebling Sts.) | Brooklyn |
L to Bedford Ave. | 718-715-0430 | www.lovebrigade.com

Recently relocated to larger Williamsburg digs, this fledgling flagship
of the U.K. label has been reconceived as a hybrid boutique/showroom;
the house line of music-inspired dancefloor-ready clothing, plus about

20 love-erly lines for men, women and kids from a cavalcade of local and national designers are all worth the troop over.

Loveday31 ◐Ⓜ

-	-	-	M

Astoria | 33-06 31st. Ave. (bet. 33rd & 34th Sts.) | Queens | N/W to 30th Ave. | 718-728-4057

"Manhattanites are just discovering" this "small" boutique in Astoria, a vintage-challenged neighborhood – until now; the owner, a "former Screaming Mimi's buyer, knows her stuff", picking the perfect dresses, coats, tops and accessories for guys and dolls", including a floor-to-ceiling tower of belts.

Love Saves The Day ◐

17	18	15	M

E Village | 119 Second Ave. (7th St.) | 6 to Astor Pl. | 212-228-3802

"Still kooky after all these years" (41, to be exact), this "cluttered" East Village venue for "vintage toys, dolls", games, "cool" collectibles and clothing (plus gag gifts) remains "the perfect store for a rainy day"; even if "funky" isn't your forte, "it's worth going in and just looking around" the "narrow, tight aisles and display cases of memorabilia" guaranteed to "make you kick yourself for not saving the metal lunch box you had when growing up."

Lowell/Edwards Ⓢ

-	-	-	E

E 50s | D&D Bldg. | 979 Third Ave., 5th fl. (bet. 58th & 59th Sts.) | 4/5/6/F/N/R/W to 59th St./Lexington Ave. | 212-980-2862 | www.lowelledwards.com

Audio-visual design meets interior design at this sleek showroom cocooned on the fifth floor of the UES's D&D Building that attracts celebs and Fortune 500 types; it specializes in classy custom cabinetry that exposes exotic electronics with the click of a button, as well as "top-end" home theaters replete with nine-ft. screens and room-shaking speakers.

Lower East Side Tenement Museum Bookshop

21	-	21	M

LES | 108 Orchard St. (bet. Broome & Delancey Sts.) | B/D to Grand St. | 212-982-8420 | www.tenement.org

"Access your inner immigrant" at this "charming store", which recently relocated to the Museum's Visitors' Center, and merged its stock of books, cards, gifts and games with a New York theme; the staff gives "the impression they're not there to make money, but to remind you of a long-forgotten time."

Lowe's ◐

21	19	17	M

Gowanus | 118 Second Ave. (Hamilton Pl.) | Brooklyn | F/G to Smith/9th Sts. | 718-249-1151
Staten Island | 2171 Forest Ave. (bet. Grandview Ave. & Samuel Pl.) | 718-682-9027
800-445-6937 | www.lowes.com

"Blows Home Depot away with a helpful staff" "you don't have to search for", "easy-to-navigate" aisles and "variety" vow "DIY sorts" wowed by this "more civilized" "welcome alternative" chain with links in Gowanus and Staten Island; decorate or "build your house and find all the supplies" you need, from hammers and hasps to "small appliances, home furnishings and organizing products"; still, a handful wish there was "more lumber and real construction hardware" in stock and insist "service depends on which employee you ask."

Luca Luca
25 | 24 | 25 | VE

E 60s | 690 Madison Ave. (62nd St.) | 4/5/6/F/N/R/W to 59th St./
Lexington Ave. | 212-753-2444
E 70s | 1011 Madison Ave. (78th St.) | 6 to 77th St. | 212-288-9285
www.lucaluca.com

"Sexy, yet appropriate; fun, but timeless", this Italian "favorite" designed
by Luca Orlandi – whose front-row fans include Mary J. Blige and the
Williams twins – specializes in dresses for "big galas" in brocade, taffeta and chiffon, as well as "feminine, comfortable" suits that Luca
"great for work"; some say the wares are "pricey, even for Madison
Avenue", but an "extremely friendly" staff helps offset sticker shock.

NEW Luceplan
23 | 21 | 20 | E

SoHo | 49 Greene St. (bet. Broome & Grand Sts.) | C/E to Spring St. |
212-966-1399 | www.luceplan.com

"Light up your life" by considering this "illuminating" newcomer's
"cool" "cutting-edge" lighting from Italy that looks more like "one-of-
a-kind" "art" from over a dozen different designers; the gleaming
white minimalist SoHo outpost is a "great place for making enlightened choices", albeit at blinding prices.

NEW Lucia Nenickova Ⓜ
21 | 22 | 21 | E

Gramercy | 72½ Irving Pl. (bet. 18th & 19th Sts.) | 4/5/6/L/N/Q/R/
W to 14th St./Union Sq. | 212-777-0810 | www.lucianenickova.com

After apprenticing with craftswoman Barbara Shaum and starting her
own collection, Czech-born owner-designer Lucia Nenickova opened
this "tiny gem" "hidden away" from Gramercy Park to showcase her
"gorgeous" handmade, hand-stitched, hand-dyed organic processed
leather goods; "if you're a bag person, this is the place" to find that ostrich clutch or cowhide tote, and if snap-closure belts or flat strappy
sandals are your thing, you can also expect a "chic, great look."

Lucien Pellat-Finet
- | - | - | VE

G Village | 14 Christopher St. (Gay St.) | 1 to Christopher St./Sheridan Sq. |
212-255-8560 | www.lucienpellat-finet.com

Sporting "cutting-edge" intarsias with hemp-leaf and skull-and-
crossbones designs, the "best-quality sweaters around" abound at
this art-filled Greenwich Village shop, which also offers luxe bed covers, belts and silk umbrellas, all in luscious candy colors or Gothic
hues; they don't call this designer 'the king of cashmere' for nothing,
but the "unbelievable prices" mean you better cash in the crown jewels before you arrive.

Lucky Brand Jeans ◑
23 | 21 | 22 | E

E 60s | 1151 Third Ave. (67th St.) | 6 to 68th St. | 646-422-1192
Flatiron | 172 Fifth Ave. (22nd St.) | N/R/W to 23rd St. | 917-606-1418
SoHo | 38 Greene St. (Grand St.) | A/C/E to Canal St. | 212-625-0707
SoHo | 535 Broadway (Spring St.) | 6 to Spring St. | 212-680-0130
W 70s | 216 Columbus Ave. (70th St.) | 1/2/3 to 72nd St. | 212-579-1760
NEW Boerum Hill | 135 Smith St. (bet. Bergen & Dean Sts.) | Brooklyn |
F/G to Bergen St. | 718-488-7071
800-964-5777 | www.luckybrandjeans.com

For "great-looking", "well-fitting" "made in the USA" jeans that suit
"everyone from the bird-legged bean pole" guy to the "luscious, curvy"
hottie aiming for a "rock-chick-meets-new-country" look, "steer" over

to this national chain; let the "easygoing" "urban cow"-hands round you up a pair, plus other items designed with "good taste", and you'll agree it's "worth the extra cost for how great your butt looks."

Lucky Kid ☻

| - | - | - | E |

SoHo | 127 Prince St. (Wooster St.) | N/R/W to Prince St. | 212-466-0849 | 800-964-5777 | www.luckybrandjeans.com

SoHo browsers who have the good fortune to stumble upon Lucky Brand Jeans' sibling for pint-sized trendsetters are rewarded with a cool-looking shop decorated with green-and-white leaf frond-patterned wallpaper and whimsical window displays; lucky kids, from babies to toddlers to children up to size 12, hit pay dirt with funky, laid-back looks including rocker tees, hoodies, denim jackets and jeans.

Lucky Wang

| ▽ 25 | 22 | 19 | E |

Chelsea | 82 Seventh Ave. (bet. 15th & 16th Sts.) | 1/2/3 to 14th St. | 212-229-2900
G Village | 799 Broadway (bet. 10th & 11th Sts.) | 4/5/6/L/N/Q/R/W to 14th St./Union Sq. | 212-353-2850
866-353-2850 | www.luckywang.com

"At last!" sigh the fortunate few who've happened upon this Greenwich Village–Chelsea twosome where the "adorable" Asian-inspired kiddie creations like miniature kimonos packaged sushi-style come in "wonderful colors"; with such "funky-chic" finds, the only hitch is that there "isn't enough" of the stuff in the smaller Broadway original.

Ludivine ☻

| - | - | - | E |

G Village | 172 W. Fourth St. (Jones St.) | A/B/C/D/E/F/V to W. 4th St. | 646-336-6576 | www.boutiqueludivine.com

Parisienne to the core, this Greenwich Village find has light pink walls that serve as a feminine backdrop for insouciant styles that are somewhat reminiscent of what actress Julie Delpy wore in *Before Sunset* while marathon-chatting with Ethan Hawke; along with Les Prairies de Paris' strictly tailored coats, Tsumori Chisato's boldly printed dresses and Vanessa Bruno's floaty camis, you'll find shoes and totes to round out the *c'est magnifique* chic of owner Ludivine Gregoire's divine taste.

Lulu Guinness

| 24 | 25 | 19 | E |

W Village | 394 Bleecker St. (bet. Perry & W. 11th Sts.) | 1 to Christopher St./Sheridan Sq. | 212-367-2120 | www.luluguinness.com

"What a hoot" – "how can you not love" this "British eccentric's" "fabulously" "quirky" handbags, shoes and makeup cases, all showcased at her "funky", "friendly" West Village shop boasting "great window displays"; the "whimsical contents" are the "perfect" "pick-me-up" – like "a breath of fresh air on a hot summer day" – but the willpowerless should beware a lulu of a bill as they may "spend lots of money for lots of fun"; N.B. she's also added a new line of luxe bedding.

lululemon athletica ☻

| - | - | - | E |

W 60s | 1928 Broadway (64th St.) | 1 to 66th St./Lincoln Ctr. | 212-712-1767 | www.lululemon.com

Guy and gal yoginis with a yen for Zen essentials zone in on ultra-fashionable down-dog-wear and cycling and running garb too at this Canadian company's West 60s flagship; the colorful, dry wick cropped pants, leggings, sweats, fitted hoodies, tights, tanks, even tu-

nics flatter the bod with the extra boost of organic and natural fabrics –
and you can pack it all up in a funky, locker-size gymbag; N.B. a new
branch is slated to open in Union Square.

L'Uomo ●

▽ 24 | 21 | 20 | VE

W Village | 383 Bleecker St. (Perry St.) | 1 to Christopher St./Sheridan Sq. |
212-206-1844

As one might deduce from the name, which translates from Italian
as 'the man', most of the slightly "avant-garde" offerings at this
West Village boutique come with a Euro bent; choose from a selection
of Baldessarini, CP and Stone Island or, if indecision strikes, the
"owner knows what looks good on everyone"; N.B. plans are afoot to
relocate in 2008.

Lush ●

23 | 23 | 22 | M

Flatiron | 7 E. 14th St. (bet. 5th Ave. & University Pl.) | L/N/R/W/Q/
4/5/6 to Union Sq. | 212-255-5133
Garment District | 1293 Broadway (bet. 33rd & 34th Sts.) | B/D/F/N/
Q/R/V/W to 34th St./Herald Sq. | 212-564-9120
SoHo | 531 Broadway (bet. Prince & Spring Sts.) | 6 to Spring St. |
212-925-2323
W 70s | 2165 Broadway (bet. 76th & 77th Sts.) | 1 to 79th St. | 212-787-5874
Elmhurst | Queens Ctr. | 90-15 Queens Blvd. (bet. 57th & 59th Aves.) |
Queens | G/R/V to Grand Ave./Newtown | 718-699-8969
www.lush.com

"The best British import since the Beatles" cheer fans of these "funky,
playful" chain links where "quirky" toiletries like Vegan Karma soap,
Cynthia Sylvia Stout Shampoo and famous Bath Bombs in "flavors
you'd never think of" are stacked in colorful "deli-style displays"; but
delicate types decry "gimmicky" products and "smelly", "overpowering" premises that "assault the senses."

Lyell

- | - | - | E

NoLita | 173 Elizabeth St. (bet. Kenmare & Spring Sts.) | J/M/Z to
Bowery | 212-966-8484 | www.lyellnyc.com

Emma Fletcher pleases ladylike stylesetters who like a hint of nostalgia in their Victorian pleated blouses and a touch of silver-screen class
in a cinched-waist jacket; with its delicate 1940s-era wallpaper and
tiled floor, her pearl of a shop on the SoHo-NoLita border reflects the
hip, yet old-fashioned vibe of her femme-fabulous designs.

☑ Lyric Hi-Fi, Inc. ▨

28 | 25 | 23 | VE

E 80s | 1221 Lexington Ave. (bet. 82nd & 83rd Sts.) | 4/5/6 to 86th St. |
212-439-1900 | www.lyricusa.com

Enter "the inner sanctuary for high-end sound and video" at this "conservative" yet state-of-the-art store on the UES; some say the audio
"high priests" on staff "can be forbidding", but beyond that "stuffy" facade awaits "expert" advice and "outstanding recommendations" on
"top-tier" equipment, the likes of which has even seduced Bill Clinton.

M.A.C. Cosmetics

26 | 24 | 20 | M

Flatiron | Flatiron Bldg. | 1 E. 22nd St. (B'way) | N/R/W to 23rd St. |
212-677-6611 ●
Harlem | 202 W. 125th St. (bet. Adam Clayton Powell &
Frederick Douglass Blvds.) | A/B/C/D to 125th St. | 212-665-0676 ●

(continued)

(continued)

M.A.C. Cosmetics

SoHo | 113 Spring St. (bet. Greene & Mercer Sts.) | 6 to Spring St. | 212-334-4641

W 60s | 148 Columbus Ave. (bet. 66th & 67th Sts.) | 1 to 66th St./ Lincoln Ctr. | 212-769-0725 ◗

Brooklyn Heights | 152 Montague St. (bet. Clinton & Henry Sts.) | Brooklyn | 1/2/4/5/M/N/R to Court St./Borough Hall | 718-596-1994 ◗

800-387-6707 | www.maccosmetics.com

"Once you go M.A.C. you don't go back" maintain mavens of this makeup chain "mecca" that attracts actors, artists and drag queens alike with "a vast array" of products in a "rainbow of colors" that "last long and wear well" at "prices that will not break your budget"; however, service is "highly variable" as some of the staffers seem "too self-obsessed to actually serve customers", while others apply "clown"-quality cosmetic jobs.

☑ MacKenzie-Childs

25 | 27 | 22 | E

E 50s | 14 W. 57th St. (bet. 5th & 6th Aves.) | N/R/W to 5th Ave./59th St. | 212-570-6050 | 888-665-1999 | www.mackenzie-childs.com

It's a "visual frenzy" at this Midtown purveyor of clashingly colored and patterned ceramics, painted furniture and other "feminine and frilly" products for the home like ramekins that resemble cupcakes, black-and-white check fondue sets and "quirky" chairs decorated with fish; the "very expensive" "eye candy" here has its admirers, but cynics sniff "wasn't this a fad whose time has passed?"

☑ Macy's ◗

19 | 15 | 12 | M

Garment District | 151 W. 34th St. (bet. B'way & 7th Ave.) | 1/2/3/A/C/E to 34th St./Penn Station | 212-695-4400 | 800-289-6229 | www.macys.com
Additional locations throughout the NY area

You can do "all your shopping under one roof" at this block-long "Herald Square landmark", "riding the old wooden escalators" to peruse the "affordable accessories", "a corridor of cool" cookware, "a nice variety" of cosmetics and clothing and "good bets in beds and mattresses"; "if you can't find it here, you're not looking hard enough" – but look hard you will, given "too many tourists", "mostly non-helpful help" and "chaotic" aisles; cynics sigh "if only Macy's ran its store like it runs the Thanksgiving Day parade" – still, even though it's "often maddening", NYC "couldn't live without it."

Madura

24 | 25 | 21 | E

E 80s | 1162 Madison Ave. (bet. 85th & 86th Sts.) | 4/5/6 to 86th St. | 212-327-2681 | www.madurahome.com

This family-owned French firm makes an "excellent addition to home stores on the UES" by offering "colorful" ready-made curtains with "coordinated household items" like bedspreads and tablecloths that are not your "typical" "Bed Bath & Beyond" look; the "helpful" and "efficient" staff enables you to navigate the somewhat "complicated" concept.

Magic Windows

27 | 20 | 19 | E

E 80s | 1186 Madison Ave. (87th St.) | 4/5/6 to 86th St. | 212-289-0028 | www.magic-windows.com

"If you want to drop a bundle on your little bundle", this "Upper East Side institution" has "got it all"; no high-fashion hocus-pocus here, just "ducky duds" that range from "high-quality" layette pieces to "adorable" "special-occasion" outfits for girls and "very European boys stuff" to dreamy prom dresses for your teen; still, a handful huff that the "sales staff could lower their noses a notch."

Magnificent Costume Jewels 🗷 Ⓜ

| 22 | 21 | 20 | E |

By appointment only | inquiries: 212-996-3540 | www.magnificentcostumejewels.com

One of the city's top-secret sources for faux estate pieces like copies of "the queen's jewels" is this costume king housed in the owner's Upper East Side apartment; the "large selection" is "constantly changing", and even those "on Cinderella's budget" can find duplicates of "one-of-a-kind designs" here; N.B. by appointment only.

Maison Martin Margiela

| - | - | - | VE |

W Village | 803 Greenwich St. (bet. Jane & W. 12th Sts.) | A/C/E/L to 14th St./8th Ave. | 212-989-7612 | www.maisonmartinmargiela.com

"The quintessential enfant terrible of fashion finally gets an outpost to showcase his exquisitely constructed pieces of art" – deceptively simple designs boasting unexpected details like snipped banding, raw edges and asymmetrical closures; the presentation in the West Village space is "reflective of the Margiela image" (bright lights, all-white and off-kilter), and while some giggle at the "wacked-out" mens- and womenswear, it's "well worth the bankruptcy" to those who believe in "inspirational, not aspirational" clothing.

Make Up For Ever 🗷

| ▽ 28 | - | 20 | M |

G Village | 8 E. 12th St. (bet. 5th Ave. & University Pl.) | 4/5/6/L/N/Q/R/W to 14th St./Union Sq. | 212-941-9337 | 877-757-5145 | www.makeupforever.com

Geared to "the professional makeup artist as well as the everyday girl or boy", the cosmetics at this "user-friendly" store, relocated from SoHo to the Village, boast "high amounts of pigment and lots of staying power" – maybe not enough to last forever but supporters swear sufficient "to last all night long without turning funny or runny."

Maleeka Ⓜ

| - | - | - | E |

Downtown | 327 Atlantic Ave. (bet. Hoyt & Smith Sts.) | Brooklyn | F/G to Bergen St. | 718-596-0991 | www.maleeka.com

With its entrancing windows and cabinets filled with ornamented slippers and glittering jewelry from faraway lands including the owner's native Pakistan, this dreamscape on Atlantic Avenue evokes the vibrancy of a Bollywood flick; completing the picture: colorful clothing from an array of contemporary European and American lines like Harkham and Olga Kapustina that change with the season.

Malia Mills Swimwear

| 26 | 21 | 23 | E |

E 70s | 1031 Lexington Ave. (bet. 73rd & 74th Sts.) | 6 to 77th St. | 212-517-7485 🗷

NoLita | 199 Mulberry St. (bet. Kenmare & Spring Sts.) | 6 to Spring St. | 212-625-2311

W 70s | 220 Columbus Ave. (70th St.) | 1/2/3 to 72nd St. | 212-874-7200 800-685-3479 | www.maliamills.com

"Bathing suit shopping has been redesigned" at this eponymous designer's trio where the "dreaded experience of trying on bikinis" becomes an opportunity "to make any woman feel good" about her "unique" shape; the "mix-and-match" selection "flatters" "different" bodies, even "lumpy" ones, plus the "warm staff" further "justifies" the "expensive" prices, helping you "find just the right top and bottom" in "lovely colors" and "fabrics that hold up nicely"; N.B. the company has added new sportwear pieces that can double as beach coverups.

Malin + Goetz ●

▽ 22	24	23	E

Chelsea | 177 Seventh Ave. (bet. 20th & 21st Sts.) | 1 to 23rd St. | 212-463-7368 | www.malinandgoetz.com

Matthew Malin (ex Kiehl's) and Andrew Goetz's "real up-and-coming-brand" of "high-quality" unisex face, body and haircare products has "such nice packaging" that "you almost hate to break the seal", but once you do the "goods are incomparable" – especially the peppermint scrub seen in many an upscale Manhattan bathroom; the futuristic, all-white Chelsea space also features a lab on the premises, which adds to its modern apothecary aura.

M&J Trimming

25	19	20	M

Garment District | 1008 Sixth Ave. (bet. 37th & 38th Sts.) | B/D/F/N/Q/R/V/W to 34th St./Herald Sq. | 212-391-6200 | 800-965-8746 | www.mjtrim.com

Do-it-yourselfers "drool over the choices" at this 71-year-old Garment District "candy store for trimmings" that "looks like it was designed by Willy Wonka", with "zillions" of "colorful, enticing" ribbons, crystals, "beads, buttons and notions" stacked all the way up to the 30-ft. ceiling; ok, it's "not inexpensive but it's certainly consumer-friendly", since "everything's easy to find" and the "knowledgeable", "non-harassing staff" "allows you to wander while you envision your creations."

Manhattan Center for Kitchen & Bath

-	-	-	E

Flatiron | 29 E. 19th St. (bet. B'way & Park Ave.) | N/R/W to 23rd St. | 212-995-0500 | www.mckb.com

This "beautiful" 10,000-sq.-ft., two-story showroom in the Flatiron District features products from over 84 manufacturers, including the highly coveted Euro brands Aga and Liebherr, in categories ranging from high-end appliances and custom cabinetry to tile and stone, plumbing fixtures and home theater equipment; the megalith is a joint venture between Brooklyn's Drimmers and Kitchen Expressions.

Manhattan Saddlery ⊠

-	-	-	E

Gramercy | 117 E. 24th St. (bet. Lexington & Park Aves.) | 6 to 23rd St. | 212-673-1400 | www.manhattansaddlery.com

Saddle up and run for the roses at this Gramercy haunt, a standby since 1912 where equestrian enthusiasts pony up greenbacks aplenty for stylish barnyard fashions from jodhpurs, bridles and tack to outfits for the track; there's no need to be a horse whisperer, though, since helpful "salespeople" will take you by the reins and "spend" plenty of time guiding you to the best for fox hunts, steeplechases and polo matches.

⊿ Manolo Blahnik ⊠

28	28	24	VE

W 50s | 31 W. 54th St. (bet. 5th & 6th Aves.) | E/V to 5th Ave./53rd St. | 212-582-3007

"Carrie Bradshaw made us all dream" about investing in "foot candy" with "fabulously high heels" from the Midtown "house of the famous and expensive" designer shoes, but "even if you're not sexy and single", "true shoe addicts" insist "you'll glide on air when you slip into" the "ultimate" "must-have" stilettos that will definitely "deplete your Swiss bank account"; "every woman should experience the royal treatment of shopping" at this "pinnacle" of "luxury" – does there "live a dame who wouldn't if she could"?

NEW Manrico Cashmere — | - | - | VE

E 70s | 922 Madison Ave. (73rd St.) | 6 to 77th St. | 212-794-4200 | www.manrico.com

Recently moved to new, monochromatic Madison Avenue digs – a bi-level black, white and gray space, adorned with art deco antiques (which are for sale) and custom-made armoires – this Italian maker offers the cashmere-conscious a collection of mens- and womens-wear, ranging from the classic (feather-light sweaters, scarves) to the clever (five-pocket blue jeans); those who truly go for the goat's hair won't be able to resist the bed linens, made of a unique, super-thin blend.

Marc and Max ● — | - | - | E

W Village | 342 Bleecker St. (bet. Christopher & W. 10th Sts.) | 1 to Christopher St./Sheridan Sq. | 212-647-1688 | www.marcandmax.com

This petite and unpretentious West Village shop is well-stocked with lingerie and loungewear from the likes of Cosabella, Huit, Princess Tam Tam and Wolford, including racks of camisoles so stylish you may not want to hide them under your clothing; a small selection of fine jewelry helps make it a perfect girlie stop when shopping on the Bleecker Street strip.

Marc by Marc Jacobs ● 25 | 24 | 20 | E

NEW W Village | 382 Bleecker St. (Perry St.) | 1 to Christopher St./Sheridan Sq. | 212-929-0304
W Village | 403-5 Bleecker St. (W. 11th St.) | 1 to Christopher St./Sheridan Sq. | 212-924-0026
www.marcjacobs.com

Those jonesin' for some Jacobs start off at this "trendy-to-the-max" women's store (at 403-5 Bleecker Street) and it's new, neighboring men's-only offshoot to get a taste of the "cute clothes, cute bags, cute everything" from this controversial designer's "colorful and fresh" diffusion line; the staff "is such fun" that the "serious prices come as a bit of a shock", but guys and "girls with a sense of humor" are "hooked" on these "quirky" re-Marc-able pieces.

Marc by Marc Jacobs Accessories ● 28 | 26 | 21 | E

W Village | 385 Bleecker St. (Perry St.) | 1 to Christopher St./Sheridan Sq. | 212-924-6126 | www.marcjacobs.com

"Love is all I can say!" avow acolytes who anoint this boldface designer the "god of accessories" and covet his "cherished" bags, truly the "holy grail for fashionistas"; you'll "want everything" at Bleecker Street's "funky yet chic" "hipster heaven" (oftentimes boasting "terrific windows" that make political points) because the shoes, gloves, leather goods and perfumes are also the "most lovely of lovelies" and "worth every penny"; N.B. it now exclusively carries Marc by Marc Jacobs accessories, which may outdate the scores.

NEW Marc Ecko Cut & Sew ●

| - | - | - | M |

Chelsea | 147 Eighth Ave. (bet. 17th & 18th Sts.) | A/C/E/L to 14th St./ 8th Ave. | 212-206-8351 | www.marceckocollection.com

The half-naked woman sculpted onto the door handle of this Chelsea upstart is a dead giveaway that you're not in traditional menswear turf anymore; welcome to the new showcase for enterprising founder/ creative director Marc Ecko's affordable signature collection, a Gotham-goes-Gothic librarylike setting tweaked with skull wallpaper, a fantasy-land mural and a tree growing through the atrium roof – an apt backdrop for edgy urban-guy offerings like printed hoodies, velvet blazers, tuxedo shirts, novelty jeans and funky, screenprinted T-shirts.

Marc Jacobs

| 27 | 25 | 20 | VE |

SoHo | 163 Mercer St. (bet. Houston & Prince Sts.) | N/R/W to Prince St. | 212-343-1490 | www.marcjacobs.com

On your Marc, get set, go to this "cool, casual mecca" in SoHo "for all things achingly hip and modern with a vintage twist" from the designer whose "amazing" American sportswear is defined as "the epitome of NYC chic" by "tall, skinny supermodels" and "very, very rich skater dudes"; housing both mens- and womenswear, the loftlike space is "a great place to blow your rent", although some say you may "need a raise and cosmetic surgery to be comfortable shopping here" ("unless you're a movie star, don't expect any service").

Marie-Chantal ⊠

| 25 | 24 | 17 | VE |

E 80s | 1192 Madison Ave. (bet. 87th & 88th Sts.) | 4/5/6 to 86th St. | 212-828-7300 | www.mariechantal.com

"Cute setup, cute clothing" characterizes this quaint East 80s boutique, home to the Greek Princess and über-socialite/shopper Marie-Chantal's children's collection; her designs slow down the hands of time with "*très chic*", age-appropriate fashions that actually let kids be kids; so even if the staff exhibits some "attitude from hell" and the "exquisite" garb costs a king's ransom, your offspring will feel like royalty.

Mariko ⊠

| - | - | - | E |

E 70s | 998 Madison Ave. (bet. 77th & 78th Sts.) | 6 to 77th St. | 212-472-1176 | www.marikopalmbeach.com

Several generations of Upper East Side blue bloods and social climbers alike have relied on this costume-jewelry shop for its stash of pedi-greed and pricey "knockoffs", from fake pearl ropes and beaded chokers to very Schlumberger-like enamel bangles and Verdura-inspired cross-decorated cuff bracelets; some say one thing that's genuine though is the staff's "attitude."

Marimekko

| 24 | 23 | 21 | E |

E 70s | 1262 Third Ave. (bet. 72nd & 73rd Sts.) | 6 to 68th St. | 212-628-8400 | 800-527-0624 | www.kiitosmarimekko.com

"Bright", "bold", "eye-catching prints" characterize this East 70s haven for fans of the Finnish brand, whose "forever '60s" aesthetic "inspires" nostalgia for "fun stuff for the home", "adorable accessories and clothing", "fabrics by the yard" and now bed linens too; "it's hard not to smile when you see" the "rainbow" of colors; still, "for the price of a couple" of "super-cool" women's frocks you could "be on your way to Helsinki."

| | QUALITY | DISPLAY | SERVICE | COST |

Market NYC Ⓜ
▽ 20 | 18 | 20 | M

NoLita | 268 Mulberry St. (bet. Houston & Prince Sts.) | B/D/F/V to B'way/Lafayette St. | 212-580-8995 | www.themarketnyc.com
Hip-hunters dedicated to scouting out "unique items" that "distinguish them from the pack" make this "awesome" NoLita bazaar their "first stop"; held only on Saturday and Sunday in a school gym, this "best-kept secret" fashion collective presents "funky, original" "jewelry, bags and tees" by young designers who are "excited to tell you about their product" and may even "give you a better price" than what's at retail.

Mark Ingram Bridal Atelier ☒
27 | - | 26 | E

E 50s | 110 E. 55th St. (bet. Lexington & Park Aves.) | 4/5/6/F/N/R/W to 59th St./Lexington Ave. | 212-319-6778 | www.bridalatelier.com
Owner "Mark Ingram knows his stuff", in fact, he and his "very mellow", "outstanding staff" at this "low-key, upscale", by-appointment-only bridal atelier (now in the East 50s) "treat you like the special lady you are", "offering input" to "ensure you won't look like a big bonbon" on your wedding day; it's an "excellent place" to view a "beautifully edited selection" of "high-quality gowns" that includes "designers not a lot of others carry", like Angel Sanchez, Karl Lagerfeld and Monique Lhuillier.

Marmalade ◐
- | - | - | M

LES | 172 Ludlow St. (bet. Houston & Stanton Sts.) | F/V to Lower East Side/2nd Ave. | 212-473-8070 | www.marmaladevintage.com
Set in a spacious, sunny storefront on the Lower East Side, this vintage clothing store serves up a sweet collection of casual clothes that convey a curiously contemporary quality, even though they date from the '50s to the '80s; there are also lots of midpriced accessories and shoes (remember Pappagallo?) – mostly for her, though there's a small assortment for him and the kiddies too.

Marni
▽ 24 | 25 | 21 | VE

SoHo | 161 Mercer St. (bet. Houston & Prince Sts.) | N/R/W to Prince St. | 212-343-3912 | www.marni.com
Boasting milky-glass floors and silvery tree-limb fixtures, this "slick environment showcases lovingly dreamed-up womenswear" – plus "inventive" clothing for men and kids – from Milanese designer Consuelo Castiglioni; her loosely fitted dresses and duster coats are "definitely a distinctive look", but a big hit with the "bohemian-chic crowd" that urges "purchase early, as this SoHo location sells out of the hot items fast."

☒ Marshalls ◐
16 | 9 | 8 | I

W 100s | 105 W. 125th St. (Lenox Ave.) | 1 to 125th St. | 212-866-3963
Bronx | Bay Plaza Shopping Ctr. | 2100 Bartow Ave. (Co-Op City Blvd.) | 6 to Pelham Bay Park | 718-320-7211
Bronx | 50 W. 225th St. (bet. B'way & Kingsbridge Ave.) | 1 to 225th St. | 718-933-9062
Bensonhurst | 1832 86th St. (bet. 18th & 19th Aves.) | Brooklyn | N to 86th St. | 718-621-0784
Downtown | Atlantic Ctr. | 625 Atlantic Ave. (bet. Ft. Greene Pl. & S. Portland Ave.) | Brooklyn | 2/3/4/5/B/D/M/N/Q/R to Atlantic Ave. | 718-398-5254

(continued)

(continued)

Marshalls

Starrett City | Gateway Ctr. | 351 Gateway Dr. (bet. Fountain & Vandalia Aves.) | Brooklyn | A/C to Euclid Ave. | 718-235-8142
LIC | 48-18 Northern Blvd. (48th St.) | Queens | G/R/V to Northern Blvd. | 718-626-4700
Rego Park | 96-05 Queens Blvd. (Junction Blvd.) | Queens | G/R/V to 63rd Dr./Rego Park | 718-275-7797
Staten Island | 2485 Richmond Ave. (Richmond Hill Rd.) | 718-370-3313
888-627-7425 | www.marshallsonline.com

If you go to this discount chain with no specific needs, you "can really score a hit" among "an amazing variety of clothes and housewares", with "some of the items looking like they should cost more" (perfect for "furnishing your overpriced studio"); however, it "depends on the location" as "stores vary tremendously" – though scores suggest the "nasty treatment from employees" and the "messy" digs ("worse than the kids' room") are universal.

Marston & Langinger ☒   - | - | - | E

SoHo | 117 Mercer St. (bet. Prince & Spring Sts.) | N/R/W to Prince St. | 212-965-0434 | www.marston-and-langinger.com

It seems fitting that this veddy upscale British import that's best known for custom-made timber-and-glass conservatories opened its first stateside shop in SoHo in a 19th-century warehouse; the cavernous, yet calm, space is home to outdoor-inspired items like garden tools, textiles, tiny Christian Tortu dried rose arrangements, wire tables and planters, pastel pressed-glass plates, classic willow or contemporary furniture, stone fountains and aged teak benches.

Mary Adams The Dress Ⓜ   - | - | - | E

LES | 138 Ludlow St. (bet. Rivington & Stanton Sts.) | F/V to Lower East Side/2nd Ave. | 212-473-0237 | www.maryadamsthedress.com

Nonconformist brides and left-of-center party girls jonesing for one-of-a-kind, fanciful eveningwear head to this by-appointment shop on the Lower East Side where designer Mary Adams whips up flirty off-the-rack and custom-made confections; the gowns, minis and separates are infused with a sense of wit, fun and, at times, a bit of retro flair, playing into every woman's dress-up fantasy.

🅉 Mary Arnold Toys ☒   26 | 19 | 20 | E

E 70s | 1010 Lexington Ave. (bet. 72nd & 73rd Sts.) | 6 to 68th St. | 212-744-8510

"Save yourself the hassle" of the "big" chains and skip over to this "wonderfully old-fashioned", "friendly" East 70s toy-meister that's "been around forever"; you'll find "all of the usual suspects" crammed into the "close" quarters, from the "hottest, most cutting-edge" playthings to the "thinking child's" "goodies", including early developmental games, books, art kits and dress-up duds; the added edge: "they always have" stuff "in stock", plus "they deliver!"

Mason's Tennis Mart   ▽ 26 | 19 | 23 | E

E 50s | 56 E. 53rd St. (bet. Madison & Park Aves.) | E/V to 5th Ave./53rd St. | 212-755-5805 | www.masonstennis.com

Perhaps "the only shop a serious tennis player needs" is how swinging supporters sum up this Midtown racquet retailer, a "regular" stop thanks to its "great selection" of "unique clothes", "top-of-the-line" equipment, "solid stringing" and "affable", "helpful staffers"; if a few fault it as "too pricey", insiders advise that its January "annual sale is the best" way to score that "perfect" something at a serious markdown.

Mastic Spa ◑

| | | | E |

SoHo | 438 W. Broadway (Prince St.) | N/R/W to Prince St. | 212-219-3251 | www.masticspa.com

The Mastic tree only grows on the Greek island of Chios, and the gummy resin it exudes is believed to have healing properties; here at this family-owned SoHo spa the exotic ingredient turns up in tony treatment products like moisturizers, soaps, salts and shampoos for both sexes.

Matta

| | | | E |

NoLita | 241 Lafayette St. (bet. Prince & Spring Sts.) | 6 to Spring St. | 212-343-9399 | www.mattany.com

This spare, airy, high-ceilinged shop on Lafayette makes a big impact with its "fabulous bohemian" women's and children's clothing, delicate jewelry and home furnishings; Italian designer/co-owner Christina Gitti travels the world to find inspiration for her lightweight cotton sarongs, kurtas, tees and button-downs in lush colors and patterns and covetable quilts and pillows; compatible lines like Antipast, Lucky Fish, Velvet and Orla Kiely reflect her flair for mild-mannered chic.

Matter

| | | | E |

NEW **Little Italy** | 405 Broome St. (bet. Centre & Lafayette Sts.) | 6 to Spring St. | 212-343-2600

Park Slope | 227 Fifth Ave. (bet. Carroll & President Sts.) | Brooklyn | M/R to Union St. | 718-230-1150 **M**

www.mattermatters.com

Every "well-designed" object does Matter at this all-white, progressive Park Slope provocateur with a gallerylike feel (artwork is actually displayed to the rear) and its new Broome Street offshoot; high-concept goods like cast resin picture frames, antler-shaped ceramic table lamps and sleek glass carafes along with a well-edited selection of unabashedly cool jewelry prompt aesthetes to sigh I "always want to buy everything" here.

⊠ Maurice Villency

| 26 | - | 21 | VE |

E 50s | 949 Third Ave. (57th St.) | 4/5/6/F/N/R/W to 59th St./Lexington Ave. | 212-725-4840 | 877-845-5362 | www.villency.com

Since 1932, this luxury furniture company has offered "quality" "modern" "European design" and pieces that "last many years in top condition", "especially sofas and sectionals" in "fabulous leather" and at "high prices"; the relocated Midtown flagship still stretches a city block, boasts an in-house coffee shop and is full of salespeople that are "helpful without being pushy."

Mavi ◑

| 22 | 21 | 20 | M |

E Village | 832 Broadway (bet. 12th & 13th Sts.) | 4/5/6/L/N/Q/R/W to 14th St./Union Sq. | 917-289-0520 | 866-628-4575 | www.mavi.com

Mavens of the Mavi-lous Turkish brand maintain that this Broadway flagship, a modern steel-and-wood showroom with a rotating gallery, is a mecca for "inexpensive yet trendy jeans"; rely on a "helpful staff" to help you nail down booty-enhancing denim as well as a "good selection" of his-and-hers jackets, hoodies and casualwear.

Max Azria
- | - | - | VE

SoHo | 409 W. Broadway (Spring St.) | C/E to Spring St. | 212-991-4740 | www.maxazria.com

Women who are mad for Max and have much moolah motor to this SoHo boutique, devoted to the designer's upscale collection; taking nature as its inspiration, the small shop has an organic ambiance – it's centered around an actual tree trunk, and images of leaves and shrubbery abound amid the racks of clothes; the garments have the same flowy, loose feel as Azria's BCBG label, but are edgier and more luxurious, with higher-quality fabrics and attention to detail.

Maxilla & Mandible
∇ 25 | 22 | 20 | E

W 80s | 451 Columbus Ave. (bet. 81st & 82nd Sts.) | B/C to 81st St. | 212-724-6173 | www.maxillaandmandible.com

For an "only in NYC" experience, cut a path to this "tiny, but treasure-laden" osteological shop (strategically located a stone's throw from the American Museum of Natural History) where kids, collectors, "aspiring taxidermists and bone collectors" alike "love" to dig through the "weird" array of skeletons, fossils, insects and quarry curios "you can't see anywhere else"; "it's worth a visit, even just to look in the window."

MaxMara
25 | 24 | 22 | VE

E 60s | 813 Madison Ave. (68th St.) | 6 to 68th St. | 212-879-6100 | 🛇
SoHo |450 W. Broadway (bet. Houston & Prince Sts.) | C/E to Spring St. | 212-674-1817

"Sleek and classy", this Italian womenswear powerhouse takes a pragmatic approach in its "treasure trove" of "well-made classics" at "costly" but – given the quality – "correct prices", including "wool coats to die for", "nice-fitting" suits and other "tailored clothing" just "fashionable" enough that "you don't see yourself coming and going"; amid the "minimalist decor" of the East 60s or SoHo shops, the "clothes could sell themselves – thankfully, since the salespeople", though "attentive", do have some "attitude."

Max Studio
20 | 21 | 18 | E

SoHo | 426 W. Broadway (bet. Prince & Spring Sts.) | C/E to Spring St. | 212-431-8995 | www.maxstudio.com

No need to max out your MasterCard at this SoHo boutique, which has "an edge over its" competition with its ever-changing stock of skirts and shirts in "flowy fabrics", "fun work clothes", lean outerwear and hip sandals and boots; however, malcontents moan over the "mixed quality."

Mayle
- | - | - | E

NoLita | 242 Elizabeth St. (bet. Houston & Prince Sts.) | B/D/F/V to B'way/Lafayette St. | 212-625-0406

One of NoLita's first, this little shop is now a fixture for sweet-but-not-sugary stylemakers, who adore owner/ex-model Jayne Mayle's "original offbeat takes on classic styles"; the designer reveals her "different eye" with chic, unique, vintagey ladylike looks that also have a definite downtown edge and, *mais oui*, a "French feeling."

	QUALITY	DISPLAY	SERVICE	COST

McGuire ⊠
Murray Hill | 200 Lexington Ave. (32nd St.) | 6 to 33rd St. | 212-689-1565 | www.mcguirefurniture.com

| - | - | - | VE |

It took almost 60 years for this San Francisco–based fine furniture company, founded in '48, to open its first New York store, in Murray Hill; designers like Barbara Barry and Adam Tihany are on board, bringing an urban eye to traditionally outdoor materials like rattan and teak to produce "beautiful" high-end pieces that are at home in upscale interiors.

Me & Ro
NoLita | 241 Elizabeth St. (bet. Houston & Prince Sts.) | B/D/F/V to B'way/Lafayette St. | 917-237-9215 | 877-632-6376 | www.meandrojewelry.com

| 23 | 24 | 21 | E |

Against a backdrop of silk ceiling lamps and a floating flower pond, this small NoLita shop showcases "hip" Indian, Chinese and Tibetan jewelry "with a mystical edge" (think symbols and lotus petal motifs) in silver and gold; the rich boho look "makes you feel like a Hollywood or fashion insider", but cynics question "how something so tiny can cost so much?"

Mecox Gardens
E 70s | 962 Lexington Ave. (bet. 70th & 71st Sts.) | 6 to 68th St. | 212-249-5301 | www.mecoxgardens.com

| - | - | - | VE |

An "expensive" urban outpost of an upscale Hamptons flagship designed for those with second (and third) homes, this Upper East Side garden-inspired furnishings shop showcases a blend of antique, reproduction and custom pieces and tony tabletop accessories, like pewter-rimmed hurricane lamps; devotees declare if you're looking for the likes of a limestone frieze, this is the place.

Medici ◐
W 80s | 420 Columbus Ave. (bet. 80th & 81st Sts.) | B/C to 81st St. | 212-712-9342

| 20 | 17 | 17 | M |

It's "one of my regular stops" assert admirers who hit this Columbus Avenue standby for "stylish" footwear that's "a bit different"; the "breadth and depth can satisfy any shoe aficionado who wants a break from the mass-marketers", plus the "great prices" and "leather quality" make it a "good bet" – though you'll look like "you spent a fortune."

Meg Cohen Design Shop
SoHo | 59 Thompson St. (bet. Broome & Spring Sts.) | C/E to Spring St. | 917-805-0189 | www.megcohendesign.com

| - | - | - | E |

With its painted white brick walls and airy feel, this accessories designer's modern nook feels like an oasis of calm in SoHo; soft-touch seekers score plush cashmere finds, from feminine hoods, fingerless gloves and arm socks for her to ski caps and long skinny scarves for him, all in luscious solids or stripes; nesters zero in on bull's-eye pillows and trays with collapsible stands to create instant coffee tables.

Memorial Sloan-Kettering Cancer Center Thrift Shop ⊠
E 80s | 1440 Third Ave. (bet. 81st & 82nd Sts.) | 4/5/6 to 86th St. | 212-535-1250 | www.memorialthriftshop.org

| 22 | 17 | 15 | M |

There's "always something to buy" "and it's all for a good cause" (cancer research and patient care) at this veteran, "airy" Upper

East Side thrift store where shopping is "like picking through your rich aunt's closet" – not to mention her living room, kitchen and library – for "high-end" items; down 'n' dirty bargain-hunters find it a "little too coolly genteel", but "sometimes you get a great bargain for a quality item."

Men's Wearhouse ◑

| | 17 | 16 | 19 | M |

E 40s | 380 Madison Ave. (46th St.) | 4/5/6/7/S to 42nd St./ Grand Central | 212-856-9008 | 800-851-6744 | www.menswearhouse.com
Additional locations throughout the NY area

When in need of business attire or a "rented tux", fellas head for this menswear chain that even carries sizes to fit "nontraditional shapes"; "nice displays" of its "ordinary" but "not high-priced" clothing (suits, dress shirts, slacks, shoes, ties, outerwear) and salesmen who greet you upon arrival add up to a "pleasant shopping" experience for most, though more sensitive sorts find the floor crew "overly pushy."

Metro Bicycles

| | 20 | 15 | 20 | M |

E 80s | 1311 Lexington Ave. (88th St.) | 4/5/6 to 86th St. | 212-427-4450
E Village | 332 E. 14th St. (bet. 1st & 2nd Aves.) | 4/5/6/L/N/Q/R/W to 14th St./Union Sq. | 212-228-4344
Flatiron | 546 Sixth Ave. (15th St.) | A/C/E/L to 14th St./8th Ave. | 212-255-5100
TriBeCa | 75 Varick St. (bet. Grand & Watts Sts.) | 1 to Canal St. | 212-334-8000
W 40s | 360 W. 47th St. (9th Ave.) | A/C/E to 42nd St./Port Authority | 212-581-4500
W 90s | 231 W. 96th St. (B'way) | 1/2/3 to 96th St. | 212-663-7531
www.metrobicycles.com

Not only will you find "good prices" at this chainlet, but you'll also "get what you pay for" – namely, "quality" cycles including "medium range" models such as Raleigh, LeMond and Trek; the "helpful", "no-attitude" staffers are "patient", which one especially "needs when buying kids' bikes", and the numerous locations throughout Manhattan make it "convenient for parts" too.

Metropolitan Lumber & Hardware

| | 22 | 12 | 17 | M |

SoHo | 175 Spring St. (bet. Thompson St. & W. B'way) | C/E to Spring St. | 212-966-3466
W 40s | 617 11th Ave. (bet. 45th & 46th Sts.) | A/C/E to 42nd St./ Port Authority | 212-246-9090
Astoria | 34-35 Steinway St. (bet. 34th & 35th Aves.) | Queens | G/R/ V to Steinway St. | 718-392-4441
Corona | 108-56 Roosevelt Ave. (108th St.) | Queens | 7 to 111th St. | 718-898-2100
Jamaica | 108-20 Merrick Blvd. (109th Ave.) | Queens | E/J/Z to Jamaica Ctr. Parsons/Archer | 718-657-0100
www.themetlumber.com

Go "where the local builders buy" suggest planksters who get on board at these "convenient full-service lumberyards in Manhattan" and Queens offering a "great selection" at "fair prices"; service is "nice and old-fashioned", which means "they'll go out of their way for you" – "if you get the right person, you're set for life"; they can also help you choose tools and electrical and plumbing equipment.

☑ Metropolitan Museum of Art Store, The `25` `23` `20` `M`

E 80s | 1000 Fifth Ave. (81st St.) | 6 to 77th St. | 212-570-3894 Ⓜ
Seaport | South Street Seaport Museum | 14 Fulton St. (bet. Front &
South Sts.) | 2/3/4/5/A/C/J/M/Z to Fulton St./B'way/Nassau |
212-248-0954
Washington Heights | The Cloisters, Fort Tryon Park |
799 Fort Washington Ave. (190th St.) | A to 190th St. |
212-650-2277 Ⓜ
W 40s | Rockefeller Ctr. | 15 W. 49th St. (5th Ave.) | B/D/F/V to
47-50th Sts./Rockefeller Ctr. | 212-332-1360
800-468-7386 | www.metmuseum.org

"Dazzle your friends while supporting the arts" when you "prospect"
for gifts at Fifth Avenue's "gold standard for all museum shops" and its
three branches; the "eye-popping" selection features "fantastic
books", "high-quality reproductions", "amazing" accessories and "inspired" toys as well as "creative holiday items"; service is "knowledgeable", "prices vary" from "expensive" to "modest" and insiders suggest
checking out the clearance tables for "dirt-cheap" tchotchkes.

Metropolitan Opera Shop `24` `22` `20` `E`

W 60s | Lincoln Ctr., Metropolitan Opera Hse., north lobby | Columbus Ave.
(bet. 62nd & 65th Sts.) | 1 to 66th St./Lincoln Ctr. | 212-580-4090 |
www.metoperashop.org

The Met's lobby shop hums, especially on show nights when the culture crowd peruses an "expansive" array of CDs, DVDs, posters, accessories, jewelry and other "*bibelots*" – all "keyed to the lover of
music" (e.g. pseudo-Egyptian earrings to suggest *Aida*, kimonolike
bathrobes à la *Madame Butterfly*); at the very least, it's a "pleasant in-
termission diversion", although "helpful salespeople" and "bargains"
actually make it a fine stop for a "last-minute" gift.

Michael Anchin Glass Company `-` `-` `-` `M`

Williamsburg | 51 S. First St. (bet. Kent & Wythe Aves.) | Brooklyn | L
to Bedford Ave. | 212-925-1470 | www.michaelanchin.com

The "talented" artist-owner of this colorful, by-appointment-only
Williamsburg glass gallery hand-blows "lovely" vessels, vases, lamps
and bowls, and "you can own an original piece for a reasonable price."

NEW Michael Andrews Bespoke `22` `21` `20` `E`

LES | 20 Clinton St. (bet. Houston & Stanton St.) | F to 2nd Ave. |
212-677-1755 | www.michaelandrewsbespoke.com

Admirers of this by-appointment-only men's clothing store on the
Lower East Side assert "after you get one of their custom-tailored
creations" – whether it be a suit, shirt, overcoat or tuxedo – "you'll
never buy off-the-rack again"; after perusing the "latest fashions",
check out the luxe loafers and wingtips from bespoke shoemaker
Otabo – or just kick back at the full bar and watch the flat-screen TV.

NEW Michael Aram `26` `25` `21` `E`

Chelsea | 136 W. 18th St. (bet. 6th & 7th Aves.) | 1 to 18th St. |
212-461-6903 | www.michaelaram.com

"Finally, his own store!" exult admirers of this "talented artist" who's
inspired by Indian crafts and works mainly in metals like silver plate
and stainless steel for "unusual" "contemporary" pieces ranging from
tableware to furniture; his recently opened Chelsea flagship is housed

in a two-story skylit carriage house, a "beautiful" backdrop for "great wedding and engagement presents" at mostly "decent prices."

Michael Ashton 🖼   - | - | - | VE

E 70s | 933 Madison Ave. (74th St.) | 6 to 77th St. | 212-517-6655 | www.michaelashtonwatches.com

Passionate and worldly, the owner of this by-appointment corner shop near the Whitney Museum specializes in rare vintage watches from 1900–1990s, especially from Rolex (encompassing limited-edition Jean-Claude Killy or Paul Newman styles), Patek Philippe and Vacherin & Constantine; there's also a collection of estate jewelry, mostly art deco, along with European-cut diamond engagement rings.

✉ Michael C. Fina   26 | 23 | 20 | E

E 40s | 545 Fifth Ave. (45th St.) | 4/5/6/7/S to 42nd St./Grand Central | 212-557-2500 | 800-289-3462 | www.michaelcfina.com

Family-owned since 1935, and now located in Midtown only, this "wedding registry mecca" offers an "excellent selection" of "lovely", "high-end merchandise", from classic and contemporary fine china (Kate Spade to Spode), crystal, silver, cookware and giftware at "a discount" that is often "below regular department store prices"; however, surveyors are split on service, with pros pronouncing it "knowledgeable" and cons calling it "disorganized and slow."

Michael Kors   26 | 24 | 23 | VE

E 70s | 974 Madison Ave. (76th St.) | 6 to 77th St. | 212-452-4685 🖼
NEW **SoHo** | 101 Prince St. (bet. Greene & Mercer Sts.) | N/R/W to Prince St. | 212-965-0401
www.michaelkors.com

What some deem "the best selection of low-key luxe" lives at this *Project Runway* guru's East 70s flagship designed by architect Dan Rowen, whose subdued colors create the perfect backdrop for the boldface designer's "classic chic" silhouettes for him or her done up in "cashmere, fur and leather", plus there are also "fab shoes and bags"; the "excellent tailors" and "eye-candy" staff add to the "great experience"; N.B. the new SoHo store specializes in variously priced accessories from all three of the designer's collections – the main line, KORS and MICHAEL – plus a small sample of womenswear.

Michael's, The Consignment Shop for Women 🖼   25 | 19 | 20 | E

E 70s | 1041 Madison Ave. (bet. 79th & 80th Sts.) | 6 to 77th St. | 212-737-7273 | www.michaelsconsignment.com

"Still the UES's best resource for gently used Chanel, Hermès, etc." confide consignment acolytes about this vet (est. 1954), whose "helpful staff" supplies ladies with "designer merch at a discount" (it's also "one of the few to specialize in wedding dresses"); some bargain-hunters blanch at the cost, but fans find the "quality vs. price ratio superb", plus, it's "the only way I can wear Armani."

Michal Negrin   26 | 27 | 24 | E

E 70s | 971 Madison Ave. (bet. 75th & 76th Sts.) | 6 to 77th St. | 212-439-8414 | 800-773-4319 | www.michalnegrinnyc.com

From gilded swag molding and crystal chandeliers to painted nymphs, this East 70s yearling – the "olde timey", "feminine" vision of veteran

Israeli designer Michal Negrin and the 39th outpost in her global chain – is a Victoriana lover's delight; the emphasis is on crystal, metal and bead-encrusted baubles, but the lifestyle collection also includes hand-printed tunics, tiles and wrought-iron shelving.

Michele Varian ⊠
– | – | – | E

SoHo | 35 Crosby St. (bet. Broome & Grand Sts.) | 6 to Spring St. | 212-343-0033 | www.michelevarian.com

For "fabrics rich and luxurious in color", head to this "lovely little store" in SoHo, "where you can always find something precious", including handmade pillows, throws and duvet covers in silk, suede and leather, along with "a good collection of jewelry and tableware"; the eponymous owner-designer runs the shop and is "ever-accommodating."

Michelle New York
– | – | – | M

Boerum Hill | 376 Atlantic Ave. (bet. Bond & Hoyt Sts.) | Brooklyn | A/C/G to Hoyt/Schermerhorn Sts. | 718-643-1680

Michelle New York Brides Ⓜ
Boerum Hill | 396 Atlantic Ave. (bet. Bond & Hoyt Sts.) | Brooklyn | A/C/G to Hoyt/Schermerhorn Sts. | 718-643-1680
www.michellenewyork.com

Designer-owner Michelle Fields dresses women for their everyday lives as well as for their wedding date at her Boerum Hill duo; the spacious, loftlike womenswear shop boasts her edgy, sexy collection plus lines from around the world, funky jewelry and accessories; a few doors up brides-to-be can make an appointment, find gowns for every budget and even get ready on the big day at the on-site salon.

Mick Margo
– | – | – | E

W Village | 19 Commerce St. (bet. Bedford St. & 7th Ave. S.) | 1 to Christopher St./Sheridan Sq. | 212-463-0515 | www.mickmargo.com

Fashionistas get a "great feeling" just walking into this "quaint" West Village charmer done up with dark-wood floors, pinstriped curtains and photos of the store's namesake who happens to be the "attentive" owner's grandfather; the well-edited racks reveal finds from Alexander Wang and Hache, while the "cute" jewelry case contains a tasteful selection of bags and shoes from the likes of Deere Colhoun.

NEW Miguelina
24 | 25 | 22 | E

W Village | 347 Bleecker St. (W. 10th St.) | 1 to Christopher St./Sheridan Sq. | 212-400-3100 | www.miguelina.com

"Not to be missed" – especially when you're filled with "dread" about what to "pack for a fun trip" confirm "fashionistas" who file into Dominican Republican–born designer Miguelina Gambaccini's breezy blue-and-white Bleecker Street "find" with a Caribbean feel; choose from "flirty", "easy travel clothes" from the label's Honeymoon collection and "feminine, not saccharine" styles, including "going-out" dresses and "boudoirlike" lace-trimmed camis in "elegant fabrics" and "courageous colors" sure to "suit your personality."

Mika Inatome ⊠
– | – | – | E

TriBeCa | 93 Reade St. (bet. Church St. & W. B'way) | 1/2/3 to Chambers St. | 212-966-7777 | www.mikainatome.com

"The personalized attention" that "passionate, extremely talented" designer "Mika Inatome provides is priceless" at her TriBeCa studio where brides actually look "forward to every fitting" of their custom-crafted gowns; made from natural fabrics like Japanese or Italian silk and enhanced by touches like distinctive embroidery, hand-stitched beading and European lace, the luxe creations walk the line between timeless and contemporary, making an "already special event more memorable."

☑ Mikimoto ☒ | 29 | 26 | 25 | VE |

E 50s | 730 Fifth Ave. (bet. 56th & 57th Sts.) | N/R/W to 5th Ave./59th St. | 212-457-4600 | 888-701-2323 | www.mikimotoamerica.com

If you "live for" "pretty, perfect pearls", this elegant Fifth Avenue store hasn't lost its luster as the "prime place to go" since its founder invented the cultured variety, plus it carries everything from classic Japanese Akoya to bigger South Sea varieties; admirers assert "their reliability is worth the cost", and add after all, dahling, "you are buying an heirloom."

miks ◕ | - | - | - | M |

LES | 100 Stanton St. (bet. Ludlow & Orchard Sts.) | F/V to Lower East Side/2nd Ave. | 212-505-1982

This cheerful Lower East Side jewel box is so tiny you may bump into the creative clerk, who's styling the mannequins in the window, but that's part of the charm of exploring Japanese designer Mitsuyo Toyoda's womenswear – smart separates in a chic array of colors, some adorned with oversized buttons or polka dots; also on display are cashmere hand-knits from Peru, well-priced Topkapi leather purses and gorgeous gloves, scarves and hats.

Mimi Maternity | 19 | 18 | 20 | M |

Borough Park | 4420 13th Ave. (45th St.) | Brooklyn | D/M to Fort Hamilton Pkwy. | 718-871-9430
Staten Island | Staten Island Mall | 2655 Richmond Ave. (bet. Platinum Ave. & Richmond Hill Rd.) | 718-761-0097 ◕
877-646-4666 | www.mimimaternity.com

Moms-to-be love the "bang for the buck" at this mega maternity chain where the "looks aren't too pricey" and there's a "decent selection" of everyday wear like "basic black pants" and jeans good enough "for a few months"; but cutting-edgers who complain "it's not the most trendy" say utilize the "extremely helpful staff" and "shop wisely or you'll look like a pregnant Carol Brady."

Mimi's Closet ◕☒Ⓜ | 21 | 22 | 23 | E |

Astoria | 21-10 31st St. (21st Ave.) | Queens | N/W to Ditmars Blvd. | 718-278-4585 | www.mimiscloset.net

"Bring along a decent amount of cash" so that you won't have to "leave a gem behind" at this "quaint" blue-and-green Astoria store where former Issey Miyake assistant Mimi Yamanobe and her "knowledgeable staff" provide "excellent service" to those browsing a "small collection" of "simply sexy", whimsical frocks and tops designed by the owner, plus "NYC-made, one-of-a-kind"-looking purses, accessories and jewelry.

Mini Jake | - | - | - | E |

Williamsburg | 178 N. Ninth St. (bet. Bedford & Driggs Aves.) | Brooklyn | L to Bedford Ave. | 718-782-2005 | www.minijake.com

Big on style and selection, humongous in size and 'Mini' only in terms of name and its main audience, this offshoot of Williamsburg's Two Jakes caters to ever-discriminating parents with a storehouse of goodies; stock up on playful Dwell bedding, "great" furniture like Netto cribs, BabyBjörn diaper bags, Oeuf clothing, Dan Zanes' CDs and much, much more – everything modern moms and dads need for their little urban offspring.

Mini Minimarket ◑
`- | - | - | M`

Williamsburg | Mini Mall | 218 Bedford Ave. (bet. N. 4th & 5th Sts.) | Brooklyn | L to Bedford Ave. | 718-302-9337 | www.miniminimarket.com
Even adventurous Gothamites maintain it's "worth crossing the bridge" to get to this "ultracool" "kitschy boutique" with a red linoleum floor in the Mini Mall that "embodies the flavor of the 'Burg"; the "big draw": a "great sampling of the most current fashions", from "cute accessories", T-shirts, cards and jewelry to "hipster-fabulous" shoes, lingerie and dresses from Asian and local independent designers.

Min-K ◑
`- | - | - | M`

E Village | 334 E. 11th St. (bet. 1st & 2nd Aves.) | L to 1st Ave. | 212-253-8337
NoLita | 219 Mott St. (bet. Prince & Spring Sts.) | N/R/W to Prince St. | 212-219-2834
www.mink-nyc.com
"Every city girl needs a good frock", and shoppers deem this East Village original and its NoLita sidekick "ideal spots for scoring beautiful party dresses" that "you won't see another woman wearing"; owner Mingi Kim also parlays her "genius design" abilities into "reasonably priced" wool jumpsuits, tailored trousers and silk halter dresses – for sizes 2–6 – plus stocks a few jewels and heels, which help seal its status as a "sanctuary for funky boutique lovers."

Miriam Rigler ▣
`▽ 28 | 23 | 26 | VE`

E 60s | 41 E. 60th St. (bet. Madison & Park Aves.) | 4/5/6/F/N/R/W to 59th St./Lexington Ave. | 212-581-5519 | www.miriamriglerinc.com
This elite purveyor of evening- and weddingwear has "been around 'forever'", and now shares its East 60s digs with the Jeanmarie Gallery (hence, all the oil paintings decorating the walls); the long, narrow space is crammed with colorful "clothing that's great for women of a certain age" – indeed, dressing the mother of the bride has long been the store's specialty; but it also offers custom-made gowns, plus jewelry and accessories, for all participants in the happy day, so "if you're an old-fashioned bride with traditional class, come here."

Mish ▣
`- | - | - | VE`

E 70s | 131 E. 70th St. (bet. Lexington & Park Aves.) | 6 to 68th St. | 212-734-3500 | www.mishnewyork.com
Set in a magnificent East 70s townhouse, with a garden entrance, this tiny shop (with workrooms in back) is the home of the eponymous, bow-tied jeweler to the ladies who lunch; they adore his "very few but very beautiful" and very expensive designs – from deliciously colorful, multistrand gemstone necklaces, coral and bamboo collections, whimsical brooches and a charm bracelet or two to cuff links for men.

Mish Mish
`- | - | - | M`

E 90s | 1435 Lexington Ave. (bet. 93rd & 94th Sts.) | 6 to 96th St. | 212-996-6474
This Israeli import in the East 90s makes shopping for even the most finicky kids a snap with its well-merchandised collection of colorful

cotton separates made for easy mixing and matching; from peasant skirts and embellished T-shirts for girls to military jackets and cargo pants for boys, the fresh fashions here deliver a dose of European style – without the steep European price tags.

Missha ●

-	-	-	I

Garment District | 488 Seventh Ave. (36th St.) | 1/2/3/A/C/E to 34th St./ Penn Station | 212-239-3305
Woodhaven | Queens Ctr. | 90-15 Queens Blvd. (bet. 57th & 59th Aves.) | Queens | G/R/V to Woodhaven Blvd. | 718-271-6268

This Korean superstore duo in Manhattan and Queens is "the H&M of makeup" with over 500 products like lipsticks and eyeshadows for under $5 a pop, plus bath and body products at "bargain-basement prices"; but sophisticates sniff at settings dominated by blaring pop soundtracks and "teenybopper employees."

Missoni 🅢

26	25	22	VE

E 70s | 1009 Madison Ave. (78th St.) | 6 to 77th St. | 212-517-9339 | www.missoni.com

On Madison Avenue, a "modernist interior serves as a glass box displaying the vibrant knit garments" of the Italian label like "rare gems" (appropriate, given the "oh-so-expensive" prices); the "beautiful" signature prints and "fantasy" weaves, now designed by heir to the house Angela Missoni, "still reign" for their "originality" – but given the high-voltage hues, you better "like color."

Miss Sixty

21	20	16	E

NEW Flatiron | 901 Broadway (20th St.) | N/R/W to 23rd St. | 212-260-2690 ●
SoHo | 386 W. Broadway (bet. Broome & Spring Sts.) | C/E to Spring St. | 212-334-9772
www.misssixty.com

"You can't put a price on sexy" insist fans who flock to these "funky" chain links in SoHo and now the Flatiron District too for "fabulous" Italian jeans, "guaranteed to make anyone into a goddess"; although the "casually stylish" "urban-chic" "weekend wear" and "cute" chunky boots rock in a Sienna Miller boho kind of way, mischief-makers hiss that it's "expensive for what it is" and "should be called Miss 18" for the teen "poseurs" it attracts.

NEW Mitchell Gold + Bob Williams ●

-	-	-	E

SoHo | 210 Lafayette St. (Kenmare St.) | 6 to Spring St. | 212-431-2575 | www.mgandbw.com

Behind the cool, curved facade of hotelier André Balazs' sweeping SoHo building lies this long-standing North Carolina-based furniture company's first New York City stand-alone showroom – a two-story, 11,000-sq.-ft space; the eponymous design duo aims for a relaxed contemporary look whether it's expressed in buttery leather club chairs, slouchy slip-covered couches, chic but comfy dining chairs or dog beds in color schemes coordinating with the master bedrooms on display.

Miu Miu

25	24	20	E

E 60s | 831 Madison Ave. (bet. 69th & 70th Sts.) | 6 to 68th St. | 212-249-9660 🅢

(continued)

Miu Miu

SoHo | 100 Prince St. (bet. Greene & Mercer Sts.) | N/R/W to Prince St. | 212-334-5156
www.miumiu.com

"Prada's funky cousin" draws in '60s-style gamines, indie starlets and cool Condé Nasties at its "very friendly" SoHo flagship and its "beautifully designed" Madison Avenue branch; both boast baby-doll print dresses, "well-cut pants, couture-ish detailed shirts and fun" high-heeled platform shoes – all with an "edgy, earthy" spirit that saves it from being a chic clone of Miuccia Prada's signature line (not to mention "more affordable").

Mixona

NoLita | 262 Mott St. (bet. Houston & Prince Sts.) | B/D/F/V to B'way/Lafayette St. | 646-613-0100 | www.mixona.com

Stocked with "pretty" lacy dainties as well as sizzling bustiers, garter belts and thongs from hot tickets including Cosabella, Hanky Panky and Siren, this large and airy white-walled "fave lingerie" shop in NoLita makes a seductive prelude to that "special date"; saunter in to scan the easy-to-navigate racks for "great underwear and swimsuits too" and you may be rewarded with a "celeb sighting" at the same time.

M Missoni

SoHo | 426 W. Broadway (bet. Prince & Spring Sts.) | A/C/E to Canal St. | 212-431-6500 | www.m-missoni.com

When that craving for Italian zigzag knits with a hip bent hits, make tracks to Angela Missoni's new light, airy, well-lit SoHo boutique and scoop up the creative director's lively luxury line; the inventive coterie of colorful, patterned womenswear is actually a bit more affordable, sexy and youthful than the mother ship collection – little wonder it's caught on with boldface names like Lindsay Lohan and Mischa Barton, not to mention company muse/daughter Margherita Missoni.

NEW MNG by Mango

SoHo | 561 Broadway (bet. Crosby & Mercer Sts.) | N/R/W to Prince St. | 212-343-7012 | 866-666-4664 | www.mngshop.com

Taking a page from European mega-chains like H&M and Zara, this fast-fashion outfit from Spain stakes its claim on SoHo, filling its sleek, black-and-white 7,500-sq.-ft. space with – what else – trendy, colorful womenswear, bags and accessories with an urban edge at moderate prices; high ceilings, house music and a catwalk extending almost the entire length of the store accentuate the oh-so-Euro feel.

Modell's Sporting Goods

16 | 11 | 10 | VE

Garment District | 1293 Broadway (34th St.) | B/D/F/N/Q/R/V/W to 34th St./Herald Sq. | 212-244-4544 | 800-275-6633 |
www.modells.com
Additional locations throughout the NY area

"Anything athletic they'll have" at this ubiquitous sporting goods chain, a "true New York original" that fans feel is "the place to go" for "inexpensive supplies"; but detractors deride its "awful presentation" as a "disorganized mess" and claim the "couldn't-care-less staff" "barely knows where the products are, much less how to use them."

| | QUALITY | DISPLAY | SERVICE | COST |

Modernica ⊠
- | - | - | E

SoHo | 57 Greene St. (bet. Broome & Spring Sts.) | C/E to Spring St. |
212-219-1303 | www.modernica.net

Step off the teeming SoHo sidewalk and into this "nice place to dream
about the furniture you would buy if you had a TriBeCa loft"; the focus
is on reproductions of midcentury classics like Case Study sofas and
Noguchi coffee tables, and prices are surprisingly "ok."

NEW ModernTots
23 | 21 | 21 | E

Dumbo | 53 Pearl St. (Water St.) | Brooklyn | F to York St. | 718-488-8293 |
877-289-0453 | www.moderntots.com

There are "no cutesy blue and pink baby items" at this Dumbo
showroom – instead, you'll find "cool stuff for cool" infants, kids and
teens "with personalities" and modern design for the parents; the "very
clean"-lined furniture, from eco-friendly play tables to hardwood birch
bunk beds and baby gear like Quinny strollers, is "so stylish" you may
"want it for your living room – forget the nursery!", plus it's also a "great
place for a different gift" and "lovely toys" – "not your usual things."

Molton Brown
27 | 24 | 24 | E

E 50s | 515 Madison Ave. (53rd St.) | E/V to Lexington Ave./53rd St. |
212-755-7194 ⊠
E 60s | 1098 Third Ave. (bet. 64th & 65th Sts.) | 6 to 68th St. | 212-744-6430
SoHo | 128 Spring St. (bet. Greene & Wooster Sts.) | N/R/W to Prince St. |
212-965-1740
www.moltonbrown.co.uk

This English import offers "quietly sophisticated", "beautifully packaged" cosmetics and toiletries like "unbeatable bath oils", "the world's
best haircare products" and "shower gels to die for"; its jet-set clientele
doesn't seem to object to paying "premium prices" – but you might.

⊠ MoMA Design and Book Store
25 | 24 | 18 | E

SoHo | 81 Spring St. (Crosby St.) | 6 to Spring St. | 646-613-1367 ◗
W 50s | 11 W. 53rd St. (5th Ave.) | E/V to 5th Ave./53rd St. | 212-708-9700
W 50s | 44 W. 53rd St. (bet. 5th & 6th Aves.) | E/V to 5th Ave./53rd St. |
212-708-9669
800-793-3167 | www.momastore.org

"Midcentury modern" mavens and "design-forward" hipsters "feel like
kids in a candy store" at MoMA's "breathtaking" flagship, across-the-
street annex and the forever-"fresh" SoHo satellite; "sophisticated"
shoppers find "fabulous" furniture and housewares, "excellent books"
and "whimsical" children's items, and though it can be "hectic" and
prices "expensive", it's a "unique" resource for "stylish" gifts.

⊠ Montblanc
28 | 26 | 24 | VE

E 50s | 598 Madison Ave. (57th St.) | N/R/W to 5th Ave./59th St. |
212-223-8888
SoHo | 120 Greene St. (bet. Prince & Spring Sts.) | N/R/W to Prince St. |
212-680-1300
www.montblanc.com

Those who have a pen-chant for "absolutely exquisite" "classic" writing
instruments that "everyone wants" head to these SoHo and Madison
Avenue shops that also sell watches, leather goods and "gifts designed
for all important celebrations"; proponents praise "superb service",
but be prepared for prices as "high as your golden parachute."

	QUALITY	DISPLAY	SERVICE	COST

Montmartre
22 | 20 | 18 | E

E 80s | 1157 Madison Ave. (85th St.) | 4/5/6 to 86th St. | 212-988-8962
Financial District | 22150 World Financial Ctr., 2nd fl. (West Side Hwy.) |
R/W to Rector St. | 212-945-7858
W 60s | The Shops at Columbus Circle, Time Warner Ctr. |
10 Columbus Circle, 3rd fl. (60th St. at B'way) | 1/A/B/C/D to
59th St./Columbus Circle | 212-823-9821 ◐
W 70s | 2212 Broadway (bet. 78th & 79th Sts.) | 1 to 79th St. |
212-875-8430 ◐
www.montmartreny.com
It's "impossible to walk out empty-handed" from this "friendly" quartet
"packed" with "funky, stylish" casualwear, "bright happy-hip" "going-
out" garb and "sophisticated cocktail attire" "with an extra ladylike
oomph"; *mais oui*, it's "expensive", but the "well-edited collection" of
"wearable, trendy" "cool designers" like Elie Tahari and Nanette Lepore
reveals this outfit's "keen eye" for "what's in fashion now."

Mood Designer Fabrics ⊠
▽ 25 | 13 | 20 | M

Garment District | 225 W. 37th St., 3rd fl. (7th Ave.) | 1/2/3/A/C/E to
34th St./Penn Station | 212-730-5003 | www.moodfabrics.com
"Horizontally stacked bolts" of "eye-candy" fabrics (including closeouts
from Calvin Klein and Marc Jacobs) fill the 25,000 sq. ft. of this Garment
District behemoth, giving its clientele of clothing, stage designers and
Project Runway contestants "loads to choose from" at "low prices"; still,
a few turn moody muttering "sometimes it's hard to see what's there"
because "they have so much" – and it can be "hard to track down help."

Moon River Chattel Ⓜ
- | - | - | E

Williamsburg | 62 Grand St. (bet. Kent & Wythe Aves.) | Brooklyn | L
to Bedford Ave. | 718-388-1121 | www.moonriverchattel.com
Nesters zero in on weathered farm tables, hutches and bureaus that
"stay on the right side of the shabby-chic line", along with reproductions of classic toys and enamelware at this "sooo cute" Williamsburg
home-furnishings shop that also fills its nooks and crannies with
modern-day finds like cotton and hemp towels, comfy couches and
new lighting fixtures; head to the annex across the street for architectural salvage treasures also certain to send you over the moon.

MoonSoup
▽ 24 | 21 | 22 | M

E 50s | 1059 Second Ave. (bet. 55th & 56th Sts.) | 4/5/6/F/N/R/W to
59th St./Lexington Ave. | 212-319-3222 | www.moonsoup.net
Midtown moms are astir over this "cute, little" East 50s children's emporium, which combines play and learning classes, a party center and
"great shopping for all things kid" under one roof, including clothing, toys
and diaper bags you don't see everywhere; the selection may be "tiny",
nevertheless it can't be beat for "picking up unique gifts" in a pinch.

Morgane Le Fay
26 | 24 | 21 | VE

E 60s | 746 Madison Ave. (bet. 64th & 65th Sts.) | N/R/W to 5th Ave./
59th St. | 212-879-9700
SoHo | 67 Wooster St. (bet. Broome & Spring Sts.) | C/E to Spring St. |
212-219-7672
www.morganelefay.com
You feel like you're in a BAM New Wave Festival at this SoHo and
Madison Avenue twosome where surreal statues model a fantasy array

of apparel that's "awesome, elegant and classical, with a downtown twist" (and uptown prices); still, cynics say the gauzy gowns and separates look "just perfect for having tea in the forest with elves and fairies – but, how many times do you have tea in the forest with elves and fairies?"

Morgan Library & Museum Shop Ⓜ | 25 | 23 | 20 | E |

Murray Hill | Morgan Library | 225 Madison Ave. (36th St.) | 6 to 33rd St. | 212-590-0300 | www.themorgan.org

"So glad they're open again" cry connoisseurs of this museum shop "in the original J.P. Morgan home" in Murray Hill; "much airier than the previous" incarnation, the "hushed", "rarefied" "atmosphere induces one to spend" on a "small but exquisite selection" of "interesting" art books, "special papers and cards" and other "gift shop goodies" "for a cultured friend"; "service can be a bit leisurely" and some find "prices are on the high side – but so is the quality"; besides, "someone has to pay for the renovations" to the "redone" Morgan Library.

Morgenthal Frederics | 28 | 26 | 24 | VE |

E 60s | 699 Madison Ave. (bet. 62nd & 63rd Sts.) | 4/5/6/F/N/R/W to 59th St./Lexington Ave. | 212-838-3090
E 70s | 944 Madison Ave. (bet. 74th & 75th Sts.) | 6 to 77th St. | 212-744-9444
SoHo | 399 W. Broadway (Spring St.) | C/E to Spring St. | 212-966-0099 ●
W 60s | The Shops at Columbus Circle, Time Warner Ctr. | 10 Columbus Circle, ground fl. (60th St. at B'way) | 1/A/B/C/D to 59th St./Columbus Circle | 212-956-6402
www.morgenthalfrederics.com

"Forget contact lenses" – this "quality" quartet offers the "coolest" handcrafted frames as well as "top-of-the-line sunglasses" that will "make your face stand out"; the "soothing" David Rockwell–designed spaces and "fabulous" service (including "outstanding opticians") ensure a "pleasant experience", and even if you may "never spend more" on specs, you'll also "never want to buy them anywhere else."

🆕 Moroso | - | - | - | VE |

SoHo | 146 Greene St. (bet. Prince & W. Houston Sts.) | N/R to Prince St. | 212-334-7222 | www.moroso.it

This long-standing, family-owned Italian furniture company has trendily landed on these shores, with its new showroom sharing space with SoHo style-arbiter Moss; Patrizia Moroso collaborates with international heavies like Ron Arad, Tord Boontje and Patricia Urquiola (who also conceptualized the 3,800-sq.-ft. futuristic gallerylike space) to come up with cutting-edge tables, sofas and chairs (with pieces upholstered in prestigious Maharam textiles); but since prices are decidedly high, many devoted design disciples simply come to pay homage.

Moscot | 21 | 14 | 20 | M |

Flatiron | 69 W. 14th St. (6th Ave.) | F/L/V to 14th St./6th Ave. | 212-647-1550
LES | 118 Orchard St. (Delancey St.) | F/J/M/Z to Delancey/Essex Sts. | 212-477-3796
Forest Hills | 107-20 Continental Ave. (bet. Austin St. & Queens Blvd.) | Queens | E/F/G/R/V to Forest Hills/71st Ave. | 718-544-2200 Ⓢ
www.moscot.com

Even if it's "been around since the Flood", ok, 1920, this Lower East Side optician and its Flatiron and Forest Hills progeny Noah from "stylish", offering big names in frames from Fendi to Prada at "bargain" prices; the staff's "ready, willing and able to help", and though some soliloquize you "have to know what you're looking for", its mascots maintain it's the epitome of "what an eyewear store should be."

☑ Moss

28 | 29 | 21 | VE

SoHo | 150 Greene St. (Houston St.) | N/R/W to Prince St. | 212-204-7100 | 866-888-6677 | www.mossonline.com
"Murray Moss has an exceptional eye" and "is on top of what's hot" in high-end home furnishings, so much so that "an hour of browsing" the "museumlike" "glass cases" in this "quirky, clever", ever-mushrooming and "insanely priced" SoHo "temple of cool" "is like a college course in classic" "modern design"; voted this Survey's Tops for Display, the "outstanding selection" includes items for the kitchen, office, living and bedroom and ranges from "the silly to the fabulous" – e.g. an intricate Marcel Wanders Crochet table constructed of cotton and epoxy.

Moulin Bleu

- | - | - | E

TriBeCa | 176 Franklin St. (Hudson St.) | 1 to Franklin St. | 212-334-1130
If you're feeling kind of *bleu*, hit this TriBeCa venue for a home furnishings pick-me-up that includes a charming selection of pricey antique furniture, affordable glassware made from vintage molds, perfume bottles capped with rose-shaped stoppers, delicate dishes, scented soaps and a bounty of other gift-ready items reminiscent of the South of France.

Movado

26 | 26 | 23 | E

W 40s | Rockefeller Ctr. | 610 Fifth Ave. (bet. 49th & 50th Sts.) | B/D/F/V to 47-50th Sts./Rockefeller Ctr. | 212-218-7555 | www.movado.com
Many have "made the move" to these "simple", "sleek and statusy" watches that are "sold all over the city" but have a home store in Rockefeller Center; proponents praise the "not insanely priced" pieces and a "helpful", "patient" staff that "even sends thank-you notes" to its customers.

☑ Mrs. John L. Strong ☒

28 | 24 | 23 | VE

E 60s | 699 Madison Ave., 5th fl. (62nd St.) | 4/5/6/F/N/R/W to 59th St./Lexington Ave. | 212-838-3775 | www.mrsstrong.com
"When only the very best will do", debs and dowagers head to this statusy fifth-floor stationer on Madison Avenue founded in 1929 for "beautiful" hand-engraved invitations, letter paper, holiday cards and custom-leather accessories like albums; but "wildly expensive" prices mean the merchandise is "out of the range of most" mortals.

NEW msg

- | - | - | E

Little Italy | 66 Kenmare St. (bet. Mott & Mulberry Sts.) | J/M/Z to Bowery | 212-334-4032 | www.msgnewyorkcity.com
Decorated with a fanciful white-framed mirror and carved chandelier and filled with fashion-forward finds, mostly from independent Japanese lines (including owner-designer Mami Suzuki's house collection), this yellow-and-brick-walled boutique straddling Little Italy and NoLita feels like a special enclave; the fresh, daring clothing and funky bags from little-known names like face too, Isola and Iliann Loeb appeal to style-sleuths who want to turn heads – but don't want to see themselves coming or going.

| | QUALITY | DISPLAY | SERVICE | COST |

NEW Muji ●
– | – | – | M

SoHo | 455 Broadway (bet. Grand & Howard Sts.) | 6/J/M/N/Q/R/
W/Z to Canal St. | 212-334-2002 | www.muji.com

The cult-sensation Japanese company premieres here in a minimalist
new SoHo space that's as pared-down as the products on its neatly ordered shelves; its haikus to home design include bedding made from
fabric scraps and no-frills kitchenware, but it also offers clothing like
utilitarian tees and offbeat office supplies; acolytes pack the place like
it's a rock concert, but the four to five additional New York branches
that are planned may help quell the queues.

Mulberry
– | – | – | VE

E 50s | 605 Madison Ave. (58th St.) | N/R/W to 5th Ave./59th St. |
212-835-4700 ext. 102
W Village | 387 Bleecker St. (Perry St.) | 1 to Christopher St./Sheridan Sq. |
212-835-4700 ext. 101
www.mulberry.com

Though it's been manufacturing its long-lasting leather goods for 35
years, this British brand became a big deal when Kate Moss began tot-
ing its Bayswater bag around; now the label's making a huge splash
this side of the pond with its East 50s and West Village shops that sell
rugged-yet-sexy, oak-toned clutches and shoulder bags; in addition,
the Madison Avenue location – done up with leather and wood accents, like a sophisticated log cabin – stocks ready-to-wear clothing
for blokes and birds too.

Munder-Skiles ⊠
– | – | – | VE

E 60s | 799 Madison Ave., 3rd fl. (bet. 67th & 68th Sts.) | 6 to 68th St. |
212-717-0150 | www.munder-skiles.com

'Exterior decorator' and owner of this pricey Madison Avenue garden
furnishings shop John Danzer showcases tables, chairs, benches and
urns – many of which are modeled on historic classics from places like
Monticello – designed to make the outside of your property as enticing
as the inside.

☑ Museum of Arts & Design Store
26 | 24 | 20 | E

W 50s | 40 W. 53rd St. (bet. 5th & 6th Aves.) | E/V to 5th Ave./53rd St. |
212-956-3535 | www.madmuseum.org

It's "always a pleasure to browse" at this "beautiful" Midtown shop
showcasing "one-of-a-kind jewelry and scarves from American crafts-
people" along with "stunning glasswork", "extraordinary tableware"
and other "conversation pieces"; wallet-watchers warn "there are no
bargains", but the wowed say it's "worth it" for "gifts you won't find
anywhere else"; N.B. plans are underway to relocate to architect
Edward Durell Stone's 'Lollipop' building at 2 Columbus Circle in 2008.

Museum of Sex
19 | 20 | 18 | M

Gramercy | 233 Fifth Ave. (27th St.) | N/R/W to 28th St. | 212-689-6337 |
www.museumofsex.com

"Never realized the selling of sex could be so sophisticated" say surveyors seduced by this industrial-looking, red-and-gray Gramercy emporium stocked with underwear, "interesting books" and the "highlight: sex
toys almost pretty enough to pass as decorative works of art" (some
actually are, like the anatomically correct origami man); all the items

are "displayed in good taste" – though critics cavil the "understocked" inventory is "not risqué enough"; even so, "few museum shops sell such functional products" (just "stay away from any floor samples").

Museum of the City of New York Ⓜ | 21 | 18 | 18 | M |

E 100s | 1220 Fifth Ave. (103rd St.) | 6 to 103rd St. | 212-534-1672 ext. 3330 | www.mcny.org

"Nostalgic New Yorkers" laud this "little-known" museum shop in the East 100s celebrating "Big Apple quality" with "delightful jewelry and art objects" as well as "books and games for the whole family"; the "small but impressive" inventory, "helpful staff" and "decent prices" make it a must for folks seeking "thoughtful gifts" for "city buffs."

Mxyplyzyk | 21 | 23 | 18 | M |

W Village | 125 Greenwich Ave. (bet. Horatio & 13th Sts.) | A/C/E/L to 14th St./8th Ave. | 212-989-4300 | 800-243-9810 | www.mxyplyzyk.com

If you're in the West Village, this is the "perfect" "quick-stop" for a "quirky" "gift on the run" or "stylish tchotchkes" that run the gamut from scented candles and clocks to retro train cases and toys; space is tight and service "can be snooty", but the frugal feel the price is right.

My Glass Slipper Ⓜ | ▽ 25 | 22 | 20 | M |

Flatiron | 20 W. 22nd St., 6th fl. (bet. 5th & 6th Aves.) | N/R/W to 23rd St. | 212-627-0231 | www.myglassslipper.com

Yes, "it's all wedding shoes, all the time" at this "great concept", web-based sixth-floor shop in the Flatiron District that's "even better in person"; would-be Cinderellas engage in "discount name-brand" footsie, slipping into "everything from Vera Wang to" "surprisingly inexpensive" lesser-known finds and dance away with purses, jewelry and hosiery too; if a few snarl that this Slipper "doesn't fit all", supporters retort "they can order" whatever you want.

Myla | – | – | – | E |

E 60s | 20 E. 69th St. (bet. 5th & Madison Aves.) | 6 to 68th St. | 212-570-1590 | www.myla.com

You'd never expect so much naughtiness on a quiet Upper East Side block, but this high-end Londoner that hit New York a few years ago with a chic collection of lingerie and a handful of rechargeable adult toys in seductive designs delivers bad-girl paraphernalia aplenty; the mirrored back wall and leather-stooled fitting rooms are perfect for modeling pricey feathered mules, see-thru silk teddies and split-cup bras.

Mylo Dweck Maternity | – | – | – | E |

Bensonhurst | 364 Ave. U (bet. E. 1st & West Sts.) | Brooklyn | F to Ave. U | 718-333-0420

Style-minded moms-to-be make tracks to the recently expanded Bensonhurst shop of maternity maven Mylo Dweck, who's got a knack for finding the most sought-after fashions from name-brand lines like Childish, Japanese Weekend and Seven; sure, these designer duds come with designer prices, but sometimes you deserve to be spoiled, if only for nine months; N.B. closed Saturdays.

Myoptics | 25 | 21 | 24 | E |

Chelsea | 96 Seventh Ave. (bet. 15th & 16th Sts.) | 1/2/3 to 14th St. | 212-633-6014

(continued)

(continued)

Myoptics

E Village | 42 St. Marks Pl. (bet. 1st & 2nd Aves.) | 6 to Astor Pl. | 212-533-1577
SoHo | 123 Prince St. (bet. Greene & Wooster Sts.) | N/R/W to Prince St. | 212-598-9306
TriBeCa | 327 Greenwich St. (bet. Duane & Jay Sts.) | 1/2/3 to Chambers St. | 212-334-3123
www.myoptics.com

"Urban chic without attitude" is the appeal at this slightly "edgy" eyewear chain that offers a "fantastic" selection of frames with designer names like Oliver Peoples and Paul Smith; a befuddled few find the "presentation a bit confusing", but most report it's "fun to buy here", particularly since there are "no high-pressure sales" tactics in play.

M Z Wallace

`- | - | - | E`

SoHo | 93 Crosby St. (bet. Prince & Spring Sts.) | 6 to Spring St. | 212-431-8252 | 888-600-5559 | www.mzwallace.com

This large, airy SoHo shop showcases "beautiful", colorful, quilted fabric and canvas bags "for the independent" New Yorker who blazes her own trail, with compartments for cell phones, Metrocards and Palm Pilots, all made by owners-designers Lucy Wallace Eustice and Monica Zwirner; the dynamic duo also offers a line of "nice stuff" for men too, including briefcases, laptop totes and overnighters, each named after a movie star.

N

`- | - | - | E`

Harlem | 114 W. 116th St. (bet. Lenox & 7th Aves.) | 2/3 to 116th St. | 212-961-1036 | www.nharlemnewyork.com

Couture comes to Harlem with this pioneering two-level clothing emporium, a spacious 4,000-sq.-ft. loft space; like a mini-department store, the ground floor offers cosmetics, home furnishings by Jonathan Adler, leather goods and womenswear that ranges from Nicole Miller to Tracy Reese, from Miss Sixty to Marimekko – plus local designers and a proprietary label; downstairs, in the exposed-stone basement, boys can browse among the Hugo Boss, Ike Behar, Diesel and Denim Factor threads.

Nakedeye

`- | - | - | E`

LES | 192 Orchard St. (bet. Houston & Stanton Sts.) | F/V to Lower East Side/2nd Ave. | 212-253-4935 | www.nakedeyeoptical.com

Naked fans consider this eyewear resource "the best" and co-owner George Lee "just the kind of hip cat you want decking out your specs" so you "walk out of there looking good"; with "the coolest" frames from top-notch names like Christian Roth, and a "great" Asian-style "environment" with an art gallery and "cool furnishings", it's clear to see why it's a Lower East Side must.

Nancy & Co.

`23 | - | 21 | E`

E 80s | 1178 Lexington Ave. (bet. 80th & 81st Sts.) | 6 to 77th St. | 212-427-0770 | www.nancycony.com

"Keep up the good work!" say fans of Nan, an "old-time" "fave" that's recently relocated from Madison Avenue to Lexington; you "always find something you can't find elsewhere", be it "great quality staples", "accessories to complete the outfit" or some "funky stuff" to add to the "mix" in a "wide size range"; if a few snipe "service could be less snooty", devotees vow the "knowledgeable staff understands what looks good on you."

Nancy Koltes at Home
∇ 28 | 22 | 23 | VE

NoLita | 29-31 Spring St. (bet. Mott & Mulberry Sts.) | 6 to Spring St. | 212-219-2271 | www.nkah.com

Cognoscenti claim you'll "sleep deeply and dream imaginatively" tucked into "beautiful", "high-quality" Italian bed linens from this cozy NoLita store, which recently added a room next door stuffed with "great home stuff"; a "very helpful staff" also sells towels, throws, napkins, place mats and "wonderful down pillows and comforters."

Nanette Lepore
25 | 24 | 23 | E

SoHo | 423 Broome St. (bet. Crosby & Lafayette Sts.) | 6 to Spring St. | 212-219-8265 | www.nanettelepore.com

Free spirits favor this namesake designer's perky pink SoHo birdcage for "precious but hip" "creative togs" with a "'50s cuteness that works for today"; "universally flattering", these "demure yet sexy" threads, including "well-tailored suits" and "girlie-chic" "dresses cut really well", display a "rare attention to detail" with trims, buttons and loads of "unique" prints that make each outfit look "just totally clever."

Napapijri
- | - | - | E

SoHo | 149 Mercer St. (bet. Houston & Prince Sts.) | B/D/F/V to B'way/Lafayette St. | 212-431-4490 | www.napapijri.com

Outward-bound men, women and kids as well as city folk who aspire to the great outdoors–look converge at this Italian company's "beautiful" SoHo stomping ground stocked with "excellent casualwear and activewear" like rugged parkas, fashionable fleece and camo-patterned ski overalls; "if you want to look good" in your board shorts, "this is the place to be" – just bring lots of lira.

Natalie and Friends ●
∇ 28 | 25 | 26 | E

E 60s | 205 E. 60th St. (bet. 2nd & 3rd Aves.) | 4/5/6/F/N/R/W to 59th St./ Lexington Ave. | 212-759-9077 | www.natalieandfriends.com

For way-"cute" fashions that'll have you wishing you were "small again", head to this East 60s kids' and tweens' emporium "deliciously close to Dylan's Candy Bar", where owner Natalie Mayer is "on a first name basis with customers"; with a host of "hip" labels like Tina Neumann, and even a "store mascot, Raider" Potader, a Labrador with "a line of clothing" named after him, the only drawback is that it's "hard to make a decision."

Natan Borlam's
∇ 28 | 11 | 24 | M

Williamsburg | 157 Havemeyer St. (bet. S. 2nd & 3rd Sts.) | Brooklyn | G/L to Metropolitan Ave./Lorimer St. | 718-782-0108 | 866-782-0108 | www.boysitalansuits.com

It's well "worth the trip" to this sprawling, old-guard children's boutique, a family-owned Williamsburg fixture for over half a century; brave the "barely presentable" displays and you'll be rewarded with some of the "best buys" around on spiffy Italian suits for boys and "beautiful" fashions for infants and toddlers from big-name French labels that change with the season; N.B. closes early on Fridays and closed Saturdays.

	QUALITY	DISPLAY	SERVICE	COST

National Jean Company ●
| - | - | - | E |

NEW **E 70s** | 1375 Third Ave. (bet. 78th & 79th Sts.) | 6 to 77th St. | 212-772-2392
Sheepshead Bay | 2803 Coney Island Ave. (bet. Gerald Ct. & Avenue Y) | Brooklyn | Q to Sheepshead Bay | 718-332-7864
www.nationaljeancompany.com

With thousands of jeans from coveted labels like Cheap Monday, J Brand and True Religion in every cut imaginable filling the shelves of these chain links in the East 70s and Sheepshead Bay, what more could a style maven possibly lust for?; how about flirty dresses, sexy blouses and edgy wardrobe essentials from fashion darlings like Ella Moss, Graham & Spencer, LaRok and Madison Marcus; the Brooklyn store is smaller and the merch mix less expensive.

National Wholesale Liquidators ●
| 11 | 6 | 6 | I |

NoHo | 632 Broadway (Houston St.) | B/D/F/V to B'way/Lafayette St. | 212-979-2400
Bronx | 691 Co-Op City Blvd. (bet. Carver Loop & Peartree Ave.) | 6 to Pelham Bay Park | 718-320-7771
Bensonhurst | 2201 59th St. (Bay Pkwy.) | Brooklyn | F to Ave. N | 718-621-3993
Flushing | 71-01 Kissena Blvd. (71st Ave.) | Queens | 7 to Main St. | 718-591-3900
LIC | 35-00 48th St. (bet. Northern Blvd. & 35th Ave.) | Queens | G/R/V to 46th St. | 718-389-3311
Staten Island | 1565 Forest Ave. (Decker Ave.) | 718-815-6533
www.nationalwholesaleliquidators.com

In between "the rudest salespeople" and the "messy aisles", this "circus"-like chain has "all the charms of a bus station", but pricewise you "can't beat it for staples" "for your bedroom, bathroom, living room, dining room" and kitchen; at select locations, the "gourmet food department is worth checking out", and since 'dirt' is the operative word at this dirt-cheap discounter, "wash anything you buy here before using" it.

Naturino
| ∇ 28 | 26 | 23 | VE |

E 70s | 1410 Second Ave. (bet. 73rd & 74th Sts.) | 6 to 77th St. | 212-794-0570
E 80s | 1184 Madison Ave. (bet. 86th & 87th Sts.) | 4/5/6 to 86th St. | 212-427-0679
www.naturino.com

A household name overseas, this Italian children's footwear firm is making strides stateside, bringing a colorful cast of "very pricey", "cool" kicks for kids to its Madison Avenue and East 70s offshoots; "what a selection" cheer cohorts who choose from the namesake label as well as splurge-worthy styles from designer brands like Moschino and Oilily.

Natuzzi
| ∇ 27 | 23 | 21 | E |

SoHo | 101 Greene St. (bet. Prince & Spring Sts.) | N/R/W to Prince St. | 212-334-4335 | www.natuzzi.com

"Well-made", "attractive modern" leather furniture like sofas, daybeds and chairs handcrafted in Italy is featured at this airy, Zen-feeling SoHo showroom selling what supporters cite is an "unbeatable combination of comfort and reasonable prices" for the quality.

	QUALITY	DISPLAY	SERVICE	COST

NBA Store

| | 21 | 23 | 16 | E |

E 50s | 666 Fifth Ave. (52nd St.) | E/V to 5th Ave./53rd St. | 212-515-6221 | 877-622-0206 | www.nba.com/nycstore

Grab your "hyperactive teenage sons" and hit this "kid-friendly" Midtown mecca, an "enduring concept" for all things NBA where "excitement abounds" and you may even catch a "famous" player appearance; jump-start hoop dreams with "authentic" activewear and footwear, then whoosh down the circular ramp to shoot baskets or "play" video games; still, the "tourist"-fatigued yawn "yeah, if you're from Kansas."

Necessary Clothing ◐

| | ▽ 17 | 15 | 15 | I |

NoHo | 676 Broadway (bet. Bond & Great Jones Sts.) | B/D/F/V to B'way/Lafayette St. | 212-966-9011
SoHo | 442 Broadway (bet. Canal & Grand Sts.) | 6/J/M/N/Q/R/W/Z to Canal St. | 212-343-0515
www.necessaryclothes.com

When you're "on a budget but still want to look faboo when you go out with your girlfriends", this NoHo standby and its newly relocated SoHo sibling serves up what's necessary "for work or play" with "cute" knit shrugs, dressy capris, "surprisingly flirty and feminine" halter dresses, a tube top or two, tailored vests and velour tracksuits, all "for a fraction of the price" you pay at other Downtown emporiums nearby.

Néda ◐

| | 21 | 21 | 24 | E |

NEW Cobble Hill | 302 Court St. (Degraw St.) | Brooklyn | F to Bergen St. | 718-624-6332
Park Slope | 413A Seventh Ave. (bet. 13th & 14th Sts.) | Brooklyn | F to 7th Ave. | 718-965-0990
www.shopneda.com

This Park Slope hotbed of cool looks added another notch to its small but stylish belt with the opening of its Cobble Hill sidekick; choose from sexy tops and slinky womenswear at prices that won't scorch your wallet from labels like Harkham as well as under-the-radar names; need-a accessories to go-with? check out owner-designer Néda Meier's affordable earrings and handbags ("great for gifts").

Neighborhoodies

| | 20 | 19 | 21 | M |

Seaport | Pier 17 | 89 South St. (bet. Beekman & Fulton Sts.) | 2/3/4/5/A/C/J/M/Z to Fulton St./B'way/Nassau | 212-608-7285 ◐
NEW Dumbo | 26 Jay St. (bet. John & Plymouth Sts.) | Brooklyn | F to York St. | 718-722-7277 ▣
www.neighborhoodies.com

"What's not to love?" – this "cool" "do-it-(sort of)-yourself custom-clothing" outfit with "super-helpful" staffers and branches in Dumbo and the Seaport is the "perfect place" to get hoodies that spell out "your 'hood loyalty"; stop in for "cute" sweatshirts and tees with stitched or pressed letters, all "made right quick" – they're "great gifts" for "ex-New Yorkers who still want to flash" their roots; still, scoffers feel it had more "charm" when it was a "smaller, more personal" enterprise.

Nellie M. Boutique ◐

| | 22 | 17 | 17 | E |

E 80s | 1309 Lexington Ave. (88th St.) | 4/5/6 to 86th St. | 212-996-4410 | www.nelliem.com

We like this "cute" standby "better than some of the other small UES boutiques" reveal loyalists who laud the staff that's "generally friendlier" as well as the "assortment of T-shirts", "competitively priced jeans" and "very trendy" but a bit expensive women's designer collections; bridal parties get big-time pampering, and if you're lucky, you'll be there for one of their "spur-of-the-moment sales"; N.B. they now carry kidswear too.

Nemo Tile Company 🛇   21 | 15 | 17 | M

Flatiron | 48 E. 21st St. (bet. B'way & Park Ave. S.) | 6 to 23rd St. | 212-505-0009
Jamaica | 177-02 Jamaica Ave. (177th St.) | Queens | F to Hillside | 718-291-5969
800-636-6845 | www.nemotile.com

Since 1921, this "contractors' source" in Queens and the newer two-story showroom in the Flatiron District have offered a "good selection of tiles" for "budget-conscious bathroom renovation", along with a discount area and plumbing and accessories like mirrors, medicine cabinets and shower doors.

🖸 Neue Galerie New York   26 | 23 | 20 | E

E 80s | 1048 Fifth Ave. (86th St.) | 4/5/6 to 86th St. | 212-628-6200 | www.neuegalerie.org

Even the "gift store is a museum" at this "amazing" landmark building on upper Fifth Avenue featuring the "*wunderbar*" fine and decorative arts of Germany and Austria; the "superior silver and crafts" (replicas of work by designers such as Josef Hoffmann) and "fantastic books" are "as much of a treat" as the exhibitions (and the "first-class" restaurants, Cafe Sabarsky and the Cafe Fledermaus downstairs), but "high prices" have *nein*-sayers sniffing it's "not for the average shopper."

New Balance   27 | 20 | 22 | M

E 50s | 821 Third Ave. (50th St.) | 6 to 51st St. | 212-421-4444
W 40s | 51 W. 42nd St. (bet. 5th & 6th Aves.) | 7/B/D/F/V to 42nd St./Bryant Park | 212-997-9112
www.newbalance.com

"If you're an athlete, or work out on a regular basis", sprint over to these Midtown "runner's meccas" for "long-lasting", "high-performance shoes for the big race" and styles "light, comfortable and tough enough" for "pavement pounders"; the staff "doesn't just try to sell you the latest trend – it helps you figure out what is best for your foot and your sport."

New London Pharmacy ◑   23 | 19 | 20 | M

Chelsea | 246 Eighth Ave. (23rd St.) | E to 8th Ave. | 212-243-4987 | 800-941-0490 | www.newlondonpharmacy.com

Chelsea houses one of "the best drug stores in the city" for "one-stop shopping" for a "wide selection of top-notch products" ranging from natural and "holistic to traditional", "popular or hard-to-find" "pick-me-up treats" like toiletries and cosmetics (over 200 upscale brands); it may be a little "cramped", but "excellent" "personalized" service makes for a "pleasant" "anything-but-Duane-Reade" experience.

NEW New Museum of Contemporary Art Store Ⓜ   - | - | - | E

LES | 235 Bowery (Prince St.) | F to 2nd Ave. | 212-343-0460 | www.newmuseum.org

After perusing the three galleries of this recently reopened seven-story Bowery beacon of contemporary art, slip into its tiny lobby shop behind the metal-mesh divider; browse through books about Raymond Pettibon and Kara Walker, John Waters' porcelain plates, modern-day nesting dolls from Visionaire and espresso sets designed by SANAA, the building's architects, for Alessi, or take home coffee mugs bearing the 'Hell, Yes' rainbow, a memento of artist Ugo Rondinone's sign hanging outside on one of the building's rectilinear boxes.

New York & Company ☒

17 | 17 | 16 | M

Financial District | 83 Nassau St. (bet. Fulton & John Sts.) | 2/3/4/5/A/C/J/M/Z to Fulton St./B'way/Nassau | 212-964-2864 | 800-723-5333 | www.newyorkandcompany.com
Additional locations throughout the NY area

"Constant sales and discounts" make this the spot to get "trendy, comfortable" women's attire and accessories; still, the "sizing is significantly off-base", which doesn't bother some ladies who don't mind being an 8 rather than a 12 when they visit this affordable chain; also be aware that "it's always tough to get a dressing room."

New York Central Art Supply ☒

25 | 16 | 21 | M

E Village | 62 Third Ave. (11th St.) | 4/5/6/L/N/Q/R/W to 14th St./Union Sq. | 212-473-7705 | 800-950-6111 | www.nycentralart.com
"What an art supply shop is supposed to be" profess patrons of this "small" East Village "indie" veteran vending both the "esoteric and the ordinary" including a "mind-boggling", "top-of-the-line" array of "beautiful papers for book artists" and watercolorists; service can be "hit-or-miss" (some note it's "a cut above", others detect "arti-tude"), but the "good prices" and "interesting inventory" make it "worth a visit."

New York Doll Hospital ☒⊄

▽ 28 | 19 | 25 | E

E 60s | 787 Lexington Ave., 2nd fl. (bet. 61st & 62nd Sts.) | 4/5/6/F/N/R/W to 59th St./Lexington Ave. | 212-838-7527
When "their favorite" dollie, teddy or toy is in need of "repair or rehabilitation", little kids rush them straight to this East 60s "haven" where, with a little TLC, the "master-craftsman" "owner, Irving Chais – an "institution in-and-of himself" – nurses "modern and antique" cherished ones; this "landmark" has been a "New York tradition" for over a century, and "no one does it better" insist loyalists.

New York Elegant Fabric

- | - | - | E

W 40s | 222 W. 40th St. (bet. 7th & 8th Aves.) | 1/2/3/7/N/Q/R/S/W to 42nd St./Times Sq. | 212-302-4980
Just off Times Square and steps away from Parsons Fashion Design Center, this basters' bastion may look basic but material witnesses swear it's 20,000 sq. ft. of "lovely fabric" (specialties include European brocades and silks) proffered by "lovely people"; high-quality weaves for upholstery and draperies draw decorators and DIYers as well.

New York Golf Center

24 | 20 | 20 | E

Chelsea | Golf Club at Chelsea Piers | Chelsea Pier 59 (18th St. & West Side Hwy.) | A/C/E/L to 14th St./8th Ave. | 212-242-8899
Garment District | 131 W. 35th St. (bet. B'way & 7th Ave.) | B/D/F/N/Q/R/V/W to 34th St./Herald Sq. | 212-564-2255
888-465-7890 | www.nygolfcenter.com
With 9,000 sq. ft. of showroom, this Garment District mainstay is "the place to go" for the "best golf selection in the city"; an "excellent staff"

can caddy you through "all the major brands" from Titlest to Taylor, and while the merchandise is "on the pricey side, you get what you need"; P.S. "try out a new club" at the Chelsea Piers branch boasting an expansive "indoor driving range."

New York Look, The

20 | 17 | 15 | E

E 40s | 551 Fifth Ave. (45th St.) | 4/5/6/7/S to 42nd St./Grand Central | 212-557-0909 ◐

SoHo | 468 W. Broadway (bet. Houston & Prince Sts.) | C/E to Spring St. | 212-598-9988 ◐

W 40s | 570 Seventh Ave. (41st St.) | 1/2/3/7/N/Q/R/S/W to 42nd St./ Times Sq. | 212-382-2760 ◙

W 60s | 2030 Broadway (69th St.) | 1/2/3 to 72nd St. | 212-362-8650 ◐

W 60s | 30 Lincoln Plaza (bet. 62nd & 63rd Sts.) | 1/A/B/C/D to 59th St./ Columbus Circle | 212-245-6511 ◐

"Check out" this fashionista chain with a name "reminiscent of the '80s" and the "latest" looks for work, "trendy", "up-to-date" party dresses, shoes and "excellent costume jewelry"; while no one denies this outfit's "knack" for "quality and style", shoppers say the staff practically "air-kisses you on arrival" and can be "more aggressive than primitive cavemen" – in fact their *Glengarry Glen Ross* sales technique is a major detraction."

New York Pipe Dreams

- | - | - | E

E 80s | 1623 York Ave. (bet. 85th & 86th Sts.) | 4/5/6 to 86th St. | 866-666-6973 | www.newyorkpipedreams.com

Whether the equipment of choice is surf, skate or snow, board members are big believers in this East 80s sporting goods store, which handles a "large selection" of gear, plus all the garb and accessories that accompany these activities; "prices are good", considering the range of brands, and the store also offers sign-up services for bus trips to mountains, beaches and skate parks.

New York Public Library Shop, The Ⓜ

23 | 20 | 18 | M

E 40s | 476 Fifth Ave. (42nd St.) | 7 to 5th Ave. | 212-930-0641

Harlem | Schomburg Ctr. | 515 Malcolm X Blvd. (135th St.) | 2/3 to 135th St. | 212-491-2206 ◙

www.thelibraryshop.org

Paging all "book-lovers": the New York Public Library's "interesting" shop (and its Schomburg Center outpost) constitutes "heaven for literary" lions lured by "everything from pencils to huge coffee-table" tomes; like the "NYPL system", it's a "treasure" trove of "gifts galore" including maps, writing instruments, "innovative cards" and apparel that's "not too pricey", and though a few whisper there's "not much there", more maintain it's "worth a visit."

New York Replacement Parts Corp. ◙

22 | 10 | 20 | M

E 90s | 1456 & 1464 Lexington Ave. (bet. 94th & 95th Sts.) | 6 to 96th St. | 212-534-0818 | 800-228-4718 | www.nyrpcorp.com

"Can't find it? – they can", so for "older fixtures" that need "rare" or "replacement parts", pros head over to this "essential" plumbing showroom and supply house on the Upper East Side that "covers a range of prices"; it's always "packed" so "be prepared to wait"; N.B. closed weekends.

	QUALITY	DISPLAY	SERVICE	COST

New York Running Company ◗
24 | 24 | 23 | E

W 60s | The Shops at Columbus Circle, Time Warner Ctr. |
10 Columbus Circle, 2nd fl. (60th St. at B'way) | 1/A/B/C/D to 59th St./
Columbus Circle | 212-823-9626 | www.therunningcompany.net

"If you need shoe guidance" and a "lot of good running gear and sneakers", dash over to this Time Warner Center standby, "well situated to
Central Park"; the "excellent staff" "evaluates you on the treadmill" and "helps" "even the most serious" athlete "find shoes that match
your stride and improve efficiency"; such scrutiny "results in perfect fit, if not the perfect price."

New York Transit Museum Store
20 | 18 | 17 | M

E 40s | Grand Central, main concourse | 42nd St. (Vanderbilt Ave.) | 4/5/
6/7/S to 42nd St./Grand Central | 212-878-0106 ◗
Downtown | Boerum Pl. & Schermerhorn St. | Brooklyn | 2/4/5/M/R to
Court St./Borough Hall | 718-694-1600
www.transitmuseumstore.com

"Be true to your train line" at these Downtown and Grand Central Station
museum stores, where the "transit-themed tchotchkes" roam from
"vintage token jewelry" to "subway map mugs" to "cute" apparel covered
with the "MTA insignia"; you'll also find "great" authentic memorabilia
from retired fleets (reproduction signs, straps, tiles) and "unique"
gifts for kids – "the only thing missing is that underground aroma."

Nicholas Perricone ⊠
22 | 21 | 21 | VE

E 60s | 791 Madison Ave. (67th St.) | 6 to 68th St. | 212-734-2537 |
www.nvperriconemd.com

This "spacious and serene" Upper East Side store touts the teachings
of its dermatologist founder Dr. Nicholas Perricone, who believes
great skin comes from diet (salmon, salmon and more salmon), vitamin supplements and his own "patented" 35-piece, anti-aging treatment line that includes the likes of Amine Complex Face Lift; but foes
fume that the "overpriced" products are "so costly I thought they
would just scare my wrinkles away!"

Nicole Miller
24 | 22 | 21 | E

E 60s | 780 Madison Ave. (bet. 66th & 67th Sts.) | 6 to 68th St. | 212-288-9779
SoHo | 77 Greene St. (bet. Broome & Spring Sts.) | N/R/W to Prince St. |
212-219-1825
www.nicolemiller.com

"Relatively affordable for Madison Avenue" and SoHo too (especially
with the "faboo sales"), this duo specializes in "event dresses" and
"true-to-size" eveningwear "you can actually wear", plus a few "funky
pieces to add to your work separates"; despite the "classic cuts", this
designer "always" delivers "something original to fit the occasion",
thanks to the highly "helpful staff."

Niketown New York ◗
24 | 25 | 17 | E

E 50s | 6 E. 57th St. (bet. 5th & Madison Aves.) | 4/5/6/F/N/R/W to
59th St./Lexington Ave. | 212-891-6453 | www.nike.com

"Like an amusement park for the feet" and the bod too, this multifloor
Midtown "athlete's dream" is "so big" with so many "stylish, yet functional" sneakers and activewear items you can "make a day event out" of
"browsing"; the "cool vibe" puts "motivated" types and "couch potatoes alike" "in the work-out mood" and so may the "eager staff"; still,

the "crowd"-adverse cry it's "impossible to make a quick in/out purchase"; N.B. sneakerheads lusting for invitations to NoLita's exclusive Nike iD studio can now design their own kicks at Niketown's in-store lab.

Nili Lotan Ⓜ — | — | — | E

TriBeCa | 188 Duane St. (Greenwich St.) | 1/2/3 to Chambers St. | 212-431-7788 | www.nililotan.com

Imagine rocker Patti Smith dressing for a job interview and you'll get a sense of the crisp shirts, skinny pants and masculine-feminine tailoring offered at this "individual and interesting" Israeli designer's elegantly spare TriBeCa flagship/design studio; while "beautiful people shop here", the vibe is more art gallery than boutique, with a dry cleaner's conveyer belt circulating the "well-designed" womenswear coveted by cool Downtowners prepared to "break the bank."

99X ◐ ▽ 18 | 17 | 19 | M

E Village | 84 E. 10th St. (bet. 3rd & 4th Aves.) | 6 to Astor Pl. | 212-460-8599 | www.99xnyc.com

"Head up the stairs for the best of King's Road" British apparel advise guys who "look and feel like a trendster" shopping at this "East Village punk store" that's been "rocking" for decades; admirers mark it as a spot for one of the "best selections of Fred Perry" and Ben Sherman clothing, plus "essential mod gear" like Tuk creepers, "cool" Doc Martens and Gola trainers, and while the stock's mostly for blokes, there's a bit for birds too.

Nine West 17 | 18 | 16 | M

E 50s | 675 Fifth Ave. (bet. 53rd & 54th Sts.) | E/V to 5th Ave./53rd St. | 212-319-6893 | 800-999-1877 | www.ninewest.com
Additional locations throughout the NY area

"Without" this "solid-bet" chain, "I'd be barefoot" quip shoppers who circle the "constantly changing" racks for "on-trend footwear at prices that allow you to treat yourself to more than one pair"; "for those that can't afford the Manolos and the Choos", the "sexy", "stylish" shoes "for work and play" "make us feel almost Sarah-Jessica-y"; but naysayers not "willing to put up with" "knockoffs" "you'll see all over the city" concur it's "not worth the inexpensive price tag."

Nintendo World ◐ ▽ 25 | 25 | 22 | M

E 40s | Rockefeller Ctr. | 10 Rockefeller Ctr. (bet. 5th & 6th Aves.) | B/D/F/V to 47-50th Sts./Rockefeller Ctr. | 646-459-0800 | www.nintendoworldstore.com
Nirvana for Nintendoheads, this "slick" Rockefeller Center superstore "rocks" thanks to a "fantastic" retailtainment "setup" split between the Game Boy Advance, DS and GameCube systems; kids make a bee-line for the sampling bar or the giant gaming wall, then settle into the surround-sound gaming pods and software library; P.S. fans of former inhabitant Pokémon Center need not "miss" Pikachu and pals – they still live here in their own area.

Noisette — | — | — | E

Williamsburg | 54 N. Sixth St. (Kent Ave.) | Brooklyn | L to Bedford Ave. | 718-388-5188 | www.noisettenyc.com

This once-deserted strip of Williamsburg has become shopping central due to style-magnets like this large, seductive store, whose name means 'hazelnut' in French; it's owned by Stéphanie Deleau, whose

| | QUALITY | DISPLAY | SERVICE | COST |

"beautiful" taste in all things Gallic – Aoyama Itchome ethnic-print dresses, Bash knits, Maje frocks and coats – "is worth the cost" for seriously sleek gamines; N.B. don't miss Jerome Lagarrigue's stunning oil painting on the back wall.

Nokia ❷

| 22 | 21 | 18 | E |

E 50s | 5 E. 57th St. (bet. 5th & Madison Aves.) | N/R/W to 5th Ave./59th St. | 212-758-1980 | www.nokia.com

Fans of the Finnish brand reach "high-tech" "heaven" at this "flashy" "futuristic" three-floor Midtown flagship showcasing a "well-organized" selection of the "latest" mobile phones, accessories, electronics and other "geek stuff"; "if you have lots of bucks" head upstairs where upwards of $5,000 can buy you a customized Vertu cell, otherwise "go here to look and then go elsewhere to buy."

Nom de Guerre ❷

| ▽ 20 | 20 | 16 | E |

NoHo | 640 Broadway (Bleecker St.) | 6 to Bleecker St. | 212-253-2891 | www.nomdeguerre.net

With a name that means 'pseudonym', it's no wonder that this signless "guerrilla"-style boutique is located "underground" in a NoHo building reputed to be a "former Black Panthers' hangout"; the "cool, if limited merchandise" is just as "unexpected", from the house line of men's urbanwear to the "wildly exclusive kicks", including collaborative collections with Converse Jack Purcell and Adidas to the Comme des Garçons scents; still, snipers sling arrows at "snotty service."

Norman's Sound & Vision ❷

| - | - | - | I |

E Village | 67 Cooper Sq. (3rd. Ave., bet. 7th & 8th Sts.) | 6 to Astor Pl. | 212-473-6599 | www.normanssound.com

"Searching through the cases can be time consuming but it's so worth it" is the sound advice from admirers of owner Norman Isaacs' vision, which has created this East Village vet that's light on vinyl but heavy on "tough-to-find" jazz CDs; "overlooked deals abound."

North Face, The

| 24 | 20 | 18 | E |

SoHo | 139 Wooster St. (bet. Houston & Prince Sts.) | N/R/W to Prince St. | 212-260-1000

W 70s | 2101 Broadway (73rd St.) | 1/2/3 to 72nd St. | 212-362-1000 ❷
800-362-4963 | www.thenorthface.com

"Serious hikers" as well as "urban dwellers who want to" dress to "match their SUVs" trek to these shops in the Ansonia and in SoHo for "top-of-the-line gear" and clothing that "holds up to wear and tear"; whether you're searching for a "phat puffy" jacket or tents and backpacks, "nobody has a better selection of the brand that defines outdoor adventure"; still, a lost few "wish they were more inventive" and question the "clueless" staff.

Nort/Recon

| - | - | - | E |

NoHo | 359 Lafayette St. (bet. Bleecker & Bond Sts.) | 6 to Bleecker St. | 212-777-6102 | www.reconstore.com

At this NoHo streetwear/sneaker specialist owned by legendary graffiti artists Stash and Futura, cool-hunters stock up on apparel and bags while in-the-know Nike nuts hit the mother lode, tracking down unique kicks from the activewear label's limited-edition, imported and collaborative footwear collections.

	QUALITY	DISPLAY	SERVICE	COST

No. 6 Ⓜ
Little Italy | 6 Centre Market Pl. (bet. Broome & Grand Sts.) | 6 to Spring St. | 212-226-5759 | www.no6store.com

| ▽ - | - | - | E |

Down a Little Italy alleyway ("never even knew of this street") lies this vintage clothier, specializing in everyday, if slightly "expensive", European garb; its light-filled digs, artfully if minimally decorated with white wood floors, leather couches and painted windows, highlight the womenswear, which includes both pure old pieces (primarily from the '40s–'70s) and some reconstituted ones; Jacqueline Schnabel footwear and new accessories round out the Continental collection.

Number (N)ine
TriBeCa | 431 Washington St. (Vestry St.) | 1 to Canal St. | 212-431-8699 | www.numberniners.com

| - | - | - | E |

The interior almost outshines the clothes at this tiny TriBeCa boutique, as everything within its shadowy, draped interior seems made of 'found' objects: stereo speakers comprise the back wall and books sandwiched between wood slabs are tables; on the racks (erstwhile iron gate posts) hang casual mens- and womenswear from Japanese designer Takahiro Miyashita, whose stylings are for small-boned folks who enjoy neutral or earth-toned basics with that little extra – a tuxedo-frilled shirt here, a tab-fronted military jacket there – thrown in; N.B. closed Tuesdays.

NYC Velo ●
E Village | 64 Second Ave. (bet. 3rd & 4th Sts.) | F/V to Lower East Side/2nd Ave. | 212-253-7771 | www.nycvelo.com

| ▽ 20 | 19 | 19 | E |

This family-owned East Village cycle shop offers more than a set of wheels; enthusiasts can latch onto every aspect of the bicycle lifestyle, from "beautiful" rides by Bianchi, Ridley and Turner to clothing and gear from the likes of Campagnolo, Descente and Giro, and even turn to the "knowledgeable staff" that bikes to work everyday for advice about the right fit; stop by the lounge to mingle with messengers and commuters over a free coffee and bagel.

Oak
NEW NoHo | 28 Bond St. (bet. Bowery & Lafayette Sts.) | B/D/F/V to B'way/Lafayette St. | 212-260-7536 ●
Park Slope | 668 President St. (bet. 5th & 6th Aves.) | Brooklyn | M/R to Union St. | 718-857-2080 Ⓜ
Williamsburg | 208 N. Eighth St. (bet. Driggs & Roebling Sts.) | Brooklyn | L to Bedford Ave. | 718-782-0521 Ⓜ
www.oaknyc.com

| - | - | - | E |

While the original Oak may be long gone, another incarnation grows in Williamsburg, a cool-as-ever sibling to the Park Slope standby that sprouted up a few years ago in a two-level spare white carriage house off the main Fifth Avenue drag, while another recently put down roots in NoHo; willowy hipsters of both sexes fall for boldface and emerging designer names, including Acne Jeans, Band of Outsiders, Generra, filippa k., Helmet Lang and Opening Ceremony.

Oakley ●
SoHo | 113 Prince St. (Greene St.) | N/R/W to Prince St. | 212-673-7700 | www.oakley.com

| ▽ 21 | 23 | 21 | E |

"Making people look good under the sun" for over 30 years, this SoHo outpost of an international chain offers "stylish shades" (including a line incorporating MP3 technology) preferred by "surfer dudes" and snowboarders as well as "sleek" eyeglasses; the "great" store also offers apparel and gear for those leading a high-performance lifestyle.

Occhiali 🗷   24 | 22 | 21 | E

E 80s | 1188 Lexington Ave. (81st St.) | 6 to 77th St. | 212-639-1188

"Always satisfied" asserts the spec-set that sets its sights on this sleek, modern East 80s eyewear maven, "one of the best-designed stores in NYC", when it's time to see straight; "everything is good quality", from the funky frames to the Zeiss lenses, plus the "staff takes top-notch service to a new level", offering "polite but firm advice if you've gone astray in your choices."

Ochre   - | - | - | VE

SoHo | 462 Broome St. (bet. Greene & Mercer Sts.) | N/R/W to Prince St. | 212-414-4332 | www.ochre.net

"Amazing style" and high-quality craftsmanship mark this stateside SoHo flagship of a decade-old British home-furnishings firm known for sexy signature seating, luxe day beds and chairs in plush velvet, suede and leather, along with lighting and bespoke chandeliers; of course, this kind of posh comes at a pretty price.

Oculus 20/20 ❶   - | - | - | E

Carroll Gardens | 267 Smith St. (Degraw St.) | Brooklyn | F/G to Carroll St. | 718-554-6230

Williamsburg | 189 Bedford Ave. (bet. N. 6th & 7th Sts.) | Brooklyn | L to Bedford Ave. | 718-666-0040

www.oculus2020.com

For "beautiful frames not found anywhere else", set your sights on this eyewear duo in Carroll Gardens and Williamsburg, boasting 20/20 fashion vision; the broad selection of high-end specs focuses on spectacular names including Francis Klein, Freudenhaus and Robert Marc, so chances are "you'll pay a lot" for the luxury of looking good; N.B. the Henry Street offshoot closed and a new branch is slated to open in Red Hook, spring 2008.

Odin ❶   - | - | - | E

NoLita | 199 Lafayette St. (bet. Broome & Kenmare Sts.) | 6 to Spring St. | 212-966-0026

Odin on 11th ❶

E Village | 328 E. 11th St. (2nd Ave.) | L to 1st Ave. | 212-475-0666

www.odinnewyork.com

"The vibe is so right" at these sophisticated "little" East Village and NoLita "outfitters" for the "modern metro man" featuring timely and fashionable urban wear from labels like Umbro by Kim Jones and Comme des Garçons alongside exclusive jewelry and accessories; "look in the back" for a small but well-edited selection of "perfect" gifts for "picky" guys, such as design books, grooming products and cameras from Lomo and Holga.

NEW Ohio Knitting Mills ❶Ⓜ   22 | 19 | 20 | E

Carroll Gardens | 231 Smith St. (bet. Butler & Douglass Sts.) | Brooklyn | F/G to Bergen St. | 718-596-7103 | www.ohioknittingmills.com

Snagged from the archives of a now-shuttered Cleveland mill, this "treasure trove" of "absolutely 'virgin'", never-been-worn knit goods from 1947–1974 is displayed in a Carroll Gardens space reminiscent of its industrial roots, complete with sewing table lamps and dressmaker dummies; what an "interesting concept": owner-sculptor Steven Tatar happened upon the pristinely preserved samples while scouting for scrap metal and brought the one-off argyle sweaters, preppy vests and other "neat stuff" east, where an appetite for retro lives on.

Oilily
23 | 25 | 21 | E

E 60s | 820 Madison Ave. (bet. 68th & 69th Sts.) | 6 to 68th St. | 212-772-8686
SoHo | 465 W. Broadway (bet. Prince & W. Houston Sts.) | N/R/W to Prince St. | 212-871-0201
800-977-7736 | www.oililyusa.com

Catering to the "nonconformist" "future bohemian" "who marches to a different beat", Madison Avenue's Dutch treat with a "sweet staff" stirs the senses with its "quirky" brand of kids' clothing (and adult of-ferings too) that comes in "happy" "showstopping" colors and pat-terns sure to "brighten up a gray New York day"; though too "wacky" for some, diehards decree that their "rugrats have never looked so good"; N.B. the gigantic SoHo store sells a different merchandise mix.

Olá Baby Ⓜ
▽ 27 | 24 | 21 | E

Bay Ridge | 8511 Third Ave. (85th St.) | Brooklyn | R to 86th St. | 718-745-1190
Carroll Gardens | 315 Court St. (bet. Degraw & Sackett Sts.) | Brooklyn | F/G to Carroll St. | 718-422-1978
www.olababy.com

Stroller pushers steer straight to this "interesting" "gem" in Carroll Gardens – and its Bay Ridge sibling too – when they want to spoil their little bundle with a "fantastic variety" of ultramodern nursery furniture and bedding, including Stokke Collection items from Sweden, baby clothing, toys, books and other "cool", "unusual design-y stuff"; throw in "fair prices" and a "pleasant, helpful staff" and you've got the per-fect "neighborhood place."

O'Lampia Studio
▽ 29 | 26 | 28 | E

LES | 155 Bowery (bet. Broome & Delancey Sts.) | 6 to Spring St. | 212-925-1660 | www.olampia.com

For "unique and carefully crafted" custom lighting ranging from floor and table models to chandeliers, pendants and sconces, loyalists like this Bowery studio known for "sky-high quality without prices to match."

Olatz Ⓢ
- | - | - | VE

W Village | 45 Clarkson St. (bet. Greenwich & Hudson Sts.) | 1 to Houston St. | 212-255-8627 | www.olatz.com

Two huge sleigh beds and a dramatic black-and-white checkered floor dominate this West Village shop owned by Olatz Schnabel, the wife of the painter Julian Schnabel; "high-quality" hand-embroidered linens, towels and crib sets are offered at equally elevated prices.

Olde Good Things
▽ 18 | 14 | 21 | M

Chelsea | 124 W. 24th St. (bet. 6th & 7th Aves.) | F/V to 23rd St. | 212-989-8401
G Village | 19 Greenwich Ave. (bet. 6th & 7th Aves.) | A/B/C/D/E/F/V to W. 4th St. | 212-229-0850 ◗
888-551-7333 | www.oldegoodthings.com

The "goods" at these Chelsea and Greenwich Village salvage stores are indeed "old" and range from "outdoor fountains" and fireplace mantels to dressers, doorknobs, drawer pulls, tin mirrors, panels and "perfect period fixtures" and architectural elements for those "renovating turn-of-the-century brownstones"; the "presentation is haphazard at best" and "you are on your own" in terms of service, but there are lots of "unique artifacts" to be unearthed.

Olden Camera & Lens Company, Inc. ✉

20 | 10 | 16 | M

Garment District | 1263 Broadway, 4th fl. (bet. 31st & 32nd Sts.) | B/D/F/N/Q/R/V/W to 34th St./Herald Sq. | 212-725-1234

"Worth a stop", this Garment District "oldie but goodie" lives up to its "wonderful reputation" as a "neat place" for analogue "camera nuts" "hunting for bargains" thanks to its "good selection of lenses" and "excellent used equipment" (such as "classic" Leicas and Super 8s) sold by "intelligent salespeople" "at reasonable prices"; still, some digital devotees declare it "outdated."

Old Navy ⓘ

14 | 14 | 13 | I

Garment District | 150 W. 34th St. (bet. 6th & 7th Aves.) | B/D/F/N/Q/R/V/W to 34th St./Herald Sq. | 212-594-0115 | 800-653-6289 | www.oldnavy.com
Additional locations throughout the NY area

"Thrifty is the word" at this "no-frills" "upbeat" chain, which may provide "the best value out there" for "cheap basics" as well as "trendy pieces" for the entire family crew; you may "have to hunt forever for a size" given that everything's "so stuffed onto the racks" and the stores are often a "mob scene"; nonetheless to most it's always "worth a look."

Olive & Bette's

22 | 19 | 19 | E

E 80s | 1070 Madison Ave. (bet. 80th & 81st Sts.) | 6 to 77th St. | 212-717-9655
SoHo | 158 Spring St. (bet. W. B'way & Wooster St.) | C/E to Spring St. | 646-613-8772
W 70s | 252 Columbus Ave. (bet. 71st & 72nd Sts.) | 1/2/3 to 72nd St. | 212-579-2178 ⓘ
W Village | 384 Bleecker St. (Perry St.) | 1 to Christopher St./Sheridan Sq. | 212-206-0036 ⓘ
www.oliveandbettes.com

"Knock yourself out" at this "quirky" quartet – it's the "go-to place for what's hot for the moment" confirm fashionistas; the "mix of froufrou and basics is ideal for one-stop shopping", particularly if you're jonesing for "cute T-shirts", "in-vogue accessories" and "anything sequined" from "popular" labels; as to the "witty staff", hey, "salespeople who actually deign to help find the perfect pair of jeans make my day."

Oliver Peoples

27 | 25 | 23 | VE

E 60s | 755 Madison Ave. (bet. 65th & 66th Sts.) | 6 to 68th St. | 212-585-3433
SoHo | 366 W. Broadway (Broome St.) | N/R/W to Prince St. | 212-925-5400
888-568-1655 | www.oliverpeoples.com

"For LA style" at "NYC prices" tastemakers "go no further" than this spec-tacular, "top-notch" Uptown-Downtown duo with "courteous" service; slip on a pair of "chic shades to cruise around SoHo like a native" or check out the "hip eyewear", the "sportier" Mosley Tribes spin-off collection (a "great addition") and Paul Smith numbers; sure, "seeing is believing" when it comes to the "expensive prices", but fans insist they're the "most interesting glasses out there, bar none."

Oliver Spencer
`- - - E`

W Village | 750 Greenwich St. (11th St.) | 1 to Christopher St./Sheridan Sq. | 212-337-3095 | www.oliverspencer.co.uk

With scuffed-up antique furniture and shirts stuffed into bell jars, this intimate West Villager resembles the study of a slightly daft Victorian gent; but the clothing is all contemporary – quality sportswear from the namesake British designer whose U.K. clientele includes Paul McCartney, Daniel Day Lewis and Pierce Brosnan, plus sweaters, tees and jeans from Trovata, Engineered Garments and Rag & Bone; Sharp toiletries and a few leather goods round out the lot.

NEW OMALA ●
`∇ 20 20 22 E`

Boerum Hill | 400 Atlantic Ave. (Bond St.) | Brooklyn | A/C/G to Hoyt/Schermerhorn Sts. | 718-694-9642 | www.omalausa.com

Yoginis reach a new realm of consciousness – design consciousness, that is – at this "lovely" Atlantic Avenue haven for all things yoga; it's difficult to stay calm given the impressive selection of innovative, "expensive" yogawear, from the house brand, created to complement curves, with a special collection for Bikram devotees, to beyond-basic lines like City Lights, which may be why this good-looking leviathan also hosts free yoga and pilates classes.

OMO Norma Kamali ⌧
`22 26 24 E`

W 50s | 11 W. 56th St. (bet. 5th & 6th Aves.) | N/Q/R/W to 57th St. | 212-957-9797 | 800-852-6254 | www.normakamalicollection.com

"Diversity and quality are always an element in the style" of this truly original designer, whose museumlike Midtown store displays her wares like works of art; converts confide the wrinkle-free polyester jersey separates, pin-up girl maillots and signature "sleeping bag coats last forever" – a good thing, since there is and "will only be one Norma."

Only Hearts
`21 18 17 E`

NoLita | 230 Mott St. (bet. Prince & Spring Sts.) | 6 to Spring St. | 212-431-3694

W 70s | 386 Columbus Ave. (bet. 78th & 79th Sts.) | 1 to 79th St. | 212-724-5608

www.onlyhearts.com

"Everything is soo cute and lacy" sigh the smitten aflutter over the "beautiful lingerie" (plus some tops and leggings) at this "lovely" NoLita–West 70s twosome; whether you're scouting for "comfy" camis, come-hither thongs, a "fun bridal gift" or even "unique jewelry", the "exceptional finds make any woman happy and mend any [broken] ties with a lover"; still, "go on a day when you don't need to look at the price tags", because the cost of some scanties seems "too high."

On Stage Dance Shop ⌧
`- - - M`

Murray Hill | 197 Madison Ave. (bet. 34th & 35th Sts.) | 6 to 33rd St. | 212-725-1174 | www.onstagedancewear.com

"A bit more personal" than the boldface-name competitors with a "staff that's eager to assist", this Murray Hill shop "chock-full of dance attire" for "professional wear" outfits both Broadway performers from shows like *The Lion King* and plain ol' exercise-buffs; the leotards, unitards, skatewear and tutus are assembled on barrellike racks with ballet, salsa, jazz, flamenco and tap shoes to match.

Opening Ceremony ●

| - | - | - | E |

SoHo | 35 Howard St. (bet. B'way & Crosby St.) | N/R/W to Canal St. |
212-219-2688 | www.openingceremony.us

You're invited to an ever-changing celebration of "the most cutting-edge clothes in town" at this tri-level SoHo rite of style passage, filled with "often gorgeous, always credit-card-maxing" dresses, suits, sweatshirts and tempting T-shirts for men and women from the house line and emerging American and European designers, plus a temporary boutique-within-a-boutique upstairs devoted to Topshop, the British cheap-chic chain; chances are "few others" will be wearing this "one-off" garb "on the number 4 train."

Orange Blossom Ⓜ

| - | - | - | E |

Park Slope | 180 Lincoln Pl. (bet. 7th & 8th Aves.) | Brooklyn | B/Q to 7th Ave. | 877-466-2543 | www.orangeblossomnyc.com

Though now under new ownership, this "sweet" Park Slope shop still nurtures budding fashion plates with "cool", "creative" clothing; pick and choose from playful labels like Cakewalk, Eye Spy and Paul Frank's Small Paul line, hand-knit stuffed animals and other "fun" finds that make it a "great place to run to when you need a gift quick."

Orchard Corset Center

| - | - | - | M |

LES | 157 Orchard St. (bet. Rivington & Stanton Sts.) | F/J/M/Z to Delancey/Essex Sts. | 212-674-0786 | 877-267-2427 | www.orchardcorset.com

It's "worth a trip to the Lower East Side" for the "uplifting" New York experience at this "tiny" veteran that's been selling lingerie since 1968 (waist-cinchers are their specialty); "everything is in boxes" but that's ok since the owner and his mom "will pick the right size" "just by looking at you" – in other words, "be prepared to throw your inhibitions away."

Organic Avenue ●

| 24 | 22 | 22 | E |

LES | 101 Stanton St. (bet. Ludlow & Orchard Sts.) | F to 2nd Ave. |
212-334-4593

"Let's hear it for environmentally responsible shopping" – this "real" one-stop LES eco-emporium is "so neat" agree green-advocates who embrace everything from the "nice selection of health/earth conscious" lotions, potions and foodstuffs to wearables like hemp jackets, skinny jeans and tees made from organic, recycled or sustainable materials; still, a few granola-grumblers grouse it "probably should stick" to "edible goodies", carping the "clothes sort of evoke images of a Phish concert."

Oriental Lamp Shade Co. ☒

| 25 | 18 | 23 | E |

E 60s | 816 Lexington Ave. (bet. 62nd & 63rd Sts.) | 4/5/6/F/N/R/W to 59th St./Lexington Ave. | 212-832-8190

W 70s | 223 W. 79th St. (bet. Amsterdam Ave. & B'way) | 1 to 79th St. |
212-873-0812
www.orientallampshade.com

You can find classic lamps and the largest selection of ready-made and custom shades in hand-sewn silk, paper, linen, hide and metal at these "been-around-forever", family-run East Side and West Side siblings with an "excellent", "knowledgeable" staff; while prices are "on the expensive side", the glowing result is "worth it."

| | QUALITY | DISPLAY | SERVICE | COST |

Original Penguin ◐

- | - | - | M

W 40s | 1077 Sixth Ave. (41st St.) | 7/B/D/F/V to 42nd St./Bryant Park | 646-443-3520 | www.originalpenguin.com

The march of the penguins continues across from Bryant Park at this flagship for the venerable golf-clubhouse label (relaunched as a his-and-hers sportswear line in '03); the revisionist-retro palette "freshens up casual" clothing with a "smattering of wit"; with a staff that "makes everyone feel welcome" who wouldn't be down with OP?

Origins ◐

24 | 23 | 22 | M

E 40s | Grand Central | 42nd St. (Vanderbilt Ave.) | 4/5/6/7/S to 42nd St./Grand Central | 212-808-4141

Flatiron | Flatiron Bldg. | 175 Fifth Ave. (22nd St.) | N/R/W to 23rd St. | 212-677-9100

SoHo | 402 W. Broadway (Spring St.) | C/E to Spring St. | 212-219-9764

W 80s | 2327 Broadway (bet. 84th & 85th Sts.) | 1 to 86th St. | 212-769-0970

800-674-4467 | www.origins.com

"It even smells calm" say supporters of this skincare, bath and body chain that "knows how to cater to its clientele" with "not too pricey" "eco-conscious products" made from aromatic natural ingredients like mint and white tea, along with a mushroom-based treatment line from alternative medicine guru Dr. Andy Weil; a "knowledgeable staff" "encourages sampling", and you don't have to be a "crunchy granola type" to appreciate the "soothing, soulful" "spalike" experience here.

Orvis Company, The

25 | 23 | 22 | E

E 40s | 522 Fifth Ave. (44th St.) | 4/5/6/7/S to 42nd St./Grand Central | 212-827-0698 | 888-235-9763 | www.orvis.com

"Perfect" for the "sophisticated" "sporting set", this Midtown outpost of the 150-year-old, family-owned Vermont chain reels in "adventurous" "blue-blood types" and "outdoorsy" aspirants who "just want to look like they're going fly fishing" or hunting; no need to wade unaided through the "high-quality equipment" and "excellent" clothing (including one of the "best Barbour selections") – just turn to the "friendly" staff for "first-class fashion advice" and angling pointers too.

Z Oscar de la Renta ⊠

28 | 28 | 28 | VE

E 60s | 772 Madison Ave. (66th St.) | 6 to 68th St. | 212-288-5810 | www.oscardelarenta.com

"When you want a classy, timeless look, it's Oscar" opine the ladies who not only lunch, but party all night long – preferably in a sizzling cocktail dress or red-carpet–ready gown from the consummate designer, who still "keeps up with the moment" after more than 40 years; his "beautiful" Madison Avenue boutique offers exclusive evening collections, as well as "classic" daytime suits and extravagant accessories, all overseen by "an amazing staff."

Oska

- | - | - | M

SoHo | 415 W. Broadway (bet. Prince & Spring Sts.) | C/E to Spring St. | 212-625-2772 | www.oska.de

Collect five easy pieces – or six or seven – from the unstructured separates made by this German mens- and womenswear label; available in a rainbow of soft colors (shown to advantage in the white, boxy SoHo space) and forgiving fabrics (boiled wool, linen, corduroy), the vaguely Asian loose tunics, wide-legged pants, long skirts and shirts seem especially suited to middle-aged torsos – not to mention any soul who's sick of the super-skinny look.

NEW Osklen ⦿
`- | - | - | M`

Meatpacking | 32-36 Little W. 12th St. (Washington St.) | A/C/E to 8th Ave. | 212-727-2031
SoHo | 97 Wooster St. (Spring St.) | 6 to Spring St. | 212-219-8250
www.osklen.com

The Brazilian brand of adventure clothing and accessories hits NY with a full-fledged store in SoHo and a space within the Meatpacking shop Destination; founded by ex-sports-medicine doctor Oskar Metsavaht and looking like the love child of Eddie Bauer and Roberto Cavalli, the cool collection is aimed at surfers and snowboarders with protective casualwear, but there are still lots of skimpy bikinis for beach bunnies.

⊠ Other Music ⦿
`27 | 19 | 20 | M`

NoHo | 15 E. Fourth St. (bet. B'way & Lafayette St.) | 6 to Astor Pl. | 212-477-8150 | www.othermusic.com

"*High Fidelity* with a PhD" proclaim "indie snobs" of NoHo's "aptly named" "hip, happening" "music source" "designed to scare Top 40 types" with its "exceptional" selection of "hard-to-find" alternative and underground CDs and vinyl; if you "pay attention to the knowledgeable staff", you'll "find that next undiscovered gem" (the "more obscure the better"), and even though it's admittedly "expensive", few mind because it may be the "most influential record shop" around.

Otte ⦿
`∇ 26 | 25 | 17 | E`

W Village | 121 Greenwich Ave. (bet. Jane & W. 13th Sts.) | A/C/E/L to 14th St./8th Ave. | 212-229-9424
Williamsburg | 132 N. Fifth St. (bet. Bedford Ave. & Berry St.) | Brooklyn | L to Bedford Ave. | 718-302-3007
www.otteny.com

Devotees declare "you're guaranteed to love" the young, elegant lines like Rebecca Taylor, 3.1 Phillip Lim, Vanessa Bruno and Eberjay lingerie at the West Village shop, and chic, "up-to-the-second" finds from Acne Jeans, Velvet and Wrangler at the Williamsburg branch; all are sanely presented by color, and while the "lock on the door" can be annoying if the "staff isn't paying attention", once you're in, you'll be in fashion.

Otto
`23 | 23 | 22 | E`

Park Slope | 354 Seventh Ave. (bet. 10th & 11th Sts.) | Brooklyn | F to 7th Ave. | 718-788-6627 | www.ottobrooklyn.com

Long a side-street stop for women in-the-know, this Slope mainstay recently made the move around the corner into the Seventh Avenue limelight and now "offers more space and more of a selection of cute", "different" clothing, lingerie (from Hanro to Princess Tam-Tam), swimwear and accessories, all merchandised by owners with "excellent taste"; femme finds like dresses from S-Sung and jewelry from local designers further ensure "you won't see yourself coming and going."

Otto Tootsi Plohound ⦿
`23 | 22 | 17 | E`

Flatiron | 137 Fifth Ave. (bet. 20th & 21st Sts.) | N/R/W to 23rd St. | 212-460-8650
NoLita | 273 Lafayette St. (Prince St.) | N/R/W to Prince St. | 212-431-7299

"Entire outfits can be planned around" the "avant-garde footwear" for both sexes at this "nonconformist" Flatiron-NoLita duo; the selection is so "dizzying it'll give anyone a shoe fetish" – "whether you need something sassy, classy" or "funky", you'll find it at this "spacious" "city staple" stocked with "seriously unique" offerings from "as-of-yet-un-heard-of" labels and "veteran designer brands" alike; still, a few grumble "the only thing more preposterous than the designs are the prices."

NEW Owl's Lab
21 | 18 | 18 | E

G Village | 20 E. 12th St. (bet. 5th Ave. & University Pl.) | L/N/A/W/4/5/6 to Union Sq. | 212-633-2672 | www.owlslab.com

You would be wise, fans advise, to land at this "adorable" new Greenwich Village boutique for one-stop shopping for "trendy" top-to-toe looks from some of the touchstones of contemporary labels; start with a dress from alice + olivia or jeans from Citizens of Humanity and go on to accessories like a hat from Eugenia Kim, a cool Kooba bag or a delicate dragonfly necklace from Anne Wood.

☑ Oxxford Clothes ☒
28 | - | 27 | VE

E 50s | 717 Fifth Ave. (56th St.) | N/R/W to 5th Ave./59th St. | 212-593-0204 | www.oxxfordclothes.com

Proponents pledge their allegiance to the 102-year-old American brand at its "temple" in Midtown, where hand-tailored menswear is often customized for clients that include President Bush; the special-order crowd shells out a lot of Benjamins, but it's "ooh so worth it" for what the sartorial majority declares the "best suits made in the USA" – not to mention shirts, coats and even walking sticks.

Pan Aqua Diving
- | - | - | E

W 40s | 460 W. 43rd St. (bet. 9th & 10th Aves.) | A/C/E to 42nd St./Port Authority | 212-736-3483 | 800-434-0884 | www.panaqua.com

One of the "best dive shops in the tri-state area", this West 40s water-world offers the upscale aqua man or woman "top-of-the-line" snor-keling equipment, fins, regulators, wetsuits and swimwear – nearly everything except perhaps a pair of gills; the "knowledgeable, enthu-siastic" staff also lives the life aquatic, which means the instructors are "genuinely interested in teaching" certification classes.

P&S Fabrics
▽ 22 | 13 | 18 | I

TriBeCa | 355 Broadway (bet. Franklin & Leonard Sts.) | 1 to Franklin St. | 212-226-1534 | www.psfabrics.com

"Just steps from Chinatown", this "general-purpose sewing store" proffers a plethora of "basic items that can be hard to find in Manhattan" – and may also be the borough's "one affordable place for mainstream yarn", with "enormous selections of Lion Brand, Patons and Bernat blends" plus tools, patterns and notions; "bargain-hunters" willing to tolerate the bare-bones setting and variable service can find some "incredible values on upholstery fabrics."

Paparazzi ◑
▽ 21 | 21 | 12 | M

Gramercy | 202 E. 23rd St. (bet. 2nd & 3rd Aves.) | 6 to 23rd St. | 212-689-1968

"Pick up a gift for someone or a pick-me-up for yourself" at this "eclec-tic boutique of trinkets and treasures" near Gramercy Park, whose wares range from "subtle to outlandish, good girl to bad" clothes and jewelry, plus "good cards" and "last-minute" presents; still, like the store's namesake, the staff sometimes "breathes down your neck."

	QUALITY	DISPLAY	SERVICE	COST

Paper Presentation
25 | 20 | 19 | M

Flatiron | 23 W. 18th St. (bet. 5th & 6th Aves.) | 1 to 18th St. | 212-463-7035 | 800-727-3701 | www.paperpresentation.com

"They have it all" at this block-long Flatiron favorite with its "amazing stock" of "all things paper", from stationery and scrapbooking supplies to "do-it-yourself invitations" and business cards; "it's filled with lots of ideas and things you never knew you needed" at "bargain" prices.

Papyrus ❶
23 | 20 | 17 | M

W 40s | 11 W. 42nd St. (bet. 5th & 6th Aves.) | 7/B/D/F/V to 42nd St./ Bryant Park | 212-302-3053 | www.papyrusonline.com
Additional locations throughout the NY area

Those who prefer their greeting cards "edgier than Hallmark" prize this "convenient" Midtowner – flagship of the "crammed" chain – for its "tasteful", "original" selection (heavy on company founder Marcel Schurman's brand), along with stationery, wrapping paper and "cute extras" like stickers, frames and "little gifty things"; the "frequent-buyer program" keeps loyalists coming back as do the "great sales."

ⓩ Paragon Sporting Goods ❶
25 | 18 | 18 | M

Union Sq | 867 Broadway (18th St.) | 4/5/6/L/N/Q/R/W to 14th St./ Union Sq. | 212-255-8036 | 800-961-3030 | www.paragonsports.com

"Sports enthusiasts", "obsessive exercisers" and "ordinary" gym rats find "everything they need and then some" at Union Square's "king of sports" "supermarket" that sets the "gold standard" with its "dizzying" "A-to-Z" selection of "hiking, biking, tennis, camping and urban living goods"; weekends are so "mobbed" it can be "tough to navigate", plus a few fume "you practically have to beg" for a salesperson; nevertheless, there are plenty of "intriguing discoveries to be stumbled upon."

Parasuco ❶
21 | 20 | 18 | E

NoLita | 60 Spring St. (Lafayette St.) | 6 to Spring St. | 212-925-8858 | www.parasuco.com

"Canadian street couture" geared toward a "younger" crowd comes to NYC via this NoLita denim emporium peddling name-brand jeans and sportswear in an "opulent" chandeliered ex-bank building with "soaring" ceilings; if the "terrific" space impresses shoppers, the "under-represented label" still leads some to wonder "why everything needs to have the Parasuco name on it?"

Park Avenue Audio
24 | 19 | 20 | VE

Gramercy | 425 Park Ave. S. (29th St.) | 6 to 28th St. | 212-685-8101 | www.parkavenueaudio.com

Owned and operated by three generations of a single family, this Gramercy Park electronics store is brimming with "nice stuff", namely "high-end" entertainment equipment; the "expert" consultants enlighten customers with "honest advice" and can even team up with your interior designer to customize and install a home theater or multiroom music system that will have you curled up on the couch purring.

Parke & Ronen ❶
- | - | - | M

Chelsea | 176 Ninth Ave. (21st St.) | C/E to 23rd St. | 212-989-4245 | www.parkeandronen.com

The namesake NY-based design duo doles out seasonal collections that are "nice spins on everyday wear" for men at their one-room boutique in Chelsea; although the "body-conscious" cuts of their svelte shirts, denim and skimpy underwear leave some warning "the waistline-challenged need not shop here", alterations and custom-orders are readily available.

Paron Fabrics ⊠   20 | 13 | 18 | M

W 40s | 206 W. 40th St. (bet. 7th & 8th Aves.) | A/C/E to 42nd St./ Port Authority | 212-768-3266 | www.paronfabrics.com
Bring your "upholsterer, tailor or dressmaker" to this Times Square trove for some "wonderful buys" (e.g. "mill ends of designers' bolts"), "especially in the half-price" annex – but you'll "have to be patient to wade through all the stock"; if a handful huff it's "overrated", most insist that perks like the proprietors' "old-world knowledge" make it "well worth the trip."

Patagonia   27 | 22 | 22 | E

SoHo | 101 Wooster St. (bet. Prince & Spring Sts.) | C/E to Spring St. | 212-343-1776
W 80s | 426 Columbus Ave. (81st St.) | B/C to 81st St. | 917-441-0011
800-638-6464 | www.patagonia.com
"Must-have fleece" apparel "for every New Yorker" and "top-notch" "technical" "performance"-wear for any "outdoor adventure" draw "SUV"-owning "urban fantasizers" and "real expeditioners" alike to this activewear duo that "takes you out of SoHo" and the West 80s and "into the wilderness" with its "old-school hiking atmosphere"; made of organic and recycled materials, the "superb quality", "nothing-flashy" "clothing is legendary", if a bit pricey ("aka Patagucci"), while the "employees are knowledgeable" "users and thus great advisors."

Paterson Silks   ∇ 18 | 11 | 14 | I

W 70s | 151 W. 72nd St. (bet. Amsterdam & Columbus Aves.) | 1/2/ 3 to 72nd St. | 212-874-9510
Floral Park | 178 Jericho Tpk. (bet. Tyson & Whitney Aves.) | Queens | 718-776-5225 ⊠
www.patersonsilksus.com
"Printed cottons", wools and, yes, silks "abound" at this "no-frills" outfit in the West 70s and now Floral Park, Queens, too; the "fair prices" and a "good selection" create a "pleasant" shopping experience for DIY types.

Patina   - | - | - | E

SoHo | 451 Broome St. (bet. B'way & Mercer St.) | 6 to Spring St. | 212-625-3375
Think pink when you enter this high-walled SoHo space – the cheerful hue not only colors the ceiling, but sheds a happy patina over the small-but-select array of '30s–'60s vintage clothing, accessories and tableware; it's frequently patronized by fashion designers seeking that superb sequined clutch, fur-collared sweater or crocodile handbag.

Patricia Field ◐   ∇ 15 | - | 16 | M

NoHo | 302 Bowery (bet. Bleecker & Houston Sts.) | F/V to Lower East Side/ 2nd Ave. | 212-966-4066 | www.patriciafield.com
"If anyone knows hip, it's Pat Field" declare devotees of the "toast-of-the-town" *Sex and the City* costumer whose "wild, colorful" bazaar, a

"total throwback to 1980s new wave/punk/industrial clubwear", is now located on the Bowery; "the young and young at heart" stop by for a corset, tube top or provocative T-shirt that can "turn you into a walking fashion statement" from her own collection, plus lines like Cheap Monday, Lip Service and Nu Collective – "cutting-edge" stuff for the "next Wigstock."

Paul & Shark
27 | 25 | 22 | E

E 60s | 772 Madison Ave. (66th St.) | 6 to 68th St. | 212-452-9868 | www.paulshark.it

Aging cap'ns and younger able-bodied seamen alike love the classic, boldly colorful "yachty" threads at this East 60s flagship of the Italian chain; customers chant that "you don't need, but have to have" their "incredibly durable and well-made" nautical wear – even if the prices will hoist your credit-card bill "sky-high."

Paul Frank Store
18 | 22 | 18 | M

NoLita | 195 Mulberry St. (Kenmare St.) | 6 to Spring St. | 212-965-5079 | www.paulfrank.com

Take your "kitschy friends" to NoLita's "fanciful corner shop" and make "cute monkey faces" at Julius, the "playful" simian and his "cartoonish" pals like Bunny Girl and Skurvy the Pirate, which take center stage on "feel-good" T-shirts, undies and accessories; sure, it's "crowded", and the "staff exudes a laid-back Southern California" demeanor, but "kids and tweens love" the "quirky items" including Frank's "irreverent" Andy Warhol "stuff" with bug, banana or cow motifs.

Paul Smith
26 | 25 | 20 | VE

Flatiron | 108 Fifth Ave. (16th St.) | 4/5/6/L/N/Q/R/W to 14th St./ Union Sq. | 212-627-9770

SoHo | 142 Greene St. (W. Houston St.) | B/D/F/V to B'way/Lafayette St. | 646-613-3060

www.paulsmith.co.uk

London calling at this "exquisitely hip" Flatiron District menswear shop, a purple-hued home for the "cheeky" British designer's "dandy" striped shirts, colorful jackets and "quirky" accessories; "total style novices" and "fashion aficionados" alike "drool over" these "funky" duds, despite "the astronomical prices" ("damn exchange rate!") and a "staff that's a bit standoffish"; the younger but larger SoHo store also carries womenswear, books, home furnishings and accessories for both sexes in five distinctly styled rooms, some adorned with vintage furniture.

Paul Stuart
27 | 26 | 25 | VE

E 40s | 45th St. & Madison Ave. | 4/5/6/7/S to 42nd St./Grand Central | 212-682-0320 | 800-678-8278 | www.paulstuart.com

Men in need of "traditional looks with a touch of whimsy" buy them from the stu-ards of style at this multilevel "gold standard" in the East 40s that boasts a "broad selection" of suits, accessories and shoes, some of them custom-made; while a few fret it's "foppy" and "in need of younger appeal", most find enough "elegant" goods "across the board" here, along with "true service", to make anyone "wish for a larger budget"; P.S. the "lesser-known" women's floor makes "a nice retreat for the professional lady."

	QUALITY	DISPLAY	SERVICE	COST

Payless Shoe Source ❷

11 | 12 | 10 | I

Garment District | 484 Eighth Ave. (bet. 34th & 35th Sts.) | 1/2/3/A/
C/E to 34th St./Penn Station | 212-594-5715 | www.payless.com
Additional locations throughout the NY area

The "budget"-minded can "make out like a bandit" on the "bargain"
"faux designer shoes" – and now the real deal too, like footwear from
Abaeté designer Laura Poretzky's capsule collection, and coming up,
Lela Rose, all supplied by this chainster; if pessimists are put off by
"boxes that litter the floor, and service that's nowhere to be seen",
proponents retort if it's "good enough for Star Jones, it's good enough
for" me and the kids.

P.C. Richard & Son ❷

18 | 12 | 15 | M

Gramercy | 120 E. 14th St. (bet. Irving Pl. & 3rd Ave.) | 4/5/6/L/N/Q/R/W to
14th St./Union Sq. | 212-979-2600 | 800-369-7915 | www.pcrichard.com
Additional locations throughout the NY area

Known for its "surprisingly good" selection of "major appliances" and
"fair prices" ("you can definitely negotiate a deal"), this family-run
"warehouse" chain is the place to get "that a/c fast"; still, some cite
the "jumbled floorful" of "messy" displays and alternately "invisible"
or "pushy salespeople" as evidence that "it's not a shopping
experience to savor."

Pear ❷ Ⓜ

22 | 21 | 21 | E

NEW **LES** | 124 Ludlow St. (bet. Delancey & Rivington Sts.) | F/J/M/
Z to Delancey/Essex Sts. | 212-529-3460

Plum ❷ Ⓜ

LES | 124 Ludlow St. (bet. Delancey & Rivington Sts.) | F/J/M/Z to
Delancey/Essex Sts. | 212-529-1030
www.plumstyle.com

For "unique but wearable" designer finds from lines like Neal Sperling
and Nicholas K rarely "offered elsewhere", the fashion flock swears by
this retro-looking Lower Eastsider and its "adorable" sidekick next
door, Pear, a "welcome addition to the shoe shopping" scene boasting
plum picks from Devotee and Pour La Victoire; owner Jackie Atkins
and "all of her girls" make both boutiques so "homey" and "friendly"
that you almost "feel like you've temporarily left NYC."

☒ Pearl Paint

26 | 16 | 18 | M

Chinatown | 308 Canal St. (bet. B'way & Church St.) | 6/J/M/N/Q/R/
W/Z to Canal St. | 212-431-7932 | www.pearlpaint.com

"Artists, craftsmen and wannabes" agree: this "multifloored"
Chinatown "go-to" "institution" is "heaven on earth" supplying
"everything you need" from "poster paint to high-grade papers"; you
get a "lotta stuff for notta lotta money", which makes it a "student's
dream", and even if the contents are "cluttered", stairs a "drag" and
service sometimes "tuned out", most salute this "mother ship
of art supplies."

Pearl River Mart ❷

16 | 17 | 12 | I

SoHo | 477 Broadway (bet. Broome & Grand Sts.) | 6/J/M/N/Q/R/W/Z to
Canal St. | 212-431-4770 | 800-878-2446 | www.pearlriver.com

"Like all of Chinatown condensed into one" "spacious" store, this "inexpensive" SoHo emporium is "jam-packed" with "all things Asian",
"from Chinese cleavers", "the biggest chopstick selection this side of

Beijing" and a "food section that woks" to "funky silk" kimonos and "cute" flip-flops and doodads ("I was tempted to buy a life-size dragon's head, but common sense prevailed"); still, detractors snarl the "rude staff deters" from the fun and feel "the product displays" are in need of "feng shui"; N.B. plans are underway to add a third floor.

Peggy Pardon ●

| - | - | - | M |

LES | 153 Ludlow St. (bet. Rivington & Stanton Sts.) | F/V to Lower East Side/2nd Ave. | 212-529-3686 | www.peggypardon.com

Sure, there's not much merch, but what there is, is cherce at this LES vintage clothier; within its tiny confines, the womenswear spans decades – a Gibson Girl blouse here, a '50s sundress there – and includes a few new retro-style pieces and exotic-skin handbags; everything's in excellent condition, but should you spot a loose hem on your purchase, the owner may well whip out a needle and repair it on the spot.

P.E. Guerin ⊠

| - | - | - | VE |

W Village | 23 Jane St. (bet. 8th & Greenwich Aves.) | A/C/E/L to 14th St./8th Ave. | 212-243-5270 | www.peguerin.com

Discriminating sorts who sweat the details make a beeline to this by-appointment-only West Village studio showcasing the fine home hardware crafted by the Guerin family since 1857 at their foundries in Valencia, Spain; the extensive catalog is decidedly traditional, featuring over 25,000 samples ranging from furniture pulls, knobs, mounts and doorknockers to plumbing fixtures, but you can request custom reproductions of nearly anything, as long as it can be made in brass.

Penhaligon's

| 27 | 26 | 25 | VE |

E 70s | 870 Madison Ave. (71st St.) | 6 to 68th St. | 212-249-1771 | 877-736-4254 | www.penhaligons.co.uk

Dating back to 1870, this "terribly British" purveyor of "timelessly elegant" fragrances with names like Lavendula and Lily of the Valley is still simmering with "wonderful scents and fragrances" inspired by the English countryside; the "helpful staff" at their small UES offshoot can also show you "great candles", men's toiletries and handmade silver and leather accessories like jewelry boxes that are "perfect for presents."

Penny Whistle

| 23 | 20 | 19 | E |

W 80s | 448 Columbus Ave. (bet. 81st & 82nd Sts.) | B/C to 81st St. | 212-873-9090

"Amazing wonders await" at this "blast from the past" West 80s toy store that tickles nostalgists with its "unique", classic playthings, including pinwheels, pogo sticks, collectible dolls and craft kits; it's "fun to browse", but if you're not into lingering, the staff gets you "in and out with your holiday gifts in record time"; still, a few sing the too-"pricey" blues, grumbling "it should be renamed Dollar Whistle."

Perfumania ●

| 19 | 14 | 14 | M |

Garment District | Empire State Bldg. | 20 W. 34th St. (bet. 5th & 6th Aves.) | B/D/F/N/Q/R/V/W to 34th St./Herald Sq. | 212-736-0414 | 866-557-2368 | www.perfumania.com

There's "definitely no frills" at this "outlet" atmosphere chain that stocks women's and men's designer and drugstore perfumes at "excellent" "discount prices"; but naysayers note "they may not have what you want" and sniff at service that can be less than sweet.

Petco ●

E 80s | 147 E. 86th St. (bet. Lexington & 3rd Aves.) | 6 to 86th St. | 212-831-8001

Murray Hill | 560 Second Ave. (bet. 31st & 32nd Sts.) | 6 to 33rd St. | 212-779-4550

Union Sq | 860 Broadway (17th St.) | 4/5/6/L/N/Q/R/W to 14th St./ Union Sq. | 212-358-0692

W 90s | 2475 Broadway (92nd St.) | 1/2/3 to 96th St. | 212-877-1270

Howard Bch | 157-20 Cross Bay Blvd. (157th Ave.) | Queens | A to Howard Beach/JFK Airport | 718-845-3331

877-738-6742 | www.petco.com

19 | 17 | 13 | M

"Yes, it's a big box", but the "Home Depot of pet supplies" offers "everything you need for Fido and Fluffy" and feathered and finny friends, including "valuable services" like vaccines; though the products are more "mainstream" than "fancy" and the service "nonexistent", the "reasonable" prices are enhanced by a "great frequent buyers' program."

Peter Elliot

E 70s | 997 Lexington Ave. (72nd St.) | 6 to 68th St. | 212-570-2301

E 80s | 1070 Madison Ave. (81st St.) | 6 to 77th St. | 212-570-2300

E 80s | 1071 Madison Ave. (81st St.) | 6 to 77th St. | 212-570-1551

25 | 20 | 20 | E

Visitors to this series of "superbly edited small boutiques" leave the Upper East Side environs looking as if they're "setting off to the country house" in "high-quality" "perfectly tailored" apparel; each one curates its own niche of "something a little different" among the men's, women's and boy's wear, and while "quirky" service "makes you laugh or cry depending on your mood", most find it worthwhile "to avoid the madness of larger stores."

☑ Peter Fox Shoes

SoHo | 105 Thompson St. (bet. Prince & Spring Sts.) | C/E to Spring St. | 212-431-7426 | www.peterfox.com

28 | 25 | 25 | E

"So original and unique!" – "when you find the right style, the combination rocks" rave Fox-y ladies who find "there are no better shoes for a night of dancing" or "special occasions" than the "well-made" numbers, some "evocative of Renaissance" or Victorian footwear, sold at this designer's quaint SoHo salon; the nuptials-bound find the Italian silk satin pumps and boots "especially beautiful for weddings", while actors galore walk the Broadway boards in these "lovely" offerings.

Peters Necessities for Pets

E 70s | 236 E. 75th St. (bet. 2nd & 3rd Aves.) | 6 to 77th St. | 212-988-0769

▽ 24 | 18 | 24 | M

Devotees who "love the delivery service rarely see the store", but those who frequent this "wonderful" East 70s pet emporium hail the "hard-to-find" "specialty" foods and "interesting merchandise"; the "helpful" owner and staff also earn plaudits.

Petit Bateau

E 80s | 1094 Madison Ave. (82nd St.) | 4/5/6 to 86th St. | 212-988-8884 | www.petit-bateau.com

27 | 24 | 20 | E

For some of the "best" French "T-shirts in town" "guaranteed to make you ooh and ahh at the sight of your little cherub", sail over to this "accommodating" Madison Avenue shop, which has the market cornered on "non-fussy", "comfortable" cotton duds; you "can't beat" basics like "excellent quality" pajamas and underwear – "there's a reason

| | QUALITY | DISPLAY | SERVICE | COST |

classics are classic"; P.S. the "cuddly" children's tees are also prized by "pre-teens", teens and petite moms.

Petland Discounts ●

	QUALITY	DISPLAY	SERVICE	COST
	18	12	15	M

W 40s | 734 Ninth Ave. (50th St.) | C/E to 50th St. | 212-459-9562 | www.petlanddiscounts.com
Additional locations throughout the NY area

"Convenient" locations, "competitive prices" and a "broad array" of pet products make this chain a "weekly" stop for urbanites; though service ranges from "informed" to "clueless" and the stock can be "disorganized", the "good value" for "basics" keeps bargain-hounds happy.

Petrou 🛇Ⓜ

	QUALITY	DISPLAY	SERVICE	COST
	-	-	-	VE

E 60s | 850 Madison Ave. (bet. 69th & 70th Sts.) | 6 to 68th St. | 212-249-7111
A Euro-chic eveningwear extravaganza unfolds amid the elegant environs of upper Madison Avenue at this marble-columned boutique dedicated to the designs of Nicolas Petrou, aka Dennis Basso's creative director; his premiere collection boasts high-waisted cocktail dresses and taffeta gowns, embroidered jackets and carefully tailored coats, all handcrafted with luxurious laces, feathers and (of course) furs.

Ⓩ Pet Stop

	QUALITY	DISPLAY	SERVICE	COST
	26	21	25	M

W 80s | 564 Columbus Ave. (bet. 87th & 88th Sts.) | B/C to 86th St. | 212-580-2400 | www.petstopnyc.com

"You feel more like a friend than a customer" at this "unmatched" Upper West Side "institution" offering the "best selection" of "premium" pet products in an "enjoyable atmosphere"; the staff is "knowledgeable", the delivery service is "excellent" and on weekends you can adopt "purrfectly" "adorable" kitties.

Petticoat Lane

	QUALITY	DISPLAY	SERVICE	COST
	-	-	-	E

TriBeCa | 149 Reade St. (bet. Greenwich & Hudson Sts.) | 1/2/3 to Chambers St. | 212-571-5115 | www.bagshop.com
This TriBeCa venue (the first NYC outpost of a Westchester-based chainlet) charms customers with a "nice combination" of lingerie (from Cosabella, DKNY, Hanro, La Perla and others) and handbags (from Botkier, Rafe, Lauren Merkin and Longchamp); a small selection of belts and jewelry as well as an "always helpful" staff keep accessory obsessives returning for "little things you don't see anywhere else."

Phat Farm

	QUALITY	DISPLAY	SERVICE	COST
	16	18	14	E

SoHo | 129 Prince St. (bet. W. B'way & Wooster St.) | N/R/W to Prince St. | 212-533-7428 | www.phatfarmstore.com
"Still going strong" assert citified agrarians who flock to "Russell Simmons' urbanwear staple" in SoHo for "clothes that are the height of cool", reflecting the music entrepreneur's sartorial blend of "hip-hop" culture and Ivy League Lacoste-like look; to the rear: Kimora Lee Simmons' sexy, "very wearable" Baby Phat women's collection and cat's meow kids' offerings; still, a phew phind the "help inattentive" and "prices beyond the means of its target audience."

Phi

	QUALITY	DISPLAY	SERVICE	COST
	-	-	-	VE

SoHo | 71 Greene St. (bet. Broome & Spring Sts.) | N/R/W to Prince St. | 212-966-0076 | www.phicollection.com
Slink into this loftlike SoHo shop with its soaring ceilings, mammoth pillars and standing vases filled with mulberry leaves to soak in de-

signer Andreas Melbostad's sexy, minimalist womenswear from this edgy label backed by Susan Dell, wife of techie billionaire Michael; the clothes flatter a femme-fatale's curves with a bod-conscious cut in luxurious wools and luxe leathers, while the stratospheric prices seem in keeping with the company's provenance.

Philosophy di Alberta Ferretti ∇ 25 | 24 | 26 | VE

SoHo | 452 W. Broadway (bet. Houston & Prince Sts.) | C/E to Spring St. | 212-460-5500 | www.philosophy.it

Fashionistas don't have to know Plato to appreciate the cool sensibility of Alberta Ferretti's secondary line at this modern outpost in SoHo, which has a waterfall as a backdrop; the crowd-pleasing collection features polished suits, pretty cutwork sheaths, fluttery day-to-evening dresses and edgy inventory of accessories.

⦿ Piaget Ⓢ 28 | 28 | 27 | VE

E 50s | 730 Fifth Ave. (bet. 56th & 57th Sts.) | N/R/W to 5th Ave./ 59th St. | 212-246-5555 | www.piaget.com

"Very high-quality" Swiss dress watches that merge fine jewelry with haute horology – imagine your own fingerprint rendered in diamonds on the face – and signature gold-bracelet Polo timepieces are the focus at this East 50s store whose parent company dates back to 1874; the well-heeled warn: don't let the prices (up to $2 mil) tick you off.

Pieces of Brooklyn Ⓜ ∇ 21 | 22 | 20 | E

Prospect Heights | 671 Vanderbilt Ave. (Park Pl.) | Brooklyn | 2/3 to Grand Army Plaza | 718-857-7211 | www.piecesofbklyn.com

It's fitting that this "hip", "friendly" corner boutique in Prospect Heights is owned by a husband-and-wife team with the last name of Daring, because that's a word that sums up the men's and women's jeans, T-shirts, European designer threads and accessories; create a "style all your own" from the "eclectic" selection – you can be sure you won't see your fashion-foward pieces "all over the place."

Pier 1 Imports ◑ 15 | 18 | 15 | I

E 80s | 1550 Third Ave. (87th St.) | 4/5/6 to 86th St. | 212-987-1746
Flatiron | 71 Fifth Ave. (15th St.) | 4/5/6/L/N/Q/R/W to 14th St./ Union Sq. | 212-206-1911
800-245-4595 | www.pier1.com

"Lots of wicker" and "assorted odds and ends" like "candles and glassware galore", Christmas ornaments, baskets, pillows and picture frames make home furnishings "accessorizing cheap and simple" for those "starting out" or just looking for "staples" at these Flatiron and Upper East Side chain links; but detractors dismiss them as "cookie-cutter" "tchotchkes places" whose quality is questionable.

Pilar Rossi Ⓢ - | - | - | VE

E 60s | 784 Madison Ave. (bet. 66th & 67th Sts.) | 6 to 68th St. | 212-288-2469 | www.pilarrossi.com

Dramatic and elegant, "Ms. Rossi's clothes are styled with real women's curves in mind" assert admirers of the Brazilian eveningwear and bridal designer who find a trip to her Madison Avenue store one of the "most pleasurable shopping experiences you can have"; the glamorous get-ups include day-into-night suits, gowns in rich brocade or silk satin and sophisticated, entrance-worthy aisle-wear for that special day.

| | QUALITY | DISPLAY | SERVICE | COST |

NEW Pink Olive Boutique ▽ 24 | 24 | 21 | E

E Village | 439 E. Ninth St. (bet. Ave. A & 1st Ave.) | F/V to Lower East Side/ 2nd Ave. | 212-780-0036 | www.pinkoliveboutique.com

An eclectic mix of merch makes this brick-walled East Villager a "great place" to pick up gifts for kids, "teens – or even yourself"; owner Grace Kang, a former buyer for Bloomie's and Saks, stocks everything from "out-of-the-ordinary stationery" and picture frames to "adorable" booties, "bright" onesies and plush toys, plus getaway items like swimsuits along with bubble bath and candles for at-home escapes.

Pink Pussycat ● 19 | 19 | 19 | M

G Village | 167 W. Fourth St. (bet. 6th & 7th Aves.) | A/B/C/D/E/F/V to W. 4th St. | 212-243-0077
Park Slope | 355 Fifth Ave. (bet. 4th & 5th Sts.) | Brooklyn | F/M/R to 4th Ave./9th St. | 718-369-0088
www.pinkpussycat.com

The "grandaddy of all erotica" shops is this thirtysomething Greenwich Village "icon" (with a Park Slope spin-off) where "horny" "out-of-towners" and "giggling" "bachelorette" partiers peruse Rabbit Habit vibrators, sex toys and S&M items; but the catty counter the "dingy" digs and "low inventory" make this feline "a kitten of its former self."

Pink Slip ● ▽ 23 | 19 | 23 | M

E 40s | Grand Central | 42nd St. (Vanderbilt Ave.) | 4/5/6/7/S to 42nd St./ Grand Central | 212-949-9037 | 866-816-7465 | www.thepinkslip.com

Commuters "in a hurry" find something "mildly romantic" about buying lingerie in this Grand Central Station "little find" filled with a "quickly rotating inventory" of "beautiful" camisole sets, panties, bustiers, hosiery and sleepwear from designers like Arianne, Flirt and On Gossamer; "great" for "quick gifts" (the staff makes men feel welcome) or "last-minute personal items", its only drawback is that all "co-workers may see you" ducking in as they run for their trains.

Pinkyotto ● ▽ 21 | 20 | 20 | M

E Village | 307 E. Ninth St. (bet. 1st & 2nd Aves.) | 6 to Astor Pl. | 212-533-4028
NEW NoLita | 49 Prince St. (bet. Lafayette & Mulberry Sts.) | 6 to Spring St. | 212-226-3580
NEW Williamsburg | 204 Bedford Ave. (bet. 5th & 6th Sts.) | Brooklyn | L to Bedford Ave. | 718-387-6450
www.pinkyotto.com

The focus is on the "feminine and girlie" whether it be in frocks, smocked tops or cashmere hoodies at this private-label East Village boutique with new offshoots in NoLita and Williamsburg; "moderate prices" leave shoppers in the pink – they only wish the "fresh" looks weren't limited to such "tiny sizes."

Pintchik 20 | 12 | 18 | M

Park Slope | 478 Bergen St. (Flatbush Ave.) | Brooklyn | 2/3 to Bergen St. | 718-783-3333

Park Slope "shows its (paint) colors" at this pioneer hardware store where "you can find just about anything" including a "large assortment of flooring" and lighting; "you may not be able to see" everything, but the "informed staff" that "treats you like a neighbor" "can probably find it", so pinch some free cappuccino and popcorn while you're waiting.

Pippin ◐

- | - | - | M

Chelsea | 112 W. 17th St. (bet. 6th & 7th Aves.) | 1 to 18th St. | 212-505-5159
Practically everything decorative is for sale at this long, narrow vintage/costume jewelry shop that relocated from the LES to Chelsea, a stone's throw from where the husband-and-wife owners got their start at the 26th Street Flea Market; the display cases are filled with one-of-a-kind pieces like Bakelite bracelets and cameos dating from the late 1800s through 1970 at equally anachronistic prices.

Pir Cosmetics

- | - | - | E

NoLita | 14 Prince St. (Elizabeth St.) | 6 to Spring St. | 212-219-1290 | www.pircosmetics.com
If you're bored with beauty basics, check out this "brilliant" cosmetics boutique in NoLita specializing in "hard-to-find" luxury brands like Hamadi's shea butter hair mask and the late Kevyn Aucoin's "incredible makeup line"; the staff will "plop you down in a chair" and show you products that will "suit your skin tone, lifestyle and idiosyncrasies."

NEW Pixie Market ◐

∇ 19 | 18 | 18 | M

LES | 100 Stanton St. (Ludlow St.) | F/J/M/Z to Delancey/Essex Sts. | 212-253-0953 | www.pixiemarket.com
Compact and "cool", this "quirky" LES clothier spruced up with a geometric chandelier and a plaid bench enchants with "youth-oriented", "indie designer finds" befitting elfin queens like Liv and Zooey; from the constantly refreshed, mostly affordable stock of floaty tops, "unusual" dresses and kicky rompers culled from little-known global talents to Maud, their "interesting" house line of shoes, the well-traveled owners strive to re-create a London market feel akin to Portobello and Spitalfields.

Planet Kids ◐

18 | 13 | 13 | M

E 80s | 247 E. 86th St. (bet. 2nd & 3rd Aves.) | 4/5/6 to 86th St. | 212-426-2040
W 100s | 2688 Broadway (103rd St.) | 1 to 103rd St. | 212-864-8705
www.planetkidsny.com
"Good in a pinch", this "fun-to-browse" East Side–West Side pair of Uptown kids' supply stores fills the "need-it-now shopping" bill, squeezing a "surprisingly good selection" of "inexpensive", "cute" clothing, gear, furniture and toys into a "cramped", "limited space"; still, skeptics who wonder "what planet" the "disinterested staff" is on warn "it's every man for himself" here.

Plaza Too

21 | 21 | 21 | E

W 70s | 2231 Broadway (bet. 79th & 80th Sts.) | 1 to 79th St. | 212-362-6871
NEW W Village | 571 Hudson St. (bet. Bank & W. 11th Sts.) | A/C/E/L to 14th St./8th Ave. | 212-924-2180
www.plazatoo.com
"Gives the UWS a little oomph" – and now the West Village too – agree accessories addicts who kick up their heels over the "nicely edited shoe, bag", belt, scarf and jewelry selection that's "hip and beautiful without being pretentious" at this Westchester-based "favorite"; the "warm, friendly service is enough to keep you coming back" and so's the mix of brands like Aquatalia, Alexis Bittar, Arturo Chiang and Kate Spade suitable for "consumers of all budgets."

| | QUALITY | DISPLAY | SERVICE | COST |

Pleasure Chest ❷

| | 22 | 20 | 20 | M |

W Village | 156 Seventh Ave. S. (bet. Charles & Perry Sts.) | 1 to Christopher St./Sheridan Sq. | 212-242-2158 | 800-316-9222 | www.thepleasurechest.com

"Gay and straight" supporters of this sex shop say it peddles a "plethora of play things at palatable prices"; the "goodies to please other body parts besides your chest" range from "fantastic" to "shlock", arrayed in a "cheesy" but "not skeevy" space sporting a "window display that's one of the biggest attractions in the Village."

Pleats Please

| | – | – | – | E |

SoHo | 128 Wooster St. (Prince St.) | N/R/W to Prince St. | 212-226-3600 | www.pleatsplease.com

This glass-encased shop at a busy hub in SoHo pleases patrons with "accommodating" salespeople wearing "Issey Miyake's less-expensive" line of "crazy cuts" in super-pleated polyester that is "made to travel", so "you're always chic"; however, those unimpressed by the pressed garb growl "at this point, we've all seen it."

Poggenpohl U.S. Inc.

| | – | – | – | VE |

E 50s | A&D Bldg. | 150 E. 58th St. (bet. Lexington & 3rd Aves.) | 4/5/6/F/N/R/W to 59th St./Lexington Ave. | 212-355-3666 🛗
Union Sq | 270 Park Ave. S. (19th St.) | 4/5/6/L/N/Q/R/W to 14th St./Union Sq. | 212-228-3334
www.poggenpohl-usa.com

Founded in 1892, this luxury bath and kitchen manufacturer in Union Square and the East 50s is up to the minute with "modern", German-made products, such as high-tech aluminum, stainless-steel, wood and glass cabinetry and appliances; aesthetes applaud the "superior design", but caution it may be "too expensive for any but the super-rich", who "also have maids to keep all that stainless spotless."

🅩 Point, The ❷

| | ▽ 25 | 26 | 23 | M |

G Village | 37A Bedford St. (Carmine St.) | 1 to Houston St. | 212-929-0800 | 877-607-6468 | www.thepointnyc.com

Crafters can "have a cappuccino and peruse" the skeins "in baskets on the walls" at this "beautiful" Greenwich Village store with a "delightful cafe"; it's a "comfortable place to gather with a knitting circle", thanks to a "supportive staff" and "good" prices, though some sticklers point out the selection in this venue is "a little thin."

Poleci

| | 22 | 22 | 23 | E |

Meatpacking | 414 W. 14th St. (bet. 9th Ave. & Washington St.) | A/C/E/L to 14th St./8th Ave. | 212-229-3701 | www.poleci.com

Leave it to two LA sisters to breathe a little 'ahh' into the Meatpacking District with a striking shrine filled with "cutting-edge" womenswear; label-lovers also laud the policy (that's how the name is pronounced) of being "extremely helpful", nevertheless cynics say these "snippy bits of wrinkled fabric" "don't justify their prices."

Poltrona Frau

| | – | – | – | VE |

SoHo | 145 Wooster St. (bet. Houston & Prince Sts.) | N/R/W to Prince St. | 212-777-7592 | www.frauusa.com

"You have to be the Donald, not the apprentice" to afford the "great" leather furniture featured in this minimalist SoHo showroom for the high-end Italian company that also outfits interiors for Ferrari, Maserati and Mercedes; there are over 90 shades to choose from for sofas, chairs, beds and even tables.

Pomellato 🗷

-- | -- | -- | VE

E 60s | 741 Madison Ave. (bet. 64th & 65th Sts.) | 6 to 68th St. | 212-879-2118 | 800-254-6020 | www.pomellato.com

Milan comes to Madison Avenue with the opening of this attractive Italian fine-jewelry store showcasing its own namesake brand; signature styles include clean, colorful square-cut rings and earrings with hand-faceted semiprecious stones in smoky quartz, amethyst and blue topaz, but there's also a more ornate line of carved cameo serpent designs.

Pomme Ⓜ

-- | -- | -- | E

Dumbo | 81 Washington St. (York St.) | Brooklyn | F to York St. | 718-855-0623 | www.pommenyc.com

Sophisticated parents who prefer to dress their small fries like mini individuals turn to this Dumbo delight, a sprawling loft that doubles as a gallery/workshop space; forget overexposure – stylesetters cherry pick exclusive, globally sourced clothing for children six and under from a charming mix of traditional and edgy, new and even vintage, labels, plus jewelry from Aurelie Bidermann, wicker cradles from Nume and Momoll dollhouses and play kitchens.

🆉 Pompanoosuc Mills

25 | 21 | 24 | E

TriBeCa | 124 Hudson St. (Ericsson Pl.) | 1 to Franklin St. | 212-226-5960 | www.pompy.com

Loyalists "love the simplicity" of this "handcrafted" traditional American furniture for the bedroom, office, living and dining room that's built-to-order in Vermont; the staff at the TriBeCa showroom "is helpful and patient, without being pushy", and proponents pronounce "prices amazing" given the "silky finishes" and "superb workmanship."

Pookie & Sebastian ➊

17 | 20 | 19 | M

NEW **E 60s** | 1069 Third Ave. (63rd St.) | 6 to 59th St. | 212-991-9636
E 70s | 1488 Second Ave. (bet. 77th & 78th Sts.) | 6 to 77th St. | 212-861-0550
Murray Hill | 541 Third Ave. (36th St.) | 6 to 33rd St. | 212-951-7110
W 70s | 322 Columbus Ave. (75th St.) | B/C to 72nd St. | 212-580-5844
www.pookieandsebastian.com

This "fashion-forward" outfit "is constantly hopping", "overrun with Pookie Girls" jonesing for "stylish" jeans and the "latest knockoffs of designer pieces" including "flirty" jackets, "sparkly" party dresses and "high-style" extras with "a lot of charm"; "rabid shoppers" don't mind waiting for the "claustrophobic dressing rooms", because the "sales help is helpful and honest" – and "you can't leave without snagging a great find at a reasonable price."

POP ➊

▽ 19 | 21 | 18 | M

Williamsburg | 310 Grand St. (bet. Havemeyer & Roebling Sts.) | Brooklyn | L to Bedford Ave. | 718-486-6001 | www.shoppop.com

"By far one of my favorite stores in the neighborhood" muse Billyburg guys and gals who pop over to this lifestyle lair for the "great" "mix of inexpensive finds" and "middle-range designer" clothing, plus a "cute collection of accessories and home goods"; retro-inspired apparel lines like the LA-based BB Dakota give maximum style for the buck –

little wonder "young" customers check back often for wardrobe-freshen-uppers; N.B. there's a sibling shop in DC.

Poppet ●

| | – | – | – | E |

E Village | 350 E. Ninth St. (bet. 1st & 2nd Aves.) | 6 to Astor Pl. | 212-924-3190 | www.poppetnyc.com

There's no shortage of vintage-clothing stores in the East Village, but "somebody finally got it right" with this recently revamped poppet whose clientele ranges from NYU students to Seventh Avenue stylists; the former find moderate, midcentury blouses and dresses, while the latter love the luminous labels from the '60s–'80s (think Ozzie Clark, Zandra Rhodes and Holly Harp); the tiny, red-walled space also holds a huge shoe collection that includes a plethora of platforms; everything's cleaned, pressed and ready to wear out the door.

Poppy

| ∇ 23 | 24 | 21 | E |

NoLita | 281 Mott St. (bet. Houston & Prince Sts.) | B/D/F/V to B'way/Lafayette St. | 212-219-8934

"Stylish" women's "clothes are always in bloom" at this NoLita "shopper's paradise", which is "refreshingly spacious compared to other neighborhood boutiques", with racks and tables full of "sensual" "fashions" and "chic workplace-worthy attire" that "invite touching"; "go here whenever you need to reward" yourself – what better incentive than "very cute stuff" from hard-to-find lines, jeans from J Brand and jewelry from Moss Mills and Page Sargisson.

Porsche Design

| 26 | 26 | 22 | VE |

E 50s | 624 Madison Ave. (bet. 58th & 59th Sts.) | N/R/W to 5th Ave./59th St. | 212-308-1786 | www.porsche-design.com

"Your dollars speed out of your wallet faster than a 911 Turbo" at this "hi-tech" Madison Avenue haven with a "gallery" feel featuring "handsome", "worth-the-money" accessories that fit the sports car driver's lifestyle; "just love all things Porsche" exclaim enthusiasts who get into manly gear like sunglasses, luggage, golf products, gloves and other "cool stuff" sold by a staff that "couldn't be nicer."

Porthault ☒

| ∇ 29 | 28 | 23 | VE |

E 60s | 18 E. 69th St. (Madison Ave.) | 6 to 68th St. | 212-688-1660

"Those who want the very best" get it at this grande dame of "extremely luxurious" French linens housed in a "lovely" Upper East Side converted townhouse; it's filled with signature printed sheets, table linens, scallop-edged bath towels, home fragrances and gifts, making it a resource for "great wedding presents"; prices are a nightmare though, so "take a loan before you go."

Pottery Barn ●

| 20 | 22 | 18 | M |

E 50s | 127 E. 59th St. (Lexington Ave.) | 4/5/6/F/N/R/W to 59th St./Lexington Ave. | 917-369-0050

SoHo | 600 Broadway (Houston St.) | B/D/F/V to B'way/Lafayette St. | 212-219-2420

W 60s | 1965 Broadway (67th St.) | 1 to 66th St./Lincoln Ctr. | 212-579-8477

888-779-5176 | www.potterybarn.com

"You can always find something you need here and it will last forever" declare devotees of this "easy-to-shop-in" chain with "quality" furniture and accessories like tableware, pillows and photo frames that are "great for house presents", even if "it's for your own"; chances are "all your friends have the exact same items in their apartments", but the "affordably priced" staples and "color-coordinated" offerings "prove that a tight budget does not preclude living well."

Pottery Barn Bed & Bath ◐

- | - | - | M

Chelsea | 100-104 Seventh Ave. (bet. 16th & 17th Sts.) | 1/2/3 to 14th St. | 646-336-7160 | www.potterybarn.com

The Williams-Sonoma–owned catalog comes to life at this Chelsea outpost offering just what the name says – bed and bath furniture, fixtures and accessories; duvet covers, sheets, pillows, throws, mirrors, lamps, wall cabinets, robes, shower curtains and faucets are displayed vignette-style in the mostly white, Thomas O'Brien–designed space.

Pottery Barn Kids

- | - | - | M

E 60s | 1311 Second Ave. (69th St.) | 6 to 68th St. | 212-879-4746 | www.potterybarn.com

Tots won't mind getting sent to their rooms if they're decked out with cool furniture and knickknacks from this East 60s offshoot of the popular home chain; from French Rose to Train Junction, there's a kid-friendly decor theme to suit any style, plus a team of design experts on hand to help pull the look together; don't forget to check out the vast selection of toys including retro play kitchens, tea sets and xylophones.

Prada

26 | 26 | 21 | VE

E 50s | 45 E. 57th St. (bet. Madison & Park Aves.) | 4/5/6/F/N/R/W to 59th St./Lexington Ave. | 212-308-2332

E 50s | 724 Fifth Ave. (bet. 56th & 57th Sts.) | N/R/W to 5th Ave./59th St. | 212-664-0010

E 70s | 841 Madison Ave. (70th St.) | 6 to 68th St. | 212-327-4200 🛇

SoHo | 575 Broadway (Prince St.) | N/R/W to Prince St. | 212-334-8888 www.prada.com

"Alluring", "artful" and "A+" are some of the adjectives awarded these showcases for Miuccia Prada's "impossibly chic and polished" Italian mens- and womenswear, "sexy shoes" and "adorable accessories"; it's "the first place" to take "fashion-forward" *touristas,* especially the Rem Koolhaas–designed SoHo flagship, which feels "more like a gallery than a store"; the savvy head to "the less-touristy Madison Avenue branch" where the service is "shockingly good" as opposed to "semi-friendly" elsewhere; wherever you go, though, get ready for prices that "make your wallet bleed"; N.B. 57th Street sells shoes and bags only.

☑ Pratesi ⦸

29 | 24 | 24 | VE

E 60s | 829 Madison Ave. (69th St.) | 6 to 68th St. | 212-288-2315 | www.pratesi.com

"Upper-class" East Side boutique that showcases the family-owned, 1893 Italian firm's sheets, which "are among the best on earth"; their table linens, towels and baby layettes also offer "luxury in every sense of the word"; of course, such "exquisite" merchandise is *really* expensive", but patricians pronounce it "worth every penny."

Prato Fine Men's Wear Outlets

▽ 13 | 18 | 16 | I

Financial District | 122 Nassau St., 1st fl. (Ann St.) | 2/3/4/5/A/C/J/M/Z to Fulton St./B'way/Nassau | 212-349-4150

Garment District | 28 W. 34th St. (bet. B'way & 5th Ave.) | B/D/F/N/Q/R/V/W to 34th St./Herald Sq. | 212-629-4730 ◐

(continued)

Prato Fine Men's Wear Outlets

Garment District | 492 Seventh Ave. (bet. 36th & 37th Sts.) | 1/2/3/A/C/E to 34th St./Penn Station | 212-564-9683 ◗
Dyker Heights | 8508 Fifth Ave. (85th St.) | Brooklyn | R to 86th St. | 718-491-1234
Astoria | 30-48 Steinway St. (bet. 30th & 31st Aves.) | Queens | G/R/V to Steinway St. | 718-274-2990 ◗
888-467-7286 | www.pratomenswear.com

The "low cost" and "good selection" of formal and business attire attract thrifty men to these discount warehouses scattered around NYC, Queens and Brooklyn; the "quality varies" and style advice doesn't extend beyond the basics, but what more "do you want for the price"?

premium goods

– | – | – | E

Park Slope | 347 Fifth Ave. (bet. 4th & 5th Sts.) | Brooklyn | F/M/R to 4th Ave./9th St. | 718-369-7477 | www.premiumgoods.net

It may be pocket-sized, but this Slope sneaker specialist packs plenty of punch thanks to its premium collection of limited-edition and hard-to-track-down footwear culled from major players like Nike, Puma, Reebok and Vans, plus a small stash of street-smart silk-screened T-shirts from owner Clarence Nathan's own line; after tees and trainers, peruse the artwork from local talent on display – yes, it's for sale.

Prince & Princess ⌧

– | – | – | VE

E 70s | 41 E. 78th St. (Madison Ave.) | 6 to 77th St. | 212-879-8989 | www.princeandprincess.com

Just off Madison Avenue, this easy-to-overlook Upper East Side treasure trumpets high-end special-occasion finery that'll have your kids feeling like heirs to the throne; the crown jewels include luxe Italian-made silk party frocks for the little ladies and dapper silk suits, vests and bow ties for the lads; baby shoes and accessories supply the final flourishes.

Prince Charles III

– | – | – | E

SoHo | 98 Thompson St. (Spring St.) | C/E to Spring St. | 212-334-9102 | www.princecharlesIII.com

You don't have to be royalty to stop by this SoHo boutique to stock up on European and American men's styles that aren't overly trendy; the inventory of small labels rotates seasonally, but what has remained constant during the past decade is the unique selection of belts, socks, ties and shirts – especially in larger sizes – and the reliable eye of owner Gina Karin.

Princeton Ski Shop ◗

21 | 17 | 17 | M

Flatiron | 21 E. 22nd St. (bet. B'way & Park Ave.) | N/R/W to 23rd St. | 212-228-4400 | www.princetonski.com

Alpine enthusiasts whoosh over to this "old favorite" in the Flatiron District for a "reasonable selection" of "trendy, fashionable equipment" and clothing from "quality" names like Analog, Burton and Rossignol that are bound to make you one of the "best-dressed snow sport fans"; if a few find service "helpful" only "when you get them to focus" and the goods "pricey", most suggest waiting for the "terrific end-of-season sales", adding "if you're a serious skier, why shop anywhere else?"

🆕 Priscilla of Boston 🗷 Ⓜ `24 | 22 | 22 | E`

Garment District | 264 W. 40th St. (bet. 7th & 8th Aves.) | 1/2/3/7/N/Q/
R/S/W to 42nd St./Times Sq. | 212-997-3956 | www.priscillaofboston.com
Truly a Boston "bridal staple", this quality name seeks to take Manhattan
with its plush Garment District atelier; gals go gaga over the "gorgeous
gowns" and accessories, citing their "classic look" (though there's a
"wide selection" – from the fairly fashion-forward Melissa Sweet to the
over-the-top Platinum); still, service swings from "polite" to "pushy" –
and "make sure you have a Prince Charming to pay for it" all too.

🆕 Private Stock NY ◑Ⓜ `- | - | - | E`

Park Slope | 458 Bergen St. (bet. 5th & Flatbush Aves.) | Brooklyn | 2/3 to
Bergen St. | 718-230-0055
Dudes no longer have to scour Park Slope to find hip casualwear thanks
to the arrival of this new brick-walled beauty on Bergen Street; the ever-
changing stock features urban-essentials like cool kicks and one-off
tees, but there's lots of unexpected stuff too, from hats and jewelry to
merch from indie designers and a line of house-label clothing.

🆕 Project No. 8 ◑Ⓜ `- | - | - | E`

Chinatown | 138 Division St. (bet. Ludlow & Orchard Sts.) | F to
East Broadway | 212-925-5599 | www.projectno8.com
A clean, tranquil well-lit space just a stone's throw away from the hus-
tle and bustle of Chinatown's main drag adds to the appeal of this new
men's and women's clothing boutique with a lineup of local and international designers; "unique" pieces include shirts and knits for him
and dresses from labels like Claudia Hill for her.

Project 234 ◑ `- | - | - | M`

NoLita | 234 Mulberry St. (bet. Prince & Spring Sts.) | 6 to Spring St. |
212-334-6431
Owner Kim Phan fills her tiny NoLita gem with an artful mix of offbeat
designers including Arrogant Cat, Buddhist Punk and Lundgren and
Windinge – relatively-unheard-of labels that appeal to women who
like to express their iconoclastic tendencies with strong doses of
color; shoppers with a yen for retro-fitted fashions vie for vintage
pieces that also project distinctive style.

Psny `- | - | - | E`

SoHo | 69 W. Houston St. (bet. W. B'way & Wooster St.) | B/D/F/V to
B'way/Lafayette St. | 212-253-0630 | www.pslingnewyork.com
Done up with a cool chandelier and an orange ottoman, this sleek SoHo
shop features the Japanese company's popular baby slings, designed to
hold infants weighing up to 39 pounds; these functional little linen or
cotton helpers come in over 200 stylish options, and to go-with: sling-
rings by Me & Ro and organic cotton onesies.

Pucci `26 | 25 | 24 | VE`

E 50s | 701 Fifth Ave. (bet. 54th & 55th Sts.) | E/V to 5th Ave./53rd St. |
212-230-1135
E 60s | 24 E. 64th St. (bet. 5th & Madison Aves.) | 6 to 68th St. |
212-752-4777 🗷
www.emiliopucci.com
Revisit the "psychedelics of your youth" at either the East 60s boutique
or the Fifth Avenue flagship where the legendary Italian designer's

"swimming-in-color", "fun" fabrics are "back from the graveyard of fashion" in a big way; the "always distinctive" clothes and accessories are "sooo cute and easy-to-wear", you might well get a patented "Pucci high" after purchasing one of the signature prints"; N.B. British designer Matthew Williamson has taken over from Christian Lacroix.

NEW Pull-In
- | - | - | E

NoLita | 252 Elizabeth St. (bet. Houston & Prince Sts.) | N/R/W to Prince St. | 212-966-8914 | www.pull-in.com

I see Paris, I see France, I see Microfiber, Lycra and cotton underpants for men, women and boys at this small French import in NoLita showcasing uniquely patterned (think skulls, gnomes, Dracula and sunflowers) boxers, briefs, thongs with logoed waistbands, plus feminine items like lacey bras and thigh-high stockings; originally designed for snowboarders and surfers, the skivvies are as much about comfort as style, another reason to pull out the stops and invest in a few.

Puma
23 | 23 | 17 | M

Meatpacking | 421 W. 14th St. (bet. 9th & 10th Aves.) | A/C/E/L to 14th St./8th Ave. | 212-206-0109
SoHo | 521 Broadway (bet. Broome & Spring Sts.) | 6 to Spring St. | 212-334-7861 ◐
Union Sq | 33 Union Sq. W. (bet. 16th St. & Union Sq. W.) | 4/5/6/L/ N/Q/R/W to 14th St./Union Sq. | 212-206-7761 ◐
www.puma.com

"Pick up a pair" of "snazzy" "retro" "Euro-chic" "sneaks" in a "dazzling spectrum of colors" and "happening" athletic apparel at the two-floor SoHo showcase and you'll "stand out from the rest" and "be hip all over again"; also worth "checking out": the all-black, "super-trendy" Meatpacking District style-incubator and the Union Square branch, a self-styled 'ship container' setting in which all the fixtures are mounted on walls, suspended from the ceiling or fastened to the floor.

Purdy Girl ◐
18 | 21 | 20 | M

G Village | 220 Thompson St. (bet. Bleecker & W. 3rd Sts.) | A/B/C/ D/E/F/V to W. 4th St. | 212-529-8385
G Village | 540 LaGuardia Pl. (bet. Bleecker & W. 3rd Sts.) | 6 to Bleecker St. | 646-654-6751
W 80s | 464 Columbus Ave. (bet. 82nd & 83rd Sts.) | B/C to 81st St. | 212-787-1980
www.purdygirlnyc.com

The "name says it all" confirm fans who "feel like a true Purdy girl" dressed in the house label's "darling" "workwear with flair", "funky tees" and "bohemian stuff" from Nanette Lepore and Trina Turk; it's not only a "charming" trio, "it's magic, because it makes money fly out of my wallet" – and the "no-pressure" staff makes me "walk out smiling."

☑ Purl
28 | 25 | 22 | E

SoHo | 137 Sullivan St. (bet. Houston & Prince Sts.) | C/E to Spring St. | 212-420-8796
☑ Purl Patchwork
SoHo | 147 Sullivan St. (bet. Houston & Prince Sts.) | C/E to Spring St. | 212-420-8798
www.purlsoho.com

With a "surprisingly large selection" emphasizing natural fibers, this "little jewel" of a yarn shop in SoHo attracts local celebs plus "the hippest of the hip" who want to "sit and knit"; "charming old-world" storefront digs and a "knowledgeable staff" make for a "collegial" vibe, but claustrophobes charge the "tiny store" can "get uncomfortably crowded" – and the "gorgeous imported" skeins are "expensive" (you may need enthusiast "Julia Roberts' wallet" to "afford them"); N.B. Purl Patchwork stocks materials for quilters.

Pylones ❶ | - | - | - | I

E 60s | 842 Lexington Ave. (64th St.) | F to Lexington Ave./63rd St. | 212-317-9822

SoHo | 69 Spring St. (bet. Crosby & Lafayette Sts.) | 6 to Spring St. | 212-431-3244

W Village | 61 Grove St. (bet. Bleecker St. & 7th Ave. S.) | 1 to Christopher St./Sheridan Sq. | 212-727-2655

www.pylones-usa.com

For an inexpensive gift fix, hit this chainlet from France and scoop up brightly hued, whimsically designed knickknacks that look like they've been pulled from the pages of a children's book; the colorful mashup of household objects includes melamine plates and kitchen gadgets, stationery, desk accessories, toys and key chains, and a small pet section means you can pick up presents for pooches too.

Quiksilver Boardriders Club ❶ | 21 | 19 | 18 | M

SoHo | 519 Broadway (Spring St.) | N/R/W to Prince St. | 212-226-1193

W 40s | 3 Times Sq. (42nd St. & 7th Ave.) | 1/2/3/7/N/Q/R/S/W to 42nd St./Times Sq. | 212-840-8111

800-576-4004 | www.quiksilver.com

Natch, it's "teenage boy heaven", but this "groovy" duo stocked with "unique" hang-ten "styles for surfers and non-surfers alike" has "something for everyone"; "it's an adventure just to walk into" the Times Square tourist-magnet that emphasizes apparel over boards ("if all else fails you can always play video games"); the sprawling SoHo "favorite" carries the whole nine yards, from skis and skiwear to beach-dude duds.

Quintessentials ⧄ | 23 | 20 | 19 | E

W 80s | 532 Amsterdam Ave. (bet. 85th & 86th Sts.) | 1 to 86th St. | 212-877-1919 | www.qkb.com

A "great place to go when you are renovating", this Upper West Side "kitchen- and bath-design" destination offers a "terrific selection" of "top-of-the-line merchandise and appliances" along with "the best and most beautiful" high-end custom cabinetry, hardware, plumbing and fixtures; the "helpful" and "friendly" staffers also seem to "understand apartment spaces."

Rachel Ashwell's Shabby Chic | ▽ 23 | 27 | 22 | VE

SoHo | 83 Wooster St. (bet. Broome & Spring Sts.) | N/R/W to Prince St. | 212-274-9842 | www.shabbychic.com

Slipcover queen Rachel Ashwell combined her "California-cool" lifestyle and English upbringing to create a fashionable flea-market look consisting of comfy, oversized furniture and faded floral fabrics, all on display at her SoHo shop; while a handful huff about the "overpriced" pieces, the ever-faithful proclaim they are just "perfect for the beach house."

Rachel Riley

-	-	-	E

E 90s | 1286 Madison Ave. (bet. 91st & 92nd Sts.) | 4/5/6 to 86th St. | 212-534-7477 | www.rachelriley.com

The private-school set and their fashionable mums embrace this romantic shop on Upper Madison Avenue, the brainchild of former model Rachel Riley, a Brit who designs her lovingly detailed fashions in the Loire Valley castle she lives in; the crystal chandeliers, velvet curtains and wood-carved vitrines create a genteel backdrop for retro classics that echo decades gone by, from tartan duffle coats to argyle sweaters, while astrakhan handbags add unexpected oomph.

RadioShack ◐

16	13	15	M

E 40s | 50 E. 42nd St. (bet. Madison & Park Aves.) | 4/5/6/7/S to 42nd St./ Grand Central | 212-953-6050 | 800-843-7422 | www.radioshack.com
Additional locations throughout the NY area

"Do-it-yourselfers" are devoted to this "solid" "corner drugstore for electronics" that's "a-clutter" with "techie basics", including "the odd cable or connector", "any battery you want" and "those electronics parts you need quickly"; the less-impressed, though, find it "fine for little things" "but not for big-ticket items", as the choices are "limited" and the staff's not always "as knowledgeable as advertised."

NEW Rainbow Sandals

23	20	19	M

NoLita | 245 Elizabeth St. (bet. Houston & Prince Sts.) | 6 to Bleecker St. | 212-966-8858 | www.rainbowsandals.com

"Finally!" – you can now buy some of the "best and most comfortable flip-flops" at this NoLita newcomer instead of mail-ordering rave admirers who find these "low cost", "no-nonsense" slip-ons with arch support just right for "walking the streets of New York"; they "come in all colors" and styles for men (it's "every frat guy's go-to" spot), women and kids – in fact, the Rainbow coalition contends it's "impossible to walk out empty-handed."

Ralph Lauren

26	26	22	VE

E 70s | 867 Madison Ave. (72nd St.) | 6 to 68th St. | 212-606-2100

E 70s | 888 Madison Ave. (72nd St.) | 6 to 68th St. | 212-434-8000

SoHo | 379 W. Broadway (bet. Broome & Spring Sts.) | C/E to Spring St. | 212-625-1660

W Village | 380 Bleecker St. (bet. Charles & Perry Sts.) | 1 to Christopher St./ Sheridan Sq. | 212-645-5513 ◐

W Village | 381 Bleecker St. (bet. Charles & Perry Sts.) | 1 to Christopher St./ Sheridan Sq. | 646-638-0684 ◐

888-475-7674 | www.polo.com

"Feel like a million" ('cuz that's what you could spend) shopping these "preppy meccas" from the "king of American style", whose name's a by-word for "top-drawer basics", "tasteful, tailored" suits and gowns "evocative of another era"; the label "has several price ranges", but "whatever you end up with, the quality is usually spot-on" and the staff "is happy to help you put it all together"; if cynics sniff Ralph always produces the "same old standards", it's still "hard not to be seduced by the all-encompassing lifestyle"; P.S. the 867 Madison Avenue "mansion", with its "English-estate" "elegance", houses home furnishings that some say are even "better than the clothes."

| | QUALITY | DISPLAY | SERVICE | COST |

Ralph Lauren Boys & Girls
26 26 23 E

E 70s | 878 Madison Ave. (bet. 71st & 72nd Sts.) | 6 to 68th St. | 212-606-3376 | www.polo.com

"Stick with the classics" crow fans of the Prince of Prep's UES retail venture, which strives to make wardrobing for the shopaphobic boy or girl in your life as "painless" as possible; beef up on basics here, everything from khakis, cords and cable knit sweaters to rugbys, oxfords and barn coats, as well as "perfect attire for that special occasion", including "blazers for that party he just got invited to."

Ralph Lauren Eyewear
- - - E

E 60s | 811 Madison Ave. (68th St.) | 6 to 68th St. | 212-988-4620 | www.polo.com

For sophisticated, super-stylish specs join the upmarket set at the latest addition to Ralph World on Madison Avenue; there's lots to covet at this corner shop, from classic eyeglasses that exude the essence of RL's understated chic to wide-framed wrap and square-framed sunglasses just right for seeking refuge from the paparazzi; N.B. opticians are on hand to fill existing prescriptions but no exams are given.

Ralph Lauren Layette & Toddler
26 27 23 VE

E 70s | 872 Madison Ave. (71st St.) | 6 to 68th St. | 212-434-8099 | www.polo.com

The "first stop" for the town-and-country crowd after the stork strikes, this "absolutely darling" baby shop – just across from the designer's Madison Avenue flagship – lavishes little ones with "mini-versions" of "fabulous" "RL classics", including cashmere sweaters, madras plaid pants and those ubiquitous polo shirts; sure, it's pricey, but this "solid" "quality" "stuff" "will last."

Ray Beauty Supply ☒
24 9 19 I

W 40s | 721 Eighth Ave. (bet. 45th & 46th Sts.) | A/C/E to 42nd St./Port Authority | 212-757-0175 | 800-253-0993 | www.raybeauty.com

"One of the best, but certainly not best-looking, shops" for "all things hair" is this Hell's Kitchen retailer selling "gigantic bottles of name-brand conditioners", shampoos, dyes, dryers, curling irons and ceramic straighteners at "moderate prices"; "it's not for the weak" (the staff "looks like bikers" and the place is a "dungeon"), but it is nevertheless a "great resource" for "salon items" that's a "professional beauty secret."

Razor ◑
- - - E

Park Slope | 329 Fifth Ave. (bet. 3rd & 4th Aves.) | Brooklyn | M/R to Union St. | 718-832-0717 | www.razorny.com

No need to F train it to the city for sharp-looking menswear – just stroll over to this Fifth Avenue find that's been dressing the Slope's underserved sex for over three years; the "high-end jean" selection from premium labels like Chip & Pepper, Joe's, 1921 and Yanuk is in a growth pattern, plus there are plenty of "gems" to be found among the buttondowns, ties and accessories from European and local designers.

RCS Experience
17 15 14 E

E 50s | 575 Madison Ave. (56th St.) | E/V to 5th Ave./53rd St. | 212-949-6935 | www.rcsnet.com

There's "a lot to choose from" at this East 50s electronics outlet, including a "good range of hard-to-find-items"; "high-quality computer" connoisseurs are keen on the fact that they "don't sell any crappy lines", leading most to say they "enjoy shopping here", but some wish they could switch off the "aggressive" staff.

Rebecca & Drew

-	-	-	E

Meatpacking | 342 W. 13th St. (Hudson St.) | A/C/E/L to 14th St./8th Ave. | 212-647-8904 | www.rebeccaanddrew.com

Women who prefer their shirts crisply tailored yet cutting-edge rejoice at the bounty of button-downs offered at this modest Meatpacking District shop owned by fashion-savvy friends Drew Paluba and alice + olivia co-founder Rebecca Winn; choose a solid, striped or plaid cotton number "based on your bra size", kitted out with ruffles or grosgrain ribbons and a variety of collars – it's "almost as good as buying custom-made."

Rebecca Taylor

23	23	20	E

NoLita | 260 Mott St. (bet. Houston & Prince Sts.) | B/D/F/V to B'way/Lafayette St. | 212-966-0406 | www.rebeccataylor.com

"Cute girlie" clothes "that even a 30-year-old can get away with" hold sway at this New Zealand designer's NoLita nugget, frequented by celebs like Chelsea Clinton and Sarah Michelle Gellar; staffers are on hand to help you select "ultrafeminine" pieces that run the gamut from "fantastic pants" to "tailored suits" to "that adorable top you've been looking for."

Rebel Rebel ◗

-	-	-	M

W Village | 319 Bleecker St. (bet. Christopher & Grove Sts.) | 1 to Christopher St./Sheridan Sq. | 212-989-0770

"The best excuse for not downloading music", this "excellent" indie in the West Village "specializes in imports", with an "extra focus on Euro pop and dance" CDs, and is jammed to the gills with "classic" and "off-beat" offerings ("the selection is especially great for Anglophiles", who also love the plethora of Brit mags); in fact, the only complaint is that owner David Shebiro "needs a larger store."

Redberi ◗Ⓜ

-	-	-	E

Prospect Heights | 331 Flatbush Ave. (Park Pl.) | Brooklyn | B/Q to 7th Ave. | 718-622-1964 | www.redberi.com

"Another reason to stay in Brooklyn" brag the borough-proud who bank on owner Carlene Brown's fine-tuned sense of color and style, plucking "quirky, individual", limited-edition and handcrafted clothing, jewelry and beauty products at this beri-cool boutique; the petite Prospect Heights digs boast finds from local designers and European and Asian indies, a selection that's a tad more casual than the offerings at sidekick Blueberi in Dumbo.

Red Flower

-	-	-	M

NoLita | 13 Prince St. (bet. Bowery & Elizabeth St.) | J/M/Z to Bowery | 212-966-5301 | www.redflower.com

Fans of this flower say it's "worth the trip" to NoLita for "wonderful smelling" "unique candles" like the Moroccan Rose scented ones, along with botanically based bath and body products made out of ingredients like cherry blossoms and blood oranges; you can top off the soothing experience by taking home one of their equally evocative fragrant teas.

	QUALITY	DISPLAY	SERVICE	COST

NEW Red Toenails Ⓜ
- | - | - | E

Williamsburg | 622 Metropolitan Ave. (Lorimer St.) | Brooklyn | L to Lorimer St. | 718-387-6987 | www.redtoenails.net

Unusual cuts and recontextualized fabrics (such as toile) distinguish the clothing by local designers, including the store's own dress-centric line, at this small, relatively pricey Williamsburg boutique a few blocks east of the BQE; avant-garde watches, jewelry with vintage charms and artfully printed undies round out the small selection, plus there's a couch (and some shirts too) for patient boyfriends; N.B. open Thursday–Sunday.

Reed Space
22 | 20 | 19 | M

LES | 151 Orchard St. (bet. Rivington & Stanton Sts.) | F/J/M/Z to Delancey/Essex Sts. | 212-253-0588 | www.thereedspace.com

Yes, it may be one of those "I'm too cool" for school lifestyle shops, but there's a reason why confirm "true sneaker lovers" and hip-hunters who head to this Lower Eastsider for "lesser-known" streetwear names; what a "wonderful selection of T-shirts" – one label "to check out is brknhome – great graphic tees for men", another: FHI, plus hoodies, crewnecks, utilitarian jackets and backpacks from the likes of Addict, Qwest, Rocksmith and Swagger.

Reem Acra Ⓢ Ⓜ
▽ 29 | 29 | 28 | VE

E 60s | 14 E. 60th St. (bet. 5th & Madison Aves.) | 4/5/6/F/N/R/W to 59th St./Lexington Ave. | 212-308-8760 | www.reemacra.com

Fiancées in search of a "sinfully beautiful gown at equally sinful prices" find the "most exquisite" big-day creations at this UES salon; when you see the "magnificent embroidery" "up close" "you understand why every bride would die to have" a beaded dress or a crystal tiara (fashioned by the designer's brother, Max); the "impeccable service" is "guaranteed to make you feel like royalty", so the end result is "worth every penny."

Refinery Ⓜ
- | - | - | M

Cobble Hill | 254 Smith St. (bet. Degraw & Douglass Sts.) | Brooklyn | F/G to Bergen St. | 718-643-7861 | www.brooklynrefinery.com

"Handmade in Brooklyn, what more could you want?" quip Cobble Hill cultists who covet owner-designer Suzanne Bagdade's "great bags made from vintage" ties and "very hip, durable" fabrics (no leather), all revealing her knack for "beautiful design and craftsmanship"; the spare, sleek space also boasts clogs, jewelry from area designers and all-important 718 T-shirts for dialed-in locals.

Reinstein/Ross
▽ 28 | 26 | 21 | VE

E 70s | 29 E. 73rd St. (bet. 5th & Madison Aves.) | 6 to 68th St. | 212-772-1901 Ⓢ

SoHo | 122 Prince St. (bet. Greene & Wooster Sts.) | N/R/W to Prince St. | 212-226-4513

www.reinsteinross.com

Upper East Side and SoHo jewelry shops showcasing "carefully handmade", "excellent quality" Egyptian- and Etruscan-inspired designs, from stacks of signature gemstone-set bands and rings in different shades of gold or platinum to multicolored sapphire cuffs and necklaces; just be sure to "save your pennies" in order to shop here.

Reiss

| | 20 | 23 | 21 | E |

SoHo | 387 W. Broadway (bet. Broome & Spring Sts.) | C/E to Spring St. | 212-925-5707 ◐

W 60s | 199 Columbus Ave. (bet. 68th & 69th Sts.) | 1 to 66th St./ Lincoln Ctr. | 212-874-0245 ◐

W Village | 311 Bleecker St. (bet. Grove St. & 7th Ave. S.) | 1 to Christopher St./Sheridan Sq. | 212-488-2411
www.reiss.co.uk

"Love the presentation" at this British import, which now has three "trendy megastores" around town, each boasting a sparkling chandelier, exposed-brick walls and "fun to shop" racks filled with "interesting" Reiss' "pieces that are simple yet different" for birds (and at the Downtown destinations, blokes too); if a few squawk it's "too expensive", flush twenty- and thirtysomethings taken with the "amazing styling" of the sexy cuts "stop in every time we're in the 'hood."

Reminiscence ◐

| | 19 | 19 | 17 | M |

Flatiron | 50 W. 23rd St. (bet. 5th & 6th Aves.) | F/V to 23rd St. | 212-243-2292 | www.reminiscence.com

"Old, bold, flashy and trashy": "there's always something fun to be found" at this Flatiron "silly emporium", whose mirrored, beaded-curtained digs abound with vintage and "vintage-inspired items" ranging from "cutesy memorabilia" and "cool toys" to new Hawaiian shirts; while "it's changed since its heyday" – it's "mostly gag gifts and tchotchkes now" – "prices are manageable, if not cheap", and "if you don't find that '60s frock, you can always buy a glob of fake vomit."

Replay

| | ▽ 23 | 21 | 19 | E |

SoHo | 109 Prince St. (Greene St.) | N/R/W to Prince St. | 212-673-6300 | www.replay.it

While it's "usually quiet and often overlooked", this multifloor denim destination actually stocks a "huge choice" of what may be the "best jeans in SoHo" with a "friendly staff" to "help you navigate between dozens of styles"; "you have to know and love" this "cool" Italian label "to pay the price", but loyalists stand fast, advising "bring a lot of money" or "wait for the annual sale."

NEW REPOP Ⓜ

| | - | - | - | M |

Clinton Hill | 68 Washington Ave. (bet. Flushing & Park Aves.) | Brooklyn | C/G to Clinton/Washington Aves. | 718-260-8032 | www.repopny.com

"It's easy to lose track of time" at this Clinton Hill trove near the Brooklyn Navy Yard stocked with a "fantastic collection" of "eccentric", mostly vintage booty like Victorian picture frames, art deco jewelry, mod-era clothing and architectural salvage, all "assembled in ways that you'd never dream of, but wish you could"; the owners view the "impressive" clutter as a curatorial project, so it's fitting that they also host frequent art openings that are "worth the trip."

Restoration Hardware ◐

| | 21 | 23 | 19 | M |

Flatiron | 935 Broadway (22nd St.) | N/R/W to 23rd St. | 212-260-9479 | 800-762-1005 | www.restorationhardware.com

"Much more than just hardware" is found at this Flatiron home-furnishings store with "dependable", "well-designed", "quality furniture", lighting, bathroom fixtures, towels, bedding, cleaning products, "cool gadgets" and retro toys; it's a "little limited on styles", but "prices are fair" and the staff is "knowledgeable and helpful."

Resurrection

$-$ | $-$ | $-$ | VE

NoLita | 217 Mott St. (bet. Prince & Spring Sts.) | N/R/W to Prince St. | 212-625-1374 | www.resurrectionvintage.com

There's "sort of an arty take on vintage" mens- and womenswear at this NoLita hideaway, known among nostalgists as being "the best for Pucci, Courrèges" and other "coveted designers" from the Swinging '60s, '70s and '80s; with its "interesting mix of merch" in "remarkable" shape, "eye-catching window displays" and mod, blood-red interior, the scene is strictly "hipster central", so "don't even think about shopping here if you're not cool" or not flush (it "has gotten rather pricey").

NEW Rewind

$-$ | $-$ | $-$ | E

Gravesend | 335 Ave. U (West St.) | Brooklyn | F to Ave. U | 718-333-2288 | www.rewindbrooklyn.com

You "gotta fish around" instruct insiders who reel in used but mostly current clothing treasures from designers like Azzedine Alaïa, Chanel, Gucci and Marni, plus shoes and handbags from the likes of Miu Miu and Sergio Rossi at this consignment newcomer in Gravesend; forget bargains – this hive of haute ticket items done up with nesting tables and a white couch "tends toward the extravagant end of the vintage pricing spectrum"; N.B. closes early on Fridays and closed Saturdays.

Ricky's ●

19 | 15 | 14 | M

E 40s | 509 Fifth Ave. (bet. 42nd & 43rd Sts.) | 7 to 5th Ave. | 212-949-7230 | www.rickys-nyc.com
Additional locations throughout the NY area

These "freaky variety stores" exist because "you never know when you'll need a zebra-print boa, magenta wig, German deodorant or scented candle", along with Halloween costumes and "all the beauty products mentioned in magazines" from makeup and "top-quality hair" goop to "every lotion and potion you can think of"; then too there are those "naughty" back rooms with sex toys "without the Times Square smuttiness"; the "help is unhelpful", but that doesn't keep devotees from surrendering to "one-stop acid-trip shopping."

Rico

$-$ | $-$ | $-$ | E

Boerum Hill | 384 Atlantic Ave. (bet. Bond & Hoyt Sts.) | Brooklyn | A/C/G to Hoyt/Schermerhorn Sts. | 718-797-2077 | www.shoprico.com

Amid the amorphous sea of antiques stores lining Boerum Hill's Atlantic Avenue stands this contemporary home-design hub, offering three floors of easygoing Mitchell Gold + Bob Williams sofas, minimalist Dellarobbia rugs, sculptural Emeco chairs, handsome home theater cabinets from BDI and owner Rico Espinet's own outstanding collection of modern, sculptural lighting.

⚡ Rita's Needlepoint ⊠

26 | 21 | 23 | E

E 70s | 150 E. 79th St., 2nd fl. (bet. Lexington & 3rd Aves.) | 6 to 77th St. | 212-737-8613 | www.ritasneedlepoint.com

Needleworkers note that this Upper East Sider's "mind-boggling" selection of "beautiful hand-painted canvases" is almost certain to "contain what you're looking for" (if not, "helpful" staffers will "create your design" for you) and appreciate the "courteous" service that includes "free lessons for beginners who buy" there; though a few fret it could be more "cheerful" most agree these folks "get the point."

Rival

22 | 21 | 18 | E

(fka 225 Hudson)

SoHo | 225 Hudson St. (bet. Broome & Canal Sts.) | 1 to Canal St. | 212-929-7222 | www.rivalnyc.com

Skater boys and girls roll over to this "cool" SoHo spot to sift through the sprawling selection of "old-skool kicks" – heavy on the Nikes – and "trendy" jeans, jackets and tees, plus skate decks and snowboards, all showcased in a slick space tricked out with concrete floors, brick walls and seating made from skateboards; there's "lots to choose from", though a sticker-shocked few huff you may "spend half your car payment" on that must-have item.

RK Bridal

19 | 11 | 15 | M

Garment District | 318 W. 39th St. (bet. 8th & 9th Aves.) | A/C/E to 42nd St./Port Authority | 212-947-1155 | 800-929-9512 | www.rkbridal.com

When you want your "dream to be a princess on your wedding day to come true and you don't have much money", head to this Garment District "warehouse"; "it ain't fancy" and you need "patience" to sift through the "sea of white dresses" but the payoff is "bingo!" – "bridal and bridesmaids dresses galore" at a "large variety of price points" sold by an "accommodating staff"; P.S. "weekends are a zoo."

Roberta Freymann 🖼

- | - | - | M

E 70s | 153 E. 70th St., 2nd fl. (Lexington Ave.) | 6 to 68th St. | 212-585-3767 | www.roberta-freymann.com

"A favorite for fashion editors", this Upper East Sider on the second floor of a brownstone gives you "a lot of look for the price" with its kurta tunics, Pakistani quilts, chic bohemian clothing and accessories imported from far-flung lands, including Argentina, India and Thailand; Freymann fans praise her sharp eye, confiding you'll find items "you can't get anywhere else", and "if you could", you'd "pay a lot more."

Roberta Roller Rabbit 🖼

- | - | - | M

E 70s | 1019 Lexington Ave. (73rd St.) | 6 to 77th St. | 212-772-7200 | www.roberta-freymann.com

Boho-chic clothing boutique owner Roberta Freymann brings her ethnically oriented eye to this Indian-inspired home-furnishings' emporium in the East 70s; there are reasonably priced hand-painted armoires, chests and daybeds along with her signature hand-blocked fabrics, some of which turn up in childrenswear, and one of which inspired the offbeat name for the store.

🖾 Robert Clergerie 🖼

28 | - | 22 | VE

E 60s | 19 E. 62nd St. (bet. 5th & Madison Aves.) | N/R/W to 5th Ave./59th St. | 212-207-8600 | www.robertclergerie.com

Whether it's "chunky" wedge sandals in wild colors, "always beautiful" "classic" heels or "great" lug-soled motorcycle-style boots, the French designer's *très expensive* footwear at his transplanted East 60s boutique keeps "getting better", prompting patrons to "come back" "year after year"; the "last-forever" kicks are "comfortable" and "stylin'" – no wonder guys and gals swear you "can take them anywhere."

Robert Lee Morris Gallery

25 | 25 | 21 | E

SoHo | 400 W. Broadway (bet. Broome & Spring Sts.) | C/E to Spring St. | 212-431-9405 | 800-829-8444 | www.robertleemorris.com

"His jewelry is like artwork" "with a touch of nature", the tribal or the industrial influencing the pieces say fans of this pioneering SoHo designer and his gallerylike West Broadway haven that's headquarters for "handmade", sculptural silver cuffs and knuckle rings or more recent 18-karat gold orbital mobile necklaces.

Robert Marc

27 | 25 | 25 | VE

E 40s | 400 Madison Ave. (bet. 47th & 48th Sts.) | E/V to 5th Ave./53rd St. | 212-319-2900

E 50s | 551 Madison Ave. (bet. 55th & 56th Sts.) | N/R/W to 5th Ave./59th St. | 212-319-2000

E 60s | 782 Madison Ave. (bet. 66th & 67th Sts.) | 6 to 68th St. | 212-737-6000

E 70s | 1046 Madison Ave. (bet. 78th & 79th Sts.) | 6 to 77th St. | 212-988-9600

E 90s | 1300 Madison Ave. (bet. 92nd & 93rd Sts.) | 6 to 96th St. | 212-722-1600

SoHo | 436 W. Broadway (Prince St.) | N/R/W to Prince St. | 212-343-8300 ◑

W 60s | 190 Columbus Ave. (bet. 68th & 69th Sts.) | 1 to 66th St./Lincoln Ctr. | 212-799-4600

W Village | 386 Bleecker St. (Perry St.) | 1 to Christopher St./Sheridan Sq. | 212-242-6668 ◑

www.robertmarc.com

"If you have to wear glasses, you might as well have fun" shopping at this "outstanding" ocular octet of "well-designed" shops; the "fabulous selection of unusual frames" speaks to the "celebrity in all of us" with lots of "color options" in star-favored lines such as Freudenhaus and Lunor; sure, the wares are "costly", but the "quality is superb" and what's more, the "talented", "exacting" staff knows "just what looks best" on you – they even "try to find" specs that "fit your personality."

Roberto Cavalli

27 | 27 | 23 | VE

E 60s | 711 Madison Ave. (63rd St.) | 4/5/6/F/N/R/W to 59th St./Lexington Ave. | 212-755-7722 | www.robertocavalli.it

Get ready to frock 'n' roll at this sleek, "absolutely fabulous" Madison Avenue bi-level boutique where the Italian designer lets it rip (sometimes literally) in his-and-hers skintight, "funky, sexy stuff", from ornate leather jackets to wrap dresses in wild animal prints; true, "friends might think you're crazy when you come back with $500 jeans with paint on them, but put them on and they'll understand" "the dent you just made in your budget."

Robert Talbott ⊠

28 | 25 | 23 | VE

E 60s | 680 Madison Ave. (bet. 61st & 62nd Sts.) | N/R/W to 5th Ave./59th St. | 212-751-1200 | 800-747-8778 | www.roberttalbott.com

It's not even close to a tie when it comes to the "finest neckwear" in NYC declare devotees of this East 60s haberdasher who also laud the "phenomenal" formalwear, including "the best tuxedo shirts you can get married in"; throw in more "colorful" dress and casual shirts and a smaller women's collection combined with "personalized" service and it's an obvious "first stop" on a Madison Avenue shopping spree.

	QUALITY	DISPLAY	SERVICE	COST

ⓩ Roche Bobois
27 25 22 VE

Murray Hill | 200 Madison Ave. (35th St.) | 6 to 33rd St. | 212-889-0700 | www.rochebobois.com

This Murray Hill store is a "modern" mainstay for "top-of-the-line French furniture" to "make a home more beautiful"; "great" pieces like luxe leather sofas and headboards of amazing "quality" and design "can break the bank", but connoisseurs who aren't hide-bound calmly counter that "perfection has a price."

Rochester Big & Tall ●
26 24 24 E

W 50s | 1301 Sixth Ave. (52nd St.) | B/D/F/V to 47-50th Sts./Rockefeller Ctr. | 212-247-7500 | 800-282-8200 | www.rochesterclothing.com

"Find brands from Burberry to Ralph Lauren" at this Midtown chain link "for the man of height and girth", where "shopping is a pleasure" thanks to the "huge inventory" and "discreet" staff that "goes to great lengths" to help "chubby hubbies"; "big prices" are to be expected, but the "superior" selection and the "best tailoring" ease the sticker shock.

Rockit Scientist Records ●
- - - M

E Village | 33 St. Marks Pl. (bet. 2nd & 3rd Aves.) | 6 to Astor Pl. | 212-242-0066

Here's the prog-nosis: if "hard-to-find" progressive, psychedelic, garage, soul and '60s classics rock your world, this "hidden treasure" in the East Village will send you into orbit with one of the "best" selections of new and used CDs and vinyl; admirers are also over the moon about the "extremely knowledgeable staff", maintaining they make it a "great place to hang and talk about music."

Rogan
25 21 21 E

TriBeCa | 91 Franklin St. (bet. B'way & Church St.) | 1 to Franklin St. | 646-827-7554 | www.rogannyc.com

"Everything feels cool" at this lofty TriBeCa space with artfully rough edges (like exposed brick and metal pipes) where celebs and fashionistas pick up ultrahip dark denim that's deemed "exceptional, even for the price", as well as stylishly rumpled cashmere and silk separates from their A Ltil Btr line; furniture from recycled materials, rare books and handmade jewelry add to the all-around effortlessly chic aesthetic.

NEW Roger Vivier ⑤
28 26 23 VE

E 60s | 750 Madison Ave. (65th St.) | N/R/W to 5th Ave./59th St. | 212-861-5371 | www.rogervivier.com

"One, two buckle my shoe" choruses a "well-heeled crowd" smitten by the "mod pilgrim" "classic" (and "gorgeous" coordinating bags), all arranged in "jewellike" displays at this "charming corner" shop on Madison where the "brilliant" French footwear designer's spirit lives on; *oui*, the "always timeless and chic", "sexy, not tarty" styles offering a taste of "Paris luxe at its best" cost "an arm and a leg", but they may "last a lifetime" – and what an "elegant" way to "channel Brigitte Bardot or Catherine Deneuve" circa *Belle de Jour*.

Romp Ⓜ
- - - E

Park Slope | 145 Fifth Ave. (bet. Lincoln & St. Johns Pls.) | Brooklyn | 2/3 to Bergen St. | 718-230-4373 | www.rompbklyn.com

Not your standard-issue toy shop, this Park Slope playhouse trumpets an unusual, sophisticated medley of merchandise, such as music boxes, make-and-shoot pinhole cameras, wood drums and other curiosities, from far-flung places like Thailand, Poland and The Netherlands; modern moms also romp over for the contemporary crib linens, whimsical wallpaper and furniture from local designers.

Room & Board

24 | 27 | 21 | M

SoHo | 105 Wooster St. (bet. Prince & Spring Sts.) | 1 to Houston St. | 212-334-4343 | 800-486-6554 | www.roomandboard.com

Minneapolis-based "minimalist" "modern furnishings" company that offers "excellent quality" "beautiful things" at "reasonable prices" in their four-floor SoHo store; there's a "great choice" of "smooth, clean-lined" sofas, side chairs, tables and beds, and service is "most helpful", leading enthusiasts to exclaim "thank you for coming to New York!"

Rosen & Chadick Textiles 🗷

- | - | - | E

Garment District | 561 Seventh Ave., 2nd fl. (bet. 39th & 40th Sts.) | 1/2/3/7/N/Q/R/S/W to 42nd St. | 212-869-0142 | 800-225-3838

After more than 25 years on West 40th Street, in mid-2005 this family-owned Garment District veteran moved around the corner to sunny, airy digs; its clientele of professional designers, Broadway costumers and hobbyists has followed for the sake of its "beautiful fabrics" (e.g. custom-made linens, wools, cashmere, silks and men's suiting) and "helpful" staff.

Rothman's

23 | 19 | 22 | E

Union Sq | 200 Park Ave. S. (17th St.) | 4/5/6/L/N/Q/R/W to 14th St./Union Sq. | 212-777-7400 | www.rothmansny.com

Though perhaps "best-suited (pun intended) for those seeking traditional styles", this "Union Square institution" also stocks a "wide variety" of ultrafashionable casual- and businesswear for "grown-up guys" ready to "go that one step above the chains"; though it's no longer strictly a discounter, "you can find deals on top names" during sales, abetted by the "well-mannered staff"; N.B. the Display score may not reflect a post-Survey renovation.

Rubin Chapelle

- | - | - | VE

Meatpacking | 410 W. 14th St. (bet. 9th Ave. & Washington St.) | A/C/E/L to 14th St./8th Ave. | 212-647-8636 | www.rubinchapelle.com

Enter the brave new world of Austrian Sonya Rubin and American Kip Chapelle at their modernistic brick-walled, art-filled store in the Meatpacking District; the pair is fearless in their pursuit of a crisp minimalism in all they design for men and women, be it a svelte gown, a knit sweater or a trim suit; accessories such as buttery leather jackets, vintage bags and customized fur-lined boots round out the look.

🆉 Rubin Museum of Art Ⓜ

26 | 23 | 24 | E

Chelsea | 150 W. 17th St. (bet. 6th & 7th Aves.) | 1 to 18th St. | 212-620-5000 | www.rmanyc.org

"A beautiful little jewel" of a shop in a "charming" museum devoted to the arts of the Himalayas, this "find" offers "sumptuously designed books", lovely imported jewelry, clothing and other "unique" gift items (including "lovable stuffed yaks"); admittedly, some of the prices may be as "high" as Mt. Everest itself, but the "quality's terrific" and the staff "friendly", making it "worth a trip" to Barneys' former home in Chelsea.

	QUALITY	DISPLAY	SERVICE	COST

Ruehl ◑

| 21 | 23 | 17 | E |

W Village | 370 Bleecker St. (bet. Charles & Perry Sts.) | 1 to Christopher St./
Sheridan Sq. | 212-924-8506 | www.ruehl.com

What an "interesting retail concept: part club, part store, part cool"
quip customers of Bleecker Street's "hip", "higher-end" accessories-
only Abercrombie & Fitch spin-off who laud the "great feel" and "good
display" of leather handbags, men's bags, gloves and belts; still, an
unruly few scoff it's so "dark" you may need a "flashlight if you want to
see what you are buying" and Ruehl out the "smug" staff.

Rue St. Denis ◑

| - | - | - | E |

E Village | 170 Ave. B (bet. 10th & 11th Sts.) | L to 1st Ave. | 212-260-3388 |
www.vintagenyc.com

"Stocked with unique, unworn clothing from past eras", this East
Village vintage shop is one of the few to focus on the menfolk – offering them everything from '60s slim-cut Cardin suits to narrow '80s
ties – though femmes will find plenty to amuse them among the ruffled
skirts and open-toe pumps; aside from the bell-bottoms and European
biker gear, the clothes "eschew kitsch for subtle style"; and if some rue
the "overpriced" goods, others kvell at the "cool collection."

Rugby

| 22 | 23 | 18 | E |

G Village | 99 University Pl. (12th St.) | 4/5/6/L/N/Q/R/W to 14th St./
Union Sq. | 212-677-1895 | www.rugby.com

"Pick up one of Ralph Lauren's greatest hits, reworked and sized-down
for the college crowd" at this "amazing concept" store in Greenwich
Village; the "affordable" (compared to Ralph's other lines) clothes offer "preppy choices with a downtown edge" – i.e. "skull-and-crossbones on [corduroys], an interesting combination" – arranged in
"terrific visual displays"; staff hotties and free concerts keep "the
place packed with style-crazed young adults", and while some snap
the shop and styles are too "small", if you want "a fun alternative to
Polo", you might become "a big Rugby fan."

Rug Company, The

| - | - | - | VE |

SoHo | 88 Wooster St. (bet. Broome & Spring Sts.) | C/E to Spring St. |
212-274-0444 | www.therugcompany.info

Sure, there are traditional woven classics like Berbers at this British
import in SoHo, but it's the contemporary designs by boldface names
in interiors and fashion like Nina Campbell, Cath Kidston and Paul
Smith that generate the buzz with patterns that range from pale stalks
of bamboo to bold stripes.

Ruzzetti & Gow 🖾

| - | - | - | E |

E 70s | 22 E. 72nd St., 3rd fl. (bet. 5th & Madison Aves.) | 6 to 68th St. |
212-327-4281 | www.ruzzettiandgow.com

Tucked away on the third floor of an Upper East Side brownstone is "a
lovely place to shop" for a gleaming assortment of silver-coated seashells, vegetables and fruits, which make for tony tabletop ornaments;
the natural theme carries over into coral and rock crystal jewelry and
semiprecious stone bowls and boxes.

Sabon

| 25 | 25 | 23 | E |

Chelsea | 78 Seventh Ave. (15th St.) | 1/2/3 to 14th St. | 646-486-1809
(continued)

(continued)

Sabon

E 60s | 782 Lexington Ave. (bet. 60th & 61st Sts.) | 4/5/6/F/N/R/W to 59th St./Lexington Ave. | 212-308-5901

G Village | 434 Sixth Ave. (10th St.) | A/B/C/D/E/F/V to W. 4th St. | 212-473-4346 ●

NEW **SoHo** | 123 Prince St. (bet. Greene & Wooster Sts.) | N/R/W to Prince St. | 212-982-0968 ●

SoHo | 93 Spring St. (B'way) | N/R/W to Prince St. | 212-925-0742 ●

W 50s | 1371 Sixth Ave. (bet. 55th & 56th Sts.) | F to 57th St. | 212-974-7352

W 70s | 2052 Broadway (70th St.) | 1/2/3 to 72nd St. | 212-362-0200 ●
866-697-2266 | www.sabonnyc.com

This Israeli bath and body chain with branches around town features a handmade, natural product line that includes jewel-colored and studded soaps that are sold by the pound, "fabulous body scrubs" with Dead Sea salts and shea butter lotions and creams with "original scents" like ginger/orange that are "luscious"; they've just launched a line of bathrobes and laundry baskets too.

Sacco ●

| 22 | 19 | 20 | E |

Chelsea | 94 Seventh Ave. (bet. 15th & 16th Sts.) | 1 to 18th St. | 212-675-5180

E 50s | 118 E. 59th St. (bet. Lexington & Park Aves.) | 4/5/6/F/N/R/W to 59th St./Lexington Ave. | 212-207-3151

Flatiron | 14 E. 17th St. (bet. B'way & 5th Ave.) | 4/5/6/L/N/Q/R/W to 14th St./Union Sq. | 212-243-2070

Flatiron | 6 E. 23rd St. (bet. B'way & Madison Ave.) | N/R/W to 23rd St. | 212-777-3414

SoHo | 111 Thompson St. (bet. Prince & Spring Sts.) | N/R/W to Prince St. | 212-925-8010

W 70s | 324 Columbus Ave. (75th St.) | 1/2/3/B/C to 72nd St. | 212-799-5229
www.saccoshoes.com

Finding "fashion and function in footwear" may seem like a highfalutin demand, but it's a thoroughly "realistic" requirement for women who "live, work and play in NYC" and this "stylish" "standby" rises to the challenge, turning out "edgy" "soft-leather" shoes that are also "unbelievably comfortable"; the "quality will outlast the trend", and surprise, the "staff goes out of its way to find what you need."

Safavieh Carpets

| ∇ 26 | 19 | 21 | E |

E 50s | 238 E. 59th St. (bet. 2nd & 3rd Aves.) | 4/5/6/F/N/R/W to 59th St./Lexington Ave. | 212-888-0626

Murray Hill | 153 Madison Ave. (32nd St.) | 6 to 33rd St. | 212-683-8399

Safavieh Home Furnishings

Flatiron | 902 Broadway (bet. 20th & 21st Sts.) | N/R/W to 23rd St. | 212-477-1234
866-422-9070 | www.safaviehhome.com

You're covered because there's such a "great selection" of "tempting rugs" including "very fine quality" "antique Orientals" as well as reproductions, traditional, tribal and contemporary collections at these three Manhattan manufacturers and importers with "decent" prices; N.B. the Broadway store also carries furniture.

	QUALITY	DISPLAY	SERVICE	COST

Saipua Ⓜ
- - - M

Red Hook | 392 Van Brunt St. (bet. Coffey & Dikeman Sts.) | Brooklyn | F/G to Smith/9th Sts. | 718-624-2929 | www.saipua.com

Windows hung with old-fashioned aprons beckon you into this Red Hook nook, a Hudson Valley family's new shop for soaps made with food-grade vegetable oils, butter and herbs; the hand-cut, air-dried and cured squares, available in choices like clove geranium, rooibus tea and coffee mint, are wrapped in Florentine paper and displayed on a mantle for easy plucking; completing the scent-sational experience: seasonal flowers, also for sale here.

Saja
- - - E

NoLita | 250 Elizabeth St. (bet. Houston & Prince Sts.) | B/D/F/V to B'way/Lafayette St. | 212-226-7570 | www.sajainc.com

When the occasion calls for full-on femininity, sweep into designer Yoo Lee's boudoirlike NoLita enclave, a sliver of elegance with a bright white floor and exposed-brick wall; get your fix of "gorgeous" retro-modern dresses, girlie-girl separates and accessories, inspired by the 1920s and '30s and done up with tasteful details like French seaming, lace, beading and hand embroidery, all dispensed by a "sweet" staff.

Ⓩ Saks Fifth Avenue ●
27 | 24 | 21 | VE

E 50s | 611 Fifth Ave. (50th St.) | B/D/F/V to 47-50th Sts./Rockefeller Ctr. | 212-753-4000 | 877-551-7257 | www.saks.com

An "essential stop on any shopping spree", this Midtown mainstay "sets the standard" for "elegant" emporia because it's "not as pompous" as some, but "hasn't lost its sophistication", either; you'll see tourists, "trendy teens and socialites, side by side" savoring the "selection of mid- and upper-end fashion" for her and him, accessories and jewelry sections "reminiscent of a museum" and "super shoes", now housed in a salon so large it has its own ZIP code (10022-SHOE); and though the staff could "lower the pushiness factor a bit", "they'll check the computer for an item in your size and ship it to you."

NEW Salty Paw, The
22 | 22 | 21 | M

Seaport | 38 Peck Slip (bet. Front & South Sts.) | 2/3/4/5/A/C/J/M/Z to Fulton St./B'way/Nassau | 212-732-2275 | www.thesaltypaw.com

"Adogable! my furkids love" this brick-walled emporium applaud pet-parents who hunt down "adorable, delightful gear" from collars and travel cases to bowls and beds, plus "excellent" NYC-themed toys and apparel and custom-baked treats for their "best buds" at this "great resource" on the South Street Seaport waterfront; "forget teeny tiny sweaters" – this place "caters to large" canines ("manly" pooches "need love too!"); yip, "you pay for convenience" but it sure "makes things easy" for commuters and locals.

Salvation Army Ⓩ
11 | 6 | 8 | I

W 40s | 536 W. 46th St. (bet. 10th & 11th Aves.) | A/C/E to 42nd St./Port Authority | 212-757-2311 | www.salvationarmy.org
Additional locations throughout the NY area

The "depressing atmosphere makes you feel like a poor relation" and much of the merch has that "thrift-shop whiff", but if you "take a deep breath and search for everything as fast as you can", this historic charity's chain offers "definitely the best deal in town" on anything from

| | QUALITY | DISPLAY | SERVICE | COST |

"aging appliances" to clothes to books; converts confide the flagship "46th Street location has the most stuff" – just think of the "dusty, dingy and dark" digs as "perfect for Halloween shopping."

☑ Salvatore Ferragamo
28 | 26 | 24 | VE

E 50s | 655 Fifth Ave. (bet. 52nd & 53rd Sts.) | E/V to 5th Ave./53rd St. | 212-759-3822 | 800-628-8916 | www.salvatoreferragamo.com

Everything at this "high-end" two-story Fifth Avenue "flagship of a European icon" "screams elegance" assert Sal-ivaters who "adore" the "exquisite", "classic, always appropriate" men's and women's footwear that's "worth every penny", all proffered by a "top-notch" staff; but there's also "nothing more *bellissimo*" than the selection of "perfect scarves", "amazing ties" and "great leather accessories."

Salviati ◐
- | - | - | VE

SoHo | 422 W. Broadway (bet. Prince & Spring Sts.) | C/E to Spring St. | 212-625-8390 | www.salviati.com

In its first U.S. outpost, this Venetian glass blower dating back to 1859 offers an über-modern, orange-tiled SoHo shop done by prestigious Milanese interior designer Paola Navone; there's boldly colored barware, limited-edition vases by emerging European names and exuberant Murano-glass jewelry, all with equally eye-popping prices.

Samantha Thavasa ☒
- | - | - | E

E 70s | 965 Madison Ave. (bet. 75th & 76th Sts.) | 6 to 77th St. | 212-535-3920

Groupies who go for the glitzy, girlie, star- or heart-patterned handbags of this Japanese label rejoice in the company's first stateside location; the all-white, rhinestone-studded East 70s store features purses in vibrant colors and various styles, with the lines designed by socialites like Tinsley Mortimer well-represented; there are a few wallets as well.

Sam Flax
24 | 20 | 17 | E

E 50s | 900 Third Ave. (bet. 54th & 55th Sts.) | E/V to Lexington Ave./ 53rd St. | 212-813-6666

Flatiron | 12 W. 20th St. (bet. 5th & 6th Aves.) | F/V to 23rd St. | 212-620-3000 | 800-628-9512 | www.samflaxny.com

"Colorful" Herman Miller desks and chairs "to spice up a dull office" along with "inspirational" art supplies and a "hodgepodge of interesting" gift items are "attractively presented" at this East 50s and Flatiron duo; "don't ever submit a portfolio without checking here first" and remember it's the "last word in chic paper goods" too; there's some hue and cry about "hot and cold" service and "high" prices; nevertheless, most consider it "reliably trendy."

Samsonite Black Label
24 | 21 | 19 | E

E 60s | 838 Madison Ave. (bet. 69th & 70th Sts.) | 6 to 68th St. | 212-861-2064 | www.samsoniteblacklabel.com

"Enthusiasm reigns" at this compact, mod Madison Avenue venue, the first U.S. location for the boldface maker's worldwide spin-off brand – and no wonder: who knew "Samsonite could be so hip"?; the "very comprehensive", colorful selection, including the Vintage Collection and super-light X'Lite line, "makes you want to take a trip", while the latest luxury endeavor, a grouping from Alexander McQueen (next up: Viktor & Rolf), ensures that you'll "travel in style."

	QUALITY	DISPLAY	SERVICE	COST

Samuel's Hats ⊠   -   -   -   E

Financial District | 74 Nassau St. (John St.) | 2/3/4/5/A/C/J/M/Z to
Fulton St./B'way/Nassau | 212-513-7322 | www.samuelshats.com
"Hats off to the huge selection" at the Financial District's handmade
headpiece heaven where "expensive to moderate"–priced ladies' lids
from designers like Louise Green, Makins and Philip Treacy are available in limited quantities; whether you're looking for sleek cloches or
dressy pillboxes "you will definitely find it here" – or you can have it
custom-made; there's also a small crop of men's toppers from
Borsalino and Kangol.

S&W   18   10   10   M

Borough Park | 4217 13th Ave. (43rd St.) | Brooklyn | D/M to
Fort Hamilton Pkwy. | 718-431-2800
Williamsburg | 160 Wallabout St. (Bedford Ave.) | Brooklyn | J/M/Z to
Marcy Ave. | 718-431-2800
www.swnewyork.com
"If you don't see what you want, just ask for it – it's there" declare disciples of this discount duo in Borough Park and Williamsburg specializing in "conservative" – some say "dowdy" – womenswear; the "heavy
sales pressure" and "noise levels can overwhelm shoppers", and opponents opine "they used to have better selections."

Sanrio ☾   21   23   17   M
(aka Hello Kitty Store)

W 40s | 233 W. 42nd St. (bet. 7th & 8th Aves.) | 1/2/3/7/N/Q/R/S/
W to 42nd St./Times Sq. | 212-840-6011 | www.sanrio.com
Japan's famous feline fashionista "Hello Kitty reigns supreme" at this
slice of "heaven" in Times Square; gals of "all ages" "spend hours"
pawing through the "incredible variety of items" including "so cute"
pencil cases, purses, lip gloss, stationery and even toaster ovens featuring HK and pals My Melody, Badtz Maru and Chococat – all the
"characters we love so much" – while big spenders purr over Kimora Lee
Simmons' high-end line of diamond-encrusted watches and jewelry.

Sansha   -   -   -   M

W 50s | 888 Eighth Ave. (bet. 52nd & 53rd Sts.) | C/E to 50th St. |
212-246-6212 | www.sansha.com
"This is the place to go if you do any kind of dancing" confide movers
and shakers who lead the way to this West 50s performer's haven for
"great" handcrafted, split-sole ballet slippers as well as ballroom,
character, jazz, tap and pointe shoes at "very good prices"; leotards
and tights plus performance-ready flamenco skirts and tutus set the
stage for encore visits.

☒ Santa Maria Novella   28   25   23   VE

NoLita | 285 Lafayette St. (bet. Houston & Prince Sts.) | B/D/F/V to
B'way/Lafayette St. | 212-925-0001 | www.santamarianovellausa.com
With a gilded exterior and an imposing interior filled with an extensive
array of expensive Italian toiletries, this NoLita boutique is the place for
"absolute luxury", including heady scents such as tuber rose and over-
the-top offerings like Virgin's Milk toner for skin; the Florence-based
company's legend says it was founded by 17th-century monks, which
may be why converts call it a "heavenly" place for "divine products."

	QUALITY	DISPLAY	SERVICE	COST

Satellite
- - - E

SoHo | 412 W. Broadway (bet. Prince & Spring Sts.) | C/E to Spring St. |
212-372-0016 | www.satelliteparis.com

Morocco meets Marie Antoinette and sometimes Queen Victoria too
at this French costume jewelry import in SoHo; Sandrine Dulon's
dramatic designs incorporate semiprecious stones, elaborate beading, enamel, crystals or feathers in everything from chandelier earrings to multistrand bib necklaces, and all of the bedazzlers offer a big
bang for the buck.

Satya
21 22 22 M

NEW **NoLita** | 253 Centre St. (bet. Broome & Grand Sts.) | 6 to Spring St. |
212-966-3377 ●

NEW **W 80s** | 2265 Broadway (81st St.) | 1 to 79th St. | 212-799-5490
W Village | 330 Bleecker St. (Christopher St.) | 1 to Christopher St./
Sheridan Sq. | 212-243-7313 ●
www.satyajewelry.com

When two jewelry veterans combined their interest in things Eastern,
the result was Satya ('truth'), a "cool" West Village boutique with a
Buddha in the window; the accent is on "reasonably priced" "Indian-
inspired pieces" in silver, 24-karat gold vermeil (particularly woven-
metal cuffs and the thinnest bangles) and gemstones chosen for their
healing properties; N.B. their adjoining lifestyle store sells scarves and
soaps, plus there are now new branches in NoLita and the West 80s.

Scaredy Kat ● Ⓜ
▽ 24 23 25 M

Park Slope | 229 Fifth Ave. (bet. Carroll & President Sts.) | Brooklyn |
M/R to Union St. | 718-623-1839 | www.scaredykatstore.com

For the "best selection of hip, contemporary greeting cards" in Park
Slope and "cool weird stuff" ranging from Frida Kahlo plastic totes to
whimsical nightlights that make "fun gifts", skip over to this
buttercup-colored Fifth Avenue nook with a tongue-in-cheek
"American mom-and-pop vibe" that hints at the owners' "sense of humor"; patrons purr there's "something for every occasion" here, including announcements and notes custom-made from your photos.

Schneider's Ⓢ
▽ 25 16 19 M

Chelsea | 41 W. 25th St. (bet. B'way & 6th Ave.) | F/V to 23rd St. |
212-228-3540 | www.schneidersbaby.com

Ok, it's "cluttered" but this "gem" of a baby general store – a New York
"institution" for over 55 years, which relocated from Alphabet City to
Chelsea "digs" a few years ago – stocks a "good selection of strollers,
car seats, cribs and other basic supplies"; throw in an "incredibly helpful staff" and you've got a shop "definitely worth schlepping to."

Scholastic Store, The
24 24 21 M

SoHo | 557 Broadway (bet. Prince & Spring Sts.) | N/R/W to Prince St. |
212-343-6166 | 877-286-0137 | www.thescholasticstore.com

"Clifford and Harry Potter reside side by side" with Captain
Underpants at this "excellent, educational", always-"mobbed" SoHo
"wonderland" for little "learning minds"; the loftlike layout is stocked
solid with "engaging" toys, games, books, videos and CD-ROMs, plus
teachers can also nab "nice deals" on curriculum materials; stop in for
the "wonderful, interactive" character visits and story hour – it's a
"great way to instill [interest in] reading."

Schoolhouse Electric Co. ⌧

-	-	-	E

TriBeCa | 27 Vestry St. (Hudson St.) | 1 to Franklin St. | 212-226-6113 | www.schoolhouseelectric.com

Period-lighting lovers brighten at the sight of this TriBeCa showroom selling classic 1900–1950s fixtures and hand-blown glass shades, some out of production since the Depression; vintage molds are used to create ceiling-mounted designs, hanging pendants and wall sconces.

School Products Co., Inc. ⌧

25	16	22	M

Garment District | 1201 Broadway, 3rd fl. (bet. 28th & 29th Sts.) | N/R/W to 23rd St. | 212-679-3516 | 800-847-4127 | www.schoolproducts.com

"Definitely old-school" (founded in 1947), Berta Karapetyan's "huge", "no-atmosphere" fiber outlet near FIT is a "must-visit" for the savvy crafter; knitters "racking up" "large quantities" make a beeline for "high-quality", "bargain"-priced coned yarns left over from fashion houses, pronouncing this "Garment Center classic" a "mecca for cashmere", silk and other luxury covetables; still, a handful feel it's a "hit-or-miss" proposition – it just "depends on how lucky you are."

☒ Schweitzer Linen

27	16	21	E

E 70s | 1053 Lexington Ave. (bet. 74th & 75th Sts.) | 6 to 77th St. | 212-570-0236 ⌧

E 80s | 1132 Madison Ave. (bet. 84th & 85th Sts.) | 4/5/6 to 86th St. | 212-249-8361 ⌧

W 80s | 457 Columbus Ave. (bet. 81st & 82nd Sts.) | B/C to 81st St. | 212-799-9629

800-554-6367 | www.schweitzerlinen.com

Family-owned Uptown trio of "reasonably priced for the quality" linen stores with a "great selection" of "beautiful", "upscale", European-styled sheets that will help you "sleep better for having shopped here", along with scallop-edged, Egyptian cotton towels with a Porthault look for less; "small, cramped" quarters make it "hard to browse" and service can vary, but that doesn't keep the "discerning" from hunting for "great buys" here.

Scoop Kids ◑

23	23	18	E

Meatpacking | 875 Washington St. (bet. 13th & 14th Sts.) | A/C/E/L to 14th St./8th Ave. | 212-691-1926 | 877-726-6777 | www.scoopnyc.com

"Kids can be hip too", especially after a stop at this Meatpacking District mecca for all things child-size yet "trendy" that's "just like" Scoop for grown-ups – what an "awesome idea"; "you know what's 'in'" the moment you walk through the door: denim from Earnest Sewn, 7 for All Mankind and Joe's Jeans, novelty tops from Tory Burch and comfy basics from Juicy Couture – it's all "sooo kool but sooo expensive!"

Scoop Men's ◑

23	23	18	E

E 70s | 1277 Third Ave. (bet. 73rd & 74th Sts.) | 6 to 77th St. | 212-535-5577
Meatpacking | 873 Washington St. (bet. 13th & 14th Sts.) | A/C/E/L to 14th St./8th Ave. | 212-929-1244
www.scoopnyc.com

Anything from Scoop's sidekick for guys will "become the prized possessions of your wardrobe" insist insiders who snatch up the "latest styles" at these "easy-to-navigate" boutiques in the East 70s and "trendy Meatpacking District"; the "inventory is updated regularly, so stop in before your Thursday night date" for "great stuff" from Paul

Smith and John Varvatos, store-commissioned lines from J.Crew and Theory, plus an "excellent selection of jeans" and T-shirts; still, some dish that service is "good – if you look like you're willing to spend major dollars."

Scoop NYC ◐

23 | 22 | 16 | E

E 70s | 1273-1277 Third Ave. (bet. 73rd & 74th Sts.) | 6 to 77th St. | 212-535-5577
Meatpacking | 861 Washington St. (bet. 13th & 14th Sts.) | A/C/E/L to 14th St./8th Ave. | 212-691-1905
NEW SoHo | 473-475 Broadway (bet. Broome & Grand Sts.) | 6 to Spring St. | 212-925-3539
877-726-6777 | www.scoopnyc.com

Bring "plenty of cash" to shop at this "effortlessly cool" outfit – it's the "ultimate closet" confide fashionistas who "scoop up" the "hottest jeans", "au courant" "fun stuff" from "fabulous" labels like alice + olivia, Marc Jacobs and Theory and "accessories to make them look even better"; some claim the "candid" staff is "helpful", but detractors declare their "laser-beam stares" can "send you running"; N.B. the SoHo 'mega store' carries men's, women's and kids' clothing (plus a new fragrance line).

Scott Jordan Furniture

▽ 27 | 26 | 29 | E

SoHo | 137 Varick St. (Spring St.) | C/E to Spring St. | 212-620-4682 | www.scottjordan.com

A "knowledgeable and low-pressure staff" presides over this SoHo showroom featuring "beautifully made", "clean-lined", "handcrafted" Mission- and Shaker-style furniture in American black-cherry wood; but while there is no quibble about the "high-quality" of the pieces, some aesthetes assert they are short on "style."

Scuba Network

- | - | - | M

Chelsea | 655 Sixth Ave. (bet. 20th & 21st Sts.) | F/V to 23rd St. | 212-243-2988
E 50s | 669 Lexington Ave. (bet. 55th & 56th Sts.) | 4/5/6/F/N/R/W to 59th St./Lexington Ave. | 212-750-9160
800-688-3483 | www.scubanetwork.com

Never mind the 30-ft. octopus stationed inside the Sixth Avenue location – Cousteau wannabes gladly hand themselves over to the "friendliest staff around" at this East 50s–Chelsea outfit because the "helpful" experts take the undersea world seriously; this "great diver's resource", in business for over 20 years, has expanded from the scuba basics to include snorkels, fins and swimsuits, with prices leagues below others; P.S. "get your certification" here too.

☒ Scully & Scully

29 | 27 | 24 | VE

E 50s | 504 Park Ave. (59th St.) | 4/5/6/F/N/R/W to 59th St./
Lexington Ave. | 212-755-2590 | 800-223-3717 | www.scullyandscully.com

"Shop here" at this East 50s "classic" "Muffy/Buffy" home-furnishings destination if you have any "Republican friends who live on Park Avenue"; of course, the "lovely old-guard items" including Herend china animal figurines, sterling silver pheasants, faux sable throws and reproduction antique furniture all come at a premium price, as does the newly expanded selection of fine jewelry – a pink (sapphire) flamingo brooch, anyone?

	QUALITY	DISPLAY	SERVICE	COST

Seaman Schepps 🖾
▽ 27 | 27 | 27 | VE

E 50s | 485 Park Ave. (58th St.) | 4/5/6/F/N/R/W to 59th St./
Lexington Ave. | 212-753-9520 | www.seamanschepps.com

"Wonderful, whimsical" turban-shell earrings wrapped with gold wire,
then crowned with colored stones, are still the celebrated jeweler's
signature, and the salon-style Park Avenue store he opened in 1934 to
feature his own designs, mixing precious gems with lesser materials
such as coral or wood, remains headquarters for the "creative, exuberant" "nonpareil" pieces that were (and are) coveted by the best-
dressed-list ladies; N.B. each pricey piece is numbered.

Sean ●
▽ 24 | 24 | 26 | M

SoHo | 132 Thompson St. (bet. Houston & Prince Sts.) | C/E to Spring St. |
212-598-5980
W 70s | 224 Columbus Ave. (bet. 70th & 71st Sts.) | 1/2/3/B/C to
72nd St. | 212-769-1489
www.seanstore.com

This SoHo and West 70s pair can make almost any man "look like an
architect, or at least European" with breezy and basic French cuts
from labels such as Emile Lafaurie; the "reliably tasteful, hip" knits,
linens and shirts on the shelves come at what many consider a "good
price"; N.B. look for Sam, the seven-year-old chocolate Lab featured in
their ads, in person at the SoHo branch.

Sean John
18 | 22 | 18 | E

E 40s | 475 Fifth Ave. (41st St.) | 4/5/6/7/S to 42nd St./Grand Central |
212-220-2633 | www.seanjohn.com

The pseudonym-loving hip-hop entrepreneur parlays his fame and his
name into the fashion game with this marble-and-mahogany mecca
across from the NY Public Library; the too-cool-for-school menswear –
from jeans to suits to leather or suede sneakers – is "stylish and affordable" say aficionados aching for a bit of his inimitable lifestyle, but
skeptics sigh "why Diddy is doing this, I'll never know"; N.B. if bling is
your thing, ladies, check out the Sean by Sean Combs line.

🗹 Seaport Yarn 🖾⇱
28 | 15 | 23 | M

Seaport | 135 William St., 5th fl. (bet. Fulton & John Sts.) | 2/3/4/5/
A/C/J/M/Z to Fulton St./B'way/Nassau | 212-220-5230 |
800-347-2662 | www.seaportyarn.com

A "den for knitaholics" stashed in a "hard-to-find" fifth-floor space near
the South Street Seaport, this 3,700-sq.-ft. office suite has "every nook"
and cubicle "crammed" full of "awesome yarns" and a "tremendous
selection of books, kits and supplies"; some shoppers say it's "difficult
to find things" in the "disorganized" environs, but "knowledgeable",
"no-attitude" staffers will "helpfully lead you to the right room."

Searle ●
24 | 22 | 18 | E

E 60s | 1051 Third Ave. (62nd St.) | 4/5/6/F/N/R/W to 59th St./
Lexington Ave. | 212-838-5990
E 60s | 1142 Third Ave. (67th St.) | 6 to 68th St. | 212-988-8361
E 60s | 635 Madison Ave. (60th St.) | 4/5/6/F/N/R/W to 59th St./
Lexington Ave. | 212-750-5153
E 60s | 805 Madison Ave. (68th St.) | 6 to 68th St. | 212-628-6665
E 70s | 1035 Madison Ave. (79th St.) | 6 to 77th St. | 212-717-4022

(continued)

(continued)

Searle

E 70s | 1296 Third Ave. (74th St.) | 6 to 77th St. | 212-717-5200
E 80s | 1124 Madison Ave. (84th St.) | 4/5/6 to 86th St. | 212-988-7318
Flatiron | 156 Fifth Ave. (bet. 20th & 21st Sts.) | N/R/W to 23rd St. |
212-924-4330
www.searlenyc.com

"All the sass without the 'tude" praise pros of this "high-caliber" "NY staple for style", renowned for its "fabulous shearlings" and "lovely" jackets; forget its "dowdy" past – this outfit has "an eye for modern", "chic" looks, from its private label women's clothing "you'll reach for again and again" to its "unique" designer selection; but "pick a branch and stick with it", as "salespeople vary" from "excellent" to "pushy."

Sears

17	13	13	M

Bronx | 4720 Third Ave. (189th St.) | B/D to Fordham Rd. | 718-817-7377
Flatbush | 2307 Beverley Rd. (E. 22nd St.) | Brooklyn | 2 to Beverley Rd. |
718-826-5800 ●
Kings Plaza | Kings Plaza Shopping Ctr. | 5200 Kings Plaza
(bet. Flatbush Ave. & Ave. U) | Brooklyn | B/Q to Newkirk Ave. |
718-677-2100 ●
Flushing | 137-61 Northern Blvd. (bet. Main St. & Parsons Blvd.) |
Queens | 7 to Main St. | 718-460-7000 ●
Rego Park | 96-05 Queens Blvd. (Junction Blvd.) | Queens | G/R/V to
63rd Dr./Rego Park | 718-830-5900 ●
Staten Island | Staten Island Mall | 283 Platinum Ave. (Richmond Ave.) |
718-370-6200 ●
www.sears.com

The "old standby" that served great-gramps seems "nearly unchanged" after more than 110 years; "you cannot beat their home department" ("they back everything they sell, and now have a price-match guarantee") for washers, dryers, fridges or "anything to do with manual labor in general"; but critics counsel "buy tools and appliances here, period" – as most of the other merch is "boring" (though the "Lands' End clothing is a plus"), and many stores have "dowdy" digs, "service with a snarl" and check-out "lines longer than the Great Wall of China."

Second Chance Designer Resale, A 🖾

▽ 21	15	15	E

E 70s | 1109 Lexington Ave., 2nd fl. (bet. 77th & 78th Sts.) | 6 to 77th St. |
212-744-6041 | www.asecondchanceresale.com

Ladies "can find some lovely things" at this designer consignment store; but getting "a good deal" can be "hit-or-miss", and the "packed-to-the-gills" premises is "most unorganized", so some say this resale shop's "not worth the bother, with so many others" on the UES.

SEE Eyewear

-	-	-	M

W Village | 312 Bleecker St. (bet. Barrow & Grove Sts.) | 1 to Christopher St./
Sheridan Sq. | 212-989-7060 | www.seeeyewear.com

Ciao, high-ticket logo-splashed eyewear, hello, über-stylish, no-name specs – thanks to the arrival of this farsighted Michigan-based chain link on Bleecker Street, the hipoisie can focus on finding chic frames with an upmarket look at, gulp, affordable prices; designed by a covey of creative talents from Europe's top frame houses, the tightly edited collection ranges from aviators to wraparounds to rhinestone-speckled celebutante shades, all displayed on easy-access shelving.

	QUALITY	DISPLAY	SERVICE	COST

Seigo

▽ 28 | 26 | 27 | E

NEW **E 40s** | 762 Third Ave. (47th St.) | 4/5/6/7/S to 42nd St./ Grand Central | 212-308-3008

E 80s | 1242 Madison Ave. (bet. 89th & 90th Sts.) | 4/5/6 to 86th St. | 212-534-6275

E 90s | 1248 Madison Ave. (90th St.) | 4/5/6 to 86th St. | 212-987-0191

Their "limited-edition ties" and bow ties "make the man" maintain mavens of these Madison Avenue mainstays (with a new Third Avenue branch) who more likely than knot find a "superb selection" of "very beautiful, handmade" Asian silk neckwear in "inviting patterns" "so unique they could be framed when not worn"; for "one-of-a-kind handbags" and "interesting fashion jewelry" loop back to its ladies' accessories offshoot a few doors down.

Seize sur Vingt

25 | 23 | 20 | E

NoLita | 243 Elizabeth St. (bet. Houston & Prince Sts.) | N/R/W to Prince St. | 212-343-0476 | www.16sur20.com

"You'll feel like you're at a fancy tailor in London" at this NoLita shop, which provides "gorgeous bespoke shirts" that are custom-made in Egyptian cottons for the "hipster set", along with "spectacular" men's and women's suits, handmade Italian shoes, seven fold ties, cuff links and leather driving gloves; still, a handful huff that the staff is "standoffish, leaving inexperienced customers confused" – "maybe if you're anorexic and rich they'll look at you."

Selia Yang Ⓜ

▽ 26 | 23 | 18 | E

E Village | 324-328 E. Ninth St. (bet. 1st & 2nd Aves.) | L to 1st Ave. | 212-254-9073

TriBeCa | 71 Franklin St. (bet. B'way & Church St.) | 1 to Franklin St. | 212-941-9073 Ⓢ

www.seliayang.com

This "off-the-beaten"-wedding-path East Villager is the "ultimate for the downtown hipster bride with downtown hipster money" to burn as well as her entourage; the "gorgeous", "elegant" silk gowns "made for your special day" by the salon's owner are "unique", reflecting her "great fashion sense"; but while some praise the "one-on-one" attention, others "expected a more service-friendly" environment; N.B. the younger TriBeCa shop, which is by appointment only, sells cocktail dresses and gowns.

Selima Optique

27 | 24 | 22 | E

E 70s | 899 Madison Ave. (bet. 72nd & 73rd Sts.) | 6 to 77th St. | 212-988-6690

NoLita | 25 Prince St. (bet. Elizabeth & Mott Sts.) | N/R/W to Prince St. | 212-334-8484 ◗

SoHo | 59 Wooster St. (Broome St.) | C/E to Spring St. | 212-343-9490 ◗

Sucre ◗

W Village | 357 Bleecker St. (bet. Charles & W. 10th Sts.) | 1 to Christopher St./Sheridan Sq. | 212-352-1640

www.selimaoptique.com

"Brilliant" designer Selima Salaun offers "colorful, funky and individual" spectacles and shades at her growing eyewear empire where the "stars go to get focused" in a "party atmosphere"; the staff "really cares" (though some surveyors squint at "ditzy service"), and "if your pocketbook is up to the challenge" you'll emerge sporting the "most unusual glasses in town"; N.B. now called Sucre, the West Village branch also sells clothing and accessories.

☒ Sephora ◑

25 | **24** | **19** | **M**

E 40s | 597 Fifth Ave. (bet. 48th & 49th Sts.) | B/D/F/V to 47-50th Sts./Rockefeller Ctr. | 212-980-6534 | 877-737-4672 | www.sephora.com
Additional locations throughout the NY area

This "addictive" "candy shop for beauty junkies" offers over 100 brands (there's "something for every zit, wrinkle, stretch mark and split end"), and each has "try-before-you-buy" testers, making the chain "a great place to play" with products that range from the "reasonable" to the "pricey"; the walls are lined with men's and women's fragrances, along with tooth whiteners and brighteners – hey, they don't call it "the mother ship" of makeup for nothing.

Sergio Rossi

26 | **–** | **21** | **VE**

E 50s | 694 Fifth Ave. (bet. 54th & 55th Sts.) | E/V to 5th Ave./53rd St. | 212-956-3303 | www.sergiorossi.com

For "hugely stylish" footwear of the "utmost quality", hit this transplanted Midtown "winner" with a "sweet" staff; scoop up "godlike boots", the "best stilettos" and "sexy" sandals, plus edgy wingtips, lizard loafers and the like for men, all designed by Edmundo Castillo and team; fetishists pay a bundle for "naughty shoes that never leave the apartment – the bedroom for that matter!" while on-the-towners "always find something for special occasions."

Seven New York

▽ **26** | **22** | **19** | **E**

SoHo | 110 Mercer St. (bet. Prince & Spring Sts.) | N/R/W to Prince St. | 646-654-0156 | www.sevennewyork.com

Fashion cultists recognize the esoteric lineup at this ultramodernist SoHo provocateur where international indie designers like Raf Simons from Belgium, Germany's Bernhard Willhelm, celebrity favorite Jeremy Scott and Antwerp's Christian Wijnants are procured for hipsters of both sexes along with jeans from on-trend labels like April 77 and Ksubi; just note that these vanguard looks demand an adventurous spirit, a skinny bod and a fat wallet.

17 at 17 Thrift Shop ☒

18 | **15** | **14** | **M**

Flatiron | 17 W. 17th St. (5th Ave.) | 4/5/6/L/N/Q/R/W to 14th St./Union Sq. | 212-727-5716

"Like most thrifts, it can be hit-or-miss" at this store whose proceeds benefit the UJA-Federation of NY and Gilda's Club; "when it's hot, it's hot" with "bargains on goodies", including womenswear in a "spectrum of styles" and "high-end" costume jewelry, but "when it's not", it suffers from a "not-very-helpful staff", "dowdy" wares and prices that seem "expensive" next to "others on Thrift Shop Row" in the Flatiron District.

☒ S. Feldman Housewares

25 | **17** | **24** | **M**

E 90s | 1304 Madison Ave. (92nd St.) | 6 to 96th St. | 212-289-3961 | 800-359-8558 | www.wares2u.com

"They sold your toaster to your mom before you were born" joke jesters about this eclectic, "old-fashioned" Upper East Sider dating back to 1929 that's still going strong for housewares like cooking equipment, "unique" tabletop accessories from Alessi, Mrs. Meyer's cleaning products and Miele vacuums; "friendly and helpful" service and "free delivery" make it a particular "must at Christmastime" for many.

Sharper Image
21 | 22 | 19 | E

SoHo | 98 Greene St. (bet. Prince & Spring Sts.) | N/R/W to Prince St. | 917-237-0221

Seaport | Pier 17 | 89 South St. (Fulton St.) | 2/3/4/5/A/C/J/M/Z to Fulton St./B'way/Nassau | 212-693-0477 ◐

W 40s | Rockefeller Ctr. | 50 Rockefeller Ctr. (bet. 5th & 6th Aves.) | B/D/F/V to 47-50th Sts./Rockefeller Ctr. | 646-557-0861 ◐

W 50s | 10 W. 57th St. (bet. 5th & 6th Aves.) | F to 57th St. | 212-265-2550 ◐
800-344-4444 | www.sharperimage.com

"Not your basic electronics stores", these "gadget marts" are "fun-to-explore" just to "get a buzz" "fiddling" with the "latest" "wonderful whatchamacallits", and you might just leave with "nifty" "novelties" "you never thought you'd buy" but suddenly "can't live without" (like that robotic floor vac); still, some cynics slam the "space-age prices" and claim the "cutting-edge products" are mostly "smoke and mirrors."

Sherle Wagner International ⍟
- | - | - | VE

E 60s | 300 E. 62nd St. (2nd Ave.) | 4/5/6/F/N/R/W to 59th St./Lexington Ave. | 212-758-3300 | www.sherlewagner.com

Considered by some to be the "Rolls-Royce of bathroom" plumbing accessories, this plummy purveyor, established in 1945, provides opulent hand-painted or gold-trimmed basins, fixtures, taps, tiles, lighting and linens at its East 60s showroom; the "total collection can be a bit much", but most people could probably only afford a crystal soap dish or two anyway, since prices are shattering.

Shin Choi ◐⍟
- | - | - | E

SoHo | 119 Mercer St. (bet. Prince & Spring Sts.) | N/R/W to Prince St. | 212-625-9202 | www.shinchoi.com

For a full-on SoHo shopping experience, spacious loft space, cool vibe and all, duck into this Mercer Street standby and peruse Korean-born designer Choi's lustrous lineup; the womenswear is "understated, but flattering", ranging from special-occasion suits and sumptuous cashmeres to sexy jeans – even visitors who cry "they're out of my price range" commend the "well-styled outfits."

Shirt Store, The ⍟
22 | 18 | 22 | E

E 40s | 51 E. 44th St. (Vanderbilt Ave.) | 4/5/6/7/S to 42nd St./Grand Central | 212-557-8040 | 800-289-2744 | www.shirtstore.com

With shirt boxes stacked to the ceiling, the name really says it all as businessmen flock to this "one-stop" for all their needs at its "convenient location near Grand Central"; it's easy to nab the right fit from the 70 different ready-made sizes of "quality" button-downs, or opt for a "custom" job; P.S. "they can make you feel important by having your initials sewn on" whatever you buy.

Shoe Box ◐
23 | 19 | 17 | E

E 70s | 1349 Third Ave. (77th St.) | 6 to 77th St. | 212-535-9615

Murray Hill | 537 Third Ave. (36th St.) | 6 to 33rd St. | 212-937-5750

NEW W 70s | 2151 Broadway (75th St.) | 1/2/3 to 72nd St. | 212-877-2846
800-320-7463 | www.shoptheshoebox.com

"Followed them from Long Island" to Manhattan reveal loyalists who salute this shoe trio as a big-city "favorite"; "my heart races every time I" eye the "excellent selection" of "better quality" "designer" footwear from the likes of Marc Jacobs, Sigerson Morrison and Vaneli – "this is one busy store"; if a few fume "service is pushy", Box boosters believe they're "always friendly" and turn the other heel because the "fun" "merchandise keeps coming."

NEW Shoe Market ◑

18	17	17	M

Williamsburg | 160 N. Sixth St. (Bedford Ave.) | Brooklyn | L to Bedford Ave. | 718-388-8495

"Amazing" fashion-forward shoes for men, women and kids without the steep price tag – that's the gambit that places Mini Minimarket's new Williamsburg sidekick at the top of bargainistas' must-shop list; green curtains, comfy chairs and a "super-friendly" staff create a laid-back setting for trying on kicks from names generally not often "found in other local" shops, like Jeffrey Campbell, Sven clogs, Matiko and Tretorn.

Shoe Mine Ⓜ

-	-	-	E

Park Slope | 463 Seventh Ave. (bet. 16th St. & Windsor Pl.) | Brooklyn | F to 7th Ave. | 718-369-2624 | www.shoemine.com

Footwear fiends dig the "large selection" of way-funky shoes from names like Frye and Kors by Michael Kors showcased in this silver-ceilinged Park Slope haunt; relax on the leather ottomans and contemplate the many splendors of hand-painted clogs from Holland and Switzerland and feminine finds from Chie Mihara and Repetto, then pick up unusual womenswear and accessories to go with; N.B. Monday by appointment only.

Shoe New York, The

∇ 24	23	21	E

NoLita | 262 Mott St. (bet. Houston & Prince Sts.) | 6 to Spring St. | 212-226-7366 | www.theshoeny.com

After creating a sensation with his women's footwear at his shop The Shoe, located in Chongdamdong, the avant-garde enclave of Seoul, Korean star Jae-min Lee brought his vision to the Manhattan market, opening this "chic" NoLita "hot spot"; the edgy emporium features his brightly colored, "fashion-forward" styles, plus bags, belts and clothing from other lines; N.B. you can also order versions with customized heels.

Shoofly

∇ 26	21	19	E

TriBeCa | 42 Hudson St. (bet. Duane & Thomas Sts.) | 1/2/3 to Chambers St. | 212-406-3270 | www.shooflynyc.com

A favorite stomping ground of mini-stylehounds-in-training, this "fabulous" TriBeCa tot shop has laced up a loyal following by stocking "funky" footwear from Europe's premier labels, among them Buckle My Shoe and Aster; the accessorizing action doesn't end with the shoes: there's also an "interesting" array of "great tights" and hair tchotchkes.

Shooz ◑

19	18	20	M

Chelsea | 128 Seventh Ave. (bet. 17th & 18th Sts.) | 1 to 18th St. | 212-727-7446

"Gotta get my Shooz" gush groupies of this Chelsea standby, which stocks "sassy shoes for everyone" from laid-back labels, including Dansko, El Naturalista and United Nude, along with what may be the "best collection of Wellies this side of the pond"; the "helpful", "knowledgeable staff" is sure to send you out the door stylishly shod and with "comfortable feet" to boot.

	QUALITY	DISPLAY	SERVICE	COST

Shop
▽ 20 | 23 | 21 | E

LES | 105 Stanton St. (Ludlow St.) | F/V to Lower East Side/2nd Ave. |
212-375-0304 | iloveshop.com

It may feel like you're visiting your "über-trendy, Lower East Side-
dwelling older sister's closet", with a "few surprises thrown in" like
Siwy jeans, tops from 3.1 Philip Lim and "handmade items by indie
designers" like Sass & Bide at this girlie boutique; the "fun stuff" also
includes "groovy jewelry", lingerie and bags, plus a "no-attitude staff."

Shvitz ●
- | - | - | E

SoHo | 128 Thompson St. (bet. Houston & Prince Sts.) | C/E to Spring St. |
212-982-9465 | www.shvitznyc.com

Female fashionistas who like their loungewear on the luxury side visit
this small, sweet-as-icing SoHo boutique, whose pink/silver/white decor
is like a little girl's dream boudoir (there's even a pink Mac) – all the
better to offset the bright togs by the likes of Juicy, Jet and PRIMP that fill
the cool-and-cute requirement to a tee, tank or sweatsuit; buyers can
also order up crystallized monograms (on the store-brand clothes).

Sicis ⊠
▽ 25 | 25 | 21 | E

SoHo | 470 Broome St. (Greene St.) | 6 to Spring St. | 212-965-4100 |
www.sicis.com

"Great place and space" enthuse admirers of this 13,000-sq.-ft. SoHo
showcase for a long-standing manufacturer of Italian mosaics; "imaginative", "impeccably designed and executed" tiles in glass, marble
and metal are displayed in a striking three-story landmark building
with futuristic decor.

Sid's
▽ 21 | 16 | 20 | M

Downtown | 345 Jay St. (Willoughby St.) | Brooklyn | A/C/F to Jay St./
Borough Hall | 718-875-2259

Skip the "hassle" of the big guns and head to this "classic local" in
Downtown Brooklyn – it's the "kind of hardware store you could spend
all day in", staffed with people hardwired to "help you"; no wonder
DIYers are hooked – they cut wood in the lumberyard, and stock "every
kind of nail, light bulb" and garden tool under the sun.

Sigerson Morrison
25 | 23 | 19 | E

NEW **E 70s** | 985 Madison Ave. (76th St.) | 6 to 77th St. | 212-734-2100
NoLita | 28 Prince St. (Mott St.) | 6 to Spring St. | 212-219-3893
www.sigersonmorrison.com

Urban "chic" rules at designers Kari Sigerson and Miranda Morrison's
minimalist mecca in NoLita as well as their new haunt nestled near the
Carlyle Hotel, both proffering "perfect shoes" for "stylish" gamines "in
every color of the rainbow"; cultists covet the "understated cool" aesthetic, stocking up on "kitten heels", "amazing flats", "pointy-toed"
boots and "edgy" bags; sure, it's "pricey", but if you're serious about
your SMs, snap up the "pair you want before it goes on sale", otherwise it "will be long gone."

Signoria ⊠
25 | 23 | 22 | E

E 60s | 764 Madison Ave. (bet. 65th & 66th Sts.) | 6 to 68th St. |
212-639-1121 | www.signoria.com

At its Madison Avenue outpost, this long-standing, family-owned firm
from Florence furnishes "very fancy" linens for both the bed and table

that some wags wager are "too nice to use"; other "good quality items" include towels and bath mats.

ⓩ Simon Pearce

27 | 25 | 23 | E

E 50s | 500 Park Ave. (59th St.) | 4/5/6/F/N/R/W to 59th St./ Lexington Ave. | 212-421-8801 | www.simonpearce.com

"Solid", "simple and functional" glass like barware, bowls, lamps, cake plates and candlesticks make for good gifts say supporters of this Park Avenue purveyor that also offers "unique" inscribed pottery and engraved items; respondents remark on the "uncompromising quality" (even "the seconds are worth checking out"), and are thankful for "prices that don't make you fearful of using" the pieces.

ⓩ Simon's Hardware & Bath 🖻

26 | 21 | 19 | E

Gramercy | 421 Third Ave. (bet. 29th & 30th Sts.) | 6 to 28th St. | 212-532-9220

NEW LIC | 51-17 35th St. (Gale Ave.) | Queens | 7 to 33rd St. | 718-706-7636

888-274-6667 | www.simonshardwareandbath.com

There are "no hammers" at this Gramercy stalwart (with a new Long Island City cousin) - just a "superb selection" of "gorgeous bathroom fixtures", shower systems, tiles, door and cabinet hardware for "every knob and handle in your apartment", all "artistically displayed"; if a handful huff that "service is sometimes a challenge" and pout about "stratospheric prices", those who've been Simon-ized declare "if you're doing home improvement, stop here" – "they have the best of everything", so "it's priced accordingly."

Sir

- | - | - | E

NEW NoLita | 396 Broome St. (bet. Centre & Mulberry Sts.) | 6 to Spring St. | 212-226-3559

Boerum Hill | 360 Atlantic Ave. (bet. Bond & Hoyt Sts.) | Brooklyn | A/C/G to Hoyt/Schermerhorn Sts. | 718-643-6877

www.sirbrooklyn.com

Gamine mademoiselles like Kate Hudson who prefer their threads "hip, but not self-consciously so" amble over to this two-room Boerum Hill shop (or its new NoLita sidekick) where "promising designer" Joanna Baum, a R.I.S.D. grad, peddles her vintage-y jackets, filmy bias-cut dresses and "wonderfully tactile" washed-silk blouses; complete the look with jewelry from co-owner Nicole Rowars' Shee line, plus cool-girl bags and shoes.

Sisley ●

20 | 20 | 18 | M

G Village | 753 Broadway (8th St.) | 6 to Astor Pl. | 212-979-2537

W 60s | The Shops at Columbus Circle, Time Warner Ctr. | 10 Columbus Circle, 2nd fl. (60th St. at B'way) | 1/A/B/C/D to 59th St./Columbus Circle | 212-823-9567

www.sisley.com

You "feel like you're sipping Campari and soda in Capri" upon donning the "sexy Euro styles" at Benetton's slightly "naughty cousins", each a "one-stop shop" for guys and gals seeking "work gear that turns into night gear"; "if you're looking for sophisticated" staples "at fair prices" that are "a nice diversion from what everyone else is wearing", you may find them at these "simple settings" in the Village and the Time Warner Center, manned by an "attentive" crew.

Skechers ●

19	18	15	M

Garment District | 140 W. 34th St. (bet. 6th & 7th Aves.) | B/D/F/N/
Q/R/V/W to 34th St./Herald Sq. | 646-473-0490
W 40s | 3 Times Sq. (42nd St., bet. B'way & 6th Ave.) | 1/2/3/7/N/
Q/R/S/W to 42nd St./Times Sq. | 212-869-9550
Astoria | 31-01 Steinway St. (31st Ave.) | Queens | G/R/V to 46th St. |
718-204-0040
Elmhurst | Queens Pl. | 88-01 Queens Blvd. (bet. 55th & 56th Aves.) |
Queens | G/R/V to Grand Ave./Newtown | 718-699-2773
800-678-5019 | www.skechers.com

"The go-to spot for funky" footwear, this "friendly" chainster has got
your back when it comes to filling the "what's-in-style-at-reasonable-
prices" niche agree "tweens", "teens" and twentysomethings; but while
fans find the "walking-on-clouds" soles make for "happy feet", cynics
cool their heels elsewhere, lamenting this outfit with "earsplitting music"
and "strange" offerings is "long past having any hip factor."

Sleep ●

▽			
▽ 22	20	19	E

Williamsburg | 110 N. Sixth St. (bet. Berry St. & Wythe Ave.) | Brooklyn |
L to Bedford Ave. | 718-384-3211 | www.sleepbrooklyn.com

Everything to give you sweet dreams is the draw at this Williamsburg
bedding resource; the split-level, spiral staircase space has a boudoir
feel, with luxe lingerie and sleepwear from the likes of Elle
Macpherson and Princess Tam-Tam cohabiting with "unique"
Egyptian cotton duvet and sheet "ensembles"; "it's an excellent place
to spend any cash weighing your pocket down."

Slope Sports

-	-	-	M

Park Slope | 70 Seventh Ave. (bet. Berkeley & Lincoln Pls.) | Brooklyn |
B/Q to 7th Ave. | 718-230-4686 | www.slopesports.com

Though the name might imply skiing, this small shop for runners, cyclists, walkers and outdoor enthusiasts takes its name from its Park
Slope environs; stop in before clocking time on the Prospect Park track
and purchase performance apparel from labels like Hind, Pearl Izomi
and Sugoi, plus sneakers from major players like Asics and Brooks.

Smiley's ☒⇗

16	14	18	I

Woodhaven | 92-06 Jamaica Ave. (bet. 92nd St. & Woodhaven Blvd.) |
Queens | J/Z to Woodhaven Blvd. | 718-849-9873 | www.smileysyarns.com

Bargainistas salute this Queens stitchers stop, renowned since 1935
for its "cheap, and I mean *cheap*, prices" on a wide array of "mid-
to low-end" "synthetics and blends"; "special sales" often make it "worth
the trip" to Woodhaven ("check online" first), though fiber snobs sniff
"you get what you pay for" at this "acrylic nightmare"; P.S. "you can
make out like a bandit" at the annual 'Yarn Riots' held at area hotels.

Smith & Hawken ●

24	25	20	E

SoHo | 394 W. Broadway (bet. Broome & Spring Sts.) | C/E to Spring St. |
212-925-1190 | 800-776-3336 | www.smithandhawken.com

Root around "for gifts for your favorite gardener" at this "perfect"
SoHo shop offering plants, pots, bulbs, books and "last-a-longtime
tools"; fans of the brand also "love the teak furniture" and "big selection of Christmas ornaments and garlands", all sold by a "helpful
staff"; city dwellers sigh the experience "makes you want to move to
the suburbs and have a yard."

| | QUALITY | DISPLAY | SERVICE | COST |

Smith on Sullivan Ⓜ
▽ 20 | 19 | 18 | E

G Village | 171 Sullivan St. (bet. Bleecker & W. Houston Sts.) | A/B/C/D/E/F/V to W: 4th St. | 212-529-2040

"Very funky" fashions concur iconoclasts drawn to Karen Smith's brick-walled atelier on the SoHo-Village border; the owner-designer/sculptor creates her collection on-site, frequently adding new, "inventive" designs, like recycled handcrafted cashmere and wool sweaters, "flattering", free-floating printed dresses and "happening headbands" to the madcap mix; you won't see yourself coming or going on Sullivan – or anywhere else – in fact, some swear these creations are way "ahead of their time."

Ⓩ Smythson of Bond Street Ⓢ
28 | 27 | 24 | VE

W 50s | 4 W. 57th St. (5th Ave.) | F to 57th St. | 212-265-4573 | 866-769-8476 | www.smythson.com

For "bespoke stationery to say 'I've made it'", "luxurious" leather accessories like agendas, albums, passport covers, jewelry boxes and organizers with "unique color options" and gold and silver stamping, along with "luxurious" bags, briefcases and wallets, Anglophiles head to this "English import" on West 57th Street; needless to say, the holder of four royal warrants exclusively purveys products that go for a king's ransom; N.B. the Decor score may not reflect a recent refurb.

NEW Soapology ❶
22 | 23 | 20 | M

W Village | 67 Eighth Ave. (bet. Greenwich Ave. & W. 13th St.) | A/C/E/L to 14th St./8th Ave. | 212-255-7627

"I adore this store" bubble "soap lovers" who are drawn into this new West Village bath and body boutique, a haven for the scent-sensitive since the natural and/or organic products come fragrance free as well as with the option of adding a choice of over 30 aromas; the practical may point out that "Dove gets me just as clean", but sybarites salute this "breath of fresh air" at moderate prices.

SOHO Ⓢ Ⓜ
▽ 20 | 18 | 16 | E

NoLita | 228 Mott St. (bet. Prince & Spring Sts.) | 6 to Spring St. | 212-219-3734 | www.sohoenamel.com

At this small husband-and-wife-owned NoLita jewelry shop, the ancient Etruscan art of enameling is given an elegant contemporary edge when a "unique" collection of handmade bangles, earrings and necklaces is textured to look like marble, snakeskin, leopard spots or tiger stripes, then dusted with gold and dressed up with diamonds.

Solstice
- | - | - | E

E 40s | 500 Fifth Ave. (42nd St.) | 7 to 5th Ave. | 212-730-2500
SoHo | 107 Spring St. (Mercer St.) | 6 to Spring St. | 212-219-3940 ❶
W 60s | The Shops at Columbus Circle, Time Warner Ctr. | 10 Columbus Circle, 3rd fl. (60th St. at B'way) | 1/A/B/C/D to 59th St./Columbus Circle | 212-823-9590 ❶
866-246-9043 | www.solsticestores.com

With over 1,000 styles to choose from, you're guaranteed a "great selection" of sunglasses at this "pleasant" chain specializing in classic and cutting-edge designers; the "friendly" staff can help you find a fit, both facially and "fashion"-wise, in a "welcoming" atmosphere.

Some Odd Rubies ◐

	QUALITY	DISPLAY	SERVICE	COST
	-	-	-	E

LES | 151 Ludlow St. (bet. Rivington & Stanton Sts.) | F/V to Lower East Side/ 2nd Ave. | 212-353-1736 | www.someoddrubies.com

In "tiny" Lower East Side digs, this "seriously cool store" owned by actress Summer Phoenix and her "nice" friends, Odessa Whitmire and Ruby Canner, sparkles with a carefully "edited" selection of retro shoes and jewelry; the "great goods" also spotlight reworked vintage must-haves, some of which "look way more expensive than they are", plus some new pieces from local designers.

Something Else

	QUALITY	DISPLAY	SERVICE	COST
	23	21	20	E

Bensonhurst | 2051 86th St. (bet. 20th & 21st Aves.) | Brooklyn | D/M to 20th Ave. | 718-372-1900
Boerum Hill | 144 Smith St. (Bergen St.) | Brooklyn | F/G to Bergen St. | 718-643-3204 ◐
Park Slope | 208 Fifth Ave. (Union St.) | Brooklyn | M/R to Union St. | 718-230-4063 ◐

"Bensonhurst babes [and dudes] know how to work it with style" and so do Boerum Hill and Park Slope trendseekers hot for premium denim from Joe's Jeans, AG Adriano Goldschmied and Citizens for Humanity and "great" pieces from labels like Ben Sherman, Free People and Triple Five Soul; add in "cool" Adidas and Puma "sneaks" and Dolce Vita shoes and you've got a shopping experience that's, like, wow, something else.

Sonia Rykiel ⌷

	QUALITY	DISPLAY	SERVICE	COST
	26	24	22	VE

E 70s | 849 Madison Ave. (bet. 70th & 71st Sts.) | 6 to 68th St. | 212-396-3060 | www.soniarykiel.com

Style-savvy surveyors know "why French women are thin" – it's so they can slip into the "inventive" knits from this venerable Parisienne, whose women's collection of cashmere coats and silken sweaters is instantly wearable; while some find the attitude in the East 70s boutique "a little intimidating", most "love every item", "including the designer fragrances."

Sons + Daughters

	QUALITY	DISPLAY	SERVICE	COST
	-	-	-	E

E Village | 35 Ave. A (bet. 2nd & 3rd Sts.) | F/V to Lower East Side/ 2nd Ave. | 212-253-7797 | www.sonsanddaughtersinc.com

Wander off the beaten path to this refreshing East Village emporium, where you can easily whittle away hours exploring the eclectic selection of organic and fair-trade clothing, toys and other wares originating from far corners of the globe; it's also a great place to get "nifty gifts you don't see in other stores", like BRIO trains, vintage dollhouses and made-to-order Moroccan slippers.

⎅ Sony Style

	QUALITY	DISPLAY	SERVICE	COST
	26	26	18	E

E 50s | Sony Plaza | 550 Madison Ave. (bet. 55th & 56th Sts.) | E/V to 5th Ave./53rd St. | 212-833-8800 | www.sonystyle.com

"This is what an electronics store should look like" testify techheads taken with this "beautiful flagship store" in the East 50s, "a marvelous showcase" for all the "latest versions" of Sony's "coolest" equipment (about which the salespeople "know all the ins and outs"); though it's "entertaining" to "play with the new and fun products", deal-finders feel it's "strictly for browsing", saying you can "buy it cheaper elsewhere."

| | QUALITY | DISPLAY | SERVICE | COST |

Sophia Eugene ◐
— | — | — | M

W Village | 37 Cornelia St. (Bleecker St.) | A/B/C/D/E/F/V to W. 4th St. | 212-488-2124 | www.sophiaeugene.com

West Villagers applaud couturier Christopher Crawford's teensy atelier with its ornate dressing room fashioned by a Broadway set designer; the in-store drama begins with his eclectic print separates, continues with kittenish sweaters and finishes with a few fancy frocks from his Christopher Deane collection at twice-yearly sample sales; tucked in a corner, but not to be upstaged, is vintage costume jewelry that's fit to be tried.

Soula Ⓜ
— | — | — | M

Boerum Hill | 185 Smith St. (bet. Warren & Wyckoff Sts.) | Brooklyn | F/G to Bergen St. | 718-834-8423
NEW **Park Slope** | 184 Fifth Ave. (bet. Berkeley & Lincoln Pls.) | Brooklyn | M/R to Union St. | 718-230-0038
www.soulashoes.com

A "treat for the feet on Smith Street" – and now Park Slope's Fifth Avenue too – this "welcoming" duo owned by a former Barneys NY buyer "sparkles" with men's and women's "shoes you just have to have" from labels like Audley, Cydwoq, Frye and Tretorn and bags from Orla Kiely; the "merchandise is as hip as it gets", plus the designs "value comfort as much as style" and they're all displayed on open wooden shelves for easy browsing.

⊠ Sound by Singer
27 | 22 | 21 | VE

Union Sq | 18 E. 16th St. (bet. 5th Ave. & Union Sq. W.) | 4/5/6/L/N/Q/R/W to 14th St./Union Sq. | 212-924-8600 | www.soundbysinger.com

The "audiophile's heaven" on earth, this "terrific place" in Union Square boasts 10 showrooms decked out in such "interesting lines" as Arcam, Burmester and Zanden and staffed by "people [who] really care about sound"; "those who can afford it" report that the "high-end products and service" blow away the competition "by a large margin", while the rest of us can always "go in and drool."

Sound City Ⓧ
— | — | — | M

W 40s | 58 W. 45th St. (bet. 5th & 6th Aves.) | B/D/F/V to 47-50th Sts./Rockefeller Ctr. | 212-575-0210 | www.soundcityny.com

There's no denying that this Midtown electronics emporium in the West 40s has the goods, whether you want to heat things up with the newest speakers or cool down with a remote-controlled air conditioner; true, it may be topsy-turvy and garishly lit, but there's a reason it's known for "great bargains."

Space Kiddets Ⓧ
26 | 18 | 22 | E

Flatiron | 26 E. 22nd St. (bet. B'way & Park Ave.) | N/R/W to 23rd St. | 212-420-9878 | www.spacekiddets.com

For the "coolest kids' clothes this side of hip" from labels that fashionistas-in-training "want so badly", take off for this Flatiron emporium, home to one of the "most original collections" under the sun including "extra-special" rocker tees and toy robots; sure, it's "jam-packed" – but the "service is beyond expectation", "sales are excellent" and your offspring may be the most "imaginatively" dressed "tyke on the block."

	QUALITY	DISPLAY	SERVICE	COST

NEW Space.NK apothecary
25 | 25 | 21 | E

SoHo | 99 Greene St. (Spring St.) | 6 to Spring St. | 212-941-4200
W 70s | 217 Columbus Ave. (70th St.) | 1/2/3/B/C to 72nd St. |
212-362-2840 ●
www.spacenk.com

"Beauty aficionados rejoice" at the arrival of this "cool" new "clean and modern" "British import", an "absolute treasure trove" in SoHo and the Upper West Side for "hard-to-find" "cult European brands" of cosmetics and face, bath and body lotions and potions like Eve Lom cleanser; "packaging so pretty" also ensures that the "posh" products make for great gifts.

Space107 ⑤Ⓜ
- | - | - | E

W Village | 107 Horatio St. (bet. Washington & West Sts.) | A/C/E/L to 14th St./8th Ave. | 212-206-7599 | www.space107.com

Redesigned furniture originals from the 1920s–1970s are displayed in vignettes throughout the gallerylike setting of this West Village space, giving it the air of an impeccable designerati's digs; owner Amir Dinkha starts with pieces from big names like Karl Springer, Paul Evans and Milo Baughman and then polishes, refinishes or reupholsters them with unique and poshly priced results.

Spence-Chapin Thrift Shops
16 | 14 | 12 | M

E 80s | 1473 Third Ave. (bet. 83rd & 84th Sts.) | 4/5/6 to 86th St. | 212-737-8448
E 90s | 1850 Second Ave. (bet. 95th & 96th Sts.) | 6 to 96th St. | 212-426-7643
www.spence-chapin.org

From silk scarves to furniture to mens- and womenswear "finds", "classy castoffs can be yours" at this "cluttery" charity-store pair on the Upper East Side – and often "for very little, especially when they have sales"; pity that the "staff is sometimes more busy socializing with each other than focusing on clients."

Spoiled Brats ●
▽ 24 | 19 | 25 | M

W 40s | 340 W. 49th St. (bet. 8th & 9th Aves.) | C/E to 50th St. | 212-459-1615 | www.spoiledbratsnyc.com

Spoiled Hell's Kitchen Homo sapiens are hip to this "very service-oriented" pet store where the "great staff" "gets you whatever you want"; the "broad assortment" of "high-end, human-grade" food and "quirky" accessories may be a tad "pricey" for some, but the "shopping experience is enhanced by fragrant candles and soaps" that satisfy its "upscale" clientele; P.S. it also offers "good" kitty adoption assistance.

Sports Authority ●
17 | 14 | 11 | M

E 50s | 845 Third Ave. (51st St.) | 6 to 51st St. | 212-355-9725
Flatiron | 636 Sixth Ave. (19th St.) | 1 to 18th St. | 212-929-8971
Forest Hills | 73-25 Woodhaven Blvd. (Metropolitan Ave.) | Queens | G/R/V to 67th Ave. | 718-896-3826
Woodside | 51-30 Northern Blvd. (Newtown Rd.) | Queens | G/R/V to Northern Blvd. | 718-205-4075
888-801-9164 | www.thesportsauthority.com

"Big-box pickings mean" you'll find a "wide variety of sporting goods" from jerseys and athletic shoes to rackets and bats agree advocates of this athletic outfit; opponents opine that it "tries to be too many things" but instead "falls short" and leans toward the "middle-of-the-road"; even when "the products are there, the service isn't" always – "finding help is like going on a safari" through the "messy racks."

Spring Ⓜ
- | - | - | E

Dumbo | 126A Front St. (Jay St.) | Brooklyn | F to York St. | 718-222-1054 | www.spring3d.net

Part gallery, part spare showcase, this curated Dumbo loftspace traffics in "quirky, interesting" tchotchkes like piggy banks and rubberband vases as well as one-of-a-kind accessories, jewelry, light fixtures, paintings and tabletop items from emerging artists and designers; never mind that the "practicality factor" is sometimes minimal – each piece is high-concept, plus the owners' "hearts are in the right place."

ⓩ Spring Flowers
28 | 21 | 17 | VE

E 50s | 538 Madison Ave. (bet. 54th & 55th Sts.) | E/V to 5th Ave./ 53rd St. | 212-207-4606
E 60s | 1050 Third Ave. (62nd St.) | 6 to 68th St. | 212-758-2669
E 70s | 907 Madison Ave. (bet. 72nd & 73rd Sts.) | 6 to 68th St. | 212-717-8182
www.springflowerschildren.com

For your little "Cinderella's ball gown, a more perfect closet could not be found" believe boosters who throw bouquets to this East Side child-renswear chain, which sets the standard for special-occasion outfits with its "beautiful" "heirloom quality" party frocks and made-to-order flower-girl dresses and tot-sized tuxedos; still, a few thorny types tut "prices are not realistic" and service is "snobby."

NEW Sprout Home
▽ 25 | 23 | 21 | E

Williamsburg | 44 Grand St. (bet. Kent & Wythe Sts.) | Brooklyn | L to Bedford Ave. | 718-388-4440 | www.sprouthome.com

Nurture your nature instincts at this groundbreaking Williamsburg newcomer aimed at urban gardeners; the expansive brick-walled space boasts a green staircase and an outdoor space, the perfect modern landscape for displaying everything from rare ornamental trees and organic herbs and veggies to birdhouses and feeders, fun plant kits like the Eggling, stone furniture, faux wood planters made of resin and melamine plates for dining alfresco.

Staples ❶
19 | 16 | 13 | M

W 80s | 2248 Broadway (81st St.) | 1 to 79th St. | 212-712-9617 | 800-378-2753 | www.staples.com
Additional locations throughout the NY area

A "reliable workhorse" "for anything office-related", this "no-frills" "super-chain" "wins over" one-stop shoppers with its "breadth of merchandise" – from computers and printers to humble "paper clips and ballpoint pens purchased *en masse*" – as well as its "superb no-hassle returns policy"; still, those who say the "inattentive" staffers "seem like they were born yesterday" suggest you "stick with the online" option.

Star Struck ❶
20 | 17 | 17 | M

G Village | 47 Greenwich Ave. (bet. 6th & 7th Aves.) | 1/2/3 to 14th St. | 212-691-5357 | www.starstruckvintage.com

This "neighborhood classic" – it's been in the Village for nearly 30 years – is a crammed-to-the-gills vintage venue offering oldies but good-ies for men, women and kids, ranging from mid-'50s dresses to Western wear to "a good selection of ironic tees"; "like so many of these stores, it can be hit-or-miss", "but really worth it" if you grab a "great bargain."

Stefano Ricci ⊠

QUALITY	DISPLAY	SERVICE	COST
∇ 27	25	25	VE

E 50s | 407 Park Ave. (bet. 54th & 55th Sts.) | E/V to 5th Ave./53rd St. | 212-371-3901 | www.stefanoricci.com

"Feel like you've walked into a Stradivarius violin, lined with fragrant silks", glossy walnut woods and crocodile-upholstered furniture, when you enter this elite, "extravagant" East 50s men's store rooted in the Florentine tailoring tradition; the quality suiting, fine ties and glitzy accessories appeal to the "hip aristocrat", "mogul, sheik or pasha in every man"; you can bet "big bucks are required", but few there are who don't "find everything in this shop exactly to their liking."

Steinlauf & Stoller ⊠

QUALITY	DISPLAY	SERVICE	COST
-	-	-	M

Garment District | 239 W. 39th St. (bet. 7th & 8th Aves.) | 1/2/3/7/ N/Q/R/S/W to 42nd St./Times Sq. | 212-869-0321 | 877-869-0321 | www.steinlaufandstoller.com

"You'll want to enroll in FIT after a trip" to this Garment District notions mecca that seamsters seek out for its 1,000-plus tailoring aids including fastenings, pads, trims, threads and pieces of workroom equipment – but no fabric; the 60-year-old venue's old-fashioned vibe makes it feel like you're "stepping back in time", but you can also shop 21st-century-style via the website.

Stella Dallas ●

QUALITY	DISPLAY	SERVICE	COST
-	-	-	M

G Village | 218 Thompson St. (bet. Bleecker & W. 3rd Sts.) | A/B/C/ D/E/F/V to W. 4th St. | 212-674-0447

Ten Feet Single ●
(fka Stella Dallas)

Williamsburg | 285 N. Sixth St. (Meeker Ave.) | Brooklyn | G/L to Metropolitan Ave./Lorimer St. | 718-486-9482

"Long may she reign" cheer converts of this "quirky" queen of the vintage Village shops, which since 1970 has "specialized in women's apparel from the '40s and '50s" ("great for the domestic diva looking for a glam housedress and apron to match"); "reasonable prices keep 'em coming back" to explore the ever-changing stock boasting cowboy boots and pretty petticoats; Billyburg sibling Ten Feet Single traffics in some similar items, plus surfboards and guys' garb.

Stella Gialla ●

QUALITY	DISPLAY	SERVICE	COST
25	24	22	E

Glendale | 80-28 Cooper Ave. (bet. 80th St. & Metropolitan Ave.) | Queens | 718-894-0919 | www.stellagialla.com

"Queens got fashion!" exclaim fans of this "neighborhood hot spot", a "gem" of a boutique owned by two female FIT grads where you can find those "jeans that are sold out everywhere else", a "designer dress that won't bankrupt you", a hot handbag not carried in mainstream stores or the gals' own private-label looks; an "excellent" staff and a pretty pink vintage setting with beaded curtains add to its stellar status.

Stella McCartney

QUALITY	DISPLAY	SERVICE	COST
26	25	20	VE

Meatpacking | 429 W. 14th St. (bet. 9th & 10th Aves.) | A/C/E/L to 14th St./8th Ave. | 212-255-1556 | www.stellamccartney.com

If you're "reed thin", you'll fit right in at this "gorgeous", "fashionably trendy Meatpacking District" boutique, which offers pure "luxe for 'it'" girls" who hog the arty dressing rooms trying on the eponymous designer's "clean-lined" trousers, Savile Row–styled jackets and little sack dresses that "are the reason you ask for a raise"; while it's an "elevating experience" to visit, critics castigate the "slowest and strangest salespeople around."

Stephen Kahan 🏷️
▽ 27 | 25 | 25 | VE

E 60s | 25 E. 61st St. (Madison Ave.) | 4/5/6/F/N/R/W to 59th St./Lexington Ave. | 212-750-3456

Admirers of this long-standing Upper East Side shop site its "unbelievable jewels"; not at all surprising since the emphasis is on classic, signed estate pieces from leading lights like David Webb, Cartier, Van Cleef & Arpels, Chaumet, Tiffany and Bulgari, and all of them come at equally dazzling prices.

Stephen Russell 🏷️
27 | 25 | 24 | VE

E 70s | 970 Madison Ave. (76th St.) | 6 to 77th St. | 212-570-6900 | www.stephenrusselljewelry.com

"May all my future presents come from here" wish worshipers of this "so Madison Avenue, so lovely to look at" luxury jeweler where "exquisite" "things of beauty" run from about $1,500 to the millions and include rare Victorian and art deco period pieces and the house's signature Edwardian-style wedding bands and engagement rings.

Ⓩ Stereo Exchange ◐
26 | 20 | 21 | VE

NoHo | 627 Broadway (bet. Bleecker & Houston Sts.) | B/D/F/V to B'way/Lafayette St. | 212-505-1111 | www.stereoexchange.com

Techheads "looking for first-rate equipment", from speakers and turntables to "the best home-theater" components, say this NoHo electronics extravaganza is "forever ahead of its time", adding that "nobody can argue with the expertise" of the "smart, low-pressure salespeople"; even though the "prices are as high as the quality" of products offered, regulars recommend you at least "go to learn" and "converse with the jet set of the stereo world."

Sterling Place
- | - | - | E

Downtown | 363 Atlantic Ave. (bet. Bond & Hoyt Sts.) | Brooklyn | A/C/G to Hoyt/Schermerhorn Sts. | 718-797-5667
NEW Park Slope | 352 Seventh Ave. (bet. 10th & 11th Sts.) | Brooklyn | F to 7th Ave. | 718-499-4800
www.sterlingplace.com

Hit the home furnishings jackpot at this spacious Downtown Brooklyn standby and new Park Slope offshoot, both filled with well-crafted essentials, antiques, furniture and gizmos for the house, garden and office; gift everyone on your list with finds like French corkscrews, Laguiole cheese knifes or Chinese fortune sticks, add pizzazz to your living room with merino throws and satin pillows or express yourself with Italian leather journals and embossed note cards.

Ⓩ Steuben 🏷️
29 | 28 | 25 | VE

E 60s | 667 Madison Ave. (61st St.) | N/R/W to 5th Ave./59th St. | 212-752-1441 | 800-783-8236 | www.steuben.com

"When you want to be remembered", buy a gift from this "museumlike" East 60s store boasting "exquisitely crafted" "glass masterpieces" that include vases, bowls, barware, animals and apples;

admirers of the century-old source for "the best American crystal" croon about "class all the way" and cite "charming service", but caution that the pieces are "breakable and so is your bank account"; N.B. you can also purchase limited-edition works from select artists including noted sculptor Michele Oka Doner.

Steve Madden ● 16 | 17 | 15 | M

E 80s | 150 E. 86th St. (bet. Lexington & 3rd Aves.) | 4/5/6 to 86th St. | 212-426-0538
Garment District | 41 W. 34th St. (bet. 5th & 6th Aves.) | B/D/F/N/Q/R/V/W to 34th St./Herald Sq. | 212-736-3283
SoHo | 540 Broadway (bet. Prince & Spring Sts.) | N/R/W to Prince St. | 212-343-1800
Bayside | Bay Terrace Shopping Ctr. | 211-49 26th Ave. (bet. 2nd & 3rd Sts.) | Queens | 7 to Main St. | 718-224-4880
Queens Village | Queens Ctr. | 90-15 Queens Blvd. (bet. 57th & 59th Aves.) | Queens | R/V to Woodhaven Blvd. | 718-592-8580
Staten Island | Staten Island Mall | 2655 Richmond Ave. (bet. Platinum Ave. & Richmond Hill Rd.) | 718-494-6459
800-747-6233 | www.stevemadden.com

This "crazy, fast-paced" "teenybopper"-targeted chain "has its finger on the pulse of what hip young thangs want for traipsing around the city", be it "funky" platforms", boots with "tons of style" or moccasin-inspired loafers and the like for dudes; some styles may be "a little on the trashy side", but loads are "good to party in", and hey, they're so "reasonable" you "don't have worry if you'll ever wear them again!"

Steven ● 18 | 19 | 17 | M

NEW E 70s | 1333 Third Ave. (77th St.) | 6 to 77th St. | 212-288-8250
Garment District | 488 Seventh Ave. (36th St.) | 1/2/3/A/C/E to 34th St./Penn Station | 212-564-9254
SoHo | 529 Broadway (bet. Prince & Spring Sts.) | N/R/W to Prince St. | 212-431-6021
W Village | 355 Bleecker St. (bet. Charles & W. 10th Sts.) | 1 to Christopher St./Sheridan Sq. | 212-206-6842
www.stevemadden.com

The "large selection" of "funky", "good quality" shoes at this chain walks the "Steve Madden for grown-ups" line, and much like its better-known, teen-oriented sibling, it's "always über-crowded"; detractors quibble that it "tries too hard to be higher class", but instead falls short, turning out "sometimes uncomfortable" "middle-of-the-road" offerings that are neither "lowbrow" or "go-for-it" splurges.

Steven Alan 24 | 23 | 19 | E

TriBeCa | 103 Franklin St. (bet. Church St. & W. B'way) | 1 to Canal St. | 212-343-0692

Steven Alan annex

NoLita | 229 Elizabeth St. (bet. Houston & Prince Sts.) | 6 to Spring St. | 212-226-7482
W Village | 69 Eighth Ave. (W. 13th St.) | A/C/E/L to 14th St./8th Ave. | 212-242-2677

Steven Alan Outlet

W 80s | 465 Amsterdam Ave. (82nd St.) | 1 to 79th St. | 212-595-8451
www.stevenalan.com

"Brilliant auteur" Steven Alan curates "hip" his-and-hers collectibles from "emerging, offbeat, but accessible designers" at his "fashion landmark" in TriBeCa, an "urban general store" where Downtown-types scoop up house-label woven shirts along with "hot" looks from A.P.C., Geren Ford and Isabel Marant, Earnest Sewn jeans, Rachel Comey boots, "excellent jewelry" and Sharp face cream; the smaller NoLita and West Village annex shops are also "laid-back yet chic", showcasing those "great button-downs", while the Amsterdam Avenue outlet sells discounted merch.

☑ Stickley, Audi & Co.
28 | – | 24 | E

Chelsea | 207 W. 25th St. (7th Ave.) | 1/2/3 to 23rd St. | 212-337-0700 | www.stickley.com

While the emphasis at its showroom, in new Chelsea digs, is on "beautiful", "dark Mission-style" furniture made of "solid cherry or oak" and built "to last for the next 100 years", the Audi family also sells a "broad selection" of other lines like Craftsman Leather, as well as Oriental rugs; the "heirloom quality comes at prices to match", but some "good bargains" can be had at their sales.

☑ Stitches East ☒
26 | 22 | 17 | E

E 50s | Park Avenue Plaza | 55 E. 52nd St. (bet. Madison & Park Aves.) | 6 to 51st St. | 212-421-0112

Unexpectedly located "in an office building lobby", this "fancy" Eastside store is "worth finding"; its floor-to-ceiling cubbyholes contain an "excellent selection" of yarns (from basic to novelty), and the spacious room also stocks patterns, tools and needlepoint equipment; it's "pricey", though – "as warranted by its location" – and some surveyors sigh the "knowledgeable" staffers "could use a sense of humor."

☑ St. John
28 | 27 | 24 | VE

E 50s | 665 Fifth Ave. (53rd St.) | E/V to 5th Ave./53rd St. | 212-755-5252 | www.stjohnknits.com

"A pleasure to shop in", this spacious Fifth Avenue flagship for a 45-year-old label still sets the gold standard for "investment" clothes, with "classically timeless" knits whose "flattering", "easy fit" is "forgiving" even "when the pounds sneak up on you"; once seen as "going after the over-50 cruise crowd", the "styles have gotten younger" – and the signing of Angelina Jolie as the label's face in advertising campaigns should ramp up the "glitz" quotient.

St. Marks Sounds ●⊘
19 | 15 | 17 | I

E Village | 20 St. Marks Pl., 2nd fl. (bet. 2nd & 3rd Aves.) | 6 to Astor Pl. | 212-677-3444

Since 1979, this "classic used CD emporium" in the East Village has been attracting alt-finders with "obscure titles at great prices"; even if a handful sound off that its "heyday is past", more maintain this second-story "scavenger hunt's" "deep catalog" and "caring" staff make it a "must" – especially since they're now stocking vinyl again.

Straight from the Crate ●
13 | 9 | 13 | I

E 60s | 1114 First Ave. (61st St.) | 4/5/6/F/N/R/W to 59th St./Lexington Ave. | 212-838-8486

E 80s | 1251 Lexington Ave. (bet. 84th & 85th Sts.) | 4/5/6 to 86th St. | 212-717-4227

Flatiron | 50 W. 23rd St. (bet. 5th & 6th Aves.) | N/R/W to 23rd St. | 212-243-1844

(continued)

Straight from the Crate

Gramercy | 140 E. 14th St. (bet. Irving Pl. & 3rd Ave.) | 4/5/6/L/N/Q/R/W to 14th St./Union Sq. | 212-358-8575
Murray Hill | 464 Park Ave. S. (bet. 31st & 32nd Sts.) | 6 to 33rd St. | 212-725-5383
www.straightfromthecrate.com

This string of "super-cramped" and "super-cheap" shops offers a "good assortment" of "contemporary furnishings" – dressers, bookcases and shelving – that will "solve your storage or limited space issues"; but the worldly warn shop here only if "dorm-room style" is what you aspire to.

Strawberry ⚫   11 | 12 | 10 | I

E 40s | 129 E. 42nd St. (Lexington Ave.) | 4/5/6/7/S to 42nd St./Grand Central | 212-986-7030 | www.strawberrystores.com
Additional locations throughout the NY area

Calling "the young and on-the-go" to this budget chain where shoppers "rummage through" the racks in "cramped quarters" searching for "disposable" "trendy items for that weekend night out"; yes, you get what you pay for here, including "inexperienced clerks" and a "mess of clothes thrown on the floor", not to mention "onetime-wear" quality levels, but to most this doesn't matter much when you factor in the "cheapie prices."

Strider Records ⊠   - | - | - | M

G Village | 22 Jones St. (bet. Bleecker & W. 4th Sts.) | A/B/C/D/E/F/V to W. 4th St. | 212-675-3040

Platters matter at this "vintage" Greenwich Villager vaunted for its strictly vinyl vault of jazz, popular music, soul, R&B and rock 'n' roll; you'll find everything from Louis Armstrong 78s to Chuck Berry 45s to British Invasion and new wave LPs, and the staff will record your requests for rare "collectors' items."

⦿ String ⊠   27 | - | 24 | E

E 80s | 130 E. 82nd St. (bet. Lexington & Park Aves.) | 4/5/6 to 86th St. | 212-288-9276 | www.stringyarns.com

"The Bergdorf's of knitting stores", this recently relocated Upper East Side "jewel" specializes in the "highest-quality materials" (including what may well be New York's "best selection of cashmere and other luxury yarns"); it's not surprising that "prices are much higher than elsewhere", but "if cost is not a concern" buy your yarn here and as a bonus the "attentive" staff will "design and write you a custom pattern" for "anything you want to make."

Stuart & Wright ⚫⊠   - | - | - | E

Fort Greene | 85 Lafayette Ave. (bet. S. Elliott Pl. & S. Portland Ave.) | Brooklyn | C to Lafayette Ave. | 718-797-0011 | www.stuartandwright.com

Don't let the vintage French Garment Cleaners sign outside throw you off track – it's merely a remnant of this Fort Greene fashion haunt's past life – just duck inside and say *oui* to the urban-chic casualwear housed in its welcoming white-and-reclaimed-blond-wood space; the style-sleuth owners, both Steven Alan alums, zero in on the right stuff: labels like Band of Outsiders and Neal Sperling for guys, Isabelle Marant, Lyell and United Bamboo for women, plus A.P.C. and Unis for both.

| | QUALITY | DISPLAY | SERVICE | COST |

Stuart Weitzman ☻ | 27 | 24 | 23 | E |

E 50s | 625 Madison Ave. (bet. 58th & 59th Sts.) | N/R/W to 5th Ave./
59th St. | 212-750-2555
W 60s | The Shops at Columbus Circle, Time Warner Ctr. |
10 Columbus Circle, ground fl. (60th St. at B'way) | 1/A/B/C/D to
59th St./Columbus Circle | 212-823-9560
www.stuartweitzman.com

"Stewie is the best" confirm "well-heeled New Yorkers" who "feel like
Cinderella" in the namesake designer's "feminine, ultimately wearable" footwear that "lasts forever"; "playful" window displays and a
"great selection" of "expensive but sooo comfortable" "shoes for every reason and season" (and "cute bags too") make it "worth the trip
to his" Madison Avenue and Time Warner Center locales; here's the
kicker: the "impeccable" staff "bends over backwards" to "find you
just the right" style.

Stubbs & Wootton ☒ | ▽ 26 | 27 | 23 | E |

E 70s | 1034 Lexington Ave. (74th St.) | 6 to 77th St. | 212-249-5200 |
877-478-8227 | www.stubbsandwootton.com

"If you want your feet noticed, step out" in "the most comfortable city
shoes around" order Wasps who Wootton go anywhere but this East 70s
corner shop to purchase "unusual, comfy" European-made slippers,
loafers, heels, mules, slides, espadrilles and now boots too in tapestry,
needlepoint, brocade, velvet or leather, tendered with "old-fashioned
service"; they're all "showstoppers", and the "clever designs" "ensure
you'll have one for every mood"; N.B. monogramming available.

Studio Museum in Harlem Gift Shop Ⓜ | - | - | - | M |

Harlem | 144 W. 125th St. (bet. Lenox & 7th Aves.) | 2/3 to 125th St. |
212-864-4500 | www.studiomuseum.org

An "extension of the museum" dedicated to African and African-
American art, this "small" shop features "good exhibition-related"
books and catalogs; it also offers a "varied selection" of "fun T-shirts",
"holiday gifts", jewelry and textiles as well as "cultural items" celebrating the history of Harlem.

Studio NYC Shoes ☻ | 19 | 19 | 18 | M |

E 40s | 501 Lexington Ave. (47th St.) | 6 to 51st St. | 212-935-3336
E 60s | 1126 Third Ave. (bet. 65th & 66th Sts.) | 6 to 68th St. | 212-517-5550
NEW Murray Hill | 432 Third Ave. (30th St.) | 6 to 33rd St. | 212-532-8555

"Every girl needs a day" at this "fun" Eastside footwear trio with a
"neighborhood feel" swear shoe hounds who fall head over heels for
the "great selection" from "trendy" but "affordable" labels like
Seychelles, Jeffrey Campbell and Report, paired with "impeccable service" to boot; all "of-the-moment looks" are here at a "variety of price
points" – though a few quip "they only hold up for about as long as
they're in style."

Stussy NY | ▽ 20 | 20 | 19 | E |

SoHo | 140 Wooster St. (bet. Houston & Prince Sts.) | N/R/W to
Prince St. | 212-995-8787 | www.stussy.com

What started as a small line of T-shirts by a California surfer is now a
young "classic" at age 27, representing West Coast style on the cob-
blestone streets of SoHo; established status notwithstanding, it's still
"home to graffiti writers, skaters" and other subculturists in need of

what students of steez consider the "coolest-in-town" tees, shoes, sunglasses and hoodies.

Suarez

27 | - | 24 | E

W 50s | 5 W. 56th St. (5th Ave.) | F to 57th St. | 212-315-3870 | www.suarezny.com

It's "impossible to walk out without" buying one of the "unique" purses or "excellent" designer "knockoffs" at this family-owned "sleeper of the handbag world" (recently relocated to the West 50s) where the "quality workmanship" extends to the nice "variety" of Italian leather accessories; though antisocial shoppers snap the "pushy" staff "doesn't leave you alone", others enjoy the "personal", "friendly" service.

Sub Chrono ◑

22 | 22 | 20 | E

E 40s | Worldwide Diamond Tower | 584 Fifth Ave. (bet. 47th & 48th Sts.) | B/D/F/V to 47-50th Sts./Rockefeller Ctr. | 212-921-7073 | www.subchrono.com

Both sports fans and budget-constrained Breitling lovers hit this Midtown flagship near Rockefeller Center for serious men's and women's Swiss-made watches for pilots and divers alike; "excellent value and variety" keep these tickers on top for pocket-watchers.

Sugar ◑

▽ 22 | 21 | 23 | M

E Village | 110 E. Seventh St. (bet. Ave. A & 1st Ave.) | 6 to Astor Pl. | 212-420-6499 | www.sugarshopping.com

Every girl likes a little sugar in her life and the savvy get a fashionable dose of it at this "funky East Village boutique"; indulge in the sweet satisfaction of finding "exciting", smart stuff for work, play or evening, "including Hudson jeans", feminine frocks, well-cut cords and "original" jackets; the "knowledgable" "staff is ready when you are", but do visit early and often, since "they don't overstock on items" – and what there is, "goes fast."

Suite New York ⬚

- | - | - | VE

E 50s | 625 Madison Ave. (58th St.) | N/R/W to 5th Ave./59th St. | 212-421-3300 | www.suiteny.com

While this expensive East 50s contemporary furniture and lighting showroom may be a relative newcomer to the market, the owners – Kris Fuchs and Maria Isabel Sepulveda, formerly of the iconic store Troy – decidedly are not; they have harvested haute home furnishings from the boldest names in European and American design (think Wegner, Jacobsen and Lissoni) in a Chris Kraig–designed loftlike space to bring a little downtown edge to clients' uptown digs.

NEW Suite Orchard Ⓜ

23 | 17 | 18 | E

LES | 145A Orchard St. (Rivington St.) | F/V to Lower East Side/2nd Ave. | 212-533-4115 | www.suiteorchard.com

This new sister-owned boutique on the Lower East Side cultivates hard-to-find women's clothing labels like Jovovich-Hawk, plus the sibling's own private collection, Soni & Cindi, specializes in some rock-influenced looks like edgy blazers; gray-and-white striped walls and mirrored expanses add a crisp, sophisticated accent to the space.

Super Runners Shop

26 | 20 | 25 | M

E 40s | Grand Central, main concourse | 42nd St. (Vanderbilt Ave.) | 4/5/6/7/S to 42nd St./Grand Central | 646-487-1120 ◑

(continued)

(continued)

Super Runners Shop

E 70s | 1246 Third Ave. (72nd St.) | 6 to 68th St. | 212-249-2133
E 80s | 1337 Lexington Ave. (89th St.) | 4/5/6 to 86th St. | 212-369-6010
W 70s | 360 Amsterdam Ave. (77th St.) | 1 to 79th St. | 212-787-7665
www.superrunnersshop.com

"Quality, service, fit – that's what it's all about" at this "one-stop" "legend" that equips "hard-core" marathoners and "weekend warriors" with the "correct pair of sneaks" and apparel from labels like Asics, Saucony and Nike; the "trained staff" of "accomplished runners" "examines your stride as you walk" – and may even let you "test drive a pair around the block"; it's "not cheap", but loyalists go the distance, declaring "I won't buy athletic shoes anywhere else."

Supreme

`- | - | - | E`

SoHo | 274 Lafayette St. (bet. Houston & Prince Sts.) | B/D/F/V to B'way/Lafayette St. | 212-966-7799 | www.supremenewyork.com

Expect the wheel deal at SoHo's minimalist, white-and-chrome "skateboarders' oasis" where "hipsters" of all stripes congregate to work on their boards, watch action-packed video clips and peruse the artist-rendered equipment and wicked apparel; get in the game, or just look the part, with ramp-ready sweaters, hoodies, tees, sneakers and such from the house label plus brands like Girl Chocolate, Anti-Hero and City Stars.

Sur La Table ●

`26 | 23 | 20 | E`

SoHo | 75 Spring St. (bet. Crosby & Lafayette Sts.) | 6 to Spring St. | 212-966-3375 | www.surlatable.com

Founded in Seattle's Pike Place Market in 1972, it took this kitchenware chain well over 30 years to make it to New York, but now local culinary connoisseurs call its 5,000-sq.-ft. SoHo space a "welcome addition" to the Apple; the "great selection" of "attractively displayed" barware, bakeware, "quality pots and pans", appliances, utensils, "neat gadgets" and tabletop accessories appeal to "everyone from the master chef to the take-out queen."

Surprise! Surprise!

`15 | 10 | 13 | I`

E Village | 91 Third Ave. (12th St.) | L to 3rd Ave. | 212-777-0990 | www.surprisesurprise.com

This East Village stalwart offers "affordable furniture for temporary living", plus a "jumble" of "cheap" housewares ranging "from window blinds to hampers and everything in between" that "seems geared to the yearly influx of NYU students and their dorm rooms"; however, cynics snipe that the only surprise is the "dumpy" setting and "nothing-special" merch.

Susan van der Linde ⊠

`- | - | - | VE`

E 50s | 36 E. 57th St. (bet. 5th & Madison Aves.) | N/R/W to 5th Ave./59th St. | 212-758-7500 | www.svdl.com

Ladies of means can't help but flip their lids at this East 57th Street salon because van der Linde, a much-celebrated milliner, dreams up some of the chicest and most unique hats, shoes and handbags within city limits; the treasures are all artfully displayed within an elegant, 1930s parlor-style setting, outfitted with gilded mirrors and antique chairs, making every woman who shops here feel perfectly pampered.

Suzanne Couture Millinery ⊠

▽ 27 | 24 | 26 | VE

E 60s | 27 E. 61st St. (bet. Madison & Park Aves.) | 4/5/6/F/N/R/W to 59th St./Lexington Ave. | 212-593-3232 | www.suzannemillinery.com

While the bridal veils and "handcrafted couture hats" festooned with feathers, mesh or jewels and "styled for you by elegant Suzanne" are "priced for a queen – hey, think she buys her hats here" too? – the cap-crazed consider these *chapeaux* some of the "most chic, creative designs" around; "for a special occasion", head to the old-world-style East 60s brownstone and "treat yourself to the best there is."

Swallow

- | - | - | E

Carroll Gardens | 361 Smith St. (2nd St.) | Brooklyn | F/G to Carroll St. | 718-222-8201 | www.swallowglass.com

Over 100 artists are represented at this eclectic Smith Street gallery selling a wide assortment of handcrafted glass, ceramics, furniture and jewelry; some locals call it the "best place in Brooklyn to pick up a last-minute wedding gift", and the expertly edited offerings mean there is something for serious spendthrifts and wallet-watchers as well.

Swarovski

25 | 25 | 22 | E

E 40s | Rockefeller Ctr. | 30 Rockefeller Ctr. (bet. 49th & 50th Sts.) | B/D/F/V to 47-50th Sts./Rockefeller Ctr. | 212-332-4300

E 50s | 625 Madison Ave. (bet. 58th & 59th Sts.) | N/R/W to 5th Ave./59th St. | 212-308-1710

E 50s | 731 Lexington Ave. (bet. 58th & 59th Sts.) | 4/5/6/F/N/R/W to 59th St./Lexington Ave. | 212-308-9560 ●

NEW **W 60s** | The Shops at Columbus Circle, Time Warner Ctr. | 10 Columbus Circle, ground fl. (60th St. at B'way) | 1/A/B/C/D to 59th St./Columbus Circle | 212-823-9890

Staten Island | Staten Island Mall | 2655 Richmond Ave. (bet. Platinum Ave. & Richmond Hill Rd.) | 718-477-0469 ●

888-207-9873 | www.swarovski.com

"All that glitters is not gold" – in this quintet's case it's faceted Austrian crystal that "can really put a sparkle in your eye and on your lapel, finger or wrist"; there are other gleaming items like "small glass figurines" and tabletop accessories, but most maintain the bijoux are the best bling "for those who can't afford Harry Winston."

Swatch ●

20 | 22 | 18 | M

E 40s | Grand Central | 42nd St. (Vanderbilt Ave.) | 4/5/6/7/S to 42nd St./Grand Central | 212-297-9192

NoHo | 640 Broadway (Bleecker St.) | 6 to Bleecker St. | 212-777-1002

SoHo | 438 W. Broadway (Prince St.) | N/R/W to Prince St. | 646-613-0160

W 40s | 1528 Broadway (45th St.) | 1/2/3/7/N/Q/R/S/W to 42nd St./Times Sq. | 212-764-5541

W 70s | 100 W. 72nd St. (Columbus Ave.) | 1/2/3 to 72nd St. | 212-595-9640

Elmhurst | Queens Ctr. | 90-15 Queens Blvd. (bet. 57th & 59th Aves.) | Queens | G/R/V to Grand Ave./Newtown | 718-760-7083

888-631-6037 | www.swatch.com

There's a "funky" and "fun" "Willy Wonka" quality to these watches that "come in a dizzying variety of styles and colors" and "tickle almost everyone's fancy" since they are "cheap" but "work well"; proponents also point out that "you don't have to worry about being mugged wearing one because these babies have no street value."

	QUALITY	DISPLAY	SERVICE	COST

Sweet Tater
18 | 16 | 16 | M

NoLita | 280 Mulberry St. (bet. Houston & Prince Sts.) | B/D/F/V to B'way/
Lafayette St. | 212-219-6400 | www.sweettater.net

"My lucky day" deem surveyors who've "stumbled upon" this sweet li'l
NoLita shop stuffed with an "eclectic assortment of clothes and accessories", which range from "funky" oldies to the house line of short
dresses; some foes find it hard to "withstand the help's sideways
glances", but others maintain they "tell the truth about how you look."

SwimBikeRun ◑
– | – | – | E

W 50s | 203 W. 58th St. (bet. B'way & 7th Ave.) | N/Q/R/W to 57th St. |
212-399-3999 | www.sbrmultisports.com

This Midtown sports trifecta is staffed with "friendly" experts "that
actually do triathlons" and "go above and beyond" attest admirers
who "go in to just look and end up buying half the store"; fans "love"
the "cool layout" and the "great" apparel and gear for, what else,
swimming, biking and running; you need to be an Iron Man to handle
the "expensive" prices, but hey, "you get what you pay for."

Swiss Army
23 | 20 | 21 | M

SoHo | 136 Prince St. (W. B'way) | N/R/W to Prince St. | 212-965-5714 |
www.swissarmy.com

"Funny how we love the simple things in life like our Swiss Army
watches" declare legions of fans who fall for the "efficient", "reasonably
priced" "quality" timepieces at this SoHo haunt; but this "been-
around" forever brand is "much more than" just chronographs, "top-
notch" multitools and, of course, knives – you'll also find "great-looking"
luggage and apparel from companion line Victorinox.

Syms ◑
18 | 11 | 12 | I

E 50s | 400 Park Ave. (54th St.) | 6 to 51st St. | 212-317-8200
Financial District | 42 Trinity Pl. (Rector St.) | R/W to Rector St. |
212-797-1199
www.syms.com

Whether Midtown or Downtown, "locals go" to this discount "delight" –
"an old favorite" for clothes for the whole family, though some say you
"do much better on men's than women's"; the apparel's all "organized
by size", which "makes it a pleasure" (despite the "drab layout") "to
pick through the plethora of racks"; however, some stock is "shopworn"
or "unmarked irregulars", so "inspect items closely for flaws."

Taffin
– | – | – | VE

By appointment only | inquiries: 212-421-6222

Born into an aristocratic and artistic family (his uncle is French fashion
icon Hubert de Givenchy), James Taffin de Givenchy has been produc-
ing an "exquisite and exclusive" fine jewelry collection for over 10
years; viewable by appointment only, his voluptuous, often playful and
definitely inspired designs are based around colorful gemstones including favorite mandarin garnets, fire opals, red spinels and peridots.

Tah-Poozie ◑
∇ 18 | 20 | 17 | M

G Village | 50 Greenwich Ave. (bet. Charles & Perry Sts.) | 1 to
Christopher St./Sheridan Sq. | 212-647-0668

"Indulge your inner quirk" at this Greenwich Villager serving up "the
best gags for cheap in NYC"; "get your rubber duckies and fridge mag-

nets" along with "kitschy doodads for your home or office"; "anyone who has children, nieces or nephews should shop here" for "goofy gifts" that'll "leave 'em asking 'where did you get that?'"

Z Takashimaya 28 | 28 | 23 | VE

E 50s | 693 Fifth Ave. (bet. 54th & 55th Sts.) | E/V to 5th Ave./53rd St. | 212-350-0100 | 800-753-2038

"Exquisite things in an exquisite setting" summarizes the scene at the "beautiful if austere" Midtown outpost of a Japanese chain; the mostly "modern" "high-end home goods and clothing" chosen "with an obvious Asian eye" are admittedly "an acquired taste" ("fine to browse, not much to buy" foes feel); but "beauty addicts stock up" on cosmetics brands "not usually found in the U.S.", and "vase fetishists" fawn over the "breathtaking floral" department; besides, the "laid-back help" and "Zen surroundings will automatically lower your blood pressure – until you see the prices"; P.S. there's also tea "in their lovely cafe" or in the sixth-floor tea bar.

Z Talbots 22 | 21 | 21 | M

E 50s | 525 Madison Ave. (bet. 53rd & 54th Sts.) | E/V to 5th Ave./53rd St. | 212-838-8811
E 50s | 527 Madison Ave. (bet. 53rd & 54th Sts.) | E/V to 5th Ave./53rd St. | 212-371-5030
E 70s | 1251-1255 Third Ave. (72nd St.) | 6 to 68th St. | 212-988-8585 ◐
Seaport | Pier 17 | 189-191 Front St. (bet. Fulton & John Sts.) | 2/3/4/5/A/C/J/M/Z to Fulton St./B'way/Nassau | 212-425-0166
W 80s | 2289-2291 Broadway (bet. 82nd & 83rd Sts.) | 1 to 79th St. | 212-875-8753 ◐
800-825-2687 | www.talbots.com

"If you're looking for preppy, look no further" than this "all-time favorite" chain proffering "excellent-quality" women's "classics" like "beautifully cut slacks" and "wrinkle-resistant shirts"; it's "not for the young and hip" and it may "have a reputation for matronly styling", but admirers say that only means its "lasts-for-years" clothing "never goes out of style", and they also laud the "affordable" prices; N.B. the 527 Madison branch houses the men's collection.

Talbots Kids and Babies 24 | 23 | 22 | E

E 50s | 527 Madison Ave. (54th St.) | E/V to 5th Ave./53rd St. | 212-758-4152
E 70s | 1523 Second Ave. (79th St.) | 6 to 77th St. | 212-570-1630
800-992-9010 | www.talbots.com

"Your little ones will look like they come from money" in the "preppy" apparel on parade at these East 50s and 70s "classic" "counterparts" to the adult chain; whether you're looking for "wonderful quality" "everyday stuff" or "party clothes", "they get it right" maintain parents who "don't want their children to have that J.Lo look at seven."

Z T. Anthony Ltd. 28 | 26 | 25 | VE

E 50s | 445 Park Ave. (56th St.) | 4/5/6/F/N/R/W to 59th St./Lexington Ave. | 212-750-9797 | www.tanthony.com

The "classic signature luggage that Gwyneth Paltrow made chic" and Donald Trump totes has actually "been around forever" and for good reason: the "beautiful coordinated sets", "elegant" duffel and wheeled styles and "gorgeous" garment bags at this "oh-so-proper" Park

Avenue standby "always make you stand out when traveling"; expect "leather in all its glory" and "classy" canvas pieces, all offering "quality second to none", plus a staff that "treats you like you are royalty."

☒ Target ◐ | 17 | 17 | 13 | I |

Bronx | 40 W. 225th St. (I-87) | 1 to 225th St. | 718-733-7199
Downtown | Atlantic Terminal | 139 Flatbush Ave. (bet. Atlantic & 4th Aves.) | Brooklyn | 2/3/4/5/B/D/M/N/Q/R to Atlantic Ave. | 718-290-1109
Starrett City | Gateway Ctr. | 519 Gateway Dr. (bet. Fountain & Vandalia Aves.) | Brooklyn | A/C to Euclid Ave. | 718-235-6032
College Point | 135-05 20th Ave. (Whitestone Expwy.) | Queens | 7 to Main St. | 718-661-4346
Elmhurst | Queens Pl. | 88-01 Queens Blvd. (bet. 55th & 56th Aves.) | Queens | G/R/V to Grand Ave./Newtown | 718-760-5656
Staten Island | 2900 Veterans Rd. (N. Bridge St.) | 718-701-6205
800-440-0680 | www.target.com
Believers bellow this "neatly organized" outer-borough behemoth is the "best of the bargain mega-stores" for its "literally soup-to-nuts" variety; wheel down the "wide aisles" and "buy your outfit or outfit your home" with "lines created by designers" – like fashions from Alice Temperley (and soon to come: Rogan) and the 500-piece housewares collection from Aero's Thomas O'Brien; if critics carp "you get tired traveling the immense space to find help", converts counter "what it [lacks] in service is balanced by its selections and prices", leaving only one question: "when will the bull's-eye land in Manhattan?"

Tarina Tarantino | ▽ 22 | 24 | 20 | E |

SoHo | 117 Greene St. (Prince St.) | C/E to Spring St. | 212-226-6953 | www.tarinatarantino.com
You'll think pink at this rosy SoHo outpost named for an LA-based costume jewelry designer, who combines Swarovski crystal and Lucite in everything from eye-poppingly girlie multibead bracelets to oversized bib necklaces and drop earrings; for the even-more flamboyant, there are Barbie pendants and other pieces featuring Hello Kitty cartoon characters and storybook favorite *Alice in Wonderland*.

Taryn Rose | 25 | - | 22 | VE |

E 60s | 681 Madison Ave. (bet. 61st & 62nd Sts.) | N/R/W to 5th Ave./59th St. | 212-753-3939 | www.tarynrose.com
"Oh, to have a closet full of these shoes!" sigh admirers who swear that once you fall for the "like-butter" men's and women's offerings, this "serene" shop, relocated to the East 60s, "can be addictive"; trained as an orthopedic surgeon, the namesake designer creates "elegant" footwear that's "cute and good for your feet at the same time"; needless to say, such "extreme comfort" comes at an "extreme cost."

Tarzian True Value | 21 | 14 | 21 | M |

Park Slope | 193 Seventh Ave. (bet. 2nd & 3rd Sts.) | Brooklyn | F to 7th Ave. | 718-788-4120
"Got a brownstone? they've got what you need" at this "great" family-owned hardware store that's "provided for Park Slope throughout its renovation boom" – and decades before that, offering "a good selection of electronic and lighting" items, paint; plumbing supplies and garden tools "in a relatively small space"; natch, loyalists latch onto the "nice vibe" and "helpful staff" that "knows where everything is."

	QUALITY	DISPLAY	SERVICE	COST

Tarzian West
21 | 17 | 20 | E

Park Slope | 194 Seventh Ave. (2nd St.) | Brooklyn | F to 7th Ave. | 718-788-4213

"It's a bit crowded" and the towering piles of product make you "feel as though things are about to fall on you", but Park Slopers salute this neighborhood kitchen and bath store that "will satisfy most immediate needs", whether it's bakeware, cookware, cutlery or gadgets; locals like the fact that it "eliminates the need to trek into the city."

té casan ●
– | – | – | E

SoHo | 382 W. Broadway (bet. Broome & Spring Sts.) | C/E to Spring St. | 212-584-8000 | www.tecasan.com

From the moment you mount the spiral staircase of SoHo's champagne-colored 7,500-sq.-ft. showcase owned by a Spanish iconoclast, it's clear you're not in been-there-done-that footwear territory anymore; groupings of unique, limited-edition shoes from a rotating coterie of international designers – whose names may be unfamiliar but whose credentials speak volumes – are arranged like *objets d'art,* and you can even try on the wild wedges in your own dressing room 'pod'; after your Cinderella moment, dash downstairs for a cuppa at the on-site T Salon.

Ted Baker
25 | 22 | 22 | E

SoHo | 107 Grand St. (Mercer St.) | 6/J/M/N/Q/R/W/Z to Canal St. | 212-343-8989 | www.tedbaker.co.uk

This dual-entrance SoHo boutique (one leads to womenswear, the other to men's) surprises with its "cute designs to spice up your wardrobe", like "great shirts" that come with complementary cuff links, floaty dresses and crease-resistant suits, including the famed Party Animal Teflon-treated tuxedo; each dressing room has a fantasy mural, so you can envision wearing these "European-style clothes" anywhere abroad.

Ted Muehling ⊠Ⓜ
▽ 29 | 29 | 26 | E

SoHo | 27 Howard St. (bet. B'way & Lafayette St.) | 6/J/M/N/Q/R/W/Z to Canal St. | 212-431-3825 | www.tedmuehling.com

"No boyfriend or husband can go wrong buying" "beautiful", "timeless" jewelry from this SoHo designer whose striking "handcrafted" pieces – like pinecone or pussy willow earrings – are inspired by nature and "organic" forms; the "serene" shop also features his "incredible" porcelain and glass *objets* as well as gems by Gabriella Kiss.

Ⓩ Tekserve ●
26 | 16 | 23 | M

Chelsea | 119 W. 23rd St. (bet. 6th & 7th Aves.) | F/V to 23rd St. | 212-929-3645 | www.tekserve.com

Experience "Apple nirvana" at this "one-of-a-kind" Chelsea store whose renown rests with its reputation as the "quintessential" "computer rehab" "spot of choice for most Manhattan Mac owners"; "bring a book", though, and "expect to take a number" as "waits can be interminable"; P.S. the "quirky setting" includes a glass-enclosed pro audio and video room with original doors from the Las Vegas Sands Hotel.

Temperley
– | – | – | VE

SoHo | 453 Broome St., 2nd fl. (Mercer St.) | N/R/W to Prince St. | 212-219-2929 | www.temperleylondon.com

Visitors "love everything" about this light-filled, columned, second-story SoHo loft where British designer Alice Temperley houses her lavishly bedecked dresses and drapey feminine separates with a fin-de-siècle flair and attention to embroidered and beaded detail – all of which may account for their appeal to romantic icons like Gwyneth Paltrow and Kate Winslet; add in the accessories, and "shopping here is amazing."

☑ Tender Buttons ⊠⊅ | 28 | 26 | 21 | E |

E 60s | 143 E. 62nd St. (bet. Lexington & 3rd Aves.) | 4/5/6/F/N/R/W to 59th St./Lexington Ave. | 212-758-7004

"Virtually a museum of buttons", this genteel, garden-level Upper East Sider "abounds" with "imported, antique" and "unusual" toggles and studs that make it "heaven to put the finishing touch on a jacket or sweater"; while it's "terribly hard to choose" among the "treasures" ("if you can't find what you're looking for here, it doesn't exist"), it's certainly "easy to see" the "splendid collection" in the uncluttered setting.

Tent and Trails | 25 | 9 | 21 | M |

Financial District | 21 Park Pl. (bet. B'way & Church St.) | A/C to Chambers St. | 212-227-1760 | 800-237-1760 | www.tenttrails.com

"Undeniably" one of the "best camping retailers" around, this "folksy" "grandpappy of sporting goods" is a "unique" Financial District "experience" for "outdoor groupies"; whether you're hiking to Central Park or pitching a tent in Kilimanjaro, you'll discover a bonanza of backpacking "treasure" – as long as you rely on the "knowledgeable staff", because the "crowded" quarters feel like a crazy "Tibetan bazaar."

Ten Thousand Things | – | – | – | VE |

Meatpacking | 423 W. 14th St. (bet. 9th & 10th Aves.) | A/C/E/L to 14th St./8th Ave. | 212-352-1333

Way west on 14th Street, designers Ron Anderson and David Rees produce "simple, delicate" and "pricey" jewelry like signature cluster earrings and necklaces using gems ranging from keshi pearls to raw ruby skipping stones; N.B. there are also pieces from five other designers.

TG-170 ◐ | ▽ 20 | 17 | 18 | E |

LES | 170 Ludlow St. (bet. Houston & Stanton Sts.) | F/V to Lower East Side/2nd Ave. | 212-995-8660 | www.tg170.com

The trek Downtown to this spacious, chandeliered Lower East Side style pioneer is well worth the mileage for the "hip and eclectic selection" of "one-of-a-kind" women's threads from labels like Corey Lynn Calter, Karen Walker and less well-known designers; the "crisp aesthetic" of the clothes, jewelry and what may be the "largest assortment of messenger bags you'll ever see" "make this a neighborhood favorite."

Theory | 23 | 22 | 21 | E |

Meatpacking | 38 Gansevoort St. (bet. Greenwich & Hudson Sts.) | A/C/E/L to 14th St./8th Ave. | 212-524-6790

SoHo | 151 Spring St. (bet. W. B'way & Wooster St.) | 6 to Spring St. | 212-226-3691

W 70s | 230 Columbus Ave. (bet. 70th & 71st Sts.) | 1/2/3 to 72nd St. | 212-362-3676

www.theory.com

"Hip, but classic" "work attire" is not just theory but reality at this retail trio filled with an "always changing, always tempting" array of "no-fail outfits" in basic twill, gabardine and crepe; in particular, patrons praise "the perfectly fitting pants", provided you're a tall, "thin girl"; but "even if the trousers are cut for stick insects", the "staff tries to be honest", so "you won't regret buying the next day"; N.B. the Meatpacking District behemoth also carries menswear.

37=1 Atelier Ⓜ
- | - | - | E

SoHo | 37 Crosby St. (bet. Broome & Grand Sts.) | N/R/W to Prince St. | 212-226-0067 | www.jeanyu.com

Discriminating stylesetters, celebs and the well-endowed who can pay "an arm and a leg" for wispy silk chiffon lingerie, filmy see-through dresses and glamorous satin halter gowns rely on designer Jean Yu for those champagne-worthy occasions; devotees can buy the willowy wearable art off the rack in the slinky SoHo space or "make an appointment" to have the meticulously crafted creations made to measure.

Thomas Pink
26 | 24 | 22 | E

E 50s | 520 Madison Ave. (53rd St.) | E/V to 5th Ave./53rd St. | 212-838-1928
NEW Financial District | 63 Wall St. (Hanover St.) | 2/3 to Wall St. | 212-514-7683 ⑤
W 40s | 1155 Sixth Ave. (44th St.) | 1/2/3/7/N/Q/R/S/W to 42nd St./ Times Sq. | 212-840-9663
W 60s | The Shops at Columbus Circle, Time Warner Ctr. | 10 Columbus Circle, ground fl. (60th St. at B'way) | 1/A/B/C/D to 59th St./Columbus Circle | 212-823-9650 ⓞ
888-336-1192 | www.thomaspink.com

Channeling the Jermyn Street school of shirtmaking, this British brand is a "mecca for Anglophiles" who want to "impress the boss" with "the finest off-the-rack shirt you can buy"; pink is just one of many "bright and lovely colors" available in a "vast selection of stripes, solids" and "unrivaled patterns" and displayed in "classy windows"; however, panners proclaim "they should blush [bright red] at their prices" and that often the "staff is less than helpful."

Thomasville ⓞ
23 | 21 | 19 | E

Bayside | 217-04 Northern Blvd. (217th St.) | Queens | 7 to Main St. | 718-224-2715 | www.thomasville.com

For more than a century, this North Carolina native with a Bayside showroom has crafted traditional living room, dining room and bed-room furniture in styles that range from French country to Shaker to Mission and more, including the popular Hemingway collection; the "quality makes them well-worth the high price."

Thom Browne. ⑤
- | - | - | VE

TriBeCa | 100 Hudson St. (Franklin St.) | 1 to Franklin St. | 212-633-1197 | www.thombrowne.com

Addressing a growing fan base, the menswear designer inspired by the bureaucratic look of the late '50s-early '60s – super-slim suits, short jackets and cropped trousers (Brad Pitt's been photographed wearing a pair) – houses his line in a sprawling TriBeCa space done up with a retro-office feel; acolytes call the distinctive custom-tailored togs "near perfect in every way" – plus there are also ready-to-wear ties, shirts and Corgi cashmeres for walk-ins (though not required, appointments are recommended).

Thos. Moser Cabinetmakers

▽ 29 | 29 | 25 | VE

E 60s | 699 Madison Ave., 2nd fl. (bet. 62nd & 63rd Sts.) |
F to Lexington Ave./63rd St. | 212-753-7005 | 800-708-9016 |
www.thomasmoser.com

The covetous confess it's "hard to keep your hands off the exquisite furniture in this Madison Avenue shop" where signed and dated Shaker, Scandinavian and Asian-influenced pieces "primarily in American black-cherry" are displayed; "prices are expensive, but justifiable" as the "workmanship is worth every cent."

NEW Threads

- | - | - | M

E 70s | 1451 Second Ave. (76th St.) | 6 to 77th St. | 212-737-0104 |
www.potterybarnkids.com

With a setting somewhat reminiscent of its mother ship and a selection of infants' clothing in soothing pastels and white, this East 70s newcomer – the latest addition to the Pottery Barn family – feels as comfy as a blankie; choose from essentials like sweet organic-cotton cardigans, overalls and crib-perfect suede moccasins and cashmere-blend booties, most at moderate prices.

NEW 3.1 Phillip Lim

27 | 25 | 22 | E

SoHo | 115 Mercer St. (bet. Prince & Spring Sts.) | N/R/W to Prince St. |
212-334-1160 | www.31philliplim.com

"Phabulous" proclaim Phillipo-philes of the fashion darling who has, "finally, a boutique" on Mercer Street, "a great space" as chic as his "architectural", "cutting-edge" yet "wearable" staples for men and women; a "pleasant" staff also impresses, but while Lim's "hyped as an affordable alternative to designerwear, he's still expensive" budget stylistas sigh; even so, it's "a small price to pay for fashion cred."

3r Living ⊠

- | - | - | M

Park Slope | 276 Fifth Ave. (bet. 1st St. & Garfield Pl.) | Brooklyn | M/R to Union St. | 718-832-0951 | www.3rliving.com

Husband-and-wife-team Samantha Delman-Caserta and Mark Caserta make sure that all products in this "inventive, funky" Park Slope lifestyle store reflect the 3r's: reuse, recycle, reduce; the collection includes sustainable offerings for body, baby, home and even pets, and the goods – from bike-chain bracelets and solar daypacks to pro-green T-shirts and Mrs. Meyer's Clean Day products – prove that the eco-friendly way of life doesn't have to be "just for hippies."

Tibi

- | - | - | E

SoHo | 120 Wooster St. (bet. Prince & Spring Sts.) | N/R/W to Prince St. |
212-226-5852 | www.tibi.com

"Embrace your girlieness" at this SoHo must-stop where the power of prettiness is captured by American designer Amy Smilovic's "feminine frocks", puffy-sleeved jackets and "cute" knit vests; "you can't beat it" if you're looking for "great quality", and you're welcome to lounge awhile in the loftlike space's mod sofas, taking in the eye-popping green, black and yellow color scheme that dominates the floral murals, zany couches and catchy prints.

⊠ Tiffany & Co.

28 | 27 | 24 | VE

E 50s | 727 Fifth Ave. (57th St.) | N/R/W to 5th Ave./59th St. |
212-755-8000

(continued)

Tiffany & Co.

NEW **Financial District** | 37 Wall St. (bet. Nassau & William Sts.) | 2/3 to Wall St. | 212-514-8015 ⑤

800-843-3269 | www.tiffany.com

"Any child, adult or ancient would love something" from Fifth Avenue's "American icon", whether it's "classic" silver, diamond or gold jewelry – including signature Elsa Peretti and Paloma Picasso pieces, plus a Frank Gehry line – sterling, china and crystal for "memorable" wedding presents or the "best baby gifts"; despite "hordes of tourists" and mixed comments on service ("tops" vs. "unless you're dressed to impress get ready to answer your own questions"), "who doesn't covet the little blue box?" N.B. the Wall Street branch opened in autumn 2007.

Tiny Doll House ⑤

| | | | E |

E 70s | 314 E. 78th St. (bet. 1st & 2nd Aves.) | 6 to 77th St. | 212-744-3719 | www.tinydollhousenyc.com

"I could spend an entire day" here – you "go inside and become six years old again" sigh house-hunters mesmerized by this "not-to-be-missed" East 70s destination for decadent dream homes, along with all of the little incidentals of life in miniature – everything from, say, pint-sized Persian rugs, lobster dinners and stiletto shoes to Starbucks coffee cups, radiators and Le Corbusier chairs.

Tiny Living ◗

| | | | M |

E Village | 125 E. Seventh St. (bet. Ave. A & 1st Ave.) | L to 1st Ave. | 212-228-2748 | www.tinyliving.com

This affordable East Village shop lives up to its name by specializing in small-scaled, flexible furniture and accessories for the kind of cramped living room, kitchen, bath and office spaces that are so typical of Manhattan apartments; not only are there slim sofas, collapsible tables, chairs and even vases, many of the pieces are multipurpose and/or do double duty as storage as well.

Tip Top Kids

| 26 | 18 | 21 | E |

W 70s | 149 W. 72nd St. (bet. B'way & Columbus Ave.) | 1 to 79th St. | 212-874-1003 | 800-925-5464 | www.tiptopshoes.com

"When your kid's sneakers are suddenly too small", stride over to this "old-fashioned", "conveniently located" West 70s shoe shop steps away from the grown-ups' standby, where the expert fitters "actually know how to measure feet" – a "rarity" nowadays; gravitate toward the "good selection" of "excellent quality" footwear "favorites" from mainstream labels like Timberland and Merrell or take the leap with budding brands like Blundstone, Keen and Umi.

Tip Top Shoes

| 25 | 18 | 22 | M |

W 70s | 155 W. 72nd St. (bet. Amsterdam & Columbus Aves.) | 1/2/3 to 72nd St. | 212-787-4960 | 800-925-5464 | www.tiptopshoes.com

"Tip-top style and selection" assert admirers who stock their closets with an "excellent range" of "solid, comfortable" footwear from "international makers" galore from this "quintessential neighborhood store" that sets the "gold standard for shoe shopping on the Upper West Side"; the "window display calls me in whenever I walk by", while the "very accommodating staff" tends to my "weary feet", "fitting them correctly"; still, a handful huff the help is "grumpy" and caution it's "busy, busy, busy" on weekends.

☒ T.J. Maxx ⦿   16 | 10 | 8 | I

Flatiron | 620 Sixth Ave. (bet. 18th & 19th Sts.) | 1 to 18th St. | 212-229-0875
College Point | 136-05 20th Ave. (Parsons Blvd.) | Queens | 7 to Main St. | 718-353-2727
Staten Island | 1509 Forest Ave. (bet. Crystal & Decker Aves.) | 718-876-1995
Staten Island | 2530 Hylan Blvd. (New Dorp Ln.) | 718-980-4150
800-285-6299 | www.tjmaxx.com

"Savvy shoppers will be willing to overlook" the "time-consuming check-out lines" in order to "get an entire wardrobe for the price of one luxury item" at this "land of bargains" that also offers housewares, jewelry, luggage and other "great things mixed in with junk"; "spilling out onto the floor", the "picked-over merch is "poorly organized" and often "not that clean, but hey, when you find a $15 Tahari shirt that retailed for $100, what's a little dirt?"

Todd Hase   - | - | - | VE

SoHo | 261 Spring St. (bet. Hudson & Varick Sts.) | C/E to Spring St. | 212-871-9075 | www.toddhase.com

Known for his updates of classic furniture, designer Todd Hase's SoHo store features chaises, chairs, settees and sofas made with old-world techniques and upholstered in soft, neutral tones of mohair and silk that recall French design of the '30s and '40s; leather lamps add another quietly luxurious accent.

☒ Tod's   29 | 25 | 21 | VE

E 60s | 650 Madison Ave. (bet. 59th & 60th Sts.) | N/R/W to 5th Ave./59th St. | 212-644-5945 | www.todsonline.com

"Whether or not you" get behind the wheel, "your wardrobe must include a pair" of the "cute" signature "driving mocs" with "pebbled soles" that'll "spoil you for anything else" attest touters who feed their fetish for "clean-cut" shoes and "gorgeous bags" at this Madison Avenue flagship; if a few feel flustered by the "haughty" staff, even they admit the payoff is some of the "most comfortable" footwear "on the face of the earth" fashioned from "fabulous soft leather" ("like butter!"); N.B. the Display score may not reflect a dramatic renovation – leather-wrapped columns and steel cases – that tripled the store size.

☒ Toga Bikes   26 | 19 | 24 | E

NEW **E 60s** | 1153 First Ave. (63rd St.) | 4/5/6/N/Q/R/W to 59th St. | 212-759-0002
W 60s | 110 West End Ave. (64th St.) | 1 to 66th St./Lincoln Ctr. | 212-799-9625
www.togabikes.com

A pedal pusher since 1971, this West 60s standby and its new sibling straight across town are not only "sisters to Gotham Bikes Downtown", but "excellent places" for "enthusiasts and neophytes alike" to buy wheels; the "no-bull" staff "loves what it sells", including Cannondale road bikes and specialized all-terrain rides, and also "tinkers with every new piece of equipment you add"; all bicycles have guaranteed lifetime service, which might explain the crowds (hint: "don't go on weekends").

Tokio 7 ●
▽ 26 | 14 | 11 | M

E Village | 64 E. Seventh St. (bet. 1st & 2nd Aves.) | 6 to Astor Pl. | 212-353-8443

It's a "good, solid resale shop" pronounce patrons of this long, low-ceilinged East Villager "chock-full" of male and female "basic, midrange" "designerwear that's definitely wearable", plus some "quirky" "higher-end goodies" at "fair prices" – and sometimes even "cheap" ones, "if you think wearing someone else's Marc Jacobs top from last year is worth 50% off the original cost."

Tokyo Joe ●
22 | 15 | 15 | M

E Village | 334 E. 11th St. (bet. 1st & 2nd Aves.) | L to 1st Ave. | 212-473-0724

This East Village "walk-in closet of a store" "looks dingy from the outside, but inside it's filled with wonderful" designer his-and-hers re-treads, many "looking practically new"; the quarters can be close, "but the finds are worth the heat", especially those "at prices so low you'll have to put on your glasses to check that you aren't seeing things."

NEW Tom Ford ⊠
28 | 26 | 22 | VE

E 70s | 845 Madison Ave. (70th St.) | 6 to 68th St. | 212-359-0300 | www.tomford.com

Acolytes adore this "labyrinth of luxury" from the "world's hottest man" and "former Gucci maestro", whose first namesake flagship is a "castle" of "sartorial splendor" for the "modern male" on Madison Avenue; the "amazing", "finally-all-of-Tom's-creations-under-one-roof" collection includes "sexy" suits, eveningwear and dressing gowns, along with leather accessories and scents, which are displayed in a grand glass 'fragrance chamber'; but detractors declare it "pretentiousness defined" with "stratospherically priced" pieces proffered by a "beyond-snooty" staff in a "forbidding" albeit "unforgettable" atmosphere, replete with maids, butlers and the high-gloss vibe of Old Hollywood.

Tommy Hilfiger
20 | 20 | 18 | E

SoHo | 372 W. Broadway (Broome St.) | C/E to Spring St. | 917-237-0983
NEW **W Village** | 375 Bleecker St. (bet. Charles & Perry Sts.) | 1 to Christopher St./Sheridan Sq. | 646-638-4813 ●
www.tommy.com

Hilfiger Denim ●
NEW **SoHo** | 500 Broadway (bet. Broome & Spring Sts.) | N/R/W to Prince St. | 212-334-0042 | www.hilfigerdenim.com

Designer Tommy Hilfiger "has really stepped it up" at this "sleek" SoHo shop, delivering three floors of "classic, clean and preppy" his-and-hers "hip" wardrobe essentials infused with "European style" that are just right for "work or going out for a fine dinner"; but while it's "nice that it's all under one roof", critics cavil that the collection can "run hot and cold, depending on the season"; N.B. the new Bleecker street store is higher-end womenswear only, while Hilfiger Denim is more jeans-oriented.

Tory Burch
21 | 25 | 19 | E

NoLita | 257 Elizabeth St. (bet. Houston & Prince Sts.) | B/D/F/V to B'way/Lafayette St. | 212-334-3000 | www.toryburch.com

"Tory hits the mark" maintain mavens of this "hot, hip boutique" – a NoLita "must-stop" for the "must-haves" – that "feels like a glam '70s living room"; it's "all presentation" protest pessimists who "don't understand the buzz" about this socialite/designer's colorful wares, but "well-maintained fortysomethings" find her "original yet wearable" Me Decade–inspired pieces "perfect workday" attire and applaud the "special" wardrobe standouts that even "take you into night."

Tourneau
27 | 24 | 21 | VE

E 50s | 500 Madison Ave. (52nd St.) | E/V to 5th Ave./53rd St. | 212-758-6098
Garment District | 200 W. 34th St. (7th Ave.) | 1/2/3/A/C/E to 34th St./ Penn Station | 212-563-6880
W 60s | The Shops at Columbus Circle, Time Warner Ctr. | 10 Columbus Circle, ground fl. (60th St. at B'way) | 1/A/B/C/D to 59th St./Columbus Circle | 212-823-9425 ◑

Tourneau TimeMachine

E 50s | 12 E. 57th St. (Madison Ave.) | N/R/W to 5th Ave./59th St. | 212-758-7300
www.tourneau.com

"If you can't find it here you don't want it" assert admirers of this tony ticker chain with perhaps "the most complete selection" of the "top time pieces" in town (the TimeMachine outpost bills itself as the world's largest watch store); while opinions on service range from "spotty" and "snobby" ("if they think you can't afford it, they're not interested") to "knowledgeable", the staff is "willing to negotiate prices"; so "do your research" and note that there are "terrific pre-owned deals" and they also "take trade-ins."

Tous
22 | 21 | 21 | E

SoHo | 109 Greene St. (Prince St.) | N/R/W to Prince St. | 212-219-1444 | www.tous.com

"Tous-lovers" can "bear-ly contain themselves" at this "friendly' SoHo "paradise" that hails from Spain, scooping up "not too expensive" 18-karat gold and enamel, freshwater pearl or sterling silver bracelets, earrings or pendants for kids ("good for the Bat Mitzvah set") and more sophisticated, "interesting" pieces for adults (yes, men too), all boasting the "trademark teddy" design; but there's more than "cute" jewelry – admirers also applaud the "hip, young" handbags and "excellent leather goods" "for people of all ages."

Town Shop
25 | 14 | 25 | M

W 80s | 2273 Broadway (bet. 81st & 82nd Sts.) | 1 to 79th St. | 212-787-2762 | www.townshop.com

It "might not be the most glamorous store", but this "all-pink", "family-run" Upper West Side "institution" is the "last of the real lingerie shops" offering an "impressive array" of brand names and employing "no-nonsense" "expert" corsetieres who "size you up in a second" with "fitting savvy that's beyond compare" ("yes, you were probably wearing the wrong bra"); sure, the staff's approach is "hands-on", but it'll "hook you up" with undies that provide the "support you've always wanted."

Toy Space
23 | 21 | 24 | E

Park Slope | 426 Seventh Ave. (bet. 14th & 15th Sts.) | Brooklyn | F to 7th Ave. | 718-369-9096

"Let your soul wander back in time" at this Park Slope funhouse where the "neat" nostalgic selection of "classic, hard-to-find toys" from decades gone by "remind you of your childhood"; from "gyroscopes, baby grand pianos" and Radio Flyer wagons to build-your-own-sports-car sets, this is "*the* place" to go when you're "searching for something special" – "if you can't find it here, you can't find it anymore."

Toys "R" Us ❷

20 | 20 | 14 | M

W 40s | 1514 Broadway (44th St.) | 1/2/3/7/N/Q/R/S/W to 42nd St./ Times Sq. | 646-366-8800 | 800-869-7787 | www.toysrus.com
Additional locations throughout the NY area

"Don't miss this show on Broadway" rave fans of Times Square's towering "toy universe" flagship offering a "carnival"-like "experience" complete with a "fantastic" Ferris wheel, an "unbelievable" animatronic T. rex, "awesome" Barbie playhouse, NYC landmarks done up in Legos and a Candyland sweet shop; though Scrooges dub it the "*Romper Room* of the suburbs" and grimace over "throngs" of "over-stimulated" kids and "numbingly long lines", enthusiasts counter the "consolation is the hug you get from your child."

Tracy Feith

▽ 22 | 28 | 22 | VE

NoLita | 209 Mulberry St. (bet. Kenmare & Spring Sts.) | 6 to Spring St. | 212-334-3097

You "gotta love it" – a "surfer dude designing fab ladies' gear" grin groupies who haunt this NoLita shop filled with "dresses made to fit you like a glove" in "colorful patterns" and "awesome fabrics" for those who "like to stand out at parties"; however, you may be hanging 10 on your own as the staff sometimes sends out a "don't-be-intrusive" vibe.

Tracy Reese

25 | 25 | 23 | E

Meatpacking | 641 Hudson St. (bet. Gansevoort & Horatio Sts.) | A/C/E/L to 14th St./8th Ave. | 212-807-0505 | www.tracyreese.com

"The ambiance alone will wow you" at this "airy" va-va-voom boutique in the "über-hip Meatpacking District", showcasing the rapidly rising American designer known for her "adorable, grown-up yet girlie pieces for uptown and downtown types alike"; whether doing "womanly" work garb or a "kicky" party dress, "Reese has a great eye", imbuing garments with a vintage-modern mix of silk, satin and velvet, as well as ribbons and lace; the result is "a little pricey – but oh-so-pretty"; N.B. don't neglect her bed linen collection either.

Training Camp ❷

- | - | - | M

Garment District | 1412 Broadway (bet. 39th & 40th Sts.) | 7/B/D/F/ V to 42nd St./Bryant Park | 212-398-3930
W 40s | 1079 Sixth Ave. (41st St.) | 7/B/D/F/V to 42nd St./Bryant Park | 212-921-4430
W 40s | 25 W. 45th St. (bet. 5th & 6th Aves.) | 7/B/D/F/V to 42nd St./ Bryant Park | 212-840-7842
Canarsie | 1498 Rockaway Pkwy. (Flatlands Ave.) | Brooklyn | L to Canarsie/Rockaway Pkwy. | 718-876-6383
Staten Island | 1351 Forest Ave. (bet. Jewett & Veltman Aves.) | 718-273-9689
Staten Island | Staten Island Mall | 2655 Richmond Ave. (bet. Platinum Ave. & Richmond Hill Rd.) | 718-370-2893
Staten Island | 540 Bay St. (bet. Prospect & Sands Sts.) | 718-876-6383
www.trainingcampstores.com

"Every sneaker junkie in-the-know heads" to this military-themed "staple" with a "relaxed atmosphere" for the "hottest" kicks from

Avirex, Phat Farm and Royal Elastics along with Nike Air Jordan and Bo Jackson Air Trainer finds; "whether you're looking for comfort or just want style, they have everything for everyone", and what's more, "when they have stuff on sale, it's really a sale."

Transit ◐ | 17 | 17 | 14 | M

NoHo | 665 Broadway (bet. Bleecker & Bond Sts.) | 6 to Bleecker St. | 212-358-8726

"Grab your Metrocard" and "pass through" the "old-school turnstiles" at this multifloor NoHo standby, "one of the better places to go for midpriced" "urban streetwear" for the "hip-hop crowd" from labels like Rocawear; don't forget to "check out the sneaker" wall filled with "cool" kicks including "hard-to-find" classics – the "transit train" vibe makes "you feel like you just stepped onto a subway platform."

Trash and Vaudeville ◐ | 16 | 18 | 14 | M

E Village | 4 St. Marks Pl. (bet. 2nd & 3rd Aves.) | 6 to Astor Pl. | 212-982-3590

"Hey, ho, let's go" to this "legendary" "CBGBs of clothing", housing "a treasure trove" of "awesome rock" paraphernalia and "great club wear", including, what else, "Ramones tees", bondage collars, rubber pants "with zippers and rings", "naughty mesh things" and the "occasional beautiful corset"; "hats off" to this "museum to punk" for being "one of the last remnants of the East Village as it used to be", and for providing a "unique experience", especially for "tourists."

NEW Travessia ◐ Ⓜ | - | - | - | M

LES | 176 Stanton St. (bet. Attorney & Clinton Sts.) | F to Delancey St. | 212-477-7772 | www.travessia-nyc.com

The flirtation between fashion and art is no passing fancy at this new lifestyle retailer in the Lower East Side, where rotating exhibits hang next to a "good selection" of mainly hard-to-find Japanese and Danish women's clothing labels; there's also a selection of accessories, shoes and a smattering of unisex items for men.

Treehouse Ⓜ | - | - | - | M

Williamsburg | 430 Graham Ave. (bet. Frost & Withers Sts.) | Brooklyn | L to Graham Ave. | 718-482-8733 | www.treehousebrooklyn.com

Reawaken your childhood sense of wonder (and memories of camp crocheting classes) at this former speakeasy, now a cozy shop filled with nooks and a knitted tree; the inventory is a mix of vintage clothes, quirky mens- and womenswear (from lines like Feral Childe, Bobbi and Papi's Mami) and tweet treasures in totes and home furnishings – most from local designers; craft classes and knitting circles also keep this Williamsburg corner crowded; N.B. closed Tuesdays too.

Treillage Ⓢ | - | - | - | VE

E 70s | 418 E. 75th St. (bet. 1st & York Aves.) | 6 to 77th St. | 212-535-2288 | www.treillageonline.com

For more than a decade, "decorators have flocked" to this Upper East Side, garden-inspired furnishings shop owned by interior designer Bunny Williams and antiques dealer John Rosselli; "unique" items, such as cast-stone bird baths from the 1920s and vintage French melon pots make for pretty pictures, but unless you are an "upscale client", these "beautiful" pieces may prove über-"expensive."

NEW Tribbles Home & Garden

| 25 | 24 | 22 | E |

TriBeCa | 217 W. Broadway (Franklin St.) | 1 to Franklin St. | 212-965-8480 |
www.tribbleshomeandgarden.com

A "wonderful addition to the neighborhood" is what supporters of sisters Cara Stone-Pfeifer and Elizabeth Rad's new one-stop TriBeCa shop say about their "beautifully displayed" "eclectic" home goods ranging from "kitchen gadgets" to items for entertaining and gift-giving; while there's a florist and potted plants up front, it's the eco-friendly personal products that may leave you with a "green thumb."

Tribeca Girls ⓜ

| - | - | - | E |

TriBeCa | 171 Duane St. (bet. Greenwich & Hudson Sts.) | 1/2/3 to Chambers St. | 212-925-0049 | www.tribecagirls.com

"Top fashions for the littlest fashionista in your house", ranging from novelty T-shirts to colorful hoodies and kicky minis, fill the racks of this spacious TriBeCa yearling that caters to girls sizes 2T–14; the on-trend looks from prized labels like Diesel, Junk Food and Paul Frank are "sure-to-please" stylin' girls and their footstep-following younger sisters.

Trico Field

| - | - | - | E |

SoHo | 65 W. Houston St. (Wooster St.) | B/D/F/V to B'way/Lafayette St. | 212-358-8484

The Japanese invasion of SoHo presses on with this inviting Houston Street shop, a thoughtfully merchandised, rectangular-shaped childrenswear find owned by Fith, an Asian powerhouse company; shoppers have a field day choosing sophisticated styles for fashionable kids, particularly boys, from wooden shelves and a chunky table, creating outfits with durable essentials like jean jackets, cargo pants, striped boatnecks and rugged button-down shirts, most made from natural fabrications.

Trina Turk

| - | - | - | E |

Meatpacking | 67 Gansevoort St. (bet. Greenwich & Washington Sts.) | A/C/E/L to 14th St./8th Ave. | 212-206-7383 | www.trinaturk.com

Like an oasis in the desert, West Coast designer Trina Turk's Meatpacking District boutique rejuvenates fashionistas thirsting for form-fitting sweaters and flattering frocks in Palm Springs shades and mod patterns; reminiscent of Big Sur, the '70s-styled white space boasts splashes of color and was designed by Jonathan Adler, whose ceramics the store carries, along with a small collection of menswear.

Triple Five Soul

| 21 | 20 | 18 | E |

SoHo | 290 Lafayette St. (bet. Houston & Prince Sts.) | B/D/F/V to B'way/Lafayette St. | 212-431-2404

Williamsburg | 145 Bedford Ave. (N. 9th St.) | Brooklyn | L to Bedford Ave. | 718-599-5971 ◗
www.triple5soul.com

"Love it!" say the "trendy young" things who flock to this SoHo-Williamsburg duo to scoop up "surprisingly innovative" hoodies, velour sweatpants, boyfriend jeans and satin parkas that "ooze coolness"; if you dig the "New York grunge-casual skateboarder" look, these "excellent cutting-edge" his-and-hers threads with an "unbelievable fit" are the "epitome of hipster" "urban" "fashion", plus there's plenty of music and art in store to keep your Triple Five Soul enlightened.

ⓏTrixie and Peanut ●Ⓜ

| 27 | 28 | 24 | VE |

Flatiron | 23 E. 20th St. (bet. B'way & Park Ave.) | 4/5/6/L/N/Q/R/W to 14th St./Union Sq. | 212-358-0881 | www.trixieandpeanut.com

A "beautiful" barks-and-mortar incarnation of an "amazing" online re-tail-er, this "upscale boutique" for animal companions has become a Flatiron "favorite" for "fabulous" apparel, carriers and "doggy jewelry" that "make your pet stand out in a crowd"; the staff supplies "great service", and "as long as you're not afraid of spending more money on your pooch than yourself", it's "as good as it gets."

ⓃⒺⓌ Trixie & Tilda Ⓜ

| ▽ 25 | 21 | 21 | M |

Downtown | 407 Atlantic Ave. (Bond St.) | Brooklyn | A/C/G to Hoyt/Schermerhorn Sts. | 718-643-2100 | www.trixieandtilda.com

"Friendly" fashion industry veteran Emmi Haddock named this cute Atlantic Avenue jewelbox after her daughters, Beatrix and Mathilda, and fills it with "unique" girls' and tween-size clothing from labels like Splendid and Small Paul – the kind of stuff her kids, and like-minded budding stylesetters – like to wear; the inviting digs, done up with turquoise walls and a funky dressing room curtain, also make tiny customers feel right at home.

Troy Ⓩ

| - | - | - | VE |

Gramercy | 99 Madison Ave. (bet. 29th & 30th Sts.) | 6 to 28th St. | 212-941-4777 | 888-941-4777 | www.troysoho.com

"I'd rather live without furnishings than live without Troy" proclaim proponents of this airy, iconic and expensive store; its Gramercy Park site showcases a large collection of "cool" contemporary beds, coffee tables, chairs and couches from American and European designers like Fritz Hansen, Living Davani and Porro, along with the namesake owner's home-accessories collection that combines exotic wood with sterling silver in items like bowls and napkin rings.

True Religion

| - | - | - | E |

SoHo | 132 Prince St. (Wooster St.) | N/R/W to Prince St. | 212-966-6011 | www.truereligionbrandjeans.com

A mainstay in the pages of *US Weekly,* this beloved-by-celebs denim brand from LA takes on SoHo; the rough-hewn and woody space complements the vintage feel of the artfully worn-in duds (including T-shirts, flannels and hoodies) but the real stars are the pricey premium jeans including low-rise styles adorned with signature curve-hugging back pockets and distinctive horseshoe stitching; N.B. plans are afoot to open branches in the Time Warner Center, on the Upper East Side and in Union Square.

TSE Ⓩ

| 26 | - | 22 | VE |

SoHo | 120 Wooster St. (bet. Prince & Spring Sts.) | C/E to Spring St. | 212-472-7790 | www.tsecashmere.com

Oh, Tse can you see how "stylish" the stock is, a "sorbet assortment" of colors and "contemporary" silhouettes that ensures these luxurious knits are "not your grandma's cashmere"; admittedly "the prices are thick for such thin ply", but the "pleasant" staff makes you believe "if you could own one of these sweaters for every day of winter, your life would be complete"; N.B. it was set to move to the above SoHo address in winter 2008.

Tucker Robbins ⌧

	QUALITY	DISPLAY	SERVICE	COST
	-	-	-	VE

E 50s | 139 E. 57th St., 4th fl. (bet. Lexington & 3rd Aves.) | 4/5/6/F/
N/R/W to 59th St./Lexington Ave. | 212-355-3383 Ⓜ
LIC | 33-02 Skillman Ave. (33rd St.) | Queens | 7 to 33rd St. | 718-764-0222
www.tuckerrobbins.com

Named after their eponymous and unusual owner – a former monk
turned designer – these East 50s and Long Island City spaces showcase "interesting" furniture from around the world, which is made primarily from recycled wood and inspired by traditional Asian and
African forms, leading loyalists to say it looks like "like no one else's";
N.B. the East 50s branch is by appointment only – with Tucker himself.

Tuesday's Child

	QUALITY	DISPLAY	SERVICE	COST
	▽ 26	16	19	E

Flatbush | 1904 Ave. M (E. 19th St.) | Brooklyn | Q to Ave. M | 718-375-1790
Midwood | 2771 Nostrand Ave. (bet. Ave. N & Kings Hwy.) | Brooklyn |
Q to Kings Hwy. | 718-252-8874
888-244-5388 | www.tuesdayschild.com

It's "been around forever", but this Midwood mecca hasn't lost its
edge when it comes to whipping the wardrobes of city kids into ship-
shape; with a brand roster that reads like a who's who of "designer
names" (Burberry, Dolce & Gabbana and Sonia Rykiel to name a few),
"it's the right place to find high-priced" togs with "some regular
European clothes mixed in"; if you don't have a fat wallet, check out
the Avenue M outlet.

⊠ TUMI

	QUALITY	DISPLAY	SERVICE	COST
	28	23	23	VE

E 40s | Grand Central | 42nd St. (Vanderbilt Ave.) | 4/5/6/7/S to 42nd St./
Grand Central | 212-973-0015 ◗
E 50s | 520 Madison Ave. (54th St.) | E/V to 5th Ave./53rd St. |
212-813-0545
NEW **E 80s** | 1100 Madison Ave. (bet. 82nd & 83rd Sts.) | 4/5/6 to
86th St. | 212-288-8802
SoHo | 102 Prince St. (bet. Greene & Mercer Sts.) | N/R/W to Prince St. |
646-613-9101
W 40s | Rockefeller Ctr. | 53 W. 49th St. (bet. 5th & 6th Aves.) | B/D/
F/V to 47-50th Sts./Rockefeller Ctr. | 212-245-7460
W 60s | The Shops at Columbus Circle, Time Warner Ctr. |
10 Columbus Circle, ground fl. (60th St. at B'way) | 1/A/B/C/D to
59th St./Columbus Circle | 212-823-9390 ◗
800-322-8864 | www.tumi.com

"Luggage for road warriors" sums up this "classy, unobtrusive" outfit
renowned for its "extremely well-designed", "nothing short of fabulous" finds in "catchy au courant colors" and "gorgeous patterns"; "for
those who appreciate workmanship and durability", these pieces "can
take a beating", "survive the flight" and possibly even "last the rest of
your life and beyond"; in short, "it's the only suitcase" to own and well
"worth the investment."

Tupli ⌧Ⓜ

	QUALITY	DISPLAY	SERVICE	COST
	-	-	-	VE

E 60s | 780 Madison Ave., 2nd fl. (bet. 66th & 67th Sts.) | 6 to 68th St. |
212-472 2576 | www.tupli.com

There are unique, exquisite European-style custom-made shoes for
every woman at this by-appointment-only Madison Avenue atelier
where partners Kathy Myczkowski and Tamara Chubinidze strive to
create a knockout pair just for you – as long as you don't mind shelling

out lots of green; the staff researches your personal style, a mold is made of your foot for the best fit and, voilà: weeks later, your sole mate arrives.

☑ Turnbull & Asser ☒

28 | 27 | 25 | VE

E 50s | 42 E. 57th St. (bet. Madison & Park Aves.) | 4/5/6/F/N/R/W to 59th St./Lexington Ave. | 212-752-5700 | 877-887-6285 | www.turnbullandasser.com

"Dapper only begins to describe" the "superb English offerings" at this multidepartment "bespoke club" housed in a five-story townhouse on East 57th Street; since 1885, this "serious", "professional" haberdasher has "maintained the integrity" of its "classic, clean" dress shirts, suits and cashmere sweaters that run the gamut from banker to "dandy", and from lord to lady; service is highly "courteous", but beware – the bill for even a couple of the "great ties" may be "more expensive than the best dinner you ever had."

Two Jakes ☑

▽ 21 | 14 | 20 | M

Williamsburg | 320 Wythe Ave. (bet. Grand & S. 1st Sts.) | Brooklyn | L to Bedford Ave. | 718-782-7780 | www.twojakes.com

Within the 10,000-sq.-ft. industrial garagelike setting of this home-and office-furnishings store along the Williamsburg waterfront, there are "great vintage finds in wonderful condition" from Bisley to bludot, Offi to Emeco and Herman Miller to Knoll, along with new offerings like the owners' own J-line sofas and club chairs; N.B. check out sidekick Mini Jake for kids' furniture, bedding and more.

212 Kids

23 | 22 | 21 | E

E 80s | 230 E. 83rd St. (bet. 2nd & 3rd Aves.) | 4/5/6 to 86th St. | 212-535-4131 | www.212kids.com

For the child "who has everything" or that "last-minute birthday gift", dialed-in shoppers pop over to this "perfect little neighborhood" "playland" in the East 80s; it's always "well-stocked" with "plenty" of "unique" toys, both "oldies but goodies and newer" items, including "dress-up clothes", magic sets and science kits – and if they don't have it, "they'll get it for you"; throw in delivery service, gift-wrapping and a "kid-friendly" vibe, and it's no wonder the wowed vow it's a "keeper."

202

23 | 24 | 19 | E

Chelsea | Chelsea Mkt. | 75 Ninth Ave. (bet. 15th & 16th Sts.) | 1 to 18th St. | 646-638-0115

We "love" that her "sweet" 202 Cafe is "right in the middle of it all – very innovative and truly the future of retail" predict prognosticators who praise Nicole Farhi's Chelsea Market "one-stop" concept shop where a "great variety" of the British-based designer's clothing for men and women, "beautiful furniture", home accessories and "unique gifts" comingle; "anything you buy would get compliments" confide brunchers and browsers who frequent this pretty, if admittedly "pricey" place.

UGG Australia

- | - | - | E

SoHo | 79 Mercer St. (bet. Broome & Spring Sts.) | 6 to Spring St. | 212-226-0602 | www.uggaustralia.com

Just when you thought the sheepskin trend had reached its expiration date, the California-based brand founded by a Down Under surfer stakes its claim on SoHo, unveiling footwear, accessories and outerwear for the entire family in woodsy-colored digs; get your fill of fuzzy-wuzzy styles with the classic boot, lined flip-flops, slippers, even handbags, then dip into the smart selection of espadrilles, sandals and tote bags.

Uniqlo ◐ | - | - | - | I

SoHo | 546 Broadway (bet. Prince & Spring Sts.) | N/R/W to Prince St. | 917-237-8800 | www.uniqlo.com

"Never do laundry again - just give the dirty stuff away and buy more" maintain mavens of this massive Japanese manufacturer, whose multifloor SoHo flagship features a dizzying array of "cheap" casual cashmeres, cottons and cords "in a glow of colors" and ever-changing capsule collections from edgy designer labels like Alice Roi and Cloak; yes, the garments "aren't the highest quality", but given that the line for the men's fitting room is as long as at the women's, clearly everyone enjoys the "disposable clothing at its finest."

Unis | - | - | - | E

NoLita | 226 Elizabeth St. (bet. Houston & Prince Sts.) | N/R/W to Prince St. | 212-431-5533 | www.unisnewyork.com

This tiny but tempting NoLita shop draws the generation of guys and gals who like their sportswear cut with nonchalant chic - and know designer-owner Eunice Lee delivers just that in blousy shirts, cargo-style trousers, military-inspired coats and teensy-strap dresses with a vintage feel.

Unisa | 20 | 21 | 18 | M

E 60s | 701 Madison Ave. (bet. 62nd & 63rd Sts.) | 4/5/6/F/N/R/W to 59th St./Lexington Ave. | 212-753-7474 | www.unisa.com

For those seeking "a good quality shoe" in "a conservative-chic style" that's "not too flashy", this East 60s chainlet link serves up "fun designs at palatable prices"; not only are there "lots of flats and little heels", you may uncover the "best knockoffs in town", from "metallic slides" to "comfortable" mules, mocs and boots.

United Colors of Benetton | 20 | 20 | 17 | M

(aka Benetton)

E 40s | 601 Fifth Ave. (bet. 48th & 49th Sts.) | E/V to 5th Ave./53rd St. | 212-317-2501 ◐

Flatiron | 133 Fifth Ave. (20th St.) | N/R/W to 23rd St. | 212-420-5700 ◐

G Village | 749 Broadway (bet. Astor Pl. & 8th St.) | N/R/W to 8th St. | 212-533-0230 ◐

Seaport | Pier 17 | 10 Fulton St. (bet. Front & South Sts.) | 2/3/4/5/A/C/J/M/Z to Fulton St./B'way/Nassau | 212-509-3999 ◐

W 60s | The Shops at Columbus Circle, Time Warner Ctr. | 10 Columbus Circle, 2nd fl. (60th St. at B'way) | 1/A/B/C/D to 59th St./Columbus Circle | 212-245-5117 ◐

Bay Ridge | 409 86th St. (bet. 4th & 5th Aves.) | Brooklyn | R to 86th St. | 718-748-1555

Borough Park | 4610 13th Ave. (bet. 46th & 47th Sts.) | Brooklyn | D/M to Fort Hamilton Pkwy. | 718-853-3420

Astoria | 31-17 Steinway St. (bet. B'way & 31st Ave.) | Queens | G/R/V to Steinway St. | 718-721-3333

Forest Hills | 71-27 Austin St. (71st Rd.) | Queens | E/F/G/R/V to Forest Hills/71st Ave. | 718-544-7117 ◐

www.benetton.com

Those nostalgic for their last "trip to Italy" head to this "'80s outpost" for "bright, happy" men's and women's apparel whose "clean looks" seem somewhat "original by American standards" and sport prices "any new professional can afford"; still, foes complain of "uninspiring" designs and a "bad return policy" – each store is independently owned, so you must take merchandise back to the location where you bought it.

United Colors of Benetton Kids ❷
(aka UCB Kids)

21	22	18	M

W 60s | The Shops at Columbus Circle, Time Warner Ctr. | 10 Columbus Circle, 2nd fl. (60th St. at B'way) | 1/A/B/C/D to 59th St./Columbus Circle | 212-823-9569 | www.benetton.com

Proponents of "cute", "reasonably priced" children's clothes that "you won't see all of your friends' kids in" are united in their support of this Italian-style stallion's tot-oriented offshoot, with a "fabulous" Time Warner Center location next to sibling Sisley; snap up sassy school togs, winter jackets, activewear and accessories, available in a rainbow of "great colors" and patterns.

Urban Angler ⌧

–	–	–	E

Chelsea | 206 Fifth Ave., 3rd fl. (bet. 25th & 26th Sts.) | N/R/W to 23rd St. | 212-689-6400 | 800-255-5488 | www.urbanangler.com

Chelsea's fly-fishing mecca draws greenhorns and old salts alike with its "blue-ribbon quality" selection that "makes you proud" to be an angler; it's "nice to have a complete gear shop" in the "canyons of Manhattan" where you can pick up Sage rods, Abel reels, waders and a healthy dose of advice about local waters from "professionals"; P.S. sign up for casting lessons in nearby Madison Square Park with "appropriately named" owner Jon Fisher.

⦾ Urban Archaeology ⌧

25	24	19	VE

E 50s | 239 E. 58th St. (bet. 2nd & 3rd Aves.) | 4/5/6/F/N/R/W to 59th St./Lexington Ave. | 212-371-4646
TriBeCa | 143 Franklin St. (bet. Hudson & Varick Sts.) | 1 to Franklin St. | 212-431-4646
www.urbanarchaeology.com

For a "unique" collection of rescued and replica plunder, renovators recommend these TriBeCa and East 50s salvage shrines; "unusual handmade tiles", lighting, plumbing, pediments and statuary make them "fun places to scout", so the only dig is that sky-high prices mean that most can only "look, but not buy."

Urban Outfitters ❷

17	19	13	M

Chelsea | 526 Sixth Ave. (14th St.) | F/L/V to 14th St./6th Ave. | 646-638-1646
E 50s | 999 Third Ave. (bet. 59th & 60th Sts.) | 4/5/6/F/N/R/W to 59th St./Lexington Ave. | 212-308-1518
E Village | 162 Second Ave. (bet. 10th & 11th Sts.) | 6 to Astor Pl. | 212-375-1277
G Village | 374 Sixth Ave. (Waverly Pl.) | A/B/C/D/E/F/V to W. 4th St. | 212-677-9350
G Village | 628 Broadway (bet. Bleecker & Houston Sts.) | B/D/F/V to B'way/Lafayette St. | 212-475-0009
W 70s | 2081 Broadway (72nd St.) | 1/2/3 to 72nd St. | 212-579-3912
Rego Park | Queens Ctr. | 90-15 Queens Blvd. (bet. 57th & 59th Aves.) | Queens | G/R/V to Woodhaven Blvd. | 718-699-7511
800-282-2200 | www.urbanoutfitters.com

"Bohemian clothes" and "the funkiest" apartment kitsch bring budding hipsters who want to "look like an Olsen twin" to this "fun" chain;

the feel's "overpriced Salvation Army" and service is mostly "subpar", but that doesn't keep the novelty books, "mass-produced vintage tees", "trenderrific" shoes and such from flying off the shelves.

NEW Urban Zen 🖎   - | - | - | E

W Village | 705 Greenwich St. (bet. Charles & W. 10th Sts.) | 1 to Christopher St./Sheridan Sq. | 212-206-3999 | www.urbanzen.org

Last year, Donna Karan opened a temporary shop during an alternative-health forum in the West Village; it proved so popular it's become permanent – a large sculpture-adorned space where almost everything, from the teakwood tables to the ceramics, is for sale (part of the proceeds go to funding programs at various institutions and charities); the emphasis, though, is on the Urban Zen men's and women's line – flowy separates, made of natural or recycled fabrics that are ideal for mixing, matching and layering; jewelry and organic COMO Shambhala toiletries round out the collection.

Utowa   20 | 25 | 18 | E

Flatiron | 17 W. 18th St. (bet. 5th & 6th Aves.) | 1 to 18th St. | 212-929-4800 | 866-929-4800 | www.utowa.com

"Selling everything from flowers to clothes to makeup" (the founder is the late Shu Uemura's son), this "astronomically beautiful", brightly lit Flatiron venue offers an "eclectic mix" of goods, including "perfectly styled" womenswear ("think Yamamoto instead of Chanel") and some men's; but while "high on concept, it's low on quality" quibble critics, who also complain of "overeager or cannot-be-bothered salespeople."

Utrecht   24 | 17 | 18 | M

Chelsea | 237 W. 23rd St. (bet. 7th & 8th Aves.) | 1 to 23rd St. | 212-675-8699 ◗
E Village | 111 Fourth Ave. (bet. 11th & 12th Sts.) | 4/5/6/L/N/Q/R/W to 14th St./Union Sq. | 212-777-5353
800-223-9132 | www.utrecht.com

"*Viva* Utrecht!" – a "favorite of art students", this "reliable, important standby" in the East Village stocks "quality products at reasonable prices" including its own "top-notch brand" of paints and brushes, plus "tools and materials galore"; the landscape may be a bit "cluttered" (don't expect "fancy displays"), but the staff's "knowledgeable" and the selection's "grand" at this 50-year-old "neighborhood resource"; N.B. artists across town can cruise the younger Chelsea branch.

☑ Valentino 🖎   28 | 27 | 25 | VE

E 60s | 747 Madison Ave. (65th St.) | 6 to 68th St. | 212-772-6969 | www.valentino.com

After 45 years of creating "gorgeous grown-up clothes" including red-carpet-worthy gowns ("always the specialty") favored by the likes of luminaries such as Julia Roberts and Ashley Judd and "luscious" tailored jet-set suits, this legendary Italian designer recently retired and passed the baton to new womenswear designer Alessandra Facchinetti and menswear designer Ferruccio Pozzoni; if you're "serious about something fabulous", the "elegant" collections "with prices to match" are still sure to please at this "spacious", limestone-floored Madison Avenue shop.

| | QUALITY | DISPLAY | SERVICE | COST |

Valley

LES | 48 Orchard St. (bet. Grand & Hester Sts.) | B/D to Grand St. | 212-274-8985 | www.valleynyc.com

A little bit of California makes its way to this large LES store, where West Coast sisters Nina and Julia Werman bring together a smart mix of LA-based lines like Mike + Chris, Sweet Tater and Borne displayed alongside clog boots and moccasins; the spirit of the San Fernando Valley lives in the woody environment that includes a lounge area and a spa for manicures and Brazilian wax treatments – so shoppers can look slick as they slip into the hip clothes.

◙ Van Cleef & Arpels ▣   29 | 28 | 28 | VE

E 50s | 744 Fifth Ave. (57th St.) | N/R/W to 5th Ave./59th St. | 212-644-9500 | www.vancleef.com

"Exquisite" "drool jewelry" for "people made of money" sums up this estimable French firm, right next to Bergdorf's, whose celebrated clientele has ranged from The Duchess of Windsor (who suggested the zipper necklace that continues today) to Catherine Zeta-Jones; "truly classical beauties" here include the signature Alhambra quatrefoil (clover) necklace and "gorgeous", invisibly set floral gemstone pieces updated from their '20s and '30s origins; while a few sniff "snooty", most fans praise the "accommodating service"; N.B. a recent centennial face-lift that adds an art deco chandelier and fireplace to the stunning space may outdate the above Display score.

Vanessa Noel ▣   - | - | - | VE

E 60s | 158 E. 64th St. (Lexington Ave.) | 6 to 68th St. | 212-906-0054

Celebs like Gwyneth Paltrow and Katie Couric take on the town in "trendy, but not way out" handmade-in-Italy pumps, sandals and slingbacks from this designer's couture line, while mere mortals fall for the more affordable collection and brides scoop up "particularly good wedding shoes" at this East 60s townhouse; as you slip into "sexy" styles at the store, take note: your seat may match your feet, as Noel oftentimes uses the same fabrics for both.

Varda   ▽ 27 | 21 | 21 | E

SoHo | 147 Spring St. (bet. W. B'way & Wooster St.) | C/E to Spring St. | 212-941-4990

W 70s | 2080 Broadway (71st St.) | 1/2/3 to 72nd St. | 212-873-6910 ◗

www.vardashoes.com

"These shoes are a treat" for the feet confirm fans who cool their heels at this his-and-hers duo Up- and Downtown, a veritable "savior" stocked with "comfortable and long-lasting" footwear that "never goes out of style"; for the ladies, "perfect boots", pointy pumps, ankle-strap sandals, and for the guys, luxe loafers, wing tips and hand-stitched moccasins, all "flattering", and, of course, "well-made" in Italy.

Variazioni   17 | 18 | 15 | E

NEW NoLita | 214 Mulberry St. (Spring St.) | 6 to Spring St. | 212-941-5577 ◗

W 80s | 2389 Broadway (bet. 87th & 88th Sts.) | 1 to 86th St. | 212-595-1760 ◗

W 80s | 2395 Broadway (88th St.) | 1 to 86th St. | 212-595-8810

Variazioni is the spice of life at these trio of women's boutiques, boasting a "quirky mix" of "NYC hip" finds, including "perfect" denim, plus cashmere and shearling galore; "trendy, yet timeless" "pretty things" "abound", in fact, "you just may find a gem" assert admirers who also single out the "end-of-season blow-out sales" and confide that while the staff seems "pushy", they "know what they're talking about."

VeKa Bridal Couture

NoLita | 284 Mulberry St. (bet. Houston & Prince Sts.) | 6 to Bleecker St. | 212-925-9044 | www.vekacc.com

"Modern" bridalwear that flies in the face of convention is the mainstay of this NoLita nuptials nook that showcases "excellent dresses by a select" handful of designers in a spare space done up with antique chandeliers; while these fanciful, neo-couture designs court romance, contemporary simplicity, from architectural lines to accents like waist-clinching obis, is also key to the sexy, edgy "impressive" ensembles.

Venture

E 80s | 1156 Madison Ave. (bet. 85th & 86th Sts.) | 4/5/6 to 86th St. | 212-288-7235 | 888-388-2727

Upper East Siders venture that this long-standing stationer is a "handy" and "practical" "all-rounder" with everything from "Crane's to stickers for the kids", writing instruments, invitations, art supplies and leather goods from the likes of Longchamp; but they also call the service "unhelpful" and the store "a bit unkempt."

Vera Wang Bridal Salon ⑤

E 70s | 991 Madison Ave. (77th St.) | 6 to 77th St. | 212-628-3400 | www.verawang.com

"Dreamy", with a "royal feel", Vera Wang's Madison Avenue salon (appointments preferred) is a matrimonial "must" if your "budget is on the large side"; the "dresses are divine" (you won't "look like a high school homecoming float"), the "lighting flattering" and the "dressing rooms larger than most NYC bedrooms", plus the staff has "a keen sense of what flatters every figure", "guiding you through the world of lace and silhouettes"; even budget-minded to-bes sigh if you "try on the wonderful designs then buy" elsewhere, "you'll always have that day of splendor."

Vera Wang Maids on Madison ⑤

E 70s | 980 Madison Ave., 3rd fl. (bet. 76th & 77th Sts.) | 6 to 77th St. | 212-628-9898 | www.verawang.com

"If you're going to be in a wedding", "make an appointment" at this "super-luxurious", "top-notch" Madison Avenue salon where the designer "strikes again", this time with a "wide array of colors and shapes to suit" everyone in your party; "despite Vera's reputation for being expensive", many of these "beautiful, classic dresses" "look so un-bridesmaidy they could be worn again", and what's more, the "impeccable service makes you feel like the only girl in the store!"

Vercesi Hardware

Gramercy | 152 E. 23rd St. (bet. Lexington & 3rd Aves.) | 6 to 23rd St. | 212-475-1883 | www.vercesihardware.com

"Last of the great old-fashioned hardware stores" insist hammer-wielders about this "comprehensive", "independent" Gramercy "treasure" "crammed with good stuff" "where they greet you by name" and "practically come home to assist with a repair"; that "personal touch" means the staff "will find the exact nail you asked for, then explain why you need a bolt instead."

Verdura ⑤

E 50s | 745 Fifth Ave. (bet. 57th & 58th Sts.) | N/R/W to 5th Ave./ 59th St. | 212-758-3388 | www.verdura.com

Between the rich Fifth Avenue penthouse feel, the "witty and creative jewelry" and the service – "they treat every customer like royalty" – it feels as if "Fulco Verdura were still around", whipping up deliciously colorful, Byzantine-inspired Maltese-cross cuffs and pieces like the wrapped-heart brooch and diamond bow-tied peridot ear clips that exude "elegance"; wistful worshipers sigh "oh, to win the Lottery."

Veronique

E 90s | 1321 Madison Ave. (93rd St.) | 6 to 96th St. | 212-831-7800 | 888-265-5848 | www.veroniquematernity.com

An oasis for pregnant women who "want to sport the latest" fashions, this Upper East Sider stocks a "great selection" of designer items like Chaiken cords, Diane von Furstenberg wrap dresses and Chip & Pepper jeans "so chic" you'd "hardly know they're maternity clothes"; though the prices are "high", it's the "best of the bunch."

Versace

E 50s | 647 Fifth Ave. (bet. 51st & 52nd Sts.) | E/V to 5th Ave./53rd St. | 212-317-0224 | www.versace.com

Exhibitionist fashionistas who are "tall, thin and have a big bank account" are in "heaven, heaven, heaven" browsing in the multistoried Fifth Avenue flagship where the selection of "sexy" silhouettes in colorful silks and prints is "pretty outrageous"; while "intimidating at first glance", "the salespeople are always happy to help" ("they treated my son like he was a Trump").

Verve ◐

W 70s | 282 Columbus Ave. (bet. 73rd & 74th Sts.) | 1/2/3 to 72nd St. | 212-580-7150

W Village | 338 Bleecker St. (bet. Christopher & W. 10th Sts.) | 1 to Christopher St./Sheridan Sq. | 212-675-6693

W Village | 353 Bleecker St. (bet. Charles & W. 10th Sts.) | 1 to Christopher St./Sheridan Sq. | 212-691-6516

"Up-to-the-minute NYC girls" strut into these "continually restocked" "treasure troves" "overflowing" with "great goodies" and "always wind up leaving with some fabulous find"; the 'V' in 'Verve' is for variety", as in "funky jewelry" and "luscious, unusual" accessories from "local and European designers" "you haven't heard about yet, but will" at a "refreshing range" of prices; P.S. the shoes at 338 Bleecker "are to die for."

Vespa

SoHo | 13 Crosby St. (bet. Grand & Howard Sts.) | 6/J/M/N/Q/R/W/ Z to Canal St. | 212-226-4410 | www.vespasoho.com Ⓜ

Bronx | 3522 Webster Ave. (Gun Hill Rd.) | 2/5 to Gun Hill Rd. | 718-654-3300 | www.vespabronx.com ◐⑤

"The coolest" of cool, Piaggio USA showcases its mod motor scooters in a rainbow of "snazzy" colors and styles at this sleek, Euro-chic transportation boutique on the edge of SoHo and at a Bronx locale too; kick your "hip" quotient into high gear with a classic LX edition, replete with customized details, and if you really want to look *bellissimo* in transit, add an eye-catching helmet made by Italian craftsmen.

Victoria's Secret ❶ — 18 | 21 | 18 | M

Garment District | 1328 Broadway (34th St.) | B/D/F/N/Q/R/V/W to 34th St./Herald Sq. | 212-356-8380 | 800-888-1500 | www.victoriassecret.com
Additional locations throughout the NY area

Yes, the "Starbucks of lingerie" is "definitely for the masses", but for "Victoria's addicts", this "must-visit" chain is like "dipping your hand into a cookie jar" and emerging with "whipped cream and a cherry on top"; scout the "perfectly ordered" displays for "slinky sleepwear", a "tantalizing array of undergarments" or "something racy for that special night" and "leave feeling sexy from just being inside"; but while some tout the "tag-team" staff that even makes men feel "comfortable", others insist that service is "over-solicitous."

Vilebrequin — 27 | 25 | 22 | E

E 80s | 1070 Madison Ave. (81st St.) | 6 to 77th St. | 212-650-0353
SoHo | 436 W. Broadway (Prince St.) | C/E to Spring St. | 212-431-0673
888-458-0051 | www.vilebrequin.com

Sentimentalists say there's "nothing cuter than seeing a father and son in matching" bathing trunks from this "adorable, French" swimwear pair in SoHo and the East 80s; "if you have it to spend, it doesn't get any better" – the "colors are bright, the quality amazing" and ze "unique" look is very "St. Tropez meets East Hampton" with "tons of tropical prints that aren't cheesy or loud" to choose from.

Village Tannery ❶ — 21 | 15 | 19 | M

NoHo | 7 Great Jones St. (Lafayette St.) | 6 to Bleecker St. | 212-979-0013
W Village | 173 Bleecker St. (bet. MacDougal & Sullivan Sts.) | A/B/C/D/E/F/V to W. 4th St. | 212-673-5444
www.villagetannery.com

"If you need anything leather" to carry your essentials, canter over to this NoHo–West Village duo that's "been around forever"; the "low-key vibe suits the down-to-earth" feel of the "distinctive", "well-priced" artisan-made totes, backpacks, duffels, briefcases and handbags scattered about; P.S. "they can make any design you have in mind", plus you can catch a glimpse of the workshop at the Great Jones store.

V.I.M. 🗷Ⓜ — 14 | 11 | 11 | I

Harlem | 2239 Third Ave. (bet. 121st & 122nd Sts.) | 4/5/6 to 125th St. | 212-369-5033
Additional locations throughout the NY area

"Breeze in and breeze out" of this sneaker- and jean-centric chain, which makes sure its V.I.M. (Very Important Merchandise) includes "a good, basic collection of everyday wear, with a bit of jazz added in" from "trendy" brands like Fubu and Puma, all at "cheap prices"; "leave pretentiousness at the door", and scout out the basement for "cool" kicks.

Vintage Thrift Shop ❶ — 22 | 21 | 22 | M

Gramercy | 286 Third Ave. (bet. 22nd & 23rd Sts.) | 6 to 23rd St. | 212-871-0777

"Loaded with nostalgic items", this "cozy" thrift store near Gramercy Park is "great for the prop designer" (many shop here) "and those who long for another era"; they'll find it represented by the "mostly high-end merchandise", including "art deco armchairs", "shabby-chic" clothing, "good glassware", books and jewelry; usually the wares are "well presented", but it can be "messy", so maybe, some say, it's better if you "don't go (more for me)"; N.B. closed Saturdays.

⦿ Virgin Megastore ☻ 23 | 21 | 15 | M

Union Sq | 52 E. 14th St. (B'way) | 4/5/6/L/N/Q/R/W to 14th St./Union Sq. | 212-598-4666
W 40s | 1540 Broadway, level 2 (bet. 45th & 46th Sts.) | 1/2/3/7/N/Q/R/S/W to 42nd St./Times Sq. | 212-921-1020
www.virgin.com

Megastore virgins beware: the recently refurbed "multifloor" Times Square "mother ship" can be "a little dizzying", what with "really 21st-century" listening stations, a story-high video screen and "hordes" of tourists checking out the "impressive" offerings from CDs to DVDs to clothing; the Union Square outpost is "more civilized" with a "fabulous" selection of imports, and even if they're "not the cheapest", you're "almost guaranteed" to get satisfaction at these "temples of sound."

Vitra - | - | - | VE

Meatpacking | 29 Ninth Ave. (bet. 13th & 14th Sts.) | A/C/E/L to 14th St./8th Ave. | 212-463-5750 | www.vitra.com

"A leader in modern furnishings" for the home and office, this "cool" Swiss-owned company with a Meatpacking District showroom has a "museumlike quality" that's "fitting, considering many of the pieces displayed *are* in a museum" and priced accordingly; three "dramatic" levels display designs from different eras and re-editions of '30s and '40s classics like George Nelson clocks and Jean Prouvé chairs.

Vivaldi Boutique 23 | 20 | 20 | E

E 70s | 1388 Third Ave. (79th St.) | 6 to 77th St. | 212-734-2805 | www.vivaldi-ny.com

Upper East Side socialites sing the praises of the "well-edited collection" – ranging from European suits from Rena Lange and Christian Lacroix to Reem Acra's glamorous, gala-worthy gowns to more decorous mother-of-the-bride dresses – at this long-standing clothing salon; the "classy yet not snobby staff" will have you looking "damn good", but you will pay the price for it.

Vivienne Tam ▽ 24 | - | 22 | E

SoHo | 40 Mercer St. (Grand St.) | 6 to Spring St. | 212-966-2398 | www.viviennetam.com

There's a "cool vibe" emanating from the namesake designer's womenswear with "signature Asian flair"; though it recently moved to different digs in SoHo, a simple but brightly lit space adorned with an entire intricately carved, wooden tea house, "it's still nice to look through the merch", marveling at the "intricate" designs and "lush fabrics", especially the trademark printed velvets and stretch mesh tops.

Vogel ⊠ - | - | - | VE

SoHo | 19 Howard St. (bet. B'way & Lafayette St.) | 6/J/M/N/Q/R/W/Z to Canal St. | 212-925-2460 | www.vogelboots.com

"Makes you want to go horseback riding" exclaims a certain stratum of society that gallops over to this SoHo "classic" that's been cherished for its handiwork since 1879 and chosen repeatedly to outfit the U.S.

Olympic equestrian team; from the outside it may seem "fuddy-duddy"-ish, but inside it's a "high-end" stomping ground where sporting folk order custom-made, über-expensive English riding boots, jodhpur-style (short) booties and alligator belts.

Von Dutch

| - | - | - | M |

SoHo | 109-111 Spring St. (bet. Greene & Mercer Sts.) | 6 to Spring St. | 212-965-8886 | www.vondutch.com

Catering to California-casual car culturists (both real and wannabe), this LA-born brand has just opened a pit stop in SoHo, where guys and gals can fill up on tees, trucker hats, bomber sunglasses and other samples of highway chic; the dimly lit environs also contain a logo-crazed line of tops and jeans sold only at this outpost.

Walter Steiger ⊠

| 28 | 27 | 25 | VE |

E 50s | 417 Park Ave. (55th St.) | E/V to Lexington Ave./53rd St. | 212-826-7171 | www.walter-steiger.com

"When you want the very best" his-and-hers footwear at Steigering prices, stride over to this designer's "luxurious" Park Avenue boutique and treat yourself to "beautiful, so well-made" shoes fashioned from "incredibly soft leather that tenderly hug your foot"; "love every minute of shopping here" sigh sybarites who extol the "excellent service" and can't help but fall for the "terrific styles", exotic skins and interesting details; N.B. check out the recently added line of women's handbags.

Warren Edwards ⊠

| 28 | 27 | 26 | VE |

E 60s | 107 E. 60th St. (Park Ave.) | 4/5/6/F/N/R/W to 59th St./ Lexington Ave. | 212-223-4374 | www.warrenedwards.com

The "true couture fan can create the exact shoes" of his or her "dreams" following a "personal consultation with Warren" himself or "salespeople that know their stuff" at this East 60s stomping ground where you can also gobble up "gorgeous", "terrific-looking" handmade footwear from the bi-annual collections; sure, "prices are off the charts, but so are the designs and quality", and you get to shop alongside two fox terriers who scamper about, completing the Wasp tableau.

ⓩ Waterworks ⊠

| 28 | 28 | 21 | VE |

E 50s | 225 E. 57th St. (bet. 2nd & 3rd Aves.) | 4/5/6/F/N/R/W to 59th St./Lexington Ave. | 212-371-9266
Flatiron | 7 E. 20th St. (bet. B'way & 5th Ave.) | N/R/W to 23rd St. | 212-254-6025
SoHo | 469 Broome St. (Greene St.) | C/E to Spring St. | 212-966-0605
www.waterworks.com

"Elegant bath fittings for apartments and lofts alike" can be found at these "exquisite" stores whose "marvelous presentation" of "excellent quality", "gorgeous bathroom tiles, sinks", faucets, fixtures and furnishings is "first class"; of course, the "self-important staff" and "stratospheric" prices "will bring the Waterworks to your eyes", even if you are buying "for that seven-figure fixer-upper."

Watts on Smith Ⓜ

| - | - | - | E |

Carroll Gardens | 248 Smith St. (bet. Degraw & Douglass Sts.) | Brooklyn | F/G to Carroll St. | 718-596-2359 | www.wattsonsmith.com

Unassuming but charming, this menswear standby channels the "relaxed style" of its Carroll Gardens neighborhood; the modern space is small but the fashion is major, with coveted labels like Fred Perry, Oliver Spencer, Paul Smith, Trovata and Modern Amusement sharing space alongside established lines like Wrangler and Vans.

Wedding Library ●☒Ⓜ 25 21 21 E

E 70s | 43 E. 78th St. (bet. Madison & Park Aves.) | 6 to 77th St. | 212-327-0100 | www.theweddinglibrary.com

"An oasis for stressed-out brides" and a resource for "anything wedding"-related (except the gown) is "packed into this beautiful brownstone" on the Upper East Side; multitaskers maintain it's "great for everything from planning your city" nuptials "to buying trinkets" and "cute accessories" for the wedding party, plus there's a "good selection of bridesmaid's dresses"; the icing on the cake: the staff is "nothing but lovely."

⚡ Wempe ☒ 29 27 26 VE

E 50s | 700 Fifth Ave. (55th St.) | E/V to 5th Ave./53rd St. | 212-397-9000 | 800-513-1131 | www.wempe.com

This European-style emporium in Midtown gets high marks as "a museum" for an aristocratic array of some of "the best watches anywhere", "from the merely expensive to collectibles priced in the stratosphere"; touters tick off other pluses like "tip-top service" and "the best repair department in New York."

Wendy Mink Ⓜ - - - E

LES | 72 Orchard St. (bet. Broome & Grand Sts.) | B/D to Grand St. | 212-260-8758 | www.wendyminkjewelry.com

East meets West at the designer-owner's Lower East Side namesake, a "wonderful example of a neighborhood store" with a TriBeCa studio where a team of 10 Tibetan women craft fine gold, silver and semiprecious stone jewelry; the collection (both Wendy's and other artisans') includes chandelier earrings from gold filigree to quartz fountain styles, tassel and chain-link necklaces and delicate charms representing faith, hope and charity.

WeSC ● - - - E

SoHo | 282 Lafayette St. (bet. Houston & Prince Sts.) | B/D/F/V to B'way/Lafayette St. | 212-925-9372 | www.wesc.com

Even if you don't quite get the meaning of the insiderish acronym that stands for We Are the Superlative Conspiracy, you're sure to grasp the style inherent in the skateboarder- and snowboard-inspired attire for guys and gals at this huge Lafayette Street site from the globally expanding Swedish company; the airy, wood-paneled setting is just as sleek as the hoodies, vests, cardigans and premium denim all displayed on leather tabletops.

NEW West ● - - - E

W 70s | 147 W. 72nd St. (bet. Amsterdam & Columbus Aves.) | 1/2/3 to 72nd St. | 212-787-8595

Uptown standby Tip Top makes its foray into the fashion arena with this fresh new lifestyle outpost with an urban feel on West 72nd Street, just steps from its pair of adult and kids' footwear shops; the long, large space is crammed to capacity with streetwear essentials like hoodies, tees and track jackets, along with a slew of sneakers from brands like Creative Recreation, Nike and Vans.

	QUALITY	DISPLAY	SERVICE	COST

West Elm
| | 17 | 23 | 18 | M |

Chelsea | 112 W. 18th St. (bet. 6th & 7th Aves.) | 1 to 18th St. | 212-929-4464 ●
Dumbo | 75 Front St. (Main St.) | Brooklyn | F to York St. | 718-875-7757
866-937-8356 | www.westelm.com

A "simple" but "sophisticated" "urban vibe" permeates these Williams-Sonoma–owned stores in Chelsea and Dumbo with "appealingly displayed", "affordable" furniture and "trendy" accessories like lamps and pillows in offbeat colors that are geared to "young New York professionals"; but a rising chorus of skeptics suggests "you get what you pay for", warning "what looks glam in the catalog" is actually "hit-or-miss" in real life in the "quality" department.

West Side Kids
| | 24 | 20 | 20 | M |

W 80s | 498 Amsterdam Ave. (84th St.) | 1 to 86th St. | 212-496-7282
Shoppers in search of "a special something for a special little person" swing by this "wonderful" West 80s "mom-and-pop" "independent" shop, always well stocked with a "fantastic" selection of toys "for all ages" from top brands like Lego and Playmobil; procrastinators in need of a present pronto can count on the "excellent" staff to conjure up the "perfect" gift and "wrap it too" in "10 minutes" flat.

Wet Seal ●
| | 10 | 13 | 11 | I |

Garment District | Manhattan Mall | 901 Sixth Ave. (bet. 32nd & 33rd Sts.) | B/D/F/N/Q/R/V/W to 34th St./Herald Sq. | 212-216-0622
G Village | 42 W. 14th St. (bet. 5th & 6th Aves.) | F/L/V to 14th St./ 6th Ave. | 646-336-6914
www.wetseal.com

The "racks and racks of inexpensive, trendy clothes" – going-out tops, flirty skirts and such, plus funky accessories – at this cheapie chain draw "teenyboppers" in droves to these Garment District and Village links; the of-the-moment offerings are perhaps "not the best quality", but then most buyers are "only going to throw them out" after a few wearings anyway.

What Comes Around Goes Around ●
| | ▽ 26 | 22 | 18 | E |

SoHo | 351 W. Broadway (bet. Broome & Grand Sts.) | A/C/E to Canal St. | 212-343-9303 | www.nyvintage.com

. . . "And you hope it comes to you" declare devotees of this SoHo shop that sells a century's worth (1880–1980) of vintage and vintage-inspired clothing for men, women and children; after 13 years, it's "still great for cowboy stuff" including boots and fringed shirts, plus veteran Levis from the legendary denim bar, but a few feel it's "not as good" in the newer women's designer salon and deem prices "ridiculous" – unless "you have the disposable income to buy used rock T-shirts at 12 times the original" cost.

ⓩ Whiskers ●
| | 27 | 18 | 25 | M |

E Village | 235 E. Ninth St. (bet. 2nd & 3rd Aves.) | 6 to Astor Pl. | 212-979-2532 | 800-944-7537 | www.1800whiskers.com
It's "worth the trip to the East Village" to shop at the "Whole Foods for four-legged kids", where the staff "advocates holistic pet care"; you'll also find "lots of toys, treats and homeopathic remedies" "packed in a small space", and if the "preachy nature of the place" gives paws to some, more maintain "they know their stuff" – and the "price is right."

	QUALITY	DISPLAY	SERVICE	COST

White House Black Market ❶
Flatiron | 136 Fifth Ave. (bet. 18th & 19th Sts.) | 4/5/6/L/N/Q/R/W to 14th St./Union Sq. | 212-741-8685
NEW Elmhurst | Queens Ctr. | 90-15 Queens Blvd. (bet. 57th & 59th Aves.) | Queens | G/R/V to Grand Ave./Newtown | 718-271-6572
Glendale | The Shops at Atlas Park | 71-03 80th St. (Cooper Ave.) | Queens | 718-326-0235
www.whiteandblack.com

- - - M

It's taken years for this national chain to land in NYC, but now fans of the classic womenswear that's true to its name (ahem, everything is in black and white) can find branches in the Flatiron District as well as Queens; shop for elegant tops, suits, eveningwear and jeans in well-appointed digs done up with pseudo-Victorian touches.

White on White 🖼
Murray Hill | New York Design Center Bldg. | 200 Lexington Ave. (32nd St.) | 6 to 33rd St. | 212-213-0393 | www.whiteonwhiteny.com

- - - VE

"Everything is so feminine" at this "inviting" home-furnishings shop now in Murray Hill; it's a showcase for classic Swedish style like reproduction and antique Gustavian pieces, embroidered textiles, china, bedding and baby items mostly – as the name states – in various shades of white; all is serene and "pristine" "until you look at the prices."

Whitney Museum Store 🅼
E 70s | 945 Madison Ave. (75th St.) | 6 to 77th St. | 212-570-3614 | www.whitney.org

21 17 16 M

Whether you browse the "great book selection" on the ground floor or the restaurant-adjacent shop below, the offerings are of "good quality" at this "venerable" UES American art museum; fans find "creative gifts" including housewares and toys for "every taste", but the blasé "yawn", bemoaning the "limited" merchandise and "crowded" conditions.

William Barthman
Financial District | 176 Broadway (bet. John St. & Maiden Ln.) | 2/3/4/5/A/C/J/M/Z to Fulton St./B'way/Nassau | 212-732-0890 🖼
Gravesend | 1118 Kings Hwy. (Coney Island Ave.) | Brooklyn | N to Kings Hwy. | 718-375-1818
800-727-9725 | www.williambarthman.com

▽ 26 23 24 E

Since 1884, this traditional Financial District and Gravesend gift establishment has offered a "beautiful selection" of the "best" brands: baubles from Bulgari and David Yurman, Lalique crystal, Lladró porcelains, watches and Montblanc pens; admirers also applaud "exceptional" service "that goes the extra mile", including "excellent repairs."

🆉 Williams-Sonoma
Chelsea | 110 Seventh Ave. (bet. 16th & 17th Sts.) | 1 to 18th St. | 212-633-2203 ❶
E 50s | 121 E. 59th St. (bet. Lexington & Park Aves.) | 4/5/6/F/N/R/W to 59th St./Lexington Ave. | 917-369-1131 ❶
E 80s | 1175 Madison Ave. (86th St.) | 4/5/6 to 86th St. | 212-289-6832
W 60s | The Shops at Columbus Circle, Time Warner Ctr. | 10 Columbus Circle, ground fl. (60th St. at B'way) | 1/A/B/C/D to 59th St./Columbus Circle | 212-823-9750 ❶
800-541-2233 | www.williams-sonoma.com

26 26 22 E

With "foodie eye candy" everywhere, this "classic cook's paradise" and national chain "has it all", "from blenders to bread makers", copper and stainless-steel pots and pans, linens and accessories, gourmet oils, infusions and "I-didn't-know-I-needed-that gadgets"; "pristine" layouts and a "friendly" staff also make it "great" for "housewarming and wedding gifts" – just note that "the products somehow find their way into your basket while your money finds its way out of your wallet."

William-Wayne & Co.   ▽ 26 | 22 | 22 | M

E 60s | 846-850 Lexington Ave. (bet. 64th & 65th Sts.) | 6 to 68th St. | 212-737-8934 ☒
G Village | 40 University Pl. (9th St.) | N/R/W to 8th St. | 212-533-4711
800-318-3435 | www.william-wayne.com

"If you need something" "lovely" "for your home" or for a gift, "you'll find it here" at these Greenwich Village and Upper East Side shops stocked with tasteful tableware, mirrors, linens and other accessories "chosen with a discerning eye"; devotees declare the "selection" "great", although Wasp-weary wags lament the "Muffy/Buffy"-style merch, particularly the proliferation of the signature "monkey-themed products."

Willoughby's ◑   20 | 15 | 16 | M

Garment District | 298 Fifth Ave. (31st St.) | N/R/W to 28th St. | 212-564-1600 | 800-378-1898 | www.willoughbys.com

More than 100 years old (though only four in its current location), this "great camera store" in the Garment District is still a "standard for photographers", offering some of the "best discounts in the city", especially if you "aren't afraid to bargain"; the inventory is "spread out and well presented", but some savvy sorts say "be careful" of certain "slick salesmen looking for a quick sale."

Wink   21 | 21 | 21 | E

NEW E 70s | 1050 Lexington Ave. (bet. 74th & 75th Sts.) | 6 to 77th St. | 212-249-2033
SoHo | 155 Spring St. (bet. W. B'way & Wooster St.) | C/E to Spring St. | 212-334-3646 ◑
W 60s | 188 Columbus Ave. (bet. 68th & 69th Sts.) | 1 to 66th St./Lincoln Ctr. | 212-877-7727 ◑
www.winknyc.com

"Always on-trend", this "cute" trio stocks so many "of-the-moment accessories" "you cannot walk in without buying something", be it "cool, trendy" earrings from Kipepeo, skimmers from Seychelles, slouch boots from Fornarina, handbags from Moni Moni or "unique finds"; in the wink of an eye, the "friendly staff" including the owner, former model Ilse Werther, can help you "pull together" a "gorgeous" look.

Wolford   28 | 22 | 22 | VE

E 50s | 619 Madison Ave. (bet. 58th & 59th Sts.) | 4/5/6/F/N/R/W to 59th St./Lexington Ave. | 212-688-4850 ☒
E 70s | 997 Madison Ave. (bet. 77th & 78th Sts.) | 6 to 77th St. | 212-327-1000 ☒
SoHo | 122 Greene St. (Prince St.) | N/R/W to Prince St. | 212-343-0808
NEW W 60s | The Shops at Columbus Circle, Time Warner Ctr. | 10 Columbus Circle, ground fl. (60th St. at B'way) | 1/A/B/C/D to 59th St./Columbus Circle | 212-265-7814
800-965-3673 | www.wolford.com

"Legends are made" of stockings this "superb" sigh "happy girlfriends" and smitten socialites who love the "latest styles" of this Austrian company's "unique", "superb quality" hosiery, "sexy" bodysuits and underthings; the quartet's luxe merch "costs a pretty penny" but it's "worth the price" – "at least my legs think so" – plus it "lasts and lasts!"; N.B. check out the new limited-edition designer lines from Armani and Valentino.

Wonk

– | – | – | E

Dumbo | 68 Jay St. (bet. Front & Water Sts.) | Brooklyn | F to York St. | 718-596-8026
Williamsburg | 160A N. Fourth St. (bet. Bedford & Driggs Aves.) | Brooklyn | L to Bedford Ave. | 718-218-7750 ◗
www.wonknyc.com

Contemporary furniture in wood or lacquer finishes – from seating, shelving and desks to cabinets and dressers – is the focus at this Dumbo-Billyburg duo; space-starved urbanites hone in on pieces with storage room, like the popular Mod Quad coffee table with concealed cubbies.

Wool Gathering

▽ 24 | 21 | 20 | E

E 80s | 318 E. 84th St. (bet. 1st & 2nd Aves.) | 4/5/6 to 86th St. | 212-734-4747 | www.thewoolgathering.com

If you "yearn for wonderful yarns" but "aren't sure what you want or need" drop in for a consultation at this "quiet", "hospitable" shop "tucked away" in a vintage East 80s building, where the "very friendly" owner will provide "lots of help with a project"; given the "great selection" of materials plus the option of custom ordering, it's "terrific for experts" too; N.B. there are also lessons for novices.

Woolworks Needlepoint 🖼🚫

24 | 19 | 19 | E

E 70s | 1045 Lexington Ave., 2nd fl. (bet. 74th & 75th Sts.) | 6 to 77th St. | 212-861-8700

"Everything you need" for "serious" "projects" can be found at this "teensy", long-standing second-floor needlepoint nook on the Upper East Side, a "wonderful" and "convenient" one-stop shop for "fine yarns", needles and patterns that also offers private tutorials and finishing services; while the store stocks a variety of floral, animal and geometric designs, the staff is also happy to customize an original motif or translate a pre-made drawing into a needlepoint canvas.

World of Disney ◗

22 | 25 | 20 | E

E 50s | 711 Fifth Ave. (55th St.) | E/V to 5th Ave./53rd St. | 212-702-0702 | www.worldofdisney.com

"Great for a Disney fix when neither California nor Florida is in your immediate" travel plans, this funland brings all of the "magic" of Walt's "theme park" to Fifth Avenue, with its "eye-candy presentation" of character "stuff" and "special" attractions like meet-and-greets with "perky" Mickey and friends, a Mr. Potato Head station and pirate-themed parties; everything's "ridiculously overpriced" but it even "brings a smile to a curmudgeon's face" – "ya gotta love" the "mouse house."

World of Golf, The

24 | 18 | 20 | E

E 40s | 147 E. 47th St. (bet. Lexington & 3rd Aves.) | 6 to 51st St. | 212-755-9398
Financial District | 74 Broad St. (bet. Beaver & Stone Sts.) | 4/5 to Bowling Green | 212-385-1246 🖼
800-499-7491 | www.theworldofgolf.com

A "golf fanatic's" hole-in-one "heaven" housing a "great range" of the latest putters and irons for the links (Callaway, Cobra, MacGregor) as well as "nice" clothes for the clubhouse confirm fans of this East 40s flagship and its Financial District offshoot; lower your handicap at either location with staff pros that analyze your swing – "they know their stuff" and "almost always have what you need."

⊠ Yarn Co., The ⌖Ⓜ | 26 | 18 | 14 | E |

W 80s | 2274 Broadway, 2nd fl. (bet. 81st & 82nd Sts.) | 1 to 79th St. | 212-787-7878 | 888-927-6261 | www.theyarnco.com

"It's hip to knit" at this "bustling" second-floor West 80s "hideaway" run by a pair of best friends known for their trendy *Yarn Girls* pattern books; fans love to "stitch and schmooze" amid an "inspiring" range of "high-end" materials, but foes frown at "cramped" conditions, "top-dollar" pricing and a "snooty", "cliquish" attitude toward newcomers ("you want to stab someone with a needle"); P.S. it "turns into a mosh pit on Saturdays."

Yarn Connection, The ⌖ | 22 | 15 | 22 | M |

Murray Hill | 218 Madison Ave. (bet. 36th & 37th Sts.) | 6 to 33rd St. | 212-684-5099 | www.theyarnconnection.com

Take "a quick walk from Grand Central" to this Murray Hill "knitters' haven" showcasing a "diverse" selection of "top-brand yarns" at "not-bad" prices (with "excellent" deals in the "great sale section"); staffers are "knowledgeable" and "patient" to boot, but needleworkers note "if you've got claustrophobia, go elsewhere" – the "tiny" shop feels "cluttered" even with its high ceilings and large front window.

Yarn Tree, The ◗ | – | – | – | M |

Williamsburg | 347 Bedford Ave. (3rd St.) | Brooklyn | J/M/Z to Marcy Ave. | 718-384-8030 | www.theyarntree.com

Would-be artists and artisans eager not only to knit and crochet but also to felt, dye, spin and weave wend their way to this "warm" natural-fiber yarn boutique near the Williamsburg Bridge, where "true fiber expert" owner Linda LaBelle teaches classes (six people tops) that are "thorough" and "well worth the money"; N.B. late hours (till 10 PM Monday-Thursday) allow for after-work visits but note that it's closed Fridays.

Yellow Door | – | – | – | E |

Midwood | 1308 Ave. M (bet. 13th & 14th Sts.) | Brooklyn | Q to Ave. M | 718-998-7382 | www.theyellowdoor.com

A "go-to" "giftware oasis" for 40 years, this big "beautiful" Midwood standby lures shoppers with some of the "most coveted brands" in china, crystal and silver, including Baccarat, Lladró, Orrefors and Waterford; the selection of "expensive and inexpensive" jewelry, from cubic zirconia studs to gems from La Nouvelle Bague, Penny Preville and SeidenGang, is also golden, plus the "sincere" staff is on hand to help.

Yellow Rat Bastard ◗ | 16 | 17 | 13 | M |

SoHo | 478 Broadway (bet. Broome & Grand Sts.) | 6/J/M/N/Q/R/W/Z to Canal St. | 212-334-2150

Elmhurst | Queens Ctr. | 90-15 Queens Blvd. (bet. 57th & 59th Aves.) | Queens | G/R/V to Grand Ave./Newtown | 718-393-2030

877-935-5728 | www.yellowratbastard.com

"If you're looking for trend and funk, you'll find it at the Bastard", a "common stomping ground" for "urban guerrillas", "punk" skaters, "hip-hoppers" and "suburban" tweens and teens alike in SoHo and

Elmhurst; "you know what you're getting" at this "underground sta-ple": "witty T-shirts" and "cool" threads from Ecko, Penguin and Vans, all piled high inside a "graffiti"-strewn, warehouselike space with mu-sic pumping "so loud you have to shout over it"; N.B. the Broadway original plans to relocate across the street.

Yigal Azrouel   - | - | - | VE

Meatpacking | 408 W. 14th St. (bet. 9th Ave. & Washington St.) | A/C/E/L to 14th St./8th Ave. | 212-929-7525 | www.yigal-azrouel.com

"Don't let the secret out" that within the "loungey atmosphere" of this Meatpacking District shop, with its crystal chandelier and brick walls, are some of the "best [evening] dresses in the city" – an assortment of "ultrasexy and feminine showstoppers", favored by the likes of Natalie Portman and Cynthia Nixon; whether you prefer a sleek suit or a slinky gown, the "fit is amazing."

Ylli ◐   - | - | - | E

Williamsburg | 482 Driggs Ave. (N. 10th St.) | Brooklyn | L to Bedford Ave. | 718-302-3555 | www.yllibklyn.com

Gleaming wood floors, exposed beams and space between the racks lend this loftlike Williamsburg showcase a feel that's more SoHo than boho; the selection also walks the line between youthful and sophisti-cated, with jeans from Paige Premium and Goldsign, plus local labels like Objet Trouves, coveted lines like Daftbird and Love by Ya-Ya for her and hip threads from Barking Irons, NSF and Trovata for him, along with finds from Loomstate and Vince for both.

Yohji Yamamoto   27 | 27 | 24 | VE

SoHo | 103 Grand St. (Mercer St.) | C/E to Spring St. | 212-966-9066 | www.yohjiyamamoto.co.jp

"What the thinking artist/architect wears" can be found at this artwork-filled SoHo standby featuring the collections of Japanese designer Yohji Yamamoto, aka "a god" to "discerning" types for his "impeccable tai-loring of genius fabrics"; the clothes can be "costume-y" ("admirable and unwearable" some say), "but the more sober" architectural pieces become "wardrobe staples" if you're "unself-conscious – and have a fat wallet", plus you'll find "great sneakers" from the Y-3 line, an Adidas collaboration – which will have its own shop in early 2008 near another eponymous showcase, both in the Meatpacking District.

Yoko Devereaux   - | - | - | E

Williamsburg | 338 Broadway (bet. Keap & Rodney Sts.) | Brooklyn | J/M/Z to Marcy Ave. | 718-302-1450 | www.yokod.com

You'll never meet Yoko at this Williamsburg haunt – it's a made-up name, after all – but if you're a stylish guy or even a "tailored hipster", sooner or later you'll become familiar with this "alterna-chic mens-wear" line, the brainchild of founder-designer Andy Salzer; track down this stark sub-rosa shop with an off-kilter boys' club feel, then stake your claim on cool essentials like fleece cardigans, houndstooth pants and one-button blazers, plus collaborative limited-editions from names like In God We Trust.

Yoya   ▽ 27 | 28 | 19 | VE

W Village | 636 Hudson St. (bet. Horatio & Jane Sts.) | A/C/E/L to 14th St./8th Ave. | 646-336-6844

(continued)

Yoya Mart

W Village | 15 Gansevoort St. (Hudson St.) | A/C/E/L to 14th St./8th Ave. | 212-242-5511
www.yoyashop.com

"Virtual museums for children's clothing", this dynamic duo, located just blocks apart on the West Village/Meatpacking District border, has shoppers spellbound over its "stunningly original" selection of "chichi" fashions "almost too pretty to touch"; the huge Hudson Street shop is *the* place to find great, new lines" like Lucy Sykes and imps & elfs, plus you'll find the latest gotta-have-it gadgets at its sibling nearby.

Yves Delorme ⑤

| 28 | 27 | 23 | E |

E 70s | 985 Madison Ave. (bet. 76th & 77th Sts.) | 6 to 77th St. | 212-439-5701 | www.yvesdelorme.com

Luxe-linen lovers run for covers to this stateside venture from the venerable Paris-based company nestled next to the Carlyle Hotel; white cabinets and a marble floor set the stage for "beautiful" goods, including Egyptian cotton sheets in rich colors or "feminine" florals reminiscent of the French countryside and jacquard-woven tablecloths, as well as caned Louis XVI headboards, mahogany sleighbeds and silk pillows.

Yves Saint Laurent Rive Gauche

| 26 | 26 | 24 | VE |

E 50s | 3 E. 57th St. (bet. 5th & Madison Aves.) | N/R/W to 5th Ave./59th St. | 212-980-2970
E 70s | 855 Madison Ave. (71st St.) | 6 to 68th St. | 212-988-3821
www.ysl.com

"There's nothing gauche" about this venerable French label, whose "elegant", "impeccably tailored" men's and women's clothes in "gorgeous fabrics" are "well worth the price if it fits your budget"; whether in the East 50s or the East 70s, the "friendlier-than-you'd-think" staff "takes care of you as if you're a celebrity", making sure you find the Mombasa bag, waist-cinching suit or platform shoes "that you want more than one should want an article of clothing."

Zaba ⑤Ⓜ

| - | - | - | E |

TriBeCa | 85 Franklin St. (Church St.) | 1 to Franklin St. | 212-226-6355 | www.zababoutique.com

Shoppers in search of something a bit off the beaten path hop into this TriBeCa treasure trove, whose name is Polish for 'frog', to snap up unusual children's clothing, toys, bedding, gifts and other finds from little-known international labels, among them Viva la Pepa, Bholu, Safiras and Fig Organic – all displayed in an atmosphere that's blissfully free of the fuss found in many of the city's other high-end kids' shops.

☑ Zabar's ●

| 26 | 17 | 17 | M |

W 80s | 2245 Broadway (80th St.) | 1 to 79th St. | 212-787-2000 | 800-697-6301 | www.zabars.com

"If you can get past the foodies downstairs" at this "legendary" gourmet store and "mainstay of the Upper West Side", you'll be privy to "the best-known secret in New York", which is that "the best selection" of "the cheapest cookware, gadgets", appliances and utensils is found on its mezzanine; it can be "crowded", "cramped" and "chaotic" and "if your feelings get hurt easily don't ask for help", but beaming bargain-hunters shrug that just "adds to the NYC charm" of the experience.

| | QUALITY | DISPLAY | SERVICE | COST |

Zachary's Smile ☽
∇ 24 | 24 | 19 | M

G Village | 9 Greenwich Ave. (bet. Christopher & W. 10th Sts.) | 1 to Christopher St./Sheridan Sq. | 212-924-0604
NoHo | 317 Lafayette St. (bet. Bleecker & Houston Sts.) | 6 to Bleecker St. | 212-965-8248
www.zacharyssmile.com

Fans smile upon this colorful Villager, which offers "oodles of cool vintage" his-and-hers garments; spanning the 1940s–'80s, the stock includes famed labels (Puccis to the rear), "affordable dresses", and "great lingerie and shoes", including cowboy boots; small wonder actresses Sarah Jessica Parker and Gretchen Mol have been spotted among the racks; N.B. its NoHo sib carries "original pieces" made from old fabrics.

Zales Jewelers ☽
12 | 14 | 15 | M

Garment District | 142 W. 34th St. (bet. B'way & 7th Ave.) | 1/2/3/A/C/E to 34th St./Penn Station | 646-473-0727 | 800-311-5393 | www.zales.com
Additional locations throughout the NY area

With more than 2,300 outposts, "the fast food of jewelry" carries "a lot of inexpensive" pieces from cubic zirconia to the real (diamond) thing, but most surveyors sniff at the chain's "tawdry" quality, "tacky" styles and "pushy salespeople" "who act like your favorite long-lost cousin."

Zara ☽
18 | 19 | 15 | M

E 50s | 689 Fifth Ave. (54th St.) | E/V to 5th Ave./53rd St. | 212-371-2555
E 50s | 750 Lexington Ave. (59th St.) | 4/5/6/F/N/R/W to 59th St./Lexington Ave. | 212-754-1120
Flatiron | 101 Fifth Ave. (bet. 17th & 18th Sts.) | 4/5/6/L/N/Q/R/W to 14th St./Union Sq. | 212-741-0555
Garment District | 39 W. 34th St. (6th Ave.) | B/D/F/N/Q/R/V/W to 34th St./Herald Sq. | 212-868-6551
SoHo | 580 Broadway (bet. Houston & Prince Sts.) | N/R/W to Prince St. | 212-343-1725
www.zara.com

Everyone's "favorite" chain from Spain, this men's and women's standby offers "reasonable", "right-on-trend" styles for "young professionals on a budget"; the organization by color "saves a lot of time" when browsing collections that most consider "well made for the price" and "terrific for the long-legged" gal, if "not a woman with hips."

Zarin Fabrics and Home Furnishings
23 | 13 | 16 | M

LES | 318 Grand St. (bet. Allen & Orchard Sts.) | F/J/M/Z to Delancey/Essex Sts. | 212-925-6112 | www.harryzarin.com

Decorators and DIYers are wild about this 71-year-old LES fabric discounter that "always has what you need" (including "wondrous" name-brand wares) at "great prices"; browsers do best "when not looking for something specific" amid the vast environs, while the "overwhelmed" rely on "knowledgeable" staffers; N.B. the Display score doesn't reflect a recent expansion to showcase its house-label furniture line.

Z'Baby Company
24 | 21 | 19 | E

E 70s | 996 Lexington Ave. (72nd St.) | 6 to 68th St. | 212-472-2229
W 70s | 100 W. 72nd St. (Columbus Ave.) | 1/2/3/B/C to 72nd St. | 212-579-2229 ☽
www.zbabycompany.com

"For superb baby presents" and "cute, cute, cute" "creative" European clothes for the "special" babies, tots and tweens "in your life", head over to these "trendy" East 70s–West 70s twins, "well laid-out" and solidly stocked with a "sophisticated" selection of wardrobe wows that are definitely "not the norm"; it's "a little on the pricey side" but there's always the "legendary sales" when bargain-hunters "clean up."

Z Chemists ●

	25	20	20	E

W 50s | 40 W. 57th St. (bet. 5th & 6th Aves.) | F to 57th St. | 212-956-6000 | www.zchemists.com

Zitomer ●

E 70s | 969 Madison Ave. (bet. 75th & 76th Sts.) | 6 to 77th St. | 212-737-5560 | 888-219-2888 | www.zitomer.com

"Crowded and chaotic", this expensive Upper East Side über-drugstore (with a Midtown Z Chemists offshoot) "has a little bit of everything for everyone" from "the crème de la crème" of beauty products to perfumes and candles; in addition, there's Zittles for children's clothing and toys and a pet boutique called Z-Spot with an "almost scarily complete" collection of pampered puppy paraphernalia that includes pearl necklaces.

Zero/Maria Cornejo ●

	-	-	-	VE

NoLita | 225 Mott St. (bet. Prince & Spring Sts.) | 6 to Spring St. | 212-925-3849
W Village | 807 Greenwich St. (Jane St.) | A/C/E/L to 14th St./8th Ave. | 212-620-0460
www.mariacornejo.com

Offering "a wonderful reprieve" from the often-frazzling "SoHo shopping experience" is this grottolike NoLita store/studio nearby and its lovely West Village sibling showcasing the sensual styles of Chilean designer Maria Cornejo; her "simple, elegant looks" – bubble-hemmed dresses, cowl-neck tops, dramatic coats and draped Venus gowns – "push the design envelope without ripping it to shreds", a reason why loyal clients are said to include Sofia Coppola, Cindy Sherman and Marisa Tomei.

Zoë ●

	-	-	-	E

Dumbo | 70 Washington St. (bet. Front & York Sts.) | Brooklyn | F to York St. | 718-237-4002 | www.shopzoeonline.com

This 3,400-sq.-ft. mucho-modern sleek Dumbo sibling of the same-named Princeton, NJ, mother ship wins over fashionistas with its cultivated mix of high-end collections and contemporary lines; shoppers make the rounds, perusing showstopping pieces from Mayle, Rozae Nichols and Tsumori Chisato on circular wheeled racks, then moving on to wardrobe essentials from A.P.C., Clu and Rag & Bone, plus 19 brands of denim, bags from Anna Corinna and footwear from Chloé and Loeffler Randall.

Zoomies

	▽ 29	26	28	E

W Village | 434 Hudson St. (bet. Leroy & Morton Sts.) | 1 to Houston St. | 212-462-4480 | www.zoomiesnyc.com

"Extremely pampered pets and owners" zoom in on this Village boutique offering "high style for Buster" in the form of apparel, bedding and accessories, some designed by the former fashion exec co-owner; "dogs love" the "fresh-baked", "gourmet" cookies and treats made by a French chef, and even if it's a *peu* "expensive", it's a "bonus that the staff truly aims to please."

INDEXES

LOCATION MAPS

Locations

Includes store names, merchandise type (where necessary) and Quality ratings. ⛿ indicates highest ratings, popularity and importance.

Manhattan

CHELSEA

(24th to 30th Sts., west of 5th; 14th to 24th Sts., west of 6th)

Alexandros	*Furs*	-
Angel St. Thrift Shop	*Vintage*	17
Arcadia	*Toiletries*	25
⛿ Balenciaga	*Designer*	29
Barking Zoo	*Pets*	25
Barneys CO-OP	*Mens/Womenswear*	24
Birnbaum & Bullock	*Bridal*	-
BoConcept	*Home*	17
Bowery Kitchen	*Appliances*	22
Brooklyn Industries	*Mens/Womenswear*	20
Burlington Coat	*Discount*	15
⛿ buybuy BABY	*Baby Gear*	23
Camouflage	*Menswear*	24
⛿ Carlyle Convertibles	*Home*	26
Chelsea Garden Ctr.		23
⛿ City Quilter	*Fabrics*	28
Comme des Garçons	*Designer*	26
Container Store	*Home*	22
Dave's Army Navy	*Menswear*	21
DaVinci Art Supply		23
Door Store	*Home*	17
Ellen Christine	*Accessories*	-
Family Jewels	*Vintage*	-
Fisch for the Hip	*Vintage*	26
Gerry's	*Mens/Womenswear*	24
Giraudon	*Shoes*	22
NEW Gus Modern	*Home*	20
Habu Textiles		-
Here Comes Bridesmaid		17
Housing Works Thrift		20
Jazz Record Center		-
Jensen-Lewis	*Home*	19
Karim Rashid Shop	*Home*	-
Kleinfeld	*Bridal*	25
Knoll	*Home*	-
Kremer Pigments	*Art*	29
La Cafetière	*Home*	-
LaCrasia Gloves		25
Lightforms	*Lighting*	23
⛿ Loehmann's	*Discount*	20
Lucky Wang	*Childrenswear*	25
Malin + Goetz	*Toiletries*	22
NEW Marc Ecko	*Menswear*	-

NEW Michael Aram	*Home*	26
Myoptics	*Eyewear*	25
New London Pharm.	*Toiletries*	23
New York Golf		24
Olde Good Things	*Home*	18
Parke & Ronen	*Menswear*	-
Pippin	*Jewelry*	-
Pottery Barn Bed/Bath		-
⛿ Rubin Museum		26
Sabon	*Toiletries*	25
Sacco	*Shoes*	22
Schneider's	*Childrenswear*	25
Scuba Network		-
Shooz	*Shoes*	19
⛿ Stickley, Audi & Co.	*Home*	28
⛿ Tekserve	*Computers*	26
202	*Designer*	23
Urban Angler	*Sports*	-
Urban Outfitters	*Mens/Womenswear*	17
Utrecht	*Art*	24
West Elm	*Home*	17
⛿ Williams-Sonoma	*Home*	26

CHINATOWN

(Canal to Pearl Sts., east of B'way)

Canal Hi-Fi	*Electronics*	16
⛿ Pearl Paint	*Art*	26
NEW Project No. 8	*Mens/Womenswear*	-

EAST 40s

Airline Stationery		21
⛿ Allen Edmonds	*Shoes*	28
Ambassador Luggage		22
American Girl Place	*Toys*	24
⛿ Ann Taylor Loft	*Womenswear*	20
Aveda	*Toiletries*	26
Barami	*Womenswear*	16
BCBG Max Azria	*Designer*	22
Bloom	*Jewelry*	24
Botticelli	*Shoes*	25
⛿ Bridge Kitchenware		28
⛿ Brooks Brothers	*Mens/Womenswear*	24
⛿ Build-A-Bear	*Toys*	22
Caché	*Womenswear*	18
Caswell-Massey	*Toiletries*	25
Cellini	*Jewelry*	27

Charles Tyrwhitt | *Menswear*	26
Children's Gen. Store | *Toys*	27
Clarks | *Shoes*	23
Crabtree & Evelyn | *Toiletries*	23
Crouch & Fitzgerald | *Luggage*	26
Douglas Cosmetics	22
Erwin Pearl | *Jewelry*	20
Esprit | *Mens/Womenswear*	17
Fila | *Activewear*	23
For Eyes | *Eyewear*	23
Fossil | *Watches*	19
Grand Central Racquet	-
Innovation Luggage	20
J.Crew | *Mens/Womenswear*	20
Johnston & Murphy | *Shoes*	25
☑ Joon | *Stationery*	26
Jos. A. Bank | *Menswear*	18
Joseph Edwards | *Watches*	22
J. Press | *Menswear*	23
K&G Fashion | *Discount*	15
Kavanagh's | *Vintage*	-
Kenneth Cole NY | *Designer*	21
Lacoste | *Mens/Womenswear*	24
Laila Rowe | *Accessories*	14
Links of London | *Jewelry*	24
Men's Wearhse. | *Menswear*	17
☑ Michael C. Fina | *China/Crystal*	26
New York Look | *Womenswear*	20
New York Public Library	23
New York Transit Mus.	20
Nintendo World | *Toys*	25
Origins | *Toiletries*	24
Orvis | *Activewear*	25
Paul Stuart | *Menswear*	27
Pink Slip | *Hose/Lingerie*	23
RadioShack | *Electronics*	16
Ricky's | *Toiletries*	19
Robert Marc | *Eyewear*	27
Sean John | *Designer*	18
Seigo | *Accessories*	28
☑ Sephora | *Toiletries*	25
Shirt Store | *Menswear*	22
Solstice | *Eyewear*	-
Strawberry | *Womenswear*	11
Studio NYC Shoes	19
Sub Chrono | *Watches*	22
Super Runners Shop	26
Swarovski | *Jewelry*	25
Swatch | *Watches*	20
☑ TUMI | *Luggage*	28
UnitedColors/Benetton | *Mens/Womenswear*	20
World of Golf	24

Abercrombie | *Tween/Teen*	18
Alain Mikli | *Eyewear*	28
☑ A La Vieille Russie | *Jewelry*	29
Alexandros | *Furs*	-
☑ Allen Edmonds | *Shoes*	28
Amsale | *Bridal*	27
Anne Fontaine | *Designer*	27
☑ Ann Sacks | *Tile*	27
☑ Apple Store | *Electronics*	27
☑ Artistic Tile	26
a. testoni | *Shoes*	27
Audemars Piguet | *Watches*	29
Aveda | *Toiletries*	26
A/X | *Mens/Womenswear*	19
☑ Baccarat | *Home*	29
Bally | *Handbags*	28
☑ Banana Republic | *Mens/Womenswear*	20
☑ B&B Italia | *Home*	27
Barami | *Womenswear*	16
bebe | *Womenswear*	17
☑ Belgian Shoes	28
☑ Bergdorf | *Dept. Store*	29
☑ Bergdorf Men's | *Dept. Store*	28
☑ Bernardaud | *Home*	29
Blanc de Chine | *Designer*	24
☑ Bloomingdale's | *Dept. Store*	23
Bochic | *Jewelry*	-
BoConcept | *Home*	17
☑ Bottega Veneta | *Designer*	29
Botticelli | *Shoes*	25
Bric's | *Luggage*	27
☑ Brioni | *Designer*	28
British Amer. Hse. | *Menswear*	22
☑ Brooks Brothers | *Mens/Womenswear*	24
☑ Buccellati | *Home/Jewelry*	29
Bulgari | *Jewelry*	28
Burberry | *Designer*	27
Camera Land	22
☑ Cartier | *Jewelry*	29
Cassina USA | *Home*	-
Cellini | *Jewelry*	27
☑ Chanel | *Designer*	29
City Sports | *Sneakers*	20
Clarks | *Shoes*	23
☑ Coach | *Handbags*	26
Cole Haan | *Shoes*	25
Concord Chemists | *Toiletries*	23
Conran Shop | *Home*	23
Container Store | *Home*	22
Crabtree & Evelyn | *Toiletries*	23
☑ Crate & Barrel | *Home*	21

Dana Buchman | *Designer*	25
Davis & Warshow | *Bath Fixtures*	23
DeBeers | *Jewelry*	27
Z Dempsey & Carroll	27
DeNatale Jewelers	26
Destination Maternity	22
Dior Homme | *Designer*	26
Z Dior New York | *Designer*	28
Domenico Vacca | *Designer*	-
Door Store | *Home*	17
Dunhill | *Accessories*	27
Eileen Fisher | *Womenswear*	24
Einstein-Moomjy | *Home*	24
Emporio Armani | *Designer*	23
Eres | *Hose/Lingerie*	28
Z Ermenegildo Zegna | *Designer*	28
Escada | *Designer*	27
NEW ê Shave | *Toiletries*	23
Façonnable | *Mens/Womenswear*	27
FAO Schwarz | *Toys*	25
Fendi | *Designer*	27
Florsheim Shoe	20
Z Fogal | *Hose/Lingerie*	28
NEW Franck Muller | *Watches*	27
Fratelli Rossetti | *Shoes*	27
Furla | *Handbags*	25
Furry Paws | *Pets*	21
Gant | *Menswear*	22
Geox | *Shoes*	23
NEW Gilan | *Jewelry*	25
Golfsmith	23
Gruen Optika | *Eyewear*	25
Gucci | *Designer*	27
Gym Source | *Sports*	26
Hammacher | *Electronics*	25
Z H&M | *Mens/Womenswear*	12
Z Harry Winston | *Jewelry*	29
Hastings Tile/Bath	26
Z Henri Bendel | *Dept. Store*	26
H. Herzfeld | *Menswear*	26
Hickey Freeman | *Menswear*	27
H.L. Purdy | *Eyewear*	27
Homer | *Home*	-
Honora | *Jewelry*	-
Z H. Stern | *Jewelry*	28
H2O Plus | *Toiletries*	23
Ideal Tile	20
Il Makiage | *Toiletries*	23
Innovative Audio | *Electronics*	29
Jacob & Co. | *Jewelry*	24
James Robinson | *Jewelry/Home*	29
Jay Kos | *Menswear*	-
Jimmy Choo | *Shoes*	28
Johnston & Murphy | *Shoes*	25

Z Joon | *Stationery*	26
Jubilee | *Shoes*	16
NEW Just Cavalli | *Designer*	25
Kenneth Cole NY | *Designer*	21
Kiton | *Designer*	-
Kreiss Collection | *Home*	26
Lacoste | *Mens/Womenswear*	24
Lederer de Paris | *Handbags*	25
Levi's Store | *Jeans*	23
Linda Dresner | *Womenswear*	25
Links of London | *Jewelry*	24
Louis Vuitton | *Designer*	27
Lowell/Edwards | *Electronics*	-
Z MacKenzie-Childs | *Home*	25
Mark Ingram Bridal	27
Mason's Tennis Mart	26
Z MauricE Villency | *Home*	26
Z Mikimoto | *Jewelry*	29
Molton Brown | *Toiletries*	27
Z Montblanc | *Stationery*	28
MoonSoup | *Childrenswear*	24
Mulberry | *Handbags*	-
NBA Store | *Activewear*	21
New Balance | *Sneakers*	27
Niketown | *Activewear/Sneakers*	24
Nine West | *Shoes*	17
Nokia | *Electronics*	22
Z Oxxford Clothes | *Menswear*	28
Z Piaget | *Watches*	28
Poggenpohl U.S. | *Home*	-
Porsche Design | *Accessories*	26
Pottery Barn | *Home*	20
Prada | *Designer*	26
Pucci | *Designer*	26
RCS Experience | *Electronics*	17
Robert Marc | *Eyewear*	27
Sacco | *Shoes*	22
Safavieh | *Home*	26
Z Saks Fifth Ave. | *Dept. Store*	27
Z Salvatore Ferragamo | *Designer*	28
Sam Flax | *Art*	24
Scuba Network	-
Z Scully & Scully | *Home*	29
Seaman Schepps | *Jewelry*	27
Sergio Rossi | *Shoes*	26
Z Simon Pearce | *Home*	27
Z Sony Style | *Electronics*	26
Sports Authority	17
Z Spring Flowers | *Childrenswear*	28
Stefano Ricci | *Designer*	27
Z Stitches | *Knit/Needlepoint*	26
Z St. John | *Designer*	28
Stuart Weitzman | *Shoes*	27

Z Georg Jensen | *Home/Jewelry*	29
Z Ghurka | *Luggage*	29
Z Giorgio Armani | *Designer*	29
Z Giuseppe Zanotti | *Shoes*	28
Z Graff | *Jewelry*	28
Gruen Optika | *Eyewear*	25
Gucci | *Designer*	27
Z Hermès | *Designer*	29
Issey Miyake | *Designer*	25
NEW Ivanka Trump | *Jewelry*	-
Jacadi | *Childrenswear*	27
Janovic Plaza | *Hardware*	22
Jeri Cohen Jewelry | *Jewelry*	27
Jimmy Choo | *Shoes*	28
Z J. Mendel | *Furs*	28
J.M. Weston | *Shoes*	26
Z John Lobb | *Shoes*	29
Z Joon | *Stationery*	26
Joseph | *Designer*	23
Judith Ripka | *Jewelry*	25
Just Bulbs | *Lighting*	24
Kraft | *Bath Fixtures*	26
Krizia | *Designer*	-
La Boutique Resale	23
La Brea | *Gifts/Novelties*	18
Lalaounis | *Jewelry*	29
Z Lalique | *Home*	29
NEW Lambertson | *Handbags*	-
Lana Marks | *Handbags*	28
Z La Perla | *Hose/Lingerie*	28
Lara Hélène | *Bridal*	-
Le Chien Pet Salon	23
Z Leiber | *Accessories*	28
Léron | *Bed/Bath*	29
Le Sabon & Baby Too | *Toiletries*	23
NEW Leviev | *Jewelry*	27
Lexington Luggage	21
Lingerie on Lex	24
Longchamp | *Handbags*	26
Z Loro Piana | *Mens/Womenswear*	29
NEW Louis Féraud | *Designer*	28
Luca Luca | *Designer*	25
Lucky Brand Jeans	23
MaxMara | *Designer*	25
Miriam Rigler | *Bridal*	28
Miu Miu | *Designer*	25
Molton Brown | *Toiletries*	27
Morgane Le Fay | *Designer*	26
Morgenthal Frederics | *Eyewear*	28
Z Mrs. John L. Strong | *Stationery*	28
Munder-Skiles | *Garden*	-
Myla | *Sex Toys*	-

Natalie & Friends | *Childrenswear*	28
New York Doll | *Toys*	28
Nicholas Perricone | *Toiletries*	22
Nicole Miller | *Designer*	24
Oilily | *Children's/Womenswear*	23
Oliver Peoples | *Eyewear*	27
Oriental Lamp Shade | *Lighting*	25
Z Oscar de la Renta | *Designer*	28
Paul & Shark | *Menswear*	27
Petrou | *Designer*	-
Pilar Rossi | *Bridal*	-
Pomellato | *Jewelry*	-
Pookie/Sebastian | *Womenswear*	17
Porthault | *Bed/Bath*	29
Pottery Barn Kids | *Home*	-
Z Pratesi | *Bed/Bath*	29
Pucci | *Designer*	26
Pylones | *Gifts/Novelties*	-
Ralph Lauren Eyewear	-
Reem Acra | *Bridal*	29
Z Robert Clergerie | *Shoes*	28
Robert Marc | *Eyewear*	27
Roberto Cavalli | *Designer*	27
Robert Talbott | *Menswear*	28
NEW Roger Vivier | *Shoes*	28
Sabon | *Toiletries*	25
Samsonite | *Luggage*	24
Searle | *Womenswear*	24
Sherle Wagner | *Bath Fixtures*	-
Signoria | *Bed/Bath*	25
Z Spring Flowers | *Childrenswear*	28
Stephen Kahan | *Jewelry*	27
Z Steuben | *Home*	29
Straight from Crate | *Home*	13
Studio NYC Shoes	19
Suzanne Couture | *Accessories*	27
Taryn Rose | *Shoes*	25
Z Tender Buttons	28
Thos. Moser Cabinets | *Home*	29
Z Tod's | *Shoes*	29
Z Toga Bikes	26
Tupli | *Shoes*	-
Unisa | *Shoes*	20
Z Valentino | *Designer*	28
Vanessa Noel | *Shoes*	-
Warren Edwards | *Shoes*	28
William-Wayne | *Home*	26

EAST 70s

Adrien Linford | *Home*	22
Alain Mikli | *Eyewear*	28
NEW Allegra Hicks | *Designer*	24
Amadeo/Scognamiglio | *Jewelry*	20

Searle | *Womenswear*	24
Second Chance | *Vintage*	21
Selima/Sucre | *Eyewear*	27
Shoe Box	23
Sigerson Morrison | *Shoes*	25
Sonia Rykiel | *Designer*	26
🔁 Spring Flowers | *Childrenswear*	28
Stephen Russell | *Jewelry*	27
Steven | *Shoes*	18
Stubbs & Wootton | *Shoes*	26
Super Runners Shop	26
🔁 Talbots | *Mens/Womenswear*	22
Talbots Kids/Babies	24
NEW Threads | *Childrenswear*	-
Tiny Doll House | *Toys*	-
NEW Tom Ford | *Designer*	28
Treillage | *Home*	-
Vera Wang Bridal	27
Vera Wang Maids | *Bridal*	27
Vivaldi Boutique | *Womenswear*	23
Wedding Library	25
Whitney Museum	21
Wink | *Accessories*	21
Wolford | *Hose/Lingerie*	28
Woolworks Needlepoint	24
Yves Delorme | *Bed/Bath*	28
Yves Saint Laurent | *Designer*	26
Z'Baby Co. | *Childrenswear*	24
Z Chemists/Zitomer | *Toiletries*	25

EAST 80s

Agnès B. | *Designer*	23
Anik | *Womenswear*	21
Artbag | *Handbags*	24
NEW Baby Cottons | *Childrenswear*	26
Bambini | *Childrenswear*	27
🔁 Barbour/Peter Elliot | *Mens/Womenswear*	28
🔁 Best Buy | *Electronics*	20
Betsey Johnson | *Designer*	21
Bis Designer Resale	-
Blacker & Kooby | *Stationery*	25
Calling All Pets	24
🔁 Canine Styles	26
Catimini | *Childrenswear*	26
Cécile et Jeanne | *Jewelry*	24
Chuckies | *Shoes*	25
Circuit City | *Electronics*	19
Clarins | *Toiletries*	26
Cosmophonic Sound | *Electronics*	-
Council Thrift Shop	18
Designer Resale	24
Didi's Children's | *Toys*	-
E.A.T. Gifts | *Toys*	23

Emmelle | *Womenswear*	21
Encore | *Vintage*	20
Eric | *Shoes*	24
G.C. William | *Tween/Teen*	20
Gentlemen's Resale	24
Great Feet | *Childrenswear*	22
Greenstones | *Childrenswear*	26
Gruen Optika | *Eyewear*	25
Guggenheim Museum	22
Gymboree | *Childrenswear*	22
Hippototamus | *Childrenswear*	22
H.L. Purdy | *Eyewear*	27
Housing Works Thrift	20
Infinity | *Tween/Teen*	22
Jaded | *Jewelry*	25
J.J. Marco | *Jewelry*	24
Jonathan Adler | *Home*	26
Kidville | *Childrenswear*	22
Kieselstein-Cord | *Accessories*	28
La Brea | *Gifts/Novelties*	18
L'Artisan Parfumeur | *Toiletries*	26
Laytner's Linen	20
LeSportsac | *Handbags*	20
Lester's | *Childrenswear*	24
Little Eric | *Children's Shoes*	25
Livi's Lingerie	20
🔁 Lyric Hi-Fi | *Electronics*	28
Madura | *Home*	24
Magic Windows | *Childrenswear*	27
Magnificent Costume | *Jewelry*	22
Marie-Chantal | *Designer*	25
Mem. Sloan-Kettering | *Vintage*	22
Metro Bicycles	20
🔁 Met. Museum of Art	25
Montmartre | *Womenswear*	22
Nancy & Co. | *Womenswear*	23
Naturino | *Childrenswear*	28
Nellie M. | *Womenswear*	22
🔁 Neue Galerie NY	26
New York Pipe Dreams | *Sports*	-
Occhiali | *Eyewear*	24
Olive & Bette's | *Womenswear*	22
Petco | *Pets*	19
Peter Elliot | *Menswear*	25
Petit Bateau | *Childrenswear*	27
Pier 1 Imports | *Home*	15
Planet Kids | *Children's*	18
🔁 Schweitzer Linen	27
Searle | *Womenswear*	24
Seigo | *Accessories*	28
Spence-Chapin Thrift	16
Steve Madden | *Shoes*	16
Straight from Crate | *Home*	13
🔁 String | *Knit/Needlepoint*	27

Trash & Vaudeville | *Mens/Womenswear*	16
Urban Outfitters | *Mens/Womenswear*	17
Utrecht | *Art*	24
Z Whiskers | *Pets*	27

FINANCIAL DISTRICT

(South of Murray St.)

Boomerang Toys	-
Z Century 21 | *Discount*	22
Compact Impact | *Electronics*	-
DeNatale Jewelers	26
Z DSW | *Shoes*	21
Erwin Pearl | *Jewelry*	20
NEW Flight Club | *Sneakers*	21
Z Hermès | *Designer*	29
Hickey Freeman | *Menswear*	27
Z J&R Music | *Electronics*	24
Kenjo | *Watches*	25
Montmartre | *Womenswear*	22
New York & Co. | *Womenswear*	17
Prato Fine Men's Wear	13
Samuel's Hats	-
Syms | *Discount*	18
Tent and Trails | *Sports*	25
Thomas Pink | *Menswear*	26
Z Tiffany & Co. | *Jewelry*	28
William Barthman | *Jewelry*	26
World of Golf	24

FLATIRON DISTRICT

(14th to 24th Sts., 6th Ave. to Park Ave. S., excluding Union Sq.)

Z ABC Carpet & Home	25
Z ABC Carpets/Rugs	25
Abracadabra | *Toys*	21
Academy Records	24
Z Adorama Camera	26
A.I. Friedman | *Art*	24
Alkit ⊦ *Cameras/Video*	23
Z Ann Sacks | *Tile*	27
Z Anthropologie | *Womenswear/Home*	20
Arden B. | *Womenswear*	17
Z Artistic Tile	26
Aveda | *Toiletries*	26
A/X | *Mens/Womenswear*	19
Banana Republic Men	21
Z Bang & Olufsen | *Electronics*	28
BCBG Max Azria | *Designer*	22
Beads of Paradise | *Jewelry*	22
bebe | *Womenswear*	17
Beckenstein Fabrics	-
Z Bed Bath & Beyond	20

Z Best Buy | *Electronics*	20
Blackman | *Bath Fixtures*	26
Bridal Garden	18
Z Charles P. Rogers | *Bed/Bath*	26
Classic Sofa	23
Club Monaco | *Mens/Womenswear*	18
Design Within Reach | *Home*	24
Domain | *Home*	20
Eileen Fisher | *Womenswear*	24
Eisenberg Eisenberg | *Menswear*	22
Essentials | *Toiletries*	20
Z Filene's Basement | *Discount*	18
Fishs Eddy | *Home*	18
NEW Free People | *Womenswear*	-
Fresh | *Toiletries*	26
Geox | *Shoes*	23
G-Star Raw | *Jeans*	23
Z Home Depot	19
Innovation Luggage	20
Intermix | *Womenswear*	24
J.Crew | *Mens/Womenswear*	20
Jennifer Convertibles | *Home*	13
Jo Malone | *Toiletries*	27
NEW Journelle | *Hose/Lingerie*	-
Juicy Couture | *Designer*	20
Kate Spade | *Accessories*	24
Kenneth Cole NY | *Designer*	21
Z Kidding Around | *Toys*	26
Z Krup's Kitchen/Bath	26
Levi's Store | *Jeans*	23
LF Stores | *Womenswear*	17
Z Ligne Roset | *Home*	28
Lucky Brand Jeans	23
Lush | *Toiletries*	23
M.A.C. Cosmetics	26
Manhattan Ctr. | *Appliances*	-
Metro Bicycles	20
Miss Sixty | *Womenswear*	21
Moscot | *Eyewear*	21
My Glass Slipper | *Bridal*	25
Nemo Tile	21
Origins | *Toiletries*	24
Otto Tootsi Plohound | *Shoes*	23
Paper Presentation | *Stationery*	25
Paul Smith | *Designer*	26
Pier 1 Imports | *Home*	15
Princeton Ski Shop	21
Reminiscence | *Vintage*	19
Restoration Hardware | *Home*	21
Sacco | *Shoes*	22
Safavieh | *Home*	26
Sam Flax | *Art*	24
Searle | *Womenswear*	24

17 at 17 Thrift | *Vintage* — 18
Space Kiddets | *Childrenswear* — 26
Sports Authority — 17
Straight from Crate | *Home* — 13
Z T.J. Maxx | *Discount* — 16
Z Trixie & Peanut | *Pets* — 27
UnitedColors/Benetton | *Mens/Womenswear* — 20
Utowa | *Mens/Womenswear* — 20
Z Waterworks | *Bath Fixtures* — 28
White Hse. Black Mkt. | *Womenswear* — -
Zara | *Mens/Womenswear* — 18

GARMENT DISTRICT

(30th to 40th Sts., west of 5th)

Aerosoles | *Shoes* — 18
Aldo | *Shoes* — 16
Alixandre Furs — 24
Am. Eagle | *Tween/Teen* — 17
babyGap | *Childrenswear* — 22
Z B&H Photo-Video — 27
Z B&J Fabrics — 26
Barami | *Womenswear* — 16
Z Billabong | *Activewear/Swimwear* — 21
Blades Board & Skate — 23
Brookstone | *Electronics* — 21
Capitol Fishing | *Sports* — -
Charlotte Russe | *Tween/Teen* — 10
Cheap Jack's | *Vintage* — 14
Children's Place — 16
Claire's Accessories — 8
Z Daffy's | *Discount* — 17
Dr. Jay's | *Activewear* — 18
Enzo Angiolini | *Shoes* — 20
Express | *Womenswear* — 16
Florsheim Shoe — 20
Foot Locker | *Sneakers* — 21
Forever 21 | *Womenswear* — 10
42nd St. Photo — 21
Z Gap | *Mens/Womenswear* — 18
GapKids | *Childrenswear* — 21
Gerry Cosby | *Sports* — 25
Hyman Hendler | *Fabrics* — 28
J.J. Hat Center — 27
KB Toys — 16
Kmart | *Mass Merch.* — 12
LaDuca Shoes — -
Lady Foot Locker | *Sneakers* — 22
Lush | *Toiletries* — 23
Z Macy's | *Dept. Store* — 19
M&J Trimming | *Fabrics* — 25
Missha | *Toiletries* — -
Modell's Sport — 16

Mood | *Fabrics* — 25
New York Golf — 24
Olden Camera/Lens — 20
Old Navy | *Mens/Womenswear* — 14
Payless Shoe — 11
Perfumania | *Toiletries* — 19
Prato Fine Men's Wear — 13
NEW Priscilla of Boston | *Bridal* — 24
RK Bridal — 19
Rosen & Chadick | *Fabrics* — -
School Products | *Knit/Needlepoint* — 25
Skechers | *Shoes* — 19
Steinlauf & Stoller | *Fabrics* — -
Steve Madden | *Shoes* — 16
Steven | *Shoes* — 18
Tourneau | *Watches* — 27
Training Camp | *Sneakers* — -
Victoria's Secret | *Hose/Lingerie* — 18
Wet Seal | *Tween/Teen* — 10
Willoughby's | *Cameras/Video* — 20
Zales Jewelers — 12
Zara | *Mens/Womenswear* — 18

GRAMERCY PARK

(24th to 30th Sts., east of 5th; 14th to 24th Sts., east of Park)

Casual Male XL | *Menswear* — 19
City Opera Thrift — 22
Door Store | *Home* — 17
Furry Paws | *Pets* — 21
Housing Works Thrift — 20
Jam Paper | *Stationery* — 18
NEW Lucia Nenickova | *Accessories* — 21
Manhattan Saddlery | *Sports* — -
Museum of Sex — 19
Paparazzi | *Gifts/Novelties* — 21
Park Ave. Audio | *Electronics* — 24
P.C. Richard & Son | *Appliances* — 18
Z Simon's Hardware — 26
Straight from Crate | *Home* — 13
Troy | *Home* — -
Vercesi Hardware — 23
Vintage Thrift Shop — 22

GREENWICH VILLAGE

(Houston to 14th Sts., west of B'way, east of 7th Ave. S.)

Z Aedes De Venustas | *Toiletries* — 27
Albertine | *Womenswear* — -
Alphabets | *Gifts/Novelties* — 19
Apartment 48 | *Home* — 21
Arthur's Invitations | *Stationery* — 21

Bag House	*Luggage*	23
Bleecker Bob's	*Music/DVDs*	20
Bleecker St. Records	23
🅩 Broadway Panhandler	*Cookware*	27
🅩 Canine Styles	26
Catherine Angiel	*Jewelry*	25
Claudine	*Womenswear*	22
C.O. Bigelow	*Toiletries*	26
David Z.	*Shoes*	19
🆕🅔🆆 Diana Broussard	*Shoes*	22
Disc-O-Rama	*Music/DVDs*	20
environment337	*Home*	-
Eskandar	*Designer*	-
Estella	*Childrenswear*	25
Fat Beats	*Music/DVDs*	-
Furry Paws	*Pets*	21
Generation Records	25
Gerry's	*Mens/Womenswear*	24
Gotta Knit	21
House of Oldies	*Music/DVDs*	-
🆕🅔🆆 Hus	*Mens/Womenswear*	-
Ibiza Kidz	*Childrenswear*	23
Ibiza NY	*Womenswear*	21
Jonathan Adler	*Home*	26
Joyce Leslie	*Womenswear*	8
Jubilee	*Shoes*	16
🅩 Kate's Paperie	*Stationery*	27
kid o.	*Toys*	22
Kmart	*Mass Merch.*	12
Kuhlman	*Mens/Womenswear*	20
Laina Jane	*Hose/Lingerie*	-
La Petite Coquette	*Hose/Lingerie*	26
Lucien Pellat-Finet	*Designer*	-
Lucky Wang	*Childrenswear*	25
Ludivine	*Womenswear*	-
Make Up For Ever	28
Olde Good Things	*Home*	18
🆕🅔🆆 Owl's Lab	*Womenswear*	21
Pink Pussycat	*Sex Toys*	19
🅩 Point	*Knit/Needlepoint*	25
Purdy Girl	*Womenswear*	18
Rugby	*Mens/Womenswear*	22
Sabon	*Toiletries*	25
Sisley	*Mens/Womenswear*	20
Smith on Sullivan	*Designer*	20
Star Struck	*Vintage*	20
Stella Dallas/Ten Feet	*Vintage*	-
Strider Records	-
Tah-Poozie	*Gifts/Novelties*	18
UnitedColors/Benetton	*Mens/Womenswear*	20
Urban Outfitters	*Mens/Womenswear*	17

Wet Seal	*Tween/Teen*	10
William-Wayne	*Home*	26
Zachary's Smile	*Vintage*	24

HARLEM/EAST HARLEM

(110th to 157th Sts., excluding Columbia U. area)

B. Oyama Homme	*Menswear*	-
Carol's Daughter	*Toiletries*	24
Champs	*Sports*	17
Davis & Warshow	*Bath Fixtures*	23
Demolition Depot	*Home*	-
🆕🅔🆆 Head/Heels	*Shoes*	21
K&G Fashion	*Discount*	15
M.A.C. Cosmetics	26
N	*Mens/Womenswear*	-
New York Public Library	23
Studio Museum/Harlem	-
V.I.M.	*Jeans*	14

LITTLE ITALY

(Canal to Kenmare Sts., Bowery to Lafayette St.)

Built by Wendy	*Designer*	-
Matter	*Home*	-
🆕🅔🆆 msg	*Womenswear*	-
No. 6	*Vintage*	-

LOWER EAST SIDE

(Houston to Canal Sts., east of Bowery)

Adriennes	*Bridal*	24
Alife	*Sneakers*	24
Altman Luggage	24
A.W. Kaufman	*Hose/Lingerie*	26
🅩 Babeland	*Sex Toys*	27
Bblessing	*Menswear*	21
Bike Works NYC	-
Blibetroy	*Handbags*	-
Bowery Lighting	21
DeMask	*Sex Toys*	22
Dolce Vita	*Shoes/Womenswear*	23
Don the Verb	*Vintage*	16
Doyle & Doyle	*Jewelry*	25
Dulcinée	*Vintage*	-
Earnest Cut & Sew	*Jeans*	25
Edith Machinist	*Womenswear*	-
Ekovaruhuset	*Womenswear*	-
Foley + Corinna	*Womenswear*	21
Freemans Sporting	*Menswear*	-
Frock	*Vintage*	-
Hairy Mary's	*Vintage*	-
🅩 Harris Levy	*Bed/Bath*	26
🆕🅔🆆 Honey/Rough	*Womenswear*	21

Joe's Fabrics	-
Jutta Neumann	*Shoes*	-
Kaight	*Womenswear*	-
Lighting By Gregory	24
Lolli/Reincarnation	*Vintage*	20
Lower E. S. Tenement Museum	21
Marmalade	*Vintage*	-
Mary Adams The Dress	*Bridal*	-
NEW Michael Andrews	*Menswear*	22
miks	*Womenswear*	-
Moscot	*Eyewear*	21
Nakedeye	*Eyewear*	-
NEW New Museum	-
O'Lampia Studio	*Lighting*	29
Orchard Corset Center	-
Organic Ave.	*Mens/Womenswear*	24
Pear/Plum	*Shoes/Womenswear*	22
Peggy Pardon	*Vintage*	-
NEW Pixie Mkt.	*Womenswear*	19
Reed Space	*Mens/Womenswear*	22
Shop	*Womenswear*	20
Some Odd Rubies	*Vintage*	-
NEW Suite Orchard	*Womenswear*	23
TG-170	*Womenswear*	20
NEW Travessia	*Womenswear*	-
Valley	*Womenswear*	-
Wendy Mink	*Jewelry*	-
Zarin Fabrics	23

MEATPACKING DISTRICT

(Gansevoort to 15th Sts., west of 9th Ave.)

NEW Adam	*Mens/Womenswear*	-
Ⓩ Alexander McQueen	*Designer*	28
Ⓩ Apple Store	*Electronics*	27
Artsee	*Eyewear*	-
auto	*Home*	-
B8	*Menswear*	-
Boucher	*Jewelry*	20
Buckler	*Menswear*	-
Carlos Miele	*Designer*	-
Catriona Mackechnie	*Hose/Lingerie*	-
Charles Nolan	*Designer*	-
DDC Lab	*Jeans*	-
Dernier Cri	*Womenswear*	-
Design Within Reach	*Home*	24
Destination	*Accessories*	23

Diane von Furstenberg	*Designer*	24
Earnest Cut & Sew	*Jeans*	25
Ed Hardy	*Mens/Womenswear*	21
Elizabeth Charles	*Womenswear*	-
NEW Helmut Lang	*Designer*	-
Henry Beguelin	*Designer*	-
NEW Iris	*Shoes*	23
Jean Shop	-
Jeffrey	*Mens/Womenswear*	28
Ⓩ La Perla	*Hose/Lingerie*	28
NEW Osklen	*Mens/Womenswear*	-
Poleci	*Designer*	22
Puma	*Activewear/Sneakers*	23
Rebecca & Drew	*Designer*	-
Rubin Chapelle	*Designer*	-
Scoop Kids	*Childrenswear*	23
Scoop Men's	*Menswear*	23
Scoop NYC	*Womenswear*	23
Stella McCartney	*Designer*	26
Ten Thousand Things	*Jewelry*	-
Theory	*Mens/Womenswear*	23
Tracy Reese	*Designer*	25
Trina Turk	*Designer*	-
Vitra	*Home*	-
Yigal Azrouel	*Designer*	-

MURRAY HILL

(30th to 40th Sts., east of 5th)

Ⓩ Bang & Olufsen	*Electronics*	28
bebe	*Womenswear*	17
BoConcept	*Home*	17
Bridal Reflect.	20
City Sports	*Sneakers*	20
DataVision	*Electronics*	21
David Z.	*Shoes*	19
ddc domus design	*Home*	27
Eneslow	*Shoes*	28
Etcetera	*Gifts/Novelties*	-
Furry Paws	*Pets*	21
Ⓩ Lord & Taylor	*Dept. Store*	22
McGuire	*Home*	-
Morgan Library	25
On Stage Dance	-
Petco	*Pets*	19
Pookie/Sebastian	*Womenswear*	17
Ⓩ Roche Bobois	*Home*	27
Safavieh	*Home*	26
Shoe Box	23
Straight from Crate	*Home*	13
Studio NYC Shoes	19
White on White	*Home*	-
Yarn Connection	22

NOHO

(Houston to 4th Sts., Bowery to B'way)

Adidas | *Activewear/Sneakers*	23
American Apparel | *Mens/Womenswear*	19
Andy's Chee-Pees | *Vintage*	15
Atrium | *Mens/Womenswear*	25
☑ Best Buy | *Electronics*	20
Blades Board & Skate	23
☑ Blick Art Materials	25
Bond No. 9 | *Toiletries*	28
Bond 07/Selima | *Womenswear*	-
Caravan | *Mens/Womenswear*	20
Classic Kicks | *Sneakers*	25
☑ Crate & Barrel | *Home*	21
Daryl K | *Designer*	23
David Z. | *Shoes*	19
Edge nyNoHo | *Mens/Womenswear*	24
Eye Candy | *Jewelry*	24
French Connect. | *Mens/Womenswear*	20
NEW Helio | *Electronics*	20
Ina | *Vintage*	25
In Living Stereo | *Electronics*	-
KD Dance & Sport | *Activewear*	-
Nat'l Whse. Liquid | *Discount*	11
Necessary Clothing | *Tween/Teen*	17
Nom de Guerre | *Menswear*	20
Nort/Recon | *Sneakers*	-
Oak | *Mens/Womenswear*	-
☑ Other Music	27
Patricia Field | *Mens/Womenswear*	15
☑ Stereo Exchange | *Electronics*	26
Swatch | *Watches*	20
Transit | *Menswear*	17
Village Tannery | *Luggage*	21
Zachary's Smile | *Vintage*	24

NOLITA

(Houston to Kenmare Sts., Bowery to Lafayette St.)

alice + olivia | *Womenswear*	22
NEW Amalia | *Womenswear*	20
Barker Black | *Shoes*	25
Belle/Sig. Morrison | *Shoes*	22
Blue Bag | *Handbags*	-
Cadeau | *Maternity*	25
Calvin Tran | *Designer*	-
Calypso | *Womenswear*	23
Calypso Bijoux | *Jewelry*	25
Calypso Home	-
Chip & Pepper | *Jeans*	23
Christopher Totman | *Designer*	-
Coclico | *Shoes*	-
C. Ronson | *Womenswear*	16
Crumpler Bags	24
Dinosaur Designs | *Jewelry*	-
Dö Kham | *Accessories*	22
Duncan Quinn | *Designer*	-
EMc2 | *Womenswear*	23
Erica Tanov | *Womenswear*	-
Femmegems | *Jewelry*	17
Fresh | *Toiletries*	26
Good, Bad & Ugly | *Womenswear*	-
Groupe | *Menswear*	-
Helen Ficalora | *Jewelry*	-
Henry Lehr | *Jeans*	24
Highway | *Handbags*	-
Hollywould | *Shoes*	24
I Heart | *Womenswear*	-
Ina | *Vintage*	25
In God We Trust | *Womenswear*	-
Jamin Puech | *Handbags*	-
NEW Jane Eadie | *Jewelry*	-
John Fluevog Shoes	23
Just Shades | *Lighting*	24
Kipepeo | *Accessories*	-
Ksubi | *Jeans*	22
Le Labo | *Toiletries*	-
Lilith | *Designer*	25
Lilliput | *Childrenswear*	-
Linda Derector | *Eyewear*	-
Lord Willy's | *Menswear*	-
Lyell | *Designer*	-
Malia Mills Swimwear	26
Market NYC | *Womenswear*	20
Matta | *Womenswear*	-
Mayle | *Designer*	-
Me & Ro | *Jewelry*	23
Min-K | *Womenswear*	-
Mixona | *Hose/Lingerie*	-
Nancy Koltes Home | *Bed/Bath*	28
Odin | *Menswear*	-
Only Hearts | *Hose/Lingerie*	21
Otto Tootsi Plohound | *Shoes*	23
Parasuco | *Jeans*	21
Paul Frank | *Tween/Teen*	18
Pinkyotto | *Womenswear*	21
Pir Cosmetics	-
Poppy | *Womenswear*	23
Project 234 | *Womenswear*	-
NEW Pull-In | *Hose/Lingerie*	-
NEW Rainbow Sandals | *Shoes*	23
Rebecca Taylor | *Designer*	23
Red Flower | *Toiletries*	-
Resurrection | *Vintage*	-

Saja | *Designer*	–
☑ Santa Maria Novella | *Toiletries*	28
Satya | *Jewelry*	21
Seize sur Vingt | *Mens/Womenswear*	25
Selima/Sucre | *Eyewear*	27
Shoe New York	24
Sigerson Morrison | *Shoes*	25
Sir | *Designer*	–
SOHO | *Jewelry*	20
Steven Alan | *Mens/Womenswear*	24
Sweet Tater | *Vintage*	18
Tory Burch | *Designer*	21
Tracy Feith | *Designer*	22
Unis | *Designer*	–
Variazioni | *Womenswear*	17
VeKa Bridal Couture	–
Zero/Maria Cornejo | *Designer*	–

SOHO

(Canal to Houston Sts., west of Lafayette St.)

Active Wearhouse	18
Add Accessories	20
Adidas | *Activewear/Sneakers*	23
☑ Aero | *Home*	26
AG | *Jeans*	26
Agatha Ruiz | *Designer*	24
Agent Provocateur | *Hose/Lingerie*	27
Agnès B. | *Designer*	23
Alessi | *Home*	25
Alexis Bittar | *Jewelry*	25
Amarcord Vintage	–
Am. Eagle | *Tween/Teen*	17
Anna Sui | *Designer*	23
Anne Fontaine | *Designer*	27
☑ Anthropologie | *Womenswear/Home*	20
Anya Hindmarch | *Handbags*	25
A.P.C. | *Designer*	21
☑ Apple Store | *Electronics*	27
Arden B. | *Womenswear*	17
Armani Casa | *Home*	25
Artemide | *Lighting*	27
Atelier NY | *Menswear*	–
Aveda | *Toiletries*	26
A/X | *Mens/Womenswear*	19
☑ Babeland | *Sex Toys*	27
Banana Republic Men	21
☑ B&B Italia | *Home*	27
Barbara Bui | *Designer*	27
Barneys CO-OP | *Mens/Womenswear*	24

Bathing Ape | *Sneakers*	21
BCBG Max Azria | *Designer*	22
BDDW | *Home*	–
Beau Brummel | *Menswear*	22
Bellora | *Home*	26
Ben Sherman | *Mens/Womenswear*	23
Betsey Johnson | *Designer*	21
Bicycle Habitat	23
Big Drop | *Mens/Womenswear*	21
NEW Billionaire Boys | *Sneakers*	–
Bisazza | *Tile*	–
☑ Bloomingdale's | *Dept. Store*	23
Blue in Green | *Menswear*	21
BoConcept | *Home*	17
Boffi SoHo | *Appliances*	–
☑ Bose | *Electronics*	27
Brooklyn Industries | *Mens/Womenswear*	20
Buckler | *Menswear*	–
Burberry | *Designer*	27
Burton Store | *Sports*	25
By Boe | *Jewelry*	–
Calvin Klein Underwear	21
Calypso | *Womenswear*	23
Calypso Kids/Home	26
Camper | *Shoes*	23
Cappellini | *Home*	–
Catherine Malandrino | *Designer*	24
Catherine Memmi | *Home*	–
NEW CB2 | *Home*	–
Cécile et Jeanne | *Jewelry*	24
☑ Chanel | *Designer*	29
Chelsea Girl | *Vintage*	–
Christopher Fischer | *Designer*	23
Clarins | *Toiletries*	26
Clio | *Home*	–
Cloak | *Designer*	–
Club Monaco | *Mens/Womenswear*	18
Costume National | *Designer*	26
NEW Cotélac | *Mens/Womenswear*	–
Crew Cuts | *Childrenswear*	–
NEW Curve | *Womenswear*	19
Custo Barcelona | *Menswear*	21
D & G | *Designer*	24
David Lee Holland | *Jewelry*	–
David Z. | *Shoes*	19
Davis & Warshow | *Bath Fixtures*	23
DC Shoes	22
☑ Dean & Deluca | *Cookware*	26
Design Within Reach | *Home*	24
Desiron | *Home*	22
Diesel | *Jeans*	23

Diesel Denim Gallery	24
Diesel Kids	25
DKNY	*Designer*	21
Doggystyle	*Pets*	-
Domenico Vacca	*Designer*	-
Dosa	*Designer*	24
Dunderdon Wkshp.	*Menswear*	-
Dusica Dusica	*Shoes*	-
Ed Hardy	*Mens/Womenswear*	21
Eileen Fisher	*Womenswear*	24
Elie Tahari	*Designer*	24
Emporio Armani	*Designer*	23
EMS	*Sports*	26
Eres	*Hose/Lingerie*	28
Esprit	*Mens/Womenswear*	17
FACE Stockholm	*Toiletries*	22
Facial Index	*Eyewear*	-
Federico de Vera	*Home/Jewelry*	-
NEW 55DSL	*Mens/Womenswear*	19
Flou	*Bed/Bath*	-
Flying A	*Mens/Womenswear*	17
Forever 21	*Womenswear*	10
Fort St. Studio	*Home*	-
45rpm/R	*Jeans*	23
Fragments	*Jewelry*	25
French Connect.	*Mens/Womenswear*	20
Garrard & Co.	*Jewelry*	-
George Smith	*Home*	-
Z Georg Jensen	*Home/Jewelry*	29
Giggle	*Childrenswear*	25
Girl Props	*Accessories*	11
Global Table	*Home*	-
G-Star Raw	*Jeans*	23
Guess	*Jeans*	21
Hastens	*Bed/Bath*	-
Hat Shop	24
Helen Wang	*Designer*	-
NEW hickey	*Menswear*	-
Hogan	*Shoes*	26
Hugo Boss	*Designer*	26
Hunting World	*Luggage*	-
IC Zinco	*Mens/Womenswear*	-
IF	*Mens/Womenswear*	-
Il Bisonte	*Handbags*	27
NEW Ilori	*Eyewear*	-
Ina	*Vintage*	25
Ingo Maurer Light	*Lighting*	-
Intermix	*Womenswear*	24
NEW Irregular Choice	*Shoes*	-
IS: Ind. Stationery	*Stationery*	-
Jack Spade	*Luggage*	25
Jaime Mascaró	*Shoes*	21

J.Crew	*Mens/Womenswear*	20
Jean Shop	-
Jill Platner	*Jewelry*	-
Jill Stuart	*Designer*	22
J. Lindeberg	*Menswear*	26
Joan Michlin Gallery	*Jewelry*	27
Joël Name Optique	*Eyewear*	-
John Varvatos	*Designer*	26
Jonathan Adler	*Home*	26
Joseph	*Designer*	23
Julian & Sara	*Childrenswear*	-
NEW Karen Millen	*Womenswear*	-
Kartell	*Home*	-
Kate Spade	*Accessories*	24
Z Kate's Paperie	*Stationery*	27
Kenneth Cole NY	*Designer*	21
Key	*Womenswear*	-
Kid Robot	*Toys*	-
Kiki/Montparnasse	*Hose/Lingerie*	25
Kiosk	*Gifts/Novelties*	19
Kirna Zabête	*Womenswear*	27
NEW Korres	*Toiletries*	-
Lacoste	*Mens/Womenswear*	24
Lady Foot Locker	*Sneakers*	22
Z La Perla	*Hose/Lingerie*	28
L'Artisan Parfumeur	*Toiletries*	26
Les Petits Chapelais	*Childrenswear*	25
LeSportsac	*Handbags*	20
Levi's Store	*Jeans*	23
LF Stores	*Womenswear*	17
Z Ligne Roset	*Home*	28
Lilliput	*Childrenswear*	-
Links of London	*Jewelry*	24
L'Occitane	*Toiletries*	25
Longchamp	*Handbags*	26
Louis Vuitton	*Designer*	27
Lounge	*Mens/Womenswear*	19
NEW Luceplan	*Lighting*	23
Lucky Brand Jeans	23
Lucky Kid	*Childrenswear*	-
Lush	*Toiletries*	23
M.A.C. Cosmetics	26
Marc Jacobs	*Designer*	27
Marni	*Designer*	24
Marston & Langinger	*Home*	-
Mastic Spa	*Toiletries*	-
Max Azria	*Designer*	-
MaxMara	*Designer*	25
Max Studio	*Designer*	20
Meg Cohen Design	*Accessories*	-
Metropolitan Lumber	22

Michael Kors	*Designer*	26	Rachel Ashwell's	*Home*	23
Michele Varian	*Home*	–	Ralph Lauren	*Designer*	26
Miss Sixty	*Womenswear*	21	Reinstein/Ross	*Jewelry*	28
NEW Mitchell Gold	*Home*	–	Reiss	*Mens/Womenswear*	20
Miu Miu	*Designer*	25	Replay	*Jeans*	23
M Missoni	*Designer*	–	Rival	*Sneakers*	22
NEW MNG/Mango	*Womenswear*	–	Robert Lee Morris	*Jewelry*	25
Modernica	*Home*	–	Robert Marc	*Eyewear*	27
Molton Brown	*Toiletries*	27	Room & Board	*Home*	24
Z MoMA Store	*Museum Shop*	25	Rug Company		–
Z Montblanc	*Stationery*	28	Sabon	*Toiletries*	25
Morgane Le Fay	*Designer*	26	Sacco	*Shoes*	22
Morgenthal Frederics	*Eyewear*	28	Salviati	*China/Crystal*	–
NEW Moroso	*Home*	–	Satellite	*Jewelry*	–
Z Moss	*Home*	28	Scholastic Store	*Toys*	24
NEW Muji	*Home*	–	Scoop NYC	*Mens/Womenswear*	23
Myoptics	*Eyewear*	25	Scott Jordan	*Home*	27
M Z Wallace	*Handbags*	–	Sean	*Menswear*	24
Nanette Lepore	*Designer*	25	Selima/Sucre	*Eyewear*	27
Napapijri	*Activewear*	–	Seven NY	*Womenswear*	26
Natuzzi	*Home*	27	Sharper Image	*Electronics*	21
Necessary Clothing	*Tween/Teen*	17	Shin Choi	*Designer*	–
New York Look	*Womenswear*	20	Shvitz	*Womenswear*	–
Nicole Miller	*Designer*	24	Sicis	*Bath Fixtures/Tile*	25
North Face	*Activewear*	24	Smith & Hawken	*Garden*	24
Oakley	*Eyewear*	21	Solstice	*Eyewear*	–
Ochre	*Home*	–	**NEW** Space.NK	*Toiletries*	25
Oilily	*Children's/Womenswear*	23	Steve Madden	*Shoes*	16
Olive & Bette's	*Womenswear*	22	Steven	*Shoes*	18
Oliver Peoples	*Eyewear*	27	Stussy NY	*Menswear*	20
Opening Ceremony	*Mens/Womenswear*	–	Supreme	*Activewear*	–
Origins	*Toiletries*	24	Sur La Table	*Cookware*	26
Oska	*Mens/Womenswear*	–	Swatch	*Watches*	20
NEW Osklen	*Mens/Womenswear*	–	Swiss Army	*Accessories*	23
Patagonia	*Activewear*	27	Tarina Tarantino	*Jewelry*	22
Patina	*Vintage*	–	té casan	*Shoes*	–
Paul Smith	*Designer*	26	Ted Baker	*Designer*	25
Pearl River Mart	*Home*	16	Ted Muehling	*Jewelry*	29
Z Peter Fox Shoes	*Shoes*	28	Temperley	*Designer*	–
Phat Farm	*Mens/Womenswear*	16	Theory	*Mens/Womenswear*	23
Phi	*Designer*	–	37=1 Atelier	*Hose/Lingerie*	–
Philosophy/A.Ferretti	*Designer*	25	**NEW** 3.1 Phillip Lim	*Designer*	27
Pleats Please	*Designer*	–	Tibi	*Designer*	–
Poltrona Frau	*Home*	–	Todd Hase	*Home*	–
Pottery Barn	*Home*	20	Tommy Hilfiger/Denim	*Designer*	20
Prada	*Designer*	26	Tous	*Accessories*	22
Prince Charles III	*Menswear*	–	Trico Field	*Childrenswear*	–
Psny	*Childrenswear*	–	Triple 5 Soul	*Mens/Womenswear*	21
Puma	*Activewear/Sneakers*	23	True Religion	*Jeans*	–
Z Purl	*Knit/Needlepoint*	28	TSE	*Designer*	26
Pylones	*Gifts/Novelties*	–	**Z** TUMI	*Luggage*	28
Quiksilver	*Activewear/Swimwear*	21	UGG Australia	*Shoes*	–

Uniqlo | *Mens/Womenswear*	-
Varda | *Shoes*	27
Vespa | *Sports*	-
Vilebrequin | *Swimwear*	27
Vivienne Tam | *Designer*	24
Vogel | *Shoes*	-
Von Dutch | *Mens/Womenswear*	-
Z Waterworks | *Bath Fixtures*	28
WeSC | *Mens/Womenswear*	-
What Comes Around | *Vintage*	26
Wink | *Accessories*	21
Wolford | *Hose/Lingerie*	28
Yellow Rat | *Tween/Teen*	16
Yohji Yamamoto | *Designer*	27
Zara | *Mens/Womenswear*	18

SOUTH STREET SEAPORT

Abercrombie | *Tween/Teen*	18
Brookstone | *Electronics*	21
Express Men | *Menswear*	20
Firefly | *Childrenswear*	25
Guess | *Jeans*	21
NEW Helio | *Electronics*	20
J.Crew | *Mens/Womenswear*	20
Leontine | *Womenswear*	-
Z Met. Museum of Art	25
Neighborhoodies | *Mens/Womenswear*	20
NEW Salty Paw | *Pets*	22
Z Seaport Yarn	28
Sharper Image | *Electronics*	21
Z Talbots | *Mens/Womenswear*	22
UnitedColors/Benetton | *Mens/Womenswear*	20

TRIBECA

(Canal to Murray Sts., west of B'way)

Anbar | *Shoes*	21
A Uno/Walk | *Shoes/Womenswear*	24
NEW Babesta | *Childrenswear*	23
Babylicious | *Childrenswear*	-
Baker Tribeca | *Home*	28
Z Bed Bath & Beyond	20
Blue Bench | *Children's Furniture*	-
Boomerang Toys	-
Z Brooks Brothers | *Mens/Womenswear*	24
Bu & the Duck | *Childrenswear*	26
NEW Butterflies/Zebras | *Womenswear*	23
Calypso | *Womenswear*	23
Capucine | *Maternity*	-
Design Within Reach | *Home*	24

Disrespectacles | *Eyewear*	27
Donzella | *Home*	-
Dudley's Paw | *Pets*	-
Dune | *Home*	-
NEW Edon Manor | *Shoes*	-
Z Fountain Pen | *Stationery*	28
Goldy/Macki | *Womenswear*	22
Gotham Bikes | *Sports*	24
Issey Miyake | *Designer*	25
Kidville | *Childrenswear*	22
Koh's Kids | *Childrenswear*	-
Metro Bicycles	20
Mika Inatome | *Bridal*	-
Moulin Bleu | *Home*	-
Myoptics | *Eyewear*	25
Nili Lotan | *Designer*	-
Number (N)ine | *Designer*	-
P&S Fabrics	22
Petticoat Lane | *Hose/Lingerie*	-
Z Pompanoosuc Mills | *Home*	25
Rogan | *Jeans*	25
Schoolhouse Electric | *Lighting*	-
Selia Yang | *Bridal*	26
Shoofly | *Childrenswear*	26
Steven Alan | *Mens/Womenswear*	24
Thom Browne. | *Designer*	-
NEW Tribbles Home/Gdn.	25
Tribeca Girls | *Childrenswear*	-
Z Urban Archaeology | *Home*	25
Zaba | *Childrenswear*	-

UNION SQUARE

(14th to 17th Sts., 5th Ave. to Union Sq. E.)

Agnès B. | *Designer*	23
Am. Eagle | *Tween/Teen*	17
Babies "R" Us	19
Circuit City | *Electronics*	19
Z Country Floors | *Tile*	26
David Z. | *Shoes*	19
Diesel | *Jeans*	23
Disc-O-Rama | *Music/DVDs*	20
Z DSW | *Shoes*	21
Esprit | *Mens/Womenswear*	17
Z Filene's Basement | *Discount*	18
Forever 21 | *Womenswear*	10
JackRabbit Sports | *Activewear*	24
Z Paragon | *Sports*	25
Petco | *Pets*	19
Poggenpohl U.S. | *Home*	-
Puma | *Activewear/Sneakers*	23
Rothman's | *Menswear*	23
Z Sound by Singer | *Electronics*	27
Z Virgin | *Music/DVDs*	23

subscribe to ZAGAT.com

WASHINGTON HTS./INWOOD

(North of W. 157th St.)
- ☑ Met. Museum of Art 25

WEST 40s

Alcone	Toiletries	23
alice + olivia	Womenswear	22
☑ Allen Edmonds	Shoes	28
☑ Arthur Brown	Stationery	27
☑ Best Buy	Electronics	20
☑ Billabong	Activewear/Swimwear	21
Bra*Tenders	Hose/Lingerie	-
Champs	Sports	17
Colony Music	24
☑ Crane & Co.	Stationery	27
Delphinium	Home	24
Dykes Lumber	24
Giorgio Fedon 19	Accessories/Handbags	-
Gothic Cabinet Craft	Home	15
☑ Harvey Electronics	28
☑ International Photo	26
Metro Bicycles	20
Metropolitan Lumber	22
☑ Met. Museum of Art	25
Movado	Watches	26
New Balance	Sneakers	27
New York Fabric	Fabrics	-
New York Look	Womenswear	20
Original Penguin	Menswear	-
Pan Aqua Diving	Sports	-
Papyrus	Stationery	23
Paron Fabrics	20
Petland Discounts	18
Quiksilver	Activewear/Swimwear	21
Ray Beauty Supply	Toiletries	24
Salvation Army	Vintage	11
Sanrio	Toys	21
Sharper Image	Electronics	21
Skechers	Shoes	19
Sound City	Electronics	-
Spoiled Brats	Pets	24
Swatch	Watches	20
Thomas Pink	Menswear	26
Toys "R" Us	20
Training Camp	Sneakers	-
☑ TUMI	Luggage	28
☑ Virgin	Music/DVDs	23

WEST 50s

Aaron Faber	Jewelry/Watches	26
American Folk Art	23
☑ Anthropologie	Womenswear/Home	20

Arche	Shoes	25
Ascot Chang	Menswear	25
Beverly Feldman	Shoes	20
Blockbuster	Music/DVDs	16
Bolton's	Discount	14
Brookstone	Electronics	21
Capezio	Activewear	24
Charles Tyrwhitt	Menswear	26
Club Monaco	Mens/Womenswear	18
delfino	Handbags	22
Erwin Pearl	Jewelry	20
Eve's Garden	Sex Toys	24
Fortunoff	Home/Jewelry	24
Frank Stella	Menswear	22
French Connect.	Mens/Womenswear	20
Hippototamus	Childrenswear	22
Innovation Luggage	20
J.Crew	Mens/Womenswear	20
☑ Kate's Paperie	Stationery	27
Kenjo	Watches	25
Lee's Art Shop	25
Lee's Studio	Home	23
Leonard Opticians	26
☑ Manolo Blahnik	Shoes	28
☑ MoMA Store	Museum Shop	25
☑ Museum Arts/Design	26
OMO Norma Kamali	Designer	22
Rochester Big/Tall	Menswear	26
Sabon	Toiletries	25
Sansha	Activewear	-
Sharper Image	Electronics	21
☑ Smythson	Stationery	28
Suarez	Handbags	27
SwimBikeRun	Sports	-
Z Chemists/Zitomer	Toiletries	25

WEST 60s

American Folk Art	23
Aveda	Toiletries	26
A/X	Mens/Womenswear	19
BCBG Max Azria	Designer	22
bebe	Womenswear	17
☑ Bed Bath & Beyond	20
☑ Best Buy	Electronics	20
☑ Bose	Electronics	27
☑ Brooks Brothers	Mens/Womenswear	24
Caché	Womenswear	18
Club Monaco	Mens/Womenswear	18
Cole Haan	Shoes	25
Crabtree & Evelyn	Toiletries	23
Danskin	Activewear	23

Domain	*Home*	20
Eileen Fisher	*Womenswear*	24
Esprit	*Mens/Womenswear*	17
Ethan Allen	*Home*	23
FACE Stockholm	*Toiletries*	22
Fresh	*Toiletries*	26
Furry Paws	*Pets*	21
🅩 Gracious Home	25
Gruen Optika	*Eyewear*	25
Hugo Boss	*Designer*	26
Innovation Luggage	20
Intermix	*Womenswear*	24
Jacadi	*Childrenswear*	27
J.Crew	*Mens/Womenswear*	20
J.W. Cooper	*Accessories*	-
Kangol	*Accessories*	23
🅩 Kiehl's	*Toiletries*	27
Lancôme	*Toiletries*	26
lululemon	*Activewear*	-
M.A.C. Cosmetics	26
Met. Opera Shop	24
Montmartre	*Womenswear*	22
Morgenthal Frederics	*Eyewear*	28
New York Look	*Womenswear*	20
New York Running	*Sneakers*	24
Pottery Barn	*Home*	20
Reiss	*Mens/Womenswear*	20
Robert Marc	*Eyewear*	27
Sisley	*Mens/Womenswear*	20
Solstice	*Eyewear*	-
Stuart Weitzman	*Shoes*	27
Swarovski	*Jewelry*	25
Thomas Pink	*Menswear*	26
🅩 Toga Bikes	26
Tourneau	*Watches*	27
🅩 TUMI	*Luggage*	28
UnitedColors/Benetton	*Mens/Womenswear*	20
United Colors/Kids	*Childrenswear*	21
🅩 Williams-Sonoma	*Home*	26
Wink	*Accessories*	21
Wolford	*Hose/Lingerie*	28

WEST 70s

Am. Museum/Nat.Hist.	22
🅩 Bang & Olufsen	*Electronics*	28
Barneys CO-OP	*Mens/Womenswear*	24
Beacon Paint	22
Beau Brummel	*Menswear*	22
Berkley Girl	*Tween/Teen*	21
Betsey Johnson	*Designer*	21
Blades Board & Skate	23
Bloch	*Activewear*	-

Bra Smyth	*Hose/Lingerie*	25
Brief Encounters	*Hose/Lingerie*	-
Cardeology	*Stationery*	19
Clarins	*Toiletries*	26
NEW Crocs	*Shoes*	-
Design Within Reach	*Home*	24
Eileen Fisher	*Womenswear*	24
Emmelle	*Womenswear*	21
FACE Stockholm	*Toiletries*	22
🅩 Filene's Basement	*Discount*	18
G.C. William	*Tween/Teen*	20
Granny-Made	*Childrenswear*	24
Housing Works Thrift	20
Jewish Museum	25
Jubilee	*Shoes*	16
Kenneth Cole NY	*Designer*	21
La Boutique Resale	23
La Brea	*Gifts/Novelties*	18
L'Artisan Parfumeur	*Toiletries*	26
🅩 Loehmann's	*Discount*	20
Lucky Brand Jeans	23
Lush	*Toiletries*	23
Malia Mills Swimwear	26
Montmartre	*Womenswear*	22
North Face	*Activewear*	24
Olive & Bette's	*Womenswear*	22
Only Hearts	*Hose/Lingerie*	21
Oriental Lamp Shade	*Lighting*	25
Paterson Silks	*Fabrics*	18
Plaza Too	*Accessories*	21
Pookie/Sebastian	*Womenswear*	17
Sabon	*Toiletries*	25
Sacco	*Shoes*	22
Sean	*Menswear*	24
Shoe Box	23
NEW Space.NK	*Toiletries*	25
Super Runners Shop	26
Swatch	*Watches*	20
Theory	*Mens/Womenswear*	23
Tip Top Kids	26
Tip Top Shoes	25
Urban Outfitters	*Mens/Womenswear*	17
Varda	*Shoes*	27
Verve	*Handbags/Shoes*	24
NEW West	*Shoes*	-
Z'Baby Co.	*Childrenswear*	24

WEST 80s

Allan & Suzi	*Vintage*	20
🅩 Avventura	*China/Crystal*	26
Bicycle Renaissance	21
Böc	*Womenswear*	19
Cardeology	*Stationery*	19

Chico's	Womenswear	20
Circuit City	Electronics	19
Club Monaco	Mens/Womenswear	18
C.P.W.	Childrenswear	22
Door Store	Home	17
Essentials	Toiletries	20
Eye Man	Eyewear	25
Frank Stella	Menswear	22
Greenstones	Childrenswear	26
Gruen Optika	Eyewear	25
Gymboree	Childrenswear	22
Harry's Shoes	24
Harry's Shoes/Kids	-
Hippototamus	Childrenswear	22
Kidville	Childrenswear	22
Laina Jane	Hose/Lingerie	-
Laytner's Linen	20
Lightforms	Lighting	23
Maxilla & Mandible	Toys	25
Medici	Shoes	20
Origins	Toiletries	24
Patagonia	Activewear	27
Penny Whistle	Toys	23
☑ Pet Stop	26
Purdy Girl	Womenswear	18
Quintessentials	Appliances	23
Satya	Jewelry	21
☑ Schweitzer Linen	27
Staples	Electronics	19
Steven Alan	Mens/Womenswear	24
☑ Talbots	Mens/Womenswear	22
Town Shop	Hose/Lingerie	25
Variazioni	Womenswear	17
West Side Kids	Toys	24
☑ Yarn Co.	26
☑ Zabar's	Cookware	26

WEST 90s

Albee Baby Carriage	25
Metro Bicycles	20
Petco	Pets	19

WEST 100s

(See also Harlem/East Harlem)

Kim's Mediapolis	Music/DVDs	24
Liberty House	Childrenswear	25
☑ Marshalls	Discount	16
Planet Kids	Children's	18

WEST VILLAGE

(Houston to 14th Sts., west of 7th Ave. S., excluding Meatpacking District)

| Annelore | Designer | - |
| Bathroom | Toiletries | 27 |

Beasty Feast	Pets	24
Belly Dance Maternity	-
blush	Womenswear	21
Bond No. 9	Toiletries	28
☑ Bonpoint	Childrenswear	28
Brooklyn Industries	Mens/Womenswear	20
Brunello Cucinelli	Designer	-
Butik	Womenswear	-
Calypso	Womenswear	23
Castor & Pollux	Womenswear	-
Catherine Malandrino	Designer	24
Cherry	Vintage	-
☑ Christian Louboutin	Shoes	28
City Cricket	Childrenswear	-
Crumpler Bags	24
Cynthia Rowley	Designer	23
Darling	Womenswear	-
Disrespectacles	Eyewear	27
Flight 001	Luggage	24
Fresh	Toiletries	26
Geminola	Womenswear	-
Greenwich Letterpress	Stationery	26
Hable Construction	Home	-
Housing Works Thrift	20
Intermix	Womenswear	24
Irma	Womenswear	-
James Perse	Mens/Womenswear	24
NEW Jessie James	Womenswear	-
NEW John Bartlett	Designer	23
Juicy Couture	Designer	20
Kaas GlassWorks	Home	-
Kids Rx	Toiletries	-
Kim's Mediapolis	Music/DVDs	24
☑ Leather Man	Sex Toys	26
Le Fanion	Home	-
NEW Little Marc	Childrenswear	-
Lord Willy's	Menswear	-
Lulu Guinness	Handbags	24
L'Uomo	Menswear	24
Maison Martin Margiela	Designer	-
Marc and Max	Hose/Lingerie	-
Marc/Marc Jacobs	Designer	25
Marc Jacobs Access.	28
Mick Margo	Womenswear	-
NEW Miguelina	Designer	24
Mulberry	Handbags	-
Mxyplyzyk	Home	21
Olatz	Bed/Bath	-

Olive & Bette's	*Womenswear*	22
Oliver Spencer	*Menswear*	-
Otte	*Womenswear*	26
P.E. Guerin	*Hardware*	-
Plaza Too	*Accessories*	21
Pleasure Chest	*Sex Toys*	22
Pylones	*Gifts/Novelties*	-
Ralph Lauren	*Designer*	26
Rebel Rebel	*Music/DVDs*	-
Reiss	*Mens/Womenswear*	20
Robert Marc	*Eyewear*	27
Ruehl	*Accessories*	21
Satya	*Jewelry*	21
SEE Eyewear	-
Selima/Sucre	*Eyewear*	27
NEW Soapology	*Toiletries*	22
Sophia Eugene	*Designer*	-
Space107	*Home*	-
Steven	*Shoes*	18
Steven Alan	*Mens/Womenswear*	24
Tommy Hilfiger/Denim	*Designer*	20
NEW Urban Zen	*Mens/Womenswear*	-
Verve	*Handbags/Shoes*	24
Village Tannery	*Luggage*	21
Yoya/Yoya Mart	*Childrenswear*	27
Zero/Maria Cornejo	*Designer*	-
Zoomies	*Pets*	29

Bronx

ABC Carpet/Outlet	*Home*	21
Athlete's Foot	*Sneakers*	20
Casual Male XL	*Menswear*	19
Davis & Warshow	*Bath Fixtures*	23
Dykes Lumber	24
Kmart	*Mass Merch.*	12
Z Loehmann's	*Discount*	20
Z Marshalls	*Discount*	16
Nat'l Whse. Liquid	*Discount*	11
Sears	*Dept. Store*	17
Z Target	*Mass Merch.*	17
Vespa	*Sports*	-

Brooklyn

BAY RIDGE

Z Century 21	*Discount*	22
Circuit City	*Electronics*	19
hip-squeak	*Childrenswear*	23
Joyce Leslie	*Womenswear*	8
KB Toys	16
Olá Baby	*Children's Furniture*	27
UnitedColors/Benetton	*Mens/Womenswear*	20

BENSONHURST

Babies "R" Us	19
Z Best Buy	*Electronics*	20
Kohl's	*Mass Merch.*	-
Z Marshalls	*Discount*	16
Mylo Dweck	*Maternity*	-
Nat'l Whse. Liquid	*Discount*	11
Something Else	*Mens/Womenswear*	23

BOERUM HILL

NEW Blue Ribbon	*Gifts/Novelties*	-
Brooklyn Industries	*Mens/Womenswear*	20
Flight 001	*Luggage*	24
GRDN Bklyn	*Garden*	23
Hollander/Lexer	*Menswear*	-
NEW Homage	*Sports*	19
Knit-A-Way	-
Lucky Brand Jeans	23
Michelle	*Bridal/Womenswear*	-
NEW OMALA	*Activewear*	20
Rico	*Home*	-
Sir	*Designer*	-
Something Else	*Mens/Womenswear*	23
Soula	*Shoes*	-

BOROUGH PARK

Jacadi	*Childrenswear*	27
Mimi Maternity	19
S&W	*Discount*	18
UnitedColors/Benetton	*Mens/Womenswear*	20

BROOKLYN HEIGHTS

Abitare	*Home*	-
Design Within Reach	*Home*	24
Heights Kids	*Childrenswear*	-
Housing Works Thrift	20
M.A.C. Cosmetics	26

CANARSIE

Casual Male XL	*Menswear*	19
Training Camp	*Sneakers*	-

CARROLL GARDENS

Area	*Childrenswear*	-
Brooklyn General	*Knit/Needlepoint*	-
Debbie Fisher	*Jewelry*	-
environment337	*Home*	-
Flirt	*Womenswear*	-
Hasker	*Home*	-
Living 5th/7th/Smith	*Home/Womenswear*	-

Oculus 20/20 | *Eyewear* —
NEW Ohio Knit. | *Vintage* 22
Olá Baby | *Children's Furniture* 27
Swallow | *Home* —
Watts on Smith | *Menswear* —

CLINTON HILL

Circuit City | *Electronics* 19
NEW REPOP | *Vintage* —

COBBLE HILL

A Brooklyn Table | *Home* —
Bird | *Womenswear* 25
Dear Fieldbinder | *Womenswear* —
Diane T | *Womenswear* —
Green Onion | *Childrenswear* 24
Home & Haven 22
LF Stores | *Womenswear* 17
Lily | *Womenswear* 24
Néda | *Womenswear* 21
Refinery | *Handbags* —

CONEY ISLAND

Z Loehmann's | *Discount* 20

DITMAS PARK

Belle & Maxie | *Childrenswear* —

DOWNTOWN

Acorn | *Toys* —
Bark | *Home* —
Burlington Coat | *Discount* 15
Butter | *Womenswear* 23
Carol's Daughter | *Toiletries* 24
Consignment | *Vintage* —
Dig Garden 23
Door Store | *Home* 17
Z DSW | *Shoes* 21
Goodwill | *Vintage* 12
Layla | *Home* —
Maleeka | *Womenswear* —
Z Marshalls | *Discount* 16
New York Transit Mus. 20
Sid's | *Hardware* 21
Sterling Pl. | *Home* —
Z Target | *Mass Merch.* 17
NEW Trixie/Tilda | *Tween/Teen* 25

DUMBO

Blueberi | *Womenswear* —
BoConcept | *Home* 17
halcyon | *Music/DVDs* —
Half Pint | *Baby Gear* —
Loopy Mango | *Womenswear* —
NEW ModernTots | 23
   Children's Furniture

Neighborhoodies | 20
   Mens/Womenswear
Pomme | *Childrenswear* —
Spring | *Accessories* —
West Elm | *Home* 17
Wonk | *Home* —
Zoë | *Womenswear* —

DYKER HEIGHTS

Casual Male XL | *Menswear* 19
Prato Fine Men's Wear 13

EAST NEW YORK

Athlete's Foot | *Sneakers* 20

FLATBUSH

Canal Jean 17
Sears | *Dept. Store* 17
Tuesday's Child | *Childrenswear* 26

FORT GREENE

Addy/Ferro | *Mens/Womenswear* —
Carol's Daughter | *Toiletries* 24
Cloth | *Womenswear* —
NEW Head/Heels | *Shoes* 21
Hot Toddie | *Childrenswear* —
Stuart/Wright | —
   Mens/Womenswear

GOWANUS

Lowe's | *Hardware* 21

GRAVESEND

Cantaloup/Luxe | *Womenswear* 22
Lester's | *Childrenswear* 24
NEW Rewind | *Vintage* —
William Barthman | *Jewelry* 26

GREENPOINT

NEW Alter | *Mens/Womenswear* —
Dalaga | *Mens/Womenswear* 19
NEW HH Design | *Handbags* 20

KINGS PLAZA/ MARINE PARK

Am. Eagle | *Tween/Teen* 17
Express Men | *Menswear* 20
Forever 21 | *Womenswear* 10
Guess | *Jeans* 21
Joyce Leslie | *Womenswear* 8
Lady Foot Locker | *Sneakers* 22
Limited, The | *Womenswear* —
Limited Too | *Tween/Teen* 16
Sears | *Dept. Store* 17

MIDWOOD

Diva | *Tween/Teen* —
Drimmers | *Appliances* 24

Katz/Cradle | *Children's Furniture*	-|
Tuesday's Child | *Childrenswear*	26|
Yellow Door | *Home/Jewelry*	-|

MILL BASIN

Casual Male XL | *Menswear*	19|
Joyce Leslie | *Womenswear*	8|

PARK SLOPE

a. cheng | *Designer*	19|
Area | *Childrenswear*	-|
NEW Asha Veza | *Womenswear*	-|
Beacon's Closet | *Vintage*	19|
Bird | *Womenswear*	25|
Brooklyn Industries | *Mens/Womenswear*	20|
NEW Brklyn Merc. | *Home*	21|
NEW Bump | *Maternity*	-|
Clay Pot | *Home/Jewelry*	26|
Cog & Pearl | *Accessories*	21|
Diana Kane | *Womenswear*	-|
Dykes Lumber	24|
Eidolon | *Womenswear*	-|
Firefly | *Childrenswear*	25|
Flight 001 | *Luggage*	24|
Flirt | *Womenswear*	-|
4PlayBK | *Tween/Teen*	-|
Goldy/Macki | *Womenswear*	22|
JackRabbit Sports | *Activewear*	24|
Kiwi | *Womenswear*	22|
Lily | *Womenswear*	24|
Lion in Sun | *Stationery*	24|
Living 5th/7th/Smith | *Home/Womenswear*	-|
NEW Lola | *Womenswear*	22|
Loom | *Accessories/Womenswear*	23|
Matter | *Home*	-|
Néda | *Womenswear*	21|
Oak | *Mens/Womenswear*	-|
Orange Blossom | *Childrenswear*	-|
Otto | *Womenswear*	23|
Pink Pussycat | *Sex Toys*	19|
Pintchik | *Hardware*	20|
premium goods | *Sneakers*	-|
NEW Private Stock | *Menswear*	-|
Razor | *Menswear*	-|
Romp | *Toys*	-|
Scaredy Kat | *Gifts/Novelties*	24|
Shoe Mine	-|
Slope Sports	-|
Something Else | *Mens/Womenswear*	23|
Soula | *Shoes*	-|
Sterling Pl. | *Home*	-|

Tarzian True Value | *Hardware*	21|
Tarzian West | *Home*	21|
3r Living | *Home*	-|
Toy Space	23|

PROSPECT HEIGHTS

Brooklyn Museum	22|
NEW Corduroy Kid | *Childrenswear*	24|
Hooti Couture | *Vintage*	21|
Pieces | *Mens/Womenswear*	21|
Redberi | *Womenswear*	-|

RED HOOK

Brooklyn Collective | *Womenswear*	-|
Chelsea Garden Ctr.	23|
NEW Erie Basin | *Jewelry*	-|
Saipua | *Toiletries*	-|

SHEEPSHEAD BAY

National Jean Company	-|

STARRETT CITY

Babies "R" Us	19|
Z Bed Bath & Beyond	20|
Circuit City | *Electronics*	19|
Z Marshalls | *Discount*	16|
Z Target | *Mass Merch.*	17|

SUNSET PARK

Z Costco Warehse. | *Discount*	22|
Lady Foot Locker | *Sneakers*	22|

WILLIAMSBURG

A&G Merch | *Home*	21|
About Glamour | *Mens/Womenswear*	-|
Academy Records	24|
Amarcord Vintage	-|
Archangela | *Shoes*	-|
Beacon's Closet | *Vintage*	19|
Bettencourt | *Hardware*	-|
Brooklyn Industries | *Mens/Womenswear*	20|
Buffalo Exchange | *Vintage*	17|
Built by Wendy | *Designer*	-|
Catbird | *Jewelry/Womenswear*	-|
CB I Hate Perfume | *Toiletries*	-|
Challengher | *Womenswear*	-|
NEW 5 in 1 | *Womenswear*	-|
Flying Squirrel | *Childrenswear*	-|
Fresh Kills | *Home*	-|
Future Perfect | *Home*	-|
In God We Trust | *Womenswear*	-|
Jumelle | *Womenswear*	-|
KCDC Skate | *Sports*	22|

Lisa Levine	*Jewelry*	-
Love Brigade | *Mens/Womenswear*	-
Michael Anchin	*Home*	-
Mini Jake	*Children's Furniture*	-
Mini Minimkt.	*Accessories*	-
Moon River Chattel	*Home*	-
Natan Borlam's	*Childrenswear*	28
Noisette	*Womenswear*	-
Oak	*Mens/Womenswear*	-
Oculus 20/20	*Eyewear*	-
Otte	*Womenswear*	26
Pinkyotto	*Womenswear*	21
POP	*Mens/Womenswear*	19
🆕 Red Toenails | *Mens/Womenswear*	-
S&W	*Discount*	18
🆕 Shoe Market	18
Sleep	*Bed/Bath*	22
🆕 Sprout Home	*Garden*	25
Stella Dallas/Ten Feet	*Vintage*	-
Treehouse	*Mens/Womenswear*	-
Triple 5 Soul | *Mens/Womenswear*	21
Two Jakes	*Home*	21
Wonk	*Home*	-
Yarn Tree		-
Ylli	*Mens/Womenswear*	-
Yoko Devereaux	*Designer*	-

Queens

ASTORIA

f.y.e.	*Music/DVDs*	18
Loveday31	*Vintage*	-
Metropolitan Lumber		22
Mimi's Closet	*Womenswear*	21
Prato Fine Men's Wear		13
Skechers	*Shoes*	19
UnitedColors/Benetton | *Mens/Womenswear*	20

BAYSIDE

Am. Eagle	*Tween/Teen*	17
Chico's	*Womenswear*	20
Steve Madden	*Shoes*	16
Thomasville	*Home*	23

COLLEGE POINT

Babies "R" Us		19
Circuit City	*Electronics*	19
🔁 Target	*Mass Merch.*	17
🔁 T.J. Maxx	*Discount*	16

CORONA

| Metropolitan Lumber | | 22 |

ELMHURST

Am. Eagle	*Tween/Teen*	17
A/X	*Mens/Womenswear*	19
Bare Escentuals	*Toiletries*	25
bebe	*Womenswear*	17
🔁 Bed Bath & Beyond		20
🔁 Best Buy	*Electronics*	20
Champs	*Sports*	17
Charlotte Russe	*Tween/Teen*	10
Clarks	*Shoes*	23
Club Monaco | *Mens/Womenswear*	18
🔁 DSW	*Shoes*	21
Forever 21	*Womenswear*	10
Fossil	*Watches*	19
Geox	*Shoes*	23
Lady Foot Locker	*Sneakers*	22
Limited Too	*Tween/Teen*	16
Lush	*Toiletries*	23
Skechers	*Shoes*	19
Swatch	*Watches*	20
🔁 Target	*Mass Merch.*	17
White Hse. Black Mkt. | *Womenswear*	-
Yellow Rat	*Tween/Teen*	16

FLORAL PARK

| Paterson Silks | *Fabrics* | 18 |

FLUSHING

Athlete's Foot	*Sneakers*	20
Blackman	*Bath Fixtures*	26
🔁 Filene's Basement	*Discount*	18
Grand Central Racquet		-
Joyce Leslie	*Womenswear*	8
KB Toys		16
Nat'l Whse. Liquid	*Discount*	11
Sears	*Dept. Store*	17

FOREST HILLS

Ethan Allen	*Home*	23
Jubilee	*Shoes*	16
Moscot	*Eyewear*	21
Sports Authority		17
UnitedColors/Benetton | *Mens/Womenswear*	20

FRESH MEADOWS

| Kohl's | *Mass Merch.* | - |

GLENDALE

Gymboree	*Childrenswear*	22
Stella Gialla	*Womenswear*	25
White Hse. Black Mkt. | *Womenswear*	-

HOWARD BEACH

Petco | Pets   19

JACKSON HEIGHTS

f.y.e. | Music/DVDs   18
KB Toys   16

JAMAICA

Athlete's Foot | Sneakers   20
Metropolitan Lumber   22
Nemo Tile   21

LITTLE NECK

Eneslow | Shoes   28

LONG ISLAND CITY

Z Best Buy | Electronics   20
Z Costco Warehse. | Discount   22
David's Bridal   13
Dykes Lumber   24
Z Marshalls | Discount   16
Nat'l Whse. Liquid | Discount   11
Z Simon's Hardware   26
Tucker Robbins | Home   -

MASPETH

Davis & Warshow | Bath Fixtures   23

MIDDLE VILLAGE

Kmart | Mass Merch.   12

QUEENS VILLAGE

Blackman | Bath Fixtures   26
Steve Madden | Shoes   16

REGO PARK

Z Bed Bath & Beyond   20
Circuit City | Electronics   19
Z Loehmann's | Discount   20
Z Marshalls | Discount   16
Sears | Dept. Store   17
Urban Outfitters | 17
    Mens/Womenswear

RIDGEWOOD

Joyce Leslie | Womenswear   8
KB Toys   16

WOODHAVEN

Missha | Toiletries   -
Smiley's | Knit/Needlepoint   16

WOODSIDE

Sports Authority   17

Staten Island

Am. Eagle | Tween/Teen   17
Z Apple Store | Electronics   27
Bath & Body Works | Toiletries   19
BCBG Max Azria | Designer   22
bebe | Womenswear   17
Z Bed Bath & Beyond   20
Bellini | Children's Furniture   23
Z Best Buy | Electronics   20
Brookstone | Electronics   21
Z Build-A-Bear | Toys   22
Burlington Coat | Discount   15
Caché | Womenswear   18
Casual Male XL | Menswear   19
Champs | Sports   17
Charlotte Russe | Tween/Teen   10
Circuit City | Electronics   19
Z Costco Warehse. | Discount   22
Crabtree & Evelyn | Toiletries   23
Emily's | Womenswear   25
Esprit | Mens/Womenswear   17
Ethan Allen | Home   23
Forever 21 | Womenswear   10
Guess | Jeans   21
Gymboree | Childrenswear   22
Joyce Leslie | Womenswear   8
KB Toys   16
Kmart | Mass Merch.   12
Kohl's | Mass Merch.   -
Lady Foot Locker | Sneakers   22
Limited, The | Womenswear   -
Limited Too | Tween/Teen   16
Lowe's | Hardware   21
Z Marshalls | Discount   16
Mimi Maternity   19
Nat'l Whse. Liquid | Discount   11
Sears | Dept. Store   17
Steve Madden | Shoes   16
Swarovski | Jewelry   25
Z Target | Mass Merch.   17
Z T.J. Maxx | Discount   16
Training Camp | Sneakers   -

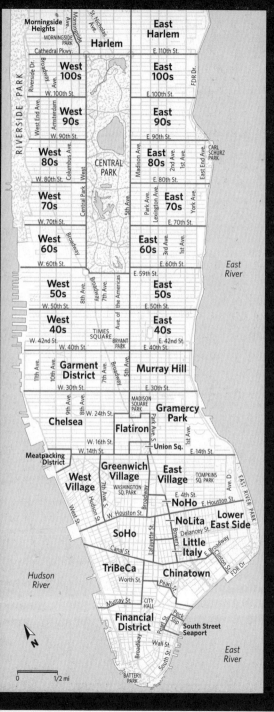

MANHATTAN NEIGHBORHOODS

Morningside Heights
MORNINGSIDE PARK
Cathedral Pkwy.
Harlem
East Harlem
E. 110th St.

West 100s
W. 100th St.
East 100s
E. 100th St.

West 90s
W. 90th St.
East 90s
E. 90th St.

West 80s
W. 80th St.
CENTRAL PARK
East 80s
E. 80th St.
CARL SCHURZ PARK

West 70s
W. 70th St.
East 70s
E. 70th St.

West 60s
W. 60th St.
East 60s
E. 60th St.

East River

West 50s
W. 50th St.
East 50s
E. 50th St.

West 40s
TIMES SQUARE
W. 42nd St.
BRYANT PARK
W. 40th St.
East 40s
E. 42nd St.
E. 40th St.

Garment District
W. 30th St.
Murray Hill
E. 30th St.

MADISON SQUARE PARK
Chelsea
W. 24th St.
Flatiron
Gramercy Park

W. 16th St.
W. 14th St.
Union Sq.
E. 14th St.

Meatpacking District
Greenwich Village
WASHINGTON SQ. PARK
East Village
TOMPKINS SQ. PARK

West Village
E. 4th St.
NoHo
E. Houston St.
Lower East Side

W. Houston St.
NoLita
Delancey St.

SoHo
Little Italy

Canal St.
Chinatown

TriBeCa
Worth St.

Hudson River

Murray St.
CITY HALL
Peck Slip

Financial District
South Street Seaport

Wall St.

BATTERY PARK

East River

0   1/2 mi

RIVERSIDE PARK

St. Nicholas Ave.
Morningside Ave.
Riverside Dr.
West End Ave.
Amsterdam
Columbus Ave.
Central Park West
Broadway
5th Ave.
Madison Ave.
Park Ave.
Lexington Ave.
3rd Ave.
2nd Ave.
1st Ave.
York Ave.
East End Ave.
FDR Dr.

8th Ave.
7th Ave.
Ave. of the Americas
Broadway
5th Ave.

11th Ave.
10th Ave.
9th Ave.
8th Ave.
7th Ave.
Broadway
Park Ave. S.
1st Ave.

Hudson St.
West St.
7th Ave. S.
Broadway
Lafayette St.
Bowery
Clinton St.
FDR Dr.
EAST RIVER PARK
Ave. D
Pearl St.
Broadway
Broadway
South St.
Pitt St.

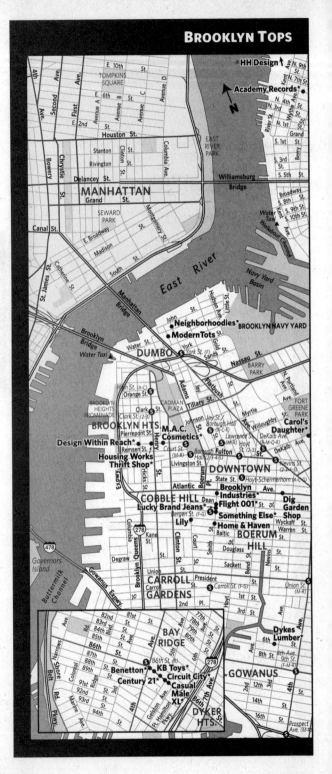

HH Design ↑

Academy Records*

N

E. 10th St.
TOMPKINS SQUARE PARK
E. 6th St.
Houston St.
Stanton St.
Rivington
Delancey St.

MANHATTAN
Grand St.

SEWARD PARK

Canal St.
E. Broadway
Madison St.
South St.

EAST RIVER PARK

Williamsburg Bridge

East River

Navy Yard Basin

Neighborhoodies*
ModernTots*

BROOKLYN NAVY YARD

Manhattan Bridge

Brooklyn Bridge

Water Taxi

DUMBO
York St. (F)

BARRY PARK

FORT GREENE PARK

High St. (A-C)
Orange St.
Clark St. (2-3)
CADMAN PLAZA
Tillary St.

BROOKLYN HEIGHTS PROMENADE

BROOKLYN HTS.
M.A.C. Cosmetics*

Carol's Daughter*

Design Within Reach*

Housing Works Thrift Shop*

Borough Hall (M-R)
Court St. (M-R)
Borough Hall (2/3-4-5)
Fulton

DOWNTOWN

State St.
Hoyt-Schermerhorn (A-C-G)

Atlantic Ave.

COBBLE HILL
Lucky Brand Jeans*
Lily*

Brooklyn Industries*
Flight 001*
Something Else*
Home & Haven*

Dig Garden Shop*

BOERUM HILL

478

Governors Island

Buttermilk Channel

CARROLL GARDENS

Carroll St. (F-G)

Union St. (M-R)

GOWANUS

BAY RIDGE

Benetton*
Century 21*
Circuit City*
Casual Male XL*

KB Toys*

Dykes Lumber*

DYKER HTS.

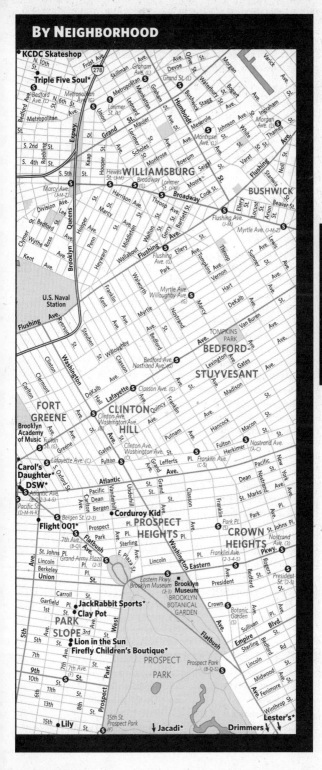

KCDC Skateshop
N. 10th
Triple Five Soul*
Bedford Ave.
N. 6th St.
Metropolitan
S. 2nd St.
S. 4th St.

WILLIAMSBURG
BUSHWICK
Broadway

U.S. Naval Station

TOMPKINS PARK
BEDFORD-STUYVESANT

FORT GREENE
Brooklyn Academy of Music

CLINTON HILL

Carol's Daughter*
DSW*

Flight 001*
Corduroy Kid
PROSPECT HEIGHTS
CROWN HEIGHTS

Brooklyn Museum
BROOKLYN BOTANICAL GARDEN

JackRabbit Sports*
Clay Pot
PARK SLOPE
Lion in the Sun
Firefly Children's Boutique*

PROSPECT PARK

Lily
Jacadi*
Drimmers
Lester's*

Merchandise

Includes store names, locations, and Quality ratings. **Z** indicates highest ratings, popularity and importance.

ACCESSORIES

(See also Department Stores)

Barbara Feinman	E Vill	23
Bird	multi.	25
Blueberi	Dumbo	-
Claire's Accessories	multi.	8
Z Coach	multi.	26
Cog & Pearl	Park Slope	21
Dear Fieldbinder	Cobble Hill	-
Destination	Meatpacking	23
Diane T	Cobble Hill	-
Dunhill	E 50s	27
Eidolon	Park Slope	-
Ellen Christine	Chelsea	-
Giorgio Fedon 19	W 40s	-
Girl Props	SoHo	11
Hat Shop	SoHo	24
NEW HH Design	Greenpt	20
Jack Spade	SoHo	25
NEW Jessie James	W Vill	-
J.J. Hat Center	Garment	27
Kangol	W 60s	23
Kate Spade	multi.	24
Kieselstein-Cord	E 80s	28
Kiki/Montparnasse	SoHo	25
Kipepeo	NoLita	-
LaCrasia Gloves	Chelsea	25
Laila Rowe	multi.	14
Z Leiber	E 60s	28
Loom	Park Slope	23
Loopy Mango	Dumbo	-
NEW Lucia Nenickova	Gramercy	21
Lulu Guinness	W Vill	24
Maleeka	Downtown Bklyn	-
Marc Jacobs Access.	W Vill	28
Max Azria	SoHo	-
Meg Cohen Design	SoHo	-
Mini Minimkt.	W'burg	-
Mulberry	multi.	-
Plaza Too	multi.	21
Porsche Design	E 50s	26
Pucci	multi.	26
Redberi	Prospect Hts	-
NEW Roger Vivier	E 60s	28
Ruehl	W Vill	21
Z Salvatore Ferragamo	E 50s	28
Samuel's Hats	Financial	-
Seigo	multi.	28

Selima/Sucre	W Vill	27
Stella Gialla	Glendale	25
Stuart/Wright	Ft Greene	-
NEW Suite Orchard	LES	23
Susan van der Linde	E 50s	-
Tory Burch	NoLita	21
Tous	SoHo	22
Tracy Reese	Meatpacking	25
Triple 5 Soul	multi.	21
Valley	LES	-
Versace	E 50s	26
Verve	multi.	24
Wink	multi.	21
Zachary's Smile	multi.	24

ACTIVEWEAR

Adidas	multi.	23
Z Billabong	multi.	21
Bloch	W 70s	-
Capezio	multi.	24
Crunch	multi.	15
Danskin	W 60s	23
Equinox Energy	multi.	22
Fila	E 40s	23
NEW Homage	Boerum Hill	19
JackRabbit Sports	multi.	24
KCDC Skate	W'burg	22
KD Dance & Sport	NoHo	-
Lady Foot Locker	multi.	22
lululemon	W 60s	-
Modell's Sport	multi.	16
Napapijri	SoHo	-
NBA Store	E 50s	21
Neighborhoodies	multi.	20
New Balance	multi.	27
New York Running	W 60s	24
Niketown	E 50s	24
North Face	multi.	24
NYC Velo	E Vill	20
NEW OMALA	Boerum Hill	20
On Stage Dance	Murray Hill	-
Orvis	E 40s	25
Z Paragon	Union Sq	25
Patagonia	multi.	27
Princeton Ski Shop	Flatiron	21
Quiksilver	multi.	21
Rival	SoHo	22
Sansha	W 50s	-
Slope Sports	Park Slope	-

Sports Authority	multi.	17
Super Runners Shop	multi.	26
Supreme	SoHo	-
SwimBikeRun	W 50s	-
NEW West	W 70s	-

APPLIANCES

Bowery Kitchen	Chelsea	22
Drimmers	Midwood	24
Gracious Home	multi.	25
Gringer & Sons	E Vill	25
Home Depot	multi.	19
Krup's Kitchen/Bath	Flatiron	26
Manhattan Ctr.	Flatiron	-
P.C. Richard & Son	multi.	18
Poggenpohl U.S.	multi.	-
Quintessentials	W 80s	23
Sears	multi.	17

ART SUPPLIES

A.I. Friedman	Flatiron	24
Blick Art Materials	NoHo	25
DaVinci Art Supply	Chelsea	23
Kremer Pigments	Chelsea	29
Lee's Art Shop	W 50s	25
New York Central Art	E Vill	25
Pearl Paint	Chinatown	26
Sam Flax	multi.	24
Utrecht	multi.	24

BABY GEAR

Albee Baby Carriage	W 90s	25
Babies "R" Us	multi.	19
buybuy BABY	Chelsea	23
Half Pint	Dumbo	-
Heights Kids	Bklyn Hts	-
Kidville	multi.	22
Mini Jake	W'burg	-
NEW ModernTots	Dumbo	23
MoonSoup	E 50s	24
Planet Kids	multi.	18
Psny	SoHo	-
Schneider's	Chelsea	25

BATH FIXTURES/TILES

Ann Sacks	multi.	27
Artistic Tile	multi.	26
Bisazza	SoHo	-
Blackman	multi.	26
Boffi SoHo	SoHo	-
Country Floors	Union Sq	26
Davis & Warshow	multi.	23
Hastings Tile/Bath	E 50s	26
Home Depot	multi.	19

Ideal Tile	E 50s	20
Kraft	E 60s	26
Krup's Kitchen/Bath	Flatiron	26
Manhattan Ctr.	Flatiron	-
Nemo Tile	multi.	21
New York Replacement	E 90s	22
Pottery Barn Bed/Bath	Chelsea	-
Quintessentials	W 80s	23
Restoration Hardware	Flatiron	21
Sherle Wagner	E 60s	-
Sicis	SoHo	25
Sid's	Downtown Bklyn	21
Simon's Hardware	multi.	26
Urban Archaeology	multi.	25
Waterworks	multi.	28

BED/BATH

ABC Carpet & Home	Flatiron	25
ABC Carpet/Outlet	Bronx	21
Abitare	Bklyn Hts	-
NEW Ankasa	E 60s	24
Armani Casa	SoHo	25
Bark	Downtown Bklyn	-
Bed Bath & Beyond	multi.	20
Bellora	SoHo	26
Bergdorf	E 50s	29
Bloomingdale's	multi.	23
Calypso Home	NoLita	-
Charles P. Rogers	Flatiron	26
NEW Charlotte Moss	E 60s	25
Conran Shop	E 50s	23
E. Braun & Co.	E 60s	-
Flou	SoHo	-
Frette	E 60s	29
Gracious Home	multi.	25
Harris Levy	LES	26
Hastens	SoHo	-
Home & Haven	Cobble Hill	22
Kreiss Collection	E 50s	26
La Cafetière	Chelsea	-
Layla	Downtown Bklyn	-
Laytner's Linen	multi.	20
Léron	E 60s	29
Lulu Guinness	W Vill	24
Macy's	multi.	19
Madura	E 80s	24
MauricE Villency	E 50s	26
Nancy Koltes Home	NoLita	28
Olatz	W Vill	-
Pier 1 Imports	multi.	15
Porthault	E 60s	29
Pottery Barn	multi.	20
Pottery Barn Bed/Bath	Chelsea	-

Z Pratesi	E 60s	29
Rachel Ashwell's	SoHo	23
Restoration Hardware	Flatiron	21
Z Schweitzer Linen	multi.	27
Signoria	E 60s	25
Sleep	W'burg	22
Thomasville	Bayside	23
Z Waterworks	multi.	28
West Elm	multi.	17
Yves Delorme	E 70s	28

BRIDAL

Adriennes	LES	24
Amsale	E 50s	27
Z Barneys NY	E 60s	27
Z Bergdorf	E 50s	29
Birnbaum & Bullock	Chelsea	-
Blue	E Vill	-
Bridal Garden	Flatiron	18
Bridal Reflect.	Murray Hill	20
Z Carolina Herrera	E 70s	28
Clea Colet	E 70s	26
David's Bridal	LIC	13
Here Comes Bridesmaid	Chelsea	17
Jane Wilson-Marquis	E 70s	-
Kleinfeld	Chelsea	25
Lara Hélène	E 60s	-
Z Macy's	multi.	19
Mark Ingram Bridal	E 50s	27
Mary Adams The Dress	LES	-
Michelle	Boerum Hill	-
Mika Inatome	TriBeCa	-
Miriam Rigler	E 60s	28
My Glass Slipper	Flatiron	25
Z Peter Fox Shoes	SoHo	28
Pilar Rossi	E 60s	-
NEW Priscilla of Boston	Garment	24
Reem Acra	E 60s	29
RK Bridal	Garment	19
Z Saks Fifth Ave.	E 50s	27
Selia Yang	multi.	26
Suzanne Couture	E 60s	27
VeKa Bridal Couture	NoLita	-
Vera Wang Bridal	E 70s	27
Vera Wang Maids	E 70s	27
Wedding Library	E 70s	25

CABINETRY

Boffi SoHo	SoHo	-
Elgot	E 60s	25
Z Home Depot	multi.	19
Z Krup's Kitchen/Bath	Flatiron	26

| Manhattan Ctr. | Flatiron | - |
| Poggenpohl U.S. | multi. | - |

CAMERAS/VIDEO

Z Adorama Camera	Flatiron	26
Alkit	Flatiron	23
Z B&H Photo-Video	Garment	27
Camera Land	E 50s	22
42nd St. Photo	Garment	21
Olden Camera/Lens	Garment	20
Willoughby's	Garment	20

CHILDREN'S BEDDING/LAYETTE

Heights Kids	Bklyn Hts	-
Jacadi	multi.	27
Mini Jake	W'burg	-
Olá Baby	multi.	27
Pottery Barn Kids	E 60s	-
Ralph Lauren Layette	E 70s	26

CHILDRENSWEAR

(See also Department Stores)
Acorn	Downtown Bklyn	-
Area	multi.	-
NEW Babesta	TriBeCa	23
NEW Baby Cottons	E 80s	26
babyGap	multi.	22
Babylicious	TriBeCa	-
Bambini	E 80s	27
Belle & Maxie	Ditmas Pk	-
Z Bonpoint	multi.	28
Bu & the Duck	TriBeCa	26
Calypso Kids/Home	SoHo	26
Catimini	E 80s	26
Children's Place	multi.	16
City Cricket	W Vill	-
NEW Corduroy Kid	Prospect Hts	24
C.P.W.	W 80s	22
Crembebè	E Vill	-
Crew Cuts	SoHo	-
Diesel Kids	SoHo	25
Diva	Midwood	-
Estella	G Vill	25
Firefly	multi.	25
flora and henri	E 70s	23
Flying Squirrel	W'burg	-
GapKids	multi.	21
Giggle	multi.	25
Granny-Made	W 70s	24
Great Feet	E 80s	22
Green Onion	Cobble Hill	24
Greenstones	multi.	26
Gymboree	multi.	22
Heights Kids	Bklyn Hts	-

Hippototamus | multi.	22
hip-squeak | Bay Ridge	23
Ibiza Kidz | G Vill	23
Jacadi | multi.	27
Julian & Sara | SoHo	-
Kidville | multi.	22
Koh's Kids | TriBeCa	-
Le Sabon & Baby Too | E 60s	23
Les Petits Chapelais | SoHo	25
Lester's | multi.	24
Liberty House | W 100s	25
Lilliput | multi.	-
NEW Little Marc | W Vill	-
Little Stinkers | E Vill	-
Lucky Kid | SoHo	-
Lucky Wang | multi.	25
Magic Windows | E 80s	27
Marie-Chantal | E 80s	25
Mish Mish | E 90s	-
MoonSoup | E 50s	24
Natalie & Friends | E 60s	28
Natan Borlam's | W'burg	28
Oilily | multi.	23
Orange Blossom | Park Slope	-
Petit Bateau | E 80s	27
NEW Pink Olive | E Vill	24
Planet Kids | multi.	18
Pomme | Dumbo	-
Prince/Princess | E 70s	-
Rachel Riley | E 90s	-
Ralph Lauren Boys/Girls | E 70s	26
Ralph Lauren Layette | E 70s	26
Roberta Roller Rabbit | E 70s	-
Scoop Kids | Meatpacking	23
Shoofly | TriBeCa	26
Sons + Daughters | E Vill	-
Space Kiddets | Flatiron	26
Z Spring Flowers | multi.	28
Talbots Kids/Babies | multi.	24
NEW Threads | E 70s	-
Tribeca Girls | TriBeCa	-
Trico Field | SoHo	-
Tuesday's Child | multi.	26
United Colors/Kids | W 60s	21
World of Disney | E 50s	22
Yoya/Yoya Mart | W Vill	27
Zaba | TriBeCa	-
Z'Baby Co. | multi.	24

CHINA/CRYSTAL

(See also Department Stores)

A Brooklyn Table | Cobble Hill	-
Z Avventura | W 80s	26
Z Baccarat | E 50s	29

Bardith | E 70s	-
Z Bernardaud | E 50s	29
NEW Charlotte Moss | E 60s	25
Z Christofle | E 60s	27
Daum | E 60s	27
Z Lalique | E 60s	29
Z Michael C. Fina | E 40s	26
Z Moss | SoHo	28
Salviati | SoHo	-
Z Simon Pearce | E 50s	27
Z Steuben | E 60s	29
Swarovski | multi.	25
Z Tiffany & Co. | multi.	28
Vera Wang Bridal | E 70s	27
Yellow Door | Midwood	-

COOKWARE

Alessi | multi.	25
Z Bed Bath & Beyond | multi.	20
Z Bloomingdale's | E 50s	23
Bowery Kitchen | Chelsea	22
Z Bridge Kitchenware | E 40s	28
Z Broadway Panhandler | G Vill	27
NEW CB2 | SoHo	-
Z Crate & Barrel | multi.	21
Z Dean & Deluca | SoHo	26
Gabay's Home | E Vill	15
Z Gracious Home | multi.	25
Z Macy's | multi.	19
Sears | multi.	17
Z S.Feldman House. | E 90s	25
Sur La Table | SoHo	26
Tarzian West | Park Slope	21
Z Williams-Sonoma | multi.	26
Z Zabar's | W 80s	26

DEPARTMENT STORES

Barneys CO-OP | multi.	24
Z Barneys NY | E 60s	27
Z Bed Bath & Beyond | multi.	20
Z Bergdorf | E 50s	29
Z Bergdorf Men's | E 50s	28
Z Bloomingdale's | multi.	23
Z Gracious Home | multi.	25
Z Henri Bendel | E 50s	26
Jeffrey | Meatpacking	28
Z Lord & Taylor | Murray Hill	22
Z Macy's | multi.	19
Z Saks Fifth Ave. | E 50s	27
Sears | multi.	17

DESIGNER CLOTHING

(See also Department Stores)

a. cheng | multi.	19
Agatha Ruiz | SoHo	24

MERCHANDISE

Agnès B. | **multi.**	23	Eskandar | **G Vill**	-
🅱 Akris | **E 60s**	29	Etro | **E 60s**	28
Alessandro Dell'Acqua | **E 60s**	26	Gianfranco Ferré | **E 70s**	27
🅱 Alexander McQueen | **Meatpacking**	28	🅱 Giorgio Armani | **E 60s**	29
		Gucci | **multi.**	27
NEW Allegra Hicks | **E 70s**	24	Helen Wang | **SoHo**	-
Alpana Bawa | **E Vill**	-	**NEW** Helmut Lang | **Meatpacking**	-
Anna Sui | **SoHo**	23		
Anne Fontaine | **multi.**	27	Henry Beguelin | **Meatpacking**	-
Anne Klein | **E 60s**	-	🅱 Hermès | **multi.**	29
Annelore | **W Vill**	-	Hugo Boss | **multi.**	26
🅱 Asprey | **E 70s**	28	Issey Miyake | **multi.**	25
🅱 Balenciaga | **Chelsea**	29	Jackie Rogers | **E 70s**	-
Barbara Bui | **SoHo**	27	Jill Stuart | **SoHo**	22
BCBG Max Azria | **multi.**	22	Jil Sander | **E 70s**	25
Betsey Johnson | **multi.**	21	**NEW** John Bartlett | **W Vill**	23
Blanc de Chine | **E 50s**	24	John Varvatos | **SoHo**	26
🅱 Bottega Veneta | **E 50s**	29	Joseph | **multi.**	23
🅱 Brioni | **E 50s**	28	Juicy Couture | **multi.**	20
Brunello Cucinelli | **W Vill**	-	**NEW** Just Cavalli | **E 50s**	25
Built by Wendy | **multi.**	-	Kenneth Cole NY | **multi.**	21
Burberry | **multi.**	27	Krizia | **E 60s**	-
Calvin Klein | **E 60s**	25	Lee Anderson | **E 70s**	-
Calvin Tran | **NoLita**	-	Lilith | **NoLita**	25
Carlos Miele | **Meatpacking**	-	**NEW** Louis Féraud | **E 60s**	28
🅱 Carolina Herrera | **E 70s**	28	Louis Vuitton | **multi.**	27
Catherine Malandrino | **multi.**	24	Luca Luca | **multi.**	25
🅱 Celine | **E 60s**	28	Lucien Pellat-Finet | **G Vill**	-
🅱 Chanel | **multi.**	29	Lyell | **NoLita**	-
Charles Nolan | **Meatpacking**	-	Maison Martin Margiela | **W Vill**	-
Chloé | **E 70s**	26		
Christopher Fischer | **SoHo**	23	Marc/Marc Jacobs | **W Vill**	25
Christopher Totman | **NoLita**	-	Marc Jacobs | **SoHo**	27
Cloak | **SoHo**	-	Marni | **SoHo**	24
Comme des Garçons | **Chelsea**	26	Max Azria | **SoHo**	-
Costume National | **SoHo**	26	MaxMara | **multi.**	25
C. Ronson | **NoLita**	16	Max Studio | **SoHo**	20
Cynthia Rowley | **W Vill**	23	Mayle | **NoLita**	-
Dana Buchman | **E 50s**	25	Michael Kors | **multi.**	26
D & G | **SoHo**	24	**NEW** Miguelina | **W Vill**	24
Daryl K | **NoHo**	23	Missoni | **E 70s**	26
Dior Homme | **E 50s**	26	Miu Miu | **multi.**	25
🅱 Dior New York | **E 50s**	28	M Missoni | **SoHo**	-
DKNY | **multi.**	21	Morgane Le Fay | **multi.**	26
Dolce & Gabbana | **E 60s**	27	Nanette Lepore | **SoHo**	25
Domenico Vacca | **multi.**	-	Nicole Miller | **multi.**	24
Donna Karan | **E 60s**	25	Nili Lotan | **TriBeCa**	-
Dosa | **SoHo**	24	Number (N)ine | **TriBeCa**	-
Duncan Quinn | **NoLita**	-	OMO Norma Kamali | **W 50s**	22
Elie Tahari | **SoHo**	24	🅱 Oscar de la Renta | **E 60s**	28
Emanuel Ungaro | **E 60s**	28	Paul Smith | **multi.**	26
Emporio Armani | **multi.**	23	Petrou | **E 60s**	-
🅱 Ermenegildo Zegna | **E 50s**	28	Phi | **SoHo**	-
Escada | **E 50s**	27	Philosophy/A.Ferretti | **SoHo**	25

| Pleats Please | **SoHo** | -
| Poleci | **Meatpacking** | 22
| Prada | **multi.** | 26
| Pucci | **multi.** | 26
| Rachel Riley | **E 90s** | -
| Ralph Lauren | **multi.** | 26
| Rebecca & Drew | **Meatpacking** | -
| Rebecca Taylor | **NoLita** | 23
| Roberto Cavalli | **E 60s** | 27
| Rubin Chapelle | **Meatpacking** | -
| Saja | **NoLita** | -
| Sean John | **E 40s** | 18
| Shin Choi | **SoHo** | -
| Sonia Rykiel | **E 70s** | 26
| Sophia Eugene | **W Vill** | -
| Stefano Ricci | **E 50s** | 27
| Stella McCartney | **Meatpacking** | 26
| ☑ St. John | **E 50s** | 28
| Ted Baker | **SoHo** | 25
| Temperley | **SoHo** | -
| Thom Browne. | **TriBeCa** | -
| **NEW** 3.1 Phillip Lim | **SoHo** | 27
| Tibi | **SoHo** | -
| **NEW** Tom Ford | **E 70s** | 28
| Tommy Hilfiger/Denim | **multi.** | 20
| Tory Burch | **NoLita** | 21
| Tracy Feith | **NoLita** | 22
| Tracy Reese | **Meatpacking** | 25
| Trina Turk | **Meatpacking** | -
| TSE | **SoHo** | 26
| 202 | **Chelsea** | 23
| Unis | **NoLita** | -
| ☑ Valentino | **E 60s** | 28
| Versace | **E 50s** | 26
| Vivienne Tam | **SoHo** | 24
| Yigal Azrouel | **Meatpacking** | -
| Yohji Yamamoto | **SoHo** | 27
| Yoko Devereaux | **W'burg** | -
| Yves Saint Laurent | **multi.** | 26
| Zero/Maria Cornejo | **multi.** | -

DISCOUNT STORES/ MASS MERCHANTS

| Anbar | **TriBeCa** | 21
| ☑ B&H Photo-Video | **Garment** | 27
| ☑ Best Buy | **multi.** | 20
| Bolton's | **multi.** | 14
| Burlington Coat | **multi.** | 15
| ☑ Century 21 | **multi.** | 22
| Circuit City | **multi.** | 19
| ☑ Costco Warehse. | **multi.** | 22
| ☑ Daffy's | **multi.** | 17
| ☑ DSW | **multi.** | 21
| ☑ Filene's Basement | **multi.** | 18

| Gabay's Home | **E Vill** | 15
| Gabay's Outlet | **E Vill** | 20
| ☑ J&R Music | **Financial** | 24
| K&G Fashion | **multi.** | 15
| Kmart | **multi.** | 12
| Kohl's | **multi.** | -
| ☑ Loehmann's | **multi.** | 20
| ☑ Marshalls | **multi.** | 16
| Nat'l Whse. Liquid | **multi.** | 11
| Payless Shoe | **multi.** | 11
| Petland Discounts | **multi.** | 18
| Prato Fine Men's Wear | **multi.** | 13
| S&W | **multi.** | 18
| Staples | **multi.** | 19
| Syms | **multi.** | 18
| ☑ Target | **multi.** | 17
| ☑ T.J. Maxx | **multi.** | 16

ELECTRONICS

| ☑ Apple Store | **multi.** | 27
| ☑ Bang & Olufsen | **multi.** | 28
| ☑ Best Buy | **multi.** | 20
| ☑ Bose | **multi.** | 27
| Brookstone | **multi.** | 21
| Camera Land | **E 50s** | 22
| Canal Hi-Fi | **Chinatown** | 16
| Circuit City | **multi.** | 19
| Compact Impact | **Financial** | -
| Cosmophonic Sound | **E 80s** | -
| DataVision | **Murray Hill** | 21
| 42nd St. Photo | **Garment** | 21
| Hammacher | **E 50s** | 25
| ☑ Harvey Electronics | **W 40s** | 28
| **NEW** Helio | **multi.** | 20
| In Living Stereo | **NoHo** | -
| Innovative Audio | **E 50s** | 29
| ☑ J&R Music | **Financial** | 24
| Lowell/Edwards | **E 50s** | -
| ☑ Lyric Hi-Fi | **E 80s** | 28
| Nokia | **E 50s** | 22
| Park Ave. Audio | **Gramercy** | 24
| P.C. Richard & Son | **multi.** | 18
| RadioShack | **multi.** | 16
| RCS Experience | **E 50s** | 17
| Sharper Image | **multi.** | 21
| ☑ Sony Style | **E 50s** | 26
| ☑ Sound by Singer | **Union Sq** | 27
| Sound City | **W 40s** | -
| Staples | **multi.** | 19
| ☑ Stereo Exchange | **NoHo** | 26
| ☑ Tekserve | **Chelsea** | 26

EYEWEAR

| Alain Mikli | **multi.** | 28
| Artsee | **Meatpacking** | -

MERCHANDISE

Cohen Optical	**multi.**	19
Disrespectacles	**multi.**	27
Eye Man	**W 80s**	25
Fabulous Fanny's	**E Vill**	-
Facial Index	**SoHo**	-
For Eyes	**E 40s**	23
Gruen Optika	**multi.**	25
H.L. Purdy	**multi.**	27
NEW Ilori	**SoHo**	-
Joël Name Optique	**SoHo**	-
Leonard Opticians	**multi.**	26
Linda Derector	**NoLita**	-
Morgenthal Frederics	**multi.**	28
Moscot	**multi.**	21
Myoptics	**multi.**	25
Nakedeye	**LES**	-
Oakley	**SoHo**	21
Occhiali	**E 80s**	24
Oculus 20/20	**multi.**	-
Oliver Peoples	**multi.**	27
Ralph Lauren Eyewear	**E 60s**	-
Robert Marc	**multi.**	27
SEE Eyewear	**W Vill**	-
Selima/Sucre	**multi.**	27
Solstice	**multi.**	-

FABRICS

Z B&J Fabrics	**Garment**	26
Beckenstein Fabrics	**Flatiron**	-
Brooklyn General	**Carroll Gdns**	-
NEW Brklyn Merc.	**Park Slope**	21
Z City Quilter	**Chelsea**	28
Habu Textiles	**Chelsea**	-
Hyman Hendler	**Garment**	28
Joe's Fabrics	**LES**	-
M&J Trimming	**Garment**	25
Mood	**Garment**	25
New York Fabric	**W 40s**	-
P&S Fabrics	**TriBeCa**	22
Paron Fabrics	**W 40s**	20
Paterson Silks	**multi.**	18
Z Purl	**SoHo**	28
Rosen & Chadick	**Garment**	-
Steinlauf & Stoller	**Garment**	-
Z Tender Buttons	**E 60s**	28
Zarin Fabrics	**LES**	23

FURNITURE/HOME FURNISHINGS

BABIES'/CHILDREN'S

Albee Baby Carriage	**W 90s**	25
Bellini	**multi.**	23
Z buybuy BABY	**Chelsea**	23
Giggle	**multi.**	25

Katz/Cradle	**Midwood**	-
kid o.	**G Vill**	22
Mini Jake	**W'burg**	-
NEW ModernTots	**Dumbo**	23
Olá Baby	**multi.**	27
Pomme	**Dumbo**	-
Z Pompanoosuc Mills	**TriBeCa**	25
Pottery Barn Kids	**E 60s**	-
Room & Board	**SoHo**	24
Schneider's	**Chelsea**	25
White on White	**Murray Hill**	-

GENERAL

A&G Merch	**W'burg**	21
Z ABC Carpet & Home	**Flatiron**	25
Z ABC Carpets/Rugs	**Flatiron**	25
ABC Carpet/Outlet	**Bronx**	21
Abitare	**Bklyn Hts**	-
A Brooklyn Table	**Cobble Hill**	-
Adrien Linford	**multi.**	22
Z Aero	**SoHo**	26
Alessi	**multi.**	25
NEW Ankasa	**E 60s**	24
Z Anthropologie	**multi.**	20
Apartment 48	**G Vill**	21
Armani Casa	**SoHo**	25
auto	**Meatpacking**	-
Baker Tribeca	**TriBeCa**	28
Z B&B Italia	**multi.**	27
Bark	**Downtown Bklyn**	-
BDDW	**SoHo**	-
Z Bergdorf	**E 50s**	29
Z Bloomingdale's	**E 50s**	23
BoConcept	**multi.**	17
NEW Brklyn Merc.	**Park Slope**	21
Calypso Home	**NoLita**	-
Cappellini	**SoHo**	-
Z Carlyle Convertibles	**multi.**	26
Cassina USA	**E 50s**	-
Catherine Memmi	**SoHo**	-
NEW CB2	**SoHo**	-
NEW Charlotte Moss	**E 60s**	25
Classic Sofa	**Flatiron**	23
Clay Pot	**Park Slope**	26
Clio	**SoHo**	-
Conran Shop	**E 50s**	23
Container Store	**multi.**	22
Z Crate & Barrel	**multi.**	21
ddc domus design	**Murray Hill**	27
Demolition Depot	**Harlem**	-
Design Within Reach	**multi.**	24
Desiron	**SoHo**	22
Domain	**multi.**	20

subscribe to ZAGAT.com

Donzella	**TriBeCa**	_
Door Store	**multi.**	17
Dune	**TriBeCa**	_
Einstein-Moomjy	**E 50s**	24
environment337	**multi.**	_
Ethan Allen	**multi.**	23
Federico de Vera	**SoHo**	_
Fishs Eddy	**Flatiron**	18
F.M. Allen	**E 70s**	_
Fort St. Studio	**SoHo**	_
Fortunoff	**W 50s**	24
Fresh Kills	**W'burg**	_
Future Perfect	**W'burg**	_
George Smith	**SoHo**	_
Global Table	**SoHo**	_
Goodwill	**multi.**	12
Gothic Cabinet Craft	**multi.**	15
NEW Gus Modern	**Chelsea**	20
Hable Construction	**W Vill**	_
Hasker	**Carroll Gdns**	_
Home & Haven	**Cobble Hill**	22
Homer	**E 50s**	_
Jennifer Convertibles	**multi.**	13
John Derian	**E Vill**	26
Jonathan Adler	**multi.**	_
Kaas GlassWorks	**W Vill**	_
Karim Rashid Shop	**Chelsea**	_
Kartell	**SoHo**	_
Knoll	**Chelsea**	_
Kraft	**E 60s**	26
Kreiss Collection	**E 50s**	26
La Cafetière	**Chelsea**	_
LaoLao Handmade	**E Vill**	_
Laytner's Linen	**multi.**	20
Lee's Studio	**W 50s**	23
Le Fanion	**W Vill**	_
Z Ligne Roset	**multi.**	28
Living 5th/7th/Smith	**multi.**	_
Z MacKenzie-Childs	**E 50s**	25
Z Macy's	**multi.**	19
Madura	**E 80s**	24
Marimekko	**E 70s**	24
Marston & Langinger	**SoHo**	_
Matter	**multi.**	_
Z MauricE Villency	**E 50s**	26
McGuire	**Murray Hill**	_
Mem. Sloan-Kettering	**E 80s**	22
Michael Anchin	**W'burg**	_
NEW Michael Aram	**Chelsea**	26
Michele Varian	**SoHo**	_
NEW Mitchell Gold	**SoHo**	_
Modernica	**SoHo**	_
Moon River Chattel	**W'burg**	_
NEW Moroso	**SoHo**	_

Z Moss	**SoHo**	28
Moulin Bleu	**TriBeCa**	_
NEW Muji	**SoHo**	_
Mxyplyzyk	**W Vill**	21
N	**Harlem**	_
Natuzzi	**SoHo**	27
Ochre	**SoHo**	_
Olde Good Things	**multi.**	18
Pearl River Mart	**SoHo**	16
P.E. Guerin	**W Vill**	_
Pier 1 Imports	**multi.**	15
Poltrona Frau	**SoHo**	_
Z Pompanoosuc Mills	**TriBeCa**	25
Pottery Barn	**multi.**	20
Rachel Ashwell's	**SoHo**	23
NEW REPOP	**Clinton Hill**	_
Restoration Hardware	**Flatiron**	21
Rico	**Boerum Hill**	_
Roberta Roller Rabbit	**E 70s**	_
Z Roche Bobois	**Murray Hill**	27
Room & Board	**SoHo**	24
Rug Company	**SoHo**	_
Ruzzetti & Gow	**E 70s**	_
Safavieh	**multi.**	26
Salviati	**SoHo**	_
Scott Jordan	**SoHo**	27
Z Scully & Scully	**E 50s**	29
Z S.Feldman House.	**E 90s**	25
Space107	**W Vill**	_
Spring	**Dumbo**	_
NEW Sprout Home	**W'burg**	25
Sterling Pl.	**multi.**	_
Z Stickley, Audi & Co.	**Chelsea**	28
Straight from Crate	**multi.**	13
Suite New York	**E 50s**	_
Surprise! Surprise!	**E Vill**	15
Swallow	**Carroll Gdns**	_
Z Takashimaya	**E 50s**	28
Tarzian West	**Park Slope**	21
Thomasville	**Bayside**	23
Thos. Moser Cabinets	**E 60s**	29
Tiny Living	**E Vill**	_
Todd Hase	**SoHo**	_
NEW Tribbles Home/Gdn.	**TriBeCa**	25
Troy	**Gramercy**	_
Tucker Robbins	**multi.**	_
Two Jakes	**W'burg**	21
Vintage Thrift Shop	**Gramercy**	22
Vitra	**Meatpacking**	_
West Elm	**multi.**	17
White on White	**Murray Hill**	_
William-Wayne	**multi.**	26

MERCHANDISE

Wonk | **multi.**	–
Yellow Door | **Midwood**	–

FURS

Alexandros | **multi.**	–
Alixandre Furs | **Garment**	24
☑ Bergdorf | **E 50s**	29
☑ Bloomingdale's | **E 50s**	23
Dennis Basso | **E 60s**	24
Fendi | **E 50s**	27
☑ J. Mendel | **E 60s**	28
☑ Saks Fifth Ave. | **E 50s**	27

GARDEN

Chelsea Garden Ctr. | **multi.**	23
Dig Garden | **Downtown Bklyn**	23
☑ Gracious Home | **multi.**	25
GRDN Bklyn | **Boerum Hill**	23
☑ Home Depot | **multi.**	19
Lexington Gardens | **E 70s**	–
Mecox Gardens | **E 70s**	–
Moon River Chattel | **W'burg**	–
Munder-Skiles | **E 60s**	–
Smith & Hawken | **SoHo**	24
NEW Sprout Home | **W'burg**	25
☑ Takashimaya | **E 50s**	28
Treillage | **E 70s**	–
NEW Tribbles Home/Gdn. | **TriBeCa**	25

GIFTS/NOVELTIES

(See also Museum Shops)

Abracadabra | **Flatiron**	21
Alphabets | **multi.**	19
NEW Blue Ribbon | **Boerum Hill**	–
Delphinium | **W 40s**	24
Dylan's Candy | **E 60s**	22
Etcetera | **Murray Hill**	–
Kiosk | **SoHo**	19
La Brea | **multi.**	18
Loom | **Park Slope**	23
Met. Opera Shop | **W 60s**	24
Paparazzi | **Gramercy**	21
Papyrus | **multi.**	23
Pylones | **multi.**	–
Sanrio | **W 40s**	21
Scaredy Kat | **Park Slope**	24
Sterling Pl. | **multi.**	–
Tah-Poozie | **G Vill**	18

HANDBAGS

(See also Department Stores)

Add Accessories | **SoHo**	20
Anya Hindmarch | **multi.**	25
Artbag | **E 80s**	24
Bally | **E 50s**	28

Barneys CO-OP | **multi.**	24
☑ Barneys NY | **E 60s**	27
Blibetroy | **LES**	–
Blue Bag | **NoLita**	–
☑ Bottega Veneta | **E 50s**	29
Butter | **Downtown Bklyn**	23
☑ Chanel | **multi.**	29
Chloé | **E 70s**	26
☑ Christian Louboutin | **multi.**	28
☑ Coach | **multi.**	26
Crouch & Fitzgerald | **E 40s**	26
delfino | **multi.**	22
☑ Dior New York | **E 50s**	28
Dolce & Gabbana | **E 60s**	27
Dooney & Bourke | **E 60s**	25
NEW Edon Manor | **TriBeCa**	–
Fendi | **E 50s**	27
Fratelli Rossetti | **E 50s**	27
Furla | **multi.**	25
Gucci | **multi.**	27
Henry Beguelin | **Meatpacking**	–
☑ Hermès | **multi.**	29
NEW HH Design | **Greenpt**	20
Highway | **NoLita**	–
Hogan | **SoHo**	26
Il Bisonte | **SoHo**	27
Jamin Puech | **NoLita**	–
Jumelle | **W'burg**	–
Kate Spade | **multi.**	24
Kipepeo | **NoLita**	–
NEW Lambertson | **E 60s**	–
Lana Marks | **E 60s**	28
Lederer de Paris | **E 50s**	25
☑ Leiber | **E 60s**	28
LeSportsac | **multi.**	20
Lolli/Reincarnation | **LES**	20
Longchamp | **multi.**	26
Louis Vuitton | **multi.**	27
NEW Lucia Nenickova | **Gramercy**	21
Lulu Guinness | **W Vill**	24
Marc Jacobs Access. | **W Vill**	28
Miu Miu | **multi.**	25
Mulberry | **multi.**	–
M Z Wallace | **SoHo**	–
Petticoat Lane | **TriBeCa**	–
Prada | **multi.**	26
Refinery | **Cobble Hill**	–
NEW Roger Vivier | **E 60s**	28
☑ Salvatore Ferragamo | **E 50s**	28
Samantha Thavasa | **E 70s**	–
Seigo | **E 80s**	28
Sergio Rossi | **E 50s**	26
Steve Madden | **multi.**	16

Store	Rating
Steven | **multi.**	18
Suarez | **W 50s**	27
Ⓩ T. Anthony | **E 50s**	28
Taryn Rose | **E 60s**	25
Ⓩ Tod's | **E 60s**	29
Versace | **E 50s**	26
Verve | **multi.**	24
Village Tannery | **multi.**	21
Wink | **multi.**	21
Yves Saint Laurent | **multi.**	26

HARDWARE

Store	Rating
Beacon Paint | **W 70s**	22
Bettencourt | **W'burg**	-
Dykes Lumber | **multi.**	24
Ⓩ Gracious Home | **multi.**	25
Ⓩ Home Depot | **multi.**	19
Janovic Plaza | **multi.**	22
Lowe's | **multi.**	21
Metropolitan Lumber | **multi.**	22
P.E. Guerin | **W Vill**	-
Pintchik | **Park Slope**	20
Sears | **multi.**	17
Sid's | **Downtown Bklyn**	21
Ⓩ Simon's Hardware | **multi.**	26
Tarzian True Value | **Park Slope**	21
Vercesi Hardware | **Gramercy**	23

HOSE/LINGERIE

(See also Department Stores)

Store	Rating
Agent Provocateur | **SoHo**	27
A.W. Kaufman | **LES**	26
Azaleas | **E Vill**	-
Beneath | **E 70s**	22
Bonne Nuit | **E 70s**	24
Bra Smyth | **multi.**	25
Bra*Tenders | **W 40s**	-
Brief Encounters | **W 70s**	-
Calvin Klein Underwear | **SoHo**	21
Catriona Mackechnie | **Meatpacking**	-
Diana Kane | **Park Slope**	-
Eres | **multi.**	28
Ⓩ Fogal | **E 50s**	28
Girly NYC | **E Vill**	21
Intimacy | **E 90s**	28
NEW Journelle | **Flatiron**	-
Kiki/Montparnasse | **SoHo**	25
Laina Jane | **multi.**	-
Ⓩ La Perla | **multi.**	28
La Petite Coquette | **G Vill**	26
Lingerie on Lex | **E 60s**	24
Livi's Lingerie | **E 80s**	20
Marc and Max | **W Vill**	-
Mixona | **NoLita**	-

Store	Rating
Myla | **E 60s**	-
Only Hearts | **multi.**	21
Orchard Corset Center | **LES**	-
Otto | **Park Slope**	23
Petticoat Lane | **TriBeCa**	-
Pink Slip | **E 40s**	23
NEW Pull-In | **NoLita**	-
Sleep | **W'burg**	22
37=1 Atelier | **SoHo**	-
Town Shop | **W 80s**	25
Victoria's Secret | **multi.**	18
Wolford | **multi.**	28

JEANS

Store	Rating
Abercrombie | **multi.**	18
AG | **SoHo**	26
Atrium | **NoHo**	25
Barneys CO-OP | **multi.**	24
Ⓩ Bloomingdale's | **multi.**	23
Canal Jean | **Flatbush**	17
Cantaloup/Luxe | **multi.**	22
Chip & Pepper | **NoLita**	23
DDC Lab | **Meatpacking**	-
Diesel | **multi.**	23
Diesel Denim Gallery | **SoHo**	24
Dunderdon Wkshp. | **SoHo**	-
Earnest Cut & Sew | **multi.**	25
45rpm/R | **multi.**	23
Ⓩ Gap | **multi.**	18
G-Star Raw | **multi.**	23
Guess | **multi.**	21
NEW Helmut Lang | **Meatpacking**	-
Ⓩ Henri Bendel | **E 50s**	26
Henry Lehr | **NoLita**	24
Jean Shop | **multi.**	-
Ksubi | **NoLita**	22
Levi's Store | **multi.**	23
Lounge | **SoHo**	19
Lucky Brand Jeans | **multi.**	23
Mavi | **E Vill**	22
Miss Sixty | **multi.**	21
National Jean Company | **multi.**	-
Oak | **multi.**	-
Old Navy | **multi.**	14
Parasuco | **NoLita**	21
Razor | **Park Slope**	-
Replay | **SoHo**	23
Rogan | **TriBeCa**	25
Scoop Men's | **multi.**	23
Scoop NYC | **multi.**	23
Stuart/Wright | **Ft Greene**	-
Tommy Hilfiger/Denim | **SoHo**	20
Transit | **NoHo**	17

MERCHANDISE

True Religion	**SoHo**	–
V.I.M.	**multi.**	14
What Comes Around	**SoHo**	26
Ylli	**W'burg**	–

JEWELRY

COSTUME/ SEMIPRECIOUS

Add Accessories	**SoHo**	20
Alexis Bittar	**SoHo**	25
Beads of Paradise	**Flatiron**	22
Boucher	**Meatpacking**	20
By Boe	**SoHo**	–
Calypso Bijoux	**NoLita**	25
Cog & Pearl	**Park Slope**	21
Debbie Fisher	**Carroll Gdns**	–
Dinosaur Designs	**NoLita**	–
Erwin Pearl	**multi.**	20
Femmegems	**NoLita**	17
Fragments	**multi.**	25
☑ Henri Bendel	**E 50s**	26
Jaded	**E 80s**	25
NEW Jane Eadie	**NoLita**	–
Jennifer Miller Jewelry	**E 70s**	–
Kipepeo	**NoLita**	–
Magnificent Costume	**E 80s**	22
Mariko	**E 70s**	–
Marni	**SoHo**	24
Michal Negrin	**E 70s**	26
Néda	**multi.**	21
Satellite	**SoHo**	–
SOHO	**NoLita**	20
Swarovski	**multi.**	25
Tarina Tarantino	**SoHo**	22
Tous	**SoHo**	22
Yellow Door	**Midwood**	–

FINE

Aaron Basha	**E 60s**	25
Aaron Faber	**W 50s**	26
Amadeo/Scognamiglio	**E 70s**	20
☑ Barneys NY	**E 60s**	27
☑ Bergdorf	**E 50s**	29
Bloom	**E 40s**	24
☑ Bloomingdale's	**E 50s**	23
Bochic	**E 50s**	–
Breguet	**E 60s**	29
☑ Buccellati	**E 50s**	29
Bulgari	**multi.**	28
Butter	**Downtown Bklyn**	23
Camilla Bergeron	**E 60s**	–
☑ Cartier	**multi.**	29
Catbird	**W'burg**	–
Catherine Angiel	**G Vill**	25
Cécile et Jeanne	**multi.**	24

Chanel Jewelry	**E 60s**	27
NEW Charlotte Moss	**E 60s**	25
☑ Chopard	**E 60s**	29
Chrome Hearts	**E 60s**	28
Clay Pot	**Park Slope**	26
Damiani	**E 60s**	–
David Lee Holland	**SoHo**	–
David Webb	**E 60s**	25
David Yurman	**E 60s**	25
DeBeers	**E 50s**	27
de Grisogono	**E 60s**	–
DeNatale Jewelers	**multi.**	26
Diana Kane	**Park Slope**	–
Elizabeth Locke	**E 70s**	29
NEW Erie Basin	**Red Hook**	–
Fortunoff	**W 50s**	24
Fragments	**multi.**	25
Garrard & Co.	**SoHo**	–
☑ Georg Jensen	**multi.**	29
NEW Gilan	**E 50s**	25
☑ Graff	**E 60s**	28
Hannah Clark	**E Vill**	–
☑ Harry Winston	**E 50s**	29
Helen Ficalora	**NoLita**	–
Honora	**E 50s**	–
☑ H. Stern	**E 50s**	28
NEW Ivanka Trump	**E 60s**	–
Jacob & Co.	**E 50s**	24
Jennifer Miller Jewelry	**E 70s**	–
Jeri Cohen Jewelry	**E 60s**	27
Jill Platner	**SoHo**	–
J.J. Marco	**E 80s**	24
Joan Michlin Gallery	**SoHo**	27
Judith Ripka	**E 60s**	25
Kieselstein-Cord	**E 80s**	28
Lalaounis	**E 60s**	29
☑ Lalique	**E 60s**	29
NEW Leviev	**E 60s**	27
Links of London	**multi.**	24
Lisa Levine	**W'burg**	–
☑ Lord & Taylor	**Murray Hill**	22
☑ Macy's	**multi.**	19
Me & Ro	**NoLita**	23
☑ Michael C. Fina	**E 40s**	26
☑ Mikimoto	**E 50s**	29
Mish	**E 70s**	–
☑ Piaget	**E 50s**	28
Pomellato	**E 60s**	–
Reinstein/Ross	**multi.**	28
Robert Lee Morris	**SoHo**	25
☑ Saks Fifth Ave.	**E 50s**	27
Satya	**multi.**	21
Seaman Schepps	**E 50s**	27
Stephen Kahan	**E 60s**	27

MERCHANDISE

Destination Maternity | E 50s	22
Liz Lange Maternity | E 70s	23
Mimi Maternity | multi.	19
Mylo Dweck | Bensonhurst	-
Veronique | E 90s	26

MENSWEAR

(See also Mens/Womenswear, Department Stores)

Alife | LES	24
Ascot Chang | W 50s	25
Atelier NY | SoHo	-
B8 | Meatpacking	-
Banana Republic Men | multi.	21
Bblessing | LES	21
Beau Brummel | multi.	22
Ben Sherman | SoHo	23
☑ Bergdorf Men's | E 50s	28
NEW Billionaire Boys | SoHo	-
Blue in Green | SoHo	21
Borrelli Boutique | E 60s	-
B. Oyama Homme | Harlem	-
British Amer. Hse. | E 50s	22
Buckler | multi.	-
Camouflage | Chelsea	24
Casual Male XL | multi.	19
Charles Tyrwhitt | multi.	26
Dave's Army Navy | Chelsea	21
☑ Davide Cenci | E 60s	29
NEW Den | E Vill	22
Dunderdon Wkshp. | SoHo	-
Eisenberg Eisenberg | Flatiron	22
Express Men | multi.	20
Frank Stella | multi.	22
Freemans Sporting | LES	-
Gant | E 50s	22
Groupe | NoLita	-
H. Herzfeld | E 50s	26
NEW hickey | SoHo	-
Hickey Freeman | multi.	27
Hollander/Lexer | Boerum Hill	-
Jay Kos | E 50s	-
J. Lindeberg | SoHo	26
Jos. A. Bank | E 40s	18
J. Press | E 40s	23
Lord Willy's | multi.	-
L'Uomo | W Vill	24
NEW Marc Ecko | Chelsea	-
Men's Wearhse. | multi.	17
NEW Michael Andrews | LES	22
99X | E Vill	18
Nom de Guerre | NoHo	20
Odin | multi.	-
Oliver Spencer | W Vill	-
Original Penguin | W 40s	-

☑ Oxxford Clothes | E 50s	28
Parke & Ronen | Chelsea	-
Paul & Shark | E 60s	27
Paul Stuart | E 40s	27
Peter Elliot | multi.	25
Prato Fine Men's Wear | multi.	13
Prince Charles III | SoHo	-
NEW Private Stock | Park Slope	-
Razor | Park Slope	-
Robert Talbott | E 60s	28
Rochester Big/Tall | W 50s	26
Rothman's | Union Sq	23
Scoop Men's | multi.	23
Sean | multi.	24
Shirt Store | E 40s	22
Stussy NY | SoHo	20
Transit | NoHo	17
☑ Turnbull & Asser | E 50s	28
Vilebrequin | multi.	27
Watts on Smith | Carroll Gdns	-

MENS/WOMENSWEAR

(Stores carrying both; see also Department Stores)

Abercrombie | multi.	18
About Glamour | W'burg	-
NEW Adam | Meatpacking	-
Addy/Ferro | Ft Greene	-
NEW Alter | Greenpt	-
American Apparel | multi.	19
Am. Eagle | multi.	17
A.P.C. | SoHo	21
A/X | multi.	19
☑ Banana Republic | multi.	20
☑ Barbour/Peter Elliot | E 80s	28
Barneys CO-OP | multi.	24
Bathing Ape | SoHo	21
Big Drop | multi.	21
Billy Martin's | E 60s	27
NEW Blue & Cream | E Vill	-
Brooklyn Industries | multi.	20
☑ Brooks Brothers | multi.	24
Caravan | NoHo	20
Club Monaco | multi.	18
NEW Cotélac | SoHo	-
Custo Barcelona | SoHo	21
Dalaga | Greenpt	19
Diesel | multi.	23
Dö Kham | NoLita	22
Dr. Jay's | multi.	18
Ed Hardy | multi.	21
Esprit | multi.	17
Façonnable | E 50s	27
NEW 55DSL | SoHo	19
Flying A | SoHo	17

French Connect. | **multi.**	20
🅉 Gap | **multi.**	18
Gerry's | **multi.**	24
🅉 H&M | **multi.**	12
NEW Hus | **G Vill**	-
IC Zinco | **SoHo**	-
IF | **SoHo**	-
In God We Trust | **multi.**	-
James Perse | **W Vill**	24
J.Crew | **multi.**	20
Jeffrey | **Meatpacking**	28
J. McLaughlin | **multi.**	22
Kiton | **E 50s**	-
Kohl's | **multi.**	-
Kuhlman | **G Vill**	20
Lacoste | **multi.**	24
🅉 Loro Piana | **E 60s**	29
Lounge | **SoHo**	19
Love Brigade | **W'burg**	-
NEW Muji | **SoHo**	-
N | **Harlem**	-
Neighborhoodies | **multi.**	20
Oak | **multi.**	-
Old Navy | **multi.**	14
Opening Ceremony | **SoHo**	-
Organic Ave. | **LES**	24
Oska | **SoHo**	-
NEW Osklen | **multi.**	-
Phat Farm | **SoHo**	16
Pieces | **Prospect Hts**	21
POP | **W'burg**	19
NEW Project No. 8 | **Chinatown**	-
NEW Red Toenails | **W'burg**	-
Reed Space | **LES**	22
Reiss | **multi.**	20
Rugby | **G Vill**	22
Scoop NYC | **SoHo**	23
Seize sur Vingt | **NoLita**	25
Sisley | **multi.**	20
Something Else | **multi.**	23
Steven Alan | **multi.**	24
Stuart/Wright | **Ft Greene**	-
🅉 Talbots | **multi.**	22
Theory | **multi.**	23
Thomas Pink | **multi.**	26
Trash & Vaudeville | **E Vill**	16
Treehouse | **W'burg**	-
Triple 5 Soul | **multi.**	21
Uniqlo | **SoHo**	-
UnitedColors/Benetton | **multi.**	20
Urban Outfitters | **multi.**	17
NEW Urban Zen | **W Vill**	-
Von Dutch | **SoHo**	-
WeSC | **SoHo**	-
Ylli | **W'burg**	-
Zara | **multi.**	18

MUSEUM SHOPS

American Folk Art | **multi.**	23
Am. Museum/Nat.Hist. | **W 70s**	22
AsiaStore/Asia Society | **E 70s**	24
Brooklyn Museum | **Prospect Hts**	22
Cooper-Hewitt | **E 90s**	24
El Museo Del Barrio | **E 100s**	20
Frick Collection | **E 70s**	22
Guggenheim Museum | **E 80s**	22
🅉 International Photo | **W 40s**	26
Jewish Museum | **multi.**	25
Lower E. S. Tenement Museum | **LES**	21
🅉 Met. Museum of Art | **multi.**	25
🅉 MoMA Store | **multi.**	25
Morgan Library | **Murray Hill**	25
🅉 Museum Arts/Design | **W 50s**	26
Museum of Sex | **Gramercy**	19
Museum/City of NY | **E 100s**	21
🅉 Neue Galerie NY | **E 80s**	26
NEW New Museum | **LES**	-
New York Public Library | **multi.**	23
New York Transit Mus. | **multi.**	20
🅉 Rubin Museum | **Chelsea**	26
Studio Museum/Harlem | **Harlem**	-
Whitney Museum | **E 70s**	21

MUSIC/DVDS

Academy Records | **multi.**	24
🅉 Best Buy | **multi.**	20
Bleecker Bob's | **G Vill**	20
Bleecker St. Records | **G Vill**	23
Blockbuster | **multi.**	16
Colony Music | **W 40s**	24
Disc-O-Rama | **multi.**	20
Etherea | **E Vill**	-
Fat Beats | **G Vill**	-
f.y.e. | **multi.**	18
Generation Records | **G Vill**	25
halcyon | **Dumbo**	-
House of Oldies | **G Vill**	-
Jammyland | **E Vill**	-
🅉 J&R Music | **Financial**	24
Jazz Record Center | **Chelsea**	-
Kim's Mediapolis | **multi.**	24
Met. Opera Shop | **W 60s**	24
Norman's Sound/Vision | **E Vill**	-
🅉 Other Music | **NoHo**	27
Rebel Rebel | **W Vill**	-

Rockit Sci. Records	**E Vill**	—
St. Marks Sounds	**E Vill**	19
Strider Records	**G Vill**	—
Z Virgin	**multi.**	23

PETS

American Kennels	**E 60s**	17
Barking Zoo	**Chelsea**	25
Beasty Feast	**W Vill**	24
Calling All Pets	**multi.**	24
Z Canine Styles	**multi.**	26
Doggystyle	**SoHo**	—
Dudley's Paw	**TriBeCa**	—
Furry Paws	**multi.**	21
Le Chien Pet Salon	**E 60s**	23
Petco	**multi.**	19
Peters Necessities/Pets	**E 70s**	24
Petland Discounts	**multi.**	18
Z Pet Stop	**W 80s**	26
NEW Salty Paw	**Seaport**	22
Spoiled Brats	**W 40s**	24
Z Trixie & Peanut	**Flatiron**	27
Z Whiskers	**E Vill**	27
Zoomies	**W Vill**	29

SEX TOYS

Z Babeland	**multi.**	27
DeMask	**LES**	22
Eve's Garden	**W 50s**	24
Kiki/Montparnasse	**SoHo**	25
Z Leather Man	**W Vill**	26
Museum of Sex	**Gramercy**	19
Myla	**E 60s**	—
Pink Pussycat	**multi.**	19
Pleasure Chest	**W Vill**	22

SHOES: CHILDREN'S

(See also Department Stores)

Area	**multi.**	—
Belle & Maxie	**Ditmas Pk**	—
NEW Corduroy Kid	**Prospect Hts**	24
Eneslow	**multi.**	28
Flying Squirrel	**W'burg**	—
Geox	**multi.**	23
Great Feet	**E 80s**	22
Harry's Shoes/Kids	**W 80s**	—
Ibiza Kidz	**G Vill**	23
Lester's	**multi.**	24
Little Eric	**E 80s**	25
Little Stinkers	**E Vill**	—
Naturino	**multi.**	28
Oilily	**multi.**	23
NEW Pink Olive	**E Vill**	24
Rachel Riley	**E 90s**	—

Shoofly	**TriBeCa**	26
Skechers	**multi.**	19
Tip Top Kids	**W 70s**	26
Z'Baby Co.	**multi.**	24

SHOES: MEN'S/WOMEN'S

(See also Department Stores)

Aerosoles	**multi.**	18
Aldo	**multi.**	16
Z Allen Edmonds	**multi.**	28
Anbar	**TriBeCa**	21
Archangela	**W'burg**	—
Arche	**multi.**	25
a. testoni	**E 50s**	27
A Uno/Walk	**TriBeCa**	24
Bally	**E 50s**	28
Barbara Shaum	**E Vill**	—
Barker Black	**NoLita**	25
Z Belgian Shoes	**E 50s**	28
Belle/Sig. Morrison	**NoLita**	22
Berluti	**E 70s**	—
Beverly Feldman	**W 50s**	20
Botticelli	**multi.**	25
Butter	**Downtown Bklyn**	23
Camper	**SoHo**	23
Z Christian Louboutin	**multi.**	28
Chuckies	**multi.**	25
Church's Shoes	**E 60s**	25
Clarks	**multi.**	23
Claudia Ciuti	**E 70s**	25
Cole Haan	**multi.**	25
NEW Crocs	**W 70s**	—
David Z.	**multi.**	19
DC Shoes	**SoHo**	22
NEW Diana Broussard	**G Vill**	22
Dolce Vita	**LES**	23
Z DSW	**multi.**	21
Dusica Dusica	**SoHo**	—
NEW Edon Manor	**TriBeCa**	—
Eneslow	**Murray Hill**	28
Enzo Angiolini	**Garment**	20
Eric	**multi.**	24
Florsheim Shoe	**multi.**	20
Fratelli Rossetti	**E 50s**	27
French Sole	**E 70s**	24
Galo	**multi.**	22
Geox	**multi.**	23
Giraudon	**Chelsea**	22
Z Giuseppe Zanotti	**E 60s**	28
Harry's Shoes	**W 80s**	24
NEW Head/Heels	**multi.**	21
Hollywould	**NoLita**	24
NEW Iris	**Meatpacking**	23

NEW Irregular Choice	SoHo	-
Jaime Mascaró	SoHo	21
Jimmy Choo	multi.	28
J.M. Weston	E 60s	26
John Fluevog Shoes	NoLita	23
Z John Lobb	E 60s	29
Johnston & Murphy	multi.	25
Jubilee	multi.	16
Jutta Neumann	LES	-
LaDuca Shoes	Garment	-
Z Manolo Blahnik	W 50s	28
Marc/Marc Jacobs	W Vill	25
Medici	W 80s	20
My Glass Slipper	Flatiron	25
Nine West	multi.	17
Otto Tootsi Plohound	multi.	23
Payless Shoe	multi.	11
Pear/Plum	LES	22
Z Peter Fox Shoes	SoHo	28
Plaza Too	multi.	21
Prada	multi.	26
NEW Rainbow Sandals	NoLita	23
Z Robert Clergerie	E 60s	28
NEW Roger Vivier	E 60s	28
Sacco	multi.	22
Z Salvatore Ferragamo	E 50s	28
Sergio Rossi	E 50s	26
Shoe Box	multi.	23
NEW Shoe Market	W'burg	18
Shoe Mine	Park Slope	-
Shoe New York	NoLita	24
Shooz	Chelsea	19
Sigerson Morrison	multi.	25
Skechers	multi.	19
Something Else	multi.	23
Soula	multi.	-
Steve Madden	multi.	16
Steven	multi.	18
Stuart Weitzman	multi.	27
Stubbs & Wootton	E 70s	26
Studio NYC Shoes	multi.	19
Susan van der Linde	E 50s	-
Taryn Rose	E 60s	25
té casan	SoHo	-
Tip Top Shoes	W 70s	25
Z Tod's	E 60s	29
Tupli	E 60s	-
UGG Australia	SoHo	-
Unisa	E 60s	20
Valley	LES	-
Vanessa Noel	E 60s	-
Varda	multi.	27
Verve	W Vill	24
Vogel	SoHo	-
Walter Steiger	E 50s	28
Warren Edwards	E 60s	28

SHOES: TWEEN/TEEN

(See also Department Stores)

Aldo	multi.	16
NEW Crocs	W 70s	-
David Z.	multi.	19
DC Shoes	SoHo	22
Lester's	multi.	24
Limited Too	multi.	16
NEW Rainbow Sandals	NoLita	23
Something Else	multi.	23
Steve Madden	multi.	16
Steven	multi.	18
Studio NYC Shoes	multi.	19
UGG Australia	SoHo	-

SILVER

Z A La Vieille Russie	E 50s	29
Z Asprey	E 70s	28
Z Buccellati	E 50s	29
Z Cartier	multi.	29
Z Christofle	E 60s	27
Z Georg Jensen	multi.	29
James Robinson	E 50s	29
Z Michael C. Fina	E 40s	26
Z Moss	SoHo	28
Ruzzetti & Gow	E 70s	-
Z Tiffany & Co.	multi.	28

SNEAKERS

Active Wearhouse	SoHo	18
Adidas	multi.	23
Alife	LES	24
Athlete's Foot	multi.	20
Bathing Ape	SoHo	21
NEW Billionaire Boys	SoHo	-
Champs	multi.	17
City Sports	multi.	20
Classic Kicks	NoHo	25
Dave's Quality Meat	E Vill	-
NEW Flight Club	Financial	21
Foot Locker	multi.	21
JackRabbit Sports	multi.	24
Lady Foot Locker	multi.	22
Mason's Tennis Mart	E 50s	26
Modell's Sport	multi.	16
NBA Store	E 50s	21
New Balance	multi.	27
New York Running	W 60s	24
Niketown	E 50s	24
Nort/Recon	NoHo	-
premium goods	Park Slope	-
NEW Private Stock	Park Slope	-

MERCHANDISE

Puma	**multi.**	23
Reed Space	**LES**	22
Rival	**SoHo**	22
Slope Sports	**Park Slope**	-
Sports Authority	**multi.**	17
Super Runners Shop	**multi.**	26
Tip Top Shoes	**W 70s**	25
Training Camp	**multi.**	-
Transit	**NoHo**	17
V.I.M.	**multi.**	14
NEW West	**W 70s**	-

SPORTS

Bicycle Habitat	**SoHo**	23
Bicycle Renaissance	**W 80s**	21
Bike Works NYC	**LES**	-
Blades Board & Skate	**multi.**	23
Burton Store	**SoHo**	25
Capitol Fishing	**Garment**	-
Champs	**multi.**	17
City Sports	**multi.**	20
EMS	**SoHo**	26
Gerry Cosby	**Garment**	25
Golfsmith	**E 50s**	23
Gotham Bikes	**TriBeCa**	24
Grand Central Racquet	**multi.**	-
Gym Source	**E 50s**	26
NEW Homage	**Boerum Hill**	19
JackRabbit Sports	**multi.**	24
KCDC Skate	**W'burg**	22
Larry & Jeff Bicycle	**E 70s**	-
Manhattan Saddlery	**Gramercy**	-
Mason's Tennis Mart	**E 50s**	26
Metro Bicycles	**multi.**	20
Modell's Sport	**multi.**	16
New York Golf	**multi.**	24
New York Pipe Dreams	**E 80s**	-
NYC Velo	**E Vill**	20
Orvis	**E 40s**	25
Pan Aqua Diving	**W 40s**	-
☑ Paragon	**Union Sq**	25
Princeton Ski Shop	**Flatiron**	21
Rival	**SoHo**	22
Scuba Network	**multi.**	-
Slope Sports	**Park Slope**	-
Sports Authority	**multi.**	17
Supreme	**SoHo**	-
SwimBikeRun	**W 50s**	-
☑ Target	**multi.**	17
Tent and Trails	**Financial**	25
☑ Toga Bikes	**multi.**	26
Urban Angler	**Chelsea**	-
Vespa	**multi.**	-
World of Golf	**multi.**	24

STATIONERY

Airline Stationery	**E 40s**	21
☑ Arthur Brown	**W 40s**	27
Arthur's Invitations	**G Vill**	21
Blacker & Kooby	**E 80s**	25
Cardeology	**multi.**	19
☑ Crane & Co.	**W 40s**	27
☑ Dempsey & Carroll	**E 50s**	27
☑ Fountain Pen	**TriBeCa**	28
Greenwich Letterpress	**W Vill**	26
☑ Il Papiro	**E 70s**	28
IS: Ind. Stationery	**SoHo**	-
Jam Paper	**Gramercy**	18
☑ Joon	**multi.**	26
☑ Kate's Paperie	**multi.**	27
Lion in Sun	**Park Slope**	24
☑ Montblanc	**multi.**	28
☑ Mrs. John L. Strong	**E 60s**	28
Paper Presentation	**Flatiron**	25
Papyrus	**multi.**	23
Sam Flax	**multi.**	24
Scaredy Kat	**Park Slope**	24
☑ Smythson	**W 50s**	28
☑ Tiffany & Co.	**multi.**	28
Venture	**E 80s**	22

SWIMWEAR

(See also Department Stores)

☑ Billabong	**multi.**	21
Calypso	**multi.**	23
Canyon Beachwear	**E 60s**	26
Catriona Mackechnie	**Meatpacking**	-
Eres	**multi.**	28
Heidi Klein	**E 70s**	-
J.Crew	**multi.**	20
Malia Mills Swimwear	**multi.**	26
Otto	**Park Slope**	23
Quiksilver	**multi.**	21
Vilebrequin	**multi.**	27

TOILETRIES

(See also Department Stores)

☑ Aedes De Venustas	**G Vill**	27
Alcone	**W 40s**	23
Arcadia	**Chelsea**	25
Aveda	**multi.**	26
Bare Escentuals	**multi.**	25
Bath & Body Works	**multi.**	19
Bathroom	**W Vill**	27
Body Shop	**multi.**	20
Bond No. 9	**multi.**	28
Carol's Daughter	**multi.**	24
Caswell-Massey	**E 40s**	25
CB I Hate Perfume	**W'burg**	-

Clarins | multi.	26
Clyde's | E 70s	27
C.O. Bigelow | G Vill	26
Concord Chemists | E 50s	23
Crabtree & Evelyn | multi.	23
Douglas Cosmetics | E 40s	22
NEW ê Shave | E 50s	23
Essentials | multi.	20
FACE Stockholm | multi.	22
Fresh | multi.	26
H2O Plus | E 50s	23
Jo Malone | multi.	27
Kids Rx | W Vill	-
☑ Kiehl's | multi.	27
Kiki/Montparnasse | SoHo	25
NEW Korres | SoHo	-
Lancôme | W 60s	26
L'Artisan Parfumeur | multi.	26
Le Labo | NoLita	-
Le Sabon & Baby Too | E 60s	23
L'Occitane | multi.	25
Lulu Guinness | W Vill	24
Lush | multi.	23
M.A.C. Cosmetics | multi.	26
Make Up For Ever | G Vill	28
Mastic Spa | SoHo	-
Missha | multi.	-
Molton Brown | multi.	27
N | Harlem	-
Nanette Lepore | SoHo	25
New London Pharm. | Chelsea	23
Nicholas Perricone | E 60s	22
Oliver Spencer | W Vill	-
Origins | multi.	24
Penhaligon's | E 70s	27
Perfumania | Garment	19
Pir Cosmetics | NoLita	-
Ray Beauty Supply | W 40s	24
Red Flower | NoLita	-
Ricky's | multi.	19
Sabon | multi.	25
Saipua | Red Hook	-
☑ Santa Maria Novella | NoLita	28
☑ Sephora | multi.	25
NEW Soapology | W Vill	22
NEW Space.NK | multi.	25
NEW Urban Zen | W Vill	-
Z Chemists/Zitomer | multi.	25

TOYS

Acorn | Downtown Bklyn	-
American Girl Place | E 40s	24
Blue Tree | E 90s	24
Boomerang Toys | multi.	-

☑ Build-A-Bear | multi.	22
Children's Gen. Store | multi.	27
Didi's Children's | E 80s	-
Dinosaur Hill | E Vill	24
E.A.T. Gifts | E 80s	23
FAO Schwarz | E 50s	25
Flying Squirrel | W'burg	-
Heights Kids | Bklyn Hts	-
Homboms | E 70s	-
Hot Toddie | Ft Greene	-
KB Toys | multi.	16
☑ Kidding Around | Flatiron	26
kid o. | G Vill	22
Kid Robot | SoHo	-
Kidville | multi.	22
☑ Mary Arnold Toys | E 70s	26
Maxilla & Mandible | W 80s	25
Mini Jake | W'burg	-
NEW ModernTots | Dumbo	23
MoonSoup | E 50s	24
New York Doll | E 60s	28
Nintendo World | E 40s	25
Penny Whistle | W 80s	23
Pomme | Dumbo	-
Romp | Park Slope	-
Sanrio | W 40s	21
Scholastic Store | SoHo	24
Tiny Doll House | E 70s	-
Toy Space | Park Slope	23
Toys "R" Us | multi.	20
212 Kids | E 80s	23
West Side Kids | W 80s	24
World of Disney | E 50s	22

TWEEN/TEEN CLOTHING

Abercrombie | multi.	18
Am. Eagle | multi.	17
Berkley Girl | multi.	21
Charlotte Russe | multi.	10
Diva | Midwood	-
Forever 21 | multi.	10
4PlayBK | Park Slope	-
G.C. William | multi.	20
Infinity | E 80s	22
Joyce Leslie | multi.	8
Lester's | multi.	24
Limited Too | multi.	16
Magic Windows | E 80s	27
Natalie & Friends | E 60s	28
Paul Frank | NoLita	18
Petit Bateau | E 80s	27
Phat Farm | SoHo	16
Quiksilver | multi.	21
Strawberry | multi.	11

MERCHANDISE

Tribeca Girls | TriBeCa	–
Triple 5 Soul | multi.	21
NEW Trixie/Tilda | Downtown Bklyn	25
Tuesday's Child | multi.	26
V.I.M. | multi.	14
Wet Seal | multi.	10
Yellow Rat | multi.	16

VINTAGE CLOTHING

About Glamour | W'burg	–
Allan & Suzi | W 80s	20
Amarcord Vintage | multi.	–
Andy's Chee-Pees | multi.	15
Angela's Vintage | E Vill	–
Angel St. Thrift Shop | Chelsea	17
Archangel Antiques | E Vill	–
Beacon's Closet | multi.	19
Bis Designer Resale | E 80s	–
Buffalo Exchange | W'burg	17
Centricity | E Vill	–
Cheap Jack's | Garment	14
Chelsea Girl | SoHo	–
Cherry | W Vill	–
City Opera Thrift | Gramercy	22
Consignment | Downtown Bklyn	–
Council Thrift Shop | E 80s	18
Designer Resale | E 80s	24
Don the Verb | LES	16
Dulcinée | LES	–
Edith Machinist | LES	–
Encore | E 80s	20
Eye Candy | NoHo	24
Family Jewels | Chelsea	–
Fisch for the Hip | Chelsea	26
Frock | LES	–
Gentlemen's Resale | E 80s	24
Goodwill | multi.	12
Hairy Mary's | LES	–
Hooti Couture | Prospect Hts	21
Housing Works Thrift | multi.	20
Ina | multi.	25
Jane's Exchange | E Vill	21
Kavanagh's | E 40s	–
La Boutique Resale | multi.	23
Lolli/Reincarnation | LES	20
Loveday31 | Astoria	–
Love Saves The Day | E Vill	17
Marmalade | LES	–
Mem. Sloan-Kettering | E 80s	22
Michael's/Consignment | E 70s	25
No. 6 | L Italy	–
NEW Ohio Knit. | Carroll Gdns	22
Patina | SoHo	–

Peggy Pardon | LES	–
Poppet | E Vill	–
Reminiscence | Flatiron	19
NEW REPOP | Clinton Hill	–
Resurrection | NoLita	–
NEW Rewind | Gravesend	–
Rue St. Denis | E Vill	–
Salvation Army | multi.	11
Second Chance | E 70s	21
17 at 17 Thrift | Flatiron	18
Some Odd Rubies | LES	–
Spence-Chapin Thrift | multi.	16
Star Struck | G Vill	20
Stella Dallas/Ten Feet | multi.	–
Sweet Tater | NoLita	18
Tokio 7 | E Vill	26
Tokyo Joe | E Vill	22
Vintage Thrift Shop | Gramercy	22
What Comes Around | SoHo	26
Zachary's Smile | multi.	24

WATCHES

Audemars Piguet | E 50s	29
Z Cartier | multi.	29
Cellini | multi.	27
Z Chopard | E 60s	29
Fossil | multi.	19
NEW Franck Muller | E 50s	27
Joseph Edwards | E 40s	22
Kenjo | multi.	25
Michael Ashton | E 70s	–
Movado | W 40s	26
Z Piaget | E 50s	28
Sub Chrono | E 40s	22
Swatch | multi.	20
Swiss Army | SoHo	23
Taffin | E 50s	–
Z Tiffany & Co. | multi.	28
Tourneau | multi.	27
Z Van Cleef & Arpels | E 50s	29
Z Wempe | E 50s	29
William Barthman | multi.	26
Yellow Door | Midwood	–
Zales Jewelers | multi.	12

WOMENSWEAR

(See also Mens/Womenswear, Department Stores)

Albertine | G Vill	–
alice + olivia | multi.	22
NEW Amalia | NoLita	20
Anik | multi.	21
Anna | E Vill	–
Ann Crabtree | E 90s	23
Z Ann Taylor | multi.	21

Store	Location	Rating
Z Ann Taylor Loft	**multi.**	20
Z Anthropologie	**multi.**	20
Arden B.	**multi.**	17
NEW Asha Veza	**Park Slope**	-
A Uno/Walk	**TriBeCa**	24
Barami	**multi.**	16
bebe	**multi.**	17
Betsey Bunky	**E 70s**	23
Bird	**multi.**	25
Blueberi	**Dumbo**	-
blush	**W Vill**	21
Böc	**W 80s**	19
Bond 07/Selima	**NoHo**	-
Brooklyn Collective	**Red Hook**	-
Butik	**W Vill**	-
Butter	**Downtown Bklyn**	23
NEW Butterflies/Zebras	**TriBeCa**	23
Caché	**multi.**	18
Calypso	**multi.**	23
Cantaloup/Luxe	**multi.**	22
Castor & Pollux	**W Vill**	-
Catbird	**W'burg**	-
Challengher	**W'burg**	-
Chico's	**multi.**	20
CK Bradley	**E 70s**	24
Claudine	**G Vill**	22
Cloth	**Ft Greene**	-
CoCo & Delilah	**E Vill**	-
NEW Curve	**SoHo**	19
Darling	**W Vill**	-
Dear Fieldbinder	**Cobble Hill**	-
Dernier Cri	**Meatpacking**	-
NEW Diabless	**E 60s**	-
Diana Kane	**Park Slope**	-
Diane T	**Cobble Hill**	-
Diane von Furstenberg	**Meatpacking**	24
DIGS	**E 60s**	19
D/L Cerney	**E Vill**	-
Dolce Vita	**LES**	23
NEW Edit	**E 90s**	-
Eidolon	**Park Slope**	-
Eileen Fisher	**multi.**	24
Ekovaruhuset	**LES**	-
Elizabeth Charles	**Meatpacking**	-
EMc2	**NoLita**	23
Emily's	**SI**	25
Emmelle	**multi.**	21
Erica Tanov	**NoLita**	-
Express	**multi.**	16
NEW 5 in 1	**W'burg**	-
Flirt	**multi.**	-
Foley + Corinna	**LES**	21
Forever 21	**multi.**	10
NEW Free People	**Flatiron**	-
G.C. William	**multi.**	20
Geminola	**W Vill**	-
Goldy/Macki	**multi.**	22
gominyc	**E Vill**	-
Good, Bad & Ugly	**NoLita**	-
NEW HH Design	**Greenpt**	20
NEW Honey/Rough	**LES**	21
Ibiza NY	**G Vill**	21
I Heart	**NoLita**	-
Intermix	**multi.**	24
Irma	**W Vill**	-
Jane	**E 70s**	-
NEW Jessie James	**W Vill**	-
Joyce Leslie	**multi.**	8
Jumelle	**W'burg**	-
Kaight	**LES**	-
NEW Karen Millen	**SoHo**	-
Key	**SoHo**	-
Kirna Zabête	**SoHo**	27
Kiwi	**Park Slope**	22
Leontine	**Seaport**	-
LF Stores	**multi.**	17
Liberty House	**W 100s**	25
Lily	**multi.**	24
Limited, The	**multi.**	-
Linda Dresner	**E 50s**	25
Living 5th/7th/Smith	**multi.**	-
NEW Lola	**Park Slope**	22
Loopy Mango	**Dumbo**	-
Ludivine	**G Vill**	-
Maleeka	**Downtown Bklyn**	-
NEW Manrico	**E 70s**	-
Marimekko	**E 70s**	24
Market NYC	**NoLita**	20
Matta	**NoLita**	-
Michelle	**Boerum Hill**	-
Mick Margo	**W Vill**	-
miks	**LES**	-
Mimi's Closet	**Astoria**	21
Min-K	**multi.**	-
Miss Sixty	**multi.**	21
NEW MNG/Mango	**SoHo**	-
Montmartre	**multi.**	22
NEW msg	**L Italy**	-
Nancy & Co.	**E 80s**	23
National Jean Company	**multi.**	-
Necessary Clothing	**multi.**	17
Néda	**multi.**	21
Nellie M.	**E 80s**	22
New York & Co.	**multi.**	17
New York Look	**multi.**	20
Noisette	**W'burg**	-

Oilily	**SoHo**	23	Searle	**multi.**	24
Olive & Bette's	**multi.**	22	Selima/Sucre	**W Vill**	27
Otte	**multi.**	26	Seven NY	**SoHo**	26
Otto	**Park Slope**	23	Shop	**LES**	20
NEW Owl's Lab	**G Vill**	21	Shvitz	**SoHo**	-
Patricia Field	**NoHo**	15	Sir	**multi.**	-
Pearl River Mart	**SoHo**	16	Smith on Sullivan	**G Vill**	20
Pear/Plum	**LES**	22	Stella Gialla	**Glendale**	25
Peter Elliot	**E 80s**	25	Sugar	**E Vill**	22
Pinkyotto	**multi.**	21	**NEW** Suite Orchard	**LES**	23
NEW Pixie Mkt.	**LES**	19	TG-170	**LES**	20
Pookie/Sebastian	**multi.**	17	**NEW** Travessia	**LES**	-
Poppy	**NoLita**	23	UnitedColors/Benetton	**multi.**	20
Project 234	**NoLita**	-	Utowa	**Flatiron**	20
Purdy Girl	**multi.**	18	Valley	**LES**	-
Redberi	**Prospect Hts**	-	Variazioni	**multi.**	17
Roberta Freymann	**E 70s**	-	Vivaldi Boutique	**E 70s**	23
S&W	**multi.**	18	White Hse. Black Mkt.	**multi.**	-
Scoop NYC	**multi.**	23	Zoë	**Dumbo**	-

Special Features

Listings cover the best in each category and include store names, locations and Quality ratings. ☑ indicates highest ratings, popularity and importance.

ADDITIONS

(Properties added since the last edition of the book)

A&G Merch | **W'burg**	21
About Glamour | **W'burg**	-
Adam | **Meatpacking**	-
Allegra Hicks | **E 70s**	24
Alter | **Greenpt**	-
Amadeo/Scognamiglio | **E 70s**	20
Amalia | **NoLita**	20
Ambassador Luggage | **E 40s**	22
Ankasa | **E 60s**	24
Archangela | **W'burg**	-
Asha Veza | **Park Slope**	-
Audemars Piguet | **E 50s**	29
Babesta | **TriBeCa**	23
Baby Cottons | **E 80s**	26
Barker Black | **NoLita**	25
Belle/Sig. Morrison | **NoLita**	22
Bellora | **SoHo**	26
Bettencourt | **W'burg**	-
Billionaire Boys | **SoHo**	-
Blue & Cream | **E Vill**	-
Blue Ribbon | **Boerum Hill**	-
Brklyn Merc. | **Park Slope**	21
Buffalo Exchange | **W'burg**	17
Bump | **Park Slope**	-
Butterflies/Zebras | **TriBeCa**	23
Catherine Angiel | **G Vill**	25
CB2 | **SoHo**	-
Challengher | **W'burg**	-
Charlotte Moss | **E 60s**	25
Chelsea Garden Ctr. | **multi.**	23
Claudine | **G Vill**	22
Concord Chemists | **E 50s**	23
Corduroy Kid | **Prospect Hts**	24
Cotélac | **SoHo**	-
Crocs | **W 70s**	-
Curve | **SoHo**	19
Dalaga | **Greenpt**	19
Den | **E Vill**	22
Diabless | **E 60s**	-
Diana Broussard | **G Vill**	22
Dig Garden | **Downtown Bklyn**	23
DIGS | **E 60s**	19
Don the Verb | **LES**	16
Edit | **E 90s**	-
Edith Weber | **E 70s**	-
Edon Manor | **TriBeCa**	-

Ekovaruhuset | **LES**	-
Emily's | **SI**	25
Erie Basin | **Red Hook**	-
ê Shave | **E 50s**	23
55DSL | **SoHo**	19
Firefly | **multi.**	25
5 in 1 | **W'burg**	-
Flight Club | **Financial**	21
Franck Muller | **E 50s**	27
Free People | **Flatiron**	-
Gilan | **E 50s**	25
gominyc | **E Vill**	-
Gus Modern | **Chelsea**	20
Hannah Clark | **E Vill**	-
Head/Heels | **multi.**	21
Helio | **multi.**	20
Helmut Lang | **Meatpacking**	-
HH Design | **Greenpt**	20
hickey | **SoHo**	-
Hippototamus | **multi.**	22
hip-squeak | **Bay Ridge**	23
Homage | **Boerum Hill**	19
Home & Haven | **Cobble Hill**	22
Honey/Rough | **LES**	21
Hus | **G Vill**	-
Ilori | **SoHo**	-
In God We Trust | **multi.**	-
Iris | **Meatpacking**	23
Irregular Choice | **SoHo**	-
Ivanka Trump | **E 60s**	-
Jane Eadie | **NoLita**	-
Jane's Exchange | **E Vill**	21
Jessie James | **W Vill**	-
John Bartlett | **W Vill**	23
Journelle | **Flatiron**	-
Just Cavalli | **E 50s**	25
Karen Millen | **SoHo**	-
KCDC Skate | **W'burg**	22
Kiosk | **SoHo**	19
Kiwi | **Park Slope**	22
Kohl's | **multi.**	-
Korres | **SoHo**	-
Ksubi | **NoLita**	22
Lambertson | **E 60s**	-
Leviev | **E 60s**	27
Lily | **multi.**	24
Limited, The | **multi.**	-
Little Marc | **W Vill**	-
Lola | **Park Slope**	22

Lolli/Reincarnation | **LES**	20
Louis Féraud | **E 60s**	28
Luceplan | **SoHo**	23
Lucia Nenickova | **Gramercy**	21
Magnificent Costume | **E 80s**	22
Manrico | **E 70s**	-
Marc Ecko | **Chelsea**	-
Michael Andrews | **LES**	22
Michael Aram | **Chelsea**	26
Miguelina | **W Vill**	24
Mini Jake | **W'burg**	-
Mitchell Gold | **SoHo**	-
MNG/Mango | **SoHo**	-
ModernTots | **Dumbo**	23
Moroso | **SoHo**	-
msg | **L Italy**	-
Muji | **SoHo**	-
National Jean Company | **multi.**	-
Néda | **multi.**	21
Neighborhoodies | **multi.**	20
New London Pharm. | **Chelsea**	23
Ohio Knit. | **Carroll Gdns**	22
OMALA | **Boerum Hill**	20
Organic Ave. | **LES**	24
Osklen | **multi.**	-
Otto | **Park Slope**	23
Owl's Lab | **G Vill**	21
Pear/Plum | **LES**	22
Pink Olive | **E Vill**	24
Pinkyotto | **multi.**	21
Pixie Mkt. | **LES**	19
POP | **W'burg**	19
Priscilla of Boston | **Garment**	24
Private Stock | **Park Slope**	-
Project No. 8 | **Chinatown**	-
Pull-In | **NoLita**	-
Rainbow Sandals | **NoLita**	23
Red Toenails | **W'burg**	-
Reed Space | **LES**	22
REPOP | **Clinton Hill**	-
Rewind | **Gravesend**	-
Roger Vivier | **E 60s**	28
Saipua | **Red Hook**	-
Salty Paw | **Seaport**	22
Shoe Market | **W'burg**	18
Smith on Sullivan | **G Vill**	20
Soapology | **W Vill**	22
Space.NK | **multi.**	25
Sprout Home | **W'burg**	25
Star Struck | **G Vill**	20
Stella Gialla | **Glendale**	25
Stephen Kahan | **E 60s**	27
Stephen Russell | **E 70s**	27
Sterling Pl. | **multi.**	-

Studio NYC Shoes | **multi.**	19
Sub Chrono | **E 40s**	22
Suite Orchard | **LES**	23
Susan van der Linde | **E 50s**	-
Sweet Tater | **NoLita**	18
Threads | **E 70s**	-
3.1 Phillip Lim | **SoHo**	27
Tom Ford | **E 70s**	28
Tous | **SoHo**	22
Travessia | **LES**	-
Tribbles Home/Gdn. | **TriBeCa**	25
Trixie/Tilda | **Downtown Bklyn**	25
212 Kids | **E 80s**	23
Urban Zen | **W Vill**	-
Utowa | **Flatiron**	20
Vivaldi Boutique | **E 70s**	23
West | **W 70s**	-
Zaba | **TriBeCa**	-

AVANT-GARDE

Agent Provocateur | **SoHo**	27
Alain Mikli | **multi.**	28
☑ Alexander McQueen | **Meatpacking**	28
auto | **Meatpacking**	-
☑ Balenciaga | **Chelsea**	29
☑ Barneys NY | **E 60s**	27
Bathing Ape | **SoHo**	21
Bblessing | **LES**	21
Bond 07/Selima | **NoHo**	-
Butter | **Downtown Bklyn**	23
CB I Hate Perfume | **W'burg**	-
Chrome Hearts | **E 60s**	28
Cloak | **SoHo**	-
Comme des Garçons | **Chelsea**	26
Compact Impact | **Financial**	-
Costume National | **SoHo**	26
NEW Den | **E Vill**	22
Dernier Cri | **Meatpacking**	-
Design Within Reach | **multi.**	24
Destination | **Meatpacking**	23
Dolce & Gabbana | **E 60s**	27
Edge nyNoHo | **NoHo**	24
NEW Edon Manor | **TriBeCa**	-
NEW Erie Basin | **Red Hook**	-
NEW 5 in 1 | **W'burg**	-
45rpm/R | **E 70s**	23
Fragments | **multi.**	25
Future Perfect | **W'burg**	-
Garrard & Co. | **SoHo**	-
Good, Bad & Ugly | **NoLita**	-
IF | **SoHo**	-
Ingo Maurer Light | **SoHo**	-
NEW Iris | **Meatpacking**	23

Issey Miyake | **multi.**	25
Jean Shop | **multi.**	-
Jeffrey | **Meatpacking**	28
Kiosk | **SoHo**	19
Kirna Zabête | **SoHo**	27
NEW Luceplan | **SoHo**	23
Maison Martin Margiela | **W Vill**	-
Marni | **SoHo**	24
Matter | **multi.**	-
Z MoMA Store | **multi.**	25
Z Moss | **SoHo**	28
Opening Ceremony | **SoHo**	-
Z Other Music | **NoHo**	27
Patricia Field | **NoHo**	15
Pleats Please | **SoHo**	-
Prada | **multi.**	26
NEW Project No. 8 | **Chinatown**	-
Roberto Cavalli | **E 60s**	27
Seven NY | **SoHo**	26
Smith on Sullivan | **G Vill**	20
Spring | **Dumbo**	-
Z Takashimaya | **E 50s**	28
37=1 Atelier | **SoHo**	-
Tupli | **E 60s**	-
Utowa | **Flatiron**	20
Vitra | **Meatpacking**	-
Yohji Yamamoto | **SoHo**	27
Zero/Maria Cornejo | **multi.**	-

CELEBRITY CLIENTELE

Aaron Basha | **E 60s**	25
Z ABC Carpet & Home | **Flatiron**	25
Z Aedes De Venustas | **G Vill**	27
Alain Mikli | **multi.**	28
Alessandro Dell'Acqua | **E 60s**	26
Z Alexander McQueen | **Meatpacking**	28
Alexis Bittar | **SoHo**	25
Annelore | **W Vill**	-
Z Balenciaga | **Chelsea**	29
Barker Black | **NoLita**	25
Z Barneys NY | **E 60s**	27
BDDW | **SoHo**	-
Z Bergdorf | **E 50s**	29
Z Bergdorf Men's | **E 50s**	28
Berluti | **E 70s**	-
Beverly Feldman | **W 50s**	20
Billy Martin's | **E 60s**	27
Blue Tree | **E 90s**	24
Z Bottega Veneta | **E 50s**	29
Breguet | **E 60s**	29
Burberry | **multi.**	27
Burton Store | **SoHo**	25

Butik | **W Vill**	-
Calvin Klein | **E 60s**	25
Calvin Tran | **NoLita**	-
Calypso | **multi.**	23
Camilla Bergeron | **E 60s**	-
Caravan | **NoHo**	20
Carlos Miele | **Meatpacking**	-
Z Carolina Herrera | **E 70s**	28
Catherine Malandrino | **multi.**	24
CB I Hate Perfume | **W'burg**	-
Z Chanel | **multi.**	29
NEW Charlotte Moss | **E 60s**	25
Chloé | **E 70s**	26
Z Christian Louboutin | **multi.**	28
Chrome Hearts | **E 60s**	28
Claudia Ciuti | **E 70s**	25
Damiani | **E 60s**	-
DDC Lab | **Meatpacking**	-
de Grisogono | **E 60s**	-
Dernier Cri | **Meatpacking**	-
Dior Homme | **E 50s**	26
Z Dior New York | **E 50s**	28
Dolce & Gabbana | **E 60s**	27
Domenico Vacca | **multi.**	-
Donna Karan | **E 60s**	25
Dylan's Candy | **E 60s**	22
Earnest Cut & Sew | **multi.**	25
Ed Hardy | **multi.**	21
Elizabeth Charles | **Meatpacking**	-
EMc2 | **NoLita**	23
Fat Beats | **G Vill**	-
Fendi | **E 50s**	27
Fragments | **multi.**	25
Z Fred Leighton | **E 60s**	29
Fresh | **multi.**	26
Garrard & Co. | **SoHo**	-
Geminola | **W Vill**	-
NEW Gilan | **E 50s**	25
Z Giorgio Armani | **E 60s**	29
Gucci | **multi.**	27
Hastens | **SoHo**	-
Helen Ficalora | **NoLita**	-
Henry Beguelin | **Meatpacking**	-
Z Hermès | **multi.**	29
Hogan | **SoHo**	26
Hollywould | **NoLita**	24
Hugo Boss | **multi.**	26
NEW Iris | **Meatpacking**	23
Issey Miyake | **multi.**	25
NEW Ivanka Trump | **E 60s**	-
Jacob & Co. | **E 50s**	24
Jeffrey | **Meatpacking**	28
Jennifer Miller Jewelry | **E 70s**	-

Jill Platner | **SoHo**	-
Jimmy Choo | **multi.**	28
J.M. Weston | **E 60s**	26
Jonathan Adler | **multi.**	26
Joseph | **multi.**	23
Juicy Couture | **multi.**	20
NEW Just Cavalli | **E 50s**	25
Kangol | **W 60s**	23
Key | **SoHo**	-
Kiki/Montparnasse | **SoHo**	25
Kipepeo | **NoLita**	-
Kiton | **E 50s**	-
NEW Korres | **SoHo**	-
LaDuca Shoes | **Garment**	-
Lana Marks | **E 60s**	28
La Petite Coquette | **G Vill**	26
NEW Leviev | **E 60s**	27
Longchamp | **SoHo**	26
Lord Willy's | **multi.**	-
NEW Louis Féraud | **E 60s**	28
Louis Vuitton | **multi.**	27
Lowell/Edwards | **E 50s**	-
Lulu Guinness | **W Vill**	24
Manhattan Saddlery | **Gramercy**	-
Z Manolo Blahnik | **W 50s**	28
Marc Jacobs Access. | **W Vill**	28
Marc Jacobs | **SoHo**	27
Marie-Chantal | **E 80s**	25
Marni | **SoHo**	24
Max Azria | **SoHo**	-
Mayle | **NoLita**	-
Michael Kors | **multi.**	26
Michele Varian | **SoHo**	-
Mish | **E 70s**	-
Miu Miu | **multi.**	25
Mixona | **NoLita**	-
Z Moss | **SoHo**	28
Mulberry | **multi.**	-
Oliver Peoples | **multi.**	27
Oliver Spencer | **W Vill**	-
Z Oscar de la Renta | **E 60s**	28
Petrou | **E 60s**	-
Poleci | **Meatpacking**	22
Prada | **multi.**	26
Pucci | **multi.**	26
Z Purl | **SoHo**	28
Ralph Lauren | **multi.**	26
Ralph Lauren Boys/Girls | **E 70s**	26
Ralph Lauren Eyewear | **E 60s**	-
Rebecca Taylor | **NoLita**	23
Reem Acra | **E 60s**	29
Robert Marc | **multi.**	27
Roberto Cavalli | **E 60s**	27

Rogan | **TriBeCa**	25
NEW Roger Vivier | **E 60s**	28
Rubin Chapelle | **Meatpacking**	-
Samantha Thavasa | **E 70s**	-
Z Santa Maria Novella | **NoLita**	28
Satya | **multi.**	21
Sean John | **E 40s**	18
Shin Choi | **SoHo**	-
Sir | **multi.**	-
Some Odd Rubies | **LES**	-
NEW Space.NK | **multi.**	25
Stella McCartney | **Meatpacking**	26
Swarovski | **multi.**	25
Taffin | **E 50s**	-
Tarina Tarantino | **SoHo**	22
Temperley | **SoHo**	-
Todd Hase | **SoHo**	-
Z Tod's | **E 60s**	29
NEW Tom Ford | **E 70s**	28
Trina Turk | **Meatpacking**	-
True Religion | **SoHo**	-
Tupli | **E 60s**	-
Z Urban Archaeology | **multi.**	25
Z Valentino | **E 60s**	28
Vanessa Noel | **E 60s**	-
Versace | **E 50s**	26
Vogel | **SoHo**	-
Yigal Azrouel | **Meatpacking**	-
Yohji Yamamoto | **SoHo**	27

COOL LOOS

Z ABC Carpet & Home | **Flatiron**	25
Z Apple Store | **multi.**	27
Z Asprey | **E 70s**	28
Z Bergdorf | **E 50s**	29
Burton Store | **SoHo**	25
Caravan | **NoHo**	20
Chanel Jewelry | **E 60s**	27
Charles Nolan | **Meatpacking**	-
NEW Charlotte Moss | **E 60s**	25
Earnest Cut & Sew | **multi.**	25
Ed Hardy | **multi.**	21
Fendi | **E 50s**	27
Marimekko | **E 70s**	24
N | **Harlem**	-
NEW New Museum | **LES**	-
Nili Lotan | **TriBeCa**	-
Patricia Field | **NoHo**	15
Phi | **SoHo**	-
Poleci | **Meatpacking**	22
Reiss | **SoHo**	20
Rugby | **G Vill**	22
Sophia Eugene | **W Vill**	-

SPECIAL FEATURES

☑ Frette | **E 60s**	29
Future Perfect | **W'burg**	-
Garrard & Co. | **SoHo**	-
George Smith | **SoHo**	-
Granny-Made | **W 70s**	24
Hannah Clark | **E Vill**	-
☑ Harris Levy | **LES**	26
☑ Harry Winston | **E 50s**	29
Hasker | **Carroll Gdns**	-
Hastens | **SoHo**	-
Hat Shop | **SoHo**	24
Henry Beguelin | **Meatpacking**	-
H. Herzfeld | **E 50s**	26
NEW hickey | **SoHo**	-
Hickey Freeman | **multi.**	27
Highway | **NoLita**	-
☑ Home Depot | **multi.**	19
NEW Hus | **G Vill**	-
IF | **SoHo**	-
Il Makiage | **E 50s**	23
Jacob & Co. | **E 50s**	24
Jane Wilson-Marquis | **E 70s**	-
Jay Kos | **E 50s**	-
Jean Shop | **Meatpacking**	-
Jennifer Miller Jewelry | **E 70s**	-
Jeri Cohen Jewelry | **E 60s**	27
J.J. Hat Center | **Garment**	27
J.J. Marco | **E 80s**	24
☑ J. Mendel | **E 60s**	28
J.M. Weston | **E 60s**	26
Joan Michlin Gallery | **SoHo**	27
NEW John Bartlett | **W Vill**	23
John Derian | **E Vill**	-
☑ John Lobb | **E 60s**	29
Just Shades | **NoLita**	24
Jutta Neumann | **LES**	-
J.W. Cooper | **W 60s**	-
Kaas GlassWorks | **W Vill**	-
Katz/Cradle | **Midwood**	-
Kenjo | **multi.**	25
Kiki/Montparnasse | **SoHo**	25
Kiton | **E 50s**	-
Knoll | **Chelsea**	-
Kraft | **E 60s**	26
Kreiss Collection | **E 50s**	26
☑ Krup's Kitchen/Bath | **Flatiron**	26
La Cafetière | **Chelsea**	-
LaDuca Shoes | **Garment**	-
Lalaounis | **E 60s**	29
☑ Lalique | **E 60s**	29
Lana Marks | **E 60s**	28
LaoLao Handmade | **E Vill**	-
☑ Leather Man | **W Vill**	26

Lee Anderson | **E 70s**	-
Lee's Art Shop | **W 50s**	25
Le Fanion | **W Vill**	-
☑ Leiber | **E 60s**	28
Léron | **E 60s**	29
NEW Leviev | **E 60s**	27
Lightforms | **multi.**	23
Lighting By Gregory | **LES**	24
Lion in Sun | **Park Slope**	24
Lolli/Reincarnation | **LES**	20
Longchamp | **multi.**	26
Lord Willy's | **NoLita**	-
Lowe's | **multi.**	21
NEW Lucia Nenickova | **Gramercy**	21
Lucien Pellat-Finet | **G Vill**	-
Magic Windows | **E 80s**	27
Magnificent Costume | **E 80s**	22
Manhattan Ctr. | **Flatiron**	-
Marimekko | **E 70s**	24
Mary Adams The Dress | **LES**	-
☑ MauricE Villency | **E 50s**	26
McGuire | **Murray Hill**	-
Michael Anchin | **W'burg**	-
NEW Michael Andrews | **LES**	22
NEW Michael Aram | **Chelsea**	26
Michael Kors | **multi.**	26
Michele Varian | **SoHo**	-
Michelle | **Boerum Hill**	-
Mika Inatome | **TriBeCa**	-
Miriam Rigler | **E 60s**	28
Mish | **E 70s**	-
NEW ModernTots | **Dumbo**	23
MoonSoup | **E 50s**	24
☑ Moss | **SoHo**	28
Moulin Bleu | **TriBeCa**	-
Mulberry | **multi.**	-
Munder-Skiles | **E 60s**	-
Mxyplyzyk | **W Vill**	21
Neighborhoodies | **multi.**	20
Nemo Tile | **multi.**	21
NYC Velo | **E Vill**	20
Occhiali | **E 80s**	24
Oculus 20/20 | **multi.**	-
O'Lampia Studio | **LES**	29
OMO Norma Kamali | **W 50s**	22
On Stage Dance | **Murray Hill**	-
Oriental Lamp Shade | **multi.**	25
☑ Oxxford Clothes | **E 50s**	28
Parke & Ronen | **Chelsea**	-
Paterson Silks | **multi.**	18
P.E. Guerin | **W Vill**	-
Poggenpohl U.S. | **multi.**	-
Poltrona Frau | **SoHo**	-

Pomellato | **E 60s**	–
Pomme | **Dumbo**	–
☑ Pompanoosuc Mills | **TriBeCa**	25
Porthault | **E 60s**	29
☑ Pratesi | **E 60s**	29
NEW Priscilla of Boston | **Garment**	24
Quintessentials | **W 80s**	23
Rachel Ashwell's | **SoHo**	23
Reem Acra | **E 60s**	29
Refinery | **Cobble Hill**	–
Reinstein/Ross | **multi.**	28
Roberta Roller Rabbit | **E 70s**	–
Robert Lee Morris | **SoHo**	25
Robert Marc | **multi.**	27
☑ Roche Bobois | **Murray Hill**	27
Romp | **Park Slope**	–
Rosen & Chadick | **Garment**	–
Rubin Chapelle | **Meatpacking**	–
Rug Company | **SoHo**	–
Ruzzetti & Gow | **E 70s**	–
Saipua | **Red Hook**	–
NEW Salty Paw | **Seaport**	22
Salviati | **SoHo**	–
Samuel's Hats | **Financial**	–
☑ Santa Maria Novella | **NoLita**	28
Schoolhouse Electric | **TriBeCa**	–
☑ Schweitzer Linen | **multi.**	27
Scott Jordan | **SoHo**	27
Seigo | **E 80s**	28
Seize sur Vingt | **NoLita**	25
Selia Yang | **multi.**	26
Sherle Wagner | **E 60s**	–
Shirt Store | **E 40s**	22
Shoe Mine | **Park Slope**	–
Shvitz | **SoHo**	–
Sid's | **Downtown Bklyn**	21
Signoria | **E 60s**	25
Sir | **multi.**	–
Sleep | **W'burg**	22
Smith on Sullivan | **G Vill**	20
SOHO | **NoLita**	20
Space107 | **W Vill**	–
Spring | **Dumbo**	–
Stefano Ricci | **E 50s**	27
Stephen Kahan | **E 60s**	27
Sterling Pl. | **multi.**	–
☑ Steuben | **E 60s**	29
☑ String | **E 80s**	27
Stubbs & Wootton | **E 70s**	26
Susan van der Linde | **E 50s**	–
Suzanne Couture | **E 60s**	27
Taffin | **E 50s**	–
Ted Muehling | **SoHo**	29
37=1 Atelier | **SoHo**	–
Thom Browne. | **TriBeCa**	–
Thos. Moser Cabinets | **E 60s**	29
☑ Tiffany & Co. | **E 50s**	28
Tiny Doll House | **E 70s**	–
Todd Hase | **SoHo**	–
☑ Toga Bikes | **E 60s**	26
NEW Tom Ford | **E 70s**	28
Town Shop | **W 80s**	25
Treehouse | **W'burg**	–
Treillage | **E 70s**	–
Troy | **Gramercy**	–
Tucker Robbins | **multi.**	–
Tupli | **E 60s**	–
☑ Turnbull & Asser | **E 50s**	28
☑ Van Cleef & Arpels | **E 50s**	29
Vanessa Noel | **E 60s**	–
Venture | **E 80s**	22
Vera Wang Bridal | **E 70s**	27
Vera Wang Maids | **E 70s**	27
Village Tannery | **multi.**	21
Vivaldi Boutique | **E 70s**	23
Vogel | **SoHo**	–
Walter Steiger | **E 50s**	28
Warren Edwards | **E 60s**	28
White on White | **Murray Hill**	–
Yigal Azrouel | **Meatpacking**	–
Yoya/Yoya Mart | **W Vill**	27
Yves Delorme | **E 70s**	28
Zarin Fabrics | **LES**	23

FREQUENT-BUYER PROGRAMS

Alkit | **Flatiron**	23
☑ Allen Edmonds | **E 40s**	28
Aveda | **multi.**	26
☑ Barneys NY | **E 60s**	27
☑ Bergdorf | **E 50s**	29
☑ Bergdorf Men's | **E 50s**	28
☑ Bloomingdale's | **SoHo**	23
Carol's Daughter | **multi.**	24
Casual Male XL | **multi.**	19
Chico's | **multi.**	20
Dana Buchman | **E 50s**	25
☑ DSW | **multi.**	21
Ed Hardy | **multi.**	21
Eileen Fisher | **multi.**	24
Esprit | **W 60s**	17
Harry's Shoes | **W 80s**	24
Harry's Shoes/Kids | **W 80s**	–
JackRabbit Sports | **multi.**	24
☑ Loehmann's | **multi.**	20
☑ Marshalls | **multi.**	16

SPECIAL FEATURES

Montmartre | **multi.**	22
Naturino | **multi.**	28
Petco | **multi.**	19
Poggenpohl U.S. | **multi.**	–
Prato Fine Men's Wear | **multi.**	13
Sacco | **multi.**	22
⚡ Saks Fifth Ave. | **E 50s**	27
Sharper Image | **multi.**	21
Staples | **multi.**	19
Syms | **multi.**	18
⚡ T.J. Maxx | **multi.**	16
Tourneau | **multi.**	27
Toys "R" Us | **multi.**	20
Utrecht | **E Vill**	24
Victoria's Secret | **multi.**	18
White Hse. Black Mkt. | **multi.**	–

HIP/HOT PLACES

A&G Merch | **W'burg**	21
Adidas | **multi.**	23
⚡ Aedes De Venustas | **G Vill**	27
AG | **SoHo**	26
Agent Provocateur | **SoHo**	27
Albertine | **G Vill**	–
Alessandro Dell'Acqua | **E 60s**	26
Alessi | **multi.**	25
⚡ Alexander McQueen | **Meatpacking**	28
Alexis Bittar | **SoHo**	25
alice + olivia | **multi.**	22
NEW Amalia | **NoLita**	20
Amarcord Vintage | **multi.**	–
American Apparel | **multi.**	19
Anna Sui | **SoHo**	23
⚡ Apple Store | **multi.**	27
⚡ Balenciaga | **Chelsea**	29
Barneys CO-OP | **multi.**	24
⚡ Barneys NY | **E 60s**	27
Bathroom | **W Vill**	27
BCBG Max Azria | **multi.**	22
Belle/Sig. Morrison | **NoLita**	22
NEW Billionaire Boys | **SoHo**	–
Bird | **multi.**	25
NEW Blue & Cream | **E Vill**	–
Bond 07/Selima | **NoHo**	–
⚡ Bottega Veneta | **E 50s**	29
Built by Wendy | **multi.**	–
Burberry | **multi.**	27
Burton Store | **SoHo**	25
Butter | **Downtown Bklyn**	23
Calypso | **multi.**	23
Calypso Home | **NoLita**	–
⚡ Canine Styles | **multi.**	26
Caravan | **NoHo**	20

Carlos Miele | **Meatpacking**	–
Catbird | **W'burg**	–
Catherine Malandrino | **multi.**	24
NEW CB2 | **SoHo**	–
Chloé | **E 70s**	26
⚡ Christian Louboutin | **multi.**	28
Chrome Hearts | **E 60s**	28
Cloak | **SoHo**	–
Costume National | **SoHo**	26
C. Ronson | **NoLita**	16
NEW Curve | **SoHo**	19
Dalaga | **Greenpt**	19
D & G | **SoHo**	24
Darling | **W Vill**	–
Daryl K | **NoHo**	23
Dear Fieldbinder | **Cobble Hill**	–
NEW Den | **E Vill**	22
Dernier Cri | **Meatpacking**	–
Diana Kane | **Park Slope**	–
Diane T | **Cobble Hill**	–
Diane von Furstenberg | **Meatpacking**	24
Diesel | **multi.**	23
Diesel Denim Gallery | **SoHo**	24
Dior Homme | **E 50s**	26
⚡ Dior New York | **E 50s**	28
Doggystyle | **SoHo**	–
Dolce & Gabbana | **E 60s**	27
Dylan's Candy | **E 60s**	22
Earnest Cut & Sew | **multi.**	25
Ed Hardy | **multi.**	21
Erica Tanov | **NoLita**	–
Fat Beats | **G Vill**	–
Flight 001 | **multi.**	24
Foley + Corinna | **LES**	21
NEW Free People | **Flatiron**	–
Fresh Kills | **W'burg**	–
Future Perfect | **W'burg**	–
⚡ Giuseppe Zanotti | **E 60s**	28
Good, Bad & Ugly | **NoLita**	–
Gucci | **multi.**	27
⚡ H&M | **multi.**	12
Henry Beguelin | **Meatpacking**	–
NEW HH Design | **Greenpt**	20
NEW hickey | **SoHo**	–
Hollander/Lexer | **Boerum Hill**	–
NEW Homage | **Boerum Hill**	19
I Heart | **NoLita**	–
In God We Trust | **multi.**	–
Intermix | **multi.**	24
NEW Irregular Choice | **SoHo**	–
Jack Spade | **SoHo**	25
Jacob & Co. | **E 50s**	24
NEW Jane Eadie | **NoLita**	–

Store	Location	Rating
Jean Shop	multi.	-
Jeffrey	Meatpacking	28
NEW Jessie James	W Vill	-
Jill Stuart	SoHo	22
Jimmy Choo	multi.	28
NEW John Bartlett	W Vill	23
John Derian	E Vill	-
John Varvatos	SoHo	26
Jonathan Adler	multi.	26
Juicy Couture	multi.	20
Jumelle	W'burg	-
Key	SoHo	-
Z Kiehl's	multi.	27
Kiki/Montparnasse	SoHo	25
Kirna Zabête	SoHo	27
NEW Korres	SoHo	-
Ksubi	NoLita	22
L'Artisan Parfumeur	multi.	26
LeSportsac	multi.	20
Lisa Levine	W'burg	-
Loopy Mango	Dumbo	-
Lord Willy's	multi.	-
NEW Luceplan	SoHo	23
Lulu Guinness	W Vill	24
Lyell	NoLita	-
Maison Martin Margiela	W Vill	-
Malin + Goetz	Chelsea	22
Z Manolo Blahnik	W 50s	28
Marc/Marc Jacobs	W Vill	25
Marc Jacobs Access.	W Vill	28
NEW Marc Ecko	Chelsea	-
Marc Jacobs	SoHo	27
Marni	SoHo	24
Matter	multi.	-
Mayle	NoLita	-
Me & Ro	NoLita	23
NEW Michael Aram	Chelsea	26
NEW Miguelina	W Vill	24
Mimi's Closet	Astoria	21
Mini Jake	W'burg	-
Missha	multi.	-
Miu Miu	multi.	25
NEW MNG/Mango	SoHo	-
Moon River Chattel	W'burg	-
NEW Moroso	SoHo	-
Z Moss	SoHo	28
NEW Muji	SoHo	-
Mulberry	multi.	-
N	Harlem	-
Nanette Lepore	SoHo	25
Noisette	W'burg	-
No. 6	L Italy	-
Oak	multi.	-
Oakley	SoHo	21
Odin	multi.	-
Olive & Bette's	multi.	22
Opening Ceremony	SoHo	-
Z Other Music	NoHo	27
Otte	multi.	26
Paul Frank	NoLita	18
Paul Smith	multi.	26
Phat Farm	SoHo	16
Pieces	Prospect Hts	21
Poppy	NoLita	23
Prada	multi.	26
Pucci	multi.	26
Puma	multi.	23
Rebecca Taylor	NoLita	23
Red Flower	NoLita	-
Resurrection	NoLita	-
Rico	Boerum Hill	-
Robert Marc	multi.	27
Roberto Cavalli	E 60s	27
Rugby	G Vill	22
Saja	NoLita	-
Z Santa Maria Novella	NoLita	28
Satellite	SoHo	-
Satya	multi.	21
Scoop NYC	multi.	23
Sean John	E 40s	18
Searle	multi.	24
Seize sur Vingt	NoLita	25
Selima/Sucre	multi.	27
Seven NY	SoHo	26
NEW Shoe Market	W'burg	18
Sigerson Morrison	multi.	25
Sleep	W'burg	22
Space Kiddets	Flatiron	26
NEW Space.NK	multi.	25
Stella Gialla	Glendale	25
Stella McCartney	Meatpacking	26
Steven Alan	multi.	24
Stuart/Wright	Ft Greene	-
Swarovski	multi.	25
Tarina Tarantino	SoHo	22
té casan	SoHo	-
Z Tekserve	Chelsea	26
TG-170	LES	20
Theory	multi.	23
Thom Browne.	TriBeCa	-
NEW 3.1 Phillip Lim	SoHo	27
Tory Burch	NoLita	21
Tous	SoHo	22
Tracy Feith	NoLita	22
Tracy Reese	Meatpacking	25
NEW Tribbles Home/Gdn.	TriBeCa	25

SPECIAL FEATURES

Trina Turk | **Meatpacking**	-|
Troy | **Gramercy**	-|
Uniqlo | **SoHo**	-|
Urban Outfitters | **multi.**	17|
Vespa | **multi.**	-|
Vitra | **Meatpacking**	-|
Wink | **multi.**	21|
Ylli | **W'burg**	-|
Zachary's Smile | **multi.**	24|
Zero/Maria Cornejo | **multi.**	-|
Zoë | **Dumbo**	-|

INSIDER SECRETS

Abitare | **Bklyn Hts**	-|
About Glamour | **W'burg**	-|
NEW Adam | **Meatpacking**	-|
Adriennes | **LES**	24|
Alcone | **W 40s**	23|
Alexandros | **multi.**	-|
Alife | **LES**	24|
Alixandre Furs | **Garment**	24|
Alpana Bawa | **E Vill**	-|
Amarcord Vintage | **multi.**	-|
Anbar | **TriBeCa**	21|
Anna | **E Vill**	-|
Annelore | **W Vill**	-|
NEW Asha Veza | **Park Slope**	-|
Barbara Shaum | **E Vill**	-|
Bark | **Downtown Bklyn**	-|
Bblessing | **LES**	21|
Beneath | **E 70s**	22|
Bettencourt | **W'burg**	-|
Blibetroy | **LES**	-|
Blue | **E Vill**	-|
Blue in Green | **SoHo**	21|
Bowery Kitchen | **Chelsea**	22|
B. Oyama Homme | **Harlem**	-|
Bra*Tenders | **W 40s**	-|
Built by Wendy | **multi.**	-|
NEW Bump | **Park Slope**	-|
Butik | **W Vill**	-|
NEW Butterflies/Zebras | **TriBeCa**	23|
Camilla Bergeron | **E 60s**	-|
CB I Hate Perfume | **W'burg**	-|
Challengher | **W'burg**	-|
Classic Kicks | **NoHo**	25|
Claudine | **G Vill**	22|
Cloth | **Ft Greene**	-|
Consignment | **Downtown Bklyn**	-|
David Lee Holland | **SoHo**	-|
Diva | **Midwood**	-|
D/L Cerney | **E Vill**	-|
Dosa | **SoHo**	24|

Doyle & Doyle | **LES**	25|
Duncan Quinn | **NoLita**	-|
NEW Edit | **E 90s**	-|
Edith Machinist | **LES**	-|
NEW Edon Manor | **TriBeCa**	-|
Elizabeth Charles | **Meatpacking**	-|
Ellen Christine | **Chelsea**	-|
environment337 | **G Vill**	-|
NEW Erie Basin | **Red Hook**	-|
Family Jewels | **Chelsea**	-|
NEW 5 in 1 | **W'burg**	-|
Fort St. Studio | **SoHo**	-|
45rpm/R | **multi.**	23|
Fresh Kills | **W'burg**	-|
Garrard & Co. | **SoHo**	-|
Geminola | **W Vill**	-|
Gentlemen's Resale | **E 80s**	24|
Good, Bad & Ugly | **NoLita**	-|
Greenwich Letterpress | **W Vill**	26|
halcyon | **Dumbo**	-|
NEW Head/Heels | **multi.**	21|
Heidi Klein | **E 70s**	-|
IF | **SoHo**	-|
NEW Iris | **Meatpacking**	23|
Jammyland | **E Vill**	-|
Jane | **E 70s**	-|
Jeri Cohen Jewelry | **E 60s**	27|
Jill Platner | **SoHo**	-|
Kavanagh's | **E 40s**	-|
Key | **SoHo**	-|
Kiosk | **SoHo**	19|
Kiton | **E 50s**	-|
Kremer Pigments | **Chelsea**	29|
Layla | **Downtown Bklyn**	-|
Lee Anderson | **E 70s**	-|
Le Labo | **NoLita**	-|
Leontine | **Seaport**	-|
Linda Derector | **NoLita**	-|
Lowell/Edwards | **E 50s**	-|
NEW Lucia Nenickova | **Gramercy**	21|
Lucky Wang | **multi.**	25|
Magnificent Costume | **E 80s**	22|
Mariko | **E 70s**	-|
Market NYC | **NoLita**	20|
Mary Adams The Dress | **LES**	-|
Matta | **NoLita**	-|
Michael Anchin | **W'burg**	-|
Mick Margo | **W Vill**	-|
Mika Inatome | **TriBeCa**	-|
NEW ModernTots | **Dumbo**	23|
Moulin Bleu | **TriBeCa**	-|
NEW msg | **L Italy**	-|

subscribe to ZAGAT.com

Myla	E 60s	-
Mylo Dweck	Bensonhurst	-
M Z Wallace	SoHo	-
New York Replacement	E 90s	22
Nom de Guerre	NoHo	20
Nort/Recon	NoHo	-
Number (N)ine	TriBeCa	-
NYC Velo	E Vill	20
Occhiali	E 80s	24
NEW Ohio Knit.	Carroll Gdns	22
Peggy Pardon	LES	-
P.E. Guerin	W Vill	-
Pippin	Chelsea	-
NEW Pixie Mkt.	LES	19
Pomme	Dumbo	-
premium goods	Park Slope	-
Prince Charles III	SoHo	-
NEW Private Stock	Park Slope	-
NEW Project No. 8	Chinatown	-
Project 234	NoLita	-
Psny	SoHo	-
NEW REPOP	Clinton Hill	-
Ruzzetti & Gow	E 70s	-
Saipua	Red Hook	-
Sean	multi.	24
Sir	multi.	-
Some Odd Rubies	LES	-
Susan van der Linde	E 50s	-
Swallow	Carroll Gdns	-
Taffin	E 50s	-
Temperley	SoHo	-
Tiny Living	E Vill	-
Tupli	E 60s	-
Unis	NoLita	-
Urban Angler	Chelsea	-
Utowa	Flatiron	20
Vogel	SoHo	-
Yoko Devereaux	W'burg	-

LEGENDARY

(Date company founded)

1752	Caswell-Massey	E 40s	25
1775	Breguet	E 60s	29
1781	Asprey	E 70s	28
1801	Crane & Co.	W 40s	27
1816	Baccarat	E 50s	29
1818	Brooks Brothers	multi.	24
1825	Clarks	E 40s	23
1826	Lord & Taylor	Murray Hill	22
1830	Christofle	E 60s	27
1831	Takashimaya	E 50s	28
1837	Hermès	multi.	29
1837	Tiffany & Co.	multi.	28
1838	C.O. Bigelow	G Vill	26
1847	Cartier	multi.	29
1848	Hammacher	E 50s	25
1851	A La Vieille Russie	E 50s	29
1851	Bally	E 50s	28
1851	Kiehl's	multi.	27
1852	Hastens	SoHo	-
1853	Levi's Store	multi.	23
1854	Louis Vuitton	multi.	27
1855	Charles P. Rogers	Flatiron	26
1856	Burberry	multi.	27
1856	Orvis	E 40s	25
1857	P.E. Guerin	W Vill	-
1858	Macy's	multi.	19
1860	Chopard	E 60s	29
1860	Frette	E 60s	29
1860	Ligne Roset	multi.	28
1862	FAO Schwarz	E 50s	25
1863	Bernardaud	E 50s	29
1870	Met. Museum of Art	multi.	25
1870	Penhaligon's	E 70s	27
1872	Bloomingdale's	multi.	23
1873	Church's Shoes	E 60s	25
1874	Piaget	E 50s	28
1878	Daum	E 60s	27
1878	Dempsey & Carroll	E 50s	27
1878	Salvation Army	multi.	11
1878	Wempe	E 50s	29
1879	Vogel	SoHo	-
1881	Movado	W 40s	26
1882	Danskin	W 60s	23
1883	Bellora	SoHo	26
1884	William Barthman	multi.	26
1885	Turnbull & Asser	E 50s	28
1887	Capezio	multi.	24
1887	Smythson	W 50s	28
1888	Town Shop	W 80s	25
1889	Modell's Sport	multi.	16
1890	H. Herzfeld	E 50s	26
1891	J.M. Weston	E 60s	26
1892	Abercrombie	multi.	18
1892	Poggenpohl U.S.	multi.	-
1893	Dunhill	E 50s	27
1893	Mikimoto	E 50s	29
1893	Pratesi	E 60s	29
1893	Sears	multi.	17
1894	Bulgari	multi.	28
1894	Harris Levy	LES	26
1895	Berluti	E 70s	-
1895	Swarovski	multi.	25
1896	Henri Bendel	E 50s	26
1897	ABC Carpet & Home	Flatiron	25
1897	ABC Carpets/Rugs	Flatiron	25

SPECIAL FEATURES

1897 | Swiss Army | **SoHo**	23
1898 | Eisenberg Eisenberg | **Flatiron**	22
1898 | Lederer de Paris | **E 50s**	25
1898 | Willoughby's | **Garment**	20
1899 | Beacon Paint | **W 70s**	22
1899 | Bergdorf | **E 50s**	29
1899 | Hickey Freeman | **multi.**	27
1900 | Hyman Hendler | **Garment**	28
1900 | New York Doll | **E 60s**	28
1900 | Stickley, Audi & Co. | **Chelsea**	28
1900 | Tourneau | **multi.**	27
1902 | Goodwill | **multi.**	12
1902 | J. Press | **E 40s**	23
1903 | Steuben | **E 60s**	29
1904 | Georg Jensen | **multi.**	29
1904 | Seaman Schepps | **E 50s**	27
1905 | Jos. A. Bank | **E 40s**	18
1905 | Lalique | **E 60s**	29
1905 | Simon's Hardware | **LIC**	26
1905 | Thomasville | **Bayside**	23
1906 | Aaron Basha | **E 60s**	25
1906 | Montblanc | **multi.**	28
1906 | Van Cleef & Arpels | **E 50s**	29
1908 | DeNatale Jewelers | **multi.**	26
1908 | Paragon | **Union Sq**	25
1908 | Spence-Chapin Thrift | **multi.**	16
1909 | Filene's Basement | **multi.**	18
1910 | Ermenegildo Zegna | **E 50s**	28
1910 | Léron | **E 60s**	29
1911 | Fila | **E 40s**	23
1911 | J.J. Hat Center | **Garment**	27
1911 | New York Public Library | **E 40s**	23
1912 | James Robinson | **E 50s**	29
1912 | Manhattan Saddlery | **Gramercy**	-
1913 | Prada | **multi.**	26
1914 | Chanel | **multi.**	29
1914 | Salvatore Ferragamo | **E 50s**	28
1915 | Moscot | **multi.**	21
1916 | Oxxford Clothes | **E 50s**	28
1917 | Alixandre Furs | **Garment**	24
1918 | Beckenstein Fabrics | **Flatiron**	-
1918 | Gringer & Sons | **E Vill**	25
1918 | Paterson Silks | **Floral Pk**	18
1919 | Buccellati | **E 50s**	29
1919 | Giorgio Fedon 19 | **W 40s**	-
1919 | Greenstones | **W 80s**	26
1920 | Altman Luggage | **LES**	24
1920 | Harry Winston | **E 50s**	29
1920 | Oriental Lamp Shade | **multi.**	25
1920 | Tous | **SoHo**	22
1921 | Alessi | **multi.**	25
1921 | Blackman | **multi.**	26
1921 | Gucci | **multi.**	27
1921 | Loehmann's | **multi.**	20
1922 | Allen Edmonds | **multi.**	28
1923 | Barneys NY | **E 60s**	27
1923 | Fogal | **E 50s**	28
1924 | Arthur Brown | **W 40s**	27
1924 | A.W. Kaufman | **LES**	26
1924 | Damiani | **E 60s**	-
1924 | Loro Piana | **E 60s**	29
1924 | Saks Fifth Ave. | **E 50s**	27
1925 | Bang & Olufsen | **multi.**	28
1925 | Capitol Fishing | **Garment**	-
1925 | Davis & Warshow | **multi.**	23
1925 | Fendi | **E 50s**	27
1926 | Davide Cenci | **E 60s**	29
1926 | Eneslow | **multi.**	28
1927 | Cassina USA | **E 50s**	-
1927 | Furla | **multi.**	25
1927 | Harvey Electronics | **W 40s**	28
1928 | Cole Haan | **multi.**	25
1929 | A.I. Friedman | **Flatiron**	24
1929 | a. testoni | **E 50s**	27
1929 | Mrs. John L. Strong | **E 60s**	28
1929 | S.Feldman House. | **E 90s**	25
1930 | Cappellini | **SoHo**	-
1930 | Princeton Ski Shop | **Flatiron**	21
1930 | Signoria | **E 60s**	25
1930 | Whitney Museum | **E 70s**	21
1931 | Mary Arnold Toys | **E 70s**	26
1932 | Artbag | **E 80s**	24
1932 | Ethan Allen | **multi.**	23
1932 | H.L. Purdy | **multi.**	27
1932 | MauricE Villency | **E 50s**	26
1932 | Sid's | **Downtown Bklyn**	21
1933 | Albee Baby Carriage | **W 90s**	25
1933 | Lacoste | **multi.**	24
1933 | Pearl Paint | **Chinatown**	26
1934 | Alkit | **Flatiron**	23
1934 | Boffi SoHo | **SoHo**	-
1934 | Scully & Scully | **E 50s**	29
1935 | Frick Collection | **E 70s**	22
1935 | Kraft | **E 60s**	26
1935 | Michael C. Fina | **E 40s**	26
1935 | Smiley's | **Woodhaven**	16
1936 | M&J Trimming | **Garment**	25
1936 | Olden Camera/Lens | **Garment**	20
1936 | Zarin Fabrics | **LES**	23

1938 | Kangol | **W 60s**	23
1938 | Knoll | **Chelsea**	-
1938 | Paul Stuart | **E 40s**	27
1938 | Suarez | **W 50s**	27
1939 | Gerry Cosby | **Garment**	25
1939 | Verdura | **E 50s**	28
1940 | Coach | **multi.**	26
1940 | Gabay's Outlet | **E Vill**	20
1940 | Tip Top Shoes | **W 70s**	25
1941 | Kleinfeld | **Chelsea**	25
1945 | Brioni | **E 50s**	28
1945 | Celine | **E 60s**	28
1945 | Elgot | **E 60s**	25
1945 | H. Stern | **E 50s**	28
1945 | Priscilla of Boston | **Garment**	24
1945 | Sherle Wagner | **E 60s**	-
1946 | Bridge Kitchenware | **E 40s**	28
1946 | Dior New York | **E 50s**	28
1946 | Fountain Pen | **TriBeCa**	28
1946 | Honora | **E 50s**	-
1946 | T. Anthony | **E 50s**	28
1947 | F.M. Allen | **E 70s**	-
1947 | H&M | **multi.**	12
1947 | Jewish Museum | **E 90s**	25
1947 | Pucci | **multi.**	26
1947 | Steinlauf & Stoller | **Garment**	-
1947 | Talbots | **multi.**	22
1948 | Colony Music | **W 40s**	24
1948 | David Webb | **E 60s**	25
1948 | Lester's | **multi.**	24
1948 | Lexington Luggage | **E 60s**	21
1948 | Longchamp | **SoHo**	26
1948 | Mem. Sloan-Kettering | **E 80s**	22
1948 | Puma | **multi.**	23
1949 | Adidas | **multi.**	23
1949 | Gant | **E 50s**	22
1949 | Miriam Rigler | **E 60s**	28
1949 | Pottery Barn | **multi.**	20
1949 | Wolford | **multi.**	28
1950 | Adriennes | **LES**	24
1950 | Alcone | **W 40s**	23
1950 | Kreiss Collection | **E 50s**	26
1950 | Leonard Opticians | **multi.**	26
1950 | Louis Féraud | **E 60s**	28
1950 | Ray Beauty Supply | **W 40s**	24
1950 | Robert Talbott | **E 60s**	28
1950 | Schneider's | **Chelsea**	25
1950 | Z Chemists/Zitomer | **E 70s**	25
1951 | Kiton | **E 50s**	-
1951 | Marimekko | **E 70s**	24

1952 | 'Bric's | **E 50s**	27
1952 | Chloé | **E 70s**	26
1952 | Council Thrift Shop | **E 80s**	18
1952 | Kartell | **SoHo**	-
1952 | Rosen & Chadick | **Garment**	-
1953 | Fratelli Rossetti | **E 50s**	27
1953 | Missoni | **E 70s**	26
1954 | Ann Taylor | **multi.**	21
1954 | Clarins | **multi.**	26
1954 | Encore | **E 80s**	20
1954 | Michael's/Consignment | **E 70s**	25
1954 | Shoe Box | **multi.**	23
1955 | Airline Stationery | **E 40s**	21
1955 | Ascot Chang | **W 50s**	25
1955 | Innovation Luggage | **multi.**	20
1955 | Natan Borlam's | **W'burg**	28
1955 | Original Penguin | **W 40s**	-
1955 | Utrecht | **E Vill**	24
1956 | AsiaStore/Asia Society | **E 70s**	24
1956 | Belgian Shoes | **E 50s**	28
1956 | Bisazza | **SoHo**	-
1956 | Conran Shop | **E 50s**	23
1956 | Lyric Hi-Fi | **E 80s**	28
1956 | Museum Arts/Design | **W 50s**	26
1956 | Williams-Sonoma | **multi.**	26
1957 | Camera Land | **E 50s**	22
1957 | Krizia | **E 60s**	-

ONLY IN NEW YORK

☑ ABC Carpet & Home | **Flatiron**	25
Academy Records | **multi.**	24
Alexandros | **multi.**	-
Alixandre Furs | **Garment**	24
☑ B&H Photo-Video | **Garment**	27
Capitol Fishing | **Garment**	-
Colony Music | **W 40s**	24
Demolition Depot | **Harlem**	-
Dylan's Candy | **E 60s**	22
Earnest Cut & Sew | **multi.**	25
E.A.T. Gifts | **E 80s**	23
FAO Schwarz | **E 50s**	25
Hyman Hendler | **Garment**	28
Jacob & Co. | **E 50s**	24
Jean Shop | **multi.**	-
Love Saves The Day | **E Vill**	17
Lower E. S. Tenement Museum | **LES**	21
Maxilla & Mandible | **W 80s**	25
Met. Opera Shop | **W 60s**	24
☑ MoMA Store | **multi.**	25

Morgan Library | **Murray Hill**	25
Museum/City of NY | **E 100s**	21
Z Neue Galerie NY | **E 80s**	26
New York Public Library | **multi.**	23
New York Transit | **multi.**	20
Ray Beauty Supply | **W 40s**	24
Ricky's | **multi.**	19
Z Tender Buttons | **E 60s**	28
Z Zabar's | **W 80s**	26

REGISTRY: BABY

Acorn | **Downtown Bklyn**	-
Area | **multi.**	-
Babies "R" Us | **multi.**	19
NEW Baby Cottons | **E 80s**	26
Z Bed Bath & Beyond | **SI**	20
Z Bergdorf | **E 50s**	29
Z Bloomingdale's | **SoHo**	23
Blue Bench | **TriBeCa**	-
Burlington Coat | **multi.**	15
Z buybuy BABY | **Chelsea**	23
City Cricket | **W Vill**	-
Crembebè | **E Vill**	-
Destination Maternity | **E 50s**	22
FAO Schwarz | **E 50s**	25
flora and henri | **E 70s**	23
Z Georg Jensen | **SoHo**	29
Giggle | **multi.**	25
Green Onion | **Cobble Hill**	24
Half Pint | **Dumbo**	-
Hippototamus | **multi.**	22
Ibiza Kidz | **G Vill**	23
Julian & Sara | **SoHo**	-
Katz/Cradle | **Midwood**	-
Z Kidding Around | **Flatiron**	26
kid o. | **G Vill**	22
Kidville | **multi.**	22
Le Sabon & Baby Too | **E 60s**	23
Les Petits Chapelais | **SoHo**	25
Little Stinkers | **E Vill**	-
Lucky Wang | **Chelsea**	25
Mini Jake | **W'burg**	-
Mish Mish | **E 90s**	-
NEW ModernTots | **Dumbo**	23
MoonSoup | **E 50s**	24
Natalie & Friends | **E 60s**	28
Olá Baby | **multi.**	27
Planet Kids | **multi.**	18
Pomme | **Dumbo**	-
Pottery Barn Kids | **E 60s**	-
Prince/Princess | **E 70s**	-
Ralph Lauren Layette | **E 70s**	26
Schneider's | **Chelsea**	25
Sons + Daughters | **E Vill**	-

Space Kiddets | **Flatiron**	26
Z Target | **multi.**	17
NEW Threads | **E 70s**	-
Z Tiffany & Co. | **E 50s**	28
Tiny Doll House | **E 70s**	-
Tous | **SoHo**	22
212 Kids | **E 80s**	23
Yoya/Yoya Mart | **W Vill**	27
Z'Baby Co. | **multi.**	24

REGISTRY: BRIDAL/GIFT

Z ABC Carpet & Home | **Flatiron**	25
Abitare | **Bklyn Hts**	-
A Brooklyn Table | **Cobble Hill**	-
Adrien Linford | **multi.**	22
Z Aero | **SoHo**	26
Agent Provocateur | **SoHo**	27
Area | **multi.**	-
Armani Casa | **SoHo**	25
Z Asprey | **E 70s**	28
Z Avventura | **W 80s**	26
Z Baccarat | **E 50s**	29
Bardith | **E 70s**	-
Bark | **Downtown Bklyn**	-
Z Barneys NY | **E 60s**	27
Z Bed Bath & Beyond | **multi.**	20
Bellora | **SoHo**	26
Z Bergdorf | **E 50s**	29
Z Bloomingdale's | **multi.**	23
Blue Tree | **E 90s**	24
Bonne Nuit | **E 70s**	24
Borrelli Boutique | **E 60s**	-
Boucher | **Meatpacking**	20
Z Bridge Kitchenware | **E 40s**	28
Z Broadway Panhandler | **G Vill**	27
Z Buccellati | **E 50s**	29
NEW Bump | **Park Slope**	-
Calvin Klein | **E 60s**	25
NEW CB2 | **SoHo**	-
Z Charles P. Rogers | **Flatiron**	26
Z Christofle | **E 60s**	27
Clio | **SoHo**	-
Conran Shop | **E 50s**	23
Z Crate & Barrel | **multi.**	21
Daum | **E 60s**	27
E. Braun & Co. | **E 60s**	-
environment337 | **multi.**	-
Ethan Allen | **multi.**	23
Fishs Eddy | **Flatiron**	18
Z Frette | **E 60s**	29
Z Georg Jensen | **multi.**	29
Global Table | **SoHo**	-
Z Gracious Home | **multi.**	25

☑ Harris Levy | **LES**	26
☑ Hermès | **E 60s**	29
Home & Haven | **Cobble Hill**	22
Honora | **E 50s**	-
Jensen-Lewis | **Chelsea**	19
John Derian | **E Vill**	-
Jumelle | **W'burg**	-
Kiki/Montparnasse | **SoHo**	25
La Cafetière | **Chelsea**	-
Laina Jane | **multi.**	-
☑ Lalique | **E 60s**	29
☑ La Perla | **multi.**	28
Laytner's Linen | **multi.**	20
Léron | **E 60s**	29
Longchamp | **multi.**	26
☑ MacKenzie-Childs | **E 50s**	25
☑ Macy's | **multi.**	19
Meg Cohen Design | **SoHo**	-
☑ Michael C. Fina | **E 40s**	26
☑ Moss | **SoHo**	28
Nancy Koltes Home | **NoLita**	28
Pier 1 Imports | **multi.**	15
Porthault | **E 60s**	29
Pottery Barn | **multi.**	20
☑ Pratesi | **E 60s**	29
Restoration Hardware | **Flatiron**	21
☑ Saks Fifth Ave. | **E 50s**	27
Satellite | **SoHo**	-
☑ Scully & Scully | **E 50s**	29
Sherle Wagner | **E 60s**	-
☑ Simon Pearce | **E 50s**	27
Sleep | **W'burg**	22
☑ Steuben | **E 60s**	29
☑ Takashimaya | **E 50s**	28
☑ Target | **multi.**	17
Tarina Tarantino | **SoHo**	22
37=1 Atelier | **SoHo**	-
☑ Tiffany & Co. | **E 50s**	28
Tous | **SoHo**	22
☑ TUMI | **E 80s**	28
Victoria's Secret | **multi.**	18
☑ Williams-Sonoma | **multi.**	26
William-Wayne | **G Vill**	26
Yellow Door | **Midwood**	-
☑ Zabar's | **W 80s**	26

STATUS GOODS

☑ Aedes De Venustas | **G Vill**	27
Agent Provocateur | **SoHo**	27
☑ Akris | **E 60s**	29
☑ A La Vieille Russie | **E 50s**	29
Alessandro Dell'Acqua | **E 60s**	26
☑ Alexander McQueen | **Meatpacking**	28

NEW Allegra Hicks | **E 70s**	24
☑ Allen Edmonds | **multi.**	28
☑ Ann Sacks | **multi.**	27
☑ Apple Store | **multi.**	27
Armani Casa | **SoHo**	25
☑ Asprey | **E 70s**	28
a. testoni | **E 50s**	27
Audemars Piguet | **E 50s**	29
☑ Baccarat | **E 50s**	29
☑ Balenciaga | **Chelsea**	29
☑ B&B Italia | **multi.**	27
☑ Bang & Olufsen | **multi.**	28
☑ Barbour/Peter Elliot | **E 80s**	28
Barker Black | **NoLita**	25
☑ Barneys NY | **E 60s**	27
☑ Belgian Shoes | **E 50s**	28
Bellini | **multi.**	23
☑ Bergdorf | **E 50s**	29
Berluti | **E 70s**	-
☑ Bernardaud | **E 50s**	29
Blue Tree | **E 90s**	24
Boffi SoHo | **SoHo**	-
☑ Bonpoint | **multi.**	28
☑ Bose | **multi.**	27
☑ Bottega Veneta | **E 50s**	29
Breguet | **E 60s**	29
Bric's | **E 50s**	27
☑ Brioni | **E 50s**	28
Brunello Cucinelli | **W Vill**	-
☑ Buccellati | **E 50s**	29
Bulgari | **multi.**	28
Burberry | **multi.**	27
Burton Store | **SoHo**	25
Butter | **Downtown Bklyn**	23
Calvin Klein | **E 60s**	25
Camilla Bergeron | **E 60s**	-
Cappellini | **SoHo**	-
Carlos Miele | **Meatpacking**	-
☑ Carolina Herrera | **E 70s**	28
☑ Cartier | **multi.**	29
Cassina USA | **E 50s**	-
Catherine Memmi | **SoHo**	-
Catimini | **E 80s**	26
Catriona Mackechnie | **Meatpacking**	-
☑ Celine | **E 60s**	28
Cellini | **multi.**	27
☑ Chanel | **multi.**	29
NEW Charlotte Moss | **E 60s**	25
Chloé | **E 70s**	26
☑ Chopard | **E 60s**	29
☑ Christian Louboutin | **multi.**	28
☑ Christofle | **E 60s**	27
Comme des Garçons | **Chelsea**	26

Ⓩ Mikimoto | **E 50s**	29
Mish | **E 70s**	-
Missoni | **E 70s**	26
Miu Miu | **multi.**	25
Morgenthal Frederics | **multi.**	28
NEW Moroso | **SoHo**	-
Ⓩ Moss | **SoHo**	28
Movado | **W 40s**	26
Ⓩ Mrs. John L. Strong | **E 60s**	28
Mylo Dweck | **Bensonhurst**	-
Nokia | **E 50s**	22
Oakley | **SoHo**	21
Ochre | **SoHo**	-
Olatz | **W Vill**	-
Oliver Peoples | **multi.**	27
Ⓩ Oscar de la Renta | **E 60s**	28
Ⓩ Oxxford Clothes | **E 50s**	28
Paul & Shark | **E 60s**	27
Paul Smith | **multi.**	26
P.E. Guerin | **W Vill**	-
Phi | **SoHo**	-
Ⓩ Piaget | **E 50s**	28
Pilar Rossi | **E 60s**	-
Poltrona Frau | **SoHo**	-
Porsche Design | **E 50s**	26
Porthault | **E 60s**	29
Prada | **multi.**	26
Ⓩ Pratesi | **E 60s**	29
Pucci | **multi.**	26
Ralph Lauren | **multi.**	26
Ralph Lauren Boys/Girls | **E 70s**	26
Ralph Lauren Eyewear | **E 60s**	-
Ralph Lauren Layette | **E 70s**	26
Reem Acra | **E 60s**	29
Resurrection | **NoLita**	-
Robert Marc | **multi.**	27
Roberto Cavalli | **E 60s**	27
Robert Talbott | **E 60s**	28
NEW Roger Vivier | **E 60s**	28
Ⓩ Salvatore Ferragamo | **E 50s**	28
Samsonite | **E 60s**	24
Ⓩ Santa Maria Novella | **NoLita**	28
Seaman Schepps | **E 50s**	27
Sherle Wagner | **E 60s**	-
Sicis | **SoHo**	25
Sigerson Morrison | **multi.**	25
Ⓩ Smythson | **W 50s**	28
SOHO | **NoLita**	20
Sonia Rykiel | **E 70s**	26
Ⓩ Sound by Singer | **Union Sq**	27
Stella McCartney | **Meatpacking**	26
Stephen Kahan | **E 60s**	27
Stephen Russell | **E 70s**	27

Ⓩ Stereo Exchange | **NoHo**	26
Ⓩ Steuben | **E 60s**	29
Stubbs & Wootton | **E 70s**	26
Suarez | **W 50s**	27
Sub Chrono | **E 40s**	22
Suite New York | **E 50s**	-
Taffin | **E 50s**	-
Ⓩ Takashimaya | **E 50s**	28
Ⓩ T. Anthony | **E 50s**	28
Ted Muehling | **SoHo**	29
Temperley | **SoHo**	-
Thomas Pink | **multi.**	26
Thom Browne. | **TriBeCa**	-
Thos. Moser Cabinets | **E 60s**	29
NEW 3.1 Phillip Lim | **SoHo**	27
Ⓩ Tiffany & Co. | **multi.**	28
Ⓩ Tod's | **E 60s**	29
NEW Tom Ford | **E 70s**	28
TSE | **SoHo**	26
Tupli | **E 60s**	-
Ⓩ Turnbull & Asser | **E 50s**	28
Ⓩ Valentino | **E 60s**	28
Ⓩ Van Cleef & Arpels | **E 50s**	29
Vanessa Noel | **E 50s**	-
Vera Wang Bridal | **E 70s**	27
Verdura | **E 50s**	28
Versace | **E 50s**	26
Vitra | **Meatpacking**	-
Vogel | **SoHo**	-
Walter Steiger | **E 50s**	28
Ⓩ Waterworks | **multi.**	28
Ⓩ Wempe | **E 50s**	29
Yigal Azrouel | **Meatpacking**	-
Yohji Yamamoto | **SoHo**	27
Yves Delorme | **E 70s**	28
Yves Saint Laurent | **multi.**	26
Zoë | **Dumbo**	-

TWEEN/TEEN APPEAL

Abracadabra | **Flatiron**	21
Adidas | **multi.**	23
Alphabets | **multi.**	19
American Apparel | **multi.**	19
Am. Eagle | **multi.**	17
Ⓩ Apple Store | **multi.**	27
Arden B. | **multi.**	17
Atrium | **NoHo**	25
Beacon's Closet | **multi.**	19
bebe | **multi.**	17
Ben Sherman | **SoHo**	23
Berkley Girl | **multi.**	21
Ⓩ Billabong | **multi.**	21
NEW Billionaire Boys | **SoHo**	-
Blades Board & Skate | **multi.**	23

Body Shop | **multi.**	20
Brooklyn Industries | **multi.**	20
Buffalo Exchange | **W'burg**	17
Burton Store | **SoHo**	25
Canal Jean | **Flatbush**	17
Caravan | **NoHo**	20
Cardeology | **multi.**	19
Charlotte Russe | **multi.**	10
Cheap Jack's | **Garment**	14
Claire's Accessories | **multi.**	8
CoCo & Delilah | **E Vill**	-
Compact Impact | **Financial**	-
NEW Cotélac | **SoHo**	-
NEW Crocs | **W 70s**	-
Crumpler Bags | **multi.**	24
Dave's Quality Meat | **E Vill**	-
David Z. | **multi.**	19
DC Shoes | **SoHo**	22
Diva | **Midwood**	-
Dylan's Candy | **E 60s**	22
Ed Hardy | **multi.**	21
Essentials | **multi.**	20
Express | **multi.**	16
NEW Flight Club | **Financial**	21
Flying A | **SoHo**	17
Forever 21 | **multi.**	10
4PlayBK | **Park Slope**	-
NEW Free People | **Flatiron**	-
G.C. William | **multi.**	20
Girl Props | **SoHo**	11
Guess | **multi.**	21
Hairy Mary's | **LES**	-
halcyon | **Dumbo**	-
NEW Homage | **Boerum Hill**	19
NEW Irregular Choice | **SoHo**	-
Joyce Leslie | **multi.**	8
Jubilee | **multi.**	16
Juicy Couture | **multi.**	20
NEW Karen Millen | **SoHo**	-
KCDC Skate | **W'burg**	22
Laila Rowe | **multi.**	14
Lester's | **multi.**	24
Levi's Store | **multi.**	23
LF Stores | **multi.**	17
Lily | **multi.**	24
Limited, The | **multi.**	-
Limited Too | **multi.**	16
Loom | **Park Slope**	23
M.A.C. Cosmetics | **multi.**	26
Marmalade | **LES**	-
Maxilla & Mandible | **W 80s**	25
Metro Bicycles | **multi.**	20
Mimi's Closet | **Astoria**	21
Missha | **multi.**	-
NEW MNG/Mango | **SoHo**	-
Necessary Clothing | **multi.**	17
Neighborhoodies | **multi.**	20
Niketown | **E 50s**	24
North Face | **multi.**	24
Oakley | **SoHo**	21
Z Paragon | **Union Sq**	25
Paul Frank | **NoLita**	18
Pearl River Mart | **SoHo**	16
NEW Pink Olive | **E Vill**	24
Plaza Too | **multi.**	21
Puma | **multi.**	23
Pylones | **multi.**	-
Quiksilver | **multi.**	21
NEW Rainbow Sandals | **NoLita**	23
Reminiscence | **Flatiron**	19
Rival | **SoHo**	22
Ruehl | **W Vill**	21
Rugby | **G Vill**	22
Sanrio | **W 40s**	21
Scaredy Kat | **Park Slope**	24
Scoop Kids | **Meatpacking**	23
Sean John | **E 40s**	18
Z Sephora | **multi.**	25
Something Else | **multi.**	23
Z Sony Style | **E 50s**	26
Steve Madden | **multi.**	16
Strawberry | **multi.**	11
Studio NYC Shoes | **multi.**	19
Supreme | **SoHo**	-
Tah-Poozie | **G Vill**	18
Tokio 7 | **E Vill**	26
Trash & Vaudeville | **E Vill**	16
Treehouse | **W'burg**	-
Tribeca Girls | **TriBeCa**	-
NEW Trixie/Tilda | **Downtown Bklyn**	25
Tuesday's Child | **multi.**	26
UGG Australia | **SoHo**	-
Uniqlo | **SoHo**	-
Urban Outfitters | **multi.**	17
Z Virgin | **multi.**	23
Von Dutch | **SoHo**	-
WeSC | **SoHo**	-
NEW West | **W 70s**	-
Yellow Rat | **multi.**	16

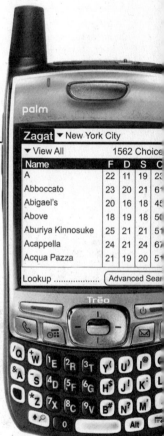